WELSH AFFAIRS
COMMITTEE

Second Report

THE PRESERVATION OF HISTORIC BUILDINGS
AND
ANCIENT MONUMENTS

VOLUME II

Minutes of Evidence
and Appendices

Ordered by The House of Commons *to be printed*
19 May 1993

LONDON: HMSO

£28.00 net

403–II

The Welsh Affairs Committee is appointed under Standing Order No 130 to examine the expenditure, administration and policy of the Welsh Office and associated public bodies.

The Committee consists of 11 Members of whom the quorum is three.

The Committee shall have power:

(a)   to send for persons, papers and records, to sit notwithstanding any adjournment of the House, to adjourn from place to place, and to report from time to time;

(b)   to appoint specialist advisers either to supply information which is not readily available or to elucidate matters of complexity within the Committee's order of reference;

(c)   to communicate to any other committee and to the Committee of Public Accounts its evidence and any other documents relating to matters of common interest; and

(d)   to meet concurrently with any other such committee for the purposes of deliberating, taking evidence, or considering draft reports.

Unless the House otherwise orders, all Members nominated to the Committee continue to be members of the Committee for the remainder of the Parliament.

The membership of the Committee since its nomination on 13 July 1992 has been as follows:

Mr Gareth Wardell (Chairman)

Mr Nick Ainger   Mr Elfyn Llwyd
(appointed 25.1.93)   Mr Peter Luff
Mr Alex Carlile   Mr Roderick Richards
Mr Jonathan Evans   Mr Mark Robinson
Mr Roger Evans   Mr Walter Sweeney
Mr David Hanson
Mr Jon Owen Jones
(discharged 25.1.93)

Mr Gareth Wardell was elected Chairman on 16 July 1992.

The cost of printing and publishing this Volume is estimated by HMSO at £29,140

TABLE OF CONTENTS
(VOLUME I)

LIST OF WITNESSES

(VOLUME II)

LIST OF MEMORANDA
INCLUDED IN THE MINUTES OF EVIDENCE

(VOLUME II)

LIST OF APPENDICES
TO THE MINUTES OF EVIDENCE
(VOLUME II)

Page

UNPRINTED MEMORANDA

Additional memoranda have been received by the following and have been reported to the House, but to save printing costs they have not been printed and copies have been placed in the House of Commons Library where they may be inspected by Members. Other copies are in the Record Office, House of Lords, and are available to the public for inspection. Requests for inspection should be addressed to the Record Office, House of Lords, London, SW1. (Tel 071-219 3074). Hours of inspection are from 9.30 am to 5.30 pm on Mondays to Fridays.

1. Union of Welsh Independents (HB 12)

2. Association of Preservation Trusts (HB 22)

3. Dr Richard Prentice (HB 25)

4. Landmark Trust (HB 31)

5. Dr Roger Wools (HB 55)

6. West Glamorgan County Council (HB 63)

7. Mid Glamorgan County Council (HB 64)

8. Gwynedd County Council (HB 65)

9. Powys County Council (HB 66)

10. Gwent County Council (HB 71)

11. South Glamorgan County Council (HB 75)

12. Mr M R Hadley (HB 77)

13. Mid Glamorgan County Council (HB 81)

14. The Revd David Kellen (HB 82)

15. D Gruffydd Jones, The University College of Wales, Aberystwyth (HB 89)

16. Alec Webster, Chairman, Hendref: Welsh Traditional Houses at Risk (HB 94)

17. The Architectural Heritage Fund (HB 96)

MINUTES OF EVIDENCE

TAKEN BEFORE THE WELSH AFFAIRS COMMITTEE

WEDNESDAY 20 JANUARY 1993

Members present:

Mr Gareth Wardell, in the Chair

Mr Roger Evans	Mr Jon Owen Jones
Mr David Hanson	Mr Mark Robinson
Mr Elfyn Llwyd	Mr Rod Richards
Mr Peter Luff	Mr Walter Sweeney

Memorandum by Cadw: Welsh Historic Monuments Executive Agency

PRESERVATION OF HISTORIC BUILDINGS AND ANCIENT MONUMENTS (HB2)

INTRODUCTION

1. The need to preserve historic buildings and ancient monuments has long been recognised by Parliament. The development of statutory protection began in 1882 with the Ancient Monuments Protection Act which safeguarded 29 monuments in England and Wales and 21 in Scotland. The protection of buildings more or less in daily use for historic or aesthetic reasons was a more recent development through the Town and Country Planning Act 1932. Current legislation (the Planning (Listed Buildings and Conservation Areas) Act 1990) offers statutory protection to individual buildings of special architectural or historic interest and provides for the designation of Conservation Areas. Legislation also has provided for assistance to owners in meeting the costs of repairing historic buildings and ancient monuments. Current measures of key relevance are:

    (a) Historic Buildings and Ancient Monuments Act 1953;

    (b) Ancient Monuments and Archaeological Areas Act 1979;

    (c) Planning (Listed Buildings and Conservation Areas) Act 1990.

2. Within the primary legislation and supporting regulations (governing for example applications for listed building consent), the Secretary of State has issued policy guidance, principally in Welsh Office Circular 61/81: Historic Buildings and Conservation Areas—Policy and Procedure, and Planning Policy Guidance Note 16: Archaeology and Planning. Other planning guidance issued by the Department also refers to the built heritage.

3. Responsibility within the Welsh Office for historic buildings and ancient monuments rests with Cadw: Welsh Historic Monuments Executive Agency which was launched on 2 April 1991. Cadw was first established in 1984 as a Division of the Welsh Office drawing in officers with skills of particular relevance to the management of the estate in care. These included the externally recruited director, Mr John Carr, now Chief Executive of the Agency. As well as the direct functions set out below, Cadw is responsible for sponsorship of the Royal Commission on Ancient and Historical Monuments (Wales). The Commission was established by Royal Warrant in 1908 to make an inventory of all historical monuments and constructions connected with or illustrative of the life of the people of Wales.

4. As with other activities of the Welsh Office, Cadw is funded through the Welsh Office's Vote structure. Programme expenditure on grants and the costs of managing the Estate in Care are partly offset by income from admissions to sites and the sale of souvenirs, publications etc. Gross programme expenditure by Cadw (excluding costs of salaries and administrative costs) over the past five years is as follows:

1988-89	1989-90	1990-91	1991-92	1992-93 (Planned)
£6,242m	£6,410m	£7,696m	£8,961m	£10,059m

THE BUILT HERITAGE OF WALES

5. Wales is particularly well blessed with ancient remains. These include the prehistoric monuments, Roman remains, castles of Welsh princes, Anglo-Norman castles, ecclesiastical buildings and relics of the Industrial Revolution. There are some 14,700 listed buildings in Wales and nearly 2,700 scheduled ancient monuments.

CONDITION OF THE BUILT HERITAGE

6. The standard of care for the most important components of Wales' built heritage is thought to be generally high. The estate in the care of the Secretary of State for Wales, properties in the ownership of organisations such as the National Trust, most Church buildings and key properties in private or local authority ownership have benefited from programmes of conservation or restoration. This is important because unlike many expressions of society's artistic past, historic architecture requires regular and painstaking repair and maintenance if it is to survive. Climate, vandalism and, on occasions, ignorance take

a toll. The place of simple, vernacular buildings has come to be more widely appreciated, and appropriate stewardship for these is becoming increasingly important as unspoiled examples become rarer. The value of Wales' historic townscapes has also become more widely appreciated and greater care is evident in a higher proportion than before. Ancient monuments in Wales have avoided many of the development pressures which similar monuments in other parts of the United Kingdom have faced. The majority of scheduled remains have fared well and the growing readiness of private owners and local authorities to support such monuments is improving this position.

HISTORIC BUILDINGS

7. Under section 1 of the Planning (Listed Buildings and Conservation Areas) Act 1990 the Secretary of State is required to compile a list of buildings that appear to him to be of special architectural or historical interest. The purpose of listing is to provide guidance to local planning authorities and to ensure that special consideration is given before a listed structure is altered or destroyed. The Department's published policy guidance (Welsh Office Circular 61/81: Historic Buildings and Conservation Areas—Policy and Procedure) guides that process.

8. The first survey of historic buildings in Wales was carried out in the 1950s and early 1960s. As a result statutory lists were provided for all local authority areas. Assessments were made drawing on criteria established by an expert committee of architects, antiquaries and historians. These are still followed though they are revised from time to time.

9. All buildings built before 1700 which survive in anything like their original condition qualify for listing, as do most buildings of the period 1700 to 1840. Between 1840 and 1914 only buildings of definite quality and character qualify and the selection is designed to include the principal works of the principal architects. Selected buildings after 1914 may also be listed. In choosing buildings, particular attention is paid to:

Special value within certain types, either for architectural or planning reasons or as illustrating social and economic history (for instance, industrial buildings, railway stations, schools, hospitals, theatres, town halls, markets, exchanges, alms houses, prisons, lockups, mills).

Technological innovation or virtuosity (for instance cast iron, pre-fabrication, or the early use of concrete).

Association with well-known characters or events.

Group value, especially as examples of town planning (for instance squares, terraces or model villages).

Wales has some 14,700 listed structures; the figure increases each week. Structures are listed by the following 3 grades:

Grade I: buildings of exceptional interest (less than 5 per cent of the buildings so far are in this grade);

Grade II*: particularly important buildings of other special interest, including buildings with internal detail;

Grade II: buildings of special interest which warrant every effort being made to preserve them.

10. Assessments of structures for listing are made by Cadw's Inspectorate of Historic Buildings. Inspectors are usually architectural historians. Two of the Inspectorate's staff are devoted to resurvey work. They are assisted by 2 contract staff with a further contract inspector due to join the team shortly. The Inspectorate also includes an Inspector of historic industrial buildings—to date Cadw is the only UK heritage body to employ one. This officer is undertaking thematic surveys such as that of the coal estate and miners' institutes. Applying the prevailing criteria 30 resurveys were undertaken prior to the establishment of Cadw. Twenty-five were completed by Cadw before it was established as an Executive Agency. Seven resurveys were published in the Agency's first year (against a target of 12), though preparatory work was completed on 4 others. For 1992–93, with a target of 12, 8 commmunities have been resurveyed and work on a further 13 is under way.

11. Before resurveying a community, the Inspectorate consults the local authorities and interested local groups such as amenity societies. Every structure in the chosen area is examined and, where appropriate, further research undertaken to establish which structures may be listable. Draft list entries drawing attention to features of interest are prepared. Once the resurvey has been completed Cadw consults a number of bodies, principally the local planning authority, on the draft list. Following resolution of any points raised during the consultation period, the list is signed and published, with a copy going to the constituency MP. Owners/occupiers are notified direct by Cadw when the list is signed, but formal notification is undertaken by the local planning authority, who receive an advance copy.

12. In addition to those working on the resurvey, another Inspector is devoted to ad hoc listing. The Agency is vigilant where buildings may be under threat and through ad hoc listing a structure can be urgently considered and listed if appropriate. In 1992–93, Cadw has a target of resolving 75 per cent of ad hoc listing requests within 120 days. In this Cadw works very closely with the local planning authorities, who have powers to provide temporary protection for unlisted structures which they believe merit it by issuing Building Preservation Notices under section 3 of the Planning (Listed Buildings and Conservation Areas) Act 1990. A

building protected by a Building Preservation Notice is treated as if it were listed. A Notice is effective for 6 months and in that period the Secretary of State must assess the structure for listing. In 1991–92, 31 Building Preservation Notices were issued of which Cadw confirmed the listing of 25 structures.

LISTED BUILDING CONTROL

13. Section 8 of the Planning (Listed Buildings and Conservation Areas) Act requires anyone who plans to alter the character or appearance of a listed building first to seek listed building consent from the local planning authority. The application (which may be made without charge) and the authority's consideration of it is tested against policy guidance issued in Welsh Office Circular 61/81. This says that attention should be given to the quality of the proposals, which wherever possible should avoid damage to historic structures. New features should be planned sympathetically. More generally, it is important that the effect of development close to listed buildings should be carefully considered and authorities are expected to take this into account. Buildings in use for worship have been exempt for listed building controls. The Government has recently announced new arrangements whereby the exemption may be limited in some cases.

14. In the case of demolition, by Direction local planning authorities must seek the views of 6 amenity groups: the Ancient Monuments Society; the Council for British Archaeology; the Georgian Group; the Society for the Protection of Ancient Buildings; the Victorian Society; and the Royal Commission on Ancient and Historical Monuments in Wales. In most cases, where a local planning authority is minded to grant consent it must refer the case to Cadw to consider if there are issues which require further consideration. If so, a case would be called in for determination. For 1992–93, the Agency's published target is to process 75 per cent of applications referred within 28 days. Applications relating to interior work to Grade II buildings (which have not been granted aided) are determined by local planning authorities without reference to Cadw.

15. All applications are considered by Cadw's professional architectural staff, who test the proposals against the guidance in Welsh Office Circular 61/81. Frequently, advice will be given to the planning authority on changes which will reduce possible impact on the listed structure. Where possible such advice is provided before an application is made. Where an application is thought to warrant further consideration, Cadw advises the Department accordingly and the process of call-in and subsequent determination is handled by the Department's Planning Division. In the event that an application is called in Cadw's professional assessment is made available to the parties concerned and, where requested, Cadw's Conservation Architect attends any public inquiry to present a professional assessment of a case.

16. The table below shows the number of applications for listed building consent received from private applicants since 1985–86 and the numbers called in for further consideration:

	Total LBC Applications Received	*Number Called In*
1985-86	376	13
1986-87	443	8
1987-88	468	19
1988-89	466	10
1989-90	542	24
1990-91	521	10
1991-92	595	5

17. All applications by local authorities for listed building and conservation area consents relating to structures in their own areas are evaluated by Cadw prior to determination by the Department. The following table shows the number of such applications received since 1985-86:

	Total LA Listed Building Consent Applications	*Total LA Conservation Area Consent Applications*
1985-86	18	16
1986-87	24	3
1987-88	31	11
1988-89	19	10
1989-90	42	11
1990-91	42	13
1991-92	36	16

CONSERVATION AREAS

18. There are currently 399 Conservation Areas in Wales. The designation of a conservation area is a planning function carried out by local planning authorities. Section 69 of the Planning (Listed Buildings and Conservation Areas) Act 1990 provides that each local authority shall, from time to time, determine which parts of its district are areas of special architectural or historic interest, the character or appearance of which it is desirable to preserve or enhance. These may be large (town centres) or small (squares, terraces and smaller

groups of buildings). Conservation areas are often centred on listed buildings but it is the character of an *area* rather than individual buildings which the legislation seeks to enhance.

19. The designation of a conservation area places a duty on the local authority when considering planning issues affecting that area to give special attention to the desirability of preserving or enhancing its character or appearance. Designation also provides control over the demolition of buildings (under section 74 of the Act, the local planning authority must give consent before buildings in conservation areas can be demolished). The thrust of this is to ensure that an area remains alive and prosperous and ensures that new development accords existing special architectural and visual qualities. Local planning authorities are advised to establish conservation area advisory committees (comprising a cross-section of local opinion) to consider applications for external works which would affect the character or appearance of the area.

REGISTER OF LANDSCAPES, PARKS AND GARDENS OF SPECIAL HISTORIC INTEREST IN WALES

20. In 1989 Cadw and ICOMOS (International Council of Monuments and Sites) agreed to fund jointly the preparation of a Register of Landscapes, Parks and Gardens of Special Historic Interest in Wales. Work began in May 1990 and the first register (for Gwent) is being prepared for publication. It is expected that it will take until 1996 to complete the Register, which is being prepared county by county. The Register is advisory only, and has no statutory status. The aim is to provide detailed information on historic parks, gardens and, to a lesser extent, landscapes, to aid their protection and conservation. It is hoped that this information will help owners, local planning authorities, developers, statutory bodies, and all who are concerned with the protection of this part of our national heritage, to make informed decisions about sites on the Register.

GRANT AID

21. Under section 4 of the Historic Buildings and Ancient Monuments Act 1953 the Secretary of State may grant aid the repair of buildings which he judges to be of outstanding architectural or historic interest. This involves an area of subjective judgement and here the Agency is guided by the Secretary of State's independent statutory advisers, the Historic Buildings Council for Wales. The Act requires that the Council is consulted before a grant is made.

22. Under section 77 of the Planning (Listed Buildings and Conservation Areas) Act 1990 the Secretary of State is empowered to assist owners with grants to undertake significant external repairs. Grant-aided works must make a significant contribution towards the preservation or enhancement of the conservation area within which the building is located. Under section 79 of the 1990 Act the Secretary of State and one or more local authorities may make grants towards buildings designated for Town Scheme purposes within a conservation area. The aim of the scheme is to improve the appearance of the historic townscape. These grants are therefore also available to help owners with external repairs, and there has been welcome growth in the numbers of Town Schemes from 6 in 1985-86 to 28 currently. This is an important area of co-operation with local authorities. The Historic Buildings Council advises on buildings to be assisted with conservation area grants and also on the establishment of Town Schemes.

23. All grant applications are evaluated by Cadw's professional architectural staff, who take advice from other professionals as appropriate; a site visit is undertaken and a report offered to the Council. The question of need for support is an important consideration and, although there are no formal means testing procedures, Cadw has introduced financial appraisals for the evaluation of commercial applications, especially in cases of large grant requirement. The Council's advice is considered by Ministers and offers are made subject to standard and any special conditions which might be thought appropriate. Conditions extend, for example, from professional supervision of work and contracts to the use of particular material. This last point is of particular importance in ensuring that works are carried out to an appropriate standard and that structures gain a real benefit and appropriate materials (such as slate) are used. Major benficiaries of grant aid include the National Trust and the Church Estate, both bodies controlling very rich examples of Wales' built heritage. In addition, private owners of some of Wales' properties are assisted. Provision for this activity has grown steadily in recent years from £2.2m in 1988-89 to £3.9m in 1992-93. In 1991-92, 309 applications were considered and 154 offers of grant made. Expenditure on Town Schemes is shared with local authorities and has grown from some £50,000 in 1985-86 to nearly £370,606 in 1991-92.

24. Grant assistance from Cadw can mesh with grant from elsewhere in the Department. For example, where a redevelopment project is taking place in an area which includes a listed building then Cadw grant can stand alongside financial assistance by means of, say, an Urban Investment Grant. The fact that Cadw is prepared to grant aid particular works within a redevelopment scheme can help to encourage other funding bodies by persuading them to join in support for the built heritage. The Agency has published targets for 1992-93 for giving decisions on historic buildings grant applications—to resolve 80 per cent of grant applications within 18 weeks and to pay 90 per cent of certified claims for payment within 6 weeks.

ANCIENT MONUMENTS OUTSIDE STATE CARE

25. Archaeological remains are irreplaceable. They are evidence of the past development of Wales' civilisation. They vary—in their type, condition and our understanding of them—from upstanding remains to ancient settlements.Some are visible only from the air. Arrangements to ensure that this national resource is effectively managed involve identification, development control and financial assistance.

IDENTIFICATION

26. Sites and monuments records for Wales currently contain around 60,000 entries varying from place names to major archaeological sites. Of these, nearly 2,700 nationally-important monuments enjoy special protection as scheduled ancient monuments under the provisions of the Ancient Monuments and Archaeological Areas Act 1979. These range from palaeolithic caves representing the earliest evidence of man's occupation of Wales to industrial sites of the Twentieth Century. Under section 1 of the 1979 Act the Secretary of State is required to compile and maintain a schedule of monuments which appear to him to be of national importance. Recommendations to add to or modify the schedule are provided by Cadw's Inspectorate of Ancient Monuments, drawing on the Secretary of State's published criteria for the identification of sites of national importance. Where such sites are identified, Cadw routinely consults owners and the planning authority before statutory protection is put in place. Schedules are maintained by Cadw on a county basis. They are published periodically, being made available to local authorities, utility companies, archaeological organisations and other interested parties.

27. A key target for the Agency is to deal with 60 scheduling actions during 1992-93 (new schedulings, revisions and descheduling). The selection of sites is guided both by ad hoc requests and by work within Cadw's systematic scheduling enhancement programme under which to date 3 groups of monuments have been examined (palaeolithic caves, medieval castles and moated sites).The programme involves drawing up specific guidelines based on the national criteria for each monument type. The first 3 exercises have concentrated on monuments where up-to-date records are available. The same is true with regional exercises currently under way to examine Offa's and Wat's Dykes, enclosures identified from the air in Dyfed, hut groups in Gwynedd and the lead mines of Mid Wales. The next all-Wales scheduling enhancement exercise will look at Roman military sites.

28. In taking this activity forward Cadw works closely with the Royal Commission on Ancient and Historical Monuments in Wales, which is the national body of survey and record. The Commission's aim is to compile and make available a comprehensive archive and national database of ancient monuments and historic buildings in Wales (the National Monuments Record) for use by individuals and bodies concerned with understanding, conserving and managing the built heritage.

29. The Commission also undertakes detailed surveys of ancient monuments and historic buildings. Currently it is working on the final stages of a survey of the castles of Glamorgan and is surveying the vernacular buildings of Radnor District. The Commission is about to embark on a survey of later religious buildings in Wales and is working, with others, on a survey of archaeological areas in the uplands of Wales, known as the Uplands Initiative. The Commission also undertakes a programme of aerial photography and funds the maintenance and enhancement of the regional sites and monuments records (SMR) held by the four Welsh Archaeological Trusts. The SMR is a database of all known sites which is an invaluable resource to historians, archaeologists, prospective developers and most important as a planning tool for District Councils in their development control role. The Commission is developing a programme in which the local SMRs, the National Monuments Record and Cadw's Scheduled Ancient Monuments records will all form part of an integrated national database of archaeological sites and historic buildings for Wales.

MONITORING

30. Monitoring of the condition of scheduled ancient monuments is an important task for the Agency and using its Field Monument Wardens, periodic assessments are made on an all-Wales basis. The latest of these, conducted in 1991, showed that the condition of the great majority of monuments remained high.

STATUTORY PROTECTION

31. Scheduling brings with it a presumption against development. However, some developments, such as programmes of conservation work, are desirable and the provision of necessary modern facilities may justify the loss of some remains. In such circumstances, a developer must seek consent from the Secretary of State for Wales—scheduled monument consent (SMC). In 1991-92 there were 89 applications for SMC. Applications are evaluated by Cadw's archaeological and architectural staff and views are sought from bodies such as the Royal Commission, Council for British Archaeology, local authorities and the regional Archaeological Trust. The Agency's target for 1992-93 is to process 75 per cent of SMC applications within 90 days. Preliminary figures show the Agency's performance is on target. Once an evaluation of an application has been made an interim decision is given enabling the applicant to submit further written representations

or to request a hearing by an independent Inspector. In 1991–92 three such hearings were held and in each case the proposed decision not to grant scheduled monument consent was upheld.

32. Local authorities also have a very important role to play in the protection of monuments through the planning system. While scheduled ancient monuments enjoy a very specific level of protection the needs of other archaeological remains and monuments are also of considerable significance, especially locally. In this last respect the Secretary of State recently issued policy guidance, Planning Policy Guidance Note 16: Archaeology and Planning, to inform local planning authorities in the conduct of this work. This explains the significance of archaeology for development planning and offers detailed advice on how archaeological issues should be addressed in the planning process. Points emphasised include early consultation with developers, the value of field evaluations, consultations with informed sources, preservation by record and planning conditions.

33. As part of the planning process local planning authorities and utility companies consult Cadw on applications which have a potential impact on scheduled ancient monuments. In 1991–92 there were 331 such referrals. This consultation allows Cadw to draw attention to any particular matter which the Agency feels should be considered. It also enables the Agency to consider if any proposals raise issues which make it desirable for a planning application to be called in for the Secretary of State's own determination.

FINANCIAL SUPPORT

34. Section 24 of the 1979 Act empowers the Secretary of State to assist owners financially with the preservation, maintenance and management of ancient monuments. In recent years there has been growing interest in the grants available and, in 1991–92, 24 schemes were assisted at a cost of £146,000. Applications are evaluated by Cadw's archaeological and conservation architectural staff. In general the Agency offers a grant of 50 per cent of the cost, this being the level at which it is judged owners are able to make a matching contribution on an investment which is unlikely to see any economic return for them. In circumstances of financial need or in respect of a monument of exceptional significance this grant rate can be exceeded.

35. It has recently been decided to grant aid archaeological work at churches receiving financial support for repair work on the recommendation of the Historic Buildings Council for Wales. This followed concern from archaeological interests, in particular the Ancient Monuments Board for Wales, that work to ecclesiastical buildings could impact upon important archaeological remains. Cadw now funds the regional Archaeological Trust to carry out an archaeological investigation before work to the church begins.

36. Under the provisions of section 17 of the 1979 Act the Secretary of State (or local authorities) may enter into a management agreement with an owner or occupier of an ancient monument. Such an agreement may be used to encourage the beneficial management of field monuments on agricultural land (eg barrows or deserted settlement sites). They may run for an agreed number of years, sometimes following a lump-sum payment to cover capital costs (eg fencing) with periodic payments to compensate an owner for additional costs incurred in maintaining a positive management regime (eg weed control and restrictions of grazing). There are currently 76 such agreements in place at an average annual cost in total of some £30,000.

GUARDIANSHIP

37. Section 12 of the 1979 Act empowers the Secretary of State to bring any ancient monument in Wales into his guardianship. Under these arrangements ownership of the monument is not affected but full responsibility for the management and maintenance of a monument is assumed by Cadw. A monument to be brought into guardianship should be of special archaeological, architectural or historic interest. Guardianship agreements are normally offered only in circumstances where it is considered that a site is in danger of being lost or is of such exceptional interest that it should be made available to a wider public to enjoy. Most recently Plas Mawr in Conwy has been brought into the Estate in Care via a guardianship agreement. Other monuments where guardianship agreements are close to completion are Dinefwr Castle, Llandeilo and Wiston Castle near Haverfordwest.

38. Cadw also exercises the power available to the Secretary of State under section 5 of the 1979 Act in respect of urgent preservation works to monuments outside the Estate in Care. This reserve power was used most recently in the case of St. Quintin's Castle, Llanblethian, a monument in private ownership which was in need of urgent attention.

ARCHAEOLOGICAL TRUSTS

39. Modern pressures on archaeological sites and the need to respond in a systematic way led, in the mid 1970s, to the establishment of four independent trusts providing archaeological expertise for the whole of Wales. The Trusts are limited liability companies with charitable status and receive core and project funding from Cadw. In 1991–92 the funds allocated to the four Trusts were:

(a) Glamorgan-Gwent	...	...	...	...	£256,289
(b) Dyfed	...	...	...	...	...	£205,642
(c) Clwyd-Powys	...	...	...	...	...	£177,118
(d) Gwynedd ...	...	...	...	...	...	£196,022

40. The role of the Trusts has extended beyond their initial task of undertaking rescue excavations and supervision of development work associated with archaeological remains. The establishment of regional sites and monuments records (SMRs) became an early priority and, amongst other functions, they now fulfil an important role in development control particularly with regard to the implementation of PPG16. Recently, Cadw has been using the Trusts to undertake assessment of the longer-term threats arising out of development. These can be used to inform the planning process and thereby help to avert threat.

41. The Trusts are also funded by the Highways Directorate of the Welsh Office (with Cadw providing archaeological advice) to undertake archaeological work associated with the Welsh Office's Trunk Road programme. They also receive funding from developers, local authorities etc and continue to provide a broadly-based archaeological service within their areas covering a wide range of activities including educational work.

42. As the Trust is often the only local source of archaeological advice available, it can sometimes become involved in advising the local authority and also in acting for the developer. To ensure that any potential conflicts of interest are avoided Cadw, with the help of the Trusts, has drawn up a Code of Practice to guide the Trusts' work in this area.

43. There can be circumstances where archaeological remains must be excavated. These have included the discovery of important, hitherto unknown remains. In such circumstances Cadw has, via the Welsh Archaeological Trusts, maintained a positive programme for such "rescue" archaeology. This funding also represents support for the key task of ensuring that the excavations are well documented and reports of the work published. Cadw funds three University-based scientific contracts covering the fields of the conservation of archaeological finds, environmental analysis and radiocarbon dating to support this post-excavation work.

UNDERWATER ARCHAEOLOGY

44. In April 1991 responsibility for the designation of historic wreck sites and the control of diving activity on these sites under the Protection of Wrecks Act 1973 was transferred from the Department of Transport to the Welsh Office and is administered by Cadw. There are four designated wreck sites in Welsh waters. Soon after the transfer of this work to Cadw a site off the Smalls, Pembrokeshire, was designated following the discovery of a Hiberno-Norse sword hilt, and it is now statutorily protected. In considering sites for statutory protection and the subsequent licensing of diving activity Cadw is advised by the Advisory Committee on Historic Wreck Sites. As part of Cadw's increasing involvement in this area the 9th Welsh Archaeological Conference held on 4 December had underwater archaeology as its theme. This is a new area of work for the Agency, which will be developed in collaboration with the Royal Commission on Ancient and Historical Monuments for Wales.

SUPPORT FOR THE VOLUNTARY SECTOR

45. The voluntary sector makes an important contribution to the welfare of and interest in the built heritage. Cadw maintains links with voluntary bodies in this field and provides financial support for a number of them:-

(a) Architectural Heritage Fund

The Architectural Heritage Fund, an independent charity set up in 1976, provides soft loans to building preservation trusts, and other organisations meeting its criteria, to enable them to carry out repairs to historic buildings. The Fund also encourages the establishment of new building preservation trusts. There are currently seven projects in Wales, to which the AHF has committed £450,000. Ministers have agreed a Welsh Office grant to the Fund in 1992–93 of £60,000.

(b) Civic Trust for Wales (CTW)

The CTW was founded in 1964 to promote quality, beauty and design standards in the environment of Welsh cities and towns. The Trust is a non-endowed charity which supports a growing network of local amenity societies throughout Wales. It acts as a focus for concern on urban environmental issues and gives advice on practical projects. Since 1988-89 an annual grant has been provided by the Department to enable the Trust to employ a Director and administrative staff in order to develop a strategy for its long-term future and to support Civic Societies in Wales. The grant for 1992-93 is £34,500. In April 1990 Cadw launched the Civic Initiatives (Heritage) Grant Scheme to provide grant aid to civic societies and other local voluntary organisations for projects which preserve, enhance or improve the physical environment and increase social awareness of the built heritage in Wales. Cadw has received 32 applications, of which 19 have been approved with grant totalling £19,715. Examples of projects assisted are photographic exhibitions, the erection of plaques and the annual Llandeilo in Bloom event.

(c) National Amenity Societies

Welsh Office Circular 61/81 directs local planning authorities to notify national amenity bodies of all applications for consent to demolish listed buildings. The societies are the Victorian Society, Georgian Group, Society for the Protection of Ancient Buildings, Ancient Monuments Society and Council for British Archaeology. Any representations which these bodies make must be taken into account by local authorities when applications for demolition are being considered. The bodies therefore have an important role to play and their work will grow as Cadw's listing resurvey programme progresses. In recognition of their work, Cadw provides an annual grant towards the costs of societies' contributions to decision-making in this area. For 1991-92 the grant to each of four of the societies was £1,100 (a 10 per cent increase on 1990-91). The Council for British Archaeology receives a slightly higher grant (£1,375 in 1991-92) because of the additional casework it undertakes in respect of ancient monuments.

ANCIENT MONUMENTS IN STATE CARE

Introduction

47. There are at present 128 monuments in the care of the Secretary of State for Wales. This estate includes prehistoric field monuments, Roman remains, medieval castles and ecclesiastical buildings and relics from the more recent industrial past. The majority of this estate passed to the Secretary of State for Wales in 1969 by a transfer of functions from the Minister of Public Building and Works. These functions were carried out on the Secretary of State's behalf by the Department of Environment until 1978. The statutory bases on which elements of the estate came into State care differ from monument to monument, from the Ancient Monuments Protection Act 1886 to the Ancient Monuments and Archaeological Areas Act 1979. The terms under which they are held in care vary from ownership to leasehold interest or guardianship (a Deed of Guardianship signed by the owner and the Secretary of State places a site into State care without a change of ownership).

Conservation Maintenance

48. Annual maintenance programmes are prepared following Quinquennial Reviews undertaken by the Agency's Superintending Conservation Architect. The next review will take place in 1994. Regular inspections by Conservation Architects and Inspectors of Ancient Monuments monitor the state of the monuments and contribute to the preparation of the annual programmes. The majority of recurrent conservation maintenance within annual programmes is carried out by a Directly Employed Labour (DEL) force of about 100 craftsmen, auxiliaries and labourers. They also undertake a large part of initial conservation works and a small part of presentation maintenance. All other maintenance and all new works are put out to contract. The DEL is organised into squads and most of the staff are mobile over a local area. The squads are grouped into three Regional Management Units (RMU) with professional and technical staff responsible for DEL and contract works. Contract works are the subject of competitive tender procedures. The progress of conservation maintenance is monitored through one of the Agency's key performance targets which, for 1992–93, is to complete 90 per cent of the approved conservation maintenance programme. Planned expenditure on conservation maintenance in 1992–93 is £1.393 million.

Development

49. The Agency is engaged in a programme of capital development across the estate. Its purpose is to improve facilities for the public and for custodial staff. The programme ranges from the creation of new visitor reception facilities and shops to the provision of such basic facilities as car parking and toilets. In most instances detailed archaeological work is required in advance of developments to ensure that ancient remains are protected or recorded. Cadw's policy on the provision of such developments is to seek to identify and acquire an existing building adjacent to the monument (so that the evolved environment is not intruded upon) or to fit them into the existing fabric. Where these opportunities do not exist, considerable care is taken on the design and location of new facilities in order to minimise the intrusion into the curtilage and the effect on the ambience of the monument.

50. Conversions of existing structures for these purposes since 1984 include those at Chepstow Castle, Tintern Abbey, Caerleon, Castell Coch, Kidwelly Castle, St. David's Bishops Palace, St. Dogmael's Abbey, Harlech, Criccieth and Caernarfon Castles and are planned at Oxwich and Denbigh Castles and Tretower

Court, where existing buildings capable of conversion have been acquired. New buildings for visitor reception since 1984 include those for Conwy and Cilgerran Castles and Rug Chapel; another is planned for Beaumaris Castle. Joint developments with the agricultural owners have been completed at Carreg Cennen and Dolwyddelan Castles. In many instances these developments have been integrated with the introduction of comprehensive interpretation, such as exhibitions, explanatory panels, three-dimensional tableaux, audio tours (for general use and for those with special needs) audio-visual displays and reconstruction in small-scale model form. Planned expenditure on development in 1992–93 is £820,000.

MONUMENT DEVELOPMENT PLANS

51. Since early 1992–93 the Agency has brought together teams of experts from the various disciplines within Cadw to prepare Monument Development Plans for properties in care. Each Plan will be evaluated with regard for conservation requirements and development potential and capital projects will be subject to financial appraisal to meet the investment guidelines set out by HM Treasury. The first phase includes 10 of the most-visited monuments. Over a five-year period all sites—however small or remote—will be subject to similar critical appraisal. In every instance, however, it is Agency policy to provide direction signing, pedestrian access and introductory information panels as a minimum. Each plan will also consider the setting of each monument in its urban or rural context.

SITE MANAGEMENT AND PRESENTATION MAINTENANCE

52. The Agency is responsible for the proper custody of monuments and the safety and care of visitors. It has an annual programme of site maintenance (eg grass cutting, fire precautions, electrical installations, painting and repairs) to keep all monuments and related facilities etc in a state which is attractive to and safe for visitors. Planned expenditure in 1992–93 is £550,000. Of the 128 sites in State care, 20 are staffed by salaried custodians, six are supervised by key keepers and 11 are managed through agreements with private, voluntary or public sector partners. Admission charges are made currently at 33 of these sites, but some of these are open free of charge in the winter. Because of the seasonal nature of visits, the 21 full-time and eight part-time established custodians are supplemented by casual relief staff. The terms of joint management agreements vary from one site to another; broadly, they are geared to the main season and the site manager receives a proportion of admission and retail sales receipts. Key keepers are engaged to provide security and to keep less popular monuments free of litter in return for an annual fee. Most of these monuments are open free of charge. The arrangements for custody and management are currently under review.

MARKETING AND MARKET RESEARCH

53. As part of the Business Planning process, the Agency engages market research consultants under contract for surveys of visitors each year. These surveys seek to identify the core market, changes in the market place, levels of satisfaction of visitors, origin of visitors (whether resident in Wales, on holiday or day trips) and demographic and socio-economic groupings. In 1986 a survey was undertaken to establish the reasons for not visiting monuments. These surveys provide information for the development of the Agency's marketing strategy, which is subject to review each year.

54. The Agency's policy on marketing expenditure is to limit such costs to approximately 15 per cent of the forecast total revenue in any one year. Its policy on promotions is to seek to capture visitors to sites from the total attracted into Wales by the wider-ranging marketing expenditure of the Wales Tourist Board and British Tourist Authority. The means of attracting visitors—whether residents or tourists—from within the Principality are focused on the widespread distribution of attractive full-colour marketing leaflets and show-cards to Tourist Information Centres and to tourist accommodation (hotels, guest houses, holiday camps, bed and breakfast houses), other attractions and through local marketing consortia. About 1 million leaflets are distributed in this way each year by a specialist contractor. Limited press advertising is also used to support this activity.

THE MARKET PLACE

55. Analysis of the origin of visitors to manned monuments in care shows that the great majority come from outside Wales, with some 20-24 per cent from overseas. Of these, most originate in North America, closely followed by Western Europe, with Australasia also providing a significant number. The British Tourist Authority's forecasts of tourism from within the UK predict a 1.2 per cent growth per annum up to 1996 with an average 5.7 per cent growth in overseas traffic to Britain. The Agency forecasts that the main area of growth to its monuments will be in the overseas market, although it is also targeting potential visitors resident in Wales and in the English conurbations. Major improvements in the M4, A5 and A55 and local improvements to the road network in Wales provide the opportunity to capture increasing numbers of day visitors.

56. Over the past few years, the tourism market in Britain has been volatile, owing to both international conflict and economic factors. While Cadw was able in its early years to increase numbers of visitors from the

1984 baseline of 1.282 million to a peak of 1.597 million in 1988-89, there has been gradual decline as a result both of these external factors and the increase in competitor attractions, resulting in attendance of 1.289 million in 1991-92. There has also been a marked change in holiday-taking patterns among UK residents which has reduced the numbers of long-holiday visits to Wales over the past 10-15 years. Cadw considers that the recent decision to permit the Wales Tourist Board to market Wales overseas will help to increase visitor numbers to monuments in care and to enhance revenue. The Agency's key target for 1992-93 is to increase market share of the numbers of visitors to the top 20 heritage sites in Wales by 1.3 per cent to 65 per cent.

57. The educational market is considered to have increasing potential. In 1991-92 such visits rose by 5 per cent to 122,000 by the provision of specially-tailored Theatre in Education programmes throughout Wales and through direct marketing to schools. Cadw has developed that approach during 1992-93 and plans to increase direct marketing efforts in subsequent years. While schools visits are free, the Agency sees educational outreach as a service to support the National Curricula, to raise awareness of the value of built heritage protection and to increase the reservoir of future visitors committed to the ideals of conservation and preservation.

58. Planned expenditure on Presentation activities is £925,000 in 1992-93. This includes the cost of educational initiatives, marketing, exhibitions and the purchase of souvenirs for resale.

REVENUE EARNING

59. The Agency operates within a net financial regime, ie its revenues in-year are retained for expenditure on operating costs. Since 1984 receipts have increased every year from £939,000 to £2.659 million in 1991-92, despite fluctuations in numbers of visitors. Receipts fall into three main categories: admissions from charging sites, souvenir and publications sales, and net Value Added Tax. In addition, the Agency administers the Heritage in Wales membership scheme, which has about 16,000 members at present. They enjoy benefits with members of similar schemes run by Historic Scotland and English Heritage. Souvenirs are specially bought in or commissioned to reflect historical attributes of the whole estate or groups of monuments (eg Cistercian Abbeys) or a particular monument (eg Castell Coch). The award-winning Cadw guidebook programme has now included all major and most minor monuments, with temporary pamphlet guides available to explain those sites for which full guides are not available. The Agency is also developing a series of themed publications (eg on The Historic Gardens of Wales and the Civil War in Wales) in conjunction with HMSO. The sale of souvenirs and publications makes an increasing contribution to the Agency's revenue (£695,000 in 1991-92).

PRICING POLICY

60. Pricing strategies are reviewed each year. For admissions charges, the Agency places its 33 charging sites in price bands which reflect (a) what it perceives the market will bear in relation to competitor attractions; (b) the level of development, interpretation and experience provided for the visitor; (c) the level of provision of general visitor facilities. Souvenirs and publications are priced according to usual retail practice with an eye on the norms for shops at other leisure attractions. Annually-conducted market research tests the public's perception of the value visitors have received from their expenditure on visits to monuments managed by Cadw. The key commercial target is to increase average spend per visitor from 163 pence in 1991–92 to 175 pence in 1992–93.

THE WAY FORWARD

61. Cadw's primary responsibility in relation to Properties in Care is to meet the Secretary of State's obligations to the statutory protection, maintenance and management of the estate in care. Conservation is the dominant theme and will continue to be afforded resources to enable future generations to take on monuments in good states of preservation. Within its present financial regime, the Agency is required to generate income in order to reduce the net cost to the Exchequer of conservation and the presentation of the estate. As the monuments in care represent one of the best-known images to encourage visitors to Wales, the Agency's forward strategy is to continue to promote them as cost-effectively as it can.

OUTLOOK

62. Over coming years, Cadw plans to proceed as quickly as possible with the listing resurvey and scheduling enhancement programmes. The need to work closely with other bodies and individuals, to support their efforts both financially and with advice, will continue to command maximum effort. The estate in care will continue to receive both careful conservation and appropriate development to improve visitors' enjoyment and understanding. Building on the publication of the Heritage Charter in spring 1993, Cadw will endeavour to provide improved service to the public and to maximise value for money for the taxpayer.

December 1992

Examination of Witnesses

MR J CARR, Chief Executive, MR R HUGHES, Director, Policy and Administration, and MR R AVENT, Principal Inspector of Ancient Monuments and Historic Buildings, Cadw: Welsh Historic Monuments Executive Agency, were examined.

Chairman

1. Mr Carr, gentlemen, may I, on behalf of the Committee, welcome you here this morning. We would be grateful, Mr Carr, if you would introduce your colleagues.

(*Mr Carr*) Thank you, Mr Chairman. I have with me Mr Richard Hughes, Director of Policy and Administration for Cadw and Mr Richard Avent, Principal Inspector of Ancient Monuments and Historic Buildings.

2. Let us look first of all, Mr Carr, at the arrangements for the monuments in the care of the Secretary of State. We understand from the evidence we have that there are currently some 128 such monuments in Wales. In terms of the situation of the estate, as it were, would you agree that the portfolio of properties you have has resulted in a large proportion of sites restricted to a small number of categories, such as castles?

(*Mr Carr*) The range of monuments, Mr Chairman, is from castles to Roman, industrial, ecclesiastical and, obviously, pre-historic sites. There are 58 castles, houses and town walls, 31 pre-historic monuments, 5 industrial, 9 Roman and 24 ecclesiastical. I think, in representation, they cover the very best examples of the remains in Wales.

3. In terms of the distinction between what is an ancient monument and what is an historic building, you include examples of ancient monuments such as Strata Florida Abbey, and the nineteenth century iron furnaces at Blaenavon, both in fact as ancient monuments. Where do you draw the line between ancient monuments and historic buildings?

(*Mr Carr*) The very simple criterion for an historic building, Mr Chairman, is whether the building has an ongoing, viable use; an ancient monument is one that is unlikely to be able to produce a viable use or dwelling. Most of the ancient monuments are, of course, roofless and are no longer capable of the original use or, in the case of industrial monuments, the original industrial use.

4. Therefore the consideration by some people of this building as an ancient monument is misplaced!

(*Mr Carr*) This is a listed building. I would imagine, Mr Chairman, it is Grade I!

5. I am glad to hear that! In terms of the criteria for selecting, accepting or rejecting new monuments for this group under the care of the Secretary of State, what criterion do you use to determine whether a building should be included under the guardianship of the Secretary of State?

(*Mr Carr*) The principal criteria, Mr Chairman, are its special architectural, archaeological and/or historic interest, or the need to conserve a particular class of monument. If it is outstanding in its own particular class, then of course we are advised by the Secretary of State's statutory advisers, the Ancient Monuments Board for Wales, who offer their view to the Secretary of State; we are consulted by Ministers and reach conclusions thereafter.

6. Is the commercial potential of the monument a major factor, or do you aim to acquire a representative portfolio?

(*Mr Carr*) The subsequent commercial viability is not a factor. As to the representative value, while we do have a very broad representation, if there were a category where we felt we were under-represented and the monument was of exceptional value, then that would also be considered for guardianship.

7. Why can it take so long for new monuments to be opened to the public? For instance, Laugharne Castle has been in your care for more than ten years and negotiations for Dinefwr Castle have taken more than ten years?

(*Mr Carr*) May I take the example of Laugharne first, Mr Chairman? I am not sure whether the Committee is familiar with its appearance ten or fifteen years ago. I was not, but Mr Avent was, and has been involved for the past ten to fifteen years. This monument was severely covered with spoil, silt, overgrowth and so forth and required several summer seasons of excavation to uncover the original remains. Indeed, what was visible when it was first taken into care has been enhanced by those excavations, since we have discovered the Tudor levels, the original Norman levels and, I understand from Mr Avent's report, the vestiges of a ringwork castle at one point. Therefore, what we have discovered in the process of the excavation is the various stages of occupation right through to when it was a romantic ruin in the 18th and 19th century.

8. What about Dinefwr Castle?

(*Mr Carr*) This is very important. As you are aware, we have not yet taken it into care, but have been conserving it for a number of years. The guardianship agreement has not yet been concluded, as the access arrangements had not been resolved until very recently. We are now in the process of determining the guardianship area and completing the guardianship deed with the owners of that castle, Dyfed Wildlife Trust. Meanwhile, the monument has received conservation attention over the past ten or fifteen years and we have prevented further despoliation of the castle.

9. Is it open to the public yet?

(*Mr Carr*) It is open to the public by arrangement. The Dyfed Wildlife Trust do arrange tours in conjunction with us, since we are concerned about the safety considerations.

10. In terms of the justification of the expenditure of state money on the maintenance of care, presumably one of the justifications is the symbolic value of the monuments to their society and culture. Could it not be said that many of Cadw's monuments in care, as portrayed in publicity, concentrate on the way the Welsh, as a nation, were put under the heel of the English and, therefore, certainly do not add to the feeling of Welsh nationhood? How do you actually justify spending state money in that way?

[**Chairman** *Cont*]

(*Mr Carr*) All the built heritage of Wales is a reflection of the history and culture of Wales, whether it is a burial chamber dating back 6,000 years or whether it is the campaign of Edward I or the campaigns of the Welsh princes. We do have in care what we describe as Welsh castles—they were initiated by the Welsh princes—and I could enumerate them if you wish, but in terms of promotion of these castles, I do not think that you would find Criccieth, for example, had any less promotion than the castles of Edward I or those of the Norman barons along the Landsker in the South.

11. Does it not remain a problem, however, when you have to decide what to add to your portfolio? Do you think you now have an imbalance in that portfolio and that possibly some of these castles are of symbolic importance to the English, in terms of what they did—a kind of imbalanced slur on what happened in history? It is selective, is it not, since one of your roles is to decide what to keep and what not to keep. Would it be a problem for you to keep rather less of these symbols and rather more of the ones which are indigenous?

(*Mr Carr*) I think you will find, Mr Chairman, that we already have in care the majority of the important Welsh stone castles. There are others, of course, which are in the care of local authorities or national parks. For example, Castell Dinas Bran above Llangollen is in the care of Clwyd and we are extensively grant-aiding the conservation work there. Carew Castle, near Pembroke, is also in the care of the National Park Authority for Pembrokeshire and we extensively grant-aid it. Pembroke Castle is in private ownership, a trust. Aberystwyth—forgive me, that is another Edward I castle—is in the care of Ceredigion Council. There is no deliberate policy concerning the cultural, social, military, or historical origin of a monument. It is its intrinsic value which governs whether or not it is taken into care. Care is very much a last resort, in that we extensively encourage local authorities, who have the same powers as the state to take monuments into care, to exercise their powers in the preservation of these monuments, with perhaps the incentive of grant-aid.

12. Why do you keep so many of these piles of stone; they are just piles of stones arranged in a certain order, are they not? What real value is there to the people of Wales in preserving them? What would be the answer to this philistine point of view?

(*Mr Carr*) I note the word, Mr Chairman! My view is that these monuments are a direct, visible expression of the history and culture of Wales, and because of their very richness, they enhance the understanding of Welsh people. Indeed, for people from overseas and for the rest of Britain, they enhance the understanding of the social, military and economic conflict which this Principality has undergone over the past several centuries.

13. Let us forget those conflicts and get on with cohesiveness. We do not want to know why we were apart in the past; we want to know how to move forward. How does this help us?

(*Mr Carr*) Every society is based on some form of change. Change is frequently the result of conflict, whether it be of a militaristic or economic nature.

14. Could you not argue that you are highlighting the sores of the past and reminding people of conflicts and experiences they wish to forget? One does not wish to be reminded continually of what happened in one's own personal experience 20 or 30 years ago, if that experience was not enjoyable or satisfying?

(*Mr Carr*) I do not think so, Mr Chairman. It is a viewpoint which has been expressed to me a number of times and something I find difficult to accept. If one takes a specific example of the castles of Edward I, which are now crumbling ruins—at least, they have been conserved and consolidated in their state of decay—I would venture to suggest that the culture of Wales, the language and spirit has survived and developed intact and these are inevitably in the landscape. I think they should be accepted as being part of the background to the Principality's history. On the basis of accepting them, we are then in the position to make progress towards the requirements of the 20th and 21st centuries. I do not think it is possible to deny the past.

Mr Llwyd

15. Following the Chairman's questions, may I just add one small point. There is a public perception that Cadw concentrates upon the more dramatic examples, such as Edwardian castles, to the detriment of places such as Dolwyddelan, in my constituency. You said it figured in publicity, but I have to tell you that few people who visit North Wales know about Dolwyddelan; they know all about Caernarfon, however?

(*Mr Carr*) Caernarfon did enjoy international publicity at the time of the investiture; it was seen by millions of television viewers throughout the world. Dolwyddelan appears prominently in our promotional literature for North Wales and this is available to visitors, to tourist information centres, bed and breakfast establishments, hotels, etc. It is my belief that, within the limits of economic prudence, all monuments in care—without exception—are given the same level of basic promotion.

16. Do you believe enough is being made of our early celtic churches, burial sites, etc—there are numerous in North Wales, hidden here and there—to reflect that part of our history?

(*Mr Carr*) There is a difficulty with some of these sites in that even though they are built of stone, they are delicate. That is not to say that we under-promote them; we make them available to people. However, I think there is a perception that people may have a greater interest in the military and domestic past, rather than in the Christian past. We promote these monuments even-handedly and we leave the choice to the public.

17. You mentioned earlier that commercial viability does not figure in your decision to take care of a site, but is it correct to say that very few of your sites are commercially viable in the true sense?

(*Mr Carr*) That is true.

18. In your document, you refer in several places—for instance, in paragraph 57—to "the market" and, rather unusually, you apply the word "market" to education as well, so clearly you are speaking the current language. There is reference to an educational market, increased direct marketing

[Mr Llwyd Cont]

efforts, etc. Do you think there is some kind of conflict between conservation and commerce in the management of an estate in care?

(Mr Carr) There is scope for conflict, but we do our utmost to avoid it, which is why we take the advice of the Ancient Monuments Board for Wales on all monument activities.

19. Have you, as a body, contemplated the disposal of some of the less profitable monuments, perhaps offering them to local management in the manner proposed by English Heritage, for example?

(Mr Carr) No, we have not. We do not consider the profitability. We are in discussion with one local authority for the removal of one site from state care into their care and, if I may, I would like to explain the circumstances. In the Rhymney Valley there is a structure called the Elliot Engine House. The fabric of the building is in the care of the Secretary of State, the machinery inside it is in the care of the local authority; so we have two cooks in the kitchen, as it were. It is our view, and the view of the local authority, that it would be best if the totality of the building was in one pair of hands. Rhymney Valley have indicated that they would be willing to take the monument into care. This is a practical management issue; it has nothing to do with commercialism.

20. You referred earlier to Castell Dinas Bran above Llangollen. I presume the relationship between yourself and the local authority, vis-a-vis that site, is perfectly adequate?

(Mr Carr) We have had lengthy discussions and I think we have a very good working relationship. We are offering grant-aid for the conservation of the monument, which they are taking up.

21. I think we all accept that you are under-resourced, and I wonder whether, in the overall plan, you had considered whether one or two sites might be managed locally by, say, local authorities or trusts. Do I take it that, hitherto, this has not been discussed by you?

(Mr Carr) We have not discussed it with local authorities. It is not something we would necessarily avoid if we could be certain that the site manager, whoever that may be, could maintain the standards of presentation we require. Conservation is another issue; we would be very concerned that any body or organisation taking over one of the sites currently in state care, had the right resources and skills to maintain the monument to the level we thought necessary.

22. In your reply to the Chairman on your portfolio of sites, you said your portfolio was representative of Wales?

(Mr Carr) It is widespread.

23. Moving from the general to the specific, could you tell me whether you have made any initial plans to take over sites such as Cosmeston, near Cardiff?

(Mr Carr) No, we have not taken that into view. That is a site which, until recently, was in the ownership of the Glamorgan-Gwent Archaeological Trust; my colleague informs me it is now in local authority care.

24. What will Cadw's role be in the development of that site? Do you foresee making an approach directly, or jointly, or grant-aiding?

(Mr Carr) If we were to receive an approach for grant-aid for works which were eligible, then we would consider it carefully. It is not a site scheduled as being of national importance.

Mr Evans

25. It has been suggested to you, with great vigour, that some of the Edwardian castles in Wales are simply heaps of stone. Would you accept that the evolution of the picturesque in the 18th century is, in fact, one of the great British influences upon European aesthetics?

(Mr Carr) Yes.

26. Would you accept the importance of Welsh people involved in that was particularly significant?

(Mr Carr) Yes.

27. How would you assess, for example, the importance of, say, some of the Edwardian castles of Wales to the Picturesque Movement and, for example, how that is reflected in paintings by Wilson and Turner?

(Mr Carr) I regret that is not a field in which I am expert.

Mr Luff

28. I suspect that our Chairman's flirtation with philistinism earlier in this session owed more to a devil's advocacy, rather than a sincerely held belief— at least I trust so! I have to confess to a certain historical illiteracy, so when I arrive at an historic site, interpretation matters to me a great deal. I wonder if you could outline your philosophy of interpretation, particularly in the light of comments we have heard from organisations such as the Victorian Society, that your guidebooks are showing a trend more towards popularism than academic information?

(Mr Carr) The balance on interpretation is not an easy one to strike. Back in the 1930s and up to the middle 1980s, the concentration on explanation of sites was on the architecture or the archaeology; the involvement of people was not given great coverage. It is our philosophy, in interpreting these monuments, to ensure that the involvement of people is given due prominence because, quite clearly, the monuments were built by people for the use of people, and for their own sense of progress. A charge of popularism is one I could not accept. Our guidebooks, for example—and I think these may be to what you are referring—have won Society for the Interpretation of British Heritage awards, as being exemplars of how to marry the historical, architectural and archaeological with the involvement and impact of people. I do not know what the Victorian Society's particular viewpoint is on this, but I believe that what we must do is engage the interest of people in an understanding of their past. Part of that is an understanding of the structures built by their forebears. We also engage the attention of the Ancient Monuments Board for Wales in assessing the presentation of those volumes and whereas, initially, as their Annual Reports for 1985, 1986 and so on suggest, they were concerned that there would be over-popularisation, they have been kind enough to say that the guide books are exceptionally good. I take great pride in that.

14 MINUTES OF EVIDENCE TAKEN BEFORE

[Mr Luff Cont]

29. How do you decide at whom guide books should be aimed? For example, when you visit many National Trust properties in England, both a child's and adult's guide is available. When you gave evidence before us last, you said specifically you do not produce guides for children. Have you any thought of reviewing that policy?

(Mr Carr) What I also said last time was that the way we approach the children's interest is through our education initiative, where we are developing, and have already developed, education literature for classrooms and, what is most vivid to children, theatre in education, where they can actually translate what they see in these crumbling piles—if I may use the Chairman's analogy - into their own experience. The guide books themselves, I think, are accessible quite readily to children over the age of ten. My ten-year-old daughter, for example, flips through them and finds elements of them absolutely fascinating, and she is not a committed conservationist!

30. I am sure she will be soon! May I move on to your relationship with other bodies, and your view of the balance of the portfolio between Cadw's role and the other agencies, organisations and individuals that effectively preserve monuments in Wales. It is quite clear that Cadw gives a great deal of useful advice to those other organisations and bodies and, of course, provides them with grant-aid in their role, but does Cadw have any feeling for what the structure or balance of care should be between local authorities, National Trust, private individuals and Cadw itself in terms of the monuments that exist in Wales?

(Mr Carr) I am not sure I fully grasp the question.

31. For example, you set out in your memorandum to this Committee your objective to increase the market share that Cadw gets of visits to historic monuments; therefore you clearly need to have attractive monuments in your care. You might have a view of what you actually want to see as your ideal distribution of monuments between your own and other bodies. You must, to an extent, be in competition with the National Trust, for example.

(Mr Carr) Our commercial activities are geared to contributing revenue towards the upkeep of the monuments. We do not take the sort of commercial view of the presentation of the monuments which one might find at, say, Alton Towers or Warwick Castle because, in our view, there is a requirement to preserve the integrity of the site in everything we do. We are not necessarily in competition with the others; it is a difficult concept to grasp, I know, but the market share key target is designed to indicate that we are maintaining our promotional efforts to a particular standard. Indeed, if one looks at it in market competitive terms, we support our rivals to a large extent, in the sense that extensive grant-aid goes to the National Trust and we are grant-aiding other major monuments such as Carew, and Pembroke from time to time. Cardiff Castle is a beneficiary of considerable grant-aid, both of ancient monument grant and the historic building grant for various works. We see ourselves as being a very significant component of the tourism industry in Wales. We have a contribution to make towards the economy of Wales. This is nothing new; it has been going on for several centuries, but I think that if we organise it in

a more structured fashion and at the same time join forces with local authorities and other monument owners in joint marketing efforts—which we do, as members of some 18 or 19 marketing consortia—then we are making a contribution to the local as well as the national economy.

32. Cadw therefore has no view of the ideal structure or tenure of the properties and buildings that should be preserved in Wales?

(Mr Carr) No, I think there is an essential freedom there. If, for example, as has happened, Clwyd County Council wish to take on Dinas Bran, then we do not have a view, provided the monument is kept in good condition.

33. May I explore this question of your support to your rivals or however you like to describe them. It has been said to us that in your promotional literature, you advertise your own monuments, but not those in the care of others—local authorities, private care, National Trust—and your memorandum makes no reference to the role of other bodies and private owners in the conservation and preservation of Welsh heritage. We have had a specific point raised with us by the Council of Welsh Districts who say this is a problem for them. They say you will not allow local authorities to advertise their properties in your literature. Is this a conscious decision; is there an advantage flowing to Wales or Cadw from doing this or is it a function of the competitive pressure between yourself and other bodies?

(Mr Carr) I would not say it was a function of competitive pressure. What I would say is that significant monuments in the ownership of others receive mention in our literature.

34. Are you saying the Council of Welsh Districts is wrong to make this point?

(Mr Carr) I think that they might well wish to reflect upon it, because we do have significant monuments not in State care mentioned in our marketing literature, and as I said, we are members of 18 or 19 marketing consortia which, in several instances, include monuments not in state care.

35. So you would see the promotion of the overall Welsh built heritage as being a function of those marketing consortia and others and not yourselves?

(Mr Carr) I think it would also be useful if we were to go beyond the simple marketing leaflets and look at the other work we do in terms of presenting, or making accessible to the public, information on monuments, both within and without state care. For example, last year we published two in a series of gazetteers to the Ancient and Field Monuments of Dyfed and Glamorgan. We also publish general books on the Civil War, for example, and on medieval Wales where many sites not in state care are mentioned and their historical and architectural attributes, etc. are open to public reading.

Chairman

36. May I develop that point further, Mr Carr? In the evidence we had from the Council of Welsh Districts, they said: "Cadw is not prepared to allow a local authority to advertise its own historic buildings in the same brochure as Cadw." Do you have any

[**Chairman** *Cont*]

brochures in which you forbid local authorities to advertise their own historic buildings, or is that statement entirely untrue.

(*Mr Carr*) I do not think it is true, Mr Chairman. We do permit entries into our own marketing leaflets. We do not produce specific advertising material at all where we offer advertising space to local authorities. With regard to our Heritage in Wales newspaper for members, we do have it in view to offer advertising space to help cover some of the costs of production, but that is something we are still considering.

Mr Richards

37. Much of a Member of Parliament's work concerns conflict of interests, very often between bodies and individuals in Wales. Indeed, more often than not, Members of Parliament do not become involved until much blood has already been spilt! As far as Cadw is concerned, there must be occasions when there are conflicts of interest, say with local authorities, other government bodies, highway authorities, etc. For example, if the Welsh Office or highway authority want to build a road somewhere and you think it is not a very good idea, what is the machinery by which you resolve that conflict before, shall we say, local people become involved in protests, etc.?

(*Mr Carr*) In the case of a highway being constructed over or through a scheduled area—and this would apply to any development on a scheduled area—the person wishing to undertake the development has to apply to the Secretary of State, via Cadw, for Scheduled Monument Consent and we consider the merits of the scheme. Our Inspectorate of Ancient Monuments will perhaps discuss with the developer a variation of the line of a road or the positioning of a pylon or telegraph pole, and frequently that discussion or negotiation can result in the monument not being affected. It can take some time to negotiate. If, however, the applicant formally applies, then Scheduled Monument Consent procedures go forward and, under the 1979 Act, we are required to consult with a variety of bodies as to their views of this particular development and its impact upon the monument. They may agree to it, provided there is a watching brief or a prior archaeological excavation, and having taken all these consultative views on board, we reach an interim decision, inform the applicant of it and offer them the opportunity of further written representations, or a public local enquiry. Thus, if a developer is intent on his project and he opts for a public local inquiry, the Secretary of State appoints an Inspector to carry forward that inquiry. He then reports to the Secretary of State who determines the outcome.

38. What about within non-governmental bodies and government itself? You might for example—and I do not know if this has ever happened—be in conflict with, shall we say, the Welsh Development Agency or the DBRW, or the Welsh Office itself, for that matter?

(*Mr Carr*) Conflict is perhaps too strong a word, but under arrangements we will discuss with the WDA what it is they wish to do. They are a non-departmental public body with a degree of freedom of action, but the same process applies to them as it would to any other applicant. In the case of Welsh

Office Highways, we broke new ground several years ago in agreeing with the Highways Group that they would fund archaeological investigation in advance of development, and I think I am correct in saying we were the first heritage body in Britain to have established that relationship with the State Highways Department.

Chairman: I think we should turn now to the considerable concern expressed to us in a number of memoranda about the condition of churches and chapels in Wales. These concerns are, first of all, the question of continuing the ecclesiastical exemption from listed building planning laws and, secondly, the condition of the increasing number of redundant churches. I will ask Mr Roger Evans to ask a few questions on that, if I may.

Mr Evans

39. There was an announcement just before Christmas that the ecclesiastical exemption was being reviewed. Did you or Cadw give advice to the Secretary of State for Wales on that issue?

(*Mr Carr*) May I make it absolutely clear that Cadw is the Secretary of State; we are part of the Welsh Office and therefore we act on his behalf. The Historic Buildings Council for Wales has considered ecclesiastical exemption and has offered advice to the Secretary of State on this matter. As you said, the Secretary of State for National Heritage and Secretary of State for Wales made a joint announcement about the decision on the future of ecclesiastical exemption just before Christmas. Both Departments will be making a joint Order in due course bringing the arrangements into effect.

40. As I understand the announcement, the way in which this is going to work is that each denomination or body will be considered on a case by case basis, to see what system they have and whether it is satisfactory?

(*Mr Carr*) On a case by case basis, not on an individual property basis.

41. But denomination by denomination?

(*Mr Carr*) Yes. If they have sufficient safeguards themselves for assessing what work should be permitted, then they will not be subject to listed building consent procedures. That is my understanding.

42. In terms of that assessment, will Cadw be playing any part in giving advice to the Secretary of State?

(*Mr Carr*) Yes.

43. It would be very surprising if Cadw or one of your officials was not giving advice. I think it would be fair to say that, in Wales, you are probably the body with the best detailed knowledge of the workings of these individual systems?

(*Mr Carr*) I think that would be correct, and indeed if it is of any interest to the Committee, I understand that one of my colleagues, the Superintending Conservation Architect, has, during the course of his 14 years with Cadw, examined some 500 ecclesiastical structures as part of his role as Architectural Assessor to the Historic Buildings Council.

[Mr Evans *Cont*]

44. May I turn, first of all, to the Church in Wales. What does Cadw identify as the critical areas in respect of ecclesiastical exemption in the Church in Wales?

(*Mr Carr*) As far as we are aware, there is a very strong diocesan structure for the care of ecclesiastical buildings in the ownership of the Representative Body.

45. The provisions of the Care of Churches and Ecclesiastical Jurisdiction Measure of 1991 in England—the principle of bringing cathedrals within the faculty jurisdiction system—has not been applied in Wales, has it?

(*Mr Carr*) No, it has not.

46. Would you see the extension of some system of control and assessment in respect of cathedrals as a requirement which the Church in Wales ought to introduce?

(*Mr Carr*) There is a faculty system which has been reviewed in Wales.

47. Has been, or is being?

(*Mr Carr*) Has been, and is continuing to be.

48. I am asking you, but I do not know whether it might be easier for Mr Hughes to answer the question if it is a matter of being briefed?

(*Mr Carr*) I regret that I do need to be reminded of some of the complexities with which this organisation has to deal, and I am content for Mr Hughes to respond to that.

49. Regarding the Church in Wales—and this concern has been expressed to us in other memoranda—the first criticism made in respect to cathedrals is that, as yet, there is no system of control comparable to the one which has just been introduced in England. Would you agree that this is an area of concern?

(*Mr Hughes*) I think it is an area which needs to be looked at in the context of the ecclesiastical exemption review which has been announced. I think the important thing to bear in mind is that the Church in Wales has long-established controls through its faculty jurisdiction system. We know, from advice we have had from the Historic Buildings Council, and from representations we have received from amenity societies, including the Victorian Society, that there are anxieties about the workings and effectiveness of those controls. The concept the government is putting forward for ecclesiastical exemption is that if the Church authorities can demonstrate that their own internal procedures are robust enough to compare with the secular procedures, then they will be allowed to retain the exemption, within the terms that the government is considering under the announcement. The question of cathedrals is one we would need to look at against that background.

50. Let us take some other examples of criticism on possible areas where the present systems of the Church in Wales are not robust enough and on which Cadw may have views, or be able to give advice. For example, in Wales, unlike in England, there is no expert body like the Council for the Care of Churches to advise Diocesan Advisory Committees, is there?

(*Mr Hughes*) No, but Diocesan Advisory Committees do have experts in architectural history; we have tried to encourage this and, for example, a member of the Historic Buildings Council serves on one Diocesan Advisory Committee and we are aware of experts who serve on others. Mr Carr referred to the work that Mr Douglas Hogg is doing as assessor to the Historic Buildings Council. He is also taking forward an education initiative, which has involved him in visiting Diocesan Advisory Committees to talk to them about their work and to help them understand the importance of sympathetic treatment of this estate which the Church in Wales has. They have an inordinate share of responsibility in the care of built heritage and we know, from our regular contacts with them, that their concern is that this care and responsibility takes away from their work in the living Church. We are trying to support them in dealing with what, I suspect, is a great problem for them.

51. We know there is an appalling lack of resources, but that is a separate matter. You speak of encouraging this expert and being aware of other experts on Diocesan Advisory Committees; surely the whole principle behind having DACs is that they should contain a representative expert in every field for which a faculty might be granted?

(*Mr Hughes*) I think when looking at the whole system of faculty jurisdiction, the Church in Wales has been considering the expertise available to it in the way you describe, but I do not yet know their conclusions.

52. Let me not continue this unnecessarily, but the criticisms which have been made to us are that, compared to the Church of England, there is a lack of a central expert body, such as the Council for the Repair of Churches, there is a lack of a comprehensive set of experts on the DACs, and there is a lack of amenity society representation on the DACs. Are these concerns which Cadw will be considering?

(*Mr Hughes*) We are certainly aware of those concerns. We know, too, that the Church in Wales's Representative Body is aware of those concerns; indeed that was one of the reasons why they went into this review of faculty jurisdiction.

53. Can you help me in respect of the free churches in Wales? Can you give me some examples or a summary as to what you see to be the position in respect of the free churches, and the effectiveness and robustness of their systems of control?

(*Mr Hughes*) I think, in this context, it is more difficult. The announcement the government made about limiting the ecclesiastical exemption, and the church's ability to retain that exemption, does depend upon the church having an organisational structure which would enable it to fulfil the terms of the draft Code of Practice that was issued. The more structured the church, the easier it is going to be for them to fulfil those terms. We are waiting to see what the response of the free churches will be, but it may be that it will not be possible for the ecclesiastical exemption to continue to be applied.

54. What examples can you give me of particular chapels or free churches which have caused Cadw particular concern recently? What are the two or three worst examples you could give of the

[Mr Evans Cont]
ecclesiastical exemption allowing something which you would never permit?

(Mr Hughes) I am afraid I cannot call to mind the sort of example I think you want. The cases I have letters about—from people like the Victorian Society, for instance—tend to relate to fixtures and fittings rather than major structural changes to the total fabric of the building. Fixtures and fittings is a difficult area within listed building controls, in any case. What I am saying is that the ecclesiastical exemption, by itself, is not the only question that arises. It may be that even if the building had been treated normally as a listed building, there would still have been arguments about the treatment of fixtures and fittings.

55. That undoubtedly is a well-known old chestnut! What about free churches being demolished or being put to inappropriate use? Have there been particular examples about which Cadw has been concerned?

(Mr Hughes) The ecclesiastical exemption only applies while the building is in use for worship, so if there is a question of a listed building being demolished, then listed building consent would have to be applied for in the normal way.

56. May I take it one stage further? The Union of Welsh Independent Churches has written to us suggesting that, as far as listed buildings are concerned, Cadw are showing a greater concern in respect of architectural, rather than historical, significance.

(Mr Carr) I would find great difficulty in agreeing with that. Our inspectors of historic buildings are art historians, or architectural historians, and they list on the basis of special interest in both those categories. If you are speaking in terms of grant-aid, then the Historic Buildings Council for Wales assesses the importance of the structure for grant-aid even-handedly on architectural and historical grounds.

57. That is a criticism you reject?
(Mr Carr) Indeed.

58. May I go on to the question of redundant churches and chapels? In respect of redundant chapels, is there not a long-standing difficulty that the trustees have a legal obligation to dispose of the site for the best possible price, and that this has led to conservation difficulties in the sense that it may conflict with the preservation aims of Cadw?

(Mr Carr) Forgive me, I have lost my train of thought. May I ask for the question to be repeated?

59. What I was suggesting was that in respect of free churches, where the trustees are charity trustees, in the event of a building going out of use, they have a legal obligation to obtain the best price for it; this is a well-known cause of problems within the United Kingdom. Has this been a particular concern to Cadw in Wales, as a result, for example, of inappropriate development applications, or pressure to do things to maximise profit in respect of these buildings or sites?

(Mr Carr) We are concerned solely with the protection of the listed structure. How it is disposed of, and to whom, is not a matter for the Secretary of State's concern.

60. Strictly speaking, you must be right, but in the sense that if you have an historic interior, the alteration to a totally inappropriate use has inevitable implications for the integrity of the interior, does it not?

(Mr Carr) Yes, it does, and that would be an aspect that would be considered during the listed building consent process.

61. Has there not been a problem in Wales in respect of dis-used chapels?
(Mr Carr) In respect of conversion?

62. As to what happens to these buildings?
(Mr Carr) There is universal concern.

63. Can you quantify that or give us some indication as to the extent of it?

(Mr Carr) No, I cannot quantify it. There is an organisation in Wales called Capel, with whom we are working, and they are currently developing a register of, in their opinion, the most significant chapels. Their findings will be considered by our historic building inspectors when they are undertaking their listing duties. I am not aware that it would even be possible to quantify the problem, as you are seeking to do.

64. When is the Capel survey due to be completed?

(Mr Carr) I am not sure. They are a voluntary body and are undertaking the work as and when they can. I should also mention to the Committee that the Royal Commission on Ancient and Historical Monuments is about to undertake a survey of ecclesiastical buildings, including chapels.

65. Before I finish the question of redundant churches, and return to the Church in Wales, there is no Redundant Churches Fund in Wales. Currently, what proposals does Cadw have to assess this problem?

(Mr Carr) If you have taken evidence from the Representative Body, you will be aware that discussions have been going on with them since 1985 on how the question of redundant churches might be addressed. We have had very lengthy discussions with them, but have not yet been able to reach a conclusion.

66. Where are the sticking points, as far as Cadw is concerned?

(Mr Carr) I think what we are concerned to do is ensure the preservation of those structures. The Representative Body has, I dare say, complex difficulties in terms of its constitution, if I may use that word.

67. The Representative Body, as it has told us, is concerned at the amount of ongoing maintenance costs and the general financial burden on the Church in Wales?

(Mr Carr) I think one needs to separate out the two issues. One of our early suggestions to Ministers, which they accepted and concerning which they have written to the Representative Body, was that we should take into care some significant examples of these churches, so that they were guaranteed protection. I think the difficulty here for the Representative Body is that some of these redundant churches are not necessarily outstanding in terms of the criteria applied by the Historic Buildings Council.

Chairman

68. One of the memoranda we received was from the Friends of Friendless Churches. I think that sums up part of the problem; many of the churches of Wales are going to become increasingly friendless, and this particular body is very concerned about that. One of the memoranda we had, referring to this particular memorandum, was from the Ancient Monuments Society, and I would like to have your view on it. They say that they are willing—that is, the Friends of Friendless Churches are willing—to perform the role of the Redundant Churches Fund in England, for Wales. In their evidence they say—and they are looking at a specific example: "The fact that extra measures are urgently required was demonstrated in 1991 by the disgraceful application to demolish the church of St Bride's, Wentloog, in Gwent with its intact and elaborate 15th century tower, as good as many in Somerset. The Friends have had to turn down the ownership of a number of churches and chapels in Wales simply through lack of funds." What I think is important to know is whether it is the case that Wales is going to lose churches of significant architectural value like this because organisations like the Friends of Friendless Churches are unable to take them over, because of financial restraints. What is your role in examples such as this?

(*Mr Carr*) If I may answer the middle point first, Mr Chairman. The Friends of Friendless Churches have successfully had 100 per cent grant-aid to two churches in Wales. In relation to the Wentloog church, we were made aware of this as being potentially redundant. It is a magnificent structure; I have visited it myself in the company of Mr Hogg, and it is conceivable that allied to the activities of the local parishioners and our own interest, the question of redundancy was changed, at least for the time being. We are open at all times to applications for grant assistance for structures of great significance.

69. With regard to chapels, we understand—again from the evidence of the Ancient Monuments Society—that there is in England an Historic Chapels Trust, which is equivalent to the Redundant Churches Fund for non-Anglican places of worship. It was established in December 1992 with co-funding from the Department of National Heritage and it hopes to take on two chapels per year, but we understand that, constitutionally, it would not be able to cover Wales. Do you think there is a clear need for some equivalent body in Wales to the Historic Chapels Trust in England?

(*Mr Carr*) There may well be, Mr Chairman. I would like to consider that point further.

70. Do you think that the initiatives that have been carried out by the Landmark Trust in examples such as the conversion of Maes yr Onen Chapel in Glasbury-on-Wye in Powys is the kind of example that should be replicated in other areas where, in fact, they have taken over, according to page 120 of their handbook: "....the neat and tidy cottage built in the first half of the 18th century on to the end of one of Wales's shrines of non-conformity, the Maes yr Onen Chapel. The chapel, converted from probably a 16th century barn in 1696, dates from the early vernacular days when any suitable building was made use of for enthusiastic worship." Is that kind of initiative one

that Cadw would fully support for the conversion of Welsh chapels?

(*Mr Carr*) In general terms we would be highly sympathetic to that. It would depend upon the nature of the works that were required to make it into a viable proposition. It is, I am given to understand, rather easier to think in terms of the conversion of chapels for alternative use, such as the one you have identified by the Landmark Trust, than it is for medieval churches or Victorian churches, for example.

71. Would you agree that at this time it is the case that the problem of what to do with disused places of worship has received no satisfactory resolution?

(*Mr Carr*) I think that could be said of many things, Mr Chairman.

72. But is this one of them?

(*Mr Carr*) I think there are, as you would know better than I, very many chapels of many denominations developed over the period of non-conformity in Britain, and Wales is particularly rich in examples of different denominations and sub-denominations. Some of these buildings are of exceptional architectural importance; some have very strong historical associations. Not all of them would be described by the Historic Buildings Council as being outstanding. Nonetheless, those that are outstanding, either architecturally or historically, are eligible for generous grant-aid—the most generous level of grant-aid, in fact, of any of the categories we have. It is 50 per cent for ecclesiastical buildings, which is rather more than is offered in England.

73. Since the trends do not seem to suggest that there is going to be a revival of enthusiastic worship in Wales in the last eight years or so of this century, would you agree that the number of buildings likely to be made redundant, in terms of chapels particularly, is going to increase and that this problem has not yet been addressed, at least with a solution at the end of it? Is that the current position?

(*Mr Carr*) I believe so, Mr Chairman. I think that increasing redundancy is inevitable, not for reasons of protection of the heritage, but for social reasons. The addressing of the problem has exercised many minds for some considerable time. I am afraid we do not have a glib or ready solution.

74. Turning to the whole question of the listing of historic buildings, there are, as far as we understand, 14,700 listed buildings in Wales and some 2,700 scheduled monuments while current monument records contain around 60,000 entries. Does Cadw have a strategic view of a ceiling or target for the quantity of scheduled monuments?

(*Mr Carr*) I think one needs to put the 60,000 identified historical sites into some sort of context. The Sites and Monument Record does indeed contain that number. Many of these are place names; there is no physical evidence on the ground. Many are find spots, where there may have been a dropping of flint or a coin or something similar; again, there is no upstanding or beneath-the-ground structure readily discernible. We have a schedule of 2,688 buildings, which does not include buildings in use, which are included in the SMRs' 60,000. If you press me on time taken, I think I have to point you to the

[Chairman *Cont*]

Uplands Initiative which we have instituted in co-operation with the Royal Commission on Ancient and Historical Monuments where we have transferred some funding to assist in assessing the upland areas which previously have not been fully recorded or examined. It is our belief that during the scheduling enhancement programme, the ultimate numbers scheduled as being of national importance—which is what you are seeking—will be approximately double. So we are looking at somewhere between 5,700 and 6,000 ultimately.

75. How many of those entries are place names?

(*Mr Carr*) I could not answer that, Mr Chairman, but perhaps Mr Avent can.

(*Mr Avent*) What we can say is that of the 60,000 entries in Sites and Monuments Records, only 20,000 of those are sites which could be considered for scheduling. The remaining entries are either place names, find spots, buildings in use or relatively modern structures which would not fall into the compass of scheduling as being of national importance.

76. Several memoranda quote a figure of 30,000 as Cadw's estimation of listed buildings which a complete re-survey would identify. Is this an accurate figure?

(*Mr Carr*) It is impossible to determine whether or not it is accurate. It is only an estimate at this stage. We shall not know the full number of buildings worthy of listing until after the re-survey is complete.

77. As an estimate, how good would you say it was?

(*Mr Carr*) I would say it was not too far adrift, bearing in mind that listing of the major historic urban areas is well advanced and approaching completion. We are now looking at the suburban areas and the rural districts. In England I believe there are half a million listed structures which are constantly being reviewed and added to; that represents something of the order of 2 per cent of all structures in England. I regret I do not have the number of structures in Wales at my fingertips, but we think the figure of somewhere around 30,000 would be the ultimate number of buildings protected by listing. I should also add that, as time passes, and as criteria are developed, more modern structures may be considered for listing and added to the list; there is a constant process of consideration of structures.

Mr Hanson

78. Amongst the evidence that has been submitted to the Committee is evidence from my own local authority, Delyn Borough Council, via the Association of Welsh Planning Officers. In the memorandum they have submitted to us they say: "Probably the greatest matter for concern, and one that needs urgent action towards its solution is the outdated nature of the statutory lists and the length of time the completion of the full national re-survey is taking." Could you give the Committee an estimate—bearing in mind the importance you put on it in your earlier answer to the Chairman—of the length of time the national re-survey is likely to take?

(*Mr Carr*) Committee members will have noted from the Executive Summary of our Corporate Plan that we consider the period of 60 years, which was the estimate, to be wholly unacceptable. We are addressing the question of how this can be accelerated. Over the past few years, the number of lists issued has increased considerably; it is still a lengthly process, but in our present Corporate Plan, which has yet to be submitted to Ministers, we are addressing this particular issue.

Chairman: We will come back to that, if we may, because we want to discuss a general point about listing and the estimate at this stage, and then come back to the whole question of listing when we talk about speed and efficiency. We would like to look at the whole question of strategic planning of local authorities.

Mr Robinson

79. First, may I say how glad I am that the Committee decided to mount this inquiry and I think the various comments already made this morning indicate not only the scale of the task that you have, but also the different demands you face from all quarters, which mean that at the end of the day you have the task of trying to ascertain the priorities and the agenda. As almost everyone who has written to us has their own agenda, you somehow have to balance that as well. Turning to your memorandum, there really was little reference to the strategic planning functions of local authorities through such instruments as County Structure Plans or National Park Plans, and in saying that, there is no direct criticism. I can understand you may have felt you needed a separate paper to cover that problem. Increasingly, however, very strong statements of intent concerning monuments and listed buildings are being inserted by planners in England, usually on advice from specialists in their own department. I certainly have seen that in my constituency in Somerset where much of what we have been discussing is very similar. There are some instances of this in Wales, such as Clwyd and the Pembrokeshire Coast National Park Draft Provisions, but the practice is far from consistent. Do you see a role for Cadw in encouraging the inclusion of such provisions within the strategic planning objectives throughout Wales and should you be acting as a catalyst?

(*Mr Carr*) We have an ongoing relationship with the authorities. They are required to produce structure plans and local plans and we are consultees for these. We are encouraged by the increasing emphasis placed upon the protection of the built heritage which is contained in those plans. I should also refer, if I may, to PPG16 which was introduced last year. Local authorities are encouraged to take on the guidance in that PPG and that, of course, has moved into the area where we are also concerned—the Rescue Archaeological Trusts. These trusts are encouraged by local authorities to do pro-active protection via identification, rather than re-active by excavation. They are encouraged to identify a planning potential and then to do an archaeological assessment in advance.

80. If you reached the conclusion that a local authority was not acting in the way you thought it should on matters such as this, would you regard it as your role to knock on the local authority's door, since of course much of this planning link is direct

[Mr Robinson *Cont*]

with the Welsh Office? Would you use the Welsh Office as your conduit? How would you get your message across?

(*Mr Carr*) We get our message across in a number of ways. One of the most recent and productive is the education initiative which we launched last year, where one of my conservation architecture colleagues addresses seminars of planning officers and planning committee members on the desirability of following guidance on the measures taken for listing and other protective measures. I answered that in my previous evidence, but I can expand on that if you wish.

81. There is, of course, a difference between encouraging awareness and urging or requiring action. When you see a situation which you believe urgently requires action, how do you tackle that?

(*Mr Carr*) We consult with colleague Departments within the Welsh Office. You will recognise that it is difficult for us in certain circumstances to take action on behalf of the Secretary of State, independent of our colleagues.

82. I think that answers my question; you feel it incumbent upon you to go through the Welsh Office, rather than go direct to local authorities. That brings me to a related subject; if I am right, conservation areas in Wales are entirely urban, although the Historic Buildings Council and the Countryside Council are consulting on extending the scheme to rural areas. Given that rural conservation areas have existed in England for some years, why do you think this is only now coming in Wales? Why the delay?

(*Mr Carr*) It is a difficult question to answer. I believe there are very severe difficulties in the designation of rural conservation areas in England.

83. Which do not exist in Wales?

(*Mr Carr*) I think that in the designation of those areas there have been complexities encountered during the identification of them. The way we are working in Wales—and you are right to say that most of our conservation areas are urban and there is an encouragingly increasing number being designated, certainly since Cadw was formed. The way we address some of the conservation issues in the countryside is through our co-operative links with the Countryside Council for Wales; indeed, we are part of the Tir Cymen exercise, the pilot exercise which is covering Merioneth, Dinefwr and Swansea and where we are looking at stewardship of the countryside with them. Our particular interest, of course, is the built heritage or, in the case of Gower, the Vile field system at Rhossili.

84. Is that a substitute for not having conservation in rural areas in Wales or are you saying that this is what you have been doing until now?

(*Mr Carr*) The majority of Wales is rural. There are very large areas of Wales which, if they were to be designated entirely as conservation areas, might cause difficulties for people who are legitimately farming there.

85. What should the policy be towards the designation of rural areas? Should there be a clearly defined policy, or do you think that is not practical?

(*Mr Carr*) It is difficult for me to answer that. What I can say is that with the Countryside Council for

Wales initiative, information is being gathered which will be of benefit to the local authorities, who are in fact the bodies who designate conservation areas. From time to time, the Historic Buildings Council may encourage designation, but it is not a specific function of ours to designate them.

86. You await the outcome with interest?

(*Mr Carr*) Indeed we do.

87. Would you like to see that activity result in the designation of more rural conservation areas?

(*Mr Carr*) I should like to see activity which encourages the protection of the built environment.

Chairman

88. In terms of historic landscapes, would you accept that there has been little strategic thinking with regard to the conservation of historic landscapes as a whole?

(*Mr Carr*) I am not sure I could answer such a direct question. What I would like to do is explain what we are doing in relation to historic landscapes.

89. Perhaps you could write to us on what you are doing on historic landscapes. Would that be possible?

(*Mr Carr*) Yes, indeed.

90. In terms of what you have been doing, would you say there has been little consultation; in particular why is it that there has been an emphasis on parks and gardens, when the greatest threat seems to be to less socially restrictive and more extensive landscapes, and those of earlier periods? Why have parks and gardens figured so largely in your activities?

(*Mr Carr*) In Wales we recognised that historic landscapes were prone to be neglected which is why, when we began our register on historic parks and gardens, we added the word "landscapes". Having done so we have discovered there were considerable difficulties in designating historic landscapes and we are in consultation with our colleagues in English Heritage—who have also encountered this difficulty—to see how the criteria for designating an historic landscape might be established. What we are doing positively in 1993, is joining up with the Countryside Council of Wales for a rapid, initial study to identify what are considered to be important landscapes, whether of the farming type, like the Vile, or whether they are historically important for military activity, or whatever. It is a very wide range and the criteria are extremely difficult to be precise about.

Chairman: Moving on now to the speed and efficiency of the listing procedure, I would like Mr Hanson to continue his line of questioning.

Mr Hanson

91. You have mentioned the current forecast of some 60 years for completion of the survey. Many of the memoranda we have received at the Committee have expressed concern about the length of time which the survey is planned and expected to take; they point to comparable situations within England and the length of time it has taken there. The memoranda have remarked on the confidence they have in Cadw staff in discharging the duty, but the

[**Mr Hanson** *Cont*]

point has been made that the fault lies with a failure to match staff allocation to policy aims. Would you agree, or care to comment upon that?

(*Mr Carr*) I would like to comment on some of the background to this. We took over from the Department of the Environment in 1981; the listing survey of Wales started in 1951, and went through to 1974. Since we have taken over, the rate of the survey has accelerated and we have taken on two contract listers. We are contemplating, subject to approval of our Corporate Plan, accelerating it even further. What I would like to say, to balance the concerns of these local authorities, is that we respond very rapidly to requests for examination of structures considered to be at risk, and to date we have already listed 130 this year. I would remind the Committee that there is also available to local authorities the mechanism of the building preservation notice, whereby they can put a preservation notice on a building which remains in force for some six months, during which time we have to say yes or no.

92. My own local authority indicates that there about 151 Grade 3 buildings in Delyn on the provisional list and to date, 22 have been totally demolished and 60 have suffered the type of unsympathetic alterations which are probably allowed, but which could have been prevented by listing. How would you advise authorities to deal with what can be, because of the delay, a reduction in the available properties for listing?

(*Mr Carr*) One of the ways they can move towards controlling the planning process is through the declaration of a conservation area where the demolition in a conservation area needs to be referred to the Secretary of State.

93. What representations have you made to the Secretary of State about staffing, to speed up the 60 year period?

(*Mr Carr*) As has already been identified, Cadw has a large number of duties to perform, and determining the balance between them is one of the exercises I go through every year. I make my representations to Ministers and I accept the decision as to how they wish me to take forward my Corporate Plan.

94. What would you see to be the best compromise in terms of the completion date for the listing, rather than 60 years?

(*Mr Carr*) I would like to see the listing re-survey completed in not more than 15 to 20 years. Ideally, I would like to see it done in less. However, we do have mechanisms to protect structures; listing is not necessarily the be all and end all.

95. So authorities such as my own in Delyn with local re-organisation could have spent the whole of their existence without a proper listing procedure?

(*Mr Carr*) There is a proper listing procedure.

96. A complete listing?

(*Mr Carr*) A complete listing of their borough area. That would apply to a number of district council areas.

97. May I raise one other issue of concern which has been reflected in submissions we have had, but has also been reflected in my own constituency experience, and that is the perception that Cadw is,

because of its base in Cardiff, remote from North Wales. There have been suggestions to decentralise Cadw's operations and provide a mid- or North Wales base, which I am sure would be welcomed in my constituency. Have you any comments upon those perceptions, and whether you believe they are valid and, if so, what the redress should be?

(*Mr Carr*) I do not think we could be considered to be remote; we have three works units, in the South East, the West and the North, where there is a presence by Cadw. My expert inspectorate staff constantly travel throughout Wales. They meet local authorities, they meet local owners and they spend a great deal of their time, as it were, on the hoof. What we also have is a system of field monument wardens who advise local farmers in particular or local land owners concerning the care and maintenance of their properties. Our educational initiative is now widespread throughout Wales; our education to schools initiative covers all eight counties and many of the districts, and many are over-subscribed, I am happy to say. We have extremely strong links with the officers of districts and counties, with the Welsh Development Agency, the Wales Tourist Board and the Countryside Council for Wales. We work extremely closely with the Rescue Trusts, and with the County Archivists, all of whom are able to convey our views. On a different level, colleagues of mine willingly give up their time in the evenings to go to address local history societies, Women's Institute groups on a specific monument or upon the work of Cadw. I do not know that we could do much more not to be distant.

Chairman

98. Going back to Mr Hanson's earlier series of points on listing—and I know Mr Evans will want to come in on that—the Council for British Archaeology say that your records of listed buildings only exist in paper files. Is that the case?

(*Mr Carr*) That is correct.

99. So you have no computerised records?

(*Mr Carr*) No.

100. Is it the case that there is no breakdown by geographical location, and when seeking information from local authorities about district totals, this often takes considerable time, or they claim not to know? Are the district totals of listed buildings easily available?

(*Mr Carr*) The re-survey lists are based on community council areas, so those are contained within a particular area—Radnor District, for example. Some of the earlier records are not brigaded by district, but they are readily accessible by our own internal staff, so that questions can be answered within moments, although perhaps not as efficiently as they might be if they were to be computerised.

101. If we asked you for a list of all the buildings in Wales that have been listed, you would be able to identify for us every listed building, separated out district by district, if we were to need it?

(*Mr Carr*) Yes, we could.

102. Do you agree with the Council for British Archaeology that because of staff shortages within Cadw there is a declared policy that new listings

[**Chairman** *Cont*]

cannot be considered unless the notified property is under immediate threat or in an area designated for revision?

(*Mr Carr*) No, Mr Chairman. I have referred to one inspector who is dedicated to ad hoc or spot listing.

103. You do not wish to change your mind about that?

(*Mr Carr*) I am reminded, Mr Chairman, that priority is given to structures which are under threat, on ad hoc listing.

104. However, it is not the case that you have a policy that new listing cannot be considered unless the notified property is under immediate threat or in an area designated for revision?

(*Mr Carr*) I regret I may have misinformed the Committee. That, indeed, is the case.

105. In terms of the evidence we had from the Assembly of Welsh Counties regarding the consequences of delay in the listing of buildings, this is what they say in paragraph 4.3: "There are in Wales very many buildings of listable quality which do not enjoy statutory protection and are therefore under-valued and very often under threat. The number of listable buildings that have been demolished in recent decades is incalculable. The problem can be grotesque; for example, in the Rhondda where an urban conglomeration which had a population of 163,000 people at its greatest extent, only possesses 17 listed buildings. The result is a commonplace attitude which often out of ignorance fails to respect the quality of the historic built environment." Do you accept the statement that there are only 17 listed buildings in the Rhondda as accurate, and that many listed buildings have been demolished in recent decades, as a result of which the quality of the historic built environment has been made the poorer?

(*Mr Carr*) I am not wholly familiar with the Rhondda, Mr Chairman. If there has been wholesale demolition, then the traditional industrial terraces, or the loss of them, will have made that area the poorer. What I would like to remind the Committee of, if I may, is that we have an industrial inspector whose specific area is the valleys of South Wales and the industrial part of Clwyd. His task is to examine those areas for listing and scheduling purposes. He is the first of his kind in Britain, because he covers both listing and scheduling, and to date he has completed a survey of the colliery buildings which were seen to be at greatest risk of loss. He is undertaking a survey of significant structures like the Miners' Institutes and will join with his colleagues in due course studying the individual community areas for listing. I regret the number of 17 is one I cannot recognise at this time - because I do not know the answer. I would imagine that following the survey of colliery structures the number will increase.

106. Before I ask Mr Evans to develop this, may I ask one or two quick questions. Looking at the role of Cadw in listed building matters, we have had evidence from the Victorian Society, and they said, taking the specific example of the Guildhall in Swansea, that Cadw had told the County Council it could gut the building, well in advance of any application for its conversion. As a result the Council

has left the building exposed to the elements and vandalism ever since. Do you accept this charge?

(*Mr Carr*) No.

107. The other point made by the same body is that specialist advice at certain times is not available from Cadw, as it is from English Heritage. For example, English Heritage has a legal department, the members of which are available to give help to local authorities when difficulties arise. There is nothing like that in Wales, and the example they have quoted is the illegal removal of a listed statue and, arguably, the illegal removal of internal fixtures from Leighton Hall in Montgomeryshire. Is it the case that you have no lawyers on your staff able to assist in that way?

(*Mr Carr*) If I may remind the Committee, we are part of the Welsh Office; we undertake the Secretary of State's duties. English Heritage are in a different position in that they are one step removed, being a non-departmental public body.

108. The other point they made—the same case, Leighton Hall—is that dry rot has been allowed to spread unchecked through Leighton Hall in recent years. Apparently Cadw does not employ any structural engineers, so again it was their Society— that is, the Victorian Society—who sent a structural engineer to examine the building. Is that the case?

(*Mr Carr*) We do not employ structural engineers on the staff. It is open to the owner of the building to engage his own professional advisers and in many instances we would advise him to do so.

Mr Evans

109. The difficulty with that is that there been a change of ownership at Leighton Hall, according to last Sunday's papers?

(*Mr Carr*) You have the better of me.

110. The crisis of Leighton Hall, according to the press report, is that moneys had been spent, but they had not been spent wisely and the dry rot problem, is an expert problem with which a structural engineer from Cadw might have been able to assist, but you were unable to give that degree of expert help?

(*Mr Carr*) Conservation architects are also experts in the identification of the presence of dry and wet rot or other structurally threatening factors.

111. May I come back to listing for a moment. I must make it absolutely clear to you, if this sounds critical, that we understand your body has only been in existence since April 1991 and that you have considerable funding limitations, so we are not necessarily saying that this is the fault of Cadw, but the problem is not just 17 listed buildings in the Rhondda. From information it has had from Cadw, the Victorian Society has analysed which parts of Wales have not been surveyed at all, and there are some utterly astonishing examples. May I begin in my part of the world? They say there are no lists at all for Torfaen. Is that so?

(*Mr Carr*) Yes.

112. If we go to the other end of Wales— Anglesey—there are lists for Beaumaris, but most of Anglesey has not been surveyed.

(*Mr Carr*) That may well be so.

[Mr Evans *Cont*]

113. I have just taken two examples from one end of Wales to the other, so to speak. What the Victorian Society points out is that with areas where there are no surveys, it is purely accidental whether a particular demolition crisis or alteration crisis comes to your attention, is it not?

(*Mr Carr*) It can be accidental, but it is not always so. The local authorities also have some responsibilities themselves. They will notify us where they are aware of a building which is under threat, and we will take appropriate action.

114. On the last occasion you came to give evidence, you told us that the spread of conservation experts in English local authorities is somewhat broader than it is in Wales. The difficulty here is that buildings of historic or architectural importance in areas which have not been surveyed may end up being demolished or irreparably damaged by alteration, without Cadw ever hearing about it until it has happened. Is this not so?

(*Mr Carr*) In theory that is possible; in practice, and to my knowledge, it is rare. Simply because a planning officer may not have a qualification in conservation does not mean he does not have sensitivity to, or knowledge of, the desirability of retaining a building.

Mr Evans: The whole purpose of listing is to be able to ensure that a listing is based upon a full survey, that nothing falls through the net, and that a decision is always taken. The scandal in Wales—and I am suggesting to you that it is a scandal—is that there are substantial areas where no survey has been completed.

Chairman

115. In other words, Mr Carr, the list you hold has large areas where you could not supply us with details, because there is no list?

(*Mr Carr*) Yes, that is so.

Mr Evans

116. Is that not a breach of the statutory responsibilities of the Secretary of State or yourself?

(*Mr Carr*) No, sir, it is not. It is a function of how long it takes to undertake such surveys.

117. Let us take it one stage further. The Victorian Society again tells us that where buildings are listed, often there is no list description available. What I understand they mean by that is that the particulars are so short they, for example, cannot tell whether it is a Victorian building that has been listed.

(*Mr Carr*) That occurred in the very early lists in the 1950s and 1960s; they were very short list entries. That is not the case now where the majority of properties listed have a description which covers all specific features, including the date of the building.

118. What proportion of the lists as a whole contain only short particulars?

(*Mr Carr*) I could not tell you that offhand. I can provide you with that information should you desire it.

Mr Evans: Could we please have it?

Chairman

119. In view of what in fact the evidence shows—and Mr Evans has brought that out very clearly—are you considering, or have you considered, using other methods of conducting the re-survey of listed buildings, to speed it up? You said in response to Mr Hanson that you would like to see this being done in 15 to 20 years. Is there any way in which you could actually do it in five by using any other methods; for example, contracting it out to private enterprise, such as architectural firms, or sponsoring or requiring local authorities to take on the relative expertise to do it themselves? Have you given consideration to that and would it be a practical alternative?

(*Mr Carr*) Yes, we have given consideration to it. You will doubtless have been advised that English Heritage approached the matter in that way when they did their rapid re-survey in the 1980s. There are difficulties with that; I understand that many of their expert inspectors are spending a considerable amount of time revising and reviewing the lists. In fact, in one or two instances, I understand - by hearsay—that some of the structures are no longer considered worthy of listing. So far as the earlier part of your question is concerned, we have considered the use of contractors; in fact, we already have two and a third has recently started work on the Wrexham re-survey and we are contemplating, within the Corporate Plan process, how we might engage more. My understanding from English Heritage is that some of the people to whom they contracted the work found it rather more difficult to be academically precise than they had originally thought and our concern is to have very high quality lists.

120. Once listing has occurred, the preservation of that building in a form that is suitable is crucial. I understand in the evidence that under Section 48 of the Planning (Listed Buildings and Conservation Areas Act) of 1990, the local authority can issue repair notices in respect of those buildings, but in the evidence we have had from them, they say this places an obligation on them to carry out the necessary work by default should the owner of the building fail to comply with the notice; the result of course is that the notice is not served. Are you finding any evidence of listed buildings which should be preserved by the serving of repairs notices and where the owner does not want to engage in grant-aided work? Are you finding any evidence of this, and is it leading to the loss of buildings of importance after the listing has taken place?

(*Mr Carr*) I will have to consult on that, Mr Chairman. I am not personally aware of buildings having been lost as a result of that, but perhaps my colleagues can assist me.

(*Mr Hughes*) I cannot think of an example offhand. The process is one of gradual deterioration. The sort of thing we are talking about here takes place over a number of years. I think that local planning authorities are reluctant, as you say, to commit the resources of their authority in a way they may be difficult to recover. The way we have tried to help in this regard is to draw to their attention the availability of grant-aid in cases of emergency. This is something English Heritage has done and we have written to local planning authorities to make this

[**Chairman** *Cont*]

point. I should say, however, that not every listed building is eligible for grant-aid under the terms of the legislation we have, but in cases where grant eligibility exists, we would do everything we could to be helpful.

Mr Evans

121. In an attempt to speed up this listing process, have you considered, for example, engaging the co-operation of local civic and amenity societies?

(*Mr Carr*) We consult them during the listing process, in any case. Most of those societies are peopled by volunteers and are a very valuable resource. We have not actually considered using individuals who might be members of those societies, other than those who we know are expert art or architectural historians.

122. I appreciate you will obviously be concerned about the level of expertise, which is essential to the listing. However, one of the biggest problems of public awareness of listed buildings or architectural, historic buildings in Wales is the fact that the Buildings of Wales series is proceeding extremely slowly, whereas in England anybody can immediately pick up their copy of Pevsner and immediately identify a particular building. Is that a perception you would share?

(*Mr Carr*) The perception I would share is that the coverage of Wales by the Penguin series—or the Pevsner series, which has now become the Penguin series—is rather less wide than I had hoped might be the case, but I do know that it has been accelerated. We have assisted towards that acceleration by offering grant-aid through our civic initiative grant scheme to the University of Wales who are the co-ordinators of the whole exercise.

123. At a stroke, I would suggest to you that one of the best ways of encouraging public awareness of the importance of historic buildings in Wales would be to complete the Welsh series. Is that something Cadw could do more to help?

(*Mr Carr*) I think we have done as much as we practically can, but we would be very glad to continue to encourage the rapid conclusion of the series and I have personally taken that stance and that view over the past two to three years.

124. Returning to the amenities societies; for example, if you take Usk in my constituency, the Usk Civic Society has published a work on the buildings of Usk which is of the highest professional standard, because they happen to have the people available to do it. Where there are local guides or local groups with the necessary expertise to assess and evaluate, would Cadw be prepared to co-operate with them—not just consult—to get expert information to you quicker, sooner and more effectively?

(*Mr Carr*) We do that in any event. We work closely with Civic Societies either directly or through the Civic Trust for Wales. We support publication of the type of volume you have identified through the same civic initiative grant scheme I mentioned and I know that my colleagues in the Historic Buildings Inspectorate welcome information from such Societies which might assist them in their day-to-day re-survey work.

Chairman

125. The National Trust tell us the impact of financial trends on the availability and timing of Historic Building Council grant-aid is viewed with concern, and they give a specific example. Until 1991/92, the Historic Building Council awarded a grant of £280,000 per year towards repairs at Penrhyn Castle. For the current financial year the figure was reduced to just under £200,000. The National Trust questions the efficacy of the co-funding to Cadw having to cover both Cadw's statutory responsibilities for its monuments in care and grant-aid towards historic buildings and scheduled monuments in the ownership of others. Is it the case that your co-funding means that examples such as Penrhyn have had a reduction in the money spent on them, and that, as a result, the conservation quality of the castle and other buildings will suffer?

(*Mr Carr*) My direct answer to that would be, no. The National Trust has been a major pensioner for historic buildings grants for a great number of years. In the case of Penrhyn they have had something like a ten-year programme to date, with many phases on that building. They happen to own many of the significant country houses in Wales and we are in the position of already giving them grant-aid towards their built estate, approaching 30 per cent, on average, over the years. This is a very significant proportion, and for reasons of equity as much as anything else, we have asked them to phase their work, and to identify the phasing on a pan-Wales basis. They will then produce for us a schedule of priorities of work so that we are then able to consider, upon the advice of the Historic Buildings Council, which particular items of work need to be done in a particular financial year. The grant rate to the National Trust is, in one or two instances, rather better than it is for the generality of grant recipients. That reflects partly the importance of the structure and partly the speed at which the work needs to be done, but I would not say the National Trust itself could feel that it is hard done by.

126. The redundant buildings study being undertaken by the West Wales Task Force, according to the Assembly of Welsh Counties, will be a field leader within Wales. It is worth noting that Cadw refused to contribute towards it. Would you like to comment on this?

(*Mr Carr*) This is a case I am not familiar with, Mr Chairman, so may I consult with one of my colleagues? I regret I cannot give you the reasons that Cadw were unable to fund it directly, but as it was already obtaining funding from the Welsh Office, I would suspect it was for reasons of what is called additionality.

127. In paragraph 43 of the evidence from the National Trust—and I appreciate you do not have this—they give examples relating to small buildings and their great concern that these are being lost and I note in this particular example they say: "A small building has recently come to light which has been described by a leading authority on vernacular buildings in Wales as an 'unflawed gem of an archaic vernacular Carmarthenshire farmhouse in an unspoilt landscape setting of outstanding merit'." It goes on to say that the property, which is late

[Chairman *Cont]*

medieval in origin, "has remained unchanged, along with its largely unimproved landscape, since the mid-19th century, yet it was unknown until a potentially disastrous fire brought it to the attention of the local authority in 1989 and, so far at least, no major source of funds for its purchase and future protection has been found." Is it a major problem that those "unflawed gems" find there is no funding for their purchase and future protection? Is this a problem for you?

(*Mr Carr*) I do not regard it as a problem in general, Mr Chairman, because there is the possibility that the Historic Buildings Council would recommend a grant towards purchase or towards its maintenance. The house in question is Aberdeunant, I think.

128. Gentlemen, thank you for coming to see us. There are some other questions we still have to ask you. Would it be acceptable if we asked for those responses in writing, Mr Carr?

(*Mr Carr*) Certainly, Mr Chairman.

129. Would you like to say anything further or correct anything we may have misunderstood, or add anything at all to this morning's session?

(*Mr Carr*) Not at this time, Mr Chairman, but should I have inadvertently misled the Committee during my evidence, I would like to have the freedom to correct the record, if that is agreeable to you.

Chairman: Of course, that is a facility available to you. Thank you all very much for coming.

Letter from the Chief Executive Cadw: Welsh Historic Monuments to the Clerk of the Committee

HISTORIC BUILDINGS AND ANCIENT MONUMENTS (HB57)

When I gave evidence to the Committee on 20 January there were a number of issues on which I undertook to come back with further information. I set out below my further responses on these points, listed by reference to the relevant question and numbers in the draft transcript of evidence.

Q 69 Historic Chapel Trust for Wales

The Committee asked if we saw the establishment of an Historic Chapels Trust in Wales as being desirable.

I think the short answer is yes: we would see such a move as being of considerable interest. To date our effort has been to see if a body might be established which might help the needs of important redundant ecclesiastical buildings—across all denominations. I think however it is important to note that, whilst Cadw may be able to assist such a move, I do not think it will be possible for us to take the lead on such an initiative.

Q 59 Disposal of Redundant Churches and Chapels

The Committee was concerned that Trustees have a legal obligation to dispose of sites for the best possible price.

It may be helpful for the Committee to know that the Redundant Churches and Other Religious Buildings Act 1969 as amended by the Charities Act 1992, Section 4—(2)(b) enables trustees to allow the Secretary of State or charitable bodies to acquire such premises by way of a gift or for a consideration less than full valuation.

Q 88/89 Historic Landscapes

The Chairman invited me to write on this issue. The identification of historical landscapes is seen as an important part of our work on the compilation of an all Welsh Register of Historic Landscapes, Parks and Gardens.

In the past year Cadw, ICOMOS and the Countryside Council for Wales have reviewed what criteria should be applied and how this work should be taken forward.

In January 1993 it was decided to undertake an all-Wales assessment to identify the most important landscapes in the Principality. The project will be jointly funded by Cadw and the Countryside Council for Wales and will be undertaken by the Deputy Director of the Gwynedd Archaeological Trust, an experienced landscape specialist who will be on secondment.

The work will involve desk-top assessments, related field work and draw in other experts in various fields. The Welsh Historic Gardens Trust, the four Welsh Archaeological Trusts, the Royal Commission on Ancient and Historical Monuments and university departments are all expected to make an important contribution.

Q 118 Shorter List Descriptions of Buildings of Architectural or Historic Importance

The Committee was concerned with shorter list descriptions which we have for some of our records for buildings of architectural or historical importance.

I think it is important for the Committee to know that the Ministry of Works and subsequently the Department of the Environment, who originally had charge of this work, had adopted a variety of approaches towards the list descriptions and, by modern standards, some must now be viewed as not being as helpful as they might be. Generally, the earlier lists were given shorthand descriptions which only aimed to produce identification of the individual structures and did not provide a definitive account of each building's special features or important historical elements. It was also the case that before 1971 descriptions were issued separately from the statutory lists which contained only the bare legal details of address and owner. The Town and Country Planning Act 1971 led to the production of combined statutory and descriptive lists. This coincided with a greater professionalism in the approach to the work as buildings were more carefully searched out and archive research was added. Since the Welsh Office has had responsibility for this work—and particularly so since Cadw was established in 1984—the emphasis has been towards the production of more informative list descriptions which contain all relevant architectural and historic facts to aid local authorities in carrying out their planning functions. Cadw has since 1984 seen some 4,400 listing entries which mirror the philosophy of fuller description. It is our intention that as the resurvey programme of the Principality is taken forward the older and less informed list descriptions will be replaced by the new fuller ones.

12 March 1993

Supplementary memorandum by Cadw: Welsh Historic Monuments Executive Agency

THE PRESERVATION OF HISTORIC BUILDINGS AND ANCIENT MONUMENTS IN WALES
(HB 58)

(Replies to additional questions for the Committee)

1. HISTORIC LANDSCAPES

What will be the status of the joint Cadw/ICOMOS register?

The register will be advisory and for the information of those concerned with forming and considering applications for planning consents.

How will it contribute to the conservation of landscapes (and parks and gardens)?

Improved information should ensure that the historic importance of sites is appreciated and thus promote a sensitive approach to their management.

What consultation has there been on the form and content of the register?

The parks and gardens element is based on similar registers which have been produced for England and Scotland. English Heritage is in the process of revising its register and the form of Cadw's register is similar to that being used for the English revision. All those parties who are contributing to the register (the Countryside Council for Wales, the National Trust, the Welsh county councils and some district councils, the Welsh Historic Gardens Trust, etc) provide advice through an advisory panel which was set up by Cadw and ICOMOS at the outset of the project. There is also close liaison with county and district authorities as work is taken forward on the preparation of each county register. The landscapes exercise will involve widespread consultation with those with an expert knowledge or interest in the subject.

2. AREAS OF ARCHAEOLOGICAL IMPORTANCE

Part 2 of the Ancient Monuments and Archaeological Areas Act permits the designation of archaeological areas. Has this legislation been implemented in Wales? If so, has it ever been used in Wales? What are the benefits of archaeological area status?

This legislation has not been implemented in Wales. Such designations are intended to provide for the notification of development proposals in such areas; to provide an opportunity for archaeological assessment and, if necessary, archaeological excavations. The alternative of voluntary arrangements entered into by developers has worked well. This approach has been strengthened by the issue of a Planning Policy Guidance Note on Archaeology (PPG 16 Archaeology and Planning) which encourages greater collaboration between local authorities and developers. The power to designate AAIs remains available and is kept in view.

Is Cadw seeking additional ways to accelerate its scheduling enhancement programme?

During the next financial year Cadw will be supplementing the work of its Inspectors and Ancient Monuments by employing a contractor, with previous scheduling experience, to work on the scheduling enhancement of Roman military sites in the Principality. It will also be reviewing the way in which contractors could be used to further accelerate this work, particularly in the assessment of major monument types.

3. OTHER ISSUES

Your memorandum states that "Grade II buildings (the lowest grade) are buildings of special interest which warrant every effort being made to preserve them". In what way does this lowest grade of historic buildings receive less protection than the highest?

All listed buildings are subject to the special provisions laid down in planning legislation for their treatment. However, in the case of interior works to a Grade II building, a local planning authority may determine an application for listed building consent without reference to Cadw. That is, unless historic buildings grant has been paid on the property.

How many Grade II buildings are lost or damaged each year?

Cadw is aware of 23 applications for listed building consent during the last 5 years which resulted in demolition of structures. No figures are collated centrally concerning damage or demolition without consent.

What has been the number and results of prosecutions in recent years under the historic buildings and ancient monuments legislation?

Local planning authorities are in the front-line on enforcement/prosecution action involving listed buildings. Cases are not routinely notified, though in the past year Cadw has corresponded with two local planning authorities about unlawful works to listed buildings which had been the subject of Prosecution and Enforcement action. In the same period, Cadw has corresponded additionally with around 30 local planning authorities regarding unlawful works.

In respect of ancient monuments, in 1983 and 1986 successful prosecutions were mounted in respect of damage to two monuments. Cadw takes the lead role because it has ready access to the necessary advice. Planning Policy Guidance Note 16 states that proceedings will be initiated where it is considered a good case can be sustained. Two cases are currently being considered by the Department in conjunction with the Crown Prosecution Service.

Have monuments or buildings been "written off", descheduled or delisted when damage has been difficult to prove or monitor? Or impossible to report?

In respect of ancient monuments, any change in their condition is monitored to establish whether or not they should remain monuments scheduled as being of national importance. Changes can arise for a number of reasons ranging from damage to natural erosion. In the past year four monuments have been descheduled.

In the past year 40 buildings have been removed from the list because they were thought not to be worthy of continued protection following alterations.

The memoranda from the Amenities Societies claim that local authorities have failed to provide proper notification to those Societies as required by statute in advance of demolition applications in respect of listed buildings. Are you aware of these claims? And are they justified?

Welsh Office Circular 61/81 (paragraph 52) states that:

"The Secretary of State has power under paragraph 7(2) of Schedule 11 to the 1971 Act to direct local planning authorities to notify specified persons of any applications for listed building consent and the decisions taken by the authority on them. *The Secretary of State hereby directs that notice of all applications for consent to demolish a listed building and of the decisions taken thereon should be given to the following bodies: the Ancient Monuments Society, the Council for British Archaeology, the Georgian Group, the Society for the Protection of Ancient Buildings, the Victorian Society, and the Royal Commission on Ancient and Historical Monuments in Wales.* The addresses of these bodies are given in Appendix III. Except in the case of the Royal Commission, the notifications of the applications should be accompanied by the relevant extract from the list describing the building. Any representations received in response to these notifications should be taken into account when the application is being considered."

The Circular goes on to say:

"It is often asked whether works which do not involve total demolition of a building should nevertheless be regarded as "works for the demolition of a building". An authoritative interpretation of the law cannot be given but attention is drawn to section 290(1) in which "building" is defined as including any part of a building."

Cadw's advice to local planning authorities in working contacts is that the amenity societies should be notified in cases of partial demolition especially where this involves key features of a building like chimneys. In examining cases, evidence of consultation with the amenity societies is sought and the matter raised with the authority if this is not forthcoming. Where an amenity society complains of non-notification this is taken up, but the definition of partial demolition can be problematical.

In relation to grants to historic buildings, what has been the balance of funding between rural and urban properties in each of the last three years?

Since 1988 the total value of historic buildings grant applications made and accepted by owners for each county in Wales was:

Clwyd	£1.737 m	(18 per cent)
Dyfed	£1.192 m	(12 per cent)
Glamorgan (Mid, South and West)	£1.142 m	(12 per cent)
Gwent	£1.779 m	(18 per cent)
Gwynedd	£2.321 m	(24 per cent)
Powys	£1.538 m	(16 per cent)
Total	£9.709 m	

Precise splits between rural and urban are difficult. However, taken on the broad basis that Dyfed, Powys and Gwynedd tend to be mainly rural counties, historic buildings grant was split fairly evenly between rural and urban areas. Clwyd, Gwent and the Glamorgans benefited by 48 per cent (£4.658 m) of the total.

Currently there are 76 management agreements with owners of ancient monuments. How many would you hope to enter into (a) in the long term and (b) in the next year?

Management agreements are viewed by the Department as an effective way of supporting the maintenance and preservation of ancient monuments. Typical examples might be field monuments—such as Bronze Age barrows—which if left unsecured might suffer, for example, from damage as a result of ploughing or animal erosion. The intention is therefore to enter into a positive programme of management with an owner for immediate protection and after care.

Seventy-six management agreements are currently in place and the Agency has a target to negotiate 20 in 1992-93. For the future the intention would be to introduce as many management agreements as can be matched with the needs of individual monuments and the willingness of owners to join in such arrangements.

Can you tell us how many grants were given for ancient monuments in private ownership in the last year? And what percentage of the total costs the owners were expected to fund?

In 1991-92 24 offers of grant were made: six to private owners and 18 to local authority owners at a total value of some £146,000. Generally grant is at a rate of 50 per cent but the Department can enhance this rate in certain circumstances.

Are management agreements the preferred instrument for assisting the owners of ancient monuments?

The Department's intention is to have in place different measures of assistance that can match the needs of individual monuments. For example standing remains such as town walls and bridges can require programmes of consolidation work. These can be costly and technically demanding. The intention in these cases is to offer grant aid under Section 24 of the 1979 Act which provides for financial assistance for the preservation and maintenance of monuments.

The needs of all monuments are not, however, as demanding and many field monuments require little more than careful control of tree and scrub growth, to secure the proper preservation of the site. In respect of this class of monument management agreements are judged to be the best approach.

Do you envisage extending the system of management agreements to all ancient monuments. If not, how is selection made?

It is not envisaged that all scheduled ancient monuments will need the assistance of a management agreement. In respect of upstanding remains grant aid under Section 24 of the Act may be more appropriate. Some monuments by their very nature require no assistance and a very welcome feature is that some private individuals already have a very positive approach to ancient monuments on their land and do not seek assistance. In cases where management agreements are thought desirable the selection is made by the identification of a site where it is hoped that a more positive approach by an occupier would benefit the monument. Preliminary selection is made by Cadw's Field Monument Wardens and then more critically assessed by Cadw's professional Inspectorate of Ancient Monuments.

March 1993

WEDNESDAY 17 FEBRUARY 1993

Members present:

Mr Gareth Wardell, in the Chair

Mr Nick Ainger	Mr Elfyn Llwyd
Mr Alex Carlile	Mr Peter Luff
Mr Jonathan Evans	Mr Mark Robinson
Mr Roger Evans	Mr Walter Sweeney

Memorandum by Council for British Archaeology

PRESERVATION OF HISTORIC BUILDINGS AND ANCIENT MONUMENTS IN WALES (HB6)

The Council for British Archaeology, founded in 1944, is made up of 356 national, regional and local societies, organisations and museums. The Council exists to promote the study of Britain's archaeology, and to improve public knowledge of and interest in Britain's past. The CBA has concern for archaeology throughout Great Britain and Northern Ireland: a concern which embraces the historic environment as a whole, including landscapes and buildings, as well as subsurface remains.

The CBA functions both at UK level and through a series of Regional Groups. CBA Wales serves the whole of the Principality. It is one of the bodies formally consulted by Cadw on Scheduled Monument Consent applications and consultations relating to archaeology. Local Planning Authorities are also required to notify CBA of applications for listed building consent which involve demolition.

We thank you for the opportunity to submit a memorandum to the Committee. Within the areas of inquiry identified by the Committee we wish to focus upon three issues which at present appear to us as being of particular importance: church archaeology, the scheduling and recording of industrial sites, and historic buildings.

Other matters which relate to the Committee's inquiry have recently been considered by the CBA. These include the need to bring portable antiquities within the law (Annex 1), and recommendations for the better management of historic landscapes (Annex 2).

SPECIFIC COMMENTS

GUARDIANSHIP MONUMENTS

1.1 We are pleased to note that the Secretary of State, through Cadw, remains willing to consider taking sites of national importance into Guardianship, as at Plas Mawr. We hope that this willingness will be sustained.

1.2 We also commend the considerable improvement in public facilities at many sites managed by Cadw, with the introduction of attractive exhibitions and the award-winning guide book programme. These developments are much more than cosmetic, for they help to widen public appreciation of Wales's heritage and to develop the potential of that heritage as a cultural and educational resource.

1.3 We urge Cadw to undertake a programme of compiling strategy plans for the long-term conservation and management of each site in the care of the Secretary of State. Such plans would provide a framework for the continuing care, management and interpretation of these nationally important sites.

CHURCH ARCHAEOLOGY

2.1 CBA Wales wishes to record its deep concern regarding the care and preservation of historic buildings in the possession of the Church in Wales. We recognise that churches are exempt from listed building and scheduled monument control for as long as they remain in ecclesiastical use, but remind the Committee that churches are subject to planning control (and hence the processes of *PPG16*), and that ancient monuments provisions can be applied to structures or deposits in church precincts. Hence, the points we wish to raise here do, we believe, fall within the scope of the Committee's concern.

2.2 Churches are important today as living places of worship and foci of communities; they are important too for their scientific, cultural and educational significance. The evidence that they contain—within, under, and around their buildings—has the potential to contribute to a wide range of historical issues. That potential will not be fulfilled if the evidence is lost, yet such evidence is all too easily destroyed by neglect, alteration of church buildings and surroundings, or ill-advised repair.

2.3   In England since 1972 these issues have been documented in exceptional detail, in a succession of reports by the CBA and the Church of England's own Council for the Care of Churches.[1]

During the last twenty years the Church of England has taken both practical and legislative steps to fulfil its own archaeological responsibilities. For example:

(a)   Almost all Diocesan Advisory Committees now have an archaeologist within their memberships, to advise on archaeological issues occasioned by applications for licences for repair or alteration.

(b)   The Care of Cathedrals Measure 1990 provides for an archaeologist to be nominated to the statutory Cathedrals Fabric Commission. The Measure requires each historic cathedral to appoint an archaeological consultant, and provides for consultation with members of the Joint Committee of National Amenity Societies.

(c)   Since 1968 the Redundant Churches Fund has existed, to care for redundant churches which are of outstanding architectural, archaeological, or historic importance.

None of these provisions exists in Wales. This is partly because of the disestablishment and limited resources of the Church in Wales; however, restricted means do not absolve other owners of listed buildings or archaeological sites and monuments from their responsibilities.

The Church of England's continued exemptions from listed building and scheduled monument control were retained, after consultation by DoE, partly on the strength of a willingness to overhaul its own internal statutory system of control. A comparable overhaul is now called for in Wales, if the case for exemption is to be reasonably sustained.

2.4 We would like to draw the attention of the Committee to the following points:

(a) Commission on Faculties

In 1990 the Representative Body of the Church in Wales set up a Commission on Faculties. Amongst other things it is reviewing provision for archaeological advice prior to church building and repair. We regard it as essential that each Diocesan Advisory Committee issuing faculties in Wales should include a professional archaeologist, with knowledge and experience of ecclesiastical archaeology, and ideally, a person well-versed in the study and the care of historic buildings. We also believe that in cases where significant implications have been recognised, there must be a mechanism to ensure that any excavation or recording is carried out to an appropriate standard.

The Church is naturally concerned about the potential cost of archaeological investigations. We would therefore like to congratulate Cadw upon recently agreeing to fund archaeology occasioned by repairs in cases where churches are in receipt of grants for repair under the Historic Buildings and Ancient Monuments Act 1953 (Section 4). We hope that Cadw will be able to consider sympathetically other applications for archaeological work on churches which may be submitted by the four Welsh Archaeological Trusts or other recognised archaeological bodies.

(b) Cathedrals

At present no Welsh cathedral has a formally accredited archaeological consultant. Some, but not all, ask for advice on an informal basis. This is unsatisfactory. We therefore recommend that the Church in Wales should be encouraged to institute mechanisms at Welsh cathedrals which parallel those operating in England under the Care of Cathedrals Measure.

(c) Redundant Churches

The current mechanism whereby churches in Wales are declared redundant is complex and can take many years. Meanwhile the church fabric may fall into disrepair and be vandalised. When a church is finally declared redundant there remains the difficulty of finding an alternative use, a problem which is particularly acute in the National Parks. The Church in Wales is still, on occasion, resorting to the harmful and defeatist measure of reducing redundant churches to safe ruins. There are currently four historic churches in Wales in the care of the Friends of Friendless Churches. However, because of the lack of a Redundant Churches Fund in Wales, there is an unknown number of other worthy buildings under threat.

We understand that for some years the Represenative Body of the Church in Wales has been in discussion with Cadw to establish a policy in respect of redundant churches in Wales. We urge that this now be brought to a speedy and successful conclusion.

---

[1]*Churches and archaeology* (1973); *The archaeological study of churches*, CBA Research Report 13 (1976); *Archaeological work in and around Anglican churches in use* (CBA/Church Information Office, 1978); *The church in British archaeology*, CBA Research Report 47 (1986); *The Anglo-Saxon church*, CBA Research Report 60 (1986).

(d) A Gazetteer of Welsh Churches

We understand that the Royal Commission on Ancient and Historical Monuments in Wales is currently discussing the need to compile a gazetteer of Welsh Church sites in order to determine their historic and potential archaeological importance. Such a project is of the greatest importance to all aspects of the future care and preservation of the historic churches in Wales. We urge that it should begin as soon as possible.

SCHEDULING AND INDUSTRIAL MONUMENTS

3.1 Cadw has an enhancement programme for identifying additional monuments which merit statutory protection, and the revision of existing designations. This we commend, but we have serious concerns that industrial sites and monuments in Wales are not receiving sufficient attention.

3.2 Considering that Wales played a significant role in the Industrial Revolution, relatively few sites have any protection, either through the use of the Ancient Monument and Archaeological Areas Act or listed building legislation. Since they are also poorly represented in the regional Sites and Monuments Records, industrial sites are currently not being given the consideration they deserve through the implementation of the recent *Policy Planning Guidance Note 16*.

3.3 In order to remedy the situation we recommend that consideration be given to:

(a) An urgent review of the statutory protection of industrial archaeological sites, with a view to enhancing the scheduling and listing of such sites.

(b) Enhancement of regional Sites and Monuments Records.

(c) The implementation of national or regional thematic studies, similar to those already being implemented in England under the Monument Protection Programme.

3.4 Owing to their nature, industrial sites—many of which are upstanding and ruinous buildings—are susceptible to the ravages of decay and ultimately collapse. To help prevent this we would recommend that consideration be given to increasing the proportion of grant aid normally given to owners for the repair of industrial monuments from the usual 50 per cent to, at least 80 per cent.

LISTING AND THE NEED FOR ACCELERATED RESURVEY

4.1 The listing of historic buildings in Wales gives us cause for concern; the total number has risen from 5,257 in 1971 to 14,372 by 1991. This increase, however, was largely the result of notifications of buildings under threat. We would like to see a more positive and strategic approach, as was adopted with the resurvey in England during the 1980s.

4.2 Between 1971 and 1991 only c56 out of 169 areas produced 'Revised Lists' of Historic Buildings. At this rate of progress it will be at least 2040 before the resurvey is completed. We call for greater resources to accelerate the work.

4.3 Records of listed buildings only exist in paper files. There is an urgent need to draw up a plan to computerise all records. For example, there is no breakdown by geographical location, and when seeking information from Local Authorities about district totals this often takes considerable time or they claim not to know.

4.4 Because of staff shortages within Cadw, there is a declared policy that new listings cannot be considered unless the notified property is under immediate threat or in an area designated for revision. We regard this as insufficient.

LOCAL AUTHORITY PERFORMANCE

5.1 Notified listed buildings applications from a number of local authorities have been compared with actual planning applications relating to listed buildings throughout 1990 and 1991. The results confirmed suspicions that many alterations, including demolition, have been made to listed buildings without notification to national amenity bodies. This was brought to the attention of the Society of Welsh District Planning Officers in May 1992. A substantive response is still awaited.

5.2 The care exercised by Local Authorities over their properties is very diverse. Some set a poor example to the public, as witnessed in several recent cases, where the public purse was given complete priority over historic value: Gwynedd County Council (8/9 High Street, Caernarfon), Swansea City Council (The Guildhall) and Vale of Glamorgan (The Esplanade). Civic Society action saved the first two, but the other was lost. We call for stronger, more enlightened control and the appointment of conservation officers within Local Authorities as a matter of course.

5.3 The absence of a dynamic listing programme appears to prevent any assessment of losses by 'creeping modification', whether with or without approval.

5.4 From our experience, grant schemes to restore empty listed buildings incur very high costs, because the buildings have often been allowed to fall into disrepair; this frequently leads to the abandonment of the works, as the applicants cannot face their share. We suggest that the clear reluctance of any Local Authority to apply sections 54 and 55 of the 1990 Act (the carrying out of emergency work to ensure the preservation of listed buildings) is contributing to these high costs.

LANDSCAPES, PARKS AND GARDENS

6.1 A Register of Landscapes, Parks and Gardens of Special Historic Interest in Wales is currently being compiled under the auspices of Cadw and the International Council on Monuments and Sites. We hope that this survey will eventually result in the introduction of an effective designation for historic landscapes which answers the needs and problems outlined in Annex 2.

Annex 1

PORTABLE ANTIQUITIES: A STATEMENT OF PRINCIPLES

The Council for British Archaeology, the Museum Association and the Society of Antiquaries of London have been concerned for many years that portable antiquities in England and Wales are accorded inadequate legal protection. Therefore the senior officers of each have met to agree the following statement of principles with the aim of securing the support of the archaeological community at large.

Dr Peter Addyman	President, Council for British Archaeology
Professor Barry Cunliffe	President, Society of Antiquaries of London
Professor Susan Pearce	President, Museums Association

DRAFT

In Britain today there is no coherent statutory provision for the management of our archaeological inheritance. Britain's archaeological inheritance is a unique resource for the study and understanding of human history. This inheritance includes structures, landscapes, evidence of people's relation with the natural environment, and moveable objects, whether situated on land or under water.

This paper considers the position in England and Wales, but the principles apply more widely. In England and Wales, only Treasure Trove, limited to certain gold and silver finds, provides any requirement for finds to be recorded or studied. There is no other legislation relating specifically to portable antiquities. This omission is illogical. It is also contrary to the public interest: an interest which rests in opportunity for public knowledge of our national history.

The case for bringing portable antiquities within the protection of law arises from the following principles:

(1) The archaeological inheritance is an entity. Archaeological structures and objects form an essential part of archaeological heritage. Therefore portable elements of our heritage should be accorded a status in law which is commensurate with their importance.

(2) The archaeological inheritance is irreplaceable. The nation should seek to ensure that all aspects of its inheritance are subject to appropriate stewardship.

(3) All archaeological material has a potential to contribute information which will help to retrace Britain's history. There is thus a valid public interest in the reporting by a finder of items which are found by chance.

(4) The purpose of such reporting is to allow competent recording of information. Such reporting should be made a legal obligation upon the finder (as is currently the case with Treasure Trove), and failure to report should be an offence.

Arising from these the following further principles may be proposed:

(5) It is generally the case that, at the time of discovery, the original ownership of archaeological material has lapsed through a break of continuity. Under English law, ownership at present generally lies with the landowner except in cases of Treasure Trove. The valid public interest in archaeological material indicates that a new owner should be assigned to it. In the national interest this owner should be the Crown.

(6) Competent authorities acting on behalf of the Crown should exercise discretion in the matter of future ownership.

(7) The Crown should wish to retain material of national or regional significance in museums, for purposes of study and public display. Where the Crown retains material, a financial award may be made to the finder and/or landowner.

(8) In the case of material which it is not in the public interest to retain, the Crown would normally wish to reassign title to the finder or landowner.

(9) The same principles should apply to material underwater as apply to remains on land.

(10) The definition of "material of archaeological interest" is a matter for the judgement of the competent authorities.

Memorandum by Ancient Monuments Society

PRESERVATION OF HISTORIC BUILDINGS AND ANCIENT MONUMENTS IN WALES (HB5)

The Ancient Monuments Society welcomes the chance to submit evidence to the Inquiry into the preservation of historic buildings and ancient monuments in Wales. This is the first Inquiry of its kind for many years and could be of pivotal importance in determining Government policy in the future.

Four main terms of reference are laid down and we shall offer observations on these, but we should also like to touch on other associated issues.

GENERAL REMARKS

There is an impression among many conservationists that Wales lags behind England in the adoption of the conservation ethos and practice. In some ways this has been and does remain true. Listing was first introduced in the 1950's whereas it began tentatively in 1944 and formally in 1947 in England. There is no separate National Trust for Wales and only one Building Preservation Trust compared with a hundred in England. There is no Redundant Churches Fund in Wales and no Welsh equivalent of the recently established Historic Chapels Trust. In the late Eighties only 20 Welsh country houses were open to the public, even including hotels. There is no architectural conservation course in any Welsh university and a sufficient shortage of conservation architects for a large number of Welsh clients to have to resort to English architects. A distressing number of Welsh local planning authorities lack Conservation Officers; indeed only a mere handful of the 900 Members of the Association of Conservation Officers work in Wales. Wales irrefutably has some catching up to do.

And yet in other ways it has led England. The inventories of listed buildings steal a march on England by being (selectively) illustrated, whilst Wales postdated Scotland but preceded England in introducing the Thirty Year Rule in the identification of listed buildings (in the protection of Brynmawr Factory built in 1946-52 and listed Grade II*). The organisation known as CAPEL was established before the equivalent Chapels Society in England.

1. PROPERTIES IN THE CARE OF THE SECRETARY OF STATE

The Society has no particularly strong views to offer on this matter other than to urge that Cadw continues to acquire through ownership or guardianship historic sites and monuments which are important architecturally or to the history of the Principality. The relative lack of enthusiasm among Welsh local authorities to extend their responsibilities and the almost complete lack of Building Preservation Trusts no doubt means that the policy of English Heritage as expressed in its Forward Strategy of offloading responsibility for more than half its monuments will not be taken as a precedent in Wales.

We have no general adverse observations to offer on the presentation of monuments on Cadw's care—indeed, we were very pleased to welcome the design of the new Visitor Reception Centre at Castell Coch, the great medievalising fantasy building by William Burges, where the idiom chosen borrows directly from the work of the latter.

2. OWNERSHIP BY THE NATIONAL TRUST, CHURCHES AND LOCAL AUTHORITIES

The holding of the National Trust in Wales is refreshingly diverse and as a general rule, very well presented. It displays an open policy towards further acquisition as is shown by the recent taking over of Plas Dinefwr in Dyfed. Its properties include some of the greatest houses and landscapes that Wales has to offer, buildings of national importance like Penrhyn, Powis Castle and Erddig, rescued in 1973-77 in one of the boldest conservation exercises of its time. Its horticultural work and the knowledge and appreciation of private owners has been greatly increased by the foundation of the Welsh Historic Gardens Trust (Plas Tyllwyd Tan y Groes, Cardigan SA43 2JD. Tel. 0239-810432) and by the compilation of a Register of Historic Parks and Gardens by Cadw along the lines of that drawn up in England (where the first survey has been finished and a second one is underway).

When Thomas Lloyd wrote his first edition of his major work on "The Lost Houses of Wales" in 1986, the outlook for a number of the major threatened properties was bleak. By the time the second edition was issued in 1989, whilst recording the losses since 1900 made the same melancholy tragic reading, the prospects had greatly improved. This was very largely through private initiative and investment (generously helped in a number of cases by Historic Buildings Council grant). The same lady who saved the great Plas Teg has now moved on to Bettisfield, formerly the property of the Hanmer family and the subject of at least three applications to demolish either completely or in part. Trevor Hall is now once again a private house and the burned out remains of Pickhill have been saved by multiple residential application. Douglas Blain continues the long programme to fully conserve Monaughty in Radnor, whilst plans were announced to create country house hotels within Soughton in Clwyd and the long-derelict Llangoed at Llyswen, Powys, a beautiful reconstruction of a much older house by Clough Williams Ellis. As in England and Scotland, the recession has stifled some hopes, but the increased commercial interest in sensitive country house conversion is welcome.

Financial difficulties are also threatening local authority initiative, most dramatically in the proposal by Clwyd County Council to sell Bodelwyddan which is only just repaired and converted, with commendable architectural skill, to provide an outstation to the National Portrait Gallery. Local authority initiatives, fortunately not so far threatened, have saved other outstanding buildings, particularly Llancaiach Fawr (where the saviour was Rhymney Valley) and Margam Castle where the ruins of the burned out mansion, the gardens and the orangery have been well conserved by the County Council.

As in England and Scotland, that outstanding organisation, the Landmark Trust has helped to adapt a number of more eccentric historic properties to provide attractive holiday accommodation.

Churches and Chapels

There are a proportionately higher number of churches and chapels in Wales than in England. In 1910 it was estimated that there were 4,716 non-conformist chapels alone. The problems and the challenges as well as the visual and historic benefit are therefore great. In the Church in Wales, there are direct parallels with the English system of control, particularly in the existence of Diocesan Advisory Committees, but none of the Welsh examples despatch their agendas and minutes to the AMS or any of the other national amenity societies (whereas some 80 per cent of the 42 DAC's in England do now do so). The decision-making process on what happens in churches in use within the Church in Wales is less open and consequently less well understood by bodies such as the AMS. We understand that the system is at present under review (under an equivalent Commission to the Faculty Jurisdiction Commission meeting under the Chairmanship of the Bishop of Chichester which conducted a review of Anglican practice almost 10 years ago). We consider it essential that the review is encouraged to ensure that decisions are taken by those experienced in and knowledgeable in the care and maintenance of historic churches.

The joint announcement by Mr Peter Brooke and Mr David Hunt on 17 December 1992, that Ecclesiastical Exemption would be substantially abolished will have considerable repercussions on the treatment of non-Anglican places of worship in use. The AMS warmly welcomes the announcement which will ensure that denominations will either have to establish systems of internal control which will involve consultation with outside bodies like the AMS and the other national amenity societies or bow to full local authority and Cadw control through the listed building consent machinery over internal and external changes. The AMS is willing to play its full part in any consultation system.

The problem of what to do with disused places of worship has so far received no such satisfactory resolution.

England enjoys the benefit of the Redundant Churches Fund established in 1969 to maintain redundant Anglican places of worship too important to be demolished or converted. It now owns almost 300 and is funded at present 70 per cent by the State and 30 per cent by the Church. The latter's contribution is met in part from the sale of the sites of demolished churches. The churches owned by the Fund are not put to systematic use but are open to the public and can be used occasionally. There is no equivalent to the RCF in Ulster, Scotland or in Wales. Discussions on the matter in Wales between the Archbishop and the State do not seem to have been conclusive and the Welsh Office is intending to tackle the problem at present through substantial, some 100 per cent, grants. This perhaps sounds more generous than it is for it presupposes the existence of receiving bodies able to take on the burden of caring for the churches on a regular basis given that HBC grants cannot be for maintenance as opposed to repair. The single greatest recipient of redundant churches in the Principality is the sister society of the AMS, the Friends of Friendless Churches, with which we have been in a working partnership since 1980. Further information on its role is given in the memorandum submitted by the Honorary Director, Dr Ivor Bulmer-Thomas. The Friends, established in 1957 and registered as a charity, will enjoy an indefinite life but at present the guaranteed annual income is only £10,000. There are no paid members of staff so all the money raised goes on the churches and the payment of professional advisers but £10,000 to be divided between 21 churches shows just how financially challenged the Friends are. The Friends are willing and anxious to perform the role for which they were established but if they are to provide the kernel for a Redundant Churches Fund for Wales they will need substantial financial assistance. The fact that extra measures are urgently required was demonstrated in 1991 by the disgraceful application to demolish the church at St Bride's, Wentlooge in Gwent, with its intact and elaborate 15th century tower as good as many in Somerset. The Friends have had to turn down the ownership of a number of churches and chapels in Wales simply through lack of funds.

Professor Anthony Jones's seminal study of "Welsh Chapels" in 1984 pinpointed a number of disused chapels of quality including Capel Carmel at Carmel Plas, Llyn in Caernarfonshire of c. 1810, and the Baptist Capel Mud at Penygraigwen near Amlwch in Anglesey of 1845. The Friends own one nonconformist chapel, the Strict and Particular Baptist Chapel of 1792 at Waddesdon in Buckinghamshire, but so far has no non-conformist property in Wales and where these pass out of use they can normally only be "saved" by a new use that can involve the ejection of all internal fittings. The Landmark Trust has been able to save one chapel at

Maesyronnen at Glasbury, converted from a barn in 1696 where it has created a "Landmark" for holiday occupation within the adjacent Minister's house. Another chapel, Capel Pen rhiw from Drefach Felindre, Carmarthenshire has been reconstructed at St Fagan's Open Air Museum which has also converted another in situ to provide a museum (Capel yr Hhen Gapel at Tre,r-ddol). Other chapels have been converted as with the Bethesda at Merthyr Tydfil, now a community centre, and the Machynlleth Tabernacle in Powys, reopened in late 1986 as a musical and cultural centre. New use will no doubt be the salvation for one of the greatest of mid-19th century chapels now under threat, St Paul's Methodist Church at Aberystwyth with its splendid portico, but already time is running out for it was the subject of an unsuccessful application to demolish in 1991. The majority of disused chapels will be saved by conversion but for the very special few preservation intact with only the most gentle of new uses is essential.

An Historic Chapels Trust, an equivalent for non-Anglican places of worship to the Redundant Churches Fund, was established in December 1992, in England with core funding from the Department of National Heritage. This hopes to take on two chapels per year. Constitutionally, however, it will not be able to cover Wales and there is a clear need for some equivalent across the border. The writer is a trustee of the new Trust, the Chairman is Sir Hugh Rossi, and the Director, Mrs Jennifer Freeman.

3. LISTING AND LISTED BUILDING CONSENT

Listing has been touched upon briefly in the General Remarks.

By March 1992 there were 14,374 listed buildings in Wales. This compares with 439,048 in England at the end of 1991, of which 6,068 were in Grade 1. The increase in Wales has been impressive in itself—the figure for 1974 was 5,297—but there is still a pressing need for the speeding up of the resurvey programme along the lines of that launched by Michael Heseltine in England in the 1980's. We understand that on present calculation the resurvey, if carried on at the present pace, will not be complete for 60 years. There should never be a time when the lists are closed and regarded as definitive. Nevertheless, a broad resurvey of all areas would reduce the number of spotlistings which understandably annoys owners and make the task of planning authorities easier and more stable. If a building is important and needs protection it would be as well to know that sooner rather than later.

In 1991 application was lodged to demolish a total of 42 listed buildings in Wales (on the basis of the figures compiled by the AMS which, like the other national amenity societies, has to be informed by law of all applications in England and Wales involving any degree of demolition at a listed building). This compares with applications to demolish 465 in England (the figure for 1990 was 455 and the figure for 1992 is likely to be 245,[1] clear evidence of the impact of the recession). Only a handful of these were successful and it is some comfort that the figures do not seem to have become appreciably worse. Only four listed buildings were the subject of successful applications to demolish in 1980-81 and only 11 in the two years 1988-90.

The system of consultation differs markedly from that in England by the requirement that all applications for listed building consent have to be referred to Cadw amounting, we understand, to 467 in 1988 and nearly 700 in more recent years. English Heritage (excluding London) sees all applications affecting Grade I and Grade II* listings but only Grade IIs involving substantial or total demolition where the local authority is minded to grant consent. The disparity is quite understandable and we strongly support it. The figures in Wales seem perfectly manageable for such an organisation and such increased centralisation is essential as long as local authorities lack the necessary expertise or commitment. Of course some local authorities are good but this is very often a factor of the quality of staff employed as is true with Delyn, Monmouth, Brecon Beacons and Clwyd County Council. There are some very successful Town Schemes as at Holywell in Clwyd and the compulsory purchase by Ceredigion District Council of the long-derelict house known as Llanina and its onward sale to a repairing new owner set an example ducked by many English authorities. However, even the best staff can be overruled or ignored by planning committees and many "Conservation Officers" are employed at a lowly status within the planning hierarchy, whilst others do not deal with development control at all but are limited to the offering of advice and the processing of grants. Cadw's efforts to encourage the employment of Conservation Officers is welcome but a good person in that post can only be the first step.

I am afraid we have no statistics on the number of Conservation Areas in Wales although the figure for England is now some 7,500. Conservation Area designation of itself brings control over the lopping, topping and felling of trees and over the total or substantial demolition of buildings and external changes like stone cladding, dormers and satellite dishes. Other damaging alterations, particularly to windows and doors, are not covered however unless the Conservation Area is subject to an Article 4 Direction. This has to be confirmed by the Secretary of State. The National Amenity Societies which held a conference on the matter in November are coming increasingly to the view that Conservation Areas without Article 4s are comparatively meaningless and that the Secretaries of State must be encouraged to permit Article 4s when requested and encourage rather than deter their designation. We feel that there is a strong argument for local authorities

---

[1]At the time of writing this figure [245] was a fair prediction although it turned out that the figure for 1992 was 281.

being able to decide on Article 4 Directions without referral to any Secretary of State, particularly as the designation of Conservation Areas in the first place is a matter for autonomous decision by the planning authority without any approval from another party.

4. GRANTS

The AMS has no reason to criticise the regime of grants offered by Cadw—indeed our sister society, the Friends of Friendless Churches has benefited from very generous donations. In one specific area the Society is very greatly concerned at general Government subsidies being used in a way that is destroying the traditional character of much Welsh vernacular architecture.

This is in the application of Improvement Grants as recently redefined. The damage has been so great and so obvious in West Wales that an architect practising in the area, Martin Davies, has written and published at his own expense an excellent book on the subject entitled "Save the Last of the Magic" of which I attach a copy to this paper. The interpretation of the grants varies from District to District but he has a great deal of evidence to show that the sizeable grant levels are being used to eject features of character which could easily be repaired to make way for standardised replacements. Some officers are actually specifying the use of cement-rich render rather than a lime render which should always be used on historic properties in stone. Cement, apart from being ugly, provides an impervious skin which prevents the wall "breathing" and thus exacerbates problems of damp and dry rot. In other areas sash window are being ripped out to be replaced by the ubiquitous plastic windows in uPVC (or as it is now known, PVCu). I enclose a copy of the letter Mr Davies wrote to the Society for the Protection of Ancient Buildings which lays out the problem. We feel very strongly that this is a case where public money is being used to destroy rather than enhance architectural character and we urge that the Committee investigate further to ensure that Improvement Grants are used only to provide improved amenities in a manner that is architecturally benign. The system itself needs changing to ensure that people are not forced to do more work than they want to in order to comply with the notorious and pre-ordained "fitness standards". The other problem is the way in which the system is implemented by inspectors who have little or no sympathy with the historic character of the cottages and houses they are dealing with. They spend as little time as possible in the property (sometimes just 10 minutes) assessing what work needs to be done and of course the easiest approach is to condemn everything. It takes longer and a greater knowledge to pick out those items which have to be replaced and those which can and ought to be repaired.

The new improvement Grant system has replaced the earlier three grants. There is now one major grant with theoretically no limit to expenditure above the householder's contribution which varies according to means testing and is sometimes nil, that is 100 per cent grant. Householders going for minor assistance frequently end up having to have their whole house practically reconstructed. Much of the work is mandatory which means that once the man with the clip pad had crossed their threshold the work has to be done or the house is condemned. This is an unacceptable and gross misuse of public money.

The Committee may also care to ensure that the range of Cadw grants matches those offered by English Heritage provided that English pitfalls are avoided. One such is the limitation of "Buildings at Risk" grants to those falling within Conservation Areas. It is particularly important that in country like Wales with so many scattered communities outside potential or existing Conservation Areas that this limitation is not repeated.

Finally, we urge the Committee to lend its voice to those criticising the present damaging and illogical rules on the payment of VAT, a problem which is of course common to all parts of the United Kingdom. At present after a number of changes, the most recent in 1989, VAT is payable on all works of repair and maintenance at listed buildings but works of alteration and extension are exempt provided they enjoy listed building consent. No concessions, sensible or otherwise, exist for unlisted buildings falling within Conservation Areas, whilst the existing changes do differentiate between residential and non-residential properties. Businesses registered for VAT carrying out VAT-able repairs can get the money back by passing it on but individuals, charities and churches cannot escape by that route. Responsible citizens should be encouraged to carry out repairs and discouraged from altering their buildings (other than to convert them benignly). At present the VAT regime encourages precisely the opposite. The prospects for change do seem to be weak given that Government's agreement through the EC both to a minimum rate of 15 per cent and to ban further exemptions. And yet the need to address this problem is overwhelming and the damage it is doing, incalculable.

Examination of Witnesses

MR RICHARD K MORRIS, Director, MR RICHARD J BREWER, Secretary, CBA Wales and MR RAYMOND F CAPLE, Listed Buildings Secretary, CBA Wales, and from the Council for British Archaeology; MR MATTHEW SAUNDERS, Secretary and DR ROGER WOOLS, Ancient Monuments Society, were examined.

Chairman

130. On behalf of the Committee I thank you very much for coming to see us this morning. The best thing to do to start with is for you to introduce yourselves.

(Mr Caple) I am Ray Caple. I am the Historic Buildings Secretary for Wales.

(Mr Brewer) I am Richard Brewer. I am honorary Secretary of CBA Wales.

(Mr Morris) I am Richard Morris, Director of the Council for British Archaeology.

(Mr Saunders) My name is Matthew Saunders and I am Secretary of the Ancient Monuments Society.

(Dr Wools) My name is Roger Wools. I am a member and I will be a Council Member of the Ancient Monuments Society this year.

131. Thank you very much. We shall start by looking at the arrangements for the property in care of the Secretary of State, the so-called estate in care, one of the things that we explored with Cadw, was whether that estate was representative in nature. In other words, was the portfolio that is currently in the care of the Secretary of State for Wales skewed in any way so that it would be a better mix if it excluded some of the property that is in it and included those that are not in it already? Does either the Council or the Society have any views on that? Do any of you have any strong views that there is a skewed distribution? Who is the one to criticise Cadw for its inability to represent the culture of Wales and who includes too many Edward I castles for example?

(Mr Saunders) Can I begin by mentioning something that may come later, but one of the quintessential Welsh building types is the chapel. It is a matter of great concern. I think I am right in saying that Cadw does not have in guardianship a chapel, which is extraordinary in a principality that has over 4,000 chapels, many of them listed and many of them under threat. That seems to be a building type which is ignored, for whatever reason.

132. Is there anything that you want to add to that at all?

(Mr Morris) The estate of the nation is skewed in England as well and probably in Scotland. The distortions that may exist in Wales are not peculiar to Wales. They are peculiar to the way in which we have collected monuments since 1882. There has been a tendency to go for the large masonry structures, like Edward I castles, at the expense of things more recent, such as chapels, industrial monuments and landscapes, which hitherto have eluded us because they are not very tangible in a material way, even though they are culturally very important. I do not think Cadw is to be criticised for having it skewed. It may be a lack of a collecting policy and that these monuments have accumulated over many decades and they are really a reflection of what people have been interested in over the past 100 years at different times.

133. In terms of the phrase "ancient monument" and the estate in care, Mr Saunders mentioned chapels and Mr Morris reaffirmed that, it is strange, is it not, that a chapel that could have been built 50 or 60 years ago could be regarded as an ancient monument if it fell out of use? The term "ancient monument" is not in any way time specific in terms of the length of time a building has been in existence. The public perception of an ancient monument would not include buildings that are comparatively recent. It is very difficult sometimes for the lay person to appreciate the term "ancient monument". How can you have a monument which is ancient that could be as recent as 40 or 50 years of age, or perhaps even more recent in terms of its genesis and its collapse?

(Mr Morris) I agree, it is a phrase with all sorts of luggage that perhaps we would wish to get rid of today. We perhaps need a new term that is more properly reflective of the idea that the historic environment comes up to yesterday.

(Mr Saunders) My own society labours under a misnomer, because we have been called the Ancient Monument Society since the 1920s, but we are concerned with buildings of all ages. We were involved, along with the Twentieth Century Society, very peripherally, in the Brynmawr factory, for example, which is the post-war grade II* star listed factory of exceptional architectural quality.

(Mr Morris) So were we. We sent somebody to the inquiry.

Chairman: Moving on to the guardianship exercise by other major owners over their property, such as the churches and the National Trust, I shall ask Mr Roger Evans to ask a series of questions on churches, whether they are in use now or whether they are redundant.

Mr Roger Evans

134. I begin by dealing with the question of the Church in Wales, which I suggest probably has slight different problems from non-conformist chapels. Can our experts point to the aspects of the arrangements for the Church in Wales which are different from those for the Church of England? Can Mr Saunders summarise this, looking at his paper at page 3 in particular?

(Mr Saunders) There is certainly a great difference, as in England, between churches that are redundant and churches that are in use. There are different legal procedures, depending upon whether a building is in use or out of use. Churches in use in Wales, as I understand it, are ruled under a faculty system which is very similar to the one in England which is being reviewed at present by a Commission on Faculties which will, no doubt, lead to reforms and a greater accessibility. It is a concern of the societies that the DAC—the diocesan advisory committees—which are discrete to each diocese perhaps are not so open as their English equivalents. The societies in general have not been formally approached as yet to make formal nominations of representatives to serve on the

[Mr Roger Evans *Cont*]

DACs in Wales, although we have been asked to nominate what are called contact points, which we found more difficult to do. We would prefer to have formal representatives.

135. DACs have become very much an established part of the English scene. Can you explain, for the benefit of the record, when these came into existence and how their functions in England have developed?

(*Mr Saunders*) There are 42 DACs in England, as I say discrete to each diocese. They came into force, I think I am right in saying, after the First World War partly to monitor the introduction of war memorials into churches. They are co-ordinated by a central organisation called the Council for the Care of Churches, set up in 1924. That is an extremely useful organisation in providing expertise to the DACs. They have experts on stained glass, woodwork, and metal work who are on stream. We would certainly hope that each DAC would also have its own expert on these very important and complicated areas.

Chairman

136. Can you just clarify for the record what DAC stands for?

(*Mr Saunders*) Diocesan advisory committee. It is a very complicated concept because it is advisory to the chancellor.

Mr Roger Evans

137. The intention of the system which came into being in the 1920s—if I may summarise it and if Mr Saunders agrees with this—was to provide in each diocese advice to the chancellor who makes the decision on the faculty for fabric alterations and had a wide range of representative expertise of all the likely areas and the kinds of things which he has to deal with.

(*Mr Saunders*) Yes.

138. The importance is the expertise in particular areas—stained glass, archaeology, architecture or whatever it happens to be. How far does the system in the Church in Wales compare in terms of providing the range of expertise that might be necessary?

(*Mr Morris*) From our point of view it is not good. I have examples here of things that have happened in churches which should have benefited from archaeological advice. I am using "archaeological" here in its broadest sense.

139. Can you give us a couple of good examples?

(*Mr Morris*) I understand that the church at Llanrhwydrys in Anglesey was refloored and replastered last year without any archaeological involvement. I am not sure that the diocese of Bangor has proper archaeological advice on its DAC. I am told there is a hole open there now as we speak which should not be there. I can go on.

140. Yes, give us two or three examples.

(*Mr Morris*) Llandeilo in Dyfed, an early Christian site with early sculpture, a curvilinear enclosure. This had a new heating system put in under its floor last year. This was discovered archaeologically by entire chance. It was not properly referred. Llanengan in Gwynedd where major repairs were done grant-aided by Cadw, but I am told not with archaeological

involvement; Clynnog Fawr in Gwynedd, repointing and again with no archaeology; St Mary Tenby, where an archaeologist on holiday last year encountered considerable works going on in the churchyard which had revealed earlier structures in the churchyard. I am not aware that this was properly programmed, so these all illustrate the tendencies of lack of archaeological advice, which was very similar to the Church of England in England in the 1950s and 1960s.

141. Is there any equivalent body in Wales to the Council for the Care of Churches in England to give centralised specialist expertise to Welsh diocesan advisory committees?

(*Mr Saunders*) I do not think there is.

(*Mr Morris*) I do not think so, although on occasions some of the Welsh dioceses will consult the English Council. They have a wonderful library and very good expertise, but this is an entirely informal arrangement and is not sufficient for what is needed.

142. For example, as I understand the composition of diocesan advisory committees, the people who go on them tend to be experts and you see Roman Catholics and even Buddhists serving on diocesan advisory committees because they are their for their professional expertise. How is the Church in Wales treated the openness of its range of experts, similar to England or differently?

(*Mr Saunders*) I get the impression that the new Commission may herald a sea change and there may be a copying of the English practice introduced under the Care of Churches measure which came into force last year, whereby there will be representatives, not mandated, but to pass the comments on from local authorities, English Heritage and the five national amenity societies, meeting through the joint committee. I hope that will be reflected in Wales and I hope similarly that either as observers or as members there will be on stream experts on the range of areas that were mentioned before, plus people with a general lay but knowledgeable concern for churches.

143. In terms of the amenity societies and you are slightly different strands, gentlemen, how does the Church in Wales compare either in referring matters to you or notifying you or giving you a direct input into the diocesan advisory committee structure?

(*Mr Morris*) Unfavourably.

(*Mr Saunders*) I have never been approached by a Welsh DAC ever.

144. What is the consensus of opinion at the moment? If the Church in Wales continued its present practice—I will have to ask them what their present commission is likely to do—and things stayed as they were at the moment, what is your recommendation should the Church in Wales continue to enjoy the ecclesiastical exemption or not?

(*Mr Morris*) We would be content that it should if it were to bring its practices and its desire for good advice into line with best practices elsewhere, the best practices in the Church of England. I think that would satisfy us. This applies to cathedrals too. We will be coming to those. If it does not do that I think there is a limit to the time that one would allow the exemption to continue before we start to campaign against it.

[Mr Roger Evans Cont]

145. Perhaps I can summarise that. As I understand what you are saying, if they pull their socks up over a reasonable period that would be admirable. But I put my question on the premise that if things remain as they are without change, is it your society's view that the ecclesiastical exemption should be withdrawn from the Church in Wales?

(Mr Morris) Yes.

146. What is the Ancient Monuments Society's view on this?

(Mr Saunders) Reluctantly, I think probably that they should lose the exemption, but I think there should be an investigation. I plead ignorance partly because of lack of feedback over exactly what happens in each of the Welsh dioceses. There should be an investigation. There should not be a unilateral withdrawal and that is what the Government have heralded by asking for replies by 31 March from each of the denominations in Wales and England to assess whether they have an internal system of control that would give them the right to continue to enjoy exemption.

147. I now want to deal with a slightly allied question on the Church in Wales. The position in respect of Welsh cathedrals, as I understand it, is as it was in England before the recent measures. In other words, there is no control over the dean and chapter of a Welsh cathedral, or the representative body.

(Mr Saunders) That is my understanding.

148. What are your societies' views on that?

(Mr Morris) There should be.

(Mr Saunders) Absolutely.

Chairman

149. Why do you think that?

(Mr Morris) Because I do not think that a dean and chapter should be free to disregard good advice or responsible stewardship of an historical complex of international importance, such as St David's. I do not think that liberty should be there. To put it positively, I think deans, chapters and their cathedrals benefit from good advice and the right level of expertise. At the moment they are free either to not seek it or to over-ride it.

Mr Roger Evans

150. Were there some classic examples in England before the new system came in which lead to the present arrangements?

(Mr Saunders) Yes.

151. Can you give us a good example of something which disturbed in England amenity societies in respect of deans and chapters really being judge, jury and executioner as far as their buildings were concerned?

(Mr Saunders) The screen at Hereford, for example, that was thrown out, other fittings that have been ejected from St Alban's Abbey, for example, and also from Hereford Cathedral and other places. I know that Dr Wools serves on an advisory committee.

(Dr Wools) I am on the fabric advisory committee for Ripon cathedral. As their advisory planning committee, we have now formed a very good relationship with the Dean and it is working very

well. But some years ago the Saxon crypt, St Wilfred's crypt in Ripon was one of the great disasters of British archaeology, where a new entrance was put down into the crypt without proper investigation. That is the cathedral to which I have been appointed recently, but I feel strongly that it would help Wales a great deal to have the expertise that is available to advise Deans and Chapters on works and the artefacts within the cathedrals.

Chairman

152. Are you saying that the fault was entirely the dean's for that catastrophe?

(Dr Wools) I do not know the circumstances. It was 20 years ago now. The Council for British Archaeology would be better to comment, but it did happen and it happened through ignorance, I think.

153. Mr Morris, these deans have this enormous liberty and here they are seeming to be dangerous beings when they are put in charge of these things. Should there be some vetting body set up before they are appointed to ensure that they are not allowed to have these liberties, otherwise the kind of thing that Dr Wools mentioned could very well happen.

(Mr Saunders) A DAC or deans' advisory committee?

(Mr Morris) The point you raise is important, which is that so often what is good and what is less good is determined by the background and proclivities of individuals. There are very good practices, no doubt, across Wales in both cathedrals and parish churches, but whether they are there or not is not down to the overall system. It is down to the good sense, wisdom and experience of individuals. I think that is a dangerous way in which to sustain conservation.

154. You do not think a booklet Guidance for Deans would be worthwhile considering?

(Mr Morris) I think that Wales on a number of fronts would benefit from advisory literature which goes into the do's and don'ts in a constructive way, not in a sanctimonious way. This has been done in England. There is an advisory leaflet on archaeology, for example, for the Church of England here. It is that sort of thing that one would like to see in Wales in order to extend enlightenment.

155. And training courses for deans?

(Mr Morris) And archdeacons too, particularly. Especially archdeacons!

156. Are they less or more dangerous than deans in this regard?

(Mr Morris) They have influence over more sites and so I would say they are more dangerous.

157. So we must not forget about these individuals?

(Mr Morris) Or more positive, depending on their attitudes.

Mr Roger Evans

158. If we can just summarise this, a dean and chapter of an English cathedral, until the recent Care of Cathedrals Measure, was entirely entitled under the ecclesiastical exemption to do what it will with the structure of its building?

[Mr Roger Evans *Cont*]

(*Mr Saunders*) Yes.

159. Without reference to any expert body being required of them or indeed requiring a permission? That was the purpose of an ecclesiastical exemption. Now in England there is a system whereby they have to take expert advice and the anomaly, as I understand it, is that in Wales there is no such similar system. Can I now move on to the question of redundant Church in Wales churches? Can you give us some indication of the relative gravity of this problem?

(*Dr Wools*) For my conservation diploma which I undertook at York university in 1973, I looked at this problem. I am sad to say that things have not moved on a great deal with regard to the Church in Wales in terms of redundant buildings. I think the Church in Wales finds it difficult to know the numbers of redundant buildings, but 20 years ago they were estimating that there were about 180 redundant churches in Wales which would be about 10 per cent. It is difficult until a survey is done on the ground to know churches that are redundant because many of them are closed, but are not declared redundant. My guess is that probably about 10 per cent. is the figure. One can see in west Wales churches closed and in ruined condition and it is extremely disturbing that there is no real mechanism to judge the churches to see whether they should be preserved, or find new uses or, as a last resort, be demolished as in England with the Redundant Churches Fund.

Chairman

160. As one goes round Wales and looks at the churches from a motorcar one would not know necessarily as one passes whether the church is still in use or whether it has already become an ancient monument?

(*Dr Wools*) Indeed. In west Wales you find quite a few churches covered in ivy and they have been closed and are redundant. It applies to chapels as well.

Mr Roger Evans

161. I want to make sure that we have understood how the English system operates. In England there is a Redundant Churches Fund which is funded 70 per cent. by the state and 30 per cent. by the Church of England, normally by demolitions and sales of property. But the point about it is that there is in England a system, if you could explain it, for assessing the relative importance of particular redundant churches. Can you explain how that operates?

(*Dr Wools*) There is an advisory body, and probably Mr Saunders knows it better than I, which advises on the architectural, historical and archaeological quality and character of the building and an assessment made about whether it should be taken into care and preserved as a monument. That is a monument to be seen and visited by people not something that is closed. It is an important part of the Redundant Churches Fund that these buildings are. open for public use and for public enjoyment, but they are preserved.

162. Can you explain to us in England what the cut-off point is because obviously there is not enough money and some churches the system will not save, but roughly what does it mean? How important in England do you have to be to be vested in the Redundant Churches Fund as a building? Can you give us a rough guide?

(*Mr Saunders*) There are at present almost 300 vestings in England. The majority are medieval but, if I can use the word, the catholicity of the approach is remarkable. They have just taken their tenth purely Victorian church into the Fund. They have some outstanding 18th century churches as well, an exceptional one in Sunderland and another in Macclesfield as well. There is no barrier statutorily on the age of the building. It is the quality of it. In fact, there is now a growing problem of post war buildings as well and inter war buildings, so there is no ban in terms of time.

163. In Wales there is no such Redundant Churches Fund whatsoever?

(*Mr Saunders*) No.

164. Why is that, as far as the amenity societies are concerned? What has gone wrong in Wales do you think and what should we do about it?

(*Mr Morris*) It is partly to do with the disestablishment of the Church in Wales and its poverty. It is probably more a question for them, but the Church of England approached this problem over many years from before the Second World War and came up with a partnership arrangement with the Treasury in which the Church of England puts a considerable amount of money, and put in more at the beginning. I am not sure that the Church in Wales feels able to do that, to go to the Government and say, "If we put in £X will you do that too?" Or if they have said that, we have not heard about it. So there is a sense of poverty there, but a sense of apathy with it. The poverty we can understand. The apathy is distressing.

165. In terms of the consequence of all this, Mr Saunders has told us of the sort of quality of building that goes into the Redundant Churches Fund in England. What happens to these kinds of buildings in Wales?

(*Mr Morris*) They fall down.

(*Mr Saunders*) They fall down or they are converted. It should be said that the Advisory Board for Redundant Churches, which is the statutory adviser to the Church Commissioners also examines conversion schemes, which obviously is a more common fate, fortunately, than demolition. They are also able to advise upon sensitive approaches to conversion, so their job is to facilitate the introduction of good uses which can act as flagships. In many parts of England the conversion of what previously had seemed to be a problem hulk of a building, if it has been converted into a use which draws the people in, which cleans it and shows it to its best advantage architecturally and archaeologically and touristically, has a tremendous fillip on the area and upon other redundant churches and chapels in the area. It is that that Wales in a large part lacks. There are some exceptional conversions, Llangollen and the tabernacle at Machynlleth, are very good examples. The Landmark Trust has converted some chapels very well into holiday accommodation, but there are large areas of Wales

[Mr Roger Evans Cont]

where there are not the sort of flagship conversions that people can go to that the developers can say that a conversion has been done successfully in one place and they can do likewise and make a legitimate return on their investment and embellish the area.

166. Can you give us three or four examples of Welsh churches which in England you would have expected to have been vested and saved in the fund or to have been converted? Can you give us some examples which we can consider as to where the system in Wales has broken down?

(*Mr Saunders*) Apart from the one I mentioned there is the church at Wentlooge, which is an extraordinary church with a fifteenth century tower as good as anything in Somerset. It is not often that one is really shocked as one tends to become a bit hard-bitten, but I was really shocked at the application which came in to demolish totally that building. That I am sure would be absolutely unheard of in England, literally unheard of. Those days are over. Those are the days of the 1960s when churches of that quality were just smashed to pieces. It is a sign of the need for a Fund or some equivalent mechanism when churches like Wentlooge are threatened.

167. Can we have two or three other examples?

(*Dr Wools*) In west Wales there is the church which is quite famous of Slebech, a very interesting Victorian church, in an interesting architectural stage of transition, that has been standing as a great landmark on this hill top alongside the road for 150 years. But it has been lying empty and deteriorating now for many, many years without any real means of finding a new use for it or considering whether it should be vested in a Fund. When I went there I was very surprised to see it because it was so much better than I had read about it. I would have thought that in England it might be considered for a Redundant Churches Fund because of its period in the nineteenth century and its size and character. There are other smaller churches in west Wales, such as Hasguard and Yerbeston, that are falling into decay, and there are small medieval churches. There may be very good uses for them. These may include "stone tents" or camping accommodation through agencies such as the YHA but not to have any agency to consider them and just to let them fall down seems to me to be quite shocking.

Chairman

168. We have heard about these examples like Wentlooge in Gwent, what do you find is the role of the Friends of Friendless Churches? Mr Saunders, you mentioned them in your memorandum in pages 3 and 4 in relation to St Bride's in Wentlooge itself. You finish off in the sentence at the top of page 4: "The Friends have had to turn down the ownership of a number of churches and chapels in Wales simply through lack of funds". Mr Morris said earlier that he could understand the poverty, but he could not understand the apathy. Obviously that does not refer to the Friends presumably because they cannot be considered apathetic, can they?

(*Mr Saunders*) No, I should make it clear that I will become the director of the Friends of Friendless Churches, so I have to be careful. The marvellous

Welshman who founded the Friends, Ivor Bulmer Thomas, in 1957, founded them expressly and raised money for them because there was no Fund in Wales. The Friends is a marvellous organisation, but it exists in Wales partly by default because the State and the Church are not doing what the State and the Church are doing in England. The five churches the Friends look after—on an income of only £10,000 a year with no paid staff—with the possible exclusion of one, would have been good enough for vesting in a redundant churches fund. We have a marvellous church at Llanfairkilgeddin which has a whole series of internationally important plaster panels in the medium called sgraffiti which was mentioned in an exhibition in London and the Church in Wales seriously proposed to demolish that church. The Victorian Society compiled an excellent report on the building which alerted everybody to its importance, but it was only the ability of the Friends to take that church over with substantial public assistance from the State that saved it, but that church should never have faced the threat of demolition in the first place. It is an exceptional building.

169. How would you gentlemen tackle this problem? Mr Carr of Cadw told us that the problem of increasing redundancy was inevitable and he had no glib or ready solution. He told us that on 20 January. Do you have a kind of blueprint for what is needed in Wales to solve this problem? You have given us some idea, Mr Saunders, in terms of what happens in England. What would you do, with the difficulties that are inherent in the equation, if you had carte blanche in Wales and you could be the man to solve the problem? How would you tackle it? Is there a solution?

(*Mr Saunders*) I will pass you over to Dr Wools later, but I will not duck your question initially. Part of the problems are fairly insoluble, are demographic, are to do with changing religious patterns which no one will be able to stop.

170. You do not think the Government are to blame in not having a population policy? You are not referring to that?

(*Mr Saunders*) No, it is nothing to do with breeding. There clearly are irreversible demographic trends and certain churches will be closed because people are leaving the villages. But in terms of money, I think just a little amount of money could have a remarkable effect. The Redundant Churches Fund is an example which can be followed, not just for narrow architectural reasons, but all its churches are open to the public. There is a terrible pejorative language talking about churches being in aspic and fossilised, etc. They are not. The churches' role is, to talk of higher things, just to exist and to be a reservoir of artefacts and a place where people were buried and married. That sense of the importance of a church carries on, even though formally it becomes redundant. The people will visit churches, even though they are redundant for pastoral reasons, and a fund in Wales could well help in terms of the attraction to tourists in the Principality. The Redundant Churches Fund has a very useful brochure so that when you go to a Fund church there is normally a guidebook available and the majority of Fund churches are open. Even where they are shut, during the working day there is a key holder normally

17 February 1993]   Mr Richard K Morris, Mr Richard J Brewer CBA,
Mr Raymond F Caple CBA, Mr Matthew Saunders
and Dr Roger Wools   *[Continued*

[Chairman *Cont]*

contactable and a plate is displayed saying where he can be contacted. For the amount of money that the state would have to provide to preserve the churches of fundable quality there could well be direct results in the leisure industry, in tourism for places to visit, to study and to understand what being Welsh is, which is what the churches sum up.

171. Dr Wools, would you like to add anything?

(*Dr Wools*) I think the solution should be a Welsh solution for a Welsh problem, but the Redundant Churches Fund in England provides a very good model indeed. I thought carefully about this recently and I wondered whether it should be set up on a diocesan basis, but I think the answer has to be on a National basis and I would have thought the Redundant Churches Fund basis was a way to start. The problem is where does the money come from? Having spoken to the Church in Wales recently, I think there is good will from their side to resolve this and they will do their best, but they need assistance. I would have thought that funding is the answer to it. I think a Redundant Churches Fund for Wales could be set up fairly quickly because it has worked so well in England and I do not see why the principle should not work well in Wales, but it is a matter of money.

172. Mr Morris, do you agree with that?

(*Mr Morris*) I agree with Dr Wools, yes. There is an extra point here which is that for the churches that are not of fundable quality more leadership is required from within the Church in Wales for active seeking of suitable alternative uses for those churches. At the moment the local passions sometimes defeat attempts to give churches a local use. I think more leadership is needed in searching for appropriate local new uses for those churches which will not ever be national monuments.

Mr Roger Evans

173. We have to move on because there are a number of subjects we must cover. The Church in Wales is always easier to focus upon simply because of the nature of its organisation. Probably you would agree that there is an appalling problem in Wales of non-conformist chapels. What are the views of the amenity societies on this issue? What has to be done?

(*Mr Saunders*) Can I begin with a new innovation in England at the end of last year which is something called the Historic Chapels Trust, of which I am a trustee. It is very early days indeed but it seems slightly curious that we have an Historic Chapels Trust starting in England before we have an Historic Chapels Trust in Wales because again it is the quintessential Welsh building type after the mine, I imagine. That is designed to act as a Redundant Churches Fund in so many words for that particular building type. I would come back to the point that many chapels are fairly robust buildings when compared with the more fragile medieval archaeologically sensitive fabric and can take other uses, provided it does not mean the wholesale ejection of internal fittings of course, but they can take new uses. I mentioned the case in Machynlleth of the tabernacle there which is a very good sensitive conversion and is partly reversible, and at Llangollen too, where the EC gave money towards the establishment of an interpretation centre in the

centre of that town. These kinds of chapels are purpose-built auditoria, after all. They are made for concerts and for meetings. They are easy to convert and they are an under-used resource in that sense. I think therefore that the solution to the "un-Fundable" chapels would be more flagship conversions to show developers, often without the need to go to public money whatsoever, what can be done in the way of office conversions, for example.

(*Mr Morris*) As for the chapels of national quality Wales could set the lead here, if there is to be a Redundant Churches Fund for Wales. It has not been set up. It could be a Redundant Churches and Chapels Fund from the start rather than have what I think is the unfortunate situation we have in England where we have one organisation for one group of churches and second for another. To simplify and rationalise would be useful.

Chairman

174. Thank you very much for that evidence. Perhaps we can move on to the listing of historic buildings, the scheduling of ancient monuments and the controls exercised largely through Cadw on planning consents and look, first of all, at the strategic view. Do you two bodies have a view about strategic targets for the size of the schedule of monuments or for the list of buildings, for example as a proportion of the total building stock, that is, the relative number of the number of the schedule of monuments and the number of the list of buildings that we should have in Wales?

(*Mr Morris*) I am not sure, and will defer to a colleague, about whether Cadw has a long-term strategic target for scheduling in the way that there is one in England under the monuments protection programme. I know they have annual targets.

(*Mr Brewer*) I am aware only of the annual target of adding about 80 monuments to the schedule each year, which I think they are achieving, according to their annual report.

(*Mr Morris*) In fact, comparing with what happens in other parts of Britain, that is good progress. But we are not aware of any strategic—if I may use that word in its proper sense—objective.

175. Do you think the target size of the list of historic buildings, for example, should be restricted to match the resources available to manage them?

(*Mr Morris*) No, I think the resources should be changed. There is no way of ducking this one. There are more listed buildings in a handful of London boroughs than there are in the whole of Wales. At the present rate of progress in Wales, entire categories of historic building are going either to have disappeared or to have been converted out of all recognition by the time that they might be listed. The time simply is not there. The fact that there has been an accelerated resurvey in England with temporary money provided for a term of years to do a particular job and get on with it is an example that should be followed in Wales and Scotland. The fact that it is not appears to put Wales at a massive disadvantage and I cannot understand why there is not more protest about it.

176. Do you find a major problem in Wales with regard to buildings that are listed that they then are not preserved or managed because of something that

[**Chairman** *Cont*]

the local authorities have told us and that we have picked up in other memoranda which is that they themselves are in a Catch 22 position? They find that if they use their statutory powers to insist that the owner of a property should maintain and manage that property up to a certain minimum standard, that if the owner is not in a position to do that the local authority will carry out the work, bill the owner and find the owner does not have the money to pay back the local authority for the work done? Are there obvious examples of listed buildings in Wales that are falling into disrepair and may even be lost because the local authority, for whatever reason, is not exercising its statutory duty to insist that the owners carry out the work they should carry out? Mr Caple, would you like to take that?

(*Mr Caple*) Yes, I encounter two or three of those every year. Two years ago Johnston Manor was reported as losing its roof. I spoke to the local authority and they said they simply could not face the cost of putting the roof on and the owner was unwilling or unable to pay for that.

177. But that is very few, is it not, three a year? We have altogether in Wales something like 14,700 listed buildings. I am not detracting from the fact that those three could be fundamentally important and we should not lose them. Nonetheless in terms of the size of the problem, if you are coming across only three a year that fall into that category, is that information as accurate as it can be? You are not suggesting that those are the only three in Wales that fall into that category, are you?

(*Mr Caple*) No, those are the ones I am aware of. I suspect that it is a much higher percentage.

(*Mr Saunders*) Thomas Lloyd has done an excellent book on just one building type, which is the country house. This is all the country houses in Wales demolished since 1900, with many more at the back still derelict and threatened. I am more than pleased to let the Committee· have this. This is just one building type, and the sort of threat that is being faced. Also I want to return to one of your earlier points, it is an important matter, the idea that listed buildings are always a problem, that they are always a call upon the public purse. English Heritage's assessment of its 400,000 listed buildings found only about 30,000 in either severe disrepair, disrepair or a matter for some concern, which is well under 10 per cent. As one walks the streets of most cities, through the centres where there will be a high proportion of listed buildings, one sees that they are normally in productive use. There is no need for the state to worry about their condition at all. There is no direct correlation between the increase in the number of listed buildings and necessarily a call upon state funds pro rata. Clearly there will be major problems, but the Grade I buildings, which are the most expensive, will have been listed already years ago.

(*Mr Morris*) I want to add to the point about threat and stress that from our perspective one of the greater threats, perhaps the greatest threat, is not gentle decay or demolition but creeping modification of the kind that is not sensitive relative to the building or to the building type and over the term of years will destroy the historic value of the building altogether so that it might as well be delisted. This is a serious problem everywhere. We believe that it is particularly serious in Wales and we are alarmed that certain local authorities appear not to take it as seriously as we think they should.

Mr Jonathan Evans

178. I should like to clarify the position in relation to the book that you are offering to us, which I already have and have read. I am wondering whether you can confirm that that is a photographic record of generally great old country houses that were at the heart of the landed estates that we had in Wales and that very many of those houses are revealed within that book to have been lost in the period between the 1920s and the 1950s when there was a substantial loss in terms of agricultural income and therefore there was not the money to keep these properties running. I think it may be the case—this is my recollection from having read it—that the rate of loss was rather less in more recent years than it was during that 1920s to 1950s period.

(*Mr Saunders*) That would be fair and this is the situation reflected in England when there were more losses in the 1950s than in practically all the other decades put together immediately after the war when requisitioned houses were given back to owners who could not afford to keep them up. I could go on with other publications as well. SAVE has published other books, including a whole series of books on country houses which cover Wales where there are five or six important Welsh examples that have been saved, such as Plas Teg and other major houses. There is a plan for Sker House. The British Historic Buildings Trust is going to take it on, so progress is being made on certain cases.

Mr Sweeney

179. There has been an increased understanding of the importance of landscapes and features such as hedgerows, lanes and ditches. What is your view on the management of landscapes and how can they best be preserved?

(*Mr Morris*) I do not want to seem pedantic, but they will not be preserved and archaeologically or culturally I do not think the aim should be to do so. They have always changed. The reason why they are interesting and why we seek to conserve or manage them positively today is because they have changed in the past. That process will always go on. To try to suppose that we could freeze a landscape would not be helpful to anybody. One of the great enlightenments of the past 30 years has been the understanding that the historic environment does not consist of a little sprinkling of pinpoint monuments and buildings that are very important, but between those it consists of large tracts of historic landscape which scientifically, culturally and economically tell us a huge amount about our ancestors and about the history of Wales going back 5,000 or 6,000 years. A whole stretch of barren Snowdonia hillside, when investigated closely, turns out to be laid out by people in the Iron Age, when the boulders were looked at and discovered that they were all put there deliberately and were not just lying around. This is a marvellously exciting discovery to make and it enriches the curriculum. It is rewriting aspects of our history. It calls for sensitive management, rather than

[**Mr Sweeney** *Cont*]

over prescriptive, negative controls. I think we need a new type of designation which is less powerful than scheduling, which is what we have at the moment, where there is an understandable reluctance to use scheduling because it is so powerful. If a robin builds a nest you have to get scheduled monument consent for it. Something that is more flexible and less prescriptive for landowners is what we need which recognises the fact that the individual parts of these landscapes may not always be intrinsically all that important. It is the totality that is important to us today.

180. Do you think that we need legislation?
(*Mr Morris*) There are two ways of looking at it. One is that we could make use of an existing mechanism, such as Tir Cymen, set aside, and make more beneficial use of that. The other is that the multiplication of yet more and more designations of different types, often with little packets of money being attached to them, being run by different Government departments is not, in the long run, a very productive path to go down and we would be better off by isolating it as an issue and saying that we need a modification to the Ancient Monuments Act to recognise the fact that there are things like historic landscapes and to give them a proper definition in law.

181. Does the Ancient Monuments Society have a view on this?
(*Mr Saunders*) We would very much follow the CBA line. It is very much an archaeological matter as well as a broader matter.
(*Mr Morris*) There is one little twist to it, if it is possible to comment, concerns recent landscapes. We are very concerned about the *Landscape Wales* initiative which, although very well intentioned and useful in all sorts of respects, is going perhaps too far too fast and will do things that we may regret. As an analogy, it is rather like having one's attic full of old things including lots of fairly recent things and one has a choice to clear it out and just put it all in a skip, which is often what is happening, or should one be selective, go through what is in the attic and decide what to keep. At the moment our industrial landscapes in Wales are suffering. In 10 or 20 years' time we shall look back with great regret at some of the over-cleansing that has gone on in the late twentieth century.

182. I take the point that you made, Mr Morris, about not wanting to preserve landscapes, but conserve them. Do you see this as part of an overall policy on perhaps achieving conservation areas? How do you integrate the conservation of a landscape with the conservation of the buildings that feature in that landscape?
(*Mr Morris*) It is a new skill that we have not yet learned. I am not sure that taking an existing designation like the conservation area and applying it to 4,000 hectares of upland field systems is necessarily the way to do it. We may need a variant of the conservation area, like a rural conservation area or landscape conservation area, in which the thrust of what the conservation area does, which at the moment prevents one from doing things, or ensures that only certain types of things can be done. With a landscape what we are trying to do is slightly

more subtle. We are trying to encourage the landowner to be more responsive to what is there. We are really reversing the polarity of conservation from telling people not to do things and encouraging them to do positive things. It is that change of conservation culture that is part of this landscape question where we need leadership from national agencies such as Cadw and English Heritage which at the moment we are not getting.

183. How do you provide that leadership when there is a lot of separate ownership of buildings, land and so on, which form part of the landscape, and therefore conflicts of interest with each person wanting to make the best use of their particular part of the land?
(*Mr Morris*) Your question is correct in the way that it suggests to me that there has to be a new kind of designation for landscapes which ought to be statutory. But within that framework the aim is not to be negative and prohibitive and making conservation seem something that people resent because it is "them" telling you what to do, but something that people want to embrace because it is interesting and they believe it to be worthwhile. This is a big utopian challenge, but I am always utopian. That opportunity exists in Wales now because it has some of the best historic landscapes in Europe.

Chairman

184. Mr Carr said in evidence to us that there were very severe difficulties in the designation of rural conservation areas in England. Do you think that conservation areas should be established in rural areas in Wales?
(*Mr Morris*) There are some in England. I am not aware of serious difficulties arising from them. Conservation areas have been designated in Swaledale, for example, where certain field patterns and field barns are the essence of that landscape and where there is a lot of prehistoric landscape in the background. I am not aware that this has given rise to serious difficulties.

185. Are you aware of any difficulties, Mr Saunders?
(*Mr Saunders*) I think there is a difference between "Rural" and "rural". The idea of a "Rural" conservation area is something which the Countryside Commission has been pushing as a new legislative concept. The concept of a conservation area has been in force since 1968 and there are certainly hundreds of them. There are 8,000 in England and an equivalent number in Wales which are centred on villages. In Staffordshire they will protect historic eighteenth century planned landscapes by declaring a conservation area. It does not really prevent much except the felling of trees and the demolition of buildings, but it concentrates the mind. It gives a red lining as it were round the area and says it is important. It is a form of spotlighting as well as protection. I am not aware of any problems, except the general problem of conservation areas, which is an urban one as well, that generally speaking they lack teeth, unless the local authorities are given Article 4 directions, which is another matter perhaps.

186. In terms of designation of areas in rural England, whether it is a capital "R" or a small "R",

[Chairman *Cont*]

you do not know of any severe difficulties in the designation of them?

(*Mr Saunders*) I do not know that I do.

Mr Ainger

187. We have spent an hour or so talking about buildings and their landscapes and so on. I do not think we have mentioned industrial archaeology at all. I notice in your paper that you express grave concern about what is going on. I understand that another semi-Government agency, the WDA, has been responsible for at least the removal of important sites such as the Six Bells colliery in a land reclamation scheme. Have you anything more to add to what you put in your paper which is vitally important because everybody knows what a church looks like and believes it should be conserved for whatever reason. But an industrial site is something totally different and those are the sites that are at the most risk at present.

(*Mr Morris*) We can give some estimate of the scale of the challenge. In Clywd, for example, where there are some 5,000 known archaeological sites and monuments, we estimate that about 25 per cent. of those 5,000 are of industrial character, yet of the 400 sites in Clywd that are scheduled protected ancient monuments, only 3 per cent. are industrial. So there is 25 per cent. of the known resource there and 3 per cent. of it is scheduled. In Dyfed, where there are nearly 25,000 sites on the sites and monuments record the comparable figure is 16.5 per cent. which are thought to be industrial and only 5 per cent. of Dyfyd's scheduled monuments are industrial. In Gwynedd the figures are up to 50 per cent. that have some industrial characteristics and only 1.5 per cent. of the monuments in Gwynedd that are scheduled are industrial. There is a massive under-representation of industrial monuments within the statutory mechanisms that we have. In Clywd I believe that only 1 per cent. of the listed buildings are industrial, so that is something that needs urgent attention because it is the often the most recent things that we lose the fastest because we do not value them as much.

188. Why are they not being scheduled? Why are they not being listed because presumably organisations like yourselves or local organisations are putting these sites up for protection?

(*Mr Morris*) Mr Saunders obviously has a large contribution on this, but perhaps I can point out that Cadw has made a very pioneering appointment and perhaps something that has not emerged in this conversation is how many pioneering initiatives Cadw has taken over the last few years. The problem is not that they are not doing it, but that they are not on the scale that is needed to do the job. This is an example of that. They have a very interesting worthwhile project on industrial re-survey, where they have abolished the old divide between scheduling and listing and having one person looking at both sides of the issue. But one person on the coal industry is not going to do all the rest. The rest will not be there by the time they get to it. It is under-resourcing.

189. You are saying that obviously because of development, because of these structures are more susceptible to decay, many of them being metal rather than stone—

(*Mr Morris*) They are valued less. In other parts of England we have had serious difficulties with the derelict land grant money being invested in the cleansing of landscapes at appalling cost to the historic environment in the long term. We have swept away everything we would have wanted to keep with everything we did not want.

190. You are saying that this is an urgent priority?

(*Mr Morris*) It is one of our two priorities.

Mr Llywd

191. Mr Morris, you referred earlier to Cadw not being able to provide the scale to do the job. Can I move on to the resurvey of communities for listed buildings? We have met Mr Carr on at least two occasions and taken evidence from him. But he stressed in his memoranda the consistency and the standard of work carried out by Cadw, but alas at present it is likely that the relisting programme will take 60 years to achieve. He hopes for a tighter timescale, but at present that is the kind of timescale we are looking at. He also questioned the quality and the subsequent management problems which arose from the accelerated pattern of the English resurveys. What is both your organisations' view of the progress and quality of Cadw's relisting programme?

(*Mr Morris*) The quality from everything I hear is good. The progress is hopelessly slow.

192. Mr Carr referred to 60 years, but he is aspiring to 15 to 20. Would you say that that too is unrealistically long?

(*Mr Morris*) I would say that that is unacceptable for the reason we have mentioned several times, which is that many of the buildings one might seek to care for will not be there or will not be recognisable, having been unhelpfully converted by the time we reach 2010.

(*Mr Saunders*) The example in England was something which could easily be followed in Wales with minimal public expense, which is the union between the private sector and the public sector. What happened under Mr Heseltine's initiative in England was the employment of about 80 people, half from the private sector, of which Dr Wools was one, to reassess the unresurveyed areas. I do not accept that the lists are deficient at all. The quality of the lists is variable, of course, but it is actually exemplary in the thoroughness with which the buildings were assessed and the exhaustiveness of the listing description or schedule. This was done within a very tight timetable with the practices bidding for the work so that it was done competitively. It has to be said rather cruelly that in a time of recession a lot of architectural practices on the English borders or in Wales would be only too delighted to put in really quite competitive bids to do this sort of work. Now is the time for Cadw to take advantage of that. But Roger was involved in that.

(*Dr Wools*) May I talk about the numbers of listed buildings? When I did my survey 10 years ago there were then about 8,500 listed buildings in Wales. In the report of the Historic Buildings Council they are saying that six were being demolished each year. That does not sound too bad, but over 20 years that would

[Mr Llywd *Cont*]

come to 120 buildings. The total for a quarter of the local authorities in Wales was 120 buildings, so a quarter of Wales would lose the lot. That gives an indication of the patchiness of the listing. At the moment it is going at about 500 a year. That is 6,000 over 14 years, or something like that, is the rate of increase. In the resurvey in which I was involved as the leader of a team we in North Yorkshire and Humberside surveyed 12,000 buildings in the three years and we had a team of eight people doing it, so that is about 500 buildings per person. I am pleased that Mr Saunders said the quality was good, but we were supervised by English Heritage and the people whom we employed were taken on specially for it and it was very well organised. There was the initiative to get it done, because we were not paid unless it was done, and every building in every parish was looked at and assessed on a national standard, so you have an evenness. One of the problems at the moment is that the lists are so uneven where they do exist. I think it is the most major thing. If a resurvey was undertaken it could be started next spring and would be finished within three years for Wales and there would probably be another 15,000 listed buildings done in that time. It would take 10 people and would probably cost Cadw about 2.5 per cent. of their annual expenditure over each year over three years and it would be done. Having been a conservation officer for six years and having dealt with the pre-Survey lists, it was a nightmare which similarly local authority officers in Wales must be facing at the moment, of lists that are inadequate, where one does not know if pieces of paper are missing. The amenity societies such as the Ancient Monument Society and the Victorian Society have terrible problems in assessing applications. I think it would save local authorities in Wales a tremendous amount of time and money and, especially at this period, Cadw could get very good value for money in that way. The 60 years is ridiculous. Over the last three or four years of the boom years so much would have been destroyed.

193. So really we need to adopt an accelerated English pattern?
(*Dr Wools*) I would have thought that if there is one thing I would wish to emphasise today before going away, that would be the main point.
(*Mr Morris*) With one difference, which would be the Welsh difference, which is that in Wales it would be computerised from the beginning and not going back over it as we are now doing in England. There are several lessons to be learned, but I would associate the CBA completely with what has just been said about the need for this and the benefits.

194. For the record this is a very important part of your evidence. Do you gentlemen know of any examples where this time lag that unfortunately tends to encompass Cadw has given rise to valuable buildings being destroyed? I say "valuable" in the obvious sense.
(*Mr Saunders*) That is difficult because the very fact they are not listed means they do not come before us formally. We could perhaps think of cases and post the details.
(*Mr Morris*) I am sure we could provide examples of the consequences.

195. I am sure that would be very helpful if you are able to do that.
(*Dr Wools*) There is just one instance where I was instrumental. The animal wall outside Cardiff castle was due for demolition and removal, perhaps 18 years ago. I was a student at Glasgow at the time. No one seemed to have been bothered by this, so I contacted the Victorian Society and the wall was then listed Grade I and it stays where it is. But I was just amazed that it had not been listed at that point. That is a rather spectacular example.

Mr Roger Evans

196. Which wall are you talking about?
(*Dr Wools*) There is a wall with sculptures by Thomas Nicholls, I think and that was due to be moved in a road widening scheme at that time. Coming down from being a student in Glasgow I saw it in the *South Wales Echo* and thought something ought to be done. Why was it not listed?

Chairman

197. You did not see the wall for sale in the *South Wales Echo*, did you?
(*Dr Wools*) It was part of a big six-lane highway improvement and that is just one example where structures, which one would have thought would be listed are not, and then events overtake them.
Chairman: If you could possibly send us a few examples that would be helpful.

Mr Llywd

198. That is the famous Wools wall, is it not?
(*Dr Wools*) That is right, yes. That is a very good example where the lists really should be brought up to date and so much of Cadw's time will be taken with spot listing that it is totally inefficient for them having each time to look at spot listing cases.

Mr Roger Evans

199. You gave a figure for the cost of covering Wales in the way you recommend of 2.5 per cent. of Cadw's budget for each of three years. Can you put a figure on that?
(*Dr Wools*) That would come out at about a quarter of a million pounds every year over three years. That is off the top of my head, but I have extrapolated from the costs of some years ago.

200. Can you give us any indication of how much effort is wasted by Cadw on the process of spot listing? Presumably spot listing, which must be a very inefficient way of doing things in management time and expense, has a cost.
(*Dr Wools*) Yes, that would be subtracted from the budget but after three years there would continue to be spot listing. One of the pleasures of conservation is that one always makes new discoveries. It will never be complete, but that would be a more efficient means of operating. There would be spare capacity within Cadw if there were an accelerated resurvey from the arrangements that now exist.

[Mr Roger Evans Cont]

201. Spot listing would become much less frequent, presumably, if the listing job could be done properly in the first place?

(Dr Wools) Yes.

Chairman

202. I want to ask you three very quick last questions. The first is, in terms of ancient monuments, rescheduling and the programme, the records as we understand it are kept by two bodies. One is the Local Sites and Monuments Records and the other is the National Monuments Record. Would it be sensible for conservation purposes for the funding of one record only to take place rather than to have two bodies doing the work, resulting in two sets of records?

(Mr Brewer) I should like to see the present system continuing and continuing to have the two. The local authorities have more and more call on the SMR under PPG16 and they will need this very much more in the future. The local SMR will be funded from this coming April by the Royal Commission. It is essential.

(Mr Morris) I should like to make a point about what is in the SMR which is that the historic environment consists not of what is nationally glittering, the gemstones of the heritage, but more particularly of what is local and typical and that we like to think of conservation as working from what is local, typical and general upwards, rather than from what is nationally important downwards. SMRs contain all kinds of information, which includes relatively trivial individual items and entries, but it is their patterns and their overall textures that are valuable. They are very important as a planning tool, as Mr Brewer has said, and it is right that local authorities or the county equivalent level should have some responsibilities for them, given that their use is at a county or regional level, and have some degree of the responsibility for their updating. They do not stand still. They are organic things where new data and new perceptions and new interpretations are being added to them every day—or should be. The resourcing of their improvement is an important consideration.

203. One of the points that both organisations raised about the role of local authorities is the lack of appropriate expertise. How would you assess the level of expertise in the local authorities? Do you have any explanation of why the situation should have arisen in Wales and not in England?

(Mr Morris) It does exist in England. Matthew Saunders may come up with an off-the peg, off-the-cuff estimate.

204. You will be inventing Dr Wools' law if you are not careful!

(Mr Morris) I am verbally challenged! But one can recognise in certain local authorities in Wales that they appear to be virtually inert from our point of view. We have not heard from Merioneth, for example, for the last three years on a single listed building. I find it difficult to believe that nothing has happened to a listed building in Merioneth for the past three years. We have heard only one in the past three years from Deeside. Conversely there are some other local authorities which we hear from every

month. These are massive discrepancies. And their explanations? My perception is that the attitudes of local authorities towards conservation, how seriously they take it, can vary for a whole range of reasons: the local government culture, where there has been a tradition of doing it well, according to personalities, whether elected members are keen on it or whether there is a very fiercely driving planning officer or conservation officer who has whipped up enthusiasm for it. It can vary according to other constraints, political pressures, the heavy breathing of economic arguments can make conservation suddenly appear rather flimsy or make it go away. There is a need for strategic leadership from national level of the kind that English Heritage to a degree has given—although we have criticised it for not doing enough here—with its buildings at risk survey which put information on a quantified basis, with its advice on development plans on conservation, putting backbone and fibre into local authorities generally, arming them with the information they need to do the job properly, barking at the heels of those who backslide and congratulating and supporting those who are successful. It is that kind of cajoling and supportive role that is needed in order to improve the situation. My impression of many Welsh local authorities is that they have precious little interest in conservation or, if they do, they do not show it to us and that that is a problem that needs remedying by strategic leadership. Making certain tasks obligatory would help. To have to have a conservation officer, for instance, seems to me to be a reasonable thing to expect a local authority to have, but it is not an obligation at the moment

Mr Roger Evans

205. Does Cadw provide the same kind of leadership which you suggested English Heritage has, and if not in what way does it not?

(Mr Morris) I think it provides it informally and there must be a lot of informal contact of that kind. I am not aware, though, of the same degree of formal encouragement that English Heritage provides.

(Mr Saunders) I know that English Heritage can and has grant-aided the employment of conservation officers at local level. I do not know whether Cadw has done the same.

Chairman

206. The last question is from me. In terms of local authorities and their legal obligations to notify the national amenity societies in advance of alteration or demolition, the Council for British Archaeology in its memorandum says in paragraph 5 that local authorities very often fail to do that. What evidence do you have to support your claim, and can you give us a few examples of where the system has failed?

(Mr Morris) I think probably the easiest thing is to send you the figures for the consultations we have had over the past three years. That will answer that point. You will see that they are very variable. Secondly, Mr Caple has had a letter from Douglas Hogg, the superintending conservation architect of Cadw, which raises a material point. He points out that under the circular 61/81, which instructs local authorities to consult, this only refers to, in Mr

[Chairman *Cont*]

Hogg's letter, "total demolition". In fact this is not our reading of that circular, nor is it the Department of the Environment's reading of it in England. The fact that Wales is one step behind, in that our circular in England has been modernised and the Welsh one has not is another matter that needs attention. Circular 61/81 ought to be renewed.

207. What is the date of the circular in England?

(*Mr Morris*) 1987, but there is another new PPG about to replace it, so 61/81 will be two steps behind within a few months.

208. As far as you know, the Welsh Office has no plans to revise that circular?

(*Mr Morris*) I do not know the answer to that question.

(*Mr Caple*) In five years they have stated regularly that they are considering the matter.

209. Yes, that is not unusual, of course, for Government departments. Very often announcements are "soon", "imminent" or "about to happen" and sometimes they do not. You view this with great concern, do you?

(*Mr Morris*) Yes, I do not see why Wales should be deprived of the better sense and better beamed advice that English local authorities have been getting for the past five years. The English circular is very cagey about demolition and does not define it, but it points out that since definition of "a building" in law can include part of a building, therefore the definition of "demolition" ought to include part-demolition and that is the basis on which most English local authorities consult. I am surprised to see such a flat statement here coming from a senior officer of Cadw saying otherwise.

210. Is there anything that you would like to leave us with in terms of any priorities? Presumably the one you have just identified, Mr Morris, is one that both the bodies here today feel very strongly about. Are there any other points that you would like us to emphasise? Perhaps there are matters we have not covered that you would like to add to what you have said already.

(*Mr Saunders*) I should like to mention something we spoke about in our memorandum which is the improvement grants situation in Wales. It is immensely frustrating to be told that the listing programme will take 60 years, we cannot afford to find a few hundred thousand pounds to go to the private sector. Yet it is my understanding that sometimes £50,000 is spent on one house ruining it for absolutely no reason whatsoever, other than that there is public money there and you are obliged to do things you do not want to do to your own house, otherwise you will not get the grant. It seems to me to be a chaotic and an indefensible misuse of public money. In fact this is the subject of an excellent book which we sent to you and which I think you have read written by a very experienced and very sensitive architect on such matters but also an architect who does modern work as well, called Martin Davies, in west Wales. He published this at his own expense because he felt so strongly about this misuse of public money. That is something which has not been raised so far, but I would say that if we are talking about a limited cake, for heaven's sake divert it from this misuse.

211. Mr Morris, is there anything you would like to add to what we have explored already?

(*Mr Morris*) Our main preoccupation is the need for better quality of advice within the Church in Wales and the free churches, the need for something which recognises the need to care for historic landscapes, the resurvey and industrial archaeology are all leading themes in our minds. They have all been well aired in this discussion.

Chairman: I am very grateful to you all, gentlemen, for coming to see us. Thank you very much.

Memorandum by The Georgian Group

PRESERVATION OF HISTORIC BUILDINGS AND ANCIENT MONUMENTS IN WALES (HB21)

1. The Group is grateful for the opportunity to submit evidence to the Committee's enquiry. We shall restrict our comments largely to the listing of historic buildings and the operation of listed building control as these are our principal concerns.

Listed Building Consent

2. All listed building applications in Wales are referred to CADW. We understand that CADW's two listed buildings inspectors have dealt with between 600 and 700 cases per annum in recent years.

3. Scrutiny by CADW is a vital part of the process of controlling listed building consents in Wales, and CADW's remit is wider than that of English Heritage—which looks only at applications affecting grade I and II* buildings and applications to demolish grade II buildings.

4. We understand that in the past this role has been questioned, and consideration given to ending CADW's involvement with the majority of cases involving grade II buildings. Such a change would be disastrous given the inadequacy of local authorities in matters of conservation and listed building control.

5. Many local authorities are poorly equipped to perform their duties in exercising listed building control. Few employ conservation officers or other specialist staff, without whom applications cannot be properly assessed nor unauthorised alterations controlled. The erratic pattern of consultations which we receive suggests that not all authorities notify the amenity societies in accordance with the Circular.

6. The problem of councils which give little importance to conservation is one which might be reviewed. Its resolution would contribute greatly to the effectiveness with which historic buildings and historic town or village-scapes are preserved.

The Statutory List

7. The statutory list is the principal source of information upon which the statutory protection of historic buildings rests. The fact that it is incomplete—and will take a further 60 years to complete at the present rate—immensely weakens the effectiveness of the legislation.

8. The incompleteness of the list, coupled with the fact that the "Buildings of Wales" series is also yet to be finished, is one reason for the lack of awareness of conservation to be found in Wales.

9. Extra resources should be found at the earliest opportunity to enable the rapid completion of the list. This would provide a proper basis for the exercise of listed building control and would greatly increase awareness of the importance of historic buildings. It would also create a pool of listing officers who would be suited for employment as conservation officers.

10. It is also important that the draft list of parks and gardens of special historic interest be completed and published as soon as possible.

Other Comments

11. The low priority given to conservation by local authorities in Wales is matched by a shortage of architects and surveyors with experience and knowledge of historic buildings. The consequence of this is that much everyday repair work may be carried out inappropriately, while even proposed alterations which are on paper sympathetic may turn out to be damaging.

12. Councils, professionals and house owners all need education. CADW should play a part in this process and might look at initiatives such as English Heritage's "Framing Opinions" campaign (which draws attention to the importance of preserving original windows etc, and is aimed at planning officers and professionals) as a model.

13. Other societies have already drawn attention to the problem of redundant chapels, and we would endorse their comments.

18 January 1993

Memorandum by the Victorian Society

PRESERVATION OF HISTORIC BUILDINGS AND ANCIENT MONUMENTS IN WALES (HB9)

(1) *The arrangements for the properties in the care of the Secretary of State, as exercised by Cadw*

Not many of these buildings fall within the scope of our Society, but there are outstanding exceptions such as Castell Coch. Two things the Society is worried about, however, are firstly, the trend towards ever larger "visitor centres", and secondly, the production of more "popular" but less informative guidebooks.

(2) *The care exercised by other major owners (such as the National Trust, the churches and local authorities) over their properties*

The Society is particularly concerned about the way historic churches are treated by the Church in Wales. We wish to point out that there is:

(a) no provision for redundant churches in Wales (which, in contrast to England, lacks either a Redundant Churches Fund or an Advisory Board for Redundant Churches);

(b) no equivalent body to the Council for Care of Churches to advise DACs and parishes on matters relating to historic churches in use;

(c) no representation of amenity societies on DACs;

(d) no DAC papers (agendas or minutes of meetings) sent to amenity societies;

(e) no contact at all of amenity societies with the faculty jurisdiction system in Wales and, as far as we know, no reform underway.

On its present performance, we believe that the Church in Wales should lose its exemption from listed building control.

The other denominations are comparable to those in England and again, unless they can institute an effective internal system of control (of which there is no sign at the present) as is now required by the Welsh Secretary, David Hunt, following the announcement on 17 December, then they too should lose the ecclesiastical exemption.

As far as the local authorities are concerned, it is difficult for the Society to form a comprehensive view especially, perhaps, as by no means all Welsh authorities are conscientious about notifying the amenity societies of listed building consent applications.

One case involving a publicly owned building which has worried the Society very deeply over the last year, however, has been that of Swansea Guildhall. This Grade II* building, which is owned by West Glamorganshire County Council, has been allowed to fall into appalling condition. The reasons for this are complex (and some of the blame must be shared by Cadw, as explained later) but, nonetheless, West Glamorganshire C.C. are now backing a scheme for its conversion to offices which shows no appreciation whatsoever for the historic character of the building.

Cardiff Castle (Grade I) is another historic building, owned by a local authority, whose standard of care with regard to the interior has left a great deal to be desired. The wonderful painted decoration designed by William Burges has been very crudely repainted in recent years. But now, we understand, a new committee has been formed to look after the castle and the building is likely to be treated more sensitively than before. Even so, in the last two years, the castle has been threatened with the addition of a large visitor centre. Fortunately this idea has been dropped as a result of lack of funds.

(3) *The listing of historic buildings, the scheduling of ancient monuments and the controls exercised (chiefly through Cadw) on planning consents in relation to them*

(a) *Listing*

The listing of historic buildings in Wales may be described as very patchy indeed (see Appendix listing the "greenbacks" supplied to our Society). The survey of historic buildings is gradually being completed and we consider the standard of the work being done in this area to be high. Inevitably, however, with only a small team of inspectors dealing with the entire area, progress is relatively slow.

The problem is, of course, that where buildings are listed but no list description is available, the chances of the building being properly treated when a listed building consent application is made for its alteration or demolition are much reduced. Under these circumstances, it is sometimes very difficult for our Society even to establish whether a building dates from our period or not. It is also undoubtedly true that there will be many buildings of listable quality in areas which have never been comprehensively surveyed. These buildings ought to be protected by listing as soon as possible:

It is self-evident that more resources need to be devoted to completing the survey of historic buildings if the work is to be carried out at a faster pace. This is essential if the standard of conservation in Wales is to be brought up to an acceptable level.

(b) *The controls exercised on planning consents*

The control of listed building consent applications is generally less rigorous in Wales than in other parts of the country. Few local authorities employ conservation officers, a clear indication that the care of historic buildings is not given a high priority. In addition to the problem created in areas where there may be listed buildings but no descriptions, there can also be difficulties for an organisation such as ours in obtaining plans. It is also fair to say that the quality of plans provided (and accepted as adequate by local authorities) is in some cases lower than it would be elsewhere.

This Society is also aware that it does not receive the same proportion of listed building consent notifications in relation to the overall number of listed buildings in Wales as we do in England. Obviously, there will be many factors which can affect such things; for example, the rate of change will be slower in rural areas where there is less development. Nonetheless, the disparity is too great to allow us to believe that all Welsh authorities are notifying the Society, as they are statutorily bound to do, of all listed building applications for demolition.

LBC applications notified to the Society in 1991

Wales   194 (this figure excludes those for Cardiff, Merthyr Tydfil, Newport and Swansea which are handled by our South Wales Group)

England   6,826

Another matter which needs to be addressed is the failure of many planning committees to recognise the value of conservation. This is crucial if historic buildings are to survive. No conservation officer can improve standards on his own; if his committee does not support him and appreciate the need to give careful consideration to the quality of proposals for the alteration and/or restoration of listed buildings, then bad decisions will result.

This brings us on to the role of Cadw. Wales is a small country and Cadw is a small organisation with few professional officers. It is not independent of the Welsh Office to the same degree as is English Heritage in relation to the Department of National Heritage. Because few local authorities have conservation officers, they depend heavily on Cadw for advice on listed building matters. But, since procedures for the treatment of listed buildings are handled more casually in Wales, that advice, which may be given informally before an application for listed building consent has been made or any of the statutory consultees have been informed, may seal the fate of a listed building. In the case of Swansea Guildhall, Cadw told the County Council that it could gut the building well in advance of any application for its conversion and, as a result, the Council has left the building exposed to the elements and to vandalism ever since.

Another point to emphasise is that specialist advice of certain kinds is not available from Cadw as it is from English Heritage. For example, English Heritage has a legal department the members of which are available to give help to local authorities when difficult cases arise. There is nothing like this in Wales. This Society has recently been involved with a case involving the illegal removal of a listed statue and, arguably, the illegal removal of internal fixtures from Leighton Hall in Montgomeryshire. Montgomeryshire District Council is very small and is certainly not wealthy. It had (and has) a major problem with the owner of this Grade II* listed building and it needs expert legal advice to deal with the situation. But Cadw has no lawyers on its staff and therefore could not help. The District Council applied to the Victorian Society for its support which, to the best of our ability, we have given. But what we were able to do cannot be compared to the kind of help the English Heritage lawyers could have provided. When it comes to enforcement action and prosecutions the support and advice of professionals is essential.

The same case highlighted the fact that structural advice is not available from Cadw either. Dry rot has been allowed to spread unchecked throughout Leighton Hall in recent years. Apparently, Cadw does not employ any structural engineers so again it was our Society which sent a structural engineer to examine the building. We also agreed to appear at any public inquiry either in respect to the urgently needed repairs of the removal of fixtures. But lethargy now seems to have overtaken all concerned. It really is too difficult a case for a small under-resourced local authority to handle on its own. The support of a fully effective central body with responsibility for historic buildings could have saved this major building, but now little short of a miracle will do so (we are told that, as a result of the dry rot, the house will have a negative value in about two years time).

(4) *The grant schemes available for the preservation of historic buildings and ancient monuments, their overall adequacy as well as the effectiveness and fairness with which they are allocated*

The Society does not have a close knowledge of the operation of grant schemes in Wales. However, again we have to say that we have the impression that there is much less grant aid available in Wales than in the rest of the country. The balance needs to be redressed.

The Royal Commission for Historical Monuments in Wales

The Society would like to mention that, up to now, this body has been far too little concerned with "polite" buildings of any period, and especially of the 19th and 20th centuries. The recent appointment of Peter White, to head the organisation may bring about a change here. We were encouraged to hear that the Commission has now appointed Olwen Jenkins to carry out a full-time research project on chapels.

CONCLUSION

The Society feels very strongly indeed that more resources should be given to the preservation of historic buildings in Wales. It is quite wrong that the standard of conservation in this area should lag behind that in the rest of the country. We urge the Welsh Affairs Committee to do everything in its power to improve the current situation.

December 1992

APPENDIX

WELSH "GREENBACKS"

This is a break-down of the lists held by Victorian Society, as provided by Cadw. It is difficult to assess the coverage, but there are areas for which we have no "greenbacks". There may be spot-listings covering some of the buildings in these areas, but there is no indication of comprehensive surveys. This list also indicates those major towns and areas for which there is no survey list, at least 50 per cent of the listing information that we hold for Wales is in the form of spot-listing, giving a very sporadic coverage.

CLWYD

Colwyn:

No lists for this area, only covered by spot-listings. Includes Abergele and Colwyn Bay

Delyn Borough:

    Holywell

    Mold

    Areas evidently not surveyed: Flint, Llanasa, Mostyn, Trelawnyd

Glyndwr District:

    Denbigh

    Llangollen

    Ruthin

    Areas evidently not surveyed: virtually whole area of district

Rhuddlan Borough:

  St. Asaph

  Area not covered: Prestatyn etc.

  Wrexham Maelor Borough:

    Wrexham

    Area not covered: Penley, Ruabon, Gresford, Goedpoeth

DYFED

Carmarthen District:

    Laugharne

    Newcastle Emlyn

  Most of area not covered

Ceredigion District:

    Aberaeron

    Aberystwyth

    Lampeter

  Most of area not covered, including Cardigan, New Quay

Dinefwr District:

    Llandovery

  Most of area not covered, including Landielo, Ammanford, Glanaman

Llanelli:

  No lists for this area

Preseli Pembrokeshire:

    Fishguard and Goodwick

    Haverfordwest

    St. Davids

    Solva

    Llanrhian

    St. Davids and the Cathedral Close

  No list for Milford Haven

South Pembrokeshire:

    Narberth

    Pembroke and Pembroke Dock

    Tenby

MID GLAMORGAN

Cynon Valley:

   No lists

Merthyr Tydfil District:

   Merthyr Tydfil

Ogwr District:

   Bridgend

   No list for Porthcawl, Maesteg

Rhondda:

   No lists

Rhymney Valley:

   No lists

Taff-Ely:

   No lists

SOUTH GLAMORGAN

Vale of Glamorgan Borough:

   Cowbridge

   Llantwit Major and St. Donat's

   No list for Barry

Cardiff City:

   Cardiff

   Cardiff Outer Communities

WEST GLAMORGAN

Llanelli Borough:

   Llanelli

Lliw Valley

   No list

Neath Borough Council:

   Neath

Port Talbot:

   No lists

The City of Swansea

GWENT

Blaenau Gwent:

   No lists

Islwyn:

   No lists

Monmouth District:

    Abergavenny

    Chepstow

    Monmouth

    Rural District of Pontypool

    Usk

Newport Borough:

    Caerleon

    Newport

Torfaen:

    No lists

GWYNEDD

Aberconwy Borough:

    Bro Machno

    Conwy and Llandudno Junction

    Llandudno

    Llanfairfechan

  Areas not listed include: Penmaenmawr, Betws-y-Coed

Arfon District

    Bangor

    Caernarfon

  Areas not listed include Bethesda

Dwyfor District:

  Porthmadog

  Most of area not listed, including Criccieth, and Pwllheli

Ynys Mon—Isle of Anglesey Borough:

    Beaumaris

  Most of area not listed

POWYS

Brecknock District:

    Brecon

    Crickhowell

    Hay on Wye

    Knighton

Montgomeryshire District:

    Llanidloes

    Machynlleth

    Montgomery

    Newtown

    Welshpool and outer Communities

Radnor District

Whitton

Llangunllo

Llandrindod Wells

Presteigne

Memorandum by The Society for the Protection of Ancient Buildings

THE PRESERVATION OF HISTORIC BUILDINGS AND ANCIENT MONUMENTS IN WALES
(HB 11)

INTRODUCTION

(1) The Society for the Protection of Ancient Buildings was founded in 1877 and is the oldest building conservation group in the United Kingdom. We are one of five "national amenity societies" that by law must be notified of all applications to demolish or partly demolish secular listed buildings in England and Wales. The SPAB concentrates on pre-Georgian buildings.

(2) We know well that the number of pre-Georgian listed secular buildings in Wales is proportionately far smaller than in England, and that development pressures are different. However in 1990 Welsh local authorities only notified us of 60 cases of demolition or part demolition of buildings of our period compared with 1,902 in England.

(3) Like the other amenity societies we have a feeling that some Welsh local authorities are not notifying us adequately, though we have no specific evidence to support this.

(4) This goes to the central issue of the proper care of historic buildings in Wales—the minimal arrangements in most Welsh local authorities for carrying out their historic buildings responsibilities.

(5) Few employ conservation officers or properly qualified planning staff. Owners of old buildings have no obvious source of advice on repairs and alterations, which can certainly lead to expensive and damaging mistakes. There seems to be little awareness of the value of surviving vernacular historic buildings in most local authorities, and in some cases among planning committees outright indifference or hostility to conservation. Enforcement of listed building law is almost never considered. Few serve or just threaten Repairs Notices, even when important historic buildings are severely decayed and on the point of collapse.

(6) Public awareness and knowledge of conservation appears far less developed in Wales than England. It often has a negative image among owners of listed buildings in Wales, who resent the restrictions. We are rarely contacted by local societies or individuals worried about a threat to a building in Wales, something which is all too common in England. This reflects the fact that the SPAB is barely known in Wales, but also seems symptomatic of a wider attitude to the historic environment.

(7) Our impression is that because of this lack of interest, technical knowlege, and local authority support, the quality of much repair and alteration work in Wales (for which listed building consent may have been given) is worse than across the border. Wales has few great buildings: its strength is in its many fine vernacular buildings, which have often survived without major alteration. Such buildings are specially vulnerable to ignorant or misdirected repairs and alterations. Proper advice, public education, and effective local authority control are urgently needed in many parts of the Principality.

COMMENTS RELATED TO THE TERMS OF REFERENCE

(i) Our main concern is that though Cadw generally copes well it is too understaffed for its wide range of responsibilities. We have no specific comments on the upkeep of buildings in the care of the Secretary of State, but think that they would benefit if Cadw had the resources to undertake research into technical problems common in Wales. Much conservation knowledge and experience is based on English buildings, materials and weather. Buildings in Wales often suffer from high levels of wind-driven rain, for example, and some specific research would be valuable. An equivalent to the research, technical and advisory service of English Heritage would strengthen Cadw in its work. Technical advisory leaflets aimed at owners and professionals could help prevent much unnecessary damage.

(ii) One of the most serious conservation issues in Wales is the growing number of redundant churches and chapels. The absence of an equivalent to the Redundant Churches Fund in England means that many important churches face the prospect of decay, unsuitable conversion or demolition. The future for chapels is even more uncertain. The lack of funding means that those that are still in use are often poorly maintained.

The shortage of skilled conservation architects and specialist building contractors in Wales means that the quality of repair work to Welsh churches eg the use of hard, cement-based mortars, rather than lime is sometimes of a questionable standard.

(iii) There has been no major resurvey of listed buildings in Wales. At the present rate it could take well into the next century before a complete resurvey is completed, by which time many important and interesting buildings will have been lost or effectively destroyed by damaging alterations. Wales, like Cornwall used to be, has relatively fewer listed buildings because vernacular buildings were underappreciated when the first listings were undertaken. The resurvey of Cornwall brought many fine buildings to light or led to a revaluing of their interest. The small scale, relatively simple, vernacular buildings of Wales reflect the social and economic conditions that prevailed in the past, and deserve proper protection.

Our views on the feebleness of many local authorities in administering planning consents and conservation responsibilities are given above.

(iv) What grants there are seem to be fairly administered, but they are in such short supply that they do little to reduce the risk to the essence of the Welsh built heritage—the ordinary and often remote vernacular building.

4 January 1993

Examination of Witnesses

MR MICHAEL CUDLIPP, Director, DR JOHN MARTIN ROBINSON, Member, Executive Committee, the Georgian Group; MRS TERESA SLADEN, Secretary, Victorian Society; MR PHILIP VENNING, Secretary, and MR JOHN SELL, Former Chairman, Society for the Protection of Ancient Buildings, examined.

Chairman

212. Good afternoon, Lady and Gentlemen. I am very sorry we have kept you so long while the previous witnesses while here, but as you heard the evidence you could see that it was very difficult for us to get through all the questions that we wanted to ask. Our apologies for that. Thank you for coming. For the purpose of the stenographers, will you please give us your name and your affiliation, starting with the Society for the Protection of Ancient Buildings.
(*Mr Sell*) My name is John Sell of the Society for the Protection of Ancient Buildings.
(*Mr Venning*) I am Philip Venning, also of the SPAB.
(*Mrs Sladen*) Teresa Sladen of the Victorian Society.
(*Mr Cudlipp*) Michael Cudlipp of the Georgian Group.
(*Dr Robinson*) John Robinson of the Georgian Group.

213. We start again with the question of the ecclesiastical exemption. The Victorian Society and Mrs Sladen believe that the Church in Wales should lose its exemption. The memoranda of the Georgian Group and the Society for the Protection of Ancient Buildings do not specifically address this point. What do you think, Gentlemen? You have the lady in the middle who is for exemption and on either side of her are two bodies that do not address the point. What does the Society for the Protection of Ancient Buildings say to that?
(*Mr Venning*) This is a slight re-run of the situation in England about 10 years ago when the same issue came up over the Church of England's faculty jurisdiction system. Our view then was that the system had certain advantages over secular listed building control, particularly the detail over interiors and a certain amount of repair work which fell outside secular procedures. The faculty system as a system had some pluses. It also had some gigantic minuses. In arguing about the English system we argued that there is scope for enormous reform, but if those reforms were adopted—and they would have

to be fairly demanding reforms—we would accept that the exemption should remain, not in perpetuity; it should remain under review. A reform system had advantages. I have to say that we know very little about the faculty system in Wales and that partly stems from points that have been made in other memoranda about the failure to involve amenity societies in any aspect, the much more closed way the system appears to operate, but from our understanding I would take a similar view that a reformed and radically changed faculty system in Wales taking in much more expertise, much more chance to consult outside experts in a much more closely modelled system on the secular one would, in our view, justify the retention of the exemption at least for a limited period of time.

214. You disagree with that, do you not, Mrs Sladen? Here is your great chance.
(*Mrs Sladen*) In our evidence we do, to be fair, say that on its current record we believe that the Church in Wales should lose the exemption.

215. So this is the last chance saloon?
(*Mrs Sladen*) Yes. It is urgently in need of reform, but if those reforms were carried out, it is possible that the Victorian Society would change its view, not necessarily, but possible.

216. What about the Georgian Group?
(*Dr Robinson*) We did not mention anything in our submission because there are not that many Georgian churches in Wales. There are one or two Georgian churches in Powys and Clywd, but it is not really a group of buildings that we have any relationship with. On the whole, certainly in England, we have supported the Victorian Society's case because many of the things in churches that come within our competence are fixtures and fittings, such as box pews, that have been put into older churches. At the moment they can be and are removed from churches. We would like to see that brought under control. This is not specifically a Georgian point, but nobody else has mentioned it, and that is the Catholic church in Wales. It is a large denomination with some important churches.

[Chairman *Cont]*

Because of liturgical renewal in the last 20 years or so a lot of Catholic fittings have been changed. I can give you an example which is St David's at Pantasaph which is a church by Thomas Henry Wyatt, built by the Earl of Denbigh and all the fittings in that were designed by Pugin and exhibited at the Great Exhibition. But quite a number of those have been removed in the last few years, screens, a tabernacle and so on.

217. Mr Cudlipp, do you want to add anything to that?

(*Mr Cudlipp*) No, I have nothing to add to that.

218. Perhaps we could move on slightly from this question to you, Mrs Sladen. In the memorandum of the Victorian Society on the first page, the penultimate paragraph, you give a very interesting example whereby you say that one case involving a publicly-owned building which has worried the Society very deeply over the last year has been that of Swansea Guildhall. You say that this "Grade II* building, which is owned by the ... County Council, has been allowed to fall into appalling condition". When Mr Carr came before us he rebutted or claimed that Cadw, according to you, told the county council that it could gut the building well in advance of any application for its conversion. He says that is not true. Do you say that it is true and that Mr Carr is wrong, or do you say that you wish to withdraw that statement in your evidence?

(*Mrs Sladen*) No, I am afraid I say Mr Carr is wrong. I cannot absolutely prove it conclusively, but I spent an hour yesterday reading through the correspondence which our very excellent caseworker in Swansea had with both Cadw and with the county council over the last three years. In fact it was announced by a member of the county council at a visit that our society had to the area about a year ago at which I was present. He said, to give you the background, that the society had been concerned about the vandalism and the water penetration in this building since 1990. He explained to the society—and there were about 50 of us there—that the reason the county council had taken no steps to prevent either of these problems was that they had already been told by Cadw that it would be all right if ultimately the building was gutted in the process of conversion. Therefore it would be a waste of money to take these measures at this stage. The society was obviously shocked by this and we wrote subsequently to Cadw and raised the question with them. We had a letter back in which Cadw said that it was sorry that we had been misinformed on this subject. We subsequently had further correspondence with Cadw and they came back with the answer that informal comments by individual members of their organisation were fully understood by local authorities to make merely informal comments and that everyone would know that within the system listed building consent would ultimately be required. In fact in the last week I have received a letter from the Secretary of State saying that he will not be calling the matter in for a public inquiry because Cadw has advised him that the proposals for the conversion of that building are perfectly satisfactory. Those proposals involve gutting it.

219. Perhaps I was unfair to you when I started off on the first page because the sentence I quote from concerning what Mr Carr said is on page 3 of your memorandum, where you say in paragraph in the last sentence: "In the case of Swansea Guildhall, Cadw told the County Council that it could gut the building well in advance of any application for its conversion and, as a result, the Council has left the building exposed to the elements and to vandalism every since". What I am interested in exploring with you is the sentence before that where you say "procedures for the treatment of listed buildings are handled more casually in Wales". What leads you to the conclusion that Wales has a more casual attitude than what is happening in England? "Casual" sometimes is a very nice term. It is nice to be casual, just trundling along quietly rather than doing something silly. But the implication here is that casualness is not a very good thing?

(*Mrs Sladen*) I think the case I have just outlined presents a fairly clear example of a rather casual way of dealing with listed building consent procedures.

220. Is the same true later on in that same page? You mention the problem of Leighton Hall where you make a slightly different point. Again you criticise Cadw here, not like your previous paragraph whereby you criticise them for not being sufficiently independent from the Welsh Office, but this time not having proper structural engineers employed within Cadw to ensure that the examination of the building is carried out properly. Do you know of many examples of either category in Wales that is either the casualness like the Guildhall or Leighton Hall where the structural engineering expert advice is not available or are these simply extreme examples that you take which are really so few in number that although they are listed and important nonetheless in terms of number there are not that many that fall into either of these categories?

(*Mrs Sladen*) I see what you are getting at. The Victorian Society operates rather differently from the other amenity societies in certain particular ways. Obviously we deal with all the listed building applications that we receive, but certain cases we pursue in a particularly vigorous way. I would say that with both Swansea Guildhall and Leighton Hall we made huge efforts. When I say it took me an hour to read the correspondence that is true. It was not my correspondence, but the correspondence over three years took me an hour to read. There had been an enormous amount of effort on the part of our case worker in Swansea in trying to solve that problem. It was all wasted in as far as we got nowhere. I cannot point to many cases where we have gone into applications in that sort of detail. Another case I could mention is Pembroke Dock which is a long running case of an important group of dockland buildings which are, to put it simply, being left to rot more or less, although their present owner is, as I understand it, quite wealthy. The local authority is anxious. He is the main employer of people in the locality. The local authority is anxious not to upset him in any way, but at the same time no higher authority has come in and taken a very tough or positive line about the preservation of those rather important buildings. When you have local interests

[**Chairman** *Cont*]
the local authority is not the best organisation to deal with the situation very often.

221. Let me take that last example, Mrs Sladen. I do not know the example at all, but if we take that in this case the problem is not that the local authority is concerned that it could end up paying the bill, because here you have what you called a wealthy local person who owns this facility, owns the listed building and that the local authority is reluctant to issue the statutory notice to that owner simply because of the owner's wealth, or is it because of the point you were making that they are afraid in some way that because this owner employs local people they are reluctant to move? Here we have an additional reason. Not any more is the reason that the local authority could pick up the tab, which is the evidence we have had so far, but another reason. Here we have a real power struggle. The local authority versus one wealthy local person, is that what you are saying?

(*Mrs Sladen*) Yes, and at that point you need an effective central authority to fight alongside you. Our society has tried both Cadw and the local authority obviously and we can get very little enthusiasm going on either side.

222. Have you a lot of correspondence between you and the local authority concerning Pembroke Dock that we could have so that we could explore that in much more detail?

(*Mrs Sladen*) We have a certain amount, not anything like as much as we have on Swansea Guildhall.

223. Would you be willing to let us look at some of that correspondence so that we may have a flavour of Pembroke Dock? We are going down to Pembrokeshire next Monday, but one of the problems we have been having is that we are not being welcomed to go to Pembroke dock to see the facility. So as we are not being welcomed with open arms to go there we do not feel that we want to engage in the act of trespass, but it would be handy if it were possible to have sight of some of that correspondence. It might help us. Mr Ainger here is the local Member there. He may wish to comment.

Mr Ainger: I can comment. I am also the local member from the county council point of view and the dockyard is still in my county council ward. I worked there from 1973 until 1992 so I know the area very well. We are not talking about an individual. We are now talking about a large publicly quoted company. You made a point about getting access. There is no problem with access. There is a public right of way. I have suggested to our adviser that perhaps we can see an excellent example of brilliant practice where the port authority converted a warehouse to offices, although they originally wanted to demolish it, and 100 yards away is the example that we have been talking about. I would urge that we do try to get to the dockyard to see the problem. It is a major problem where unfortunately the individual concerned and the company involved has an appalling record in the dockyard and it is a great shame. From their own point of view they should be taking a great deal more action on these buildings as it could be a very large financial benefit in the long run to them.

Chairman

224. Mrs Sladen, if we could have a copy of that information that would be very handy. Returning to the Guildhall in Swansea, from what you said before I thought you were levelling a very serious charge against the Secretary of State for Wales, if I understood you. You were saying that he was having bad advice from Cadw and that he was taking bad advice. Presumably what you were saying therefore is that yours was good advice and Cadw's advice was bad. What makes you feel that your advice is better than Cadw's?

(*Mrs Sladen*) I think I feel it was.

225. You feel it was?

(*Mrs Sladen*) Yes, it is a Grade II* building. There is an important distinction between a Grade II building and a Grade II* building. Being Grade II* puts it in the top 10 per cent. of historic buildings on the list. It has still, but not for very much longer, several very important interior features and the listing of an historic building covers the interior as well as the exterior. We did not suggest at any point that the whole of the interior of the building should be retained, but we did say that it had a very important staircase and a very important council chamber and some historically important cells. Otherwise we were perfectly happy for the rest of the interior of the building to go. Ultimately we sent a structural engineer to look at the building in conjunction with the local authority and he wrote a report in which he made it quite clear that in his opinion it was perfectly possible to retain those features of the building. But nonetheless, although we offered on countless occasions to meet Cadw and the county council with our structural engineer, to discuss how minor modifications to their scheme might be made neither saw fit to meet us.

226. Is it now too late to do anything at all about that building?

(*Mrs Sladen*) I believe it is because in the last week I have received a letter saying that the Secretary of State has given permission for its total gutting.

Mr Roger Evans

227. It is very difficult for us when you say in your statement that certain advice was given by Cadw and Cadw tell us the opposite, but you have also referred very clearly to a vast amount of correspondence. Would it be possible for us to have the relevant part of that bundle copied so that we can form some view as to how this argument unfolded?

(*Mrs Sladen*) Absolutely.

Chairman: That is very helpful.

Mr Roger Evans

228. And secondly, also I want to pick up on what the Chairman was putting to you when he asked why your view was better than Cadw's. I do not know at what level in the Victorian Society a view was taken in respect of Swansea Guildhall, but can you give us some idea of the level of architectural expertise available to the Victorian Society and perhaps compare that with the amount available to Cadw?

(*Mrs Sladen*) That is rather difficult. The person who was our case worker in Swansea and who very

[Mr Roger Evans *Cont*]

sadly has now left us had formerly been an inspector with English Heritage. She has now moved on and has taken a position with the Royal Commission on Historical Monuments in Wales. She was very experienced. She was our case worker for the Swansea district. The society has a number of regional branches, but all those regional branches come under the auspices of the society's main structure. When a really major problem like Swansea Guildhall occurs we have constant conversations. I spoke continuously during the last few months of the saga with Olwen Jenkins, but she previously consulted me and the chairman of the Victorian Society Peter Holick who has written two guidebooks on Wales and is particularly interested in buildings in Wales, so there had been contact between our office in London and our case worker in Swansea who has her own committee over a long period of time over this case.

Chairman

229. I want to ask you a slightly different question concerning Victorian listed structures in Wales that may be in the ownership of the British Rail Property Board. Two Members of the Committee are currently sitting on the Railways Bill. Since the British Rail Property Board is responsible for maintaining the bridges, the tunnels and viaducts on its disused railway lines, do you know of any listed Victorian structures currently in BR ownership that could become problematic as a result of the Railways Bill going through Parliament?
(*Mrs Sladen*) The short answer to that is no. Obviously I think the society will have to be looking at railway property across the country, not just in Wales with that in mind, but I am not aware of any particular examples in Wales.

230. So you cannot think of any line that Mr Evans can take to the Railways Bill that would help him along the path of regenerating and continuing his great interest in the Victorian structures? You cannot help us there?
(*Mrs Sladen*) No, I am afraid I cannot.

231. Can Mr Cudlipp?
(*Mr Cudlipp*) Can I pick up the question before and just say something slightly general, following on what Teresa was saying? We in the Georgian Group, like the Victorian Society, have considerable expertise in a very narrow area. Ipso facto on the whole we are of value to somebody like Cadw who, from their own evidence, appear to be under-resourced and who need access to cheap and willing advice. In our view, because we are very anxious to help, the situation seems to be summed up by something in their own evidence. They made very little reference in their written evidence to the amenities societies. They very proudly said that they had given us a 10 per cent. rise which is actually £100, but that is all they said about the amenity societies. I feel strongly, and I am sure my colleagues will agree, that Cadw should be talking to us more. We are very anxious to talk to Cadw. The Georgian Group is seriously thinking at the moment of putting somebody into Wales, at least part time that we hope might progress to full time, to talk to Cadw and to local authorities. In my view the whole thing is so

much a matter of education and we very much want to play our part.

Mr Roger Evans

232. Can I clarify one thing in respect of the Victorian Society's memorandum to us. You refer, Mrs Sladen, at 3(a) to "greenbacks" supplied to your society? Will you explain what a greenback is?
(*Mrs Sladen*) Yes, because they are not green in Wales, I am sorry. The lists that we have for the whole of England are all covered in green, so they are normally referred to as greenbacks. In fact the Welsh ones are white with pictures on the outside, but they are the finished lists for particular areas.

233. I assumed that, but the complaint you go on to make, as I understand it, is that the particulars given are inadequate in some instances for your society even to be able to discover the date of a listed building.
(*Mrs Sladen*) Very few of them are inadequate. What I was complaining of there is that there are some early lists which are inadequate, certainly not the bound volumes which have been bound at a later date. But one receives whole sheaths of pieces of paper as things are spot listed. Many of the very old lists are simply on pieces of paper, perhaps stapled together. Some of those very early ones are inadequate, but there is also the problem of time lag between the actual listing of a building and the appearance of the list description. What I was really referring to there was the fact that we can be told by a local authority that a listed building is threatened by alteration or demolition and find that we do not have a copy of the list description of a building and we find out that the local authority does not have a copy either. In some cases they may not know what date it is and then we really are stuck. One can make probably a lengthy telephone call and have gone through it all, sifted through sheaths of single sheets of paper where the whole area has not been surveyed and at the end of the day nobody can tell one what date the building is, but that is to do with the time lag between actual listing of the building and printing the list description.

Chairman

234. On the listed building consent procedures, you do not seem to be very happy as organisations or amenity societies with the quality of the records available to you on which you can form judgments. I also get the strong suspicion from your memoranda that you are not receiving all the consent applications for listing that you could receive from local authorities in Wales and that work on historic buildings is not being referred to you as required in law. Is that a fair point? Is that the situation or is my summing of that part incorrect?
(*Mrs Sladen*) No, I think that is fair. We simply infer that from the fact that we receive so few applications and from some areas no applications at all for listed building consent. We cannot point to instances where we have not been informed because we were not informed.

235. Mr Cudlipp, do you find the same?
(*Mr Cudlipp*) Yes, exactly the same, neither Cadw nor we can say how many Georgian buildings there

[Chairman *Cont]*

are in Wales. What we do know is that we receive no applications from many local authorities. Others are rather better. Monmouth is very good indeed, for example. But we have a feeling that if huge tracts of Wales where there is Georgian architecture never get in touch with us from one end of the year to the next, somebody must be doing something or the local authority is not requiring its work to be done properly. I do not know, but it is very odd.

236. What about you, Mr Venning?

(*Mr Venning*) I should like to refer back to the evidence given by the Ancient Monuments Society, if I am allowed to do that. It hinges very much on this wording within the circular, whether we are talking about total demolition or something more than that. I think it is fair to guess that quite a number of local authorities are taking a very narrow interpretation of the wording and are only sending on total demolition. The fact is that so many of the problems in Wales occur at a lower level, either with partial demolition or problems of very unsuitable alterations and how does one define what is an alteration and what is a demolition. Taking it one step further there are the problems of dereliction. We find that in Wales we are often involved, not because we have been formally notified but simply because attention has been drawn to a problem long before it reaches the formal notification system. But that is haphazard and random, so some cases we get deeply involved with, not because we have been notified but just by chance.

237. In terms of what we heard previously from the witnesses before regarding the seeming anomaly between the two circulars, one in England and one in Wales, are you as the three amenity societies here now very conscious of the seemingly large discrepancy in terms of time and effectiveness of these two, that is that Wales is lagging behind because the circular is not in place? Do you feel that something ought to be done about that quickly? If so, have you made representations to Cadw or the Secretary of State or both that they should get a move on? What has been the response to you? Or have you never made representations? Let us start there. What representations have you made to anyone regarding this anomaly?

(*Dr Robinson*) We in the Georgian Group have not made any representations, but it is certainly something which we ought to do because the circular is crucial, particularly in the area that we were talking about earlier about education and the lack of expertise.

238. Why have you not done that? What has been happening?

(*Dr Robinson*) I think we have been so busy dealing with the small things as they come in that we have not taken the overview there.

239. You mean you have the big things be and gone on to the small things, the minutiae, and forgotten about the really big important things?

(*Dr Robinson*) Most local authorities in England say how important this circular is, the conservation officers working in a local area, particularly the guidance in the back of the English circular which gives general rules on how buildings should be altered, and a rule of thumb to apply. That is very important and that is something that the Welsh circular should expand a great deal. The Georgian Group has tried to do it by publishing its own leaflets.

(*Mr Cudlipp*) I do not think we need feel defensive, Mr Chairman.

240. I was only kidding!

(*Mr Cudlipp*) In a way we can go only where somebody asks us to go. We can only react to information we are given. Our amenity societies are even smaller than Cadw and we operate much more largely in England simply because local authorities there are more interested. We receive more contact. Much of it is unofficial. I said to you that we are thinking of going into Wales. One thing I know very well, my family having come from South Wales, is that people in Wales are not particularly anxious for people in England to tell them how to do things. It seems to me that if we went into Wales and set up in Wales that we might start learning a lot more with face-to-face conversations. Having said that, because we find this is valuable elsewhere, if we go to see a local authority rather than correspond we have a face. They realise we are positive and are not just telling them that they must not do this for some obscure eighteenth century reason. They then come to us and they ask us questions. Even more so in Wales we obviously have a problem in that as we are all small charities our grant is £1,100 a year. In England our grant is £22,650 a year from DNH and there is a difference. If I am going to put somebody part time into Wales with a part time office, it is going to cost me about £12,500 for three days a week. I would like to feel that we could squeeze a little more money out of Cadw's resources or from the Welsh Office's resources. Even 20 per cent. of that, say £2,000 or £2,500, would be enormously helpful and we could find the rest of the money somewhere else. When we are there we can not only talk to local authorities and respond to Cadw, but we can talk to schools, to the new generation coming up about how important their heritage is and we can do all of that. A heritage is very important to Wales, we all know that, for the tourist industry, apart from anything else, but it is much more important than that. There are thousands of people in Wales living in Georgian houses. Of those thousands many do not know or care, but there are others who would care. If they were told why and how they should redecorate their houses, how they should carry out repairs on their houses in the right way by receiving leaflets—I am talking about ordinary people not grand houses—I think a lot of people would respond. If they responded that would make Cadw's whole job a lot easier.

241. Thank you for that, Mr Cudlipp. Mrs Sladen, what do you say to the circular? Have you made representations?

(*Mrs Sladen*) No we have not.

242. Not for the same reason is it?

(*Mrs Sladen*) It certainly is for the same reason in as far as we have three and a half members of staff dealing with the whole of England and Wales. We do not have time to go out to ask for more work. A few years ago we wrote to all the local authorities saying that they were not really sending us many listed building applications. We did not actually get very

[Chairman *Cont]*

many more as a result of that. But I think this communication thing is extremely important.

243. In terms of the circular, are you very conscious in the way you do your work of this difference between Wales and England consequential on the difference in the circular?
(*Mrs Sladen*) Not as conscious as we should be, I am sure. When the last English circular was updated it came to the Joint Committee of the Amenity Societies and we went through it clause by clause. Had it not appeared on our desks it seems to me very unlikely that any of us could have got our acts together, but because it was sent to us we looked at it and we make endless tiny amendments.

244. That is the English one?
(*Mrs Sladen*) This was the English one.

245. Did you ever have a copy of the Welsh one issued in 1981, as far as you know? Did it appear on your desk? It is a long time ago of course.
(*Mrs Sladen*) That was just before I joined the Victorian Society, but it seems to me very unlikely.
(*Dr Robinson*) It did not come to the Georgian Group.

246. It did not come to your group?
(*Mrs Sladen*) No.
(*Dr Robinson*) No.

247. So one of the things that is important at the very least is that the circulars are made available to the amenity societies at the time of issue so that at least you are aware of their existence?
(*Mrs Sladen*) Prior to issue.
(*Dr Robinson*) The draft, so that we have some input into the draft.
(*Mrs Sladen*) The draft, yes.

248. What about you, Mr Venning?
(*Mr Venning*) We did not either. I am not too sure that the precise wording of the two circulars makes all that much difference. I think it would help in Wales if they had the English equivalent. The problems in Wales go much more deeply than that, particularly the problems with local authorities. Local authorities throughout England and Wales handle conservation differently and there are some abysmal ones in England and no question about it.

249. Would you like to identify those?
(*Mr Venning*) I do not think I would want to put it on the record, but there are some that do not adequately notify us or, if they do, they do it in ways that make it almost impossible for us to respond in any realistic way. In singling out Wales as an area where this is a problem, we are talking about a matter of degree. There is no absolute difference between the two and there are some Welsh local authorities that are better than some English ones, but the generality is—certainly this is our impression and that of the other societies I know—that the number of notifications that we receive, the degree of detail that we are sent varies tremendously but tends to be on the poorer side simply because local authorities themselves do not to the same extent have specialist staff employed to look after listed buildings. That partly stems from the fact that Cadw has a slightly more hands on role with Grade II buildings in Wales than English Heritage does in England. I think it partly stems from economic, social and cultural

factors. Conservation is just not treated as seriously in many parts of Wales as it is in England. Public perception of conservation is rather different—at least that is our impression. Also too the inadequacy of the lists that everybody else has referred to makes the life of conservation officers, where they do exist, extremely difficult, so one has to accept that local authorities have a difficult time, but at the same time where they do have staff they themselves are very often marginalised within the structure of the local authority. The conservation officer may be a very junior person operating in a large planning department with a planning committee that is uneasy about conservation. The factors are very complicated and I would not over stress the circular as being the be all and end all. It will help, but the root of the problem is much deeper and all kinds of other issues have to be addressed.

250. You mentioned some of the abysmal local authorities in England. Would you categorise any of the local authorities in Wales as abysmal in the same way that you categorise some of those in England?
(*Mr Venning*) I would say that any that do not notify us where they is clear evidence that they should be notifying us now that is actually much harder would come into that category, or certainly those where there is no advice of any sort available to owners, where there is no conservation budget. A number of local authorities in Wales have no money at all for conservation, no staff and yet they have a statutory responsibility for listed buildings. I would say that those who do nil—and there are some— would come into the abysmal category.

Mr Roger Evans

251. I am slightly puzzled about the examples of non-notification by local authorities to you as amenity societies. I appreciate you have limited resources. I appreciate there are formidable difficulties necessarily of finding out. But if we asked you to provide us with a list of examples of non-notification, which you think you should have been notified about properly, could you give us chapter and verse in writing?
(*Mr Venning*) This question was answered by the previous delegation and the answer is no. This is merely a supposition on our part, based on statistics. Bearing in mind that some local authorities never notify us of anything and yet they have a significant number of listed buildings, we cannot believe there has been no significant work done to listed buildings during those periods.
(*Mr Sell*) I should like to add to that. I think it would be possible to provide some particular cases. The only way we can find out about those particular cases is through our members or other informants in Wales and therefore the extent to which we could inform you would be very limited. But it would be possible to give some examples, I believe.

252. The difficulty is this. We are bound by the evidence that we hear. You are telling us that there is this substantial problem. It is very difficult for us to be able to evaluate it unless you can provide us with some examples. I should have thought your membership would, from time to time if you are correct, be ringing and writing and complaining that

[**Mr Roger Evans** *Cont*]

buildings of importance have been altered or demolished and why have not SPAB and the Victorian Society done anything about it. Presumably the answer is that you have not been notified. Can you not find some examples for us?

(*Dr Robinson*) We can certainly.

(*Mr Venning*) With notice, yes, we can certainly.

(*Mrs Sladen*) We can certainly provide examples where we have been told ahead of time that we have not been notified and we have then become involved. We certainly have several of them.

Chairman

253. If you could send that information to us, we would be very grateful. Before we finish, can I ask you the same question that I asked the previous witnesses? Are there any issues that you would like to leave with us that we have not covered, that you think are important. We would not like to lose the opportunity to give that chance to you in case we have missed something of importance that you would like to comment on.

(*Dr Robinson*) From the Georgian Group's point of view, something that has not been mentioned so far today is the garden register. We are as concerned with eighteenth century landscape, parks and gardens and the setting of listed buildings as we are with the listed buildings themselves. Again and again in Wales we come across schemes, particularly in the last decade, where there have been holiday village developments or caravan sites or something which has completely wrecked the setting of a listed building or of an important landscape garden. About five years ago, in 1987, Cadw in association with ICOMOS started a register of gardens in Wales, but I do not think any of those have yet been published. Some of them are in draft and it seems to us that it would be enormously helpful if that was speeded up as well as the list. As in England the garden register is purely advisory. It does not have any statutory basis.

Mr Roger Evans

254. Can you give us any examples of historic landscapes which have been damaged by inappropriate development?

(*Dr Robinson*) I can quote one example straight off which is Lamphey Court in Pembrokeshire which is a charming early nineteenth century villa in a picturesque garden, next door to the episcopal palace which is a building in care of Cadw where a great deal of money has been spent on the restoration of those ruins, but this picturesque landscape, which is in private ownership, forms the setting of it and that house has been converted into a hotel and some unsatisfactory extensions were added in our view. Another case we have at the moment which is Nannau in Caernarfonshire a good Georgian house in a very beautiful park. When it was referred to us there was already an existing planning permission for a huge time share development which, fortunately, so far has not been executed, but that planning consent is still valid. We were not consulted at all about that the first time round. Another one is Talgarth near Towyn which is a very good example, we would say, of a landscape park which has been wrecked by

development as a holiday village. There are lots of others. We could provide a list if you wanted that.

255. Can you provide a list?

(*Dr Robinson*) Yes.

Chairman: Thank you very much.

Mr Ainger

256. Are you therefore recommending that gardens and landscapes should have the same statutory protection as buildings?

(*Dr Robinson*) We think that gardens should be protected in the same way. There seems very little point in listing a park grade I if it is purely advisory. It is better to have the information and the guidance for planning authorities, but it is something where we feel control should be statutory.

Mr Jonathan Evans

257. There is a very important house in my constituency called Penpont which has just come into the ownership through inheritance of a family who, in some way, will have to endeavour to provide an income to keep that house going. I listened with care to what you said about the preservation of gardens. There are very important gardens which have been examined as well, but it seems to me that preserving the gardens in their current form without there being any form of development at all is not likely to generate any of the income that will be necessary to ensure that that house does not ultimately collapse and find its way into the photographic record that we were offered by the previous witnesses.

(*Dr Robinson*) I think our general experience of enabling development is that it is nearly always so damaging to the listed building that it jeopardises the long term. It might provide some short term income for the preservation of a building, but in the long term enabling development in the setting of a listed building nearly always damages the long term chances of a building. What we find a lot of in Wales is quite small Georgian houses coming up which could still be lived in as houses and schemes come in for enormous extensions to make them into hotels or offices which would completely damage the quality of the listed building.

Chairman

258. Thank you. Mr Cudlipp, do you want to add anything?

(*Mr Cudlipp*) Just one short matter. I was very interested in Cadw's written evidence and also in its cross-examination. This inquiry has been very helpful to us. I will now undertake to attempt to re-establish relations with Cadw. We visited them earlier this year, but we will see whether we cannot find out from them if we can be of more help, in other words to sell ourselves to them. I will also undertake immediately to write to all those local authorities who do not apparently consult us and ask them why.

259. Thank you very much. It would be very helpful if you could let us know the answers to that. Mr Sell, you wanted to say something.

(*Mr Sell*) There are a number of points, I am afraid, but I wanted to touch on the question of historic landscapes. It seems to me that one of the

[**Chairman** *Cont*]

problems in Wales is that there is no grant scheme for historic landscapes at all in the way that there are grant schemes for historic landscapes in England. There are three types of grant available within what might be called the cultural area of historic landscapes in England. One is from English Heritage for parks and gardens on their register. One is under an organisation called Task Force Trees from the Countryside Commission which was set up to assist with the restoration of parks and gardens damaged after the 1987 and 1990 storms and there is, just recently—this is a very good initiative from the Countryside Commission—the notion of stewardship for landscapes whereby owners enter into management agreements with the Countryside Commission. They commit themselves, in return for receiving aid from the Countryside Commission, to manage landscapes and this refers to historic parks and gardens, in other words the landscapes of the country house, but it also refers to what I think is extremely important in Wales which is the other manmade landscape which Mr Morris referred to in his evidence, so it refers to both those kinds of landscape and it manages them over a period of 10 years. This seems to me to be an excellent way of encouraging and involving owners in the long-term maintenance of their historic landscapes.

260. So again an anomaly between England and Wales?

(*Mr Sell*) Yes, there is, and Cadw tell me that because of their terms of reference and because their grants are made by an historic buildings council they are unable to consider grants to historic gardens.

261. Thank you very much for that.

(*Mrs Sladen*) I think most of the points have been very well covered, but I should just like to mention the removal of fixtures from listed buildings because it is something which we have done a lot in our society during the last six months. I should like to offer you all copies of our pamphlet on the subject with a Welsh example on the front. This is the Icarus removed illegally from Leighton Hall. I should like to offer you copies because we have suggestions about how the problem could be contained. I think it requires minor legislative change. I will be meeting the members of the Arts and Heritage Committee in May to discuss a slightly updated version of this leaflet, but it presents some good suggestions for solving the problem.

Chairman: Mrs Sladen and Gentlemen, thank you very much for coming to see us. You have been very helpful towards this inquiry and we look forward to your written responses so we can have a feeling for what you have been experiencing. Thank you very much.

Memorandum by Dr Roger Wools

CONSERVATION IN WALES (HB15)

I wish to present my views to the Parliamentary Committee, which is at present considering Conservation and Heritage matters in Wales.

My name is Dr Roger Wools and I am an architect specialising in the care of historic buildings and sites. My interest in Wales derives from having lived in Cardiff for the first 20 years of my life and having written several reports on heritage matters within the Principality, particularly with regard to religious buildings. My Practice has offices in Wales at Carmarthen and Cardiff, although my representations on this occasion are purely personal.

My views have been influenced by three reports which I have written in the last 20 years.

(1) University of York Conservation Dissertation 1972–73. The Churches of Wales: the problems of the ecclesiastical exemption.

(2) Survey of the numbers of Listed Building and Grants for Historic Buildings from all Local Authorities in Wales—1979.

(3) Report on redundant religious buildings in West Wales 1992–93.

I am also a Trustee and Council Member of the Architectural Heritage Fund with a special interest in promoting Building Preservation Trusts in Wales.

WALES: THE POOR RELATION.

It is a common view amongst those working in the "Conservation Movement" that Wales is the poor relation in terms of an appreciation and commitment to conservation of the built heritage. This view may be challenged but in terms of the numbers of local authority conservation officers, Wales has few and these are not well qualified, compared with England. It was stated recently that the Association of Conservation Officers has over 900 members in England but under 20 in Wales.

Other bodies, or persons, will present comments on the numbers of Town Schemes and the Local Authority commitment to the protection and preservation of the heritage, but this second-class status for Wales is supported by the present lack of a policy or organisation with the churches and other religious denominations within Wales compared with England and also the lack, until a year or so ago, of an active Building Preservation Trust in Wales in contrast to over 100 in England.

Fortunately, the Church in Wales is making good progress in putting its house in order, but will need support from the government to catch up on the 20 years in which it has fallen behind the Church of England.

Wales is, therefore, seeing some changes for the better in this decade but there are four fundamental issues which I believe need to be addressed.

A.   LISTED BUILDINGS

The resurvey initiated by Michael Heseltine in 1984–87, in which I played part, has been of tremendous benefit to Local Authorities, owners, amenity societies and prospective developers in establishing a nearly definitive listing, which is relatively uniform across the country in terms of standards, information and presentation. Wales failed to follow this example and should be criticised for this decision. Amenity societies will give evidence that the inadequacy of the present lists for Wales matches the state of listing in England in 1982, which gave rise to the concern for relisting.

The Church in Wales may support my belief that the inadequate lists create uncertainty, confusion, considerable extra work in ascertaining if an unlisted building is worthy of listing, and is highly inefficient for CADW in the demands individual appeals for spot listing make upon its staff. The numbers of staff CADW have to devote to listing enquiries, spot listing demands and general relisting should be examined, but would appear to be small.

From my personal experience of running a team of 10 staff to relist 12,000 buildings in rural North Yorkshire and Humberside, an area 75 per cent the size of Wales, I believe competitive tenders from architectural firms would result in a cost of £0.75 million being expended over three years to bring Wales up the English standard. The resultant savings in local authority, the Welsh Office and CADW's time would be considerable and may be capable of assessment.

B.   RELIGIOUS BUILDINGS

It should be remembered that the Anglican Church in Wales was disestablished in the early 1920s and lost most of its endowments. It has been the poor relative of the Anglican communion every since and has not fully introduced the faculty procedures, inspections or redundancy procedures that the Church of England has brought forward in the last 20 years. The Church in Wales is undergoing a review of its procedures but it would appear that redundant churches present a considerable problem to this impoverished Church today.

All over Wales, mediaeval church buildings lie empty and derelict, with no procedure arrangements, such as the English Redundant Churches Fund, to save buildings of merit. It is my guess that between 5-10 per cent of all churches in Wales are presently redundant, amounting to 85-170 buildings. The formation of a Redundant Churches Fund for Wales, along the lines of the excellent English example, would be of significant help to the Church in Wales. I understand that there is a wish within the Church for this to be brought about, but that it may be the view of the Welsh Office that the 70 per cent contribution from public sources, as in England, could not be approved.

Although the administration of a RCF in Wales would be best tailored to Welsh organisations and geography, the acceptance of the principle of a 30/70 split for costs of administration would be of paramount importance in resolving the problem of derelict churches.

The view of the Welsh Office that additional grant aid through the Historic Buildings Council for Wales will adequately redress the lack of a RCF can be challenged. The amount of grant aid and the selectivity of buildings to be approved, coupled with the lack of a body to look after perhaps 50 churches preserved as monuments, argues heavily in favour of a RCF. The view of the Church in Wales should be sought at this time.

Non-conformist buildings, and other denominations in Wales, outnumber the Anglican churches, it would seem, by around 2:1. Some architectural historians may believe that most of these buildings are historically or architecturally worthless, but the recent formation of a Chapels Heritage Trust for England, along the lines of a RCF, points the way for Welsh non-conformity. It is, I understand, the principle of the CHT that the 30/70 split of funding is shared between a charitable trust and the DoE.

The Welsh Office appears not to favour support for a similar body in Wales.

C.   LOCAL AUTHORITIES

Expertise in historic buildings amongst the professions is in short supply within Wales. The introductions to the Shell Guides for Wales note the poor standards of development control amongst local authorities. The number of conservation staff in local government is limited, but the number of qualified conservation officers has been extremely low. I would ask the Committee to consider the present position, especially since tourism is potentially a substantial source of income for Welsh people and to consider the ways in which the Welsh Office could encourage local authorities to raise standards.

D. CADW

In my researches and reports over the last 20 years, it has been a common response from my contacts that the performance of CADW could be improved. As an ex-Conservation Officer, I am well aware of the often unjustified nature of this type of criticism but comments have been made that, although individual members of staff are committed and enthusiastic, the organisation as a whole is capable of being more pro-active.

As someone who has been in contact with English Heritage at many levels for over a decade, and is aware of the criticism often made of its own organisation, I believe CADW may have problems relating to resources and structure.

A familiar phrase of interviewees is that the Welsh Office and CADW are "too close", by which they mean a more distant relationship should be developed, such as with the DoE and English Heritage. In organisational terms, I believe these responses reflect a view that CADW should be given "headroom" to pursue the development of the Heritage of Wales, and be given adequate resources. I have not been able to compare the costs or staffing of CADW and English Heritage but the analysis may be of value.

SUMMARY

Wales has an extensive and valuable architectural heritage that is different to that of England, and may be more akin to that of Eire. It is important that the Welsh care for their own heritage through CADW or an equivalent, but without adequate resources for relisting at speed, or administering Listed Building control effectively, what has survived so far is in danger of being severely eroded. The speech of the Rev. Eli Jenkins at Llaregyb , praising the heritage of Wales whilst acknowledging its often modest contribution to a list of the wonders of the world is, I believe, a starting point for an appreciation of the Welsh character.

Letter from the Secretary Ancient Monuments Society to the Clerk of the Committee

PRESERVATION OF HISTORIC BUILDINGS AND ANCIENT MONUMENTS IN WALES (HB54)

Further to the writer's appearance, together with Dr Wools, in front of the Committee on 17 February, we have tried to find out examples of potentially listable buildings in the Principality demolished before they could be listed.

I am sure the Committee will understand as stated during the hearing that this has not been an easy exercise precisely because we learn about such cases through the grapevine. The statutory obligation on planning authorities is to consult us where *listed* buildings come under threat, not of course where unlisted ones do.

The range of demolition dates is broad and we fully accept those which came down a number of years ago may not be the direct victims of the failure to speed up the re-survey. We have tried to vary the building types but necessarily this selection must be dependent upon the cases that we know about.

With these caveats, we present the following cases to the Committee.

1. Blaenavon, Gwent. Chapel Row. Built in 1839 and demolished 1971 (see Photo 1).*

2. Cardiff. Congregational Chapel, Hannah Street. 1867. Demolished c 1970 (see Photo 2) designed by W G Habershon and A R Pite with J F Fawckner, 1867.

3. Llanelli, Dyfed. Westfa Felinfoel. A large Tudor Gothic house by R K Penson of c 1860 built for C W Nevill, the local iron master. Demolished 1989 or 1990 very rapidly by a large volume house building company after getting planning permission to build in the park. Would no doubt have been converted had it been listed.

4. Llanwenllynfro, Gwynedd. Llysdulas. An exceptionally important house designed by Deane & Woodward who were responsible for one of the great buildings of the Gothic Revival, the University Museum in Oxford (see Photo 3). The main house in Venetian Gothic was work of high quality by Sir T Deane and Benjamin Woodward 1856–58, with much finely executed carved stonework (animals, plants, etc) by a Mr Harrison. Though derelict in 1975, its end was a ridiculous, though not unique, scenario. It was known that the owners would demolish if the then unlisted building was "threatened" with listing, but in order to decide the point, the local authority sent officers to have a look around. The house was razed at once. Though this probably only hastened nature's work there were private negotiations going on at the time for the salvage of all the profuse stone carving, and this was all smashed.

5. Swansea. The Memorial Baptist Chapel, Walter Road. A prominent Gothic landmark with a spire demolished at great speed in the Summer of 1992. It was not apparently in bad structural condition and was sold for development soon after closure. Most certainly a victim of the failure to review the lists of Swansea which have never been completely revised since the 1950's.

6. Wrexham, Clwyd. The Seion Welsh Presbyterian Chapel, Regent Street. 1867. Demolished 1979 shortly before the revised lists for Wrexham were issued. As Sir Nikolaus Prevsner states in the "Buildings of Wales", this was "a sad loss". (see Photo 4).*

I hope these cases give the Committee a flavour of the problem.

8 March 1993

Letter from the Director CBA to the Clerk of the Committee

THE PRESERVATION OF HISTORIC BUILDINGS AND ANCIENT MONUMENTS INQUIRY
(HB 45)

We promised to submit further information in support of answers we gave to questions at last week's session of the Welsh Affairs Committee. I now enclose:

(1) A table of notifications of listed building applications received by us between 1990 and 1992. Even when variations in the comprehensiveness of listing are taken into account, this seems to illustrate a wide variation in the extent to which notifications are being made by different local authorities.

(2) A copy of a letter on this subject sent by us to the Society of Welsh District Planning Officers some ten months ago. The Society has acknowledged the letter on two occasions but has yet to provide a substantive reply which answers the points raised. (The second paragraph, incidentally, appears to have caused the Society some confusion, as they interpreted this as suggesting some special status on our part. In fact, the paragraph was intended only as a gloss on our role as a consultee under Welsh Office Circular 61/81. Perhaps my paragraph was badly drafted.)

We promised to look for examples of buildings of listable quality which have suffered as a result of lack of listing. My colleagues in Wales are seeking such examples at the moment, and I hope to contact you again when we have them.

COUNCIL FOR BRITISH ARCHAEOLOGY—WALES

NOTIFICATIONS OF LISTED BUILDING APPLICATIONS RECEIVED

	1990	1991	1992
ABERCONWY	—	—	2
ANGLESEY/YNYS MON	5	2	8
ARFON	4	2	2
BLAENAU GWENT	4	3	1
BRECON	1	1	2
BRECON N.P.	14	31	21
CARDIFF	9	7	7
CARMARTHEN	7	6	2
CEREDIGION	0	2	2
COLWYN	3	7	8
DELYN	2	—	6
DINEFWR	2	1	1
DYFED C.C.	—	2	3
GLYNDWR	1	3	1
GWYNEDD C.C.	4	1	1
LLANELLI	—	—	1
MID GLAM. C.C.	—	—	1
MONMOUTH	27	24	12
MONTGOMERY	7	1	3
NEATH	6	7	4
NEWPORT	1	6	3
OGWR	1	—	1
PEMBS. N.P.	4	3	6
PRESCELI	22	17	7
RADNOR	27	29	25
RHUDDLAN	—	—	3
RHYMNEY V.	—	6	4
S. PEMBS	4	4	3
SWANSEA	1	5	3
TAFF ELY	2	2	1
TORFAEN	—	—	2

*Photographs not printed

VALE OF GLAM.	1	2	1
WREXHAM	23	21	17
SNOWDONIA N.P.	—	1	—
WEST GLAM. C.C.	1	1	—
ALYN & DEE	—	1	—
CYNON V.	—	2	—
DWYFOR	1	2	—
GWENT C.C.	—	1	—
ISLWYN	—	3	—
MERTHYR	—	1	—
PORT TALBOT	—	1	—
CADW	2	1	—
TOTAL	191	209	164

Copy of a letter dated 1 May 1992 from the Society of Welsh District Planning Officers to the CBA

Historic Houses in Wales: Welsh Office Circular 61/81

As one of the bodies named in section 52 of Circular 61/81 to be notified of listed building applications involving demolition the Council for British Archaeology has the widest interest in the operations of this legislation. Its members provide expertise in all periods from earliest prehistory to the most recent past. The CBA is particularly concerned with the dynamic link between legislation, conservation, and the study of the past.

In Wales the CBA has been entrusted by Cadw to act as a monitor, to screen proposals to demolish or modify listed buildings and to give advice on the impact of such works upon their historic value. After a recent study of the working of this procedure CBA Wales has grave doubts as to whether it is able to fulfil this function properly. Our doubts arise because there is a wide disparity in the extent to which the various planning authorities of Wales operate within the spirit of the Circular.

This matter came to light when at an AGM of members a Summary was circulated indicating the numbers of listed building applications submitted annually by each Authority in Wales. The wide differences in numbers submitted by different Authorities had previously been assumed to represent the difference in distribution of Listed Buildings and had not been circulated. Members with an intimate knowledge of a few districts could see glaring disparities. Moreover, cases were quoted of extensive alteration to Listed Buildings which had never been notified at all.

It was suggested that the relationship between the distribution of listed buildings geographically throughout Wales be compared to the annual schedules of Applications referred to CBA. The large numbers involved and the random distribution of applications should remove problems of local bias. Unfortunately this cannot be done because it was found that Cadw have no statistics on the distribution of the total of nearly 14,000 listed buildings in Wales.

An analysis was therefore undertaken of two adjacent Districts of medium size where planning information was available. All applications concerning listed buildings were noted and compared to those notified over a period of two years. At the same time a larger number of districts was monitored, using the planning information given to Archaeological Trusts, and the same comparison made.

The results show that on average one listed building application out of every six planning applications which affected a Listed Building was referred to CBA. This covered a range of between one in three and one in a hundred. A total of twenty Districts was involved. The annual summaries of notifications over a longer period do not suggest that notifications from any particular district were unusual for these two years. Whilst LBCs might not result from every planning application, it is unlikely that they would not follow an approval, particularly as they involve no charges.

The wide disparity in percentages of cases referred is also reflected in the types of case. Some Districts refer cases from minor applications, such as satellite dishes, to major demolition, within the 30 per cent referred to CBA. The absence of any consistency in either the percentages or the types of applications notified to CBA is strongly evident. The only consistency noted is that where a qualified Conservation Architect is in post, that the Authority shows the higher rate of notification.

Section 52 also directs that "all decisions" resulting from notification shall be notified to the bodies specified. Only one Authority in Wales does this.

The percentage of the total housing stock which qualifies for Listing is much smaller in Wales than in England. The CBA would like to believe that for this reason much greater care and protection of it might be afforded by the Welsh planning systems. We note, with regret, that our concern that this is not done has been echoed by the Chairman of the Historic Buildings Committee for Wales.

The CBA believes that if the members of your Association could debate this matter openly, they would discover this wide disparity of interpretation of Circular 61/81 for themselves. If they are in agreement with the aims of the Circular we hope they would wish to make common cause with us in preventing any further unnecessary loss to Wales's historic built environment.

Letter from the Director CBA to the Clerk of the Committee (HB 53)

We promised to send further information, which is enclosed.

Attached is:

1. A list of examples of unlisted buildings, arguably of listable quality, which have been either demolished or harmed.

2. A list of examples of ecclesiastical/archaeological issues arising from the informality of the faculty control in Wales (and lack of any inbuilt archaeological advisory arrangements such as have been developed in England), lack of archaeological provision for cathedrals, and redundancy. Please note that while some of the cases may seem trivial, archaeological evidence is irreplaceable. The cumulative effect even of quite small interventions can be just as damaging, in archaeological terms, as single, large-scale disturbances.

3. A copy of a letter received from Ceredigion which explains its policy on notification to amenity bodies under Circular 61/81. For contrast, we append extracts from the English counterpart circular 8/87*.

5 March 1993

1. Examples of buildings, arguably of listable quality, which have been lost or harmed

1. *Pentregwenlais Lime Processing Works, Dyfed.* Possibly the last old operating works in Wales. Cadw pressed for an overall survey; in 1992, Dyfed Archaeological Trust given 48 hours notice of impending demolition. One block of kilns saved by emergency listing. The rest gone.

2. *Hayes Farm Windmill, South Glamorgan, Barry.* Possibly the last working mill in Vale of Glamorgan. In 1966 it stood complete with most of its machinery intact. Case for listing pressed, but today it stands, unlisted, an open shell.

3. *Bryn-y Grog Hall, Marchweil, Wrexham.* Unlisted in 1985 at time of purchase by new owner. Eventually listed (1988) as II*, by which time original staircase had been removed.

4. *Broadlands Fawr, Bridgend.* When inspected in September 1992 this 16/17C farmhouse was considered too much modified to deserve listing. The works concerned had not been carried out until late 1990.

5. *Penygroes Chapel, Tregarth, Arfon.* Apparently assessed for spot listing, but no entry to interior gained and turned down. Now at risk either from demolition or dereliction.

6. *Memorial Chapel, Walter Road, Swansea.* Good Victorian Gothic, outside resurvey area but arguably more deserving of care than some listed buildings within it. Representations urging spot listing without result. Demolished 1992.

7. *"Singleton Abbey", Swansea.* House of former Singleton Estate of Vivian family (copper magnates), work of P F Robinson, with slender Gothic tower—a fine and visible feature. House now contains Registry of University College of Swansea. Tower removed in 1980s: loss of fine landmark and architectural flourish. Rest of "Abbey" still unlisted.

2.–Churches in Wales

Examples of archaeological issues encountered at a number of churches in Wales. We believe these to be symptomatic of a wider problem. Examples are categorised under the headings used in our original memorandum.

(a) Working Churches

1. *St Beuno, Clynnog Fawr, Gwynedd (Diocese of Bangor) 1992*

The exterior of the nave of this fine late medieval church on an important earlier site was observed being repointed. There was no archaeological consultation, a faculty had not been applied for and the pointing was of poor quality.

*Not printed

2. *St Engan, Llanengan, Gwynedd (Diocese of Bangor)* 1993

Gwynedd Archaeological Trust has found out from a press release that major repair works are to be carried out on this fine sixteenth century church. Cadw is providing some of the funds but at present we are not aware that provision has been made for archaeological investigation of evidence that may be disturbed or destroyed by works of repair.

3. *St Mary, Tal-y-llyn, Gwynedd (Diocese of Bangor)* 1991

The vicar contacted Gwynedd Archaeological Trust when bones were discovered after the floor had been dug up. The trust did its best to record what it could. The repair work was being carried out with a Cadw: Welsh Historic Monuments Commission grant. There had been no prior archaeological consultation.

4. *St Rhwydrys, Llanrhwydrys, Anglesey, Gwynedd (Diocese of Bangor)* 1992

The floors in this twelfth-century church were recently replaced, together with most of the wall plaster. There was no archaeological consultation and Gwynedd Archaeological Trust only found out after the event. We understand that the architect's Qunquennial Report recommended the building works which were carried out. Because of these recommendations the vicar did not think he needed to apply for a faculty and therefore no application was received by the Diocesan Advisory Committee.

5. *St Mary, Tenby, Dyfed (Diocese of St Davids)* 1992

This is one of the largest parish churches in Wales. It is medieval with evidence of other early buildings in the churchyard. An archaeologist on holiday observed the relaying of paths across the churchyard in progress. A faculty had been granted for the work but no archaeological consultation had been sought. The Rector gave permission for the archaeologist to record what he could see in the trenches; contractors also gave vague accounts of other structures they had observed while carrying out the work.

6. *St Teilo, Llandeilo (Diocese of St Davids)* 1992

This is an important early Christian site with early sculpture and a curvelinear enclosure around the churchyard. Dyfed Archaeological Trust has received information from local people regarding the proposed clearance of part of the churchyard. As a result they have suggested a survey prior to any action being taken. They were also alerted by a local informant to the fact that a new heating system was in the process of being installed in the church which involved considerable excavation under the floor. DAT was able to carry out a day's recording and gained some information about original ground levels prior to the demolition of the earlier church and its replacement by the present structure. It is not known whether a faculty had been applied for.

7. *St Sadwrn, Llansadwrn, Dyfed (Diocese of St Davids)* c.1990

A drainage trench was inserted round the outside of the church. It is not known whether a faculty had been obtained.

8. *St Kentigern, St Asaph, Clwyd* May 1992

Clwyd Archaeology Services were contacted by the vicar prior to a service trench being dug across the churchyard. Because the church is medieval but is possibly on an older site, as is suggested by the dedication and the curvilinear churchyard, CAS recommended that geophysical survey be conducted together with the digging of two or three small test pits in order to assess archaeological potential. Further archaeological recording could then be carried out if necessary. It was noted that the church as "developer" should pay, but the local authority had no powers to insist such work was carried out. Nothing further has been heard.

(b) Cathedrals

1 *St David's* 1992

A member if the Cathedral Chapter, who also happens to be an archaeologist, has recently advised on a watching brief during the construction of a new Choir Room and services. If he had not been a member of the Chapter, there would have been no mechanism for archaeological consultation.

2 *Bangor* 1992

An archaeologist in Bangor saw scaffolding going up on the Cathedral tower. She contacted the Dean and was told that there had been no archaeological consultation concerning the forthcoming repairs. As a result of this personal contact she alerted Gwynedd Archaeological Trust, which received permission to make some observations and a photographic record.

(c) Redundant Churches

1. *Llangan, Dyfed (Diocese of St Davids)* October 1992

This church has been declared redundant and an application was originally made to Carmarthen District Council to demolish. This was rejected and an application was then made for conversion to a dwelling. The building is largely of the nineteenth century but retains fragments of medieval fabric. However, the site has considerable archaeological potential as a recently published article by Terrence James (*The Early Church in Wales and the West*) has shown. Aerial photographs of cropmarks in the adjoining field indicate earlier enclosures of (?) Iron Age date and there is an early Christian monument and a holy well nearby. Field names possibly indicate an outer ecclesiastical enclosure. Cadw has declined to list the church building or to schedule the surrounding features.

2. *St John the Baptist, Slebech, (Diocese of St Davids)* 1992

A Victorian church but with some notable fittings including a medieval tomb reset from the now ruinous medieval church. The church is now redundant; the interior is complete but deteriorating badly. Permission to remove monuments and other selected fittings to museum storage has been rejected by the local authority. A proposal to demolish has also been refused.

3. *Hasguard, Pembrokeshire National Park*

Redundant for at least twelve years. Several schemes for alternative uses have foundered, in part at least (we understand) because of hostility to secular uses expressed by local people.

3. Copy of a letter dated 22 May 1991 from Ceredigion Director of Planning to the CBA

Welsh Office Circular 61/81.

I refer to your letter of 7 March. I do consult the bodies specified in para. 52 of Circular 61/81 on all applications for the demolition of listed buildings. There are a great number of applications for listed building consent where the extent of demolition is very small in proportion to the building as a whole. In these cases it is not my practice to involve the statutory bodies. Cadw have accepted this practice. The two cases to which you refer involved the removal of chimney stacks and the demolition of a boundary wall. I would of course consult you on more substantial demolitions, even though these may not involve the demolition of a building in totality.

Letter from the Secretary of the Victorian Society to the Clerk of the Committee

LBC applications of which the Society was not notified in the normal manner. (HB56)

As was explained to the Committee, it is difficult for the amenity societies to provide information on this subject. The three cases the Society encountered in 1992 were:—

(1) Dyfed. Pembroke, 31 Church Street. (II, C.19). Application for LBC for replacement of windows with UPVC units. The Society was not notified, but then replacing windows may not be considered to involve demolition. (Local authorities are only obliged to inform us of cases involving demolition). The case was subsequently called in by the Welsh Office and the Society sent written representations.

(2) Dyfed. Tenby, Dyster Memorial Fountain, Tudor Square. (II, late C.19). This fountain was damaged by a lorry and then removed from the Square. The Society was informed sometime later and wrote to the local authority to ask whether the fountain was being repaired. We then received a retrospective LBC application for removal and resiting of fountain.

(3) Gwynedd. Criccieth, Church of St. Deiniol, (II, John Douglas). The Society was not notified of any application for LBC for the removal of the organ (case by John Douglas) from this redundant church. Because the church is redundant it is no longer exempt from secular legislation. Our letter to the local authority asking why we were not notified has gone unanswered.

Supplementary Memorandum by the Georgian Group

THE PRESERVATION OF HISTORIC BUILDINGS AND ANCIENT MONUMENTS IN WALES
(HB62)

This supplementary evidence attempts to answer some points raised by the Committee when the Group gave oral evidence. It also contains a selection of cases dealt with by the Group and a few additional comments following from the course of questions asked by the Committee.

1. *Some Important Buildings and Gardens at Risk*

Aberglasney, near Llandeilo: an older house, remodelled in the early eighteenth century, Aberglasney is derelict and unlisted. The principal feature of the spectacular grounds is a raised and arcaded terrace; there are also a yew tunnel and water garden. Like the house, the garden is derelict.

Neuadd Fawr, Cilycwm, Llandovery: and early nineteenth century house with fine stables in a magnificent setting. The roof leaks and floors have been lost.

Edwinsford, Talley, Llandeilo: a house of various dates from the seventeenth to the nineteenth century. The grounds were noted for rare specimen plants. Edwinsford is abandoned and derelict.

Nanteos, Aberwystwyth: empty after the failure of various commercial schemes for its restoration. Outbreaks of dry rot have been reported. The stables are sepatately owned and received a grant from the HBC in 1991.

Baron Hill, Anglesey: very fine late eighteenth century house by Samuel Wyatt, remodelled after a fire in the nineteenth century. It was abandoned after the war and is derelict. The gardens, partly laid out by the landscape gardener William Emes, are a wilderness.

Gwrych Castle, Abergele: an extraordinary and vast picturesque castle, mostly early nineteenth century and largely the creation of its owner, Lloyd Bamforth Hesketh, aided by the architects C. A. Busby and Thomas Rickman. Derelict after the failure of various commercial schemes.

Wynnstay, Denbighshire: Wynnstay was the greatest estate in North Wales and, although a Victorian house replaced the eighteenth century house which was destroyed by fire, the park, worked on by Capability Brown and John Evans, retains a number of notable buildings. The whole is decayed. The Nant-y-Belan Tower, designed by Wyatville, has collapsed. Ownership has been divided.

2. *Some Buildings and Gardens whose Settings are Threatened or have been Damaged by Unsuitable Development*

Nannau, Gwynedd: a fine early nineteenth century country house with a park and various ancillary buildings, all in a magnificent setting. Left by the family in the 1970s, recently empty for some years. Some dry rot. Permission was given several years ago for timeshare development in the park and there is now an application for an 86-stand caravan park which the Group has opposed.

Chirk Castle, Denbighshire: medievel castle with seventeenth and eighteenth century interiors; the park was laid out by William Emes. The Castle is owned by the National Trust but its setting is threatened by a golf course.

Lamphey Court, Pembrokeshire: an early nineteeth century villa built near the ruins of the Bishop of St. David's Palace, creating a fine picturesque landscape. Recently permitted extensions to the hotel now occupying the villa will compromise this landscape.

Talacre, Flintshire: an early nineteenth century house in the Tudor Gothic style by Thomas Jones, stables, a riding school and various garden buildings also survive. The house has recently been sold and its setting is threatened by proposed chalets.

The Bishop's Palace, St. Asaph: late eighteenth century house by Samuel Wyatt, with later additions. An inappropriate modern house for the bishop mars its setting. (The interior has also been unsympathetically subdivided.)

3. *Miscellaneous Cases*

These illustrate some of the characteristic problems referred to the Group, but the selection excludes the simpler categories of casework such as modest alterations to town houses, the conversion of agricultural buildings, although the latter are, of course, important.

Harmeston Hall, near Haverfordwest: an eighteenth century farmhouse with fine panelled interior and with several traditional barns in an upspoilt location. The Group opposed an application to envelop much of this in large hotel extensions, a scheme which would have preserved the interiors but destroyed the setting. The applicants withdrew after the application was called in.

Ynsmaengwyn, Gwynedd: a mid eighteenth century country house scandalously neglected by the local authority to whom it was given and ultimately, in the 1960s, burnt down by the fire brigade. There was a recent part-retrospective application to demolish remaining earlier service wings, neglected ever since. CADW has asked for structural engineers justification from the applicant but this is a case in which having their own engineers might help. It is alarming that a public authority, the town council, should proceed with demolition work without listed building consent.

Old Guildhall, Swansea: principally a Victorian building but with some early nineteenth century fabric. The Group expressed concern at the proposed gutting of the building and supported the Victorian Society's objection following that society's assessment of the structure. This is another example illustrating CADW's need for engineers. It is also another example of a publicly owned building which has been allowed to fall into dereliction.

Madog Tannery, Tremadog, Gwynedd: early nineteenth century tannery building, one of the first mill buildings of its type in Wales and part of a model industrial town. An application to demolish was withdrawn at inquiry stage and a trust has been established to save the building.

Blaenblodau Hall, Pencader, Dyfed: the Group was alerted to existence of this empty and unlisted early nineteenth century house by a member of the public. Although modest it is a fine house with two full height round bays to the rear elevation and characteristic broad eaves, as well as original sashes and shutters. It was unknown to the conservation officer due to its concealed location. It has now been listed grade II. How many more such houses remain unlisted? Traditional vernacular buildings are probably still more neglected.

Royal Dockyard Chapel, Pembroke Dock, Dyfed: an 1830s chapel by architect George Taylor. An application some years ago to demolish the chapel was refused but it has since been neglected and its future remains unsure. The case is complicated as the chapel is also a scheduled monument and responsibility therefore lies with CADW not the local authority. Other dockyard structures of later date are also at risk.

10-14 Bridge Street, Carmarthen: a proposal by Dyfed County Council to demolish a listed house and two other early nineteenth century houses to open views of the partially reconstructed wall of Carmarthen Castle was allowed after an appeal. The County Council had owned the buildings for some time and neglected them, but the case perhaps also provides an example of "antiquarian prejudice", in the preference shown for the castle over a group of houses which form a characteristic part of the townscape.

4. *Authorities*

Below are some examples of authorities who consult frequently and others who do so rarely. This is the most available measure we have and may not correspond to their all-round performance. There appears to be a considerable difference between east and west Wales.

Monmouth Borough Council is perhaps the most assiduous in Wales and has both a keen conservation officer and a model listed building consent application form. Notifications always contain full information. Monmouth has computerised its list. Wrexham Maelor, Brecon and Radnor also seem reasonable.

Many authorities scarcely notify and when they do so send no plans nor even an extract from the list, contrary to the advice in Welsh Office Circular 61/81. Dinefwr and Ceredigion in Dyfed and most of the authorities in Gwynedd notify very seldom.

The Committee asked for what reason we suggested that some authorities do not notify us when they should. We must reiterate that this suggestion was based mainly on extrapolation from the pattern of consultations which we receive.

Members and others do inform us of cases of which we are not notified. Whether we should be notified depends on the interpretation of Circular 61/81. Paragraph 55 suggests that demolition should be interpreted broadly: the demolition of any part of a building constitutes demolition of a listed building and should be notified. The following two examples illustrate the sort of cases which ought to be notified to the amenity societies if the Circular is interpreted in this manner.

Llandwrog, Gwynedd: an early to mid-nineteenth century estate village built by Lord Newborough of Glynllifon Park. Piecemeal alterations such as the replacement of original windows and doors by unsuitable modern substitutes have eroded a very good example of late Georgian Picturesque architecture.

Vaynol, Gwynedd: a Regency house, spectacularly sited overlooking the Menai Straights. Proposals to convert the house to flats involved partial demolition.

5. *Additional Comments*

In connection with the completion of the list we would support the suggestion that the publication of new lists should be computerised as soon as possible. Currently CADW has no means of analysing the composition of the list either in terms of date or building type.

One subject which deserves consideration is the effect of cumulative alterations on the character of listed buildings. We understand that many buildings are to be dropped from the revised list for Pembroke Dock as their character has been eroded by alteration. This is a phenomenum which may occur elsewhere and ought to be studied for the implications it has for the exercise of listed building control elsewhere.

In our initial evidence we emphasized the importance of completing the register of historic gardens. We would add that we would support some measure to give this statutory status, although we recognise that this is a contentious area.

Our selection of buildings at risk contains only a few important examples. It would be useful for CADW to undertake a survey of buildings at risk were resources available.

15 March 1992

Supplementary memorandum by the Council for British Archaeology

THE PAST IN TOMORROW'S LANDSCAPE (HB91)

INTRODUCTION

The Council for British Archaeology works to promote the study and safeguarding of Britain's historic environment, to provide a forum for archaeology opinion, and to improve public knowledge of Britain's past.

In 1988 the CBA published *A policy for the countryside* which set out our recommendations for the better care of Britain's rural heritage. That Policy has since guided the actions of the CBA and many other bodies. It has provided a touchstone at public inquiries, and it has been particularly useful in providing a point of reference in the CBA's dealings with government departments, national agencies, and other conservation bodies.

It was intended that the *Policy* should be regularly revised. This paper is the first such revision. Its immediate context is provided by the heightened public awareness of environmental issues, and by European Community and UK Government initiatives, which are transforming the framework within which vital decisions affecting the landscape are taken.

Our paper is occasioned by the absence of any strategy for the protection, management, and interpretation of Britain's landscape as a whole. The need for such a strategy arises both from the strength and variety of the forces which now threaten the fabric of Britain's past, and from the uneven character of such measures as are currently available to care for it.

The *Policy* has been drawn up by the CBA's Countryside Committee, and was approved for publication by the Council at its Annual General Meeting in 1992.

1. WHY WE NEED OUR PAST

1.1 Historic landscapes provide the framework in which we live and work. They are the link between ourselves and the past, and define our sense of place and belonging. Landscape is not just the rural countryside, but the whole range of features which survive from the past, such as field patterns, transport routes, historic buildings, or the remains of former industries. All give meaning to where and how we live.

1.2 In Britain the landscape is our main source of evidence for the development of human culture, religion, society, economy, and the use of land since the last Ice Age. Virtually all of Britain has been influenced by human activity.

1.3 Archaeology is concerned with the development of the whole landscape, not merely isolated sites within it. The need to conserve historic landscapes is inseparable from the need to protect the countryside in general. Archaeological deposits, once damaged, cannot be restored.

2. CONSERVATION AND CHANGE

2.1 Our landscape is always in a state of change, and it is neither desirable nor possible to freeze it. The aim of conservation is not to halt change, but to manage it in ways which allow us to weigh up, and regularly re-evaluate, what we regard as important.

2.2 Successful management requires the identification of basic principles. These must then be projected to those who are concerned with the care of the countryside, and put into effect in ways which strike a practical balance between regulation and positive management.

2.3 Today this balance is lacking. In order to attain it, it is essential to develop a more integrated philosophy of landscape conservation, and to avoid the needless waste which occurs when different agencies and interests with competing or duplicatory aims seek to ensure that their idea of conservation predominates.

3. FRAMEWORKS OF LAW (Annex 1)

3.1 *Britain in the world*

The archaeology of Britain can only be understood within a European context, and that of Europe belongs within the wider world. Archaeological conservation is therefore an international responsibility, for which frameworks are provided.

3.2 *Frameworks in Britain*

3.2.1 Since the late 19th century legislation and public attitudes governing rural archaeology in Britain have been based on the assumption that historic features in our landscape can be identified and protected as isolated, discrete monuments. During the last thirty years it has been realised that the landscape itself is of intrinsic historic value, and that the idea of seeking to protect small pinpoints within it does not do justice either to the range of our inheritance or to its management needs.

3.2.2 This recognition has coincided with a quantum increase in agricultural technology and production, which in some parts of Britain have imposed rapid and reductive changes upon landscapes which hitherto had developed largly through processes of accumulation.

3.2.3 Except in Northern Ireland, where the *Historic Monuments Act 1971* contains provisions not found elsewhere in the UK, legislation has not kept pace with the development of our understanding of the evidence, nor with the scale or pace of destruction. In England, Scotland and Wales, our main instrument is the *Ancient Monuments and Archaeological Areas Act 1979,* which is a thinly modernised version of Victorian thinking. Like so much else of that era, it remains appropriate for its original purpose: the protection of monuments. The conservation of historic landscapes calls for new legislation and new strategies. A re-examination of the mechanisms for the protecion of the historic environment is overdue.

3.2.4 There is no overall framework for the management of archaeology in Britain. Although public administration in the UK is highly centralised, a number of functions are devolved to territorial agencies for England, Wales, Scotland, and N. Ireland, which apply existing measures with differing degrees of emphasis. Local government, where much archaeological responsibility resides, is exercised through regional, county, borough, and district councils, and through National Park authorities.

3.2.5 The commitment of the government to the planning process as a mechanism for archaeological conservation, most recently through the various national versions of the Planning Policy Guidance *Archaeology and Planning,* is extremely welcome. This accords a pivotal role to local authorities. However, it is important that the effectiveness of this approach be closely monitored, to build upon present strengths, remedy weaknesses which emerge, and to ensure a high quality of research-based advice.

3.2.6 Diversity offers advantages, but requires a strong intellectual framework and foundation of principle if the strengths are to be realised. If there is to be a past in tomorrow's Britain, a fresh concept must be grasped: the ultimate indivisibility of the environment, and the interdependence between cultural, natural, and scenic dimensions. This paper states the principles by which the CBA believes landscape issues should now be tackled.

At the outset we call for:

— a recognised framework for the management of historic landscapes

— full statutory·status for Sites and Monuments Records (SMRs)

— improved provision for protecting the "setting" of ancient monuments, to harmonise with the treatment of setting in the planning process

— removal of the ignorance defence in cases of damage to protected sites and monuments

— greater delegation of the Secretaries of States' powers in respect of scheduled monuments, to avoid double-handling

— continued expansion of Field Monument Warden schemes to increase contact with owners and tenants

— strengthened and coherent legislation dealing with treasure hunting and portable antiquities

— PPG guidance on the protection of World Heritage Sites

— ratification of the 1970 UNESCO Convention and Valetta Convention

3.2.6 As well as seeking overhaul of the legislative framework, the CBA wishes to see an immediate review of the non-statutory criteria used for scheduling under the 1979 Act. Both principles and practice vary unacceptably across Britain.

4. AGENCIES OF CHANGE, NEEDS IN MANAGEMENT

4.1 Britain's landscape is a working place. Parts of it are changed every day. Changes in land use over the centuries have always resulted in destruction of some features and the accretion of others. But nowadays the scale of change has tipped the balance towards destruction. Some threats can be identified through planning controls and other legislative arrangements, but historic landscapes in particular suffer seriously from forces which fall outside the planning process. Agriculture, forestry, and the water industry are among the most formidable agencies of this sort.

4.1.2 The very rapidity of change is an issue in itself. Britain's historic landscapes are irreplaceable. A decision taken in a few minutes, prompted by short-term motives, can destroy a landscape which has developed over millennia. Hence, any cost-benefit analysis of the relationship between conservation and contemporary economic need must be seen in a perspective which is long enough to do it justice.

4.2 *Agriculture*

4.2.1 Most agricultural practices are not subject to planning control. Many cause damage to the archaeological heritage. These include the demolition, reconstruction and conversion of unlisted farm buildings, the construction of new farm roads, changes to boundaries, and changes in cultivation regime, in addition to the erosive effects of many cultivation processes themselves.

4.2.2 At a time of diversification in the countryside it is important that the opportunity is grasped to manage land in ways which minimise archaeological loss. The CBA believes that the starting point for improved management should be a partnership between archaeologists and those who depend on the land for their livelihood.

The CBA will suggest and support means of promoting good relations between archaeologists, owners, tenants, and users of land.

4.2.3 Where payments are being made to foster farming practices which are in the interests of countryside conservation, archaeology should be seen as one of the primary considerations in both prioritising the allocation of funds for such schemes and in the preparation of appropriate management strategies. In some cases archaeological considerations alone will justify specific management prescriptions and commensurate grant aid or incentives.

Immediate action should include

*   **adoption of archaeological criteria as a qualification for non-rotational set aside**

4.2.4 Good archaeological practice has been developed in some Environmentally Sensitive Areas (ESAs). We would like to see the extension of the best archaeological practice within ESAs to the whole of the rural United Kingdom. While different areas will have different requirements the basic principles can sustain widespread application. Therefore we believe that capital and particularly revenue payments for sensitive archaeological management should be made as part of a single, integrated system of payments for conservation.

4.2.5 Successful management requires information. The existing archaeological record does not always adequately reflect the actual archaeology of an area, and survey may be required to improve knowledge. Archaeological and landscape history considerations should always be incorporated in both the design and implementation of conservation programmes.

In the longer term the CBA urges

*   **a single integrated system of capital and revenue payments to promote and implement archaeological conservation within the larger framework of environmental conservation**

*   **greater use of Inheritance Tax exemption as an incentive to protect archaeological sites and landscapes**

*   **surveys to improve baseline data**

4.2.6 The CBA believes these policies to be economically viable, assuming suitable reforms to the Common Agricultural Policy (CAP), but we do not wish to lose sight of larger objectives in the midst of the administrative and economic complexities of the CAP. Therefore we list our policy goals:

*   Wherever practicable, sites and landscapes of archaeological importance which are being damaged by ploughing should be taken out of cultivation or cultivated by techniques where the depth of ground disturbance is less than that already caused by ploughing. This could apply to ploughing for the reseeding of pasture as well as arable.

*   Land which is of significant archaeological and/or palaeonenvironmental value, and has never been ploughed, or which has not been ploughed recently, should remain unploughed.

*   Upstanding archaeological features should be protected from gradual attrition by, for example, marginal ploughing, overstocking, stone dumping, or the use of off road vehicles. Care is required in the management of visitors. Where damage has already occurred appropriate remedial measures should be taken—though it must be remembered that this can only stabilise and not reverse damage.

4.2.7 Traditional and new methods of land use need to be assessed on their merits, both in relation to the environment and the working countryside.

The CBA will

*   **work in partnership with interested parties towards the integration of archaeological conservation within agricultural policies.**

*   **propose research into the suitability and effectiveness of specific management techniques**

4.3 *Forestry*

4.3.1 Tree planting and harvesting can damage or conceal areas or features of archaeological interest. Large plantations can wipe out the archaeological value of whole landscapes. The CBA regards it as essential that adequate protective and/or mitigatory measures which distinguish between different types of forestry should be employed where archaeological features are threatened.

Active management of forests and woodlands can provide a stable environment for archaeological conservation. However, in view of the fact that preparation of land for forestry, and associated developments such as roads, can have a devastating effect on the archaeological content of land, we believe it to be anomalous that a change of use to such purposes should normally be treated as 'permitted development' in the planning process. The CBA will press for such exemption to be removed, to ensure scrutiny of all forestry proposals. Meanwhile, the framework for archaeological conservation which is gradually being put into place for grant-aided forestry would be further improved by:

* Continuing to refuse grant aid for the planting of sites and landscapes of archaeological importance.

* Addressing the fact that in some parts of Britain archaeological information is inadequate for the assessment of planting proposals. The CBA believes that, in appropriate cases, prior archaeological assessment (if necessary including survey and evaluation) should be a requirement for grant-aided forestry schemes. The results of such assessment should be used to influence the scope and design of the eventual scheme. This would bring forestry more generally into line with the principles set out in PPG16, the Archaeology and Planning NPPG for Scotland, and European Environmental Assessment legislation. (While this is the CBA's preferred approach, we welcome the present provision in Scotland, where funding is made available for archaeological survey in advance of planting.)

* Not permitting replanting on archaeological sites and landscapes of importance which have survived the initial forestry cycle.

* Ensuring that positive management measures are employed for sites and landscapes that have been protected from planting but may remain susceptible to natural regeneration and damage during subsequent forestry work.

* Viewing the impact of forestry on the archaeological resource from a perspective that is wider than planting alone. The full effects of ancillary development such as the construction of roads and buildings, clear felling, and lowered water tables resulting from drainage should all be considered when asessing how the archaeological landscape should be protected.

The CBA will

* **press for the removal of "permitted development" status for new planting**

* **encourage the ·full use of existing measures to ensure that archaeological sites and landscapes are protected from damage caused by afforestation and ancillary development, and managed to ensure their long term survival**

* **urge that all management decisions be taken on the basis of up-to-date information on the potential archaeological impact of schemes**

* **press for the archaeological monitoring, survey and recording of areas subject to restocking**

4.3.2 Archaeological management should take account of differences in planting regimes, or the archaeological value of ancient and semi-natural woodlands and certain designed landscapes, which are an archaeological survival in their own right. Archaeological features will often have survived in such areas.

The CBA will

* **endeavour to promote understanding of the archaeological value of ancient and semi-natural woodlands, and designed landscapes**

* **encourage national and local initiatives to survey woodland areas**

* **favour traditional forms of woodland management, especially coppicing, which minimise ground disturbance in areas of archaeological sensitivity**

4.4 *Water*

4.4.1 Archaeological sites and deposits survive in a variety of marine and freshwater contexts. Remains fall into two categories—organic material of any type or period which has survived because of its water-logged condition (eg peat and wetlands), and secondly, sites which are of interest because of their association with the use of water resources, whether economic (fishtraps), transport related (eg waterfront remains or canals) or relating to the history of the provision of water supplies.

4.4.2 The environmental stability and physical survival of Britain's water environments is jeapardised by many factors. For example:

> *Open water* Archaeological sites and deposits may be affected by physical damage (eg from dredging, moorings or the wash of boats) and by pollution (such as increased nutrient levels).

> *Water table* Archaeological sites and deposits in water or waterlogged contexts are affected by changes in both surface- and ground-water levels, which may result in the desiccation or accelerated deterioration of organic matter and palaeoenvironmental evidence.

4.4.3 Water levels are affected by an increasing range and volume of demands. The management of these demands, and the proper consideration of archaeological conservation values within the management process, is therefore extremely important. Government and the water and river authorities involved in water management should be fully aware of the importance and vulnerability of archaeological sites and wetland/peatland areas, particularly waterlogged deposits.

4.4.4 In England and Wales the National Rivers Authority has a statutory responsibility towards the archaeological resource which is within its jurisdiction and which is affected by its activities. Similar responsibilities should be identified in Scotland and Northern Ireland.

4.4.5 In England and Wales water companies are subject to a code of practice on conservation. This should be extended to drainage boards and other bodies whose activities impinge upon the water environment. Similar Codes of Practice should be introduced for statutory undertakers, as appropriate, in Scotland and Northern Ireland.

The CBA will promote the protection of archaeological and palaeoenvironmental remains in wet contexts by arguing for

* **integrated river basin management**

* **adoption and continual review of the Code of Good Agricultural Practice, and in particular the guidelines concerning nutrient levels in, and chemical pollution of, open water and waterlogged deposits**

* **introduction of planning regulations to control fish farming to protect archaeological deposits from physical damage and pollution**

* **improvement of the advice contained within the Forestry Commission Water Guidelines**

* **a ban on extraction of peat from surviving peatlands**

* **extension of scheduled monument and planning control to works which affect the hydrological "setting" of sites and monuments, as a guard against dewatering**

* **periodic public review of the DoE/MAFF/Welsh Office Code of Practice on Conservation, Access and Recreation**

5. DEVELOPMENT

5.1 *Statutory and non-statutory conservation designations*

5.1.1. Britain's landscape is bespattered by a confusing range of conservation designations. These vary in the extent to which they contribute to the care of the historic landscape. In some cases there is close correlation between areas of archaeological interest and those with other conservation values. This can be welcomed—but serendipity is not necessarily the best way to achieve long-term management.

5.1.2 The scope of current designations needs review to integrate archaeological concerns with other conservation interests, to identify areas of potential conflict, and to improve liaison. Where such convergence is not possible, the aims must be prioritised.

5.1.3 At present information on archaeological, ecological and other environmental concerns tends to be held separately. There would be advantages in the integration of archaeological information into existing geographical information systems and databases, provided that adequate safeguards on the confidentiality and use of data can be ensured. Where data are networked, it is important that potential limitations and biases should be emphasised to non-specialist users.

5.1.4 In the longer term there should be a move towards the development of a method of landscape assessment which is common to nature conservation, scenic value and archaeology.

We will

* **press for the consideration of archaeological interests in the care and management of existing non-archaeological conservation designations**

* **in the longer term, press for the rationalisation of archaeological and other conservation designations, using the best practices which have emerged in ESAs and National Parks as models**

5.2 *Conservation archaeology and the planning system*

5.2.1 In England, Wales and Scotland the planning system has emerged as the government's principal instrument for archaeological conservation. We welcome the recent planning guidance on archaeology in PPG16 (Wales and England), expanding upon Circular 8/87 (England), and the NPPG and Planning Advice Note *Archaeology and Planning* (Scotland). Cognate advice is being prepared by DoE Northern Ireland.

5.2.2. Such guidance provides the framework within which the interests of our archaeological heritage can be measured against other needs, and if necessary protected from inappropriate development. However, as we have seen (Section 4, above) in quantitative terms most of the forces which erode Britain's historic environment lie outside the scope of planning control.

5.2.3. The CBA emphasises the breadth of the role to be played by local authorities in the curation and interpretation of our archaeological inheritance. This role is not only regulatory. Local, as well as national, authorities are centres for cultural leadership. The exercise of such leadership will improve public interest in archaeology, and thereby assist the aims and processes of conservation.

5.2.4 The effectiveness of the local authority depends upon the quality and scope of the information and expertise at its disposal. The maintenance and enhancement of Sites and Monuments Records (SMRs) as a direct function of local government normally at regional (in Scotland) or county (in England and Wales) level, is thus a prerequisite for use of the planning process as an instrument for archaeological conservation. County (or comparable area) services are necessary, too, to provide academic range and continuity, critical mass in expertise, and strategic view.

5.2.5 We welcome the principle of recent Environmental Assessment legislation, but are critical of its practice. The existing framework does not permit the LPA to give enough direction on the proper content of any required EA. By contrast, English Heritage's recent *Guidelines on Development Plans* provides excellent guidance.

The CBA will therefore support and urge

* **the creation and strengthening of local authority archaeological services at levels which are geographically and academically sustainable.**

* **recognition of the role of the SMR, provision of resources for it, and the strengthening of its role in the planning process**

* **inclusion of policies relating to historic landscapes, non-scheduled sites and buildings in development plans**

* **a review of the efficacy of EAs, and reinforcement of their provisions**

* **site assessments on historic landscapes**

* **establishment of research-based frameworks for local archaeology**

And more generally:

* **widening of local authority services, and their effective integration with those existing (eg museums), to embrace interpretation, education, and provision of information within the community**

* **schemes which encourage voluntary action for the study, display, and interpretation of sites, monuments, and landscapes**

* **regular reviews of the effectiveness of Town and Country Planning legislation as a means of achieving archaeological conservation**

5.3 *Conservation Areas*

5.3.1 Whilst Conservation Areas have been chiefly applied to built up areas, there is considerable potential for their designation in rural landscapes and for the extension of their use to embrace archaeological elements. Rural Conservation Areas have already been designated in, for example, the Yorkshire Dales and Orkney, and provision has been made for them in certain Structure Plans.

The CBA supports

* **Wider use of conservation areas, to protect archaeological features and landscapes through the strengthening of planning controls in rural areas**

5.4 *Permitted development*

5.4.1 A number of operations which can be destructive to archaeology, such as forestry, are classed as permitted developments under Town & Country Planning legislation. The CBA believes that these permitted development rights should be withdrawn, and the proposals concerned brought within the development control process. The treatment of archaeology within the General Development Order is inconsistent, and due for reform.

5.5 *Codes of Practice*

5.5.1 For other types of permitted development we believe it would be appropriate for interested parties to agree a voluntary Code of Practice which would protect archaeological interests.

6. Pressures on the Landscape: Problems and Examples

6.1 *Farm buildings* form one of the largest and most characteristic populations of buildings in our landscape. Their importance lies not only in their appearance but also in their contribution to understanding of the development of agriculture and rural settlement. They are increasingly victims of dereliction, or of schemes for conversion which deprive them of historical significance.

The CBA's existing policy statement *Historic farm buildings* (1988) recommends that wherever possible buildings should be retained in agricultural use. The conversion of buildings which have no agricultural future should begin with a search for uses which most nearly resemble the original use and demand least alteration to structural envelopes and interior volumes. Only when such possibilities have been thoroughly explored should uses which require more drastic changes (like domestic conversion) be entertained. The overall aim should be to moderate—not stifle—change.

The CBA will

* use its influence as a consultee on listed building applications in England and Wales to promote solutions which respect the archaeological value of buildings

* work in partnership with interested parties towards the integration of archaeological conservation within agricultural policies

* propose research into the nature of farm buildings and the degree of survival in order to better inform conservation policies

6.2 *Waste and minerals.* The exploitation of surface minerals and peat remains a significant countryside industry. Inevitably, such activities destroy historic landscapes. Local authorities are required to provide a strategy for mineral working and related development, and there is some discussion of archaeological issues in Minerals Planning Guidance.

Many archaeological sites are threatened by old mining permissions, some of which await activation.

The countryside is increasingly being used as a place for the dumping of household and industrial waste. This may be in former quarries or mounded in heaps. Such activities may have implications for the form of the historic landscape. They may also require topsoil stripping, road improvement and the construction of permanent installations to control methane.

6.3 *Derelict Land* Programmes for the restoration of derelict land form a large source of finance to local authorities and others. The types of sites or landscapes which fall into this category may be of archaeological interest in their own right. Dereliction is not solely confined to inner cities, and new priorities allow that historical conservation will also be given greater recognition in the reclamation of derelict sites.

It is often argued that the net result of such schemes is an improved, tidier landscape. In fact, the destruction of archaeological sites or landscapes cannot improve or preserve the historic environment, and over-zealous clearance may result in loss of local character.

The CBA will

press for all Environmental Assessments concerning large scale mineral working and waste disposal to take account of the implications of such proposals for the historical environment, and to include an appropriate archaeological component

oppose mineral working or waste disposal applications which affect World Heritage sites, listed buildings, significant archaeological sites or historic landscapes

seek to improve communication between Mineral Planning Authorities and archaeologists

urge the government to revoke mining consents on Scheduled Ancient Monuments, and areas of archaeological interest, without compensation

encourage conditions of working which limit or mitigate the effects of a scheme on the historic environment

oppose the unnecessry loss of historic features such as buildings, boundaries or historic mining landscapes

6.4 *Linear developments* such as pipelines, railways and roads destroy archaeological sites. Roads and railways also define new areas for development, with repercussions that may exceed the original scheme. For example, historic buildings and monuments may be preserved, but left stranded at the margins of new roads, while experience shows that ancilliary works such as bailey bridges, plant compounds, access roads and the manoeuvering of heavy machinery can cause more destruction than the primary scheme. National road traffic forecasts predict that by 2025 there will be approximately 2.5 times as much traffic on all roads as there is now. Analysis of social trends indicates that by far the greatest growth will be in the countryside. Associated planning issues such as the location of large developments near to road junctions or railheads will have a significant impact on the historic landscape.

The disbenefits of linear developments must sometimes be set against their archaeological advantages—for example, the limiting of pollution, or relief of pressure on historic buildings, bridges and subsurface remains in urban centres. Adequate data, as a basis for balanced judgement, are therefore essential.

The CBA will

press for the adoption of those routes which have least impact on the historic environment

campaign for the full integration of archaeology with other elements of Environmental Assessments in advance of all major road schemes, including alternative proposed routes

seek to clarify guidelines on concepts of setting and severance, and apply these to the evaluation of schemes

While less visually intrusive, pipelines can be equally destructive. The principles set out above should thus apply to the planning stages of such proposals, and similar mitigation strategies applied.

6.5 *Leisure developments* Much is being done both in the private and public sectors to boost the rural economy through the provision of facilities for recreation. Such developments may be of benefit to archaeology—for example by bringing more visitors to particular areas—but it is important to ensure that archaeological resources are not overwhelmed by relatively short-term leisure provision. The planting of national forests often involves increased public facilities and access to woodland areas, which often contain archaeological sites.

Golf courses can do much to destroy the historic landscape through the reshaping of topography, the alteration of water and vegetation regimes, eradication of hedges and boundaries, and drastic conversion of historic buildings. Provisions for off-road vehicles and motor bike scrambling can be equally damaging.

Metal detecting is a widespread leisure pursuit in the countryside. In England, Wales and Scotland (in contrast to N. Ireland: see Annex 1), there are no restrictions on the combing of unscheduled land or upon unscientific excavation, although some local authorities have introduced bye-laws which restrict treasure hunting on land in local authority ownership. In England and Wales, there is no obligation to report archaeological finds unless they concern items of gold or silver. In result, some sites are being damaged, and unknown quantities of archaeological material disappear unrecorded into private hands or the antiques market.

The CBA will

work to promote awareness of the need to safeguard historic landscapes in the face of pressures for leisure provision

promote the *Statement of Principles* on portable antiquities, jointly agreed between the Council, Society of Antiquities of London and Museums Association

encourage the reporting of archaeological finds

7. INTERPRETATION AND ACCESS

7.1 Archaeological sites and landscapes are an educational and recreational resource. Hence, it is highly desirable that there should be provision for public access where this is possible, and that opportunities for archaeological interpretation should be maximised (5.2.3).

7.2 However, where visitors pose risk to archaeological features the needs of conservation must take precedence. The historic environment represents the raw material for tomorrow's research and comprehension of our own history. It is necessary to accept that in any given area there will come a point beyond which it will no longer be possible to encourage public access, and that it may be necessary to restrict it.

7.3 Monuments and landscapes vary enormously in their fragility, vulnerability and capacity to withstand wear and tear. Assessments and surveys are needed to establish the appropriate and survivable levels of visitor access.

Basic principles of care and respect for the historic environment should be introduced to the young at school, and included in the Country Code.

7.4 When public money is invested in the conservation of archaeological features, consideration should be given to provision for public areas.

The CBA will

> **urge improved provision for public access to archaeological sites and landscapes where compatible with conservation objectives**
>
> **foster the widest possible curiosity, enthusiasm and respect for the fabric of Britain's past**

8. ENCOURAGING PARTICIPATION

8.1 Conservation needs people, not just experts. Without the support or—better—participation of the public, the best intentioned efforts of professionals will amount to little. The voluntary sector has a particularly important role in strengthening public feeling for and knowledge of local surroundings.

8.2 National and local government bodies cannot by themselves synthesise such emotional commitment, but they can influence the conditions in which public participation would more readily flourish. For example, relatively small allocations of funds (eg for equipment, training or coordination) coupled with advice, would have a multiplier effect upon voluntary resources. Strengthening of local government archaeological services with a specific view to providing support for community involvement would also bring benefits out of proportion to the investment required.

9. THE FUTURE

9.1 Existing measures for the protection of the historic landscape have their roots either in traditional restrictive legislation for control of single, selected and disembodied 'sites', or else in the adaptation of measures designed for other purposes. There is now an urgent need for new frameworks which provide both prescriptive and incentive measures to ensure good stewardship of Britain's landscapes.

9.2 Britain's landscapes are the raw materials for future research and education, as well as providing surroundings for recreation, the source of our minerals, and the basis of our agriculture. There will always be tensions between these needs, but the value of historic landscapes as an eductional and cultural resource has been insufficiently appreciated in the past, and is far from fully assimilated in legislation, designations and public attitudes in the present. In many parts of the UK little time remains, for less is now left than has already been destroyed. The past in Britain's landscape cannot be put back tomorrow if we destroy it today.

ANNEX 1

LEGISLATION

In Britain today there is no coherent statutory provision for the management of our archaeological inheritance.

Direct statutory protection of archaeological sites and monuments in the UK is provided by the *Ancient Monuments & Archaeological Areas Act 1979* for England, Wales and Scotland, and the *Historic Monuments Act 1971* for Northern Ireland.

Historic buildings, conservation areas, the setting of ancient monuments and the materiality of archaeological deposits within the planning process, are covered by Town and Country Planning legislation, now consolidated within the *Planning (Listed Buildings and Conservation Areas) Act 1990* (for England and Wales) and the *Town and Country Planning (Scotland) Act 1972*. In the *General Development Order (1988)* an 'archaeological site' is defined as an entry in the SMR. Formal government advice relating to this legislation is disjointed, with circulars and memoranda of different dates, and at different stages of revision, in Scotland, Wales and England.

Northern Ireland is the only part of the UK where unapproved excavation for the purpose of searching generally for archaeological objects is disallowed and where citizens are required to report archaeological material which is found by chance. In Scotland the reporting of chance finds is covered by Treasure Trove and *bona vacantia*. In England and Wales, by contrast, only Treasure Trove, limited to certain gold and silver finds, provides any requirement for finds to be recorded or studied.

Archaeological features under the sea to a distance of twelve nautical miles may be safeguarded by the *Protection of Wrecks Act 1973,* or by the 1979 Act. Materials from areas restricted under the *Protection of Wrecks Act* remain subject to general rules of ownership; if remains are removed to the surface they become wreck for the purposes of the *Merchant Shipping Act 1884.*

The *European Convention on the Protection of Archaeological Heritage* (the Valetta Convention), signed by the UK in 1992, will, if ratified, provide the larger framework within which domestic legislation operates. Conventions relating to portable antiquities include the *UNESCO Convention on Means of Prohibiting and Preventing the Illicit Import, Export and Transfer of Ownership of Cultural Propery 1970*—which remains unratified by the UK.

MONDAY 22 FEBRUARY 1993

The Committee met at Carew Castle

Members present:

Mr Gareth Wardell, in the Chair

Mr Nick Ainger	Mr David Hanson
Mr Roger Evans	Mr Walter Sweeney

Memorandum by the Historic Buildings Council for Wales
(HISTORIC BUILDINGS (HB 3)

INTRODUCTION

1. The Historic Buildings Council for Wales is the Secretary of State for Wales' independent advisory body on matters relating to historic buildings in the Principality.

2. The Council was first appointed by the then Minister of Works under Part I of the Historic Buildings and Ancient Monuments Act 1953. Under the Transfer of Functions (Building Control and Historic Buildings) Order 1966 (Statutory Instrument 1966 No. 692) and the Transfer of Functions (Wales) Order 1969 (Statutory Instrument 1969 No. 388) the functions of the Minister of Public Buildings and Works in Wales were transferred to the Secretary of State for Wales. The Council's terms of reference are copied at Annexe A.

3. Appointments to the Council are made by the Secretary of State for Wales. The size of the Council is not prescribed by legislation but clearly it is important for the Secretary of State to have a Council which reflects the various disciplines which can guide this work. A list of current members is at Annex B and of these only the Chairman is salaried (at £4,310 per annum). Cadw administers a budget to meet the Chairman's salary, members' expenses and the cost of producing an annual report. In 1991–92, the cost was £16,198. The Council's secretariat is provided by Cadw: Welsh Historic Monuments Executive Agency and includes the Council's Secretary, Assistant Secretary and Architectural Assessor. In 1991–92 this was estimated to cost £36,000

4. The full Council meets on five occasions each year both in Cardiff and at other venues around the Principality. Wherever possible meetings are associated with visits to properties to help inform the Council's advice. The Council is required by section 1(6) of the Historic Buildings and Ancient Monuments Act 1953 (as amended) to report each year to the Secretary of State. The Act also requires that a copy of the Annual Report be laid before each House of Parliament.

GRANT SCHEMES

5. The Council spends most of its time considering applications to Cadw for financial help with the preservation and conservation of historic structures on which the Agency seeks advice. Under the provisions of section 4 of the Historic Buildings and Ancient Monuments Act 1953 the Secretary of State is empowered to make grants for the repair or maintenance of buildings which appear to him to be of outstanding historic or architectural interest. Where he is minded to make such a grant the Act requires him to consult the Council first.

6. Section 77 of the Planning (Listed Buildings and Conservation Areas) Act 1990 (formerly the Town and Country Planning (Amendment) Act 1972) empowers the Secretary of State to make grants towards the cost of repairs to a structure where these will make a significant contribution towards the preservation or enhancement of the Conservation Area within which the structure is located. The Council again must be consulted before such grants are made. In undertaking this advisory role, the Council has been encouraged to note the growing number of Conservation Areas over recent years. There are currently some 399 Conservation Areas in Wales, to which some £3.268 million in grant aid has been offered by Cadw since 1985–86.

7. In preparing advice to Cadw on applications for assistance under the 1953 Act (historic buildings), it is the Council's task to determine if a structure is outstanding. This is an exacting test and each application for grant is considered rigorously. The Council's judgement is made in the light of its experience of assessing buildings of many types, taking account of architectural quality, historical association and the value of a particular structure in Wales as a representative of its type.

8. A conservation architect from Cadw, acting as the Council's architectural assessor, visits the buildings which are the subject of the applications under the 1953 Act (historic buildings) and the 1990 Act (buildings in Conservation Areas) to consider the works planned and also to form a judgement on the building's quality.

The visual impact of works is of particular importance in 1990 Act cases. His report together with other information—for example concerning the building's history—is considered by the Council.

9. The Council's advice in each case is considered by Ministers and offers of grant aid are made by Cadw subject to appropriate conditions, on which the Council offers advice. These can relate to fundamental considerations, like the desirability of professional supervision, to other important considerations such as the standard of restoration which the Council recommends is appropriate. The Council firmly believes that grant aid is best concentrated on traditional repair work of the highest quality. Given that contractors' overheads and scaffolding costs are major items in any project, the use of materials of lesser quality is shortsighted if this means that repairs must be repeated sooner than might otherwise be the case. Works of modernisation, extension, general maintenance and the provision of services are not items for which grant support is recommended.

10. The following table sets out the current guideline rates of grant that the Council draws on in recommending financial aid. These are set broadly to match the value of offers made against resources available and may exceptionally be varied to recognise especially deserving cases:

1953 Act (Historic Buildings)

Ecclesiastical
  buildings—50 per cent of eligible costs
Secular:
  (residential) 40 per cent of eligible costs
Commercial* 30 per cent of eligible costs
Local authority owned 25 per cent of eligible costs

1990 Act (Conservation Areas)

Ecclesiastical
  buildings—40 per cent of eligible costs
Secular:
  (residential) 25 per cent of eligible costs
Commercial* 20 per cent of eligible costs

(*Commercial properties are subject to a Departmental commercial assessment to establish need.)

All outstanding buildings grant-aided under the 1953 Act are subject to a condition stipulating that the public should have reasonable access (by appointment if necessary) to view the building and that the owner should make known the access arrangements. The Council's Annual Reports give guidance on access to buildings grant aided in each year.

11. With an ever increasing appreciation of the importance of the built heritage and the pressures which historic buildings can face there has been a welcome consistency in the number and quality of applications which the Council has been asked to consider. The Council welcomes the fact that the increased value of applications made to Cadw has been broadly matched by increases in the Agency's budget for the support of works to historic buildings. This has allowed the Council to continue to recommend—and see that advice accepted—enhanced assistance to important structures such as parish Churches. When it has felt it appropriate, for instance in the case of support for emergency works undertaken by local authorities, the Council has asked Cadw to draw attention to the availability of grant assistance.

12. The following table shows the trend in number of applications received and the numbers of offers of grant made since 1985-86. The total amount of grant offered in each year is also indicated.

	No. of Applications received	No. of offers made	Total amount of grant aid offered (£s million)
1985–86	291	139	1.942
1986–87	286	160	2.120
1987–88	311	171	3.239
1988–89	314	137	2.387
1989–90	278	160	2.779
1990–91	311	176	3.125
1991–92	309	154	3.225
TOTAL	2,100	1,097	18,817

13. The value of grants offered for repairs to buildings in Conservation Areas over the last 3 years was as follows:

	Secular	Churches
1989-90	£202,419	£84,055
1990-91	£531,265	£217,327
1991-92	£252,196	£211,174

14. The following breakdown shows the range of beneficiaries of grant payments in 1991-92:

Local Authorities	£292,710	9	per cent
National Trust	£306,669	9	" "
Churches	£781,851	23	" "
Private Owners	£939,932	27	" "
Other Non Profit Making	£123,744	3	" "
Town Schemes (see para 15)	£370,606	11	" "
NT Chirk Castle*	£608,023	18	" "
Final Expenditure	£3,422,635		

(*Assistance to Chirk Castle is made under a special agreement between the Welsh Office and the National Trust. The Council is not asked to advise on this expenditure specifically but members are kept in touch with progress in the Castle's restoration.)

TOWN SCHEMES

15. Under the provisions of section 79 of the 1990 Act (dealing with Conservation Areas) the Secretary of State and one or more local authorities may make grants towards individual buildings designated for Town Scheme purposes within a Conservation Area. The aim of the scheme is to act as a special joint initiative to improve the appearance of historic townscapes and 50 per cent grants are therefore available to help owners to carry out appropriate external repairs. The cost of these grants is shared by Cadw and the local authorities concerned. The council is asked to advise the Secretary of State on application for Town Schemes. Such schemes are managed by the local authorities in close collaboration with officers of Cadw. The Council receives an annual report for each scheme and, in order to inform its advice, and is critically examining the progress of existing schemes and the need for new ones.

16. The number of Town Schemes continues to grow with 28 schemes currently in operation. These are listed at Annex C. The following table shows the financial support for Town Schemes since 1985-86:

	Allocation	Grant Paid
1985-86	£72,613	£45,714
1986-87	£155,450	£94,724
1987-88	£228,350	£78,153
1988-89	£330,915	£148,348
1989-90	£342,241	£193,758
1990-91	£441,600	£400,808
1991-92	£605,816	£370,606

Variations in expenditure arise from the timing of projects, with commitments being carried forward from one year to the next.

ASSISTANCE TO THE NATIONAL TRUST

17. In advising the Secretary of State the Council records its praise for the work of the National Trust in securing the repair and restoration of some of the most important properties in Wales. The Council has considered 58 applications for grant aid from the National Trust since 1985-86. Of these, 53 resulted in offers of grant totalling £3.69 milion. Grant aid to the Trust is generally calculated at 40 per cent of eligible costs of repairs but the Council has recommended additional assistance where appropriate. The Council asks Cadw to keep under close review the balance of grant commitments to ensure that an appropriate range of projects undertaken by a variety of owners is supported. This review takes account of new demands and, in order to better advise the Secretary of State, the Council invites the Trust to provide an annual assessment of its priorities in Wales. Grant actually paid to the Trust in 1991-92 (27 per cent of the total) matched that paid to private applicants and exceeded that paid to churches by 4 per cent. The Council recogonises the strains put on the resources of the National Trust in the upkeep of houses such as Dinefwr.

ASSISTANCE FOR CHURCHES AND CHAPELS

18.—The Council considers many applications for grant aid from churches and chapels. It has always recognised the rich and varied stock in Wales of historic churches, chapels and other ecclesiastical buildings. Following a review of the state of such buildings in the mid 1970's, Parliament decided that repairs to outstanding churches, chapels and other ecclesiastical buildings (other than cathedrals) might benefit from grant support. With effect from 1 April 1978 the Council was invited to consider and recommend grant support for structural repairs to such buildings. The preservation of these is one of the Council's key objectives in advising the Secretary of State. The following table shows the number of applications from churches and chapels since 1985-86 and the grant offers recommended in response:

	No. of Applications	No. of Offers	Grant Offered (£'s million)
1985-86	44	24	0.318
1986-87	51	34	0.492
1987-88	73	40	0.561
1988-89	66	36	0.679
1989-90	53	22	0.385
1990-91	74	41	0.814
1991-92	78	43	0.613
TOTAL	439	240	3.862

19. Grant support to churches has ranged from grants for works to great churches and chapels like St Giles, Wrexham and Tabernacle, Morriston to small parish churches such as St David's, Rhulen, Builth Wells and small chapels like Caebach, Llandrindod Wells which are equally important in their rural context. The Council is aware of the high cost to Churches of keeping their buildings in a good state of repair and is encouraged by the high number of applications received in recent years for this vital part of Wales' rich heritage.

20. In its special position as independent adviser to the Secretary of State the Council has been particularly concerned about the plight of redundant churches. In 1986 it reported to Ministers on ways in which progress might be made with a scheme for the long-term care of redundant churches in Wales. The Council's report concluded that, in the absence of primary legislation on which to base a Redundant Churches Fund for Wales, Cadw should acquire, repair and maintain the best of redundant churches for which no other solution could be found. While supporting this, the Council views local care as a more satisfactory route. The Department accepted this advice and this was put to the Representative Body of the Church in Wales. The Council has been kept in touch with ensuing discussions which, latterly, have centred on the establishment of a Trust to care for redundant church buildings. The Council has been keen to recommend support for efforts by voluntary groups to take over redundant churches and has recommended 100 per cent grant assistance in two recent cases where churches were taken on by the Friends of Friendless Churches. The Council has twice commissioned reviews of the Church of Wales' redundant churches in 1985 and 1988. The Representative Body has been approached again recently with the object of producing an updated list for a further review. The results of the earlier reviews reassured the Council that no outstanding churches were under threat at the time.

21. In 1990, the White Paper "This Common Inheritance" gave a commitment that the Welsh Office would consider whether there was a need for extending the current historic buildings grant scheme to include cathedrals in Wales and the Council's advice was sought on this. The Council reviewed the architectural and historic interest of each of the Welsh cathedrals, their structural condition and likely future repair needs. The Council concluded that generally cathedrals were in good repair and better able to fund repair works than the many parish churches of Wales. But the Council recognised that in certain circumstances assistance might be appropriate. The Department is currently considering the Council's advice.

LISTING AND PLANNING CONTROL

22. The Council takes a keen interest in the indentification of buildings of special architectural or historical importance. Changes in the perception of and attitude towards the built heritage mean that the current schedule of listed buildings needs to be updated and that some areas need to be examined comprehensively for the first time. Cadw has this task in hand by way of its resurvey of the Principality and the Council has noted progress with this. The task is some way off completion and, in advising, the Council records its keenness to see it taken forward with all speed, but without support for other equally vital priorities being diminished. The Council encourages the vigilant posture which Cadw takes towards threatened structures and has itself asked for buildings to be surveyed urgently. As part of its consideration of grant cases the Council offers advice on structures which it believes merit early consideration for listing.

23. An important tool in ensuring the preservation of Wales' rich built heritage is the requirement for listed building consent for works to statutorily-protected structures. The Council is not consulted on the day-to-day conduct of this regulatory control but is aware of the guiding principles. In particular the Council welcomes the dialogue which exists between local planning authorities and Cadw's professional architectural staff. The Council supports Cadw's efforts to enhance its educational role in this area.

24. The Council is consulted on a wide range of issues including changes to planning controls, for example regarding satellite dishes and the ecclesiastical exemption from listed building controls. The Council's responses in such cases are published in its Annual Reports.

OTHER MATTERS

25. The Council interests itself in the welfare of individual problem buildings of importance attempting to encourage owners, local authorities and other interested parties to take a positive view of the possibilities. In some cases, such as Plas Teg and Pickhill Hall, the Council's efforts have borne fruit. In others, such as Sker House and Gwrych Castle work continues. Where appropriate the Council has recommended grant aid for feasibility studies and emergency repairs.

26. The Council is invited to advise the Inland Revenue on the exemption from Inheritance Tax of certain buildings of outstanding architectural or historic importance and on the question of adjoining land which will protect the setting. This involves considering not only the structure itself, but also the contents, landscape and overall historical integrity of the place. The Council is also invited to advise on management issues such as the level of permitted public access to buildings which enjoy exemption from Inheritance Tax.

27. The Council takes a keen interest in Cadw's work and its Chairman is a member of the Secretary of State's Cadw Advisory Committee. At the time Cadw was made an Agency, along with the Ancient Monuments Board for Wales the Council argued for the importance of in-house professional advisers reporting direct to the Chief Executive and this was taken into account.

28. The Council, on the establishment of the Countryside Council for Wales, wrote to the new body seeking its thoughts on principles surrounding the establishment of rural conservation areas. These would focus attention on rural areas of particular historic/architectural importance. The Council thought this could highlight, protect and conserve scattered groups of small vernacular rural buildings which are such a significant part of the Welsh scene. The matter is still under consideration, but a joint conference is one possibility.

CONCLUSION

29. The Council believes that there has been considerable progress in the protection of Wales' historic buildings. For example, with grant aid on the Council's advice, the National Trust has put into good condition several pre-eminent structures such as Erddig and Penrhyn Castles. Chirk Castle is benefiting from a major repair programme. Likewise great houses such as Tredegar Park and Plas Teg have been restored by public and private owners. Churches and chapels have received considerable assistance and there are very few amongst the more important that have not been considered by the Council for assistance over the last 15 years.

30. In the Council's subjective judgement there has been some improvement in the treatment of historic buildings and townscapes in Wales, but there is more to do. The Council advises on Conservation Area grants which seek to support local authorities' efforts to improve the appearance of historic towns. The growth of Town Schemes has made a major impact with good examples in Holywell and St Mary's Street, Cardiff, although without continued vigilance, this work can be set back by poor choice of materials in adjacent properties. Gradual erosion of the visual impact of historic townscapes, which can still occur even after declaration of Conservation Areas if control is not exercised, remains an enemy of the built heritage even though owners may be well meaning. In preparing its advice on the priorities to be addressed, the Council will continue to monitor closely Cadw's progress with its education initiative, listing resurvey and other work, and will stay in close touch with the efforts of other bodies such as the National Trust.

December 1992

Annex A

The present *terms of reference* of the Historic Buildings Council for Wales are as follows:

1. To advise the Secretary of State for Wales on the exercise of his powers under Part 1 of the Historic Buildings and Ancient Monuments Act 1953 as amended, the Planning (Listed Buildings and Conservation Areas) Act 1990 and on other general matters, namely:

(i) the making of grants and loans towards the repair or maintenance of buildings of outstanding historic or architectural interest or their contents or adjoining land and of gardens or other land of outstanding historic interest;

(ii) the acquisition by purchase, lease or otherwise, or the acceptance as a gift, of buildings of outstanding historic or architectural interest; or their contents or adjoining lands or of the contents of the buildings of which the Secretary of State is guardian under the Ancient Monuments and Archaeological Areas Act 1979, or of the contents of buildings vested in the National Trust, and on the disposal of any property so acquired or accepted;

115218 E

(iii) the making of grants towards the acquisition of buildings under section 47 of the Planning (Listed Buildings and Conservation Areas) Act 1990 by local authorities, and of buildings of outstanding historic or architectural interest by the National Trust;

(iv) the listing of buildings of special architectural or historic interest and the exercise of the Secretary of State's other functions relating to such buildings under the Town and Country Planning Acts.

2. To advise the Secretary of State for Wales on the exercise of his powers under the Planning (Listed Buildings and Conservation Areas) Act 1990 as amended, to make grants or loans towards schemes which make a significant contribution towards the preservation, or enhancement of the character or appearance of conservation areas and to make grants towards the repair of buildings included in a town scheme which are of architectural or historic interest.

3. To provide advice for the Capital Taxes Office and the Treasury on the exemption from Capital Inheritance Tax of buildings of outstanding architectural or historic interest.

4. To make representations to the Secretary of State for Wales if it appears to the Council that there is a need for immediate action under Part 1 of the Historic Buildings and Ancient Monuments Act 1953.

5. To keep under review, and to report to the Secretary of State from time to time on the general state of preservation of buildings of outstanding historic or architectural interest throughout Wales, and on ways of finding new uses for historic buildings and to make suggestions about possible uses for particular buildings when requested by the Secretary of State.

Annex B

HISTORIC BUILDINGS COUNCIL FOR WALES

LIST OF MEMBERSHIP

Chairman:

Mr Thomas O. S. Lloyd MA, FSA HBC Chairman since 1992 (member since 1985). Solicitor and author. Present appointment to HBC expires April 1995.

Members:

Professor John Eynon OBE, MA, Dip Arch (Wales), FRIBA Appointed to HBC 1967. Emeritus Professor of Architecture, University of Wales. Present HBC appointment ends September 1995.

Dr Prys Morgan, MA, DPhil, FR(HIST)S Appointed to HBC 1989. Historian, Senior Lecturer and Reader, University College of Wales, Swansea. Present HBC appointment expires September 1995.

Mr Richard Haslam, MA, FSA Appointed to HBC 1980. Author, freelance writer and consultant on architecture; member of the Royal Commission on Ancient and Historical Monuments, 1986. Present HBC appointment expires September 1994.

Mr William Lindsay Evans, MA, B.Litt, DipEd Appointed to HBC 1977. Retired Principal Lecturer in drama, NE Wales Institute of Higher Education; actor; Trustee of National Heritage Memorial Fund. Present HBC appointment ends September 1995.

Owen Lloyd George, 3rd Earl Lloyd George of Dwyfor Appointed to HBC 1971. Underwriting member of Lloyds; Trustee of Picton Castle Trust 1987. Present HBC appointment ends September 1995.

Mrs Sara Furse, DipArch (Scotland) Appointed to HBC October 1992. Chairman, Clwyd branch of the Welsh Historic Gardens Trust. Ex-member of the Committee of Management. Merseyside Improved Houses 1977-91. Present HBC appointment expires September 1995.

Dr Simon Unwin, BSc, BArch, PhD, RIBA Appointed to HBC October 1992. Lecturer Welsh School of Architecture. Present HBC appointment expires September 1995.

Annex C

CURRENT TOWN SCHEMES

CLWYD	GWYNEDD
Abergele	Caernarfon
Corwen	Conwy
Denbigh	Dolgellau
Holywell	Llandudno
Mold	Llanrwst
Wrexham	Maentwrog

DYFED
Aberaeron
Carmarthen
Laugharne
Llandeilo
Narberth
Pembroke
Tenby

SOUTH GLAMORGAN
Cardiff—Mount Stuart Square
            St. Mary Street
Llantwit Major

WEST GLAMORGAN
Neath

POWYS
Brecon

GWENT
Abergavenny
Chepstow
Monmouth
Newport

Examination of Witnesses

Mr Thomas Lloyd, Chairman, and Mr Douglas Hogg, Architectural Assessor, Historic Buildings Council for Wales were examined. Mr Richard Hughes, Secretary, Historic Buildings Council for Wales, was further examined

Chairman

262. Gentlemen, it is rather cold this afternoon but in this splendid building it is wonderful to be able to ask you a few simple questions regarding the role of the Historic Buildings Council for Wales. Mr Lloyd, for the shorthand writer's benefit, I wonder if you would like to introduce yourself and your two colleagues and state very briefly what each of your roles is in the Council please.

(*Mr Lloyd*) Thank you very much. My name is Thomas Lloyd and I am Chairman of the Historic Buildings Council for Wales. On my right is Mr Richard Hughes, who is Secretary of the Council and on my left is Douglas Hogg, who is the Council's Chief Architectural Assessor.

263. Thank you very much. In paragraph 5 of your memorandum you say that the Council spends most of its time considering applications to Cadw for financial help with the preservation and conservation of historic structures. When you consider various applications, do you adopt any strategic view regarding the range and structure of buildings which should be preserved?

(*Mr Lloyd*) In relation to applications that come to us we respond individually to each case to consider whether or not it is an outstanding building. As a Council we naturally have our own ideas of what an "outstanding" building is. "Outstanding" is the word or the criterion which buildings that come before us have to meet in order to obtain grants. For example, when you talk about a "strategic view", we do not have a set limit on the number of churches or chapels or houses which we would grant each year for example. We are reactive to the grants and applications that come to us.

264. Mr Lloyd, are you saying that you are entirely demand-led and that you leave it to those applications to come in and in terms then of the

approval, it is the consideration of each one on its merit that in effect occurs?

(*Mr Lloyd*) Yes, that is approximately the case.

265. If we look at the list of your grant offers made in 1990/91 it does seem to show a strong bias towards churches, country houses and middle to upper class town houses. Would you agree with that? "Bias" is a difficult word but I mean by that that in terms of the people that you grant aid to, knowing now that it is demand-led, as you said, what came out in the wash, as it were, at the end of the day tended to be biased—I am not suggesting that in a normative sense but in a statistical sense in terms of the results.

(*Mr Lloyd*) It is inevitable, given that our rules are to grant aid the outstanding buildings, that the better type of architecture in Wales is going to come before us. The country houses and the better churches and chapels of Wales are obviously the meat of our business along with a range of other buildings that we are eligible to help through alternative schemes such as the Conservation Area and the Town Scheme arrangements.

266. You mentioned chapels there but in the year 1991–92 23 per cent of your grant payments went to churches. Would that then include chapels?

(*Mr Lloyd*) Yes, it does.

267. How much of that 23 per cent went to the chapels?

(*Mr Lloyd*) I am sorry; I do not have the exact breakdown as between the two.

268. You could let us have those figures without too much difficulty, could you?

(*Mr Lloyd*) Yes, indeed.

269. It would be quite handy to know the split between the churches and the chapels.

(*Mr Lloyd*) Yes.

270. Thank you very much for that. In terms of the non-conformist chapels in Wales, are there any

[Chairman *Cont*]

particular problems they face when they apply for grants from you? To put it another way, are there particular problems that you have facing you in deciding whether or not to give them grant aid?

(*Mr Lloyd*) I do not think the Council feels it has any great problems in assessing the quality of the buildings that come before it. The Council has considerable experience from many applications now in the past and from the members of the Council's own expertise of the historic buildings of Wales, in being able to formulate in their own minds what an outstanding building is going to look like. That criterion is something that they are fairly sensitive to. The problem so often with chapels is that like farm houses or vernacular buildings they were not built to the high architectural standards of a church, particularly for example in the last century, when the great majority of chapels were built. A church was designed by an architect of known standing and everything within the church tended to be designed to high quality often for ritually significant purposes. Chapels were very much the creation of the local communities for their own needs and were built often without the assistance of architects and therefore it is not surprising that there are quite a large number of chapels that fall well below the outstanding criteria within which we are allowed to give grants.

271. In terms of chapels very often in terms of their association with the community it would not necessarily be the architectural quality of the building that would make that chapel outstanding. It could, for example, be that one of the great evangelical revivalist preachers of Wales who happened to have been in that chapel for a considerable period of time. In making the assessment of whether or not to grant aid would you include that and, if so, what would the trade-off be? In fact, could you have a pretty run-of-the-mill chapel but if it had been a chapel where one of those great revivalist preachers had been for a considerable period of time, would it be that you would actually grant aid it? How would you actually establish a trade-off of the criteria?

(*Mr Lloyd*) There are two parts to that question. The first part: would we know if the chapel is associated with a famous person? I am confident that the answer would be yes for two reasons: firstly because I am lucky to have as colleagues on the Council at least one extremely eminent Welsh historian and others with great knowledge in this area who would know these things as a matter of course. The second point is that if Mr Hogg was asked to go and inspect a chapel for grant purposes, I have no doubt whatsoever the person he met would tell him that someone of importance had been there. Thirdly the listing officers at Cadw (whom Mr Hogg can also sometimes turn to) who are architectural and Welsh historians will also be able to flag up further information. That is for the first part of the question. The second part is whether we would grant aid essentially a very humble building that may not appear to be of outstanding architectural interest but nonetheless we knew was important historically? We have undoubtedly grant aided in the past some very plain structures. I am just trying to think of one. In fact, Hen Gapel Robert Hughes is the one I was thinking of which was in ruins and certainly not an

outstanding building historically, I mean architecturally, but we felt without a doubt his connection with the chapel raised that building to outstanding status.

272. Are you then saying that when in fact a chapel is applying for money in this demand led way that it is very important that if one of these great revivalists ever graced the pulpit of that chapel, that would be sufficient connection to possibly make a major difference as to whether or not grant aid would be forthcoming because, indeed, a lot of these great revivalists preachers travelled around Wales. When Mr Hogg, say, would go along to a particular chapel the question that would need to be asked is not only whether in fact a minister who was an important minister had spent time being minister of that chapel, but had he been in the Cwrdd Mawr, for example, at Easter and that could make a difference? Where is the dividing line there because it must come down ultimately, I would assume, to a very fine subjective evaluation in the trade-off. Can it be consistent across the board that you are able to have a kind of trade-off that is uniform?

(*Mr Lloyd*) I would rely on the guidance of my fellow members who have all been selected and appointed by the Secretary of State on the basis of their ability to handle these sorts of questions.

Mr Evans

273. Mr Lloyd, in a sense you are the keeper of the public purse because if you are not satisfied that a building matches the "outstanding" criteria the Secretary of State can therefore no longer give any money.

(*Mr Lloyd*) Yes.

274. The key to this it seems to me is this: unless you have got a conservation area or a building that matches your "outstanding" criteria under section 4 of the 1953 Act, you are not going to get any money from the public purse?

(*Mr Lloyd*) The Historic Buildings Council was created for the purpose of dealing with important architecture in Wales. We quite often have applications from churches where it would be lovely as a matter of our own sympathies to give the money but they are outside the terms within which we can operate.

275. But the Secretary of State has no other terms either, has he, except for conservation areas?

(*Mr Lloyd*) He does not have a "lonely hearts club"—

276. I suggest that your use of language is a little unfortunate. What I would suggest is this: the importance of your advice is that unless a building is outstanding in your expert opinion it is not going to get public money from Cadw or the Welsh Office unless it is in a conservation area. That is so, is it not?

(*Mr Lloyd*) That is so.

277. What proportion of the Church in Wales churches total come within the "outstanding" criterion?

(*Mr Lloyd*) I do not think we would be in a position to know that.

[**Mr Evans** *Cont*]

278. How tight or loose a test is this? For example, how does it compare with the criterion used in England for vesting in the Redundant Churches Fund? Is it a higher or lower standard?

(*Mr Lloyd*) So far as the comparison with England is concerned there is no doubt whatsoever that we consider the line of "outstanding" to be drawn a little lower down than in England. Frequently we are giving grants to churches that I do not think would be considered eligible in England—although I am not in a position to speak for them—but we generally reckon that our grants are able to cover a broader spectrum than in England.

279. "Lower" is perhaps an unfortunate use of language by myself. In other words it is a wider and broader capacity but, for example, in England there is a criterion of architectural quality which justifies investing in the Redundant Churches Fund a redundant church. Now how does your "outstanding" criterion for spending public money compare to that criterion?

(*Mr Lloyd*) I am sorry, I do not think I quite follow your question.

280. The point in England is that if you have a redundant church, it can be vested in the Redundant Churches Fund in England if it reaches a certain quality standard. In Wales, where there is no Redundant Churches Fund, public money can save a building if it matches your "outstanding" criteria. The question I am asking you is a qualitative comparison. How high or low is your "outstanding" criterion as opposed to the criterion for vesting in the Redundant Churches Fund in England?

(*Mr Lloyd*) The trouble is I cannot really speak for the standard of churches vested in the Redundant Churches Fund in England. All I can really speak for is Wales and I think if a church was regarded by us as being outstanding in Wales we would grant aid it and if under the present arrangements that we have, perhaps on a temporary basis at the moment, for caring for redundant churches, if we consider them to be outstanding it may be that we could recommend them for 100 per cent grants as we have done in two cases.

281. But, for example, one of the matters of concern I am suggesting in Wales—following up what Mr Wardell has just asked you—is this: we have a large number of country churches and a large number of free chapels which are not in conservation areas. What proportion of that total is "outstanding"?

(*Mr Lloyd*) Well, as I said before, I do not think anyone has yet done a survey. The Historic Buildings Council certainly has not done a survey to satisfy itself how many of the churches out there in the countryside, some of which have never come to us for grant, are outstanding. We only decide if a church is outstanding when it comes to us with a grant application.

282. The difficulty then, of course—and this is the point Mr Wardell was putting to you—if it is demand led entirely and you have no real assessment of the scale of the problem in a sense, you do not know the numbers of churches which are outstanding which might or might not come to you.

(*Mr Lloyd*) I take your point but I think that all the members of the Council and myself included and certainly Mr Hogg, as Architectural Assessor, know a great number more churches in Wales than the ones that come to us. I am writing the present volume for Dyfed in the "Buildings of Wales" series at the moment and I myself have been round a very large number of churches, a large number of which have never yet come to the Council for consideration but when the Council makes a decision on their quality, one is able to bring that knowledge to bear.

283. Can I put an example to you? I do not know whether you have but probably Mr Hogg might have personal knowledge of this. Mitchel Troy in my constituency was ruled not outstanding by your body even though it is medieval I suspect substantially on the basis it was very thoroughly restored in the 1870s.

(*Mr Lloyd*) It is not a church, I am afraid, I have visited myself but I recall the application and as I recall we were interested in the number of medieval artefacts and vestiges of that period that remained in the church but particularly as a result of the restoration it lacked the integrity that we find to be better in other churches.

284. Is not the danger there that your usage of a rather narrow "integrity" basically shows a bias against 19th century buildings and 19th century restorations?

(*Mr Lloyd*) I do not think so at all.

285. That is one of the complaints the Victorian Society has been concerned to raise with us, that there is an under-appreciation of the importance of Victorian alteration and the case of Mitchel Troy it is a classic example of fairly drastic Victorian restoration but nevertheless the building at the end of the restoration is a building of some considerable architectural importance whether it matches your criterion or not.

(*Mr Lloyd*) I would disagree. We have some marvellous Victorian ecclesiastical work in Wales and I am particularly interested in it and have pursued it and I can assure you (obviously you are disappointed in this case) there are many and sufficient numbers of better instances of Victorian church work than in this case and it was the judgment of the Council with its acute corporate knowledge that it was not of outstanding interest in this context.

286. The difficulty I suggest, Mr Lloyd, is this: because you have no overall picture as to the number of buildings which are outstanding, which may or may not come to you, the difficulty for the Secretary of State is really being in any position to judge how much public money really would be required to keep in proper preservation what most people regard as an acceptable number of Welsh chapels and churches. The scale of the problem appears to be unknown.

(*Mr Lloyd*) If I could look at it from the other direction. We are granted every year a sum of money to spend on outstanding buildings and we are quite satisfied about our criteria of "outstandingness" and we are able to cover the demand.

Chairman

287. I think one of the difficulties here is that whereas you can cover the demand, since you do not know the availability in situ, as it were, of the number of buildings that may be eligible for grant that may be worthwhile, you are continually unable to really know the amount of money that would be needed to give grants to those buildings that at any moment in time are worth, and so waiting for the demand to come in without really being able to assess the need, of course, means that your job is comparatively easy because the resources that you have are not then stretched whereas if you did the survey and that survey would yield a very large number of cases then, of course you would have to turn round and say, "There is no way that our resources are able to meet this problem." So your argument seems to be that, "We are happy at the moment to go along with the demand-led situation because our resources are able to cope with that." However, if a major survey was done which actually meant that the number of cases that were received by you increased by a factor of whatever it was, then plainly the resources would not be enough. Is that a fair way of putting it? In other words the analogy is true with community care in Wales. If you had an assessment but the resources are not there there could be a problem. So you have got to be very careful of the assessment because if you assess too carefully and have too many people coming in you may in fact disappoint a lot of people whereas you are a happy company because you are not disappointing too many because you are not, in fact, being inundated with requests. The question is do you advertise, Mr Lloyd?

(*Mr Lloyd*) Could I answer because I think there is a coda to that last point. Forgive me if I suggest you seem to be pre-supposing there is a very large number of unrepaired medieval churches out in the countryside in Wales.

288. Not churches but chapels and all kinds of buildings.

(*Mr Lloyd*) Ecclesiastical buildings which are in disrepair: the fact remains that many of these churches have been very well looked after and they are not actually just waiting to be invited to have a grant given to them. The Church, particularly in recent years, has implemented a very effective quinquennial survey system and every five years these churches now are inspected and as their architects find the need for them to be repaired so they come to us with that grant application and we give grants where we deem it appropriate. So we are actually dealing all the time with a constant and regular turnover of buildings. I see no particular reason why there should suddenly be a great bulge in the conveyor belt of demand.

289. What about the advert? Do you do advertise the availability of your grant aid and, if so, where do you do it and how?

(*Mr Lloyd*) I think the first point perhaps to say is that we are not a body that faces the public directly. We are the Secretary of State's advisory body and therefore we are not a body that works by way of public pronouncements. The second point is that all architects and particularly any architect that would be working on a church would know of us, the

Historic Buildings Council, as a matter of course in his trade and as a matter of experience and would have no hesitation in coming to us.

Mr Evans.

290. If I may ask, what proportion of the grant applications are actually accepted rather than refused?

(*Mr Hughes*) Chairman, in 1991–92 there were 78 applications in respect of ecclesiastical buildings and from these 43 offers of grant were made. That would not necessarily be 43 buildings that were for the first time regarded as outstanding because we have regular customers. People phase work so that they can keep pace with the amount of resources they have to contribute to the work and so they keep coming back to us. The other thing as well is that figure would include applications relating to Conservation Areas.

291. Is there a published list of buildings that you have so far deemed to be outstanding?

(*Mr Lloyd*) We publish the annual report every year and there is a list of them.

292. To analyse what you have done over a number of years it would be a matter of abstracting that information from annual reports?

(*Mr Lloyd*) Yes, indeed.

Mr Hanson

293. I am interested in following up on the point that the Chairman made of assessing need. The Civic Trust in submissions to us says there is a lack of available statistics relating to need against which to measure applications for grant aid. What I am interested in is how you measure the need. Obviously you have a duty under your terms of reference "to keep under review, and to report to the Secretary of State from time to time on the general state of preservation of buildings of outstanding historic or architectural interest throughout Wales". How do you establish that need if you are only basing it effectively on demand-led applications?

(*Mr Lloyd*) So far as need is concerned we are able to establish need by the volume of applications that come to us. That is a fairly reasonable way of judging the need.

294. You establish need by the volume of applications that come to you but are you happy and do you believe that everybody within Wales who believes they could at least apply is aware of the facility to apply and if they so wished could apply?

(*Mr Lloyd*) I could not answer that definitely. I could not tell if every potential applicant knows that he could apply and it is possible that there are people or church bodies who have not heard about our services but on the other hand I think if they went about the repairing of their buildings properly they would be in touch with the sort of people who could push them in the right direction.

295. If you were sitting where we are sitting, are there mechanisms you would like us to consider to improve the method of application and the understanding of the role you perform so that the people for whom you ultimately provide a service could better understand the services that you provide?

[Mr Hanson *Cont*]

(*Mr Lloyd*) Forgive me, there is no intention on our part to be secretive or obscure in any way. We are a publicly recognised body. All local authorities, for example, know of our existence and if a listed building consent, for example, should come before them (as it would need to in relation to almost every building that we are likely to grant aid) those local authorities are going to know and are likely to push people in our direction.

296. In terms of the applications that you receive and consider do you feel that you are getting a reasonable geographical spread of both applicants and approvals?

(*Mr Lloyd*) Yes. Every agenda we have contains applications from buildings from all parts of Wales.

297. Can I just ask one final point on this particular area, Chairman. I am interested again in your memorandum it says that you have to keep under review and report to the Secretary of State from time to time on the general state of preservation of buildings and on ways of finding new uses for historic buildings and to make suggestions about possible uses for particular buildings when requested by the Secretary of State. On how many occasions, say in the last two years, has the Secretary of State requested you to consider applications in total? What is your total annually currently?

(*Mr Lloyd*) Every application is—

298. I know but what is the current total, I might have missed it.

(*Mr Hughes*) It is 309 in 1991–92.

Chairman

299. Just a very quick question. In terms of the need and the demand, if you have very large numbers of chapels with very small membership, very often down to a couple of dozen people, are you concerned that that kind of chapel may not even have the wherewithal to put together the kind of application to you for grant simply because the age of that congregation and the people within it simply would not know how to go about even applying for a grant and to whom? Is there a mechanism within the chapel communities, within the denominations, whereby information is disseminated to each of the chapels themselves so that should that situation arise that they can do that?

(*Mr Lloyd*) To a certain extent that is not our problem. It is not necessarily our business; it is their business. But on the other hand there is, for example, the Society called Capel which is presumably known to most chapels now and who would undoubtedly offer them help. We wish to be known as widely as possible. We have nothing to hide. We have every wish to help as many applications as we possibly can. We are in no way trying to be obscure or difficult. We are all known as members of the Historic Buildings Council and it is my passionate wish to be able to keep in repair as many historic buildings as we possibly can.

Mr Hanson

300. The applications that have been rejected say in this current financial year, are they rejected on the basis of cash or are they rejected on the basis of the status of the building?

(*Mr Lloyd*) The status of the building.

301. In all cases currently?

(*Mr Lloyd*) In all cases, yes.

Mr Evans

302. Mr Lloyd, if I could just follow this up. Is there a published list of buildings which have failed the "outstanding" criterion?

(*Mr Lloyd*) No.

303. Why not?

(*Mr Lloyd*) I do not think we have a duty to report that.

304. Are you able to supply us with a list of ones you have declined in the last few years?

(*Mr Lloyd*) Yes.

305. Looking at your most recent annual report the worrying feature, which takes up the point of need here, is that I notice there are two examples of grants in West Glamorgan, two in Mid Glamorgan and then one turns to other places like Powys and sees several pages of it. The thrust of the questioning that has been put to you is really this: does that reflect the architectural quality of these different areas; does it reflect the people who actually make grants; does it reflect a value judgment as to importance or what? Or are you perhaps not in any position to answer?

(*Mr Lloyd*) I think certainly so far as the first suggestion is concerned in Powys, for example, there is a very rich heritage of fine often half-timbered farm houses which are often superior to the typical farm houses of Glamorgan. They are fine, older buildings.

306. It cannot see a single farm house in your last report in 1990–91 in Powys. What we are talking about are churches and country houses.

(*Mr Lloyd*) If I can go on then. Certainly we have no bias towards any area. But on the other hand, for example in Clwyd we are very aware that that area has a particularly fine group of medieval churches. Therefore a church in Clwyd may have to be just a tiny bit better than a church in an area which has lesser churches to qualify. I think we are sensitive in that direction.

307. So "outstanding" there is where you are in relation to other equivalent buildings?

(*Mr Lloyd*) Marginally. I think if you had 20 particularly fine churches in a relatively small area, if the least of those 20 were to apply one might regard that as a less outstanding example of its type than if that particular church were transported to a particular area where it was a leader of its type.

Chairman

308. In terms of that question, do you in any way have in your mind a mental image of the distribution across Wales of buildings of outstanding importance which either would be geographically distributed in a way that would be uniform or do you have a pattern whereby their distribution would be based on so

[Chairman Cont]

many outstanding buildings per number of people living in a particular ward or county or district or is it done on the number of outstanding buildings per number of square miles? Do you have in your mind that kind of picture or is it a kind of haphazard situation whereby you just have a rolling situation where you will have a look at them as time evolves without really having any target or objective as to where you want to end up in the overall Welsh scene?

(Mr Lloyd) The first thing I would want to say is that the buildings of Wales are very variable. The quality of them varies from place to place with, for example, the churches of Cardiganshire by and large—obviously with honourable exceptions—not being terribly exciting. The churches of Clwyd are very good. The country houses of Dyfed are not outstanding. The country houses of Clwyd again perhaps are an extremely good group. Therefore looking at the total picture we are bound to find we have grant aided more churches in some areas than others because that is where the good churches are. What was the other aspect to your question?

309. What I really mean is that say in your office when you sit down and you look at the Welsh scene, whatever categories you use, say, on the crude criteria of the different categories of listed buildings, let us take any single classification—let us say Grade II* listed buildings—and you look at the number of these in Wales. Do you actually when it comes to the consideration of grant aid for those buildings say to yourself, "Ah well yes, we have already got six of those per hundred thousand population in one county. Now we cannot have any more because we have got enough of them. There we have got too few so we will put a couple more." So the chances of gaining grant aid for a new application, let us say for grant aid on an already listed Grade II* listed building, is far higher than elsewhere and if that is the case how does a potential applicant find that out?

(Mr Lloyd) We judge each case purely on merit. For example, some major houses come back to us year after year after year so we appear to have spent a great deal of money in that particular area. But if the next house down the road applied for a grant and we regarded it as suitable, we would give it a grant too.

310. So you do not look at the overall situation of Wales and look at the new applications in relation to the picture? You look at each application completely independent of the overall Welsh picture and simply say, "Is this particular application worthy of grant aid or not?"

(Mr Lloyd) That is correct, yes.

311. So you do not have an overall blueprint at all of the Welsh picture of what you would like to see— Let us have more of that and less of that—you do not have that? It is every single application on its merit?

(Mr Lloyd) Yes.

Mr Ainger

312. Coming back to the demand aspect, has Cadw ever indicated a upper limit of grant aid to you, a global figure for each year beyond which you cannot go or have you ever got to the stage where it is in the last three months of the financial year you have had

the communication, "Do not issue any more grants; we are very close to the limit." Are you ever aware of a budget from Cadw for grant aid?

(Mr Lloyd) Yes. We are given a commitment ration each year. The trouble is, as you will be aware, that Government spending is such that if we offer a grant in January, of course, the actual expenditure probably will not fall until the next year but Cadw on our behalf run a very sophisticated financial system for us. As for the question of whether or not we could ever break the bank, as you might say—particularly as the year draws to a close—we do take advice from Cadw as to how we are shaping up financially. If a particularly big application that we wish to make comes in then we will consider asking the applicant to phase the job over a number of years in order to spread the payment which makes it much more easy for Cadw to fund it and indeed it is usually preferable for the applicant anyway to do it slowly.

313. So there is a cash limit aspect not necessarily saying, "This is the limit,"—you may well be able to spread it over a number of years—but there is a limit indicated to you by Cadw? For instance, let us look at 1991–92, where you rejected 50 per cent of the applications. Of a total number of applications received of 309, the number of offers made was 154— effectively exactly almost 50 per cent. If the Government in its wisdom had indicated to Cadw that they wanted to expend more public money on preserving historic buildings and ancient monuments would that have affected your criteria for what was an "outstanding" building? In other words perhaps you would have grant aided 75 per cent of those applications instead of 50 per cent of those applications. What I am trying to get at does a cash limit have any bearing on the notion that you give to what is outstanding and has merit?

(Mr Lloyd) I cannot think in the period that I have been on the Council that we have ever been dissuaded from helping a building because it was going to be too expensive. We have found ways and means of structuring the financial need in order to accommodate what was required. There are occasions with certain projects—I am thinking of the Newport Transport Bridge, for example, where we have deemed the structure to be outstanding but we have realised that we can only play a small part in a major project for which other funding is available anyway so we may therefore give a lesser rate of grant because we are aware, for example, there is significant help from the WDA coming in.

314. Can I put it another way. If instead of £3.225 million, which is the grant aid you have offered in 1991–92, you had at the beginning of the financial year an indication from Cadw you probably would be able to spend £4 million and you still had 309 applications, would you still only have grant aided 154?

(Mr Lloyd) Perhaps I should have mentioned in the last question the rate of grant is fixed generally at the start of each year and that is based on the experience of the previous year. Now, that grant rate has changed over the years. About four or five years ago there was obviously great activity in the building world and we were faced with a very very large number of applications, therefore the rate across the board had to be cut down a little bit in order to

[Mr Ainger *Cont*]

accommodate the demand but no-one has ever been refused help on the basis that we could not afford it.

315. With respect, I do not think you have answered my question. If you had an extra £1 million to spend in 1991–92 indicated to you by Cadw, would that have affected your grant refusal of 155 applications?

(*Mr Lloyd*) I do not think we would ever have changed where we drew the line for "outstanding". I do not think it would be necessary. I cannot envisage circumstances where it would happen because I do not think we would be given the extra £1 million when the previous year we had not demonstrated the need.

316. It is rather a Catch 22 situation.

(*Mr Hughes*) Chairman, may I speak? What the Secretary of State is looking for from the Council is a judgment of these very difficult subjective issues about "outstandingness" and also about the contribution of works to a Conservation Area. So the Council's role is really to make those judgments and although the Council is kept in touch with the financial position (which actually runs for several years because of the length of time some of these projects take), the Council makes its recommendations and I am sure if it had to make these recommendations even if there were financial problems this would be for someone else to sort out.

Chairman

317. Do your recommendations ever get overruled?

(*Mr Lloyd*) I cannot recall one.

318. So they are all rubber-stamped are they, as it were, although that is not a very nice way of putting it. They are endorsed?

(*Mr Lloyd*) The Secretary of State has shown confidence in our decisions.

Mr Sweeney

319. You said in reply to a question from Mr Wardell, if I interpreted you correctly, that you do not advertise. Is that right?

(*Mr Lloyd*) No.

320. You said that architects are normally employed, for example, in the restoration of the church and they would certainly be aware of your existence. Would that apply also to listed buildings necessarily if someone, for example, has a listed building and has what is very much a personal scheme to restore it? Would they necessarily have access to architects' advice in knowing of your existence?

(*Mr Lloyd*) Again if it is a listed building and the owner is to do substantial work on it he is almost certain to have to get listed building consent to do it. I imagine the local authority would not be slow in suggesting that they might have a case for applying to the Historic Buildings Council.

321. You feel there is no risk by not advertising that you are losing people from the net?

(*Mr Lloyd*) I think if you saw the range of buildings that come to us, some of which really are very lowly buildings and really have no hope of gaining money

from us, you would realise that all sectors of the property owning sector of our society know about our existence.

322. You said you do not anticipate a bulge in applicants in the future. Is that right?

(*Mr Lloyd*) I do not expect it from the churches because all churches have now been inspected on a routine basis and the system is now up and running. A certain number are expected every year so in fact the number of applications coming from churches is relatively consistent. What is likely to make a difference is that if, for example, we come out of the represent recession to another tremendous boom then everyone will feel like spending money on their houses perhaps.

323. Cadw has said they anticipate the number of listed buildings to increase from about 15 to 30 thousand. What sort of impact would you expect that to have on your applications?

(*Mr Lloyd*) None at all directly because we are not tied in to giving grants to the status of a building in terms of its listing. We can grant aid and, we have on occasions I can remember, grant-aided unlisted buildings because they have not actually been listed. We usually request Cadw to list the building at the same time, I may add, and by the same token we have turned down a Grade II* building and I recall where we turned down a Grade I building because the application itself did not have the merit it required to get a grant.

324. Do you not think that the fact that a building was listed would tend to pre-dispose the owner to put in an application to you?

(*Mr Lloyd*) Well, we are a separate organisation from Cadw, the Historic Buildings Council, and the word "listing" does not come into our criteria.

325. If there is a bulge in the future would you expect that the Welsh Office would grant you any additional resources to enable you to do your job effectively?

(*Mr Lloyd*) I would have confidence that they would.

326. Coming back to the way the money is actually spent, do you monitor the use of grants that you push out and, if so, how?

(*Mr Lloyd*) Well the Historic Buildings Council makes recommendations of grant aid to the Secretary of State. The Historic Buildings Council itself does not deal with the money side of it. That is dealt with by Cadw on our behalf and they report back to us at each meeting how we are doing.

327. You are entirely reliant on Cadw to make sure that the grants you recommend are, in fact, spent properly?

(*Mr Lloyd*) All the actual expenditure side is dealt with by the secretariat, who are in Cadw, for us and they deal with inspecting the progress of the works and the side of the bills and invoices and the paying of the money.

328. You said that you make recommendations for grants on the basis of the merit of a building rather than the geographical distribution of the buildings in respect of which you receive applications. Do you analyse the geographical spread of the buildings to which grant aid is issued?

[**Mr Sweeney** Cont]

(Mr Lloyd) No, we do not feel the need to. As I think I have said before, we find that we are well-known throughout Wales and that we have applications coming in from all quarters on a regular basis. We are quite satisfied.

329. You said, and I accept, that the standard of buildings is bound to vary from one part of Wales to another. Would you be worried or concerned if you were to do a survey on the geographical spread and it showed you that there was a considerable imbalance in the areas to which grant aid is given?

(Mr Lloyd) If it did it would indicate that part that appeared to be least served by us had obviously a smaller number of outstanding buildings. The definition of "outstanding" is not definite. It is left to the Council to determine through its experience.

330. Could there be another explanation? Could it be, for example—because you have already mentioned that the level of economic activity has an influencing factor in determining whether people make grant applications—that in a poorer region of Wales that there might be buildings of considerable architectural merit but that the grants were not forthcoming because the owners could not afford to contribute towards the cost?

(Mr Lloyd) If the owner of a historic building—an outstanding historic building in this context—needs repairs done on his building it is in his interests to come to us. He would get money where he would not otherwise have got money.

331. Or he may otherwise neglect it?

(Mr Lloyd) Well, yes. If the owner of a listed building neglects his building it is likely that the local authority in due course will start to chivvy him on the subject and ask him to get repairing.

332. By that time it may well have gone beyond repair.

(Mr Lloyd) If it is a good local authority it will not have.

333. Do you not think you as a body have a responsibility to be a little bit more pro-active in seeking out these buildings and finding out where the grants ought to be going rather than simply waiting for the applications to land on your desk?

(Mr Lloyd) I do not think that is really written into our terms of reference. All I have to say is that the members of the Council are always interested in the preservation of the important architecture of Wales. Among our general discussions at meetings we often do register concern about buildings and the minutes of our meetings frequently contain records of these discussions and it is likely that we may have recommended that the secretariat or myself should write to local authorities pointing out that there is a building which concerns us. We do rather more of that than is perhaps apparent from our published annual report.

Chairman

334. There is a problem here that Mr Sweeney is putting his finger on. If you have a building that has not yet been listed and the person, in fact realises that here is an important development site for him or her to make a large sum of money on and they do not want it listed, nobody draws attention to it but in your demand-led system he is going to have his way which is that he will delay until such a time that that building is so dilapidated that it would not be listed because you could then turn round and say that even if somebody else, not the owner, draws attention to this building, "If only this had happened 20 years ago. It is such a pity now that it is too late". So there is that aspect that it is possible for Wales to lose buildings that could be of architectural value because nobody actually bothers to try and get the building listed and where the owner may have a vested interest in not having that building listed. Then you have got the other aspect that if a building is listed and the owner resents the fact that it has been listed because he did not want it listed in the first place (but let us assume that the building now is going to be saved) if the owner is poor it may very well be, as Mr Sweeney says, that he does not want to apply because he can only find a very small percentage of the total cost. It is not outstanding enough to qualify for the 100 per cent and so he is too poor to do it up. We saw a couple of buildings today in Pembroke Dock where in fact you have listed the buildings but in fact they have not been done up by the owner and the local authority may in certain circumstances not actually put the order on. So the fundamental question is first of all it could be because the buildings are left to go to wrack and ruin before the application is made and therefore the building is not going to be listed and then the other point where the owner is either too poor or too rich or anywhere in between, there may be reasons why they have no intention whatsoever of doing that building up. What is the way around that, if the local authority does not move? Do you have a role in pushing the local authority to do things or not?

(Mr Lloyd) The Historic Buildings Council has a role in advising the Secretary of State on neglected buildings. I am also empowered to write to local authorities and point their attention to these problems. Amenity societies are likely to hear of these things. Fortunately there are many people who are particularly concerned about architecture in Wales now and it is unlikely even in the remoter corners of Wales that there are really important buildings going to rot without somebody knowing about them who is able to draw them to the attention of the right person. People like myself writing the "Buildings of Wales" series travel up farm lanes and we find these buildings. I accept in the past, the more so the further back you go, this sort of thing did happen. Important buildings fell down because they were not noticed, but it is quite rare today; privacy is not what it used to be.

335. What about the local authority? Do you find some local authorities do not actually serve those notices and if they do not, do you know whether in fact the local authority commissioner has investigated such cases and whether in fact he has found maladministration on the part of local authorities who do not exercise their statutory duties for whatever reason?

(Mr Hughes) I think that the question of whether authorities serve notices or not is something the Council would see in relation to specific cases it was considering but only in that context. I do not think that in advising the Council I have ever had to draw their attention to any occasions when the local

[**Chairman** *Cont*]

authority commissioner has been drawn into a case like that.

Mr Ainger

336. Could I draw your attention, I do not know if you are aware of the case approximately five or seven miles from here of the Sisters' Houses. In 1927 there was a recommendation made they should be taken into public ownership because they were such an important medieval site and to date nothing has been done about that. Presumably you have not received any sort of application from, I presume, the private owner of that property? What would you suggest should be done to that piece of extremely important (we were certainly told in 1927) piece of architecture? Nothing is being done about it. Trees are growing through it. Ivy is taking its toll on these important buildings.

(*Mr Lloyd*) I do not mean to escape the question this way but it is not a building that would be in the Historic Buildings Council's remit because it would be an ancient monument as a long-ruined building. I do not think it is a question I can really answer because it is outwith my remit. Perhaps it is best if I leave it there but it would be a question of the local authority and/or Cadw approaching the owner to take forward these discussions.

337. As Mr Sweeney and the Chairman have said, there are many circumstances and I am not sure of the actual owner of this particular property but I assume it is a farmer, who certainly has not got the wherewithal to find 50 or 60 per cent of a significant amount of money just to make the property safe and prevent any further deterioration. There appear to be buildings that are literally falling down because the system is not geared sufficiently to be pro-active, as Mr Sweeney suggested.

(*Mr Lloyd*) In this particular case I believe that I am right in saying—and I am speaking out of my ground here—that the National Park has been in discussions with the owner initially to try and obtain a management agreement with him to do with keeping saplings at bay. But it is always a problem when an owner, who may not have owned it for very long, finds himself as the owner of a building that has been ruined for 500 years. It is quite clear that he is not at fault in the ruination of the building. In a case like this it would seem that the appropriate authority would be the National Park to come to some sort of arrangement possibly with some sort of grant scheme to ensure that it does not continue to deteriorate further and Cadw would no doubt have been involved in these discussions because no doubt it is a scheduled building (or maybe it ought to be) and it is not a case that as Chairman of the Historic Buildings Council is really within my remit.

338. Because you have not received an application?
(*Mr Lloyd*) No because it is an ancient monument.

339. Does it surprise you when the Council agrees to grant aid a particular project because it is outstanding from an architectural or historic point of view that the property has not been listed? You said earlier in answer to a question from either the Chairman or Mr Sweeney that there were occasions when you had grant aided properties that had not been listed and in fact a number of applications that

you referred to in the document that you presented to us referred to that. Does that surprise you?

(*Mr Lloyd*) No because as you are all aware our listing survey of Wales has not been completed yet.

340. But these are outstanding buildings. These are not the ones you do not consider worthy of grant aid. These are outstanding buildings of historic architecture. You are willing to grant aid them and yet they are not even listed.

(*Mr Lloyd*) The process of discovery of historic buildings will go on even after the re-survey has been completed. Indeed, it happens in England where they have done a re-survey. I was being told by a member of the Royal Commission a previously unlisted building was put straight in at Grade I. It had escaped the survey and had just been discovered. The owner of that building knew he had an important building. It would not have stopped him coming forward for a grant. The voyage of discovery is all part of architectural history.

Chairman

341. You cannot recommend any grant aid to ancient monuments, can you?

(*Mr Lloyd*) No, that is not dealt with by the Historic Buildings Council.

342. Thank you. I am just interested reading through the documentation and obviously from what you have said there is a lot of interdependence between yourself and Cadw in terms of administration of budgets and advice etc. I am interested in your opinion—it is not a leading question—could you outline to the Committee the advantages that this system of separation of powers has for (a) the people you are seeking to serve and (b) the wider taxpayer because obviously there is an interest in this. I would welcome your views on how you believe that to be a good thing and what advantages you believe that separation brings.

(*Mr Lloyd*) I think it is a good thing that we are an independent body from Cadw because we are not part of the administration and we are able to make our minds up without any of the departmental concerns that may be part of Cadw's business. We are a group of independent people drawn from all corners of Wales known hopefully for our knowledge of historic architecture and sympathy for the subject and I think that gives people's buildings a fairer day in court when it comes up for decision.

343. A difficult question—who pays the three of you? Where do you get your salary from? Who pays the cheque?

(*Mr Hughes*) Mr Lloyd's salary and the expenses of members are paid from a budget which Cadw administers but Mr Hogg and I are both officers of Cadw and act in our capacities for the Council.

344. How can you, Mr Lloyd, say that you are independent of Cadw? You can but can the two gentlemen either side of you when they are paid by Cadw? How do you as Chairman manage to ensure that your organisation acts completely independently of Cadw when in fact the pay cheque of the gentlemen on each side of you is paid for by Cadw? Is that easy?

[Chairman *Cont*]

(*Mr Lloyd*) We disregard their opinions—sometimes!

345. You do not want to re-phrase that!

(*Mr Lloyd*) You may not have heard; I said "sometimes"!

346. In terms of Mr Hogg, who kindly took us round Tenby this morning, are you the only architectural assessor that in fact the Council has, Mr Hogg?

(*Mr Hogg*) I am the Council's Principal Architectural Assessor. I have two other architects whom I share the casework with but I take an overview of the recommendations that are jointly put to the Council.

347. Are the other assessors paid by Cadw as well?

(*Mr Hogg*) Yes, because we have other work.

348. You do not find that a problem in any way in terms of your independence, do you?

(*Mr Hogg*) As I say, we do a range of work in Cadw because the amount of work in Wales demands that we have to operate in different ways. I deal with all listed buildings consents in Wales, for instance, and with my colleagues I deal with ancient monuments grants for Wales as well. So we have an overview on the state of the estate of historic structures in Wales. Therefore we are perhaps in a better position to know when difficult buildings are on the horizon and can advise the Historic Buildings Council.

349. But do you find the relationship between the Historic Buildings Council and Cadw made any more difficult by the financial arrangements? Should I say, would it be easier if the Historic Buildings Council had no funding at all from Cadw and that you were completely independent?

(*Mr Hogg*) I think the relationship is helped by our having the advantage of a panel of experts who are independent of my influence in that in judging the outstandingness of a building or the eligibility of a building for a grant it is not just me saying so to the Secretary of State—there is a panel independent of the Cadw system which is able to look critically at the recommendations that I make.

350. How easy is it for you to criticise Cadw? Is it just like biting the hand that feeds you?

(*Mr Hogg*) My interest is purely in the well-being of the craftsmanship of historic buildings in Wales. I look at it from the point of view that the operations that we work at together should operate with that formula at the top of their list of priorities. I am confident that the sort of funding going into the best buildings of Wales is something which historically seems to have operated quite well. I have been in Cadw for over 15 years now before it was called Cadw. I have a fairly long memory of the way things have been going over that period of time.

351. Tell me, Mr Lloyd, in terms of your memorandum in paragraph 28 you talk about rural conservation areas. What do you think are the advantages of such a designation?

(*Mr Lloyd*) There are sometimes two different things meant by "rural conservation area". There are the normal conservation areas which are declared by local authorities usually in towns but they are perfectly applicable to villages. Now we tend to think of those as conservation areas in rural places under the normal 1990 Act provisions. There is also another idea, I think one can say, that is floating around at the moment of a more informal conservation area which would be something thrown around a landscape in which buildings which are often incidental to that landscape would be included because it is appreciated that it is a beautiful view of long-settled historic landscape. At the moment that concept, ie an area where the conservation area is not generated by the quality of a group of buildings, is only an idea in Wales because we have not progressed along the lines of certain parts of Yorkshire, for example, where the stone walls which give such remarkable coherence to that landscape, make it a conservation area in structural terms. It is not something that is necessarily the Historic Buildings Council's entire problem. It is something that the Countryside Council for Wales might want to consider perhaps in conjunction with us but it is a concept that I think is gaining ground based on English examples although it is more difficult to apply to Wales because we do not have those close-knit built landscapes that they sometimes do in England.

352. What you are saying is that in terms of certain parts of England it is much easier to set up the rural conservation areas than in Wales?

(*Mr Lloyd*) It can be easier to see what you are aiming at in England. The famous example in Swaledale has these very small fields with these striking stone walls round them and little barns in each corner. You can see easily there—although one is talking about the rural scene—there is something there specifically that could be protected.

353. You see we have got a slight difficulty here because the Council for British Archaeology said exactly what you are saying, they cited Swaledale as an example of a conservation area but when Mr Carr came in front of us from Cadw—and this is where I am testing your independence, Mr Lloyd—he said, "There are very severe difficulties in the designation of rural conservation areas in England." Do you find there are such difficulties or are there not really? In other words could Mr Carr be mistaken because we have got a problem here in seemingly having two views that are different.

(*Mr Lloyd*) The problem from the Historic Buildings Council's point of view is how do we target grants in relatively amorphous areas of landscape? We are in the conservation area business; we have to look for work that significantly enhances an area in the very loosely knit Welsh landscape. We have to ask whether the re-building of one boundary wall and the re-roofing of one stone barn is the thing that is going to really improve that landscape. In my view (and this is where very often the difficulty arises) the threat to that area is not necessarily the roof falling off a barn, but planning permission being given for a bright white house in the middle of it, which is not our problem.

354. Are you aware of very severe difficulties in the designation of rural conservation areas in England, yes or no, before we freeze to death?

(*Mr Lloyd*) My knowledge stops at the Welsh border.

355. I thought you were quoting the Swaledale example earlier and you obviously have knowledge

[**Chairman** *Cont*]

that is extended further because Swaledale is not within the English border. On the one hand you were happy to quote Yorkshire and now in fact you rely on the fact you know nothing beyond Wales. Surely that cannot be true?

(*Mr Lloyd*) The miracle of photography has brought me images of Swaledale. I have no particular image in my mind of the particular areas which are causing such difficulty in England.

Mr Evans

356. Mr Lloyd, it is a condition of grant aid that the public have access to the building in question and has this always been the case under this arrangement?

(*Mr Lloyd*) Yes.

357. Is there a published list of each and every building that has actually received grant aid?

(*Mr Lloyd*) Our annual reports actually carry those lists and each annual report, as you will have noticed, carries a little access indicator.

358. Suppose I am a member of the public and I do not go to the library to find your annual reports, is there an easy town by town, county by county list of buildings which have received grant aid and which the public have the right to look at?

(*Mr Lloyd*) There is the "Historic Houses and Gardens Journal" that comes out every year that you can buy.

359. I can give you examples, if you really insist, of properties that have vanished from that publication because new owners do not terribly want the public to have access. Anyway those are purely commercial publications. Is there an authoritative published list area by area so that I can look up and see whether this particular house should be open to the public?

(*Mr Lloyd*) There is no list that you can purchase in a newsagent, for example, of grant aided Historic Buildings Council properties.

360. Suppose I buy a house in Tenby, which we have been looking round this morning, that 25 years ago had received a sum of money for roof grant aid. There is not, for example, a local land charge, is there?

(*Mr Lloyd*) No, it is a subject that we were discussing in our last and previous to that Historic Buildings Council meeting, that if an owner of a property who has had grant aid sells the properties, as a matter of fact the obligation to display to the public lapses.

361. It lapses?

(*Mr Lloyd*) Yes.

362. So you mean that is as soon as I have had my grant aid I sell my property to a Jersey developer it lapses?

(*Mr Lloyd*) If you did that straight away we would claw back the grant from you.

363. But if I had flown the nest? This is a very serious question. Are you suggesting these grants that ought to and intend to have a right of public access, that right of public access does not mean regardless of changes of ownership of that property? Is that really the case?

(*Mr Hughes*) Chairman, it is the case. If the property is sold within 10 years then a grant

technically becomes repayable and the Secretary of State may seek to reclaim whole or part of that grant.

Chairman: When you say "may", does he always?

Mr Ainger: Has he?

Chairman

364. Has he exercised that right. When you say the word "may", if in fact a property is sold within 10 years of the grant having been made, does he automatically exercise that right and reclaim it?

(*Mr Hughes*) When I say "may", I mean the Act gives him the power to recover the money. In certain cases the grant is re-claimed but not in every case. It would depend on the circumstances in every single case because the property will have benefited and these grants are granted on property rather than the individual.

Mr Evans

365. Is there not a most serious defect of the system that it ought to be the case that grant aid being made available should create some sort of local land charge obligation which goes on so that the owner of that property has forever the obligation to let the public in?

(*Mr Lloyd*) I think that would be counter productive in as much as our grants are made for the benefit of the building and not the owner and if a land charge were placed on the property ever after I think that would be quite a harsh proposition which would deter people from applying to us.

366. It may at least ensure that the public money was spent for the benefit of the public to have access, Mr Lloyd.

(*Mr Lloyd*) Public money is spent to keep the building standing for future generations.

367. What is the purpose of that if they cannot see the interior if that is the feature?

(*Mr Lloyd*) My experience is that owners of historic buildings in Wales are more than generous in allowing the public to see their buildings on application. It is a condition of grant that adequate publicity is given to access arrangements by the recipients of grants.

368. Do you ever check to see whether that is done?

(*Mr Lloyd*) I do not think we check on a regular basis but I am aware of numerous owners who are perfectly happy to let the public in.

369. Why have you not? If it is not for you it is obviously for Cadw. Why have you not required everybody who has received a grant over the last few decades to insert their property in a simple little booklet to be published either by you or Cadw. It would be a very simple thing to do. Why not?

(*Mr Hughes*) Chairman, can I say that the Council is concerned about the question Mr Evans raises and members of the Council have asked the secretariat to look into the possibility of publishing just the sort of list that he is talking about. I am afraid we have not come up with our proposals yet from the secretariat.

Mr Sweeney

370. Would it be fair to say that if there were to be a land charge imposed on property, as Mr Evans has said, that would tend to reduce the value of the property and therefore deter people from applying to you for a grant in the first place?

(*Mr Lloyd*) The most undesirable thing would be for people to be deterred from asking for our grant when they do have old properties. One of the advantages of the grant is that it buys our conditions into the restoration of that property and often as a result of us being able to give money we have been able to achieve a far better restoration of that property than if the owner had done it without the professional input that Mr Hogg is able to achieve.

Chairman

371. Is it a condition of that grant that the owner if he sells that property within 10 years must inform you of that fact?

(*Mr Hughes*) Yes, he should.

372. Is he under a legal obligation as a result of a contract for receiving a grant? Would not that in fact close that loophole and therefore would actually mean that automatically the Secretary of State could recover the money?

(*Mr Lloyd*) It is a condition of receiving grant aid that in the event of the sale of the property within a period of 10 years from the date the grant is offered the owner shall immediately inform the Secretary of State.

Mr Evans

373. What is the sanction for breach of that? Mr Lloyd, you are a solicitor, as I understand it, what is the sanction?

(*Mr Lloyd*) I have only been Chairman of the Council for a very short time. It would be for the Secretary of State to seek to recover the grant.

374. From the individual; not from the property if he has passed it on?

(*Mr Lloyd*) Yes.

375. You say these are conditions of the grant. Do we take it these are standard form conditions that are always applied and, if so, may we have a copy of them?

(*Mr Lloyd*) Yes.

Mr Sweeney: Would it be fair to say then that for the person who is selling the property there is going to be no greater sanction against him if he fails to disclose that he has sold it within the ten years than if he does disclose it? In other words he has not nothing to lose and everything to gain by not making a disclosure?

Mr Ainger

376. I think the answer to that is yes!

(*Mr Lloyd*) My masters have not written anything further on the subject than the conditions which I

inherited but it may be something that we should investigate further.

Chairman

377. Mr Lloyd, thank you very much for coming. Gentlemen, is there anything you would like to leave us with? I do not mean any physical documents necessarily but is there anything you would like to add to correct any impression we may have had that might be distorted or in fact an area we have not covered that you would like to mention that may be helpful to us?

(*Mr Hughes*) At the very start of the evidence, Chairman, Mr Evans was asking about the role of the Council and the Secretary of State's authority to grant things to owners of historic buildings. Can I just say the Council's advice is only in the context of the 1953 Act and the 1990 Act. So if the Council says a building is not outstanding that would not prevent funding coming from the Welsh Office under some other scheme.

Mr Evans

378. What other schemes have you in mind? What other schemes are there?

(*Mr Hughes*) I am only thinking, for example, under urban development programmes I believe that a chapel restoration and conversion scheme was assisted. I just wanted to say to the Committee that the Council's recommendations are within the context of specific legislation. The other point I wanted to make was that the size of the congregation is a piece of information that the Council is provided with so that the Council can judge whether it should be trying to give special help where there is just a small congregation, which is what you asked about, Chairman.

Chairman

379. Is there anything else, Mr Lloyd, or your colleagues?

(*Mr Lloyd*) A combination of cold and nerves did make me say something that Mr Evans quite correctly picked me up on. I meant to say "my heart bleeds". I think I mistakenly said "lonely hearts" which was not the right phrase. The wrong words came out and all I was meaning is that there are many small churches that we have to turn down because they simply do not come up to the criteria even though they are charming people and one would love to help them in an uncruel world.

Chairman: Thank you very much for coming and braving the cold.

Memorandum by the Royal Commission on Ancient and Historical Monuments in Wales

PRESERVATION OF HISTORIC BUILDINGS AND ANCIENT MONUMENTS IN WALES
(HB 13)

1. The Royal Commission on the Ancient and Historical Monuments of Wales was first established in 1908 by Royal Warrant, along with similar bodies for England and Scotland. Currently its powers are derived from a new Royal Warrant of April 1992, a copy of which is attached as appendix 1. A Chairman and ten Commissioners are appointed for initial terms of not more than five years. Membership is drawn from the disciplines and specialisms related to its work and includes historians, archaeologists and architectural historians. The current list of Commissioners is attached as appendix 2.

2. The Royal Commission is funded through the Welsh Office, whose Permanent Secretary is Accounting Officer, to whom the Secretary, as the Royal Commission's senior officer, is personally accountable. Cadw, an Agency of the Department is the sponsoring Division, and is responsible for advising Ministers on all aspects of the Royal Commission's activities, and for monitoring financial and other performance against targets. The Royal Commission's forward programme is developed through a corporate planning process, and, from 1991–92, an Annual Report will be published. The organisation's budget for the current year is £1.055 million, which includes a projected income of £10,000 from sales of publications. Staff costs are the largest call on funds, although there is a provision of £78,000 for the sponsorship of Upland survey, aerial photography and sites and monuments records. There are 36 members of staff; an organisation chart is attached as appendix 3.

3. The role of the Royal Commission is supportive rather than executive with regard to the care and preservation of historic buildings and monuments. Indeed, its role largely complements that of Cadw and is best outlined by the words of the Royal Warrant itself, "to provide for the survey and recording of ancient and historical monuments and constructions connected with or illustrative of the contemporary culture, civilisation and conditions of life of the people in Wales from the earliest times . . . by identifying, surveying, interpreting and recording all buildings, sites and monuments of archaeological, architectural and historical interest in Wales . . . by providing advice and information relevant to the preservation and conservation of such buildings . . . (etc) by establishing and maintaining national standards in surveying, recording and curating of records relative to archaeology and historical architecture". As a consequence of these and other activities the Royal Commission has a publication programme and is responsible for the maintenance and development of the National Monuments Record which is a site index, archive, and developing computer database; and for the sponsorship of the regional Sites and Monuments Records.

4. In order to carry out its work, the Royal Commission deploys an expert staff capable of surveying, interpreting and recording sites and structures of any period. In addition there is a specialist section which carries out, co-ordinates and sponsors archaeological aerial photography across Wales. A new information technology section is responsible for liaison with and sponsorship of sites and monuments records, and for the development of an extended national database, a computerised index to archaeological and historical sites and structures in Wales and, eventually, within UK. The National Monuments Record provides specialist library facilities, open to the public, and is an approved archive housing archaeological and architectural material.

5. The Royal Warrant of 1908 required the compilation of an inventory of monuments. Originally topographical volumes, these came to be substantial publications organised in themes within counties. This programme is now being drawn to a close and will cease with the publication of volumes on the later Castles of Glamorgan and the Prehistoric Earthworks of Brecknock. The Royal Commission's published work is the result of intensive research and a high level field recording; it is detailed, well illustrated and definitive, and deals with sites and structures irrespective of ownership. The most recent work on Glamorgan Castles to 1217 (HMSO 1991) deals with a number of Cadw sites among many others, while earlier publications have contributed greatly to the knowledge of rural domestic architecture across Wales. Although the policy is changing, publication remains a most important aspect of the Royal Commission's work.

6. An information base is the essential prerequisite for the effective management of any historic site, and the inventory entry has gone a long way to provide this for Cadw, as for any other owner. In giving effect to its responsibilities under the new Royal Warrant, the Royal Commission works in close collaboration with Cadw and is anxious to ensure that this working relationship, like that with other bodies, continues to develop so that maximum benefit can be obtained by adjusting the timescale and nature of its output. If, on occasion, another's requirement goes beyond the level of recording the Royal Commission can resource, then that body should reasonably be expected to fund the shortfall.

7. Other major owners are taking an increasing interest in providing surveys and information about their holdings, and making it available to a wider public through the National Monuments Record. The National Trust is well advanced with such work on all the historic elements of their building stock, whether listed or not, while the Church in Wales has also recently taken an initiative to identify in detail the nature of its holdings. The Royal Commission is able to fulfil a collaborative and supportive role in its relations with

bodies such as these, as they provide for buildings in their care. Chapels, on the other hand, of which some thousands survive, are not subject to unified management and the co-ordination of an information base is now an initiative of the Royal Commission working with, among others, Capel, which is a voluntary body. The provision of information in a structured and consistent form is seen as the prerequisite to decisions about grants, and listing, or to assist local congregations or other organisations in the management of their buildings.

8. The Royal Commission plays a part in that element of the planning process which relates to listed building consent, as it must be given the opportunity to record before permitted demolition takes place. It enjoys good working relations with both Cadw and local authorities who share listed building consent work and at the moment it is just able to meet this demand-led recording need.

9. Royal Commission staff are also approached about the recording of other "threatened" buildings and the relatively high incidence of this demand demonstrates how many potentially listable buildings are not protected. However, although an acceleration in the listing programme is clearly needed, the contribution which the Royal Commission could be called upon to make could consume its recources both in the provision of information at the outset and, after listing, when buildings granted consent required more detailed recording. On current resource levels, the Royal Commission could only meet this demand by diverting attention from other activities.

10. In conclusion, therefore, the Royal Commission's role is primarily to provide information and make it widely accessible. Several categories of buildings, such as major castles and many rural domestic buildings, have already been surveyed and published to a higher level than elsewhere in the United Kingdom. In other cases, notably chapels and other nineteenth century buildings in rural and, especially, industrial Wales, the task is only just beginning. For the future the Royal Commission is anxious to develop co-operation with other bodies and groups and where possible to harness and guide their efforts. However, to achieve this, it will depend upon its expert staff.

December 1992

APPENDIX 1

ROYAL WARRANT GIVEN ON THE SIXTH DAY OF APRIL 1992

ELIZABETH THE SECOND, by the Grace of God of the United Kingdom of Great Britain and Northern Ireland and of Our other Realms and Territories QUEEN, Head of the Commonwealth, Defender of the Faith, to

Our Right Trusty and Well-beloved:

Jenkyn Beverley Smith

Our Trusty and Well-beloved:

Michael Ross Apted
Ronald William Brunskill—Officer of Our Most Excellent Order of the British Empire
David Ellis Evans
Richard Haslam
Ralph Alan Griffiths
Daniel Gruffydd Jones
Geraint Dyfed Barri Jones
Stuart Brian Smith
Geoffrey John Wainwright—Member of Our Most Excellent Order of the British Empire

Greetings!

WHEREAS by Warrant under Our Royal Sign Manual bearing date the twenty-eighth day of September 1963 it was deemed that the Commissioners appointed to the Royal Commission on the ancient and historical monuments and constructions in Wales, now known as the Royal Commission on Ancient and Historical Monuments of Wales, should make an inventory of all the ancient and historical monuments and constructions connected with, or illustrative of, the contemporary culture, civilisation and conditions of the life of the people of Wales and Monmouthshire from the earliest times and to specify those most worthy of preservation:

AND WHEREAS We have revoked and determined and do by these Presents revoke and determine all the Warrants whereby Commissioners were appointed on the twenty-eighth day of September 1963 and on any subsequent date:

NOW KNOW YE that We reposing great trust and confidence in your knowledge and ability, have authorised and appointed, and do by these Presents authorise and appoint you, the said Jenkyn Beverley Smith (Chairman), Michael Ross Apted, Ronald William Brunskill, David Ellis Evans, Richard Haslam, Ralph Alan Griffiths, Daniel Gruffydd Jones, Geraint Dyfed Barri Jones, Stuart Brian Smith and Geoffrey John Wainwright to be Our Commissioners to provide for the survey and recording of ancient and historical monuments and constructions connected with, or illustrative of, the contemporary culture, civilisation and conditions of the life of the people in Wales and Monmouthshire from the earliest times (including ancient and historical monuments and constructions in, or or under, the sea bed within the United Kingdom territorial sea adjacent to Wales) by compiling, maintaining and curating the National Monuments Record of Wales as the basic national record of the archaeological and historical environment; by identifying, surveying interpreting and recording all buildings, sites and ancient monuments of archaeological, architectural and historical interest in Wales or within the territorial sea adjacent to Wales, in order both to enhamce and update the National Monuments Record of Wales, and also to respond to statutory needs; by providing advice and information relevant to the preservation and conservation of such buildings, sites and ancient monuments of archaeological, architectural and historical interest; by collecting and exchanging data with other record holders and providing an index to data from other sources; by promoting the public use of information available in the National Monuments Record of Wales by all appropriate means; by establishing and maintaining national standards in surveying, recording and curating of records relating to archaeology and historical architecture and providing guidance on these matters to other bodies and by exercising responsibility for the oversight of local Sites and Monuments Records:

AND We do by these Presents will and ordain that Our Commission shall consist of a Chairman and not more than 10 other persons, appointed by Us on the advice of Our First Lord of the Treasury in consultation with Our Secretary of State, the terms of appointment of Commissioners and Chairmen being determined by Our Secretary of State; and all such Commissioners and Chairmen shall hold and vacate and may be removed from office in accordance with the terms of their appointment; a Commissioner other than the Chairman shall not be appointed for a term of more than five years but shall be eligible for re-appointment; and a Commissioner may resign at any time by giving notice in writing to Our Secretary of State; a Vice-Chairman shall be appointed by the Commission from among the Commissioners, and the terms of the appointment shall be determined by the Commission; and if the Secretary of State is satisfied that a Commissioner has been absent from three consecutive meetings of the Commission without the consent of the Commission, or has become bankrupt or made an arrangement with his creditors, or is incapacitated by physical or mental illness, or is otherwise unable or unfit to discharge the function of a Commissioner, Our Secretary of State may remove him from his office:

AND We do further ordain that if a person present at a meeting has any financial interest in any matter which is the subject of consideration at that meeting he shall as soon as practicable after the commencement of the meeting disclose the fact and shall not, without the consent of the other Commissioners present at the meeting, take part in the consideration of or vote on any question with respect to it; this Our Commission may act notwithstanding a vacancy amongst its Commissioners; the validity of any proceedings of this Our Commission shall not be affected by any defect in the appointment of all or any of the Commissioners; subject as provided by this Our Warrant, the Commission may regulate its own procedure:

AND for the better effecting the purposes of this Our Commission, We do by these Presents give and grant you full power to call on persons with information likely to be needed for the National Monuments Record of Wales; to have access to or call for any books, documents, registers and records as may afford you the fullest information on the subject; to make enquiries about any premises by all other lawful ways and means whatsoever; to publish, by means of an annual report, progress made and activities undertaken; to promote or publish or assist in publishing information; to receive and spend money voted by Our United Kingdom Parliament, subject to any conditions that Our Secretary of State may from time to time impose; and to do all such other things as shall further the attainment of the purposes of this Our Commission (including in appropriate circumstances the grant-aiding of third parties):

AND We do by these Presents will and ordain that all property, rights and liabilities of Our Commission appointed under the 1963 Warrant and subsequent Warrants are hereby transferred to Our Commission appointed under this Warrant; and any agreement, transaction or other thing which has been made, effected or done by or in relation to the Commission appointed under previous Warrants, shall henceforth have effect as if made, effected or done by Our Commission appointed under this Warrant:

AND We do further ordain that anything done or being done (including anything done or being done under any enactment) by or in relation to Our Commission appointed under previous Warrants before the date of signing of this Warrant shall, so far as is required for continuing its effect on and after that date, have effect as if done by or in relation to Our Commission appointed under this Warrant; and any reference in any enactment or other document whatsoever to the Commission appointed under previous Warrants shall, unless the contrary intention appears, be construed as a reference to Our Commission appointed under this Warrant:

AND We do further ordain that all monies and property received by this Our Commission, including any money voted by Our United Kingdom Parliament, shall be applied solely towards the promotion of the purposes of Our Commission; and unless so directed by the Secretary of State with the consent of Our Treasury, no payment shall be made by the Commission to the Commissioners except repayment of reasonable and proper out of pocket expenses:

AND We do authorise and empower you to appoint, with the approval of Our Secretary of State, upon such terms as to remuneration, gratuities and otherwise as you with such approval think fit, a Secretary and such other officers on such terms as to remuneration, gratuities and otherwise as you think fit; provided always that such remuneration or other entitlement shall be in accordance with the terms approved by Our Secretary of State:

AND We do by these Presents further ordain that anything authorised or required to be done under this Warrant by Our Commission may be done by any Commissioner or officer of Our Commission who is authorised (generally or specially) for that purpose by the Commission; and every Commissioner and officer of Our Commission shall be indemnified against all costs and expenses and losses for which he may become liable by reason of any act or thing done by him in the proper discharge of his office or duty:

AND We do hereby for Us, Our heirs and Successors, grant and declare that this Our Warrant or the enrolment thereof shall be in all things valid and effectual in law according to the true intent and meaning of the same and shall be taken, construed and adjudged in the most favourable and beneficial sense and for the best advantage of this Our Commission as well as in Our Courts of Record as elsewhere, notwithstanding any non-recital, mis-recital, uncertainty or imperfection in this Our Warrant:

AND We do by these Presents will and ordain that this Our Commission shall continue to full force and virtue, and that you, Our said Commissions, or any five or more of you, may from time to time proceed in the execution thereof, and of every matter and thing therein continued, although the same be not continued from time to time by adjournment:

AND We do further ordain that you, or any five or more of you, shall report periodically on your proceedings under this Our Commission to Our Secretary of State at such times and in such manner as directed by him.

Given at Our Court at Sandringham

the sixth day of April 1992;

In the Forty-first Year of Our Reign

By Her Majesty's Command

APPENDIX 2

ROYAL COMMISSION ON THE ANCIENT AND HISTORICAL MONUMENTS OF WALES

COMMISSIONERS, DECEMBER 1992

Chairman:	Professor J B Smith, MA FRHistS
Commissioners:	Dr R W Brunskill, OBE FSA
	Professor D Ellis Evans, D Phil FBA
	Professor Ralph A Griffiths, PhD
	Daniel Gruffydd Jones Esq
	Professor G D Barri Jones, D Phil FSA
	Richard Haslam Esq, FSA
	S B Smith, Esq
	Dr G J Wainwright, MBE FSA
	Dr E Wiliam, FSA
	Vacancy
Secretary:	P R White, FSA

Examination of Witnesses

PROFESSOR JENKYN BEVERLEY SMITH, Chairman, MR PETER ROBERT WHITE, Secretary and MR ANTHONY JOHN
   PARKINSON, Head, Architectural History Branch, Royal Commission on Ancient and Historic
   Monuments in Wales, were examined.

Chairman

380. Gentlemen, we will try and make this a short
as possible. Professor Smith, I wonder if for the
shorthand writer's benefit you would be kind enough
to introduce yourself and your two colleagues to us.

(*Professor Smith*) Thank you, Chairman. My
name is Jenkyn Beverley Smith. I am Chairman of
the Royal Commission on Ancient and Historic
Monuments in Wales. On my left is Mr Peter White,
who is Secretary to the Commission and of course its
Chief Executive. On my right is Mr Anthony
Parkinson, who is Head of the Architectural History
Branch at the Commission. I might say that the two
senior colleagues here may be better able than the
Chairman to provide the detailed information that
the Committee might require.

381. Thank you very much. Your relationship with
Cadw is now based on a corporate planning process
although you also talk about "complementing
Cadw" and "close collaboration with Cadw". Could
you explain how you prepare you corporate plan,
and what is Cadw's involvement in the process?

(*Professor Smith*) The corporate plan is something
which is a comparatively new experience for us. We
might go back to the KPMG report commissioned in
1988 and the Policy Review the workings of the
Commission which was communicated to us by the
Minister of State in 1989. This laid down a
framework for the future in which it envisaged two
main heritage bodies for Wales. It was clearly
resolved not to provide any overriding single
authority but that there should be two bodies, and it
was envisaged that there would be formal and
informal liaison between them. The centrepiece of
the relationship is clearly the corporate planning
process and it is for us to prepare for Cadw a
corporate plan. The corporate plan provides for a
period of five years and, of course, according to
normal practice allocations are made for one year at
a time, but with a base line prediction, for two further
years. The plan is considered by Cadw and
recommendations on financing are then made to the
Minister of State.

382. Do you publish your corporate plan?

(*Professor Smith*) No, we have not as yet published
the corporate plan. We have published for the first
time this year what is in fact a pre-curser to the
annual report which will appear, but as yet we have
not published the corporate plan itself.

383. Are there any reasons why you would be
against publishing your corporate plan?

(*Professor Smith*) The brief answer is that I know
of none. We are responding to what was required of
us in the new Warrant. There has been no suggestion,
to my knowledge, that we should also publish the
corporate plan but I am sure it is something my
fellow commissioners would be prepared to consider.

384. Thank you. Does Cadw or the Minister of
State have the power to set you specific targets and
objectives?

(*Professor Smith*) Yes, these are quite clearly laid
down. May I say there are two relationships in fact.
With regard to the financial management, the
Secretary is responsible to the Permanent Secretary
of the Welsh Office so, apart from Cadw, we have
that responsibility and a corollary to that is we have
direct access to the appropriate Divisions within the
Welsh Office on certain matters. Guidance on what is
required of us is normally transmitted to us through
Cadw. We are subject, then, to those requirements.
They are thoroughly laid out, of course, in the
financial memorandum.

385. Thank you. In terms of those two inquiries
into the workings of the Commission in the 1980s
that led to you being given a number of new duties
and being subject to tighter financial disciplines,
could you summarise the principal problems
identified by the reports and their recommendations?

(*Professor Smith*) I think there is an academic
aspect to this, which is the first one to consider. The
three Commissions have traditionally been
concerned with the production of inventories and
these have been tackled on a county by county basis.
The English Commission, in particular, had moved
away from that to some considerable degree (even
before the KPMG survey of 1988), Scotland to a
certain extent but Wales still adhered to what was
largely an inventory- based programme. Since the
publication of that report, and more particularly the
issue of the policy review at the end of 1989, the
Commission has seen a marked reorientation. I think
the result of that is embodied in the Royal Warrant,
the essence of which is that we are now a body of
survey and record; a more clearly defined function
than we ever had before.

386. And in your words in your memorandum you
say that the Royal Commission is supportive rather
than executive with regard to the case of historic
buildings and monuments preservation?

(*Professor Smith*) That is a function which I think
the Commissioners would wish to endorse. This was
the view taken in the evidence which was presented
by the Commission during the course of that inquiry.
The Commission sees its functions then as a body
which provides the means whereby informed
judgements can be made on matters of preservation
and care, the kind of thing you are more particularly
concerned with in this inquiry. This is our function.
We are concerned, then, not with outstanding
buildings alone but with a whole range of sites and
monuments as well as outstanding buildings. With
buildings, I would say that we are concerned with two
things: with the means whereby decisions can be
made with regard to preservation and care and,
secondly, I think, we have a further responsibility of
ensuring a record of those buildings that it may not
be possible to preserve but which are part of the
social history of Wales, buildings which very often
reflect the social aspirations and the social endeavour
of the Welsh people.

[Chairman Cont]

387. In terms of the Royal Warrant and what has been since, do you still publish material?

(*Professor Smith*) We regard publication as a very important part of our activity. During the discussions leading up to the drafting of the Royal Warrant and so forth, the Commission was concerned with record, certainly, but beyond that two things: that it would be part of our function (a function which we are particularly well-qualified to undertake) to provide for the interpretation as well as the description of records. Interpretation needs necessarily to be linked with publication.

388. What proportion of your total expenditure goes on the publication programme?

(*Professor Smith*) I would say that Mr White may be able to provide the answer but until recently the publication of these inventories was the central activity of the Commission so it would be right to say that a very great deal indeed of the expenditure of the Commission would be geared to the preparation of the inventories.

(*Mr White*) Thank you, Chairman. I think, to appreciate the shift one has to see the completion of an inventory as a survey methodology where the resources come together over quite a long period of time and a substantial publication results. What actually happens now is that we survey and the result of that survey work largely forms a database and information bank which is available at a fairly early stage in the process of the publication; that is the direction in which we are shifting. We have brought along to the Committee two publications, two interpretative pieces of work, one more substantial than the other, but both representing levels of approach where individual members of staff or two or three members of staff have actually combined to bring material forward in an interpretative way; so that over time the amount and percentage of our resources going into publication will diminish to a single figure percentage because, as it were, it will be represented by an author's fee level of staff cost and then the production cost.

389. You see one of the difficulties we have in understanding what you do is that the Royal Warrant itself makes no mention of publication and in your annual report of 1991–92 on page 4 you say that indeed the need to publish inventories has been removed. So the difficulty that we have got is that on the one side you regard the publication programme as central and not simply maintained but extended and yet on the other hand the situation in terms of the Royal Warrant seem to suggest you should not have a programme at all—or am I misunderstanding the situation?

(*Professor Smith*) I think we need to distinguish between abandonment of the inventory programme, which is certainly built into the Royal Warrant, and the fact that the Royal Warrant also provides for interpretation and publication.

(*Mr White*) If I may, Chairman, if you look at the Royal Warrant at page 36 of our Annual report it actually contains the words, "To publish, by means of an annual report, progress made and activities undertaken, to promote or publish or assist in publishing information, to receive and spend money voted by Our United Kingdom Parliament." The Commissioners did discuss at great length the need to

include the power which enabled them to do that. For your reference that is paragraph 7 and buried in the middle of the paragraph.

Mr Evans

390. Professor, could I just qualify for the benefit of all of us so that we have understood precisely what you are. You are the Royal Commission on the Ancient and Historical Monuments of Wales but the meaning of "monument" for this purpose is not the same as for the scheduling of monuments is it?

(*Professor Smith*) No. The word "monument" has not been reconsidered in recent years. This is a name that we have been landed with since 1908.

391. The importance of this, for example, is that you include architectural matters and you include buildings?

(*Professor Smith*) Yes.

392. Not just monuments which do not have any roofs on them?

(*Professor Smith*) Indeed.

393. If we look at your annual report we see the buildings survey things of interest include chapels and so forth. So you are in effect, quite apart from the listing process, the other public body which is in the process of surveying and recording the whole building history of Wales?

(*Professor Smith*) Indeed.

394. Now what I am concerned to ask you is this (and this has been a matter of controversy, as I understand it in England) what is the cut-off date for antiquity for this purpose? For instance, the English survey has set the death of Queen Anne as you the cut-off date but you obviously do not follow such a cut-off date.

(*Professor Smith*) That was a definition that applied to the Welsh Commission as well. 1715 was the cut off date and that was formerly reflected in the inventory programme we are now completing. I would say there is no single cut-off date in so far as our buildings are concerned. I would say, for chapels, that I hope we shall discuss in a moment, we feel the period up to 1914 would be an appropriate point. I think it will depend really on the genre of monument we are examining.

395. For example. Cardiff Castle is an enormously important work of Victorian architectural restoration. Has that been included?

(*Professor Smith*) This is something that has been included.[1]

396. Would Cardiff City Hall be regarded as too modern or not?

(*Professor Smith*) No, not at all.

397. Could I just ask, because this is a matter of some concern to the Committee, the process of what was inventory and now is surveying and recording reflects a change in the emphasis of methodology. But how complete is what you have done? In other

---

[1]*Note by witness:* At this point the Chairman of the Commission referred to the *Inventory of Ancient Monuments in Glamorgan III, Part 1a, Early Castles,* pp162-211 where an account of Cardiff Castle from its foundation to early twentieth century building is given:

[**Mr Evans** *Cont*]

words what proportion of the total in Wales has really been surveyed in the fashion you have been talking about?

(*Professor Smith*) I have to say again that we work now from a new Royal Warrant which was issued in 1992 so these are early days for us. I think we might turn to one of the programmes that we have in mind and concentrate on one or two schemes. I think there are two projects which are very relevant. One is the uplands project which you might like the Secretary to develop and the other is chapels and churches which Mr Parkinson might describe for you.

398. Do I take it from this though that the advantage of the old county by county inventory system was that although not every area may have been covered but at least we have by the parameters then operating a fairly complete record of a particular area. What you have moved to now is approaching this by themes or by building type?

(*Professor Smith*) That was precisely the disadvantage of the inventory—that progress was slow. Glamorgan was well done and done in an accurate way but although a number of Welsh counties have been surveyed some of them date from a very early period. Pembrokeshire is a case in point, and that would have to be done on an entirely new basis. It is not very helpful in current conditions. It was felt in Scotland and England and finally in Wales, that it would not be possible in the foreseeable future to provide anything like this coverage for the whole of Wales so we have to be selective in the categories we examine.

399. The best comparison is the Victoria County History of England which was a noble effort but never got completed because it was doing everything in such detail?

(*Professor Smith*) It is a good parallel, yes.

400. But so far as the completeness of this new approach one of the features which has been concerning us in evidence is that the listing process in Wales is not going to be brought up-to-date for a very long time and is seriously incomplete in different areas. Does your selection of themes or topics reflect in any way the completeness or incompleteness of the listing arrangements or does it operate on different track?

(*Professor Smith*) The Commissioners have taken into account those categories of monuments which are, in our judgement, in greatest need of attention. Now we could list three or four that we are particularly concerned with. Churches and chapels are certainly at the top of our list and this is the area to which we are directing our resources. Equally with hospitals there is a great problem facing us in the next two or three years in Wales. The Secretary could explain that the English Commission has recently completed a rapid survey of hospitals. Schools will present us with an enormous problem within the next five years. There are Mechanics' Institutes, there are public libraries. What we propose is to identify those categories of monuments which are in most need, not simply of identification, but of surveying and, from the survey the third stage, there will be selected publication.

Chairman

401. In terms of the work you do on page 34 of your annual report 1991–92 you list your recent and forthcoming publications. What proportion of your work in them would you say could be described as a contribution to the development of the National Monuments Record of Wales, which is their principal function?

(*Professor Smith*) In their several ways each one of them is contributory.

402. Each of them. If we take ""Irish Stone Axes; a Review" or "Axe-making Traditions in Cumbrian Stone"—how do you think those are contributing to your primary function?

(*Professor Smith*) I mistook the drive of your question. These are staff publications so these are entirely works which staff members undertake in their private time. This is what they do of an evening or a Saturday afternoon. These are private initiatives.

403. For what purpose would you include these in your annual report because one would assume if they are in your annual report, they would be works that would be done in terms of their employment by the Royal Commission because otherwise your annual report, in fact, is not an annual report of what your staff do in your time but what they do outside.

(*Mr White*) Chairman, what I think the KPMG report stresses very heavily is that the three Royal Commissions are broadly staffed by people who are professionals and whose professional standing is perceived to be of importance within the organisation and outside it. All three Royal Commissions and our report, which is a first, a new venture, does follow very much the pattern of other Royal Commissions because it is important that people do realise the breadth of scholarship, and the type of work which our staff are involved in. It is important as a principle that historians on our staff working in Wales actually realise where the cultural affinities lie and therefore publish material related to other countries. That is really the purpose behind publishing this list of titles, some of which are simply very brief notes, as you will see not being very long; but we are very much a body concerned with the dissemination and discussion of information because that is the only way in which we can interpret and come hopefully to correct conclusions about the monuments and buildings within England and Wales.

404. Just checking with Mr White, are you saying that none of these publications were in fact the result of money that was paid to any of these individual (including yourself I notice) that you had time off in terms of your work with the Royal Commission to do? These are unpaid publications, no time off whatever, just as Professor Smith seemed to imply all done in private time without any contribution, financial or otherwise, from the Royal Commission?

(*Mr White*) Mr Parkinson may more easily be able to answer that but as far as I am concerned no staff time has been allocated to any of these publications.

405. So in a way what you have got here essentially is to show that in terms of the people who work in the Royal Commission this illustrates the fact that the

[Chairman Cont]

people who are in the Royal Commission do a lot of work outside and this is to show some of that work. That is essentially its purpose.

(Mr White) That is correct.

406. It is the kind of situation where if you were under a college and putting out a prospectus, sometimes you put the publications that their staff members have made in order to illustrate some of the work they are involved in?

(Mr White) That is the purpose.

(Professor Smith) It is indeed a function of this category of literature. There are other similar bodies who do the same.

407. They do this as well?

(Professor Smith) Precisely the same thing.

408. Looking at these publications, would you see yourself as a conservation body or a research organisation?

(Professor Smith) We would see ourselves as a body with a contributory role to conservation.

409. But in achieving your role as a conservation body, it is essential to do a body of research to enable you to serve?

(Professor Smith) That would the be object of much of our work.

410. Turning to your records because that is one of your key functions now under the Royal Warrant and your card file index giving access to a range of paper, map drawings and photographic material, what do you feel is the quality and consistency of the present record?

(Mr White) We are currently carrying out two investigations to determine precisely what that quality is because we are planning to transfer a good deal of that record to a machine-based system. You will appreciate that our new Warrant is not yet a year old and in the first year of the Warrant we have set ourselves two major tasks which are nearing completion. One is an assessment of the qualitative aspect particularly of the archaeological record that we hold, in addition to that held by the sites and monuments records. And the second is an examination of the information we generate, which we are putting on to paper, now and we will put on to machine later, and how far that information can be used without being fundamentally re-structured by the public or other professional users, because it is very easy with any organisation for the material coming from survey to be in a different form from the material which people may wish to consult. Material coming from survey is often not very rigorously indexed, for example. It does not necessarily conform to strict thesaurus rules. We have very much been taking stock of all that background and we have a target of being in a position to know what the situation is by the end of April this year.

411. Would you say you are under-resourced to do that job?

(Mr White) I do not know whether we are going to be under-resourced to do the re-structuring that we suspect is necessary. We certainly have sufficient resources at this particular moment to have engaged a consultant to be looking at this problem for us. We have been able to delegate a staff member to look at the quality of the archaeological records. What will

flow from those reports may indeed be that we need short-term extra resources to bring the information into a more manageable form.

412. You know, Mr White, if we popped up to Aberystwyth to see you, would you say that the records for Carmarthenshire would be far more comprehensive than, for example, the records for rural Pembrokeshire or can you give us better examples? Can you give us an illustrations of whether the records are very comprehensive and very good but another part of Wales where in fact it is at the opposite end of the spectrum, even if the opposite end of the spectrum is very close to the top end.

(Mr White) Generally speaking I think instead of looking horizontally one should look vertically, if I can express it in that way. Our investigations show, so far, some site and building types are generally rather better catered for than others and that the geographical aspect does not count for so much. So we are very very strong, for example, on vernacular buildings, strong on industrial archaeology, not so strong perhaps on some types of archaeological site, and the sites and monuments records may be stronger in their area on that type of record.

413. How many monuments and how many buildings do you currently have on the record?

(Mr White) Eighty thousand is the figure which has been arrived at. I say "arrived at" because we do have a backlog of information going into the system. The available record is 80,000 sites and buildings on the index.

414. When you say "back-log" could you tell us a little bit about that?

(Mr White) Yes, the nature of working for an inventory body is that certain information can be held back pending publication. That is the historical way of working. The consequence of that will be that although the records may exist they will not be publicly available. They would exist within the organisation. One of the problems with inventory publication is that the lead time is very long. Of course, it can be ten years or something of this order and indeed that is one of the reasons behind the change of emphasis. So that we can have the shortest possible time between buildings being inspected on the ground and at least a basic level of information about them being available for consultation.

Mr Evans

415. If that information was entered into a computer database straight away why could it not be available immediately on the basis you survey and what you find you find and what is not complete is not complete?

(Mr White) That is precisely our objective in carrying out the current investigation but computers have only been introduced to the Commission within the past year or 18 months.

Chairman

416. What is the purpose of that record? Why would you have spent all this time making that record—for what end?

(Professor Smith) The record on which we are now engaged? We have spoken about the business of

[Chairman *Cont*]

listing. You first need to identify clearly what are your building types, for example, and how many there are. We happily talk about churches and chapels, but we sometimes need to talk about more complicated forms of buildings.

417. Why would you need to know that?

(*Mr White*) Because it is necessary to define the building or clearly define the building types. The process of listing is, of course, a selective process and it is highly selective when one comes to 19th century building types. Only a fraction of all the 19th century building survivors are eligible for listing. It is to provide that foundation course for decision-making which is one of the purposes of the record. That is simply one example. Another example is that other people make choices, of course, for what they may wish to keep or not to keep. It may be a local community who may wish to make that decision. It may inform them. We are talking about a record which is freely available to the public.

418. When you say "freely available" is it regularly accessible to planning and conservation users?

(*Mr White*) Yes by letter, by telephone and by written application.

419. Can you outline briefly your current collection strategy for compiling the record, eg by type of monument or geographical area?

(*Mr White*) There are two major initiatives, one of which has just started which is organised by our archaeological branch which is to create very rapidly a database of the upland areas of Wales and that is then beginning what will be a very long haul. With industrial archaeology we are just about to embark on developing a database which is targeted on the areas which are known to be at risk, largely those subject to land re-clamation activities and so on, and we shall target those and create a database from a desk examination initially using late 19th century ordnance survey maps to compile information. The other initiative we have under way is the initiative Mr Parkinson is planning at the moment and will be getting under way in a matter of months. That is the all Wales Religious Buildings project which aims, again rapidly, to create a database so that we can use that as a platform from which others and ourselves can plan deeper initiatives, deeper work. It also of course does mean that we shall have information available for impact assessment activities for our planning colleagues.

420. We had some evidence from the Dyfed Archaeological Trust about this computer database and in paragraph 5.3 of their evidence to us (which I appreciate you will not have seen) they argue that in the consultants' report by Peat Marwick and McLintock, "that considerable stress was laid in their report on the need for the Royal Commission to employ modern information technology to its record-holding and this was accepted by ministers." They then go on to say, "It is therefore a matter of acute concern to the trusts that the necessary resources to achieve the creation of the extended national database, and in the process computerisation of co-data in the NMR, are not being made available. This is especially disappointing of view of the fact that Wales has the opportunity to create the most efficient integrated information system for historic sites and monuments in the whole of Europe." Do you accept that criticism and disappointment that follows from a lack of resources or do you think that archaeological trusts criticism is misplaced?

(*Mr White*) I think if I may say so that the sentiment which is expressed there about the extended national database and our achieving of it is one which the Commission entirely shares. It is a shared objective with the trusts. We did apply for extra funds to assist this process. The funding for the current year, I should say, is £24,000 which was transferred from Cadw to ourselves with the transfer of this function. Very rapid assessments in discussions with the trusts led us to the view that we should like to see a minimum of one person per SMR working with our staff on the development of the extended national database which presumes our being able to find some £60,000 a year. For the forthcoming year it is likely that the Commission will only be able to find half that sum of money. But you will appreciate, Chairman, if you look at the diagram on page 14 of our report when I say how much we can make available that some 70 per cent of our budget is in fact allocated to staff. So in fact the amount of flexibility we have year on year to make a change vireing the funds from one budget head to another is limited. We are beginning to make that change but I think that is the situation to which the memorandum from the Dyfed Archaeological Trust refers. We are going to make as much available as we can and we shall continue as a Commission to seek the level of funding which we feel is necessary.

Mr Ainger

421. What figure have you estimated the cost to be that the archaeological trusts would like to see for computerisation and a proper database established? How much will it cost?

(*Mr White*) For our corporate plan period as it is a long task we anticipate that each archaeological trust requires one dedicated officer to be funded to carry out that work which amounts to £15,000 or £16,000 a year per trust. That equals £60,000.

422. That is somewhere below the total because presumably there is hardware costs as well?

(*Mr White*) All but one trust in the current year have equipment which is sufficient to carry out the work of the re-structuring and cleaning up, as it were, of the data. It is a very heavily labour intensive or brain intensive job. It is not dependent at this particular stage on the provision of more equipment but it will be dependent on that provision, of course, as the equipment used by the trusts at the moment comes up for replacement or enhancement.

423. Are there eight archaeological trusts?

(*Mr White*) There are four.

424. Could I pursue this point. On my calculation approximately of what could happen this year or the current financial year you mentioned a figure of £24,000 that had been transferred over to you from Cadw. Is that correct?

(*Mr White*) Yes.

[Mr Ainger *Cont]*

425. So what are you going to do that with £24,000? How are you actually going to utilise that cash?

(*Mr White*) The £24,000 was transferred for the current financial year so that money was allocated £6,000 each for the trusts during the course of this year. The Commissioners had some discussion at their meeting last month about how we should allocate the £28,000 that we feel should be available for these purposes in the coming financial year which is the most we can afford in our budget. It was felt that we should share a proportion of that money equally among the trusts and then the rest would be targeted to try and achieve specific objectives in those SMRs who were capable of responding to the need.

426. So given that and given we are not likely to see a significant increase to public expenditure directed at your organisation how long will it take the trusts to complete what they have identified as being their high priority?

(*Mr White*) A very great deal longer. At this point I cannot give you an answer to that.

427. So you would expect therefore from what the trusts were saying, or the Dyfed Archaeological Trust were saying, that there is under-resourcing in this field?

(*Mr White*) There is under-resourcing in the SMR field but I am not entirely convinced that there is under-resourcing in the NMR field at this moment or until we have a report on the scope and nature of the record before us. We know that within the SMRs there is a great deal of work to be done in particular areas because they were formed by simply transferring a whole lot of Ordnance Survey information into their records and a good deal of that information needs checking out on the ground.

Chairman

428. Mr White, do you think in your opinion it makes sense for government funding to be directed towards two inadequate records, SMR and NMR, rather that to one adequate one?

(*Mr White*) The extended national database will be one record. The point is that we are not intending to hold, as it were, duplicate information. We have had very detailed discussions with the trusts and the idea is that it is, as it were, a federation. It is organised as a federation with the trusts concentrating very much on the local information base. I think one must appreciate that sometimes a record in a sites and monuments record may only be a scattering of flints in a field. The records officer does not have to be convinced that there is actually an occupation site there or whatever. The NMR will be much more concerned with records which are of substantial buildings and sites and it is likely that because we also have an archive that we shall be concerned to hold more detailed records on those sites where we will have additional information. The idea is that the extended national database has access points across Wales so that it will be perceived as one record over time. In order to get there we actually have to build on components which exist in individual records.

Mr Ainger

429. Chairman, could I pursue this further? You mentioned earlier that one of the priorities for you was the industrial archaeological survey and that initially you were going to be going back over 19th century ordnance survey maps and so on. How long will that take bearing in mind that I accept what the Professor was saying about the targeting of churches, chapels, hospitals, mechanical institutes and schools, but probably one of the very vulnerable areas is our industrial archaeology because it is under pressure from the position it is in in many cases. When do you expect your survey to be completed and when can we expect to see your recommendations that certain industrial sites are listed or individual buildings are listed?

(*Mr White*) The data-capture I am talking about is largely a desk exercise. The first level of activity is an office-based exercise. We can, by using other resources—we have our own aerial photography unit, for example—and having done a basic exercise, match it up against photographs in our possession without going out into the field to see whether the sites need to be visited or not. But we would give this a very high priority. I would expect to see substantial results, particularly in the areas at risk which are identified to us as the government body, over a period perhaps of three or four years.

430. Three or four years. Were you informed of the land reclamation scheme that destroyed the Six Bells colliery before bulldozers went through it?

(*Mr Parkinson*) We were.

431. So you were given an opportunity to comment?

(*Mr Parkinson*) I do not think were were given an opportunity to comment on the land reclamation scheme as such. I think we were given an opportunity to comment on the colliery buildings which I believe were listed.

432. Yes, my understanding is that they were listed. It was a WDA reclamation. Are you aware of the actual circumstances? Did you recommend anything specific before the bulldozers went through or was your advice ignored? Can you throw any light on that?

(*Mr Parkinson*) Our position perhaps needs a little bit of explanation in this. We are given the opportunity to see proposals for the demolition of listed buildings. We may decide to comment on those applications but those comments do not necessarily carry any force. They have no more force than the comments of any other interested body or interested individual.

433. Just to cut across you, do your comments go to the planning authority?

(*Mr Parkinson*) They would go to the local planning authority. They would be considered along with all the other comments from the public, from the amenity bodies and so on. Subsequent to that we are given the opportunity through statute to record listed buildings before demolition takes place and as far as I am aware we took that option up.

Chairman

434. Professor Smith, gentlemen, before we finish could I ask you is there anything you would like to say to us that we have put to you in a way that has not given you the opportunity of answering fully or is there anything we have not identified that you think we should have identified that you would like to make any comments on at all?

(*Professor Smith*) That is very kind of you, Chairman. I think we have been quite happy with what we have been able to say. The one thing you will appreciate, Chairman, is that the last two or three years have seen a marked reorientation in our work and a lot of the things we have alluded to are things that we are promising. I think we should lay stress on that. This period has seen a marked change in our whole financial structure, our management structure and all our academic programmes, if you like. That has been a great change. We might perhaps develop our discussions of the chapels and churches programme. You are clearly very concerned about chapels and we would hope very much that what we are planning for that will be seen to be relevant to the preservation work that you are mainly concerned with. I think that may be clear in our papers, but we will gladly develop that in a further submission if you think that might be helpful. We have a three-phase programme on churches and chapels that we will be very happy to explain to you at greater length. I do not know if my colleagues would like to add anything, but you are welcome to come to Aberystwyth and see us on a summer's day perhaps!

Chairman: Thank you very much indeed, gentlemen. We are very grateful.

Supplementary memoranda by Royal Commission on Ancient and Historical Monuments in Wales

I: RCAHM ALL-WALES SURVEY OF RELIGIOUS BUILDINGS (HB 49)

There are around a thousand churches in Wales of known or suspected mediaeval origin. The number of post-mediaeval foundations is unknown, but may easily be a further five hundred in the towns. Of these as many as 150 churches may be "at risk" from closure or redundancy, and very few have been adequately recorded.

The situation with regard to non-conformist chapels is much worse. The National Library of Wales has compiled a preliminary database of documentary records relating to some 5,500 chapels, which includes a number (perhaps 10 per cent) which have completely vanished. Recent monitoring of planning applications by RCAHM and others, together with casual observation, indicates the large number of buildings at risk. Most of these will be 19th C in date, but some may be earlier in origin.

Neither churches nor chapels are uniformly good examples of the architecture of their day. The number of churches and chapels listed as of architectural or historical interest is increasing. Nonetheless, not all such buildings will ever be list-worthy, and the pace of resurvey is too slow to catch all those in danger. Nor can the listing be accelerated by consulting a national database, since none yet exists.

RCAHM has therefore defined as the principal objective of this project the compilation of an architectural database of all religious buildings in Wales. This will have two purposes. Firstly, it will provide the basis for a second phase of the project in which individual buildings will be selected for more detailed recording using various criteria, with a view to publishing a series of books and papers illustrating various aspects of the architectural history of religious buildings in Wales. Secondly, it will be available for consultation by all interested organisations and could provide the basis for considered conservation strategies not only by the statutory authorities but also by the denominations themselves. For within the next decade, many other buildings will also fall into the category of "buildings at risk", and without a complete, consistent and reliable database it will be impossible to judge the importance of any one structure within a national context.

Compilation of the database will begin with collation of all available data, followed by fieldwork to complete a minimal record. The assistance of other organisations—notably Capel—will be of the greatest value both in compiling preliminary information and in undertaking initial fieldwork and recording. For although RCAHM will provide direction and much of the expertise, a good deal of the fieldwork will be carried out under contract. Subsequent phases of study and publication will be determined by the results of the first stage. The time-scale will depend on the availability of resources, but it is hoped to have the database completed in two years from the formal commencement of the project.

March 1993

II. SITES AND MONUMENTS RECORDS AND THE NATIONAL MONUMENTS RECORD
(HB 50)

The precise relationship between the regional Sites and Monuments Records (SMRs) and the National Monuments Record (NMR) has never been clearly defined, but with the issue of the new Royal Warrant in 1992, the Royal Commission (RCAHM) assumed responsibility for the "oversight" of SMRs. This new responsibility derived from the policy review which recommended *inter alia* that RCAHM be the national body for survey and record. The review placed emphasis on the need for RCAHM to give priority to the NMR as the destination of the results of its own survey work. RCAHM is developing objectives, policies and priorities for information collection and dissemination, through Corporate Planning. Hitherto there has been little relationship between the NMR and the SMRs.

Historically the SMRs and the NMR have very different pedigrees. The NMR was established following the revised Royal Warrant of 1963, when RCAHM took over Welsh material held in the National Buildings Record in London—essentially this was an archive of photographs. The newly created NMR then undertook to broaden the architectural collection to include records of archaeological sites. Starting in the mid 1960s a card index was developed based on a classification system relating to site type/function ordered by historic county. Thus the NMR became both an index and a repository of records and collections of architectural and archaeological sites. The record is publicly accessible, and provides information to individual and corporate visitors, telephone and postal queries, as well as an in-house service to RCAHM staff. Work on computerising the record is being implemented following the appointment of an Information Systems Manager in October 1991.

The SMRs were created by the four regional Archaeological Trusts from the mid 1970s. The Trusts were set up to undertake Rescue Archaeology and they perceived a need to establish their own records to provide rapid access to data on archaeological sites. SMRs were designed primarily as an index, and computerisation was given a priority. All SMRs were using computers by 1984. Although the main function of SMRs has been to provide the Trusts with information to manage and target resources, the SMRs have also been widely used by individuals, utilities, conservation bodies and Cadw to gain access to information on a regional basis. These records are, however, predominantly archaeological, and lack the architectural information which is contained in the NMR. In general it can be said that the NMR contains individual information on sites in depth, whereas the SMRs contain greater indexed information in breadth. The SMRs are not strong on architectural and industrial records, but hold a greater number of archaeological records than the NMR.

The RCAHM's policy is to provide a national index to both the NMR and SMRs through a forum of creators and users of data, called the Extended National Database (END). The name ENDEX has been coined for this index. Its development is running hand-in-hand with the RCAHM's own computerisation programme, which is being formed by an IS Strategy Study currently being carried out. Part of the work on creating ENDEX is an agreement to modify all existing database structures (SMRs, NMR and others) so that all can incorporate a common *core data*. Cadw is an active participant in this venture, but has no computerisation plans as yet. An RCAHM staff member is undertaking, in parallel, a comparative study of the archaeological records of the NMR and SMRs to gauge their relative strengths and weaknesses.

The eventual aim of the END project is to allow access to indexed information from a number of centres. This will allow regional organisations to gain access to national data for comparative purposes, and national organisations to gain access to more detailed sources held locally. The possibility of creating a national heritage database for Wales is seen as an achievable objective. The speed at which the database is developed from 1993–94 will of course be entirely dependent upon the resources RCAHM has available, particularly to grant aid the SMRs. The funds available for 1993–94 are about 50 per cent of what is required to achieve the optimum rate of development, and for future years there is currently no indication that this situation can be substantially improved.

March 1993

Letter from the Secretary of the Historic Buildings Council for Wales to the Clerk of the Committee

HISTORIC BUILDINGS (HB 79)

When my Chairman gave oral evidence to the Committee there were a few issues on which we were asked to provide further information, these were:

(1) Q 267 The Committee asked for a breakdown of the Welsh Office's financial support for Churches and Chapels provided on the Council's advice for the year 1991-92.

This information is provided in Annex A to the letter.

(2) Q 375 The Committee asked to see a copy of the standard conditions which are attached to grant aid.

These conditions are set out in Annex B to the letter. They are supplemented with an individual works report which sets out the way in which grant-aided works should be undertaken.

PAYMENTS MADE IN YEAR

Annex A

1991-92

1953 Act

Churches	...	...	...	...	591,933	(96.13%)
Chapels	...	...	...	...	23,847	(3.87%)

1990 Act

Churches	...	...	...	...	152,631	(91.91%)
Chapels	...	...	...	...	13,440	(8.09%)

Annex B

NOTES

Conditions

(i) that an architect/professional adviser is employed to prepare drawings in sufficient detail to illustrate the scheme, to prepare a specification and to supervise the work in progress:

(ii) that the works are carried out in full in accordance with a specification, which should be approved by our Architect before work commences (the enclosed note details the works eligible for grant aid which are considered necessary by our Architect, and for which this grant is offered) and that no other works are carried out without our approval:

(iii) that this offer is accepted within one month and that work should begin within three months of the date of this letter, unless otherwise agreed by us and that the date of the commencement of work is notified to this office:

(iv) that our Architect will have the right to inspect the work in progress and after completion, and that the work is carried out to his satisfaction:

(v) that should you receive any other offer of grants or subsidies towards the cost of the works, either from central or local government, or from any other source, you will notify this office immediately:

(vi) that the property is maintained in a reasonable state of repair:

(vii) that the property is adequately insured so that its repair and restoration after fire or other damage will be practicable by means of that insurance. The property must be insured whilst the grant eligible works are in progress, and you should forward evidence of insurance when accepting the grant offer. Please note also that you are obliged to maintain such adequate insurance for five full financial years (a financial year runs from April to March) after the financial year in which the works are completed. This will be the subject of a random check, and you may be called upon to provide evidence of insurance at any time within the five year period.

(viii) in the event of the sale of the property within a period of 10 years from the date grant is offered, the owner shall immediately notify the Secretary of State.

(ix) that this office is notified of any unforeseen increase in costs.

EXPLANATORY NOTES

(A) If any of the above conditions is contravened or not complied with the Secretary of State may at any time recover from you the whole of the grant or such part of it as he thinks fit (in accordance with Section 78 of the 1990 Act).

(B) Under the provisions of Section 78, the Secretary of State may also recover the whole or part of the grant if, during the period of 10 years beginning with the day on which the grant is made, you dispose of the property, or of any part of it, by way of sale, exchange of lease for a term of 21 years or more.

(C) Should you wish to make a gift of the property, directly or indirectly (but otherwise than by will), you should bear in mind that under the provisions of Section 78, the Secretary of State may recover the whole or part of the grant:

(i) from you, if you make a gift of your interest in part of the property and the recipient dispose of that interest or of any part of it by way of sale, exchange or lease for a term of 21 years or more within the 10 year period specified in Paragraph B; or

(ii) from the recipient, if you make a gift of the whole of your interest in the property and the recipient disposes of that interest or of any part of it by way of sale, exchange or lease for a term of 21 years or more within the 10 year period specified in Paragraph B.

(D) If you decide to accept this offer, payment of grant can be made either by way of a lump sum on completion of the work, or by instalments as the work proceeds. In either case, it will be necessary to submit architects' certificates, receipted accounts or invoices, fee statements, etc, or some other acceptable form of evidence of expenditure requesting payment as the works or stage works are completed. Provided that the conditions of this grant offer have been met, the schedule of work has been approved by our Architect and the work carried out to his satisfaction, grant-aid calculated on a pro-rata basis on the eligible portions of the submitted certificates, invoices, etc will subsequently be paid direct to the owner of the property unless an alternative method is requested. However, I must emphasise that it is the responsibility of the owner in the first place to meet payment of the full cost of the works together with, where appropriate, fees, VAT and any other associated costs.

(E) VAT at the appropriate rate is normally payable on the cost of repairs and architects' fees where appropriate and estimates on which this offer is based take that into account. But in certain cases, eg if the building is in use for trade or business purposes, VAT may be wholly or partly recoverable. Before grant can be paid therefore, you must certify the amount of VAT that you have been required to pay and that no part of it is recoverable.

(F) The Secretary of State reserves the right, at his discretion, to:

(a) alter or cancel this offer of grant if any of the above conditions is contravened;

(b) alter or cancel any grant offered in the light of any other offers of grant or subsidy towards the cost of works concerned which are accepted by you; and

(c) to reduce the grant if the actual cost of grant eligible works considered necessary by our Architect proves to be less than £50,000.

(G) Please note that the Historic Buildings Council is under no obligation to recommend further grant aid should the final cost of the works concerned exceed the figure quoted in this letter. You should also note that the Secretary of State's approval to the details of a scheme does not affect the necessity for the owner to comply with the Planning Acts.

WEDNESDAY 3 MARCH 1993

Members present:

Mr Gareth Wardell, in the Chair

Mr Nick Ainger   Mr Rod Richards
Mr Jonathan Evans   Mr Mark Robinson
Mr Roger Evans   Mr Walter Sweeney
Mr Elfyn Llwyd

Memorandum by the Council of Welsh Districts

THE PRESERVATION OF HISTORIC BUILDINGS AND ANCIENT MONUMENTS IN WALES
(HB 21)

1. *The arrangements for the properties in the care of the Secretary of State, as exercised by CADW.*

In the main properties are carefully and satisfactorily maintained by CADW. In some areas there appears to be an apparent lack of enthusiasm to implement ways to market properties imaginatively as tourist attractions. Criticism has been levelled that CADW is not prepared to join forces with other agencies eg, local authorities, to jointly promote and market properties in the same locality owned by the two organisations eg, castle owned by CADW and museum owned by local authority.

A further problem which has been identified is that CADW is not prepared to allow a local authority to advertise its own historic buildings in the same brochure as CADW.

The general view expressed by local authorities is that a more imaginative and outward looking approach is necessary, particularly in the field of marketing and promotion. Continued co-operation and co-ordination with the Wales Tourist Board is necessary. There is no strong view expressed that the local authorities should take over management roles in place of CADW. In view of the present financial climate it is doubtful if local authorities could afford to take on new responsibilities for historic buildings and ancient monuments.

It is however preferable that the body of nationally important buildings and sites should be cared for by a National Agency. It follows that, from time to time, the stock of buildings and sites should be added to, by acquisition or donation.

2. *The care exercised by other major owners (such as the National Trust, the churches and local authorities) over their properties.*

The care exercised by institutional owners of historic buildings and monuments does not appear to cause major problems. The position with churches, chapels and local authority owned buildings is however sometimes problematical. These bodies have frequently inherited obligations for historic buildings from an age when they enjoyed greater wealth and it is sometimes difficult for them to do justice to the buildings.

Comment has been made from some parts of Wales that there appears to be an imbalance in the level of financial assistance provided to church buildings as opposed to those of other non-conformist denominations. Continued financial support by CADW for local authority work in maintaining buildings under their control is essential.

The charging regime operated, for example, by the National Trust, required to maintain (and promote) buildings in their ownerships should be grant-aided if the level of entrance charge puts access beyond the reasonable ability of visitors/tourists/locals to pay. Profit on major sites should continue to be used to support smaller sites.

3. *The listing of historic buildings, the scheduling of ancient monuments and the controls exercised (chiefly through CADW) on planning consents in relation to them*

Views have been expressed that the listing of buildings of special architectural or historic interest is an issue where a change in policy is appropriate. It is the responsibility of the Secretary of State to compile the list and it does appear the work is carried out in a planning vacuum. It seems that when decisions are made on whether to list a building, the Secretary of State is required to take into account only the architectural or historic interest in the building to the exclusion of everything else. In particular the Secretary of State has no discretion to take into account planning proposals for the building concerned. Eleventh hour listings can therefore be triggered by planning proposals which may be at an advanced stage and can prove to be very frustrating to the local planning authority. Although Certificates for "immunity from listing" can always be applied for when an applicant thinks his unlisted building might be of "listable quality", this only partly solves the problem.

The greatest concern is expressed over the outdated nature of Statutory Lists and the length of time that is being taken to complete the full national resurvey. The fault does not appear to lie with CADW staff but with the resources allocated to the task. An improved procedure for dealing with applications for Listed Building Consent is desirable.

Whilst in most instances there appears to be a reasonable working relationship between CADW and local authorities, the administrative procedures involving listed building consent need streamlining, there appears to be two levels of consent required ie, Secretary of State and CADW and this causes unreasonable delay.

It is suggested that the pressure could be eased by producing an additional "grade" of building where notification only was given to CADW and the Local Planning Authorities were given a "duty" to have regard to the value of the building. This would reduce the processing burden and thus speed responses on more important applications. The said new "grade" of building should be as follows:

Dual classification ie, as an Ancient Monument and as a Listed Building should be rationalised.

4. *The grant schemes available for the preservation of historic buildings and ancient monuments, their overall adequacy as well as the effectiveness and fairness with which they are allocated.*

Grant aid on the whole appears to be effectively administered but the administration involved in operating town schemes is time consuming on occasions.

Concern has been expressed that local authorities are not consulted by CADW on applications for grant aid and are not informed when grant aid has been approved.

The level of grant aid available is of concern to a number of local authorities.

Townschemes are generally agreed to be a good basis for affording a local democratic input into local heritage, although the geographic extent of these areas was sometimes thought to be too confined. The criteria applied to grant aid in townschemes ensures fairness and consistency and it may be that a similar scheme could be advised for rural areas where Listed Buildings are, of course, more scattered.

5. *General comments*

Local authorities have the power to serve repair notices in respect of Listed Buildings which are falling into disrepair. In addition authorities have powers to serve Dangerous Structure notices should a building, including a listed building, be deemed to have become dangerous. The use of this notice does however place an obligation on the local authority to carry out the necessary works in default should the owner of the building fail to comply with the notice. This acts as a deterrent to local authorities serving such notices since, because of the extreme pressure on finances, they are very often genuinely unable to fund the works in default. This raises fundamental problems with the maintenance of the "stock" in the long term.

The problem of limited financial resources appears to be a general criticism which delays the decision making process and limits the injection of finance by grant aid or direct input.

Whilst Local Authorities in Wales continue to be impressed by the skill and diligence of the professional case officers in handling these matters, the deficiency in their numbers, especially in dealing with small matters, makes their performance inadequate, especially when the targets on Local Planning Authorities are considered.

15 January 1993

Examination of Witnesses

COUNCILLOR W D THOMAS, Chairman, CWD, and Member of Carmarthen District Council, DR A PYKETT, Deputy Director of Planning, Ceredigion District Council, COUNCILLOR G R COURT, CWD Labour Group Spokesman on Environment and Housing Issues, MR ANDREW HILL, Principal Planning Officer dealing with Conservation and Preservation, Cardiff City Council, MR E W BOWEN, Deputy Director of Planning, Dinefwr Borough Council, and MR GERAINT PRICE-THOMAS, ADC Under Secretary [Wales], Council of Welsh Districts, were examined.

Chairman

435. Councillor Thomas, gentlemen, could I welcome you here this morning on behalf of the Committee. We are looking at the preservation of historic buildings and ancient monuments in Wales.

Councillor Thomas, we would be very glad if you would introduce your team to us.

(*Cllr Thomas*) Thank you, Mr Wardell. I am tempted to call you Gareth because I have known you for some time. I come from Carmarthen, and I am at the moment Chairman of the Council of Welsh Districts. On my immediate left is Councillor

[**Chairman** *Cont*]

Graham Court who is the leader of Rumney Valley District Council, which might be called Caerphilly later on, and he is the Opposition Spokesman on Planning Issues as far as the Council of Welsh Districts is concerned. On my immediate right is Geraint Price-Thomas who is the Secretary of the CWD Office in Cardiff. On Geraint's right is Dr Pykett, and he is the Deputy Director of Planning at Ceredigion. On his far right is Mr Bowen who is Deputy Director of Planning at Dinefwr, and on the far left is Andrew Hill, the Principal Planning Officer at Cardiff City.

436. One of the areas we have had memoranda from in terms of evidence is the area that emphasises the perceived lack of expertise within the local planning authorities in Wales in terms of ancient monuments and historic buildings. One of the memoranda from the Ancient Monuments Society says that a distressing number of local planning authorities lack conservation officers. Do you know, Mr Price-Thomas, how many district councils in Wales have a conservation officer?

(*Mr Price-Thomas*) I suspect, Chairman, it is a limited number. I do not have that information to hand. In any event I suspect that there would be a need for specialist advice of all kinds in the complex areas of advising on ancient monuments and historic buildings under the requirements of the planning legislation. The short answer is that I suspect there is a limited number. Perhaps one of my planning officer colleagues can help in terms of that.

(*Dr Pykett*) I think it is appropriate to say that there is a distinction to be made between ancient monuments and historic buildings. Planning officers in local authorities are quite familiar with dealing with listed building matters and conservation area matters. As far as ancient monuments are concerned, the archaeology is much more significant. I think that is perhaps a rather more esoteric matter, in which many planning officers would feel out of their depth. Mr Hill has a certain role as a conservation officer, so he can describe that.

(*Mr Hill*) I am a conservation officer and an architect by training. I have a fairly high degree of expertise in dealing with listed buildings. Dr Pykett is right in saying that in terms of ancient monuments we have less expertise, but we do have direct links and consultations with the Glamorgan and Gwent Archaeological Trust where we buy in expertise as we need it. This I think happens elsewhere in Wales. There are four such trusts. Because an authority does not have a named conservation officer it does not mean they do not have expertise because it may be that an ordinary planning officer has qualifications which enable him to deal with most of the enquiries he gets about listed buildings, although he may not be called a conservation officer.

437. As far as you know, are you unique in being called a conservation officer in Wales?

(*Mr Hill*) No, there is one in the Vale of Glamorgan, and I think there is one in North Wales in one of the districts.

438. You think there are probably about three in Wales?

(*Mr Hill*) Yes.

439. Do you happen to know how that compares with, say, ten years ago?

(*Mr Hill*) Swansea has one as well. No, I do not. I think there are more because it is a subject which has been given a higher profile and more people are calling themselves conservation officers who would have called themselves planning officers with conservation expertise.

440. How do you find the best way is of getting specialist advice, not only within Cardiff City Council, but looking at it on an all Wales basis? If it comes to looking at the problems of ancient monuments, where do you go for specialist advice when it comes to planning matters?

(*Mr Hill*) Latterly we have found we can go to Cadw for advice on certain aspects of particularly difficult listed buildings. There has been a recent change of procedure in Cadw, where they now make themselves more available for giving advice to local authorities where listed buildings are concerned. I speak for my own district, but we would also pull in advice from St Fagans Folk Museum, for instance, and Dr Williams is very knowledgeable about medieval buildings. If it were an ancient monument we would go to the Glamorgan Gwent Archaeological Trust in Swansea, which we use on an agency basis from time to time.

441. When you say there has been a change in attitude in relations with Cadw, is that because Cadw is an executive agency within the Welsh Office, and therefore since the Secretary of State could get involved in planning decisions it puts Cadw in a difficult position in giving such specialist advice?

(*Mr Hill*) That has been the problem over the 12 years or so I have been involved in my present job. They were very reluctant and in fact refused to give advice prior to an application simply because of the likely clash of interests in the event of an appeal. Now the advice on listed building applications is given by the planning division of the Welsh Office, which is slightly at arm's length to Cadw itself. That has freed them, apparently, to be more forthcoming in giving advice to local authorities and to private owners of buildings.

442. Over how long a period have you noticed that change? A very short period?

(*Mr Hill*) Yes. I have noticed a change in the last 18 months. I believe one of my colleagues has the annual review of Cadw, and it says that in 1991 this change took place. I have noticed it for 18 months. I think there are still anomalies where it does not appear to be working that well, but in my case it does.

(*Mr Bowen*) Perhaps I could give you the experience of my authority in this respect. I want to disagree with my colleague from Cardiff, but the annual report refers to there being a change in attitude from May 1991, and I understand there was evidence given in a memorandum from Cadw with regard to the availability of advice to both developers, local authorities and individuals alike. I can quote examples where we have approached Cadw asking for specialist advice, and it comes back to the initial question regarding structural points that there are specialists and there are specialists. I would say planning officers generally are sensitive enough to recognise that they are dealing with a building of

3 March 1993]   COUNCILLOR W D THOMAS, DR A PYKETT,
COUNCILLOR G R COURT, MR ANDREW HILL,
MR E W BOWEN AND MR GERAINT PRICE-THOMAS   *[Continued*

[**Chairman** *Cont*]

special historical or architectural interest to ask for further advice. Now, where do we get this advice? Our experience is that Cadw declined to give that advice on the grounds that they feel it would prejudice the Secretary of State's position on any appeal. I have letters here going back to November 1991, and there is a specific building we approached Cadw about in November last year, where they declined to provide the advice that we required on the grounds that it would prejudice the Secretary of State.

Mr R Evans

443. Could we ask Mr Bowen to give us that information in writing so that we can put it to Cadw?
(*Mr Bowen*) Indeed.

Chairman

444. Dr Pykett, have you had experience similar to that of Mr Bowen?
(*Dr Pykett*) I do not have a recent directly comparable experience, no. I would say that there is still a certain amount of confusion as to whether Cadw is actually wearing the hat of the Secretary of State or whether it is wearing a separate hat. A few years ago, when I was more involved with this type of work, not infrequently one could have conflicting letters from Cadw. You would have a letter from the Architectural Adviser saying "Apropos a certain application for listed building consent, this is my opinion on this application. However, my letter cannot compromise any appeal which may subsequently be submitted, and does not constitute the formal view of Cadw". That puts the local planning authority in a difficult position. It was not sure whether it was getting the official or the unofficial view.

Mr R Evans

445. Could we have chapter and verse in writing on that sort of problem? It is much easier if you can produce us with a specific example, and then we can ask Cadw for comments on it.
(*Dr Pykett*) Yes.
(*Mr Bowen*) If you want to relate a specific example I can refer to a request we made in November 1991, asking for details in terms of technical advice. For example, English Heritage produced a series of books on this subject, and I would personally feel that that should be a role that Cadw should be fulfilling. There is a range of listed buildings, and a range of different techniques and different materials used. Even if you had an officer which you could call a conservation officer it is not certain that he would have that full range of experience available to him. The experience and the knowledge is there within Cadw and it seems we are unable to tap it.

446. I would like to go back a moment to this question of the need for specialist advice, and I think Mr Price-Thomas was saying, that under the planning legislation you have to make a whole series of decisions, some of which need specialist advice.
. Particularly under the Listed Buildings Act there are a whole series of decisions which need expert advice. Has the Secretary of State made a Schedule 4

direction in Wales at all under the 1990 Act requiring district councils to take specialist advice?
(*Mr Price-Thomas*) I cannot recall such a direction.

447. For example, where you have a local planning authority which does not have a designated conservation officer, and it may or may not have conservation experience within the authority, what happens about a simple matter like issuing a listed building repairs notice where a schedule of specification has to be given? Are there any problems arising from the lack of a conservation officer?
(*Dr Pykett*) I can give you one example. We have served probably about three listed building repair notices on listed buildings in Ceredigion, which were in a poor state of repair. We do not have a conservation officer; we do not have access to in-house advice on that matter. On the most important matter which we pursued we employed an outside architect who was a specialist in this type of work to advise the authority, although, from memory, I think we employed him after we had served the repairs notice.

448. Was that due to any difficulty in drafting the notice in the first place?
(*Dr Pykett*) No, it was not. The notice was really quite straightforward, but subsequently we were challenged in the courts and a public inquiry, and it was at that stage that we felt we ought to get more specialist advice.

449. Would it be the case that if you had more specialist advice perhaps some of the difficulties and the challenge in the courts might have been avoided?
(*Dr Pykett*) I think not, because the challenge was basically to do with the subsequent valuation of property, the owner being keen to obtain maximum value and the authority being keen to pay minimum value, which was what we in fact achieved in the end.

450. Mr Bowen, I wonder whether you can assist us on this. Have you had any experience of difficulty in serving any of these sort of notices?
(*Mr Bowen*) As with Ceredigion, we employed a specialist architect. In one example you may be dealing with a mansion and in the next may be a traditional longhouse. The approaches are entirely different. The materials required are entirely different. I feel that you will not get an officer being in a position to provide the variety of advice that is needed in those two cases.

451. That may well be right, but what we are particularly concerned about is that I understand you may not have a range of in-house conservation expertise, but is there a reluctance either to incur the expenditure on the necessary expert or expertise, or a failure by Cadw to provide the necessary expertise, or are things simply going by default?
(*Cllr Thomas*) I do not think many things go by default nowadays, because there are strong conservationists in practically every district area. What you will find I am sure is that there are conservation officers, not professional ones, but people who have been educated sufficiently well in practically every district in the Principality who are sufficiently well versed in advising the council at any particular time, and then of course the area can buy

[Mr R Evans Cont]

in the expertise either from Cadw or consult Cadw, or they can buy it in from other areas.

452. Mr Carr of Cadw gave evidence to us some time ago, for example, that it would be a matter Cadw would be opposed to giving district councils in Wales complete powers over listed buildings, simply because of the lack of in-house conservation expertise. Would you agree with that?

(Mr Price-Thomas) I think it is clear that there is a dearth of professional conservation officers in the districts of Wales. The issue, as ever, is a matter of the resources available to local government, and from your investigations on environmental health and environmental services you know Chairman of the difficulties district councils have had in bringing in necessary expertise over a whole range of services. This is why, I suspect, we are on the threshold of the enabling authority. Looking ahead to a couple of years when we do pull together the planning departments of the counties and the planning departments of the districts, I hope we will, with the numbers of unitary authorities in the early 20s, be under increasing pressure to employ in-house to a considerable extent conservation officers. I would expect to see a structure of professional conservation officers employed either directly by the new councils or certainly a stronger structure of joint availability of that advice to the new authorities.

Chairman

453. So far local authorities have not come together in groupings of any kind in order to seek that specialist advice.

(Mr Price-Thomas) It appears not, not in the way we have on various other matters such as economic development, planning, and waste management. But as my colleagues have mentioned there does appear to be a very close and effective relationship throughout Wales between the district planning authorities and the various archaeological trusts. We have correspondence with the Glamorgan Gwent Trust, which is very active in South Wales. There does seem to be an effective relationship, but at the end of the day I do not feel that it is as effective as having one's expert close at hand, preferably in-house, but if need be by way of an enabling arrangement.

Mr Llwyd

454. Gentlemen, you will all be aware of the extreme importance of issuing building preservation notices. You will also no doubt be aware of the Welsh Office directives in that regard encouraging district and borough councils to issue them. Do you consider that the lack of available ready expertise at district and borough council level is hampering the issuing of building preservation notices?

(Cllr Court) I have two documents here, and it would take Members two or three minutes to look at them. One is from Llancaiach Fawr, which some of you will have visited, and the other one is from Van Mansion being included in the private sector, and Llancaiach Fawr has been included in the public sector, so we have a private sector and a public sector. We have done what many think is a first class job. We have done it through universities; we have done it

through the council's Welsh museums, through the mid-Glamorgan and Gwent Archaeological Trust, and people have come up with the necessary expertise as we have wanted it. I do not think we have fallen short on anything. Certainly we have had no criticism from any sort of organisation, but that does not say that the conservation officer in his own right, in an authority, would not be a good thing. If you could justify it in total in every individual authority and there are 37 in Wales at this time, I would very much doubt.

Chairman

455. Coming back to Mr Llwyd's question, how many building preservation notices has Rhymney Valley served in the last three years?

(Cllr Court) We did not have to serve one on the Van Mansion.

456. Have you served any?

(Cllr Court) No, I do not think we have.

Mr Llwyd

457. The broad point I put is that it is an extremely important procedure, and if the expertise is unavailable at local level, then the procedure is not being implemented as it might be in terms of preserving these buildings. I understand what you say, but I am looking at the broader context.

(Mr Hill) The building preservation notice is a form of temporary listing. It gives a six month holding period. Most local authorities are keen to get some inkling from Cadw as to whether they, at the end of the six month period are willing to spot list the building. If they do not there is the question of compensation. If a building owner has been frustrated in his development aspirations by virtue of the six month holding time, and the building is not then listed, he can take up the position with the authority. What we have always done in Cardiff is to approach Cadw. Until recently they would never give us a categorical view whether they would list, but they would give us I suppose a nod and a wink, and I have been successful in three cases of getting a Building Preservation Notice served knowing, or having a very good indication that this will become firm at the end of the six month period. All three were spot listed. In the last 18 months or so, and we may be lucky in Cardiff, Cadw have spot listed six buildings in the city within a period ranging from six weeks to about three months from our requesting it.

458. Is that because Cadw are based in Cardiff?

(Mr Hill) I think my colleagues would say yes. My view is that whenever I ring Cadw to speak to an officer I can never get hold of them because they are in North Wales. I would not be the best person to ask. Yes, geographically I can get hold of one of them fairly quickly. We have been very impressed of late with the speed with which they have listed one or two critical buildings we have had. I did contact Cadw to see what they felt, and they went to look at the building and informed me they were going to list it. It avoided us having to make the Building Preservation Notice.

[Mr Llwyd *Cont]*

459. How confident would you have to be of the listable quality of a building before you issued a notice?

(*Mr Hill*) My authority would want me to be very confident that it was going to be listed because of the danger of compensation. Obviously, one is frustrating the development role if you make a mistake. With my qualifications I am fairly confident I could get it right, because of the nature of the buildings we have in the city. We do not have any medieval or tricky ones. Mostly they are Victorian or late Georgian. One could be fairly confident. I think most authorities need some sort of confidence or liaison with Cadw before they make a Building Preservation Notice.

460. That is not always convenient or possible.

(*Mr Hill*) It has not been because they did not have the staff to deal with it quickly.

461. You say things are improving?

(*Mr Hill*) They are in my experience.

(*Dr Pykett*) I can confirm what Mr Hill says from mid-Wales. In recent years we have served a number of Building Preservation Notices on the sort of the nod and the wink basis. Before that we had difficulty with Cadw because of the shortage of staff, but we did serve a number of Building Preservation Notices—I cannot remember how many offhand—and I think all the notices we have served have been successful in the sense that the buildings have subsequently been listed.

462. It is my understanding on referring to the Welsh Office circular that it recommended delegation of powers to do the listing to an officer. How many district councils, would you say, Mr Price-Thomas, have delegated this power to their officers as opposed to the council generally?

(*Mr Price-Thomas*) I would have to come back to you with that information, Mr Chairman.

(*Dr Pykett*) The listing is done by the Secretary of State not by the local authorities.

463. Yes, but there is a recommendation in that circular I referred to that the delegation of power to make the initial notice should be vested in an officer as opposed to the council at large. Mr Price-Thomas can write to the Committee.

(*Mr Price-Thomas*) I shall certainly come back with that information.

Chairman

464. In terms of the question of listing, is there any way in Wales that one can establish that listed buildings are at risk? Do we know how many there are? Say within Carmarthen district council, do you know how many buildings could be at risk and should be listed, but because of the slow process of listing they could be lost forever?

(*Cllr Thomas*) I do not honestly think there are many buildings at risk, especially in Carmarthen. As you know we have two or three very strong conservationists who keep an eye on everything, and that spurs the council into making sure that it does not miss out on anything at all. The delegation of responsibility which was the last question, I would imagine happens in most authorities, except in perhaps a few maybe up and down Wales who do not

have that facility. In Carmarthen we certainly have an officer who is responsible and brings any particular instance to the attention of the council, and we act accordingly on his advice.

465. How many listed buildings do you have in Carmarthen district council?

(*Cllr Thomas*) I will have to come back to you on that one.

466. You have not come here today not knowing the number of listed buildings you have in your authority, surely?

(*Cllr Thomas*) I have to admit I could not give you a figure[1].

467. Let us run through the panel, starting with Mr Bowen. How many have you?

(*Mr Bowen*) In Grade I we have about three; in Grade two star we have 24; and in Grade II we have in the region of 300. Can I come back to the question you raised with regard to listed buildings at risk. Do you mean buildings that are not listed at all?

468. That is right.

(*Mr Bowen*) In that case I would raise a point mentioned earlier. These building only come to somebody's notice if, for example, they were the subject of a planning application, or an officer happened to pass by. I would say that the experience and knowledge of planning officers throughout Wales was sufficient that they would be sensitive to the fact that the building they were passing or looking at was something special. If a problem comes his way he will go from there. The option is either to request Cadw to spot list it, or issue a building preservation notice. The experience of my authority is to pursue the former course of action. It does come back to the question of the issue of the ultimate possibility of compensation against the authority. I, as an adviser to the authority, am perhaps not confident enough to issue a BPN in those cases. You saw one example, when you visited Llandeilo area.

Mr R Evans

469. I would like to ask Councillor Court this question. He mentioned the two examples of Rhymney restoring buildings: one was Llancaiach and the other was the Van Mansion. Certainly as far as Llancaiach was concerned, that is rather a more strikingly imaginative success story than any local authority in the United Kingdom. How many listed buildings are there in your district council area?

(*Cllr Court*) I would not know. In recent months Cadw listed colliery buildings that we had agreed to knock over with British Coal and WDA and everybody else. I do not think members will know those figures. I think officers will. In the Rhymney Valley, we are a forward thinking authority in this kind of thing, and I would not think the members would know, but the officers would know.

[1]Note by Witness: There are three hundred and ninety six listed buildings in Carmarthen District, together with a further one hundred and two buildings of local interest, for which the Conservation Officer is responsible.

Chairman

470. In terms of Ceredigion, how many have you there? Councillor Court is saying that you should know.

(*Dr Pykett*) We have three Grade I buildings; we have about 50 two-star buildings; and we have about 600 or 700 Grade II buildings. I say "about" because the numbers are changing because three of our principal towns have been the subject of re-surveys, and I do not think there is anybody in the department who has yet totted up the numbers. I understand the members here will be unaware of the numbers of listed buildings in their areas.

471. Mr Hill, what about you?

(*Mr Hill*) We have 443 listed building in total; 397 are Grade II, 19 are Grade two star, five are Grade I, and 22 ecclesiastical.

472. In terms of the question of listed buildings, how many notices have you served in your respective local authorities on owners requiring them to do those buildings up? Can we take Ceredigion first?

(*Dr Pykett*) As I have said, I think we have served three repairs notices in the last 20 years. We have not served any urgent works notices. Can I make a general point? It does seem to me that the provisions of the Act are defective in the sense that the notices which authorities are able to serve are really fairly Draconian measures. The repairs notice, for example, basically, is a precursor to compulsory purchase, and there are not many authorities who are prepared to enter into compulsory purchase arrangements because they simply do not have the cash to pursue those particular lines.

473. In terms of what you said about the Draconian nature of the Act, and Mr Bowen made the same point to us, why is it that the serving of the notice could lead so quickly to having to take compulsory purchase notice action on those buildings? Why are the two things linked?

(*Dr Pykett*) They are linked by the Act. The only sanction available to an authority if a repair notice is not complied with is to compulsorily acquire the property.

474. The Act does not allow you to serve the notice on the owner, and should the owner not comply, then in fact you would do it and reclaim the money from the owner?

(*Dr Pykett*) That provision is there in the urgent works notices, but we are advised by the circular that urgent works notices should be used in cases where the repairs required are of a less substantial nature. I should mention under the urgent works notices the sanction there is that the authority can go in and do the work and charge the costs to the owner, but again that is a fairly complicated procedure which means chasing up owners who may be difficult to trace. I think authorities are reluctant to use that. It does seem to me that there is a gap in the legislation. I do not know what powers you have to make recommendations on legislation, but what I would like to suggest is that there should be a duty of care imposed on the owners of listed buildings and in the event of listed buildings not being cared for that the authority should be empowered to serve care orders, or something similar on owners. What I had in mind are cosmetic works, painting, repairs to windows,

repairs to gutterings, fairly minor and inexpensive issues, where one feels frequently that the owners are simply not looking after the building properly. There is a case I can think of in the middle of Aberystwyth where the building just looks tatty. It is a listed building and ought to be properly cared for. There is no provision under the Act that we can use to require that building to be properly cared for.

475. Are you losing buildings because of that kind of Catch 22 position, that the building has been listed and then because the local authority is reluctant to serve those notices, the building has decayed and in the end lost? We have had different pieces of evidence on that. Some witnesses have said that the number of listed buildings that have been lost are very few, and others seem to give us examples of the opposite. What do you feel as an officer?

(*Dr Pykett*) Buildings by and large are very valuable assets. In that sense they are not lost, but having said that, I suppose there are examples of industrial buildings especially, where the use has ceased, and chapels might be another example where the use has declined, where it is very difficult for the owners of these properties to produce enough finance to keep them going properly. It may be in that sense buildings are being lost.

(*Mr Bowen*) Given the limited resources that authorities have available they have to be selective. Take two very large houses within my district, one of which you visited. A repairs notice was issued in respect of the roof. The work was carried out by the authority but other jobs on the house have had to suffer. In the sense of not being open to the public or available for use it is lost, but the structure is still there.

Mr Llwyd

476. You have answered my question before I have put it. I was going to ask whether the fact that so few notices are being issued is correlated to the fact that there are no funds to meet the work if it needs to be carried out by the authority.

(*Mr Bowen*) Yes. It depends on the extent of the repairs required. A straightforward repairs notice would require a fairly detailed schedule of works, so not only do you require knowledge of the materials to be used, but from a constructional point of view there is no point asking an owner of a listed building to put a roof back on a building if the roof joists do not meet building regulations. At the same time you want to ensure that sympathetic materials are used.

Chairman

477. Mr Hill, do you want to add anything to what the other officers have said?

(*Mr Hill*) Yes. The urgent repairs notice often amounts only to making the building wind and weather proof, which can be a form of temporary boarding up of the windows or a temporary covering over the roof, most of which can make the building into an eyesore. The reason is that it often protects the integrity of the building to the detriment of the appearance of the building. That is the minimal element of the repairs notice item. The full repairs notice always has as its backstop the compulsory acquisition order which many authorities wish to

[Chairman *Cont*]

avoid, not only because of the initial cost, but they would then take on this liability.

Mr Ainger

478. Are you saying that because of the financial implications that you may well eventually find yourselves not even issuing the notices, never mind taking the next step after the notice is issued?

(*Dr Pykett*) I think that is right.

479. You said you had issued three. Are you telling us that if the resources were available you may have issued far more?

(*Dr Pykett*) Yes, I think that is right. The fact is that the primary example we can quote is that we served a notice about four years before we took compulsory purchase action because the owner of the property was disinclined to carry out the repairs that the notice specified. However, we did not have the financial muscle to acquire the property and then to repair it ourselves. It was only because a third party, who wanted to acquire the property, wanted to renovate it, and was able to do so financially, that we were able to pursue our compulsory purchase order. In fact, the service of a repairs notice is an empty threat if you do not have somebody behind you who has the financial muscle to carry out the work.

480. Dr Pykett made a recommendation in relation to small repairs. Have you any recommendation about the larger issue which we are discussing now, as to what the legislation should state?

(*Dr Pykett*) I think the difficulty with extending what I have suggested even further is that you could end up by imposing tremendous costs on bodies that really cannot afford to carry out the works necessary under a repairs notice system. It might be a chapel that has fallen into disrepair. Councillor Court has mentioned this problem with some British Coal buildings in his area. Both of those organisations I would imagine would be financially unable to carry out the requirements of the repairs notice.

481. I was thinking particularly of domestic properties that are occupied, rather than historic and industrial buildings. Have you any recommendations or suggestions for those particular buildings?

(*Dr Pykett*) Domestic properties tend not to be listed because Cadw are reluctant. I think it is a political decision. They are reluctant to expose the owners of dwellings to the problems and benefits of being in a listed building. Clearly, there are examples that counter that claim, but on the whole Cadw are reluctant to list domestic buildings. It does not frequently occur in quite that context.

482. The majority of your properties—and about 300 are listed—are not occupied?

(*Dr Pykett*) They are not domestic dwellings. Although a substantial number of them are. There is a reluctance to list that type of property.

Mr R Evans

483. I am fascinated by this last answer. Are you suggesting that, for example, in Wales the practice of listing domestic dwellings is different from that practice in England?

(*Dr Pykett*) I cannot answer that. Obviously, they are administered by different organisations so there could be different practices. I do remember when Aberystwyth was being re-listed five years ago I made various suggestions about domestic dwellings that I thought were appropriate candidates for listing, but the answer that came back to me was that Cadw was reluctant to get involved in listing long lists of domestic dwellings.

484. It is commonplace in England, and there are large numbers listed. How widespread is Cadw's reluctance in this area?

(*Dr Pykett*) I do not know how widespread it is. All I can report is my own experience. In Aberystwyth we have many listed buildings, but they tend to be hotels, guesthouses, college buildings, churches; they have tended to shy away from becoming involved in listing domestic dwellings. Just to put the balance right, let me tell you that in Aberaeron, which is somewhere you probably know, we do have a high number of listed buildings, and many of those are indeed domestic dwellings.

485. In terms of our inquiry it is a fundamental and important issue. If one looks at the issue in the United Kingdom, it may well be, if you are right, that the whole issue of Welsh listed buildings is distorted and the problems are exaggerated because what you are doing is listing the buildings which are more difficult to look after, whereas in England there are a large number of dwellings which are listed, and that is normally regarded as a good selling point by estate agents.

(*Dr Pykett*) I cannot respond to that. It is a matter for Cadw.

486. You said it was a political decision. By that presumably you mean it is a decision taken at a high level.

(*Dr Pykett*) I said I thought it might be political. It is difficult to argue the case with an individual houseowner rather than some sort of institutional owner.

487. Can any of your other gentlemen help? What Dr Pykett has said is extremely important and a matter of great concern.

(*Mr Hill*) It is one I have not heard about. Although Cardiff is mainly listed in terms of commercial and industrial properties, there are outlying residential, long barns and one or two thatched buildings on the fringe, but within the last year Cadw have re-surveyed south Cardiff as a result of the activities of the Cardiff Bay Development Corporation, and 44 buildings were added to the list including a row of 22 houses in either outright private ownership or multiple occupation. Those 22 in the dock area have been added to the list in the last year. I certainly have not heard the comment that Cadw were reluctant on policy grounds to list residential properties.

(*Mr Bowen*) I have been trying to run through my mind the buildings we have listed. I cannot say that I can agree with the comment that Dr Pykett made. Our experience is that a fair proportion of the buildings listed are residential properties. I would add that it obviously depends on the nature of each authority. As a fairly rural authority where properties are scattered, there is bound to be less commercial buildings, but I am afraid I cannot agree with Dr Pykett on the point that he raises.

Chairman

488. We want to move on and look at the re-listing programme. At the present rate the re-listing programme could take 60 years, and Mr Carr of Cadw told us that he hoped to reduce that to not more than 15 to 20 years. What do you believe is a realistic and acceptable time scale for that re-listing programme to take place?
(*Cllr Thomas*) It is going to depend substantially on the amount of money made available to local authorities. I take it that local authorities are responsible for re-listing. It would depend substantially on that and on the number of staff that these authorities can afford to have on their books.

489. No; Cadw is responsible.
(*Cllr Thomas*) Cadw is responsible for staff; I am sorry. I am getting a bit confused. I will leave it to the officers.
(*Mr Bowen*) I think, Chairman, we discussed this issue generally within our respective offices and it is a common problem. Section 1 of the Act does refer to the possibility of the Secretary of State referring to lists by other persons or bodies of persons. One suggestion that we could put forward is perhaps that whilst it is acknowledged that the authorites do not have the expertise, the authorities themselves could do the initial survey and present a dossier to Cadw to avoid say trekking through the fields of West Wales in order to find lost houses as it were. It is a possibility that the local authorities, particularly with the new unitary authorities, could have that function of providing the initial information for Cadw to do a rough assessment.
(*Mr Price-Thomas*) Certainly we would like to take that one on board for further investigation, especially during the lead in to the new unitary authorities in Wales. A 60-year period is totally unacceptable and I am sure the Committee would agree. In developing a more sophisticated planning responsibility there is potential for the new Welsh unitary authorities to take an active lead here, certainly in partnership with Cadw. It is something that I would wish the joint committees, shortly to be established in leading up to the unitary authorities, to consider quite carefully. I think we can help Cadw at the local grass roots level.

490. Mr Thomas, in the absence of any other sources of expertise, to what extent do local planning authorities depend upon the lists to indicate which buildings within their area are worthy of preservation? How important is that list?
(*Dr Pykett*) The list is very important. It is a constant reference list for planning officers dealing with all sorts of planning issues, both development control isues and forward planning issues. Indeed some difficulties are sometimes caused when CADW decides to do listing of buildings at a very late hour, and you will see in the evidence that we have submitted to you, in the memorandum that we have submitted, that we do suggest that the legislation really ought to be changed to require the Secretary of State to take into account the planning status of buildings as well as their architectural and historic interest. That comment is made partly as a reflection of change introduced by the Planning and Compensation Act of 1991 which sought to introduce a plan-led system to planning activities,

and it does seem to me, given the fact that the listed building legislation is framed within the general planning legislation framework, that the Secretary of State really ought to be required to take other planning issues into account before he decides to list buildings. The two areas where it seems to me the Secretary of State ought to take matters into account are first whether or not there is a planning permission extant on the building, and secondly policies and proposals contained within adopted plans affecting that building.

491. How long, Mr Hill, would it take for the re-listing programme to be undertaken in your area? Is there a long period of time? Is it 60 years before all the buildings in Cardiff could be listed, or do you think that as you are close to Cardiff, where they are not in North Wales, in fact they will take less time on the current schedule to list it because you are very near that list as it is?
(*Mr Hill*) I think in the case of Cardiff we have a couple of advantages. One of them is that we have got seven conservation area advisory committees which deal with conservation areas, and these people are lay people but they represent civic societies, the Victorian Society, the British Trust for Archeology, these sorts of things, together with interested local people. These people often come forward to us with their own suggestions for buildings that they have seen which they know, they have researched the history, they come to us with suggestions. In the case of Cardiff we have had the south of Cardiff re-listed because of Cardiff Bay very recently so apart from the city centre, the actual core of the city, the commercial heart, which I think needs re-listing with some additions, we are fairly complete because we have had as I said earlier six spot listings recently, which were for buildings that were under threat, so now with certain exceptions we are fairly complete. I think frankly that the whole of Wales should be re-listed and this acknowledges that some parts of Wales have never been listed at all. I think Torfaen has not got any listed buildings.

492. None at all?
(*Mr Hill*) I believe so, from the evidence that Mr Carr gave in his notes of meetings, I think somebody said that there were no buildings in Torfaen listed and he agreed.

493. And none in Rhymney Valley, Cllr Court?
(*Cllr Court*) Of course we have listed buildings.

494. No—there are no lists.
(*Cllr Court*) I would say we have lists, yes. I would be surprised if we have not got it identified in a similar way to Cardiff.

495. The Victorian Society say that there are no lists for Rhymney Valley or Torfaen. They are wrong, are they, Cllr Court?
(*Cllr Court*) I would have thought so.

496. There is a list as far as you know?
(*Cllr Court*) Yes.

Mr R Evans

497. They are only spot listed ones. What the Victorian Society is saying in the Rhymney Valley is that there has been no general survey containing a comprehensive list. There will of course be examples,

[Mr R Evans Cont]
I imagine, of buildings which have been spot listed in the Rhymney Valley, but there is no general list.

(Cllr Court) I am not sure if we have a general list but we are working towards a general list; I am aware of that.

498. But it is not your responsibility—it is CADW's.

(Cllr Court) I will say this, that when you have buildings in your area local authorities have a responsibility as Cadw does of scheduling and the district councils have to pick theirs up. When we picked up Llancaiash Fawr Mrs Williams was living in one room and the rest of the house was falling apart. We picked it up in that particular way, nobody else was going to pick it up.

499. Cllr Court, that was one of your most marvellous rescue jobs. I have been there; it is wonderful. The point to state about that is that it may well be that you have directed all your energies very successfully into that project and the other one which you have mentioned, but the point which the Victorian Society was making to us is that unless there is a general survey of all buildings which are of listable quality, it is a hit and miss business as to whether demolitions and alterations are picked up. That is the remedy.

(Cllr Court) The Rhymney Valley is not about those two schemes. We have won the European Heritage Award with Drenewydd in the North End Valley; we have also the new Tredegar engine house. There are a lot of things we have done as an authority. If Cadw have not done their work, I do not apologise for Cadw.

Mr R Evans: I am not criticising your authority. I am criticising Cadw; let us be quite clear.

Chairman

500. If we can move on to the area of archaelogical trusts, and there are as we know four in Wales, looking at the ancient monument side in particular, although the re-scheduling programme is only in its early stages the local SMR or sites and monuments records have been developed and maintained by these four trusts. As far as the records that they have in these SMRs do they supply local planning authorities with the sort of information which is lacking in respect of historic buildings?

(Mr Bowen) We work very closely with the Dyfed Archaelogical Trust which is in fact based in Carmarthen at the present time but are moving to Llandeilo. Not only do we work closely with them upon any planning applications which we feel are within a scheduled monument area or an area of archaeological interest, but we also work closely with them in the development of the authority's local plan. They have given us a tremendous amount of information in terms of sites of archaeological interest and we hope to identify a number of those in the local plan with the hope of enhancing their recognition to scheduled monument areas.

501. Do you find the same, Dr Pykett?

(Dr Pykett) Yes, I think that it is probably right to say that the links which do exist between planners and archaeologists are not as close as those which apply to listed buildings, simply because an archaeological monument or an ancient monument is subject to separate legislation, which you know about, and the involvement of the local planning authority in that is much more limited than applies to listed buildings. You may find in some of the evidence given to you that the archaeologists feel they are more distanced from the local planning authorities than they feel they ought to be really.

502. Mr Hill, how does the archaeological trust act as archaeological adviser to the local authority? How does the relationship actually work?

(Mr Hill) We have a plan in the Development Control division of the Department which shows all the areas which would be of interest archaeologically. We then circulate to the Glamorgan Gwent Archaelogical Trust any planning application which comes in dealing with those areas, and they respond to us in some cases, and they will write back saying that they have no interest in this one or they get heavily involved and we end up having meetings with the applicants and things go on from there depending on the complexity of the issue or the importance of the issue. We also have links of course with one of the professors in Cardiff University who has himself been involved in digs in our area, but mainly we work through the archaeological trust in Swansea.

503. Is there in your view, the three officers here today, any conflict between that function of the archeological trusts in advising you in terms of the existence of important archaeological remains in potential planning areas and the role of the archaeological trusts as contracted consultants to developers, in particular in relation to the onus placed on them by planning policy guidance note 16 to undertake archaeological assessments in advance of applications for planning permissions?

(Mr Hill) I think the employment of any consultant—and I choose my words carefully—because "who pays the piper calls the tune", but if a developer takes advice from an archaeological consultant prior to making an application, obtaining a report saying for instance that there will be very little disturbance, we would need to get independent evidence to ensure that that was a legitimate comment. We have as I say a chance of getting advice from two sources, quite separate sources. We have on occasion used the University of Wales. We do not find, to go back to your original question, that there is a conflict. It is very rare that developers employ people from the archaeological trust before they come to us with a planning application, so generally speaking the Gwent Archaeological Trust work directly to us as our clients.

504. But if a potential developer did use the trust then, going back to the point you made, you always get independent archaeological advice in addition?

(Mr Hill) In my authority's case it has never happened that way. What I am saying to you is that I would try to ensure that we would get independent advice. We have not had to yet.

505. Fine. What about you two gentlemen? Mr Bowen?

(Mr Bowen) I certainly would not question the integrity of the Dyfed Archaeological Trust in putting forward a report on any basis other than the archaeological content of any site. I would not see

[*Chairman Cont*]
them being influenced by the requirements of any developer to be honest.

506. Are you saying then that the developers would be wasting their money?

(*Mr Bowen*) No. The impression I have from your question is that an archaeological trust may be persuaded to provide a report which has perhaps identified a site as not as important as it really is, but the conclusion I would come to with our experience of the Dinefwr Archaeological Trust is that they are a dedicated team of individuals who would provide nothing but the true archaeological value of any site.

507. If I can develop that a little bit, say I was a developer and I went to the Dyfed Archaeological Trust for information, I would get no different information from what I could get as a member of the public by coming to you as a planning officer and asking you for what advice the archaeological trust has given you as a planning authority, would I?

(*Mr Bowen*) No. I think obviously if you went directly to the trust you would get more information. If you were a developer and placed a planning application before our authority's committee, we would consult the Dyfed Archaeological Trust and based on the initial information that they would provide we would make a recommendation accordingly. Quite probably, if consent was granted there would be a condition requiring the developer to provide an archaeological study and investigation of a site before the commencement of a development. In more cases than not we would suggest the Dyfed Archaeological Trust.

508. Dr Pykett, do you find the same?

(*Dr Pykett*) If I may, you would be a rare developer if you went straight to an archaeological trust and informed them of your development proposal. My experience is that developers run a hundred miles from archaeologists on the whole because they see them as frustrating their schemes, or having the potential to frustrate their schemes, but to get back to your original question I am not aware of any self-serving arrangement of the type you have described amongst the archaeologists.

(*Cllr Court*) I have before me a planning application—I am sure Mr Evans would be interested in it—on the Van Mansion and the consultees we used there were the normal ones in that we have the Ancient Monument Society, the Council for British Archaeology, the Georgian Group, the Society for the Protection of Ancient Buildings and the Victorian Society, so we have invited them to make their observations and it does not cost you any money.

509. But was that an ancient monument?

(*Cllr Court*) No. It was the Van Mansion. I think it is a bit of both.

510. But why would the archaeological trust be involved in that application?

(*Cllr Court*) Because they all have different types of experience. I do not think they list themselves between historical buildings and ancient museums. I do not think they break.

. (*Mr Hill*) I think the building concerned is surely listed. It is both a listed building and an ancient monument because it is pre-mediaeval.

511. In terms of conservation areas the Welsh Office circular states that "areas appropriate for designation as conservation areas will be found in almost vevery town and many villages", and there are almost 400 in Wales. Would you be in favour, Cllr Thomas, of extending the use of conservation area status to purely rural areas, as has happened in parts of England?

(*Cllr Thomas*) I certainly think, Chairman, that there are instances in the rural areas where there should be conservation areas designated them because wherever you go in the country in the rural area of Carmarthen there are bits and pieces that one would like very much to retain into the future when they are as original as they might be at this particular moment. In Carmarthen District Council at the moment we are looking very closely at planning applications within some of these villages and we are trying to do our best to protect them even at this particular moment, but being short of declaring them to be conservation areas. I think with the authority we might well end up with those conservation areas at the appropriate time.

512. Dr Pykett, would you like to see that?

(*Dr Pykett*) We have in fact designated recently, or near-designated a rural conservation area. The position is that we wanted to designate a conservation area in a village in Ceredigion and, as is our practice, we consulted the local community council, and they came back to us and they said, "Fine, but have you noticed this interesting field system which immediately adjoins the village?", which we have of course noticed. They are known as "slangs" in that part of the world, and they suggested that this area should also be incorporated within the conservation area and we agreed with that and recommended to our planning committee that the "slangs" should be included within the conservation area and they have been so included. The difficulty which does occur with this is that it does not actually do much as far as increasing controls over that particular area is concerned because of course there are no buildings to all intents and purposes, but what it does do I think is to give the area a status which it would otherwise not have enjoyed, and for that reason it seems to me to be beneficial and an appropriate use of the conservation area legislation.

513. Mr Bowen?

(*Mr Bowen*) I would have certain reservations. I can see certain situations where conservation area which you have outlined would merit such a designation, the setting up of a village conservation area for example, where the setting of the village is all-important, or where you have formal gardens laid out. That could be the type of conservation area that you have in mind. But I would be hesitant in as much as it would add to the complexity of the very variety of designation you already have. Within our authority we have an environmentally sensitive area where grants are available for various forms of farming. We have the recently introduced Countryside Council experiment which shows a new type of grant and a new type of designation, so I would have reservations because they would introduce a further designation which would have little value and where you could exercise little control other than tree felling.

Mr R Evans

514. Gentlemen, is not the core of the problem on this question of control that would you for example suggest that what is permitted within a rural conservation area might be altered? Would you wish to see greater powers?

(*Dr Pykett*) Clearly if an area was designated as a rural conservation area then as I have said it would increase it status and it would mean that any planning applications submitted in that area would be subject to closer scrutiny and examination, so I see that as being beneficial.

515. So what, for example, you are permitted to do within a conservation area under permitted development, what do you say about that for example? Would you wish for greater control of the hedgerows, agricultural operations and things of that sort?

(*Dr Pykett*) Before you are allowed permitted development you have got to have some development there to start with.

516. No; suppose for example you start knocking down this field system which is obviously fascinating. I am not quite sure how the "slang" actually operates but presumably if you are going to remove an earth feature or a wall feature, is that something which a conservation area would actually control or not, or would it be permitted development?

(*Dr Pykett*) The "slangs" are actually defined by hedges and one does not need planning permission to remove a hedge.

517. That is the point I am making. Are you suggesting for example that the normal exemption for ordinary agricultural operations, whether in fact in certain of these areas where you are suggesting a rural conservation area, we need to intervene much more closely and control a much wider range of things than traditionally we have done?

(*Dr Pykett*) Yes. I think that would be appropriate. Gradually the planning system is becoming more and more interested in agricultural activities. You will be aware, coming from a rural area, of the tremendous amount of resistance to the planners intervening in agricultural matters. I think we have managed it in this fairly small area because of local support for the idea, and I think it could work in that type of area, but like Mr Bowen I think there would be awful difficulties about extending it in any large scale or generalist way.

(*Mr Bowen*) I think there would have to be a specific feature, whether it was a field pattern or a formally laid out garden, which would merit such a designation.

Mr Ainger

518. I understand the Secretary of State may designate conservation areas himself. Are you aware if he has done any such designation in Wales?

(*Dr Pykett*) I am not aware of any, no.

(*Mr Bowen*) I am not aware of any.

(*Mr Hill*) I am not aware of it.

Chairman

519. In terms of town schemes local planning authorities have been encouraged to establish these in co-operation with Cadw. Your memorandum complains that the administration involved in town schemes is time consuming on occasions and that the geographic extent was sometimes thought to be too confined. Can you suggest how these problems might be addressed? Mr Hill?

(*Mr Hill*) First of all I would not subscribe to that view. I think the problems of a fairly tight city situation are quite different from my colleagues' problems. We have got town schemes operating and we find them very good, but the main reason for that is that the town scheme is set up for a period of five years. The money is provided by Cadw and the local authority. What it means is that the local authority, having entered into that agreement, is bound to provide a five-year rolling programme of money which means that as officers we know from one year to the next what sort of grant money we are going to have to spend on these buildings. With the five year plan that we operate on we know exactly where we are going, we can plan one year to the next, we can roll rather large schemes from one financial year to the next financial year in two phases and we find it quite the reverse, that in fact we do better in terms of staff time, knowing where we are going, what we are doing with our money, than we did with the previous system or the system that would prevail if you did not have a town scheme but where you would on an ad hoc basis just make grants available to listed building repairs. That is more time consuming with respect because when you get a town scheme operating we publicise the fact to all building owners in the area and we try and get them on our side and in many respects we get a great deal of enthusiasm from the owners about the improvements because they know it is a phased and planned manoeuvre and they know it is going to last five years. If they cannot find their own share of the money in the first year they know they might find it in the fifth year.

(*Dr Pykett*) Can I deal with the administration point? We did suggest in our recommendations to the CWD, although I see it is not reproduced here, that it would be advantageous if part of the town scheme grants which were made available from Cadw were earmarked for the administration of the scheme. The difficulty is that all the money which they earmark is to be used for the repair work involved and we are finding that it is tremendously time consuming. If there was a proportion of the grant available earmarked for the adminsitration of the scheme we feel we could employ part time administrative advice which would be very beneficial as far as the general work of the department is concerned and would allow the planning officers to do what they were actually employed to do, which is prepare local plans, rather than become too heavily involved in town scheme work. Perhaps I can just also mention the question of geographical area. I know that Cadw are very keen on having fairly tightly confined areas because they feel this is the best way of making a substantial impact with the grant monies that they are making available. I can see the advantage of that argument and the counter argument of course is that by having a large area then you are spreading the

[**Chairman** *Cont*]

paint too thinly. I think it all depends on the circumstances of the area and indeed the actual area in geographical terms which is being designated.

520. Thank you. Mr Bowen?

(*Mr Bowen*) Can I first of all say that as an authority we are very supportive of the concept of a town scheme. What we do find is that the resources allocated to such town schemes means that obviously there are fewer resources for more scattered rural buildings. As a local authority the bulk of our listed buildings are in the countryside. We find therefore that a large proportion of our listed buildings are denied an opportunity to apply for grant through the town scheme prposal where you get up to 50 per cent available as opposed to 20 per cent. We are also concerned about the length of time it takes for decisions made by the Historic Buildings Council for Wales to reach the authority. We obviously over the last few months have been planning expenditure for next year. We have applied for two town schemes and we have yet to have a formal decision whether those funds will be available for the next financial year. That is one point that we wish to make. We are also mindful of the extent of time taken to assess each application. Again it may come back to a matter of distance, but officers from Cadw visit our area less frequently than they would be able to visit town schemes closer to Cardiff and we are finding that when they do come out we have about eight or nine applications under the town scheme to consider rather than fewer if the visits were frequent. Those are the points we wish to make.

521. So they do not visit you very frequently at all, do they?

(*Mr Bowen*) In fairness they do visit us. We also take the opportunity when they do visit us to question them on possible spot listings as well, coming back to a previous point, but we find the visits are not frequent enough to ensure that a decision is made on an application quickly enough. You have to put the applicant on hold as it were until the officer is there and then the officer has to come back to ensure that the works have been carried out satisfactorily.

522. Cllr Thomas, in your memorandum you say that Cadw is not prepared to allow a local authority to advertise its own historic buldings in the same brochure as Cadw. Could you give us some examples of historic buildings that local authorities would like to advertise but have been refused permission to do so by Cadw?

(*Cllr Thomas*) It is a general statement that is made there, Chairman, in respect of that. What we are trying to say is that in order to be able to market the commodity at the end of the day it is necessary to advertise extensively and efficiently the facility that we have for the tourists in particular. I think that we should get together with Cadw whereby we join forces rather than stay apart and do things separately because we are certainly trying to attract the same people and trying to get what we can out of them in order to sustain whatever we are doing.

(*Mr Price-Thomas*) If I remember Chairman, the very same point was put to Mr Carr in his evidence to you and I recall he suggested the CWD should reflect on our written memorandum. We have done so and on the basis of further information and in fairness to Cadw the evidence I now have is that there is not quite the difficulty originally perceived in terms of Cadw refusing to have a local authority historic building provision advertised in their brochure.

523. That is not what Cllr Thomas said just now, is it Mr Price-Thomas, because he said that there is generally a problem. You have reflected. Do you want to reflect, Cllr Thomas, or are you saying in fact that that general statement stands because that is exactly the point that we had problems with? Cllr Thomas, you were saying that elected members are finding that as a general statement there is that problem. Now the CWD is saying there is not any more.

(*Cllr Thomas*) I have been led to believe that there is a problem and it is case—

524. Who led you? It is very important to know who has been leading you, Cllr Thomas.

(*Cllr Thomas*) I have been reading some of these documents, Chairman, and I find that even in Carmarthen I am sure that our tourism officer would confirm that there is some difficulty. What you have to appreciate is that the situation with Cadw has improved over the last 18 months to two years, and probably this problem has improved and is keeping improving all the time, so it is not as bad as what it used to be.

525. But it is still bad, you say, is it not, because you accepted the statement that in your memorandum and your memorandum still contains that. Let me ask you the question: when did this memorandum get written? Very recently, I assume.

(*Mr Price-Thomas*) I suspect it was about six weeks ago, Chairman, when we had the evidence of 24 of our 37 districts. Since that time—it is the second paragraph in our written memorandum—I would submit, on the basis of further evidence, that that statement is somewhat erroneous and we would want to temper that.

(*Mr Bowen*) I think, Chairman, the problem is not so much of specific examples of buildings not being permitted to be advertised but there are examples perhaps where there is a lack of co-operation between Cadw and local authorities. I think there is an example Mr Hill is aware of in Cardiff. When you know that one of the key targets for Cadw for 1992/93 is to raise their market share of the number of visitors, you are putting it on a competition level to begin with, so will they be prepared to get involved with not only the local authorities but the National Trust. You have got a key example in Llandeilo which you visited the other day, where you have got Cadw and the National Trust side by side. Will they be prepared for example to arrange a joint package for visitors and link it with other sites with local authorities and private individual in that particular area? That is a very interesting example from Cardiff.

(*Mr Hill*) We have had a recent example; this was last year. We were trying to market Cardiff Castle and St Fagans Folk Museum, the National Museum and Castell Coch, which is under the care of Cadw. We wanted to have a concessionary rover ticket so that a family could go and visit all four of these sites on the one ticket with obviously a concessionary fee, and Cadw said they were unable to join us in that venture because of their marketing arrangements, so

[Chairman *Cont]*

this is a fairly recent example that Cllr Thomas referred to where in fact there is still this problem where, rather than co-operate, they tend to compete. I think it is the way they are set up. They have to compete in a sense but where we are talking about tourism it would be far better if we could co-operate more.

526. I understand the point that Mr Bowen and you, Mr Hill, are saying about co-operation in terms of the general position, but that example you quoted was not in fact about the brochure, was it? Have you got any examples specifically whereby, even though I accept what Mr Price-Thomas has said that on reflection that was an erroneous view, have you got an example whereby Cadw has refused you permission as a city council to advertise one of your historic buildings that you wanted to in the literature they put out?

(*Mr Hill*) No, but I note that they do not in their literature on the castles of Wales advertise Cardiff Castle. I think Mr Price-Thomas referred to a system where they have a tourism trail throughout part of Wales where they do mention a number of buildings but it is mentioned in a very cursory way. In their individual "Castle of Wales" brochures they do not mention Cardiff Castle despite the fact for instance in Castell Coch that there is a very big link with the work of Burgess, the architect, who has examples of his work in both those areas. They are kept separate.

527. Now, Mr Price-Thomas, here is an example of one of the foremost castles of Wales. Did you reflect too soon? Here is a classic example. You say the statement is erroneous. Mr Hill says here is an example.

(*Mr Hill*) What I think I am trying to say and I am trying to help Mr Price-Thomas out in a sense, is that some of the literature that Cadw put out in a general way does refer to other buildings owned by other agencies such as councils or indeed the National Trust. It is in a way a passing reference that these things are mentioned. There is no overt way that they advertise or join with advertising with other agencies such as the city council. They do not do this in a major way.

528. Do they usually ask for a fee to advertise things like the castles or not?

(*Mr Hill*) No.

529. And Cardiff is not included in that. That is a very interesting example, and I am sure that if the councillors were to ask them to get more examples of that they may in fact look at that again. One last question, gentlemen, because we are running rapidly out of time, and that is in terms of the amenity societies. We find that under the terms of the Welsh Office circular the five national amenity societies should receive notice of all applications for consent to demolish a listed building. It is their belief they do not consistently receive such notices. Are they correct, Cllr Thomas?

(*Cllr Thomas*) I move this to my experts.

(*Mr Hill*) I again can speak for my own authority. I believe them not to be correct because we do circulate all our information not only to them but to many other people as well.

(*Dr Pykett*) I believe them to be incorrect as well. We are careful to try and make sure that their role is

protected where demolition of listed buildings is involved.

530. What about you, Mr Bowen?

(*Mr Bowen*) I would agree with my colleagues. We have discussed this and I think one point that was raised in the evidence that they gave you was that Merioneth for example did not consult them on one occasion. That situation can be exaplained by the fact that most of Merioneth is in Snowdonia National Park so any consultation they would have received in that district would have been via the National Park. I would also stress that they are only consulted in the cases of demolishing a listed building. It may be a fact that not many listed buildings are being demolished.

Mr Ainger

531. Chairman, could I ask for clarification on this term of "demolition"? Does this mean total demolition, removal of every trace of the building, or just partial demolition that you are supposed to consult the amenity societies on?

(*Dr Pykett*) It means both, although you are right to actually identify that as a problem because very frequently a scheme which alters a listed building may involve demolition and there has in fact I think been some litigation on this particular point. Certainly the legislation encourages prospective listed building developers to phrase their applications in such a way that the demolition element is minimised and the alteration element is maximised.

532. But from your point of view if it is a partial demolition do you consult the amenity societies?

(*Dr Pykett*) If for example we had an LBC application for an extension to a listed building which might involve the demolition of a wall and then the extension on the back of it, then our practice would be to regard that as being an extension to the listed building and not demolition of that building or indeed demolition of part of that building.

533. Are you aware of any advice that has been given out to local authorities from Cadw that they need only consult amenity societies when it is total demolition?

(*Mr Bowen*) We have got by on what is in the 1981 circular and it is interesting to note that sometimes you get conflicting advice from these amenity groups. You will get a Georgian building with subsequent Victorian alterations and you will get obviously a divergence of opinion there, so that is interesting in itself. I would agree with Dr Pykett that even if there is partial demolition we would consult these amenity societies.

534. And you are not aware of any letter or communication from Cadw indicating that your statutory position is that you only need to consult if it is total demolition?

(*Mr Bowen*) I am not aware of that, no. I think it stands on interpretation of the legislation and the circular by each individual council.

Chairman

535. Just one last question for me in relation to this point. Mr Bowen, how many listed buildings were demolished in Dinefwr in each of the last three years, say in 1990, 1991 and 1992? Take one of them if you like. It does not matter.

(*Mr Bowen*) Within the last year I would say that there has been a partial demolition of one I am aware of. Certainly we are in the process of looking at an application involving the demolition of another. The authorities have applied and obtained consent from Cadw to demolish a listed building, but very few. I cannot be specific.

536. What about you, Dr Pykett, in Ceredigion?
(*Dr Pykett*) I think the answer is one.

537. Cllr Thomas, is there anything you want to say or any of your team that we have not covered that you would like to make, that we have misunderstood something you have said that you want to clarify anything, anything at all that you want to add to anything we have said that we may have missed or that we may need some clearing up of any misunderstanding on?

(*Cllr Thomas*) I start from the left.

(*Mr Hill*) I think obviously the length of time taken to determine listed building applications by Cadw once they have been sent to Cadw. There has been criticism about this and I think with justification some years ago there was an enormous time lapse very often. What happens is that the local authority determines an application, which let us say takes a two month period. It then, if it is approved, goes to Cadw, so the whole clock starts again, much to the distress of the developers who cannot understand why it has to be a separate procedure. Frequently we were getting periods of two or three months before we got Cadw's response. This has improved considerably in the last two years or 18 months. Last year for instance 44 listed building applications were referred to Cadw from the city. In fact 75 per cent of those were responded to within seven weeks. Fifty per cent were responded to within three weeks. Many of these were small, which were for instance advertising on listed buildings, but having said that, that does demonstrate I think a very marked improvement and it is all down to the length of time it takes to process these things.

(*Cllr Court*) Can I just say something, Chairman, a slight criticism of Cadw if you like. We had a colliery closure in Penallta something like 18 months ago. British Coal and everybody else decided the site should be grassed as quickly as possible. The Coal Board said, "We will fill the shafts by October 1st and by November 1st the whole system will be a ploughed field". Then at the last minute Cadw lists the building, and for good reasons, because Penallta Colliery was the first colliery to produce its own power, so you do not have engine houses, you have power houses. It produced all its own power so you had buildings worth saving. But now we have got massive buildings, some of them 200 yards long, 70 or 80 feet high, that are going to go into dilapidation and very dangerous for children, 70 foot walls that children could fall over. The Coal Board removed from the site very quickly and then there was an immense danger to children. We have had one child

killed lower down the valley. Cadw will not be picking up the problem of somebody being killed there; it will be the local council that will have to cough up the money or even British Coal. I think if Cadw are going to protect them they must come in much earlier than what they have done, when everything is ready and everybody involved is there to knock the buildings over and make them safe. Now we have got these buildings in a major economic area, an industrial area, a by-pass going in. Our infra structure led us to believe that all this land was going to become available and at the last minute Cadw came in and stopped it. I am saying that is something we could be looking to Cadw to improve. This has happened since October or November 1991 and all the buildings are there.

Mr R Evans

538. Would that not be a matter for British Coal as the ongoing owners? It would be pretty scandalous if it was not British Coal who responsible for leaving the site in a safe condition.

(*Cllr Court*) Children have this nasty habit of getting into places like this which has hundreds of acres of surfaces. It is probably the largest colliery surface in the whole of South Wales. It was used for strewding and washing and so on and it is so massive you would have to have so many men there it would not be financially viable to British Coal to do it.

539. It may not be a question of financial viability but British Coal as the owner would be in very serious difficulties if they did not ensure that that site was safely fenced off.

(*Cllr Court*) They did not blame British Coal in Bedwas where the child was killed; they blamed the local council.

(*Dr Pykett*) Can I take up the point Mr Hill mentioned about processing of LBC applications? It does seem to me that there is a certain amount of duplication going on here which means there is delay built into the system. I know from Cadw's evidence to you, paragraph 16, that during a seven year period they called in 2.5 per cent of the applications which they considered, which presumably means that for the remaining 97.5 per cent they were satisfied with the decision of the local planning authority. On the basis of those figures it seems to me that there is an opportunity or a need I should say for improvement of the system under which LBC applications are considred. What I would like to suggest to you is that you might like to consider whether or not it would be appropriate for Cadw to be re-designated as it were as a consultee on LBC applications in the same way as other organisations are consultees on planning applications but in order to protect their position vis-a-vis listed buildings they should be empowered with a power of direction similar to that that the Director of Highways has on planning applications.

Mr R Evans

540. It has gone.
(*Dr Pykett*) It seems to me that that procedure would speed up the whole process of LBC applications and improve the role of Cadw vis-a-vis listed buildings.

Chairman

541. Mr Evans is saying that that has gone. You were not referring to the other highways direction where the county council could refuse?

(*Dr Pykett*) No, I was referring to the direction of the Secretary of State on trunk roads which is still very much there.

(*Mr Bowen*) I would agree with the point of view of Dr Pykett. We need to look at the direction of the Secretary of State not only from the point of view of acting as consultee but of making all their expertise and advice they have available to local authorities. If Cadw had the same relationship as the Highways Directorate has at the present time where you are able to approach the Highways Directorate and have advice on visibility and so on, where Cadw's advice would be available I suggest that would facilitate this consultation procedure.

(*Mr Price-Thomas*) This suggestion came up at our discussions yesterday and I am wondering whether it would be helpful to the Committee if, after the CWD had looked at the suggestion, we could let you have a supplementary memorandum on the subject.

542. It would be very useful. Cllr Thomas, can I thank you very much and your colleagues for coming today and giving evidence.

(*Mr Bowen*) May I say that all the local authorities represented here today are quite satisfied with the officers that work for Cadw. We have an excellent working relationship within the confines within which they have to operate both in terms of resources and manpower and from that point of view we are all very satisfied.

(*Dr Pykett*) I will endorse that.

(*Cllr Thomas*) May we wrap it up from this side by saying that we are happy to have been giving evidence to you. I hope you are going to find it of some use and I will be looking forward to the new unitary authorities being able to make far more of the ability to have officers responsible for conservation at that particular juncture. It is all about being able to plan these things and if we have too many officers with not quite enough to do we will be charged with pestering people who have these sorts of properties. I think we have a fair balance at the moment but I can assure you that it will be our intention as the Council of Welsh Districts to encourage improvement in conservation and conservation items. I will certainly be writing to you, Chairman, telling you how many listed buildings there are in Carmarthen. I find it difficult as a layman to have my finger on every detail.

Chairman: Of course I was not making any criticism. I look forward to hearing how many listed buildings there are in Lliw Valley. Thank you all very much for coming to see us. When we come to write our report it will move things forward in the constructive spirit within which we all work. Thank you very much.

The Representative Body of the Church in Wales

THE PRESERVATION OF HISTORIC BUILDINGS AND ANCIENT MONUMENTS IN WALES
(HB7)

The Church in Wales welcomes the opportunity to respond to your enquiry as outlined in your letter of 25th November, and because of widely held misconceptions about the Church in Wales, we provide first of all background information dealing with disestablishment and the development of the Church in Wales since that time. For ease of reference this information is contained in the introduction in the attached memorandum whilst we show in parenthesis the paragraph numbers which relate to the conclusions and recommendations we make below.

The care exercised by the Church in Wales is detailed in paragraphs 2.01 to 2.12.

We note in particular the arrangements for the Listing of churches under paragraphs 3.01 to 3.04. 4.01. 5.01 to 5.08. 5.33 to 5.35. We deal with ecclesiastical exemption between paragraphs 5.10 and 5.20.

With regard to the grant schemes that are available we note the arrangements relating to these under paragraphs 3.05 to 3.07. 5.08 and 5.09. 5.21 to 5.32. 5.36 and 5.37.

You enquire whether there are associated issues which seem to us to be relevant and we note these below.

The financial effects of disestablishment were significant and we have noted aspects of this in paragraphs 1.03 and 8.09. It is essential that this is understood by those wishing to secure the future of Listed churches, whether "living" of redundant.

The Representative Body is unable to carry the burden of maintaining and insuring a large number of redundant Listed churches which are unsaleable. As the trustee owning the vast majority of church buildings it must maintain its capital base and utilise its resources in the most effective was to assist the Parochial Ministry. (Paras 4.01 and 5.06)

In England, Parochial Church Authorities may require parish or district councils to assume responsibility for the maintenance of any churchyard which has been closed by an Order-in-Council. This power is not available to the province of Wales, thus increasing the burden upon the Church in Wales. This is despite the fact that burial facilities are provided for *all* deceased parishioners whether they are members of the Church or not.

CADW's role in consideration of this matter is crucial. It is essential that a realistic and practicable Listing policy is adopted to ensure that the best of the nation's built heritage is maintained. This means a policy of *sustainable* conservation, with a realistic assessment of the funding needs to support such policies (5.06). The absence of a comprehensive up-to-date resurvey of the present List of Buildings of Special Architectural and Historic Interest, creates many administrative difficulties and seriously hinders the possibility of realistic planning for redundancy (5.07; 5.33; 5.34). It is not reliable to equate the old A, B, C Listings with the new I, II*, II Listings (5.34), whilst the lack of notification of the establishment of Conservation Areas creates similar administrative problems (6.14).

The retention of ecclesiastical exemption is regarded by the Church in Wales as an important feature of the current legislation at no small cost to itself, and adequate time should be provided for the effective operation of the code of practice (5.10 to 5.20).

The operation of the Faculty Jurisdiction system is essential and creates considerable cost for the Church, both adminstratively and otherwise. The current recommendations will increase this cost and will continue to relieve the local planning authority of this burden. The financial and other benefits derived by local authorities should be recognised.

English Heritage now provides substantial financial assistance for the maintenance of the English Cathedrals. There is no such provision in Wales, and M.H.C. has not so far recommended that such funding be made available.

The absence of a Redundant Churches Fund, or similar mechanism for maintaining the best of Listed redundant churches, is widely criticised, and the attempts to establish satisfactory machinery are essentially marred by the absence of "new money" (5.37). It remains to be seen whether the New National Lottery will generate additional funds for such purposes. The reduction in the target numbers of Listed redundant churches eligible for inclusion in such a fund in the negotiations over the years with CADW, under-estimates and implies a misunderstanding of the essential problem (5.21 to 5.27). The funding of the maintenance and repair of a handful of the "outstanding" redundant churches is not a problem. Such buildings may be funded by CADW whether "living" or redundant. The main problem relates to those redundant churches which are Listed Grade II (or equivalent), (6.03), and are not regarded as "outstanding". These churches carry all the dis-benefits of Listing (requirements for Listed building consent when not in ecclesiastical use etc.), but do not enjoy the benefit of grant assistance from CADW. It is submitted that any redundant churches policy that fails to provide a system of sustainable concervation for these churches, will not succeed.

It is submitted that unless the policy for the preservation of redundant churches is carefully formulated and implemented, then public support (as tax payer or parishioner) will not be retained as noted in paragraph 5 of DOE circular 8/87.

Whilst the Pembrokeshire Coast National Park Department of Dyfed County Council has grasped the nettle of redundant churches and chapels in its region, by commissioning a report, there seems to be a lack of understanding or will to tackle the problem across the principality as a whole by Local and County Authorities (6.06 and 6.17). Urgent discussions to create practicable policies are necessary if the objective of the Act and policy guidance notes are to be attained. A greater awareness of the problems would be engendered by the appointment of more Conservation Officers to local authorities throughout the Principality.

At the same time, new funding for historic churches should be considered by County and Local Authorities (6.12 and 6.16). Greater flexibility must be shown by planning authorities with swift responses to Planning and Listed Building Consent Applications to avoid the worst effects of vandalism and the loss of Public Liability Insurance cover (paras 6.06-section 65).

Whilst the Planning (Listed Buildings and Conservation Areas) Act of 1990 is relatively recent, Welsh Office circular 61/81 requires revision to incorporate the significant changes both in legislation and thinking, since its preparation. (6.04; 6.05; 6.07).

The perception of unbalanced sectional interests, promoted by the individual Amenity Societies needs to be addressed, and a more unified approach to enable priorities to be set for the churches that are to be preserved, is essential. The absence of any grant giving function (or fund holding as envisaged in the National Health Service reforms), does not assist in the establishment of balanced priorities. (7.01)

The review of policies by Tai Cymru and in turn individual housing associations, would help in providing alternative residential user in redundant churches. (7.04)

Improved stewardship, both in financial terms and technical and professional skills is essential to every parish to ease the burdens on the Incumbent who must be encouraged to delegate more of the non-pastoral work to lay workers in the parish. (801)

With greater emphasis on self help in communities over the past decade, it is essential at a time of high unemployment, breakdown of family units, etc., that the pastoral role of the Incumbent should be facilitated to the greatest possible extent. This must be achieved by reducing the burden of maintaining a disproportionately large amount of the nations built heritage. (8.01; 8.02; 8.03; 8.08)

The Church in Wales must in turn develop better forecasting procedures and planning for redundancy, to enable the identification of the numbers of Listed churches which are likely to be scheduled for redundancy, and to avoid the worst risks of vandalism and other uninsurable problems when the church ceases to be used for ecclesiastical purposes.

More research is required and is being undertaken by the Church in Wales, supported by a number of case studies, whilst the framework for a trust is being considered and a more comprehensive paper will be placed before the Representative Body's Churches Group for consideration in April.

If there is not to be a Redundant Churches Fund in Wales, then the proposals suggested in the Wilding Report for the establishment of a trust to maintain selected redundant churches should be pursued (5.25). To encourage fund raising for the trust, both at a secular and ecclesiastical level, it will be necesary to make such a trust identifiably Welsh, based in Wales, and applying its resources in Wales. Such a trust might provide the vehicle for greater State and local authority funding for this specific task.

Should you require any further information or expansion of the information provided in the text please do not hesitate to contact us.

11 December 1992

THE PRESERVATION OF HISTORIC BUILDINGS AND ANCIENT MONUMENTS IN WALES

INTRODUCTION

1.01 The Reverend Canon D T W Price noted, in his "History of the Church in Wales in the 20th Century", that the "disestablishment process was started by the first Parliamentary motion in 1870 after the disestablishment of the Anglican Church of Ireland, but the Royal assent was not given to the Act to disestablish the Church of England in Wales until the 18 September 1914. The process of dis-endowment was to begin at once".

1.02 The Act of 1914 dissolved every cathedral and ecclesiastical corporation in Wales, removed the Welsh Bishops from the House of Lords, abolished the coercive force of the Church's Courts, and diverted tithes from the Church in Wales to the local authorities. Small endowments given to the Church before 1662 were taken from it.

1.03 The 1st World War delayed the implementation of the Act, and an Amending Act of 1919 preserved some of the endowments. The Treasury made a grant of £1 million to the Welsh Church Commissioners, charged with transferring the Church's endowments to the local authorities, so that the Commissioners could pay commutation capital to the Representative Body. The author comments that the value of money and of tithe had so changed since 1914 that some alteration in the financial provisions of the act of that year was essential. It was calculated that the Church had lost £48,000 a year of its income. Eventually, in 1942 and 1947 £3.5 million were transferred, most of it to the County and County Borough Councils, and the remainder, just under £1 million, to the University of Wales. The Church in Wales became a disestablished Church on the 31 March 1920. It remains in full communion with the Church of England.

1.04 At the time of disestablishment, there were 4 dioceses, Bangor, St. Asaph, St. Davids and Llandaff. Llandaff Diocese was divided to create the Diocese of Monmouth in 1921, and St. David's Diocese was divided to create the Diocese of Swansea and Brecon in 1923.

1.05 At a convention in Cardiff held between the 2 and 5 October 1917, it was resolved that two bodies be created to administer the Church. The first would be the legislative body named the Governing Body and the second, the Representative Body would hold in trust the Church's property.

1.06 The Constitution was not completed until April 1922 and has been developed through amendments and additions since that date.

1.07 The Governing Body consists of three orders namely, bishops, clerics and laity. The Standing Committee advises the Governing Body on matters of policy, including long term planning, the establishment of priorities in the use of resources and the approval of budgets.

1.08 The Representative Body was referred to in the Welsh Church Act 1914. The Representative Body is a trust corporation which received its Royal charter in April 1919. It is an exempt charity, and most of the property vested in it by the Welsh Church Commissioners is held on trust for the bishops, clergy and laity of the Church in Wales subject to the direction of the Governing Body. It also holds much property for particular parishes or purposes, and is bound by the laws relating to charitable trusts and can only act on resolutions of the Governing Body if they accord with these laws. Almost all the churches used by the Church in Wales are vested in the Representative Body, including the six cathedrals. Most of the parsonages are also vested in the Representative Body along with remaining glebeland and other property. It has long been the established policy of the Representative Body to preserve its capital base and to use its income primarily in support of the stipends and pensions of clerics.

1.09 The Executive Committee of the Representative Body is the Finance and Resources Committee. There are three principal sub-committees:—

(A)   Investment Sub-committee which is responsible for the investment of all the Representative Body's funds, either in stock and shares or in investment property.

(B)   Maintenance of Ministry Sub-committee which recommends the scale of stipends and pensions and deals with financial support for clerics.

(C)   Property Sub-committee and its Churches Group has responsibility for the policy and decisions relating to the acquisition or disposal of Church property, which does not include "investment property". It is this Sub-committee that is responsible for the Listed buildings and ancient monuments vested in the Representative Body, and lying within the Principality. The Churches Group provides grants and advice for the maintenance and repair of the churches.

THE CONSTITUTION OF THE CHURCH IN WALES

2.01   The Church in Wales employs faculty procedure, for the control of works to consecrated churches, and this is set down in the Constitution under the"Rules of the Diocesan Courts Applications For Faculties". Sections 1, 2 and 3 state:—

"Except as provided in rules 2 and 3 hereof, or in accordance either with an agreement under the Sharing of Church Buildings Act, 1969, or with permission granted under the Regulations for the administration of Churchyards vested in the Representative Body of the Church in Wales:

1.(a)   no change of use of a consecrated church, no alteration or addition to the fabric thereof, no repair or redecoration nor any step for the introduction or removal of furniture, fittings or murals, shall be commenced without the grant of a Faculty or the Certificate of an Archdeacon, as the case may be;

(b)   no change of use of and no alteration or addition to or removal from consecrated land vested in the Representative Body shall be commenced without the grant of a Faculty or the Certificate of an Archdeacon, as the case may be;

(c)   no grave-space shall be acquired in perpetuity and no corpse shall be removed from an existing grave or vault in a burial ground vested in the Representative Body, without the grant of a Faculty.

2.   Faculty procedure does not apply to the fabric of any cathedral but no alteration or addition to such fabric shall be commenced without the authority of the Representative Body.

3.   Faculty procedure does not apply to the fabric of any unconsecrated building licensed by the Bishop of the diocese for Divine Worship and vested in the Representative Body, but no alteration or addition to the fabric thereof shall be commenced without the authority of the Representative Body, and no introduction or removal of furniture or fittings therein shall be commenced without the authority of the Bishop of the diocese, who shall inform the Secretary of the Representative Body accordingly".

2.02   The Rules continue by describing the process by which petitions for faculties may be lodged with the Diocesan Registrar, and the processes by which the petitions are to be dealt with, including the use of Archdeacons' Certificates for Minor Works. Section 32 requires the Bishop to appoint an Advisory Committee for the Care of Churches, and later sections set out the way in which the advice shall be sent via the Registrar to the Chancellor for his decision. Section 48 requires all contentious proceedings, unless otherwise ordered by the Chancellor, to be heard in open Court.

2.03   The structure and functions of the Representative Body today are set down in Chapter III of the Constitution, and section 26 provides:—

"Subject as hereinafter mentioned the Representative Body shall have full powers of selling, exchanging, leasing and managing all real and personal property at any time vested in it, provided always that:—

(a) as regards any plate, furniture or other movable chattel (except such as are hereinafter mentioned in paragraph (b)) belonging to, or used in connection with the celebration of divine worship in any church, or as regards episcopal or capitular lands, glebes or sites for churches (other than sites hereinafter specially provided for), episcopal or glebe houses, ecclesiastical residences or any movable chattel held or enjoyed with or incident to the occupation of any such residence, or any school house or any land occupied therewith, the said powers of sale or exchange shall not be exercised unless authorised by a resolution of a majority of the Representative Body, present and voting, and assented to in writing by the Bishop of the diocese in which such property is situated, but it shall not be necessary for any purchaser to enquire whether such authorisation or consent has been given;

(b) the Representative Body shall not have power to sell, or exchange, lease or dispose of any consecrated site, or any church or building erected thereon, or to dispose of ornaments, vessels or instruments used in connection with any of the sacraments, unless authorised by a resolution of three-quarters of the members of the Representative Body, present and voting, and assented to in writing by the Bishop of the diocese in which such consecrated site, ornaments, vessels, or instruments are situated;

(c) all other powers of leasing and managing shall be exercised only in such manner and in accordance with such rules and regulations as may from time to time be made by the Governing Body;

(d) it shall be open to any person or body of persons in the diocese where such property is situated to make representation to the Representative Body requesting it to take action under this section".

2.04 There is in each diocese a Diocesan Conference and it is the duty of the Conference to appoint a Standing Committee, and appoint, or cause to be appointed, a Finance Board.

It is the duty of the Diocesan Board of Finance to provide a scheme whereby every church in the diocese shall be inspected at least once every 5 years, which scheme shall provide:—

"(a) for the establishment of a fund by means of contributions from parochial, diocesan or other sources;

(b) for the payment out of such fund or otherwise of the cost of the inspection of the churches in the diocese;

(c) for the appointment of architects or chartered surveyors competent to inspect the churches in the diocese;

(d) for the architect or chartered surveyor to make a report to the Diocesan Board of Finance in the case of every church inspected, and copies of the report so made shall be sent to the Archdeacon of the archdeaconry and to the Parochial Church Council of the parish in which the church is situate; and;

(e) such other detail not inconsistent with this section as the Diocesan Board of Finance deems fit."

2.05 The duties of the chuchwarden and other parochial officials are set out in Chapter VI and Section 21 imposes the duty on the incumbent and churchwardens to maintain a Log Book, Terrier and Inventory on parish property. That document will contain the details of faculties that have granted, the information arising from the Quinquennial Inspection Report and the schedule or works arising therefrom.

2.06 Chapter X of the Constitution deals with parsonages and the way in which the diocesan parsonage board is responsible for the parsonages in that diocese. The diocesan inspector is directly employed by the Representative Body and has responsibility for the repair and maintenance of the parsonages in the diocese, a number of which are Listed as being of Special Architectural and Historic Interest or lie within Conservation Areas.

2.07 Section 14 requires the inspector to survey each parsonage at least quinquennially, and upon any vacancy.

2.08 The Church Fabric Regulations make provision for the insurance of all cathedral and parochial insurances, and require the churchwardens to report annually to the Parochial Church Council on the state of repair of the church buildings, churchyards and burial grounds, and the steps which the churchwardens consider necessary to maintain the same in a proper state of repair. The churchwardens are also required to report on the current insurance cover of all parochial insurances including the provision of the advice of the church's insurances. The churchwardens are required under these Regulations to forward a copy of their annual report to the archdeacon, including details of what action is to be taken.

2.09 The Regulations for the Administration of Churchyards require the Parochial Church Council to maintain and keep all churchyards in the parish including walls, gates, fences, paths, grass and trees, and to effect suitable and adequate insurance cover to enable repair. The Regulations provide for a Churchyard Maintenance Fund which receives a proportion of fees. The Regulations define how burials shall take place, including cremated remains, and the nature of gravestones or monuments that may be erected with or without faculty approval.

2.10 There are supplementary Gravestones Regulations to deal with the request of a Parochial Church Council to tidy a churchyard, including the reordering of monuments or gravestones subject to faculty procedure.

2.11 The Redundant Churches Regulations set out the procedures following the closure of a church for public worship. In such circumstances churchwardens, at the expense of the Parochial Church Council, continue to be responsible for maintaining the building and providing insurance cover. They are also required to take reasonable steps to safeguard the fabric of the church building, including the security at all times of the doors and windows. It is the duty of the incumbent and churchwardens to send a copy of the inventory, of all the contents, to the Secretary of the Representative Body and the Diocesan Churches Committee. The Diocesan Churches Committee having consulted the Diocesan Advisory Committee, decides whether an application should be made to the Bishop to declare a church redundant. It is the Diocesan Churches Committee's responsibility, having consulted with the Parochial Church Council, to provide the Bishop with proposals for the future of the building, the necessary insurance cover for disposal of contents and the financial implications of these actions. The Bishop will only declare a church redundant three months after the date of the Diocesan Churches Committee's proposals.

2.12 On receipt of the declaration of redundancy, the Representative Body becomes responsible for the insurance and security of the church building and contents, and for the initiation of action on the Diocesan Churches Committee's proposals.

CURRENT LEGISLATION

3.01 The Planning (Listed Buildings and Conservation Areas) Act of 1990 is one of the four 1990 Acts consolidating the provisions in the Town and Country Act of 1971 relating to Listed Buildings and Conservation Areas, together with other related legislation.

3.02 Part I of the Act includes:—

> Chapter 1—the Listing of special buildings. Chapter 2 covers the authorisation of works effecting Listed buildings; Chapter 3—the rights of owners etc.; Chapter 4—enforcement; Chapter 5—the prevention of deterioration and damage; Chapter 6—miscellaneous and supplemental provisions. (It is in the last Chapter under sections 60 and 61 that exceptions for ecclesiastical buildings, redundant churches, and for ancient monuments etc., are provided).

3.03 Part II of the Act deals with Conservation Areas; Part III—General provisions and special cases. (The special case of ecclesiastical property is incorporated in section 86). Part IV provides supplemental provisions and schedules.

3.04 Section 60 of the Act prescribes that the provisions mentioned in sections 3, 4, 7-9, 47, 54 and 59 shall not apply to any ecclesiastical building which is for the time being used for ecclesiastical purposes (the section specifically excludes rectories and vicarages from this exemption).

3.05 Section 57 empowers local authorities to contribute to the preservation of Listed buildings which are situated in its area, and the contribution may be made by grant or loan. The loan may be made on an interest free basis.

3.06 The Historic Buildings and Ancient Monuments Act of 1953 sections 3A and 4 authorise the Secretary of State for Wales to make grants or loans for the upkeep of buildings of outstanding historic or architectural interest.

3.07 Section 77 of Part II of the Planning (Listed Buildings and Conservation Areas) Act of 1990 enables the Secretary of State to make grants or loans towards any relevant expenditure which has made or make a significant contribution towards the preservation or enhancement of the character or appearance of any Conservation Area situated in Wales.

HISTORIC BUILDINGS AND ANCIENT MONUMENTS OWNED BY THE CHURCH

4.01 The brief recent history of the Church in Wales noted above, explains why the churches, parsonages and other parcels of land upon which ancient monuments stand, are vested in the Representative Body. Of the 1,450 churches that are vested in the Representative Body, some 620 are Listed as being of Special Architectural and Historic Interest. Many of these lie within Conservation Areas, and other churces, which are not Listed, lie within Conservation Areas and thus fall under the provisions of Part II of the 1990 Act.

4.02 Research is being undertaken with regard to the number of parsonages which are Listed or lie within Conservation Areas. The care and maintenance of such buildings is under the supervision of Diocesan Inspectors in each diocese, who are in turn directly employed by the Representative Body. Such works are subject to the secular planning controls. The maintenance of such buildings is funded jointly by the Representative Body and the Diocesan Board of Finance. The importance of maintaining satisfactory accommodation for incumbents and their families cannot be overstated. Leaving aside the trustee duty to maintain, care and preserve any historic parsonages, there is the additional desire to maintain and enhance the value as one of the assets of the church.

4.03 This memorandum therefore concentrates on the principal area of concern which is that of churches which are Listed or lie within Conservation Areas.

CHURCH AND STATE

5.01 There can be little doubt that by far the greatest influence over the care and preservation of the historic churches by external bodies is exercised by CADW—Welsh Historic Monuments.

5.02 CADW became the first executive agency within the Welsh Office on the 2nd April 1991.

5.03 It is CADW's mission statement: "To protect, to conserve and to promote the built heritage of Wales." The agency is responsible for discharging the Secretary of State's statutory responsibilities relating to the preservation, protection and maintenance of ancient monuments, historic buildings and Conservation Areas, and for the sponsorship of the Royal Commission on Ancient and Historical Monuments (Wales). It provides advice for the Secretary of State on all policy issues relating to the built heritage and on any other issues which he may refer to it. It will promote legislation where appropriate.

5.04 In its annual report and accounts 1991–92, CADW notes that there were some 14,374 buildings Listed by March of 1992 "but many communities in Wales remain to be surveyed and CADW is seeking to accelerate the work". The report refers to the "carrot and stick" approach. The "carrot" aspect is noted as the significant grant giving scheme operated on the advice of the Historic Buildings Council for Wales. The HBCW advises CADW on applications for grant assistance and, of the total of 309 applications received during the year, the report records that 154 were approved, and the total value of grant assistance offered £2,712,112. The total paid for offers made previously was £2,817,112 against an annual budget of £3.5 million. This budget represented an increase of 9 per cent. on that for the previous financial year and itself represented 36 per cent of CADW's total budget. The report notes: "the Council continues to recognise the special need of churches", and recommended grant assistance often at 50 per cent of the cost of works; some £515,274 was offered in the year. 56 grants for external works to buildings in Conservation Areas were approved at a total value of £408,554.

5.05 CADW records, under "Target 5", the desire to complete 12 historic building listing resurveys in 1991/2. Seven were completed during the period, whilst in the two preceding years five and three were completed respectively. Under the "Key Targets" for 1992-3, 6.2. CADW aims to promote the preservation of historic buildings and ancient monuments by completing 12 resurvey lists and 60 scheduling entries.

5.06 CADW has indicated elsewhere that in due course it expects the number of Listed historic buildings in Wales, to rise from the present number of over 14,000 to around 30,000.

5.07 Recent enquiries have shown that a substantial proportion of the churches that are listed fall within the old classes of A, B and C. Rescheduling under the new classes of I, II* II is taking place, (frequently as a consequence of parishes having made application to CADW for grant assistance with the consequent need for HBC to determine whether the church may be regarded as outstanding).

5.08 Attached to this memorandum is the "Guide to Legislation on the Listing of Historic Buildings" issued by CADW (code: COO1C162H2) (APPENDIX 1), and "Grant Aid for Historic Buildings" (code: COO1D361H2) (APPENDIX 2).

5.09 When offering a grant, explanatory notes and conditions are attached to the decision letter. A typical letter (code: COO1B827TU) is attached (APPENDIX 3).

Ecclesiastical Exemption

5.10 A review of the workings of ecclesiastical exemption has been requested by the Welsh Office (in tandem with the DOE/DNH). When the Ancient Monuments Act was passed in 1913, Archbishop Davidson persuaded Parliament that the Church of England should continue to look after its own buildings. By 1976, the cost of repairs had become so high in relation to church resources, that the Government agreed to extend the state aid scheme for historic buildings to include buildings in ecclesiastical use. The scheme was restricted to parish churches and their non-conformist equivalents (cathedrals were excluded). As part of the agreement, on the introduction of state aid for churches in use, the Government agreed that it would be unnecessary to legislate on ecclesiastical exemption, whilst faculty jurisdiction was reviewed. The Welsh Office (and DOE) sought a response to a consultation paper dated February 1992. This consultation paper proposed a code of practice to establish whether a particular denomination would be able to provide evidence of control systems which would "include some of the key aspects of the secular controls, and that the imposition of further Listed building controls would therefore not be justified". (Consultation paper attached—Appendix 4).

5.11 The Church in Wales had established a Commission on Faculties, under the Chairmanship of His Honour Judge Michael Evans Q.C., following a Meeting of the Standing Committee of the Governing Body on 16 July 1991. There have been seven Meetings of the Commission, and the discussions have not only covered proposed revisions to the faculty rules but also the care of churches and the Church's response to the consultation paper on ecclesiastical exemption.

5.12 The final report of the Commission on Faculties is not yet ready for presentation to the Governing Body, but the Chairman of the Commission has already confirmed to the Governing Body the Commission's view that ecclesiastical exemption, should be retained. This view has been conveyed to CADW together with the Church's proposals for compliance with the code of practice. The Commission endorsed the General Principle set out under Part I of the Care of Churches and Ecclesiastical Jurisdiction Measure 1991 passed by the General Synod of the Church of England namely:—

"Any person or body carrying out functions of care and conservation under this Measure or under any other enactment or rule of law relating to churches shall have due regard to the role of a church as a local centre of worship and mission".

5.13 The Commission noted the copy of the letter sent to the Secretary of State by the Historic Buildings Council for Wales, reproduced on page 7 of the HBCW 34th Annual Report. As the purpose of the

Commission was to make recommendations to the Governing Body for improvements and strengthening of the faculty jurisdiction system to prevent alleged abuses, it was considered that the letter did not reflect the positive approach of the Church in Wales to these matters. Concern was also expressed about the Historic Buildings Council's reaffirmation of its view that the six Anglican Cathedrals in Wales should not, for the present, be eligible for grant aid. Having responded to the consultation paper, indicating the Church in Wales' willingness to operate the code of practice, the representations made by the Churches Main Committee, and dated 7 April 1992, were endorsed by the Church in Wales (Appendix 5). In addition to the endorsement of the Churches Main Committee's response, the Church in Wales confirmed to CADW the interim views of the Commission on Faculties which were subject to ratification by the Governing Body. The Diocesan Advisory Committees and the Courts would be independent of the local congregation and community and also of the Representative Body, the owner of the freehold of the church.

5.14 The Diocesan Advisory Committees were felt by the Commission to require additional membership to provide a wider basis of expert knowledge either within the Committee or as a resource to be called upon as necessary, (particularly where an unusual item was being considered). It has been proposed that the DAC will be composed of the Archdeacons of the diocese and not less than nine other members. The other members would be two persons appointed by the Diocesan Conference of the diocese from among the elected members of the Diocesan Conference of the diocese. In addition, not less than seven other persons appointed by the Diocesan Conference of the diocese of whom one shall be appointed after consultation with CADW, one shall be appointed after consultation with the relevant association of local authorities, and one shall be appointed after consultations with the National Amenity Societies. Other persons may be co-opted of a number not exceeding one third of the total number of the membership.

5.15 It has been proposed that the functions of the Diocesan Advisory Committee will be as follows:

1(a) To act as an advisory body on matters affecting places of worship in the diocese and, in particular, to give advice when requested by any of the persons specified in paragraph 2 below on matters relating to:

  (i) the grant of faculties;

  (ii) the architecture, archaeology, art and history of places or worship;

  (iii) the use, care, planning, design and redundancy of places of worship;

  (iv) the use and care of the contents of such places;

  (v) the use and care of churchyards and burial grounds.

(b) To review and assess the degree of risk to materials, or of loss to archaeological or historic remains or records, arising from any proposals relating to the conservation, repair or alterations or places of worship, churchyards and burial grounds and the contents of such places;

(c) To make recommendations as to the circumstances when the preparation of the following records should be made a condition of a faculty; Records relating to the conservation, repair and alteration of places of worship; churchyards and burial grounds and other material (including inspection reports, inventories, technical information and photographs) relating to the work of the Committee;

(d) To take action to encourage the care and appreciation of places of worship, churchyards and burial grounds, and the contents of such places, and for that purpose to publicise methods of conservation, repair, construction, adaptation and redevelopment;

(e) To perform such other functions as may be assigned to the Committee by any resolution of the Governing Body or the Diocesan Conference or as the Committee may be requested to perform by the Bishop or Chancellor of the Diocese.

2. The persons referred to in paragraph 1(a) above are:

(a) The Bishop of the diocese

(b) The Chancellor of the diocese

(c) The Archdeacons of the diocese

(d) The Parochial Church Councils in the diocese

(e) Intending petitioners for faculties in the diocese

(f) Persons engaged in the planning, design or building of new places or worship in the diocese, not being places within the jurisdiction of the Diocesan Court.

(g) Such other persons as the Committee may consider appropriate.

(h) The Representative Body of the Church in Wales.

5.16 It will be recalled that the Welsh Church Act, when passed in 1914 abolished the coercive powers of the Church's Courts. This has meant that arrangements for dealing with a breach of the control system and the provisions for reinstatement works have required careful consideration by the Commission on Faculties and the Commission's recommendations on this matter are awaited. It should be noted, however, that the

Representative Body, as owner of the freehold of almost all the churches, together with providing grant and other financial assistance, is in a position to exercise financial sanctions to achieve this end, subject to the approval of the Governing Body.

5.17 With regard to the supervision of work on the 6 cathedrals, the Commission has proposed that a Provincial Commission be established within the jurisdiction of the Provincial Court. This Provincial Commission would oversee the work of local advisory committees which would be constituted with persons having similar expertise to those on the newly constituted Diocesan Advisory Committees.

5.18 The monitoring of works on our churches will be achieved by requiring all works to consecrated buildings being the subject of faculty procedure. The Commission favours the removal of the use of Archdeacons' Certificates in respect of "minor works". The Commission was unable to find a satisfactory definition of a "minor work".

5.19 The Governing Body requires, through the Constitution, the maintenance by each parish of a Log Book, Terrier and Inventory for each church. The binder contains, in addition to an inventory of the contents and details of the fabric, a copy of the quinquennial inspection report prepared by the approved architect, together with the recommended schedule of works for completion during the quinquenium, and copies of the faculties granted or sought in relation thereto. The annual visitation offers a regular opportunity to check upon progress with works during the quinquenium, thus establishing a proactive rather than a reactive role in ensuring the satisfactory maintenance of the fabric of our historic churches.

5.20 The arrangements relating to ecclesiastical exemption and the care of church fabric relate to "living" churches. The Planning (Listed Buildings and Conservation Areas) Act of 1990 provides that ecclesiastical exemption only relates to ecclesiastical buildings which are "for the time being used for ecclesiastical purposes". It follows, therefore, that churches which are closed and/or redundant come under the ordinary secular controls currently incorporated in the four 1990 Acts. This memorandum is primarily concerned with Listed buildings, and those in Conservation Areas, hence the principal reference is to the Planning (Listed Buildings and Conservation Areas) Act 1990. The relationship between the Church and Local Planning Authorities is noted below. The relationship between the Church and State in respect of redundant churches is now considered.

Redundant Churches

5.21 Following the establishment of CADW, discussions took place with the Representative Body in order to try and formulate a policy for the care of redundant churches. Consideration was initially given to the establishment of a separate organisation, similar to the Redundant Churches Fund in England, which was created by statute in 1969. Following a detailed examination of the operation of such a fund, the proposal was rejected because it was considered to be an unnecessarily cumbersome administrative structure, particularly in the light of the Representative Body's ownership of almost all the churches. At that time, an analysis of the 62 redundant or closed churches, revealed that 6 were regarded as "definitely outstanding" and 21 being "possibly outstanding and worthy of preservation". Of the remainder, it was noted that 4 were possibly eligible for preservation if a Conservation Area was established.

The conclusion was reached at that time that the overall scale of the problem was small, and it was proposed that there would be a five year plan with CADW providing an assessment of the architectural/historic merits of buildings, and the Representative Body providing staff to operate the scheme and deal with overheads and insurance. It was further proposed that there would be a 70 per cent–30 per cent split between the Welsh Office and the Representative Body. It was envisaged that the Representative Body would employ two additional members of staff to execute repair and maintenance schemes identified by HBCW and, in addition, to deal with inspections, management, key keeping arrangements, insurance, intermittent use of repaired churches etc. It was understood that the matter was to be taken to the Historic Buildings Council in July of 1986.

5.22 On the 31st July 1987, the Archbishop of Wales received a letter from the Minister of State of the Welsh Office, proposing that the ownership of a number of redundant churches of special architectural or historic interest should be transferred to the Secretary of State and repaired, maintained and managed on his behalf by CADW. Discussions took place with the new Secretary at CADW to consider the new proposals, and it was confirmed that these matters would have to be considered firstly by the Representative Body's General Purposes Committee, and secondly by the Governing Body. Concern was expressed about the Representative Body's trustee position, as owner of the churches, and the need to control future occupation of the churches so that any use would not be inimical to the Governing Body and parish. The Representative Body's General Purposes Committee met in November 1987 and recorded a preference for the transfer of a long leasehold interest to CADW, rather than outright sale, in order that suitable covenants could be imposed. The covenants would, in addition, make provision for the continued use of the surrounding churchyard by the parish.

5.23 Before the fresh proposals could be considered by the Governing Body, a different policy was proposed by CADW. The new proposals favoured the Representative Body retaining the buildings with CADW making substantially enhanced grants for the repair of the fabric. It became clear, at that time, that

CADW recognised that only five churches were suitable for the enhanced grant aid, and it was envisaged that local support groups would be formed which would assume responsibility for the subsequent maintenance of the buildings following restoration.

5.24 The proposals were subsequently put to the Representative Body's newly constituted Property Sub-committee and Churches Group. The Churches Group considered the revised proposals and concluded that even if a maximum grant of 90 per cent were forthcoming for the handful of churches that were singled out, the scheme did not offer a satisfactory solution to the problem. Given that the original reason for redundancy would have been lack of support in perhaps a less favoured or sparsely populated part of the Province, it was doubted whether the support groups could be established let alone sustained. The Committee was understandably concerned about the ongoing maintenance costs and the potential liability of the Representative Body as a prudent trustee. No proposals had been put forward to deal with those redundant churches which were Listed, but not of exceptional quality (which would have been represented by the 21 redundant churches noted in the 1985 scheme). It was envisaged that the Representative Body would have a substantially increased administrative burden.

5.25 The Churches Group and Property Sub-committee considered a discussion paper to formulate counter proposals, whilst the Churches Main Committee was investigating the creation of an independent charitable trust which could acquire and preserve the best of the redundant buildings of denominations other than the Church of England. The proposal originated in the report prepared by Mr Richard Wilding on the operation and financing of the Redundant Churches Fund in England. Mr Wilding's report dealt with this topic under Chapter 10 entitled "Other Christian Denominations" and this specifically related to England and the relationship between English Heritage and the other denominations. He argued that the other denominations differed from the Church of England in at least 3 major respects:—

"(a)   They have far fewer buildings of importance from the heritage point of view;

(b)   With the exception of the Methodists, they have no central organisations which could undertake the handling of new arrangements for their redundant buildings across the country as a whole;

(c)   They have no central source of funds, analogous to the Church Commissioners, from which they could find a central contribution to the cost of running any such new arrangements.

It is also relevant that much of the property in question is held by independent charitable trusts, whose trustees would be in breach of their trust if they failed to sell their redundant buildings or sites to the highest bidder."

5.26 Mr Wilding's enquiries, of the responsible authorities, deduced that they "would not be prepared to devote any of their scarce resources to the preservation of buildings which they no longer needed, and their congregations would not understand if they did".

5.27 He concluded that if any new arrangements were to be set up, English Heritage would be the most appropriate channel for supporting them with public money, and he envisaged that the Department of the Environment (now Department of National Heritage) would undertake to fund, through English Heritage, 70 per cent of the cost of the programme which English Heritage had approved on the basis that the trust would make every effort to raise and could demonstrate good prospects of success in raising, the other 30 per cent from other trusts, foundations and individual contributions. The author acknowledged the difficulties in predicting the demand, but it is understood that progress is being made in England for the establishment of such a trust. The need for more information is clearly necessary.

5.28 The best, and most recent, statistical information was prepared by English Heritage during 1990 and 1991. The report entitled "Buildings at Risk"—a sample survey, was published earlier this year. A sample survey of some 43,000 Listed buildings was undertaken, in different parts of England, to establish the general condition of Listed buildings. It was noted that Listed buildings made up approximately 2 per cent of the building stock, and concluded from the sample that most of England's 500,000 Listed buildings were in reasonable condition.

5.29 The report concluded that occupancy was a major factor in the condition of the building, and analysed the sample into six Risk categories. Categories 1, 2 and 3 were entitled "Extreme Risk", "Grave Risk" and "At Risk" respectively. Of the 43,794 Listed buildings surveyed, 7.3 per cent were found to fall within the Risk categories of 1-3. The report concluded that neglect was a function of condition and occupancy, recording that over 40 per cent of the vacant buildings were in very bad or poor condition. The survey also associated Listing grade with the degree of risk. It concluded that Grade II Listed buildings were the most at risk.

5.30 The report, noting that there were more Listed buildings in rural areas than in urban areas, concluded that there was a higher degree of risk in the less affluent urban areas than in the more affluent rural areas. Over half of all Listed buildings were found to be in Conservation Areas. 77 per cent of all Listed buildings were found to be in Conservation Areas in urban areas, whilst 40 per cent of Listed buildings appeared to be in Conservation Areas in rural areas. Of Listed religious buildings, the report noted that 45 per cent were Listed

Grade I or II* (and for this purpose the old gradings for churches of A, B and C are treated as equivalent to Grades I, II* and II).

5.31 Table 9 of the report analyses the risk categories by original building type, and notes that in England 5 per cent of the sample of religious buildings fell within Risk categories 1-3, 14 per cent fell within Risk category 4 (vulnerable buildings), whilst 81 per cent of the sample were not considered to be at risk. Only domestic buildings provided lower percentages of buildings at risk or vulnerable buildings.

5.32 The deductions which may be drawn from these statistics, as they relate to "living" and redundant churches in Wales, are noted below.

Listing Policy of CADW

5.33 In 1984–85 10,313 buildings were Listed as being of Special Architectural and Historic Interest. The latest recorded figure for 1991–92 is 14,374. An eventual target of 30,000 Listings has been proposed by CADW, although it is recognised that with current staffing levels, such a target could not be achieved for very many years.

5.34 Of perhaps greater importance, when considering the position of places of religious worship, is the objective of re-surveying those buildings that are still Listed as A, B and C in Wales under the old categories. It is noted that under the English Heritage's categories of religious buildings at risk, Grades A, B and C are equated with the new grades of I, II* and II. There is a lack of statistical evidence, but samples taken following re-survey of churches Listed A, B and C have indicated that this equation is not safe, particularly in relation to the Listing of Victorian and later churches.

5.35 More information is being gathered and is required in the light of the findings of the English Heritage Survey.

5.36 The Historic Buildings Council for Wales provides in its 35th Annual Report (1990-91) details for the grants for outstanding secular buildings, buildings in use for worship and also grants for schemes in Conservation Areas (Appendix 6).[1]

5.37 The Historic Buildings Council for Wales also noted in its report, in the context of redundant churches, that it had continued its support for the Friends of Friendless Churches providing grant assistance for the old church of St Baglan near Caernarfon. The Report continues: "the Council noted that the redundant churches problem remained a difficult one and that progress was slow. However, the Council was pleased to note that a report on the workings of the Redundant Churches Fund in England had recommended that a similar mechanism need to be provided for non-Church of England buildings. Unfortunately, the Council noted that as the funds for this initiative were likely to be provided only under the terms of the Historic Buildings and Ancient Monuments Act of 1953 as modified for England by the National Heritage Act of 1983 none but buildings judged to be outstanding could qualify. The Council felt that as it was already able to assist congregations with the maintenance of such buildings, it was debatable whether a mechanism of the sort envisaged would assist in Wales. However, the Council resolved to give this matter careful consideration as details emerged."

5.38 CADW's Annual Report 1991-92 draws attention to its publications, which are largely interpretive and include "A Royal Palace in Wales, Caernarfon"; "St. David's Bishop's Palace"; "A Nation Under Seige".

Education has been identified as an important feature of CADW's work, and the main efforts have been concentrated on meeting the needs of the National Curriculum. The report notes that a range of publications, to aid the education initiatives, is planned to meet the needs of teachers.

5.39 English Heritage, in addition to publishing the interpretive works has also embarked on the publication of a number of excellent books and pamphlets which are of great assistance to owners, architects, surveyors and others responsible for looking after and promoting historic buildings. The "Buildings at Risk Survey" was noted above. This pamphlet may be read for example with "Emergency Repairs for Historic Buildings" by Eleanor Mitchell and the five Volume "Practical Building Conservation" series by John and Nicola Ashurst. The book on "Church Archaeology" by Warwick Rodwell, together with "Visitor's Welcome, A Manual on the Presentation and Interpretation of Archaeological Excavations" are two further publications of considerable importance the contents of which would promote the specific aims of CADW set out in the Mission Statement.

5.40 Mr J D Hogg, the Architectural Assessor for HBCW and others have made considerable personal efforts in guiding and advising Archdeacons, Quinquennial Inspecting Architects and others involved in the maintenance of the Church in Wales Historic Churches.

[1]Not printed.

CHURCH AND LOCAL AUTHORITIES

6.01 As a result of ecclesiastical exemption the principal point of contact between the Church and local planning authorities is in respect of closed and redundant churches.

6.02 CADW acknowledges the "carrot" and "stick" nature of its relationship with owners and occupiers of historic buildings. Local authorities largely rely on the stick following the provisions laid down in the Planning (Listed Buildings and Conservation Areas) Act 1990, and applied through their Planning Departments.

6.03 The conclusions drawn from the English Heritage "Buildings at Risk Survey" highlight the greatest danger to our historic buildings in the group that are unoccupied, are Grade II (and thus not outstanding); lie within less affluent urban areas and those which are least capable of reuse. Many redundant churches fall within these categories. In addition to exclusive fenestration, high naves and even taller towers and spires, the existence of a full or well-filled burial ground (with burials often adjacent to the walls of the church) can frequently prevent economical re-use.

6.04 In addition to following the legislation contained in the Planning (Listed Buildings and Conservation Areas) Act 1990, local authorities will be guided by the current Welsh Office Circular: 61/81 "Historic Buildings and Conservation Areas—Policy and Procedure."

6.05 The current Welsh Office circular contains 125 sections. The current DOE circular (8/87) contains 154 sections. Both have seven appendices. Space and time do not permit a detailed comparison of the two circulars but it is important to note certain omissions or variations from the Welsh Office circular 61/81 in relation to the DOE circular 8/87. Notable are the following passages from Introduction to the DOE circular which are absent from the Welsh Office circular:

> (4)...... "there are many cases where it is right to "conserve as found". But there are circumstances too where our architectural heritage has to be able to accommodate not only changes of use but also new building nearby......"

> (5)......"it is extremely important that public support for conservation policies should be retained. As more buildings are Listed and conservation areas designated, more people are likely to become involved with Listed Building controls. Their experience of this control will doubtless colour their view of conservation......"

Section 13 provides the general duties of English Heritage. These are absent from the Welsh Office circular (CADW not having been created in 1981).

Section 103 of the DOE's circular embraces the Skelmersdale announcement on the future of ecclesiastical exemption which succeeded the Welsh Office circular. (Neither document deals with the latest proposals for the Code of Practice in respect of ecclasiastical exemption.)

6.06 Under the heading "New Uses for Old Buildings" sections 61—66 (of 61/81) carry many of the most important policy aspects of the document. in the context of churches which are not subject to ecclesiastical exemption. There are subtle differences between the two circulars. For example, section 61 urges local authorities "to use all the powers available to them and to combine the service of notices under sections 101 and 115 of the 1971 Act with an urgent search to help owners find ways of keeping their buildings in economic use and thus in repair". In section 19 of the DOE circular "local authorities are asked to help owners find ways of keeping their buildings in economic use and thus in repair".

Section 62 makes the fundamental point "the best use for an historic building is the use for which it was designed and where ever possible this use should continue. Where this is not possible authorities are requested to find a use which will preserve the architectural and historic features of the building."

Section 63 acknowledges that the greatest problems arise when large buildings become vacant and continues: "Redundant churches pose a sensitive problem as there are many people who sincerely believe that a once consecrated building should not be used for other purposes which they regard as incompatible with years of worship. Nevertheless unless funds are available to retain the building as a museum piece, the only way of keeping it in repair is to use it and there will be occasions when an appropriate alternative use must be accepted in order to preserve both the building itself and it's contribution to the character and appearance of the area".

Section 65 encourages local authorities to be flexible in dealing with applications for changes of use and recommends that "they should, where ever possible, make a survey of such building in their area and make a provisional assessment of the types of new uses which they would be prepared to accept. . . . . . With this information available, authorities should be able to respond more quickly when applications for a change of use are submitted."

Section 60 of the Welsh Office circular notes that "there should normally be evidence that the freehold of the building has been offered for sale on the open market. There would need to be exceptional reasons to justify the offer of a lease for the imposition of restrictive covenants which would unreasonably limit the chances of finding a new use for the building." To preserve the sanctity of a surrounding burial ground, or indeed a crypt below a redundant church, the offering of the freehold on the open market proves unsatisfactory and the use of a lease is generally the only safe way in which effective convenants against unsuitable user can be employed.

6.07 In a memorandum submitted by the Department of the Environment to the House of Commons Environment Committee (H.C. 146-IIp13; Session 1986–87) the writer noted "public tastes reflected a growing awareness of the value of Victorian and early 20th Century buildings, and an appreciation of the contribution which individual buildings might make when sited attractively together". In 1988 the Secretary of State announced the use of a rolling 30 year rule in England and a competition was held to identify the best 50 candidates for listing from the period 1939-1958. There has been substantial movement in the approach to conservation and listing since Welsh Office circular 61/81 was prepared.

6.08 Consideration of a number of aspects of the Planning (Listed Buildings and Conservation Areas) Act of 1990 may help in achieving a better understanding of the present problems. For the purposes of this memorandum the assumption is made that ecclesiastical exemption is retained with the adoption of the proposed Code of Practice by the Church in Wales and thus the relationship between the Church and local authorities is examined, when ecclesiastical exemption ceases consequent upon the church being no longer in ecclesiastical use.

6.09 Section 6 of the Act enable the owner or prospective developer to secure an immediate decision on listing of a building or a guarantee against listing for the subsequent five years. This section is of particular importance when dealing with redundant churches but its value is severely restricted by the condition:

where—

(a) Application has been made for planning permission for any development involving the alteration, extension or demolition of a building; or

(b) Any such planning permission has been granted.

6.10 Section 32 of the Act provides for the service of a Listed Building Purchase Notice on the District Council. This procedure, of necessity requires the owner of the building to have received a refusal (or a conditional grant) of Listed Building Consent and the building has become incapable of reasonably beneficial use. This is a cumbersome and time-consuming procedure both in securing the initial decision and in obtaining the response of the local planning authority/District Council. In an area where vacant property is subject to vandalism, or the owner's insurers are not prepared to continue to provide public liability cover, this can allow rapid deterioration and severe risks for the owner respectively. The Act provides for the acquisition of Listed Buildings by agreement under section 52 by the County or District Council. There is considerable reluctance by such Councils to use this procedure in the case of redundant churches.

6.11 The Act enables the compulsory acquisition of listed buildings in need of repair providing a Repairs Notice is served as a preliminary to acquisition under section 47. Section 50 envisages a punitive effect in reducing compensation entitlement to the minmum where a listed building "has been deliberately allowed to fall into dis-repair for the purpose of justifying its demolition and the development or redevelopment of the site or any adjoining site". This can be a valuable sanction where the listed building has appreciable residual or commercial value but in the case of redundant churches, particularly with surrounding burial grounds there can be frequently be a negative value attaching to the building. Section 54 enables the local authority to carry out works urgently necessary for the preservation of an unoccupied listed building. Under section 55 of the local authority and the Secretary of State for Wales is enabled to recover expenses for works carried out under section 54.

6.12 The "carrot" is provided under section 57 where the local authority is empowered to contribute to preservation of Listed Buildings by grant or loan. Whilst a limited number of grants are provided by local authorities towards the expenses of the repair or maintenance of Listed churches which are in use, the provision of grants to a similar building which is redundant is extremely rare. It should be remembered that in 1942 and 1947 some £3.5 million was transferred by the Welsh Church Commissioners mostly to the County and County Borough Councils and the remainder, just under £1 million expressed in real terms today after over 45 years would be in the region of £47 million. An 8 per cent return on such a sum would amount to £3.76 million per annum. (The Nationwide Building Society House Price Index reveals an adjusted increase, over the same period, to £95 million.)

6.13 Section 60 deals with the current exceptions for ecclesiastical buildings which are in use for ecclesiastical purposes or are redundant. If ecclesiastical exemption were to be removed the administrative cost of dealing with all the specialised Listed Building Consent applications, relating to individual churches, would fall on the local planning authority.

6.14 The designation of conservation areas is set out under section 69. The designation of an area takes effect from the date of the appropriate resolution of the authority, but there is no requirement to notify owners and occupiers of premises in the area (although the owners criminal liability under sections 9 and 74 of the Act begins at the date of designation). Whilst the notice of designation may be seen in the local newspaper in the area of the local planning authority, for an owner such as the Representative Body the absence of notification of the establishment of conservation areas in the principality creates considerable administrative difficulties.

6.15 Whilst Welsh Office circular 61-81 is over 10 years old, The 1990 Act, the Planning Policy Guidance Note on Archaeology and Planning (PPG 16 (Wales)) was published in November 1991 and the Representative Body was consulted and made representations prior to its formulation.

Welsh Church Fund

6.16 There are varying approaches by local authorities to the payment of grants for the repair and maintenance of churches. For example, Gwent Councy Council, on 29th December 1989 advised the Monmouth Diocesan Board of Finance that its Welsh Church Fund Working Group had resolved that a grant of £5,000 would be paid to the Diocesan Board for that financial year. It further notified the diocese that with effect from April 1990 there would not an an annual grant to the Diocese but applications for assistance would be considered from individual churches. Other authorities have simply made grants direct to individual Parishes without involving the Diocese.

6.17 The Representative Body, anxious to establish a redundant churches policy, wrote to both the Assembly of Welsh Counties and the Association of District Councils in Wales offering to discuss the problems on a provincial basis to assist in the formulation of appropriate policies in Local and Structure plans. No response of substance has been received from either Body. The urgency of the situation however has been recognised by the Pembrokeshire Coast National Park Department of Dyfed County Council which has commissioned a redundant church study covering the churches and chapels in their region. The consultants who have been appointed are the Alex Gordon Partnership, Chartered Architects of 13 Guild Hall Square, Carmarthen and their final report is due to be delivered by 29 January 1993. The Church in Wales has already been contacted by the consultants and views have been provided in relation to its churches.

CHURCHES AND OTHER INTERESTED PARTIES

The Amenity Societies

7.01 The National Amenity Societies comprise the Ancient Monument Society, the Council for British Archaeology, the Georgian Group, the Society for the Protection of Ancient Buildings and the Victorian Society. Under Schedule 1 of the Care of Churches and Ecclesiastical Jurisdiction Measure of 1991 one of the Members to be appointed, by the Bishops Council, to the Diocesan Advisory Committee, arises following consultation with the National Amenity Societies. The Commission on Faculties appointed by the Governing Body of the Church in Wales has recommended a similar provision in respect of the Diocesan Advisory Committee in Wales, the appointment arising from the Diocesan Conference. Whilst the advice of the Amenity Societies has been valued by the Church over a number of years (in particular the advisory leaflets prepared for example by the Georgian Group and SPAB) concern has been voiced in the Dioceses and at the Governing Body about the influence exercised by the Amenity Societies. The concerns can be summarised in this way. Whilst there is a Joint Committee embracing the 5 Societies (and the Civic Trust) there is a perception of unbalanced promotion of sectional interests, which might be exacerbated by the addition of other societies. The absence of a grant giving function for repair and maintenance by the 5 Amenity Societies does not encourage a broad based selectivity of the most worthy buildings for conservation. Whether these perceptions are or are not correct is secondary, when viewed against the advice contained in DOE circular 8/87 section 5 "it is extremely important that public support for conservation policy should be retained. As more buildings are listed and conservation areas designated more people are likely to become involved with listed building control. Their experience of this control will doubless colour their view of conservation".

7.02 There is misunderstanding on both sides of this debate and it is to be hoped that better information, flowing from the revised DAC membership, will remove a number of these misunderstandings.

Friends of Friendless Churches

7.03 The Friends of Friendless Churches under the tireless guidance of the Honorary Director Mr Ivor Bulmer-Thomas has, in the absence of a Redundant Churches Fund in Wales, provided invaluable support to the Representative Body by taking over control of a number of redundant churches. With generous financial support from CADW the Friends have secured the future of such buildings as St Mary's, Llanfair Kilgeddin and St Baglan's, Llanfaglan. Resources are stretched and the demands for assistance pressing.

Tai Cymru—Housing Associations

7.04 It has been frequently stated that the key to the preservation of a redundant Listed building is to find a suitable alternative use. It is recognised that the unusual form of construction and fenestration of ecclesiastical buildings renders them difficult and costly to convert if the external features, which are often the most prominent aspects in the land or townscape, are to be preserved. The number of Listed redundant churches in commercial areas in the principality is limited and thus, most frequently, it is not an alternative commerical use that is sought but a residential one. Against a background of increasing homelessness and the wish of the Governing Body to see redundant churches use for socially beneficial purposes, it would be particularly desirable to encourage the conversion of a number of redundant churches for residential use. The very sharp decline in Local Authority expenditure in providing new residential accommodation may have been arrested by recent policy changes, however it is understood that the policy of Tai Cymru and, perforce the Housing Associations, is to pursue large scale new build projects, benefiting from perceived economies of scale. In addition, the policy of reducing the number of Housing Associations for the sake of administrative and other perceived efficiencies militates against the smaller Associations which, with the aid of skilful and ingenious architectural advice, could achieve the small scale conversions. Such redundant church conversions would perhaps be at higher unit cost but this should be examined on the broader measurement of preservation of the built heritage and the creation of residential user in such a location. The mutual benefits for Church and society are obvious and would greatly assist the "grieving process" inevitable in any parish which felt unable to maintain its church any longer.

Local Conservation Groups

7.05 Discussions have taken place between the Representative Body and a number of local conservation groups to try and secure the futures of several redundant churches. Following initial enthusiasm the promoters have frequently become discouraged when faced with a long or medium term commitment to repair and maintain a redundant church under a lease (whether or not financial assistance is available from CADW or other sources). Some trusts have been set up successfully and have been responsible for saving such churches as St Mary's, Warren, in St David's Diocese.

The Church in Wales Internal Arrangements and Miscellaneous Items

8.01 Welsh Office Circular 61/81 paragraph 62 states "The best use for an historic building is the use for which it was designed and wherever possible this use should continue". The less adaptable the building the more important this statement. The Church in Wales has a parochial system which covers the whole of the Principality and the churches in use average 2.65 per benefice and one for every 28.4 members of a congregation (or one for every 71 Easter communicants). Some benefices incorporate as many as six churches in the care of one Incumbent. Many benefices have more than one Listed church as the responsibility of that Incumbent. Many Incumbents have expressed the view that far too much of their time is taken up with the maintenance of buildings and filling in forms for grant assistance Faculty Applications, etc. Other Incumbents depute these tasks to skilled members of their congregation although it has to be pointed out that such skilled professional help is not often not available in the most hard-pressed parishes where there is a Listed church and the demand for professional help is most required. Many priests feel that there is a lack of understanding of the need to concentrate their limited time on the task for which they were ordained, namely the spiritual support and guidance of their parish.

8.02 It was felt important to question Deaneries to establish views on the number of buildings contained in individual parishes. Of the 35 Deaneries that responded, 28 said that they had too many buildings. Some responses thought that the problem was not just one of excess: "The buildings concerned are frequently in the wrong place, unsuitable for modern use and expensive to maintain and run". There is no question that generally, Deaneries feel that an enormous amount of clergy and lay resources are devoted to the maintenance of unnecessary and/or unsuitable buildings and this is a major impediment to the work of the Church both in the parish and the wider context".

8.03 A recent report "The Church in the Welsh Countryside" prepared by the Church in Wales' Board of Mission in 1992 comments:—"In most of rural Wales, Parochial Church Councils devote an extraordinary amount of their time to considering matters relating to the buildings in their care. Large sums of money which could be better spent on the work of the Church, are collected by a variety of means to maintain the buildings, though not always up to an acceptable standard. Great pride is felt in undertaking such work and clerics who are successful at it are very popular, but it might be that such pride is misplaced. With changing economic and social circumstances, there is considerable uncertainty as to whether sufficient finances to support buildings will be forthcoming in the future. Certainly the dire situation of hill farmers, who had an average income of £144 a week in 1992, just £4 above the Child Poverty Action Group's definition of poverty, would suggest that the Church should be helping them rather than the other way around".

8.04 The Representative Body shares with CADW the view, that further and better particulars of the likely pattern of redundancy across the province is the key to devising a successful redundant churches policy. Not only has it proved very difficult to forecast the numbers of churches that are likely to become redundant but more difficult still to determine whether the church to be declared redundant, is likely to be listed or lie in a conservation area and hence be a prime candidate for a new redundancy scheme.

8.05 The current redundant churches procedure visualises the parish being responsible for initiating the petition for redundancy to the Bishop and Diocesan Churches Committee responding to that request. Other anglican provinces have considered fundamental restructuring of benefices to substantially reduce the number of churches in use. A provincial initiative to this end, rather than a parochial or diocesan initiative, in one province led to serious pastoral breakdown and the scheme was abandoned. The indications are that the parish and/or diocese must formulate the policy on the basis of local need, financial constraints, stewardship provision, etc.

8.06 The needs of the parish and the diocese, to create the most effective ministry, may therefore be at odds with the wish of the State and Local Authority to see a Listed church building continue in ecclesiastical use, thereby avoiding the creation of another burden on the redundant church machinery that evolves from the current discussions.

8.07 More work in this area is required principally at Diocesan and Deanery levels. It should be added that if there were a choice in the redundancy of a number of churches, the retention of the Listed church with the surrounding burial ground, in ecclesiastical use would be of great help. The Representative Body acting as a prudent trustee would find it much simpler to dispose of an unlisted redundant church building (especially if it had no surrounding burial ground), whilst the resultant proceeds would then be available for use in accordance with the provisions in the Constitution (as amended). Furthermore, the redundant church that was Listed would not become another burden for the new redundant churches machinery.

8.08 Against a background of falling income for the Representative Body, greater demands are going to be made on individual parishes towards the maintenance of the ministry and other needs. The Constitution currently requires the parish to undertake repairs to the church and to insure the church. With the greater demands on quota, without increased giving, there will be reduced funds available for the maintenance of the fabric and insurance at a time when the demands of the faculty system require the highest possible standards (implying greater cost) and when insurance costs are rising at a disproportionately fast rate above the index or retail prices.

8.09 A circular has recently been sent out to all Church in Wales parishes seeking detailed information on the insurance of the churches to ensure that adequate insurance cover is provided, particularly in relation to Listed buildings and those in 61/81, often creates conflict with the parish and the parish is frequently supported, for the best pastoral reasons, by the Diocese.

8.11 Section 63 of Welsh Office Circular 61/81 recognises the problem when it says "Redundant churches pose a sensitive problem as there are many people who sincerely believe that once consecrated a building should not be used for other purposes which they regard as incompatible with years of worship".

APPENDIX 1

CADW: WELSH HISTORIC MONUMENTS

A GUIDE TO LEGISLATION ON THE LISTING OF HISTORIC BUILDINGS

Listing

The Secretary of State for Wales is required to compile lists of buildings of special architectural or historic interest. The administration of both local and national conservation policies is based on these lists, which are constantly under revision.

The first survey of historic buildings in Wales was carried out in the 1950s and early 1960s as a result which statutory lists were provided for all local authority areas. Following a revision of the criteria followed in choosing these buildings in 1970, a resurvey was begun and a number of revised lists issued. Since 1984, and following further revisions of the criteria, the resurvey in Wales has been carried out on a more intensive basis. Revised lists issued after 1984 show changes in style to previous lists.

How The Buildings Are Chosen

The principles of selection for these lists were orginally drawn up by an expert committee of architects, antiquaries, and historians, and are still followed although they are revised from time to time. All buildings built before 1700 which survive in anything like their original condition qualify for listing as do most buildings of between 1700 and 1840. Between 1840 and 1914 only buildings of definite quality and character qualify and the selection is designed to include the principal works of the principal architects. Selected buildings built after 1914 may also be listed. In choosing buildings, particular attention is paid to:

Special value within certain types, either for architectural or planning reasons or as illustrating social and economic history (for instance, industrial buildings, railway stations, schools, hospitals, theatres, town halls, markets, exchanges, alms houses, prisons, lockups, mills).

Technological innovation or virtuosity (for instance, cast iron, pre-fabrication, or the early use of concrete).

Association with well-known characters or events.

Group value, especially as examples of town planning (for instance, squares, terraces or model villages).

A survey is carried out by CADW's Inspectors of Historic Buildings, for each local authority area, and buildings are classified in grades to show their relative importance.

> Grade I These are buildings of exceptional interest (less than 5 per cent of the listed buildings so far are in this grade).

> Grade II* These are particularly important buildings of more than special interest.

> Grade II These are buildings of special interest, which warrent every effort being made to preserve them.

> (Note. There was previously a Grade III status which did not form part of the statutory list. Many of the buildings which were shown as Grade III when the lists were first compiled, are now considered to be of special interest by modern standards—particularly where they possess "group value". These buildings are therefore being added to the statutory lists as these are revised).

Listed Buildings and Ancient Monuments

"Listed buildings" are described in these notes as buildings listed by the Secretary of State for Wales as being of special architectural or historic insterest. They are, usually inhabited buildings, but any object or structure (eg bridges, lighthouse, lamp stands etc) may be listed.

"Scheduled ancient monuments" are buildings of other structures scheduled under The Ancient Monuments and Archaeological Areas Act 1979. They are usually unoccupied and often in ruinous condition. In any case where a listed building is also a scheduled monument and provisions of the Ancient Monuments legislation superseded those of the Planning (Listed Buildings and Conservation Areas) Act.

The Statutory List

Before 1974 it had been the practice to issue two separate types of list—a provisional list containing details of grades and descriptions of buildings and a staututory list containing only the addresses of the buildings. Local authority areas are now being resurveyed by CADW's Inspectors of Historic Buildings, and their reports are used as a basis for producing revised statutory lists in new form. Details of gradings and descriptive notes are now included in one cumulative statutory list for each local authority area. All the buildings included in the statutory list are legally subject to the provisions described in this pamphlet.

Building Preservation Notices

To protect buildings which are of special interest but which have not yet been listed District Councils and National Park Authorities have been given power to serve emergency Building Preservation Notices.

A building subject to one of these notices is protected by the same provisions as a building which has been listed. The notice is effective for a maximum of six months, unless within that period the Secretary of State lists the buildings or decides that it should not be listed.

"Spot" Listing

It is also open to anyone to bring to CADW's attention individual buildings which are threatened by unsympathetic alteration or demolition. In urgent cases, these buildings will be assessed, and (if they qualify) added to the statutory list. This emergency procedure is known as "spot" listing.

Certificate of Immunity Against Listing

The addition of a building to the statutory list at a late stage in the preparation of proposals for its alteration or demolition can cause delay and even abandonment of a redevelopment scheme as well as other difficulties and hardships. Most developers would prefer to know the listing position at the earliest possible stage. Provided, therefore, that planning permission is being sought or has been granted any person may now apply to the Secretary of State for a certificate stating that it is not intended to list the building shown in the application plans. If the certificate is granted the building cannot be listed or be the subject of a Building Preservation Notice for a period of five years. Where the building in question is assessed as being of special architectural or historic interest however, it is listed, and no certificate is issued.

Where To See The Lists

You can inspect the statutory lists at:

> CADW: Welsh Historic Monuments,
> Brunel House,
> 2 Fitzlan Road,
> Cardiff
> CF2 1UY

or at the office of the relevant county council, district council or national park authority.

PROTECTION OF BUILDINGS OF SPECIAL ARCHITECTURAL OR HISTORIC INTEREST

Listed Building Consent

The fact that a building is listed as of special architectural or historic interest does not mean that it will be preserved intact in all circumstances, but it does mean that demolition must not be allowed unless the case for it has been fully examined, and that proposed alterations or extensions must preserve the character of the building as far as possible. Anyone who wants to demolish a listed building, or to alter or extend one in any way that affects its character, must obtain listed building consent from, in the first instance the local planning authority. The procedure is similar to that for obtaining planning permission. (Details can be obtained from the planning Department of any county or district council, or national park authority).

It is an offence to demolish, alter or extend a listed building without listed building consent and the penalty can be a fine or imprisonment, or both.

Listed Building Consent and Planning Permission

Anyone wishing to redevelop a site on which a listed building stands, will need both listed building consent for the demolition and planning permission for the new building. Planning permission alone is not sufficient to authorise the demolition. Anyone wishing to alter or extend a listed building in a way which would affect its character, and whose proposed alteration amounts to development for which specific planning permission is required (as distinct from a general permission given by the General Development Order), will also need the express authorisation of planning permission as well as listed building consent.

Appeals

If an application for listed building consent is refused by the local planning authority, or granted subject to conditions, the applicants has right of appeal to the Secretary of State.

On receipt of an appeal the Secretary of State will normally hold a public local inquiry if either the applicant or the local planning authority ask him to do so. The procedure for appealing is virtually identical with the procedure for appealing against a refusal of planning permission, although the grounds of appeal which may be included are different.

Notification and Publicity

The Secretary of State must be notified by the local planning authority before they give listed building consent in most cases, and they must send him full details of the application and of the reasons why they propose to grant consent. Details of the application must be advertised locally, so that the Amenity Societies and other members of the public have an opportunity to comment. Any comments which they make must be forwarded to the Secretary of State, who will then consider whether the decision should be left to the local authority, or whether the importance of the building, and nature of views expressed, or any other circumstances warrant his "calling in" the application for his own decision.

When the Secretary of State "calls in" an application, he will arrange a public inquiry if either the applicant or the local planning authority asks for one. The Secretary of State can also direct that an inquiry will be held.

Recording of Buildings to be Demolished

If you are granted listed building consent to demolish a building you must not do so until the Royal Commission on Ancient and Historical Monuments in Wales has been given an opportunity to make a record of it. So if you propose to demolish a listed building you should tell the Royal Commission at Crown Buildings, Plas Crug, Queen's Road, Aberystwyth, Dyfed SY23 2HB, either before or immediately after you get listed building consent.

You can get a form for this purpose from the local planning authority. You must then wait for a least a month (the period runs from one to two dates—the date on which the listed building consent is given or the date on which the Royal Commission is notified, whichever is the later). During that time you must allow the

Royal Commission reasonable access to the building. If the Royal Commission completes its record of the building within one month, or states that it does not with to record it, you can then demolish the building at once, providing all other necessary consents or permission have been obtained.

Repairs

If a local authority consider that a listed building is not being properly preserved, they may serve on the owner a "repairs notice" under section 48 of the Planning (Listed Buildings and Conservation Areas) Act 1990. This notice must specify the works which the authority consider reasonably necessary for the proper preservation of the building and explain that if it is not complied with within two months, the local authority may be entitled to buy it compulsorily (with the Secretary of State's consent). If the owner deliberately neglects the building in order to redevelop the site, the local authority may not only acquire the building, but may do so at a price which excludes the value of the site for redevelopment.

If the building is unoccupied, the authority can, after giving seven days notice to the Owner, carry out as a matter of urgency, any necessary repair works and then recover the cost from the owner. Both of these powers may be exercised by the Secretary of State in exceptional cases.

Owners of listed buildings can, in some cases, get grants or loans to help them with repair or maintenance.

Conservation Areas

Whole areas of architectural or historic interest are also protected. The Planning (Listed Buildings and Conservation Areas) Act 1990 requires local planning authorities to designate "Conservation Areas". These are "areas of special architectrual or historic interest, the character or appearance of which it is desirable to preserve or enhance".

The local planning authorities and the Secretary of State must pay special attention to the character or appearance of these areas when exercising their powers of planning control.

Applications for permission to carry out development that would affect the character of these areas must be advertised, and the view expressed by the public must be taken into account by the planning authority before they decide the application.

The Town and County Amenities Act 1974 (now the Planning (Listed Buildings and Conservation Areas) Act 1990 sections 71-73) extended the powers of local authorities in relation to conservation areas (and also the preservation of historic buildings). In particular, no unlisted buildings situated in a conservation area may now be demolished without the consent of the Local Planning authority of the Secretary of State.

Grants and Loans

Grants (which in this section can be taken to include loans) are available in certain circumstances both from central government funds and from local authorities. They are always at the discretion of the body giving them; listing does not give any automatic entitlement to a grant.

Grants to Outstanding Secular Buildings

Repair grants are available for buildings of "outstanding architectural or historic interest". Grants are made towards works such as re-roofing, dry rot and other structural repairs, but not towards decoration or works of regular maintenance. Owners have to show that they would not be able to complete the work without financial help. Applications should be made to CADW, Historic Buildings Branch, Brunel House, 2 Fitzalan Road, Cardiff CF2 1UY.

Grants to Places of Worship in Use

Grants are also available to churches and other religious buildings which are of outstanding interest. Grants are made in the same way as repair grant for secular buildings and the same criteria for selection are applied. Applications should be made direct to CADW at the address above. Applicants for Church in Wales buildings should send a copy of the application to the Representation Body of the Church in Wales.

Conservation Area Grants

Conservation Area grants are available for buildings in a conservation area and are made for works which will make a "significant contribution to the preservation or enhancement of the character or appearance of a conservation area". Applications should be made to CADW.

Local Authority Grants

Local authorities may also make grants to building of architectural or historic interest but are not restricted to outstanding buildings or even to listed buildings. Grants may be made by county and district councils and enquiries should be addressed to the appropriate local authority.

Churches

Many Churches are of special architectural or historic interest, and are listed as such. But so long as they are used for ecclesiastical purposes they remain generally outside the scope of the provisions described in this pamphlet (one particular exception to this are those relating to grants and loans). Listed building consent is not required, for instance, for works to a listed ecclesiastical building which is remaining in ecclesiastical use. However, listed building consent is required for the total demolition of a listed ecclesiastical building or for the total demolition of an unlisted-ecclesiastical building in a conservation area, (except where the building is a redundant Church of the Church of England, and the demolition is in pursuance of a pastoral or redundancy scheme made under the Pastoral Measures 1968).

LIST OF STATUTES

The relevant Act of Parliament is the:

Planning (Listed Buildings and Conservation Areas) Act 1990

APPENDIX 2

GRANT AID FOR HISTORIC BUILDINGS

This leaflet describes the grants available from the Secretary of State for Wales for the repair of historic buildings and buildings within conservation areas. The Secretary of State's responsibilities in this respect are administered by Cadw (Welsh Historic Monuments) which is the historic buildings and ancient monuments division of the Welsh Office. All applications for grant are considered by the Historic Buildings Council for Wales which will make a recommendation to the Secretary of State. The Council is an independent statutory body of experts appointed by the Secretary of State for Wales.

THE GRANTS AVAILABLE

There are two schemes:

i. Grants to Outstanding Buildings†

Grant is made towards the cost of internal or external repairs to buildings of outstanding architectural or historic interest. (Works of routine maintenance, improvement or alteration are not normally eligible for grant.)

The qualifying standards are very high and only the most important buildings are usually successful. The fact that a building has been listed does not mean that it will necessarily be awarded a grant. As a general rule, most grade I and II* listed properties reach the required standard but some grade II, and even unlisted, properties may also qualify.

ii. Grants to Buildings in Conservation Areas††

Grant is available for works which are judged to make a significant contribution to the preservation or enhancement of the character or appearance of a designated conservation area. Works of routine maintenance such as painting or minor repairs would be unlikely to qualify for grant aid. Your local authority will be able to let you know whether your property lies within a conservation area.

†Section 4 of the Historic Buildings and Ancient Monuments Act 1953

†† Section 77 of the Planning (Listed Buildings and Conservation Areas) Act 1990

THE HANDLING OF THE APPLICATIONS

A completed application form and the necessary supporting information should be sent to Cadw at the address shown at the foot of this leaflet and applicants may wish to submit their applications by recorded delivery. All applications will be acknowledged on receipt and applicants are advised to contact Cadw if they are not notified within two weeks of submitting the application. The application form contains further advice about the material necessary to accompany the application. Once an application has been received, an architect from Cadw will inspect the property and complete a report on the architectural merit of the building, the works to be done and their estimated cost. Any historical associations will also be identified. The application will be considered at the next available meeting of the Council (which usually meets five times a year). The Council will take into account such factors as the importance of the building, urgency of the work and the financial contribution which the applicant might make. A decision is usually announced within six weeks of the Council meeting. Details of all grant offers may be publicised in advance of an applicant's acceptance or rejection of the offer.

GRANT CONDITIONS

These may vary depending upon the building involved and the particular works proposed, but generally conditions will be imposed to secure:—

— that where appropriate, listed building consent is obtained before grant may be paid;

— that work is not started until the application has been accepted or written permission to do so has been obtained;

— that an architect is employed to supervise the approved works, which must start within 3 months of the date of offer of grant. Any further delay may result in grant being withheld;

— final claims should be submitted not later than nine months after completion of the eligible works;

— that no variation of the approved work will be carried out without CADW's prior permission;

— that the property is kept at all times in good state of repair and is adequately maintained and insured;

— that in relation to outstanding buildings, members of the public are allowed access to the property and that the owner publicises access arrangements;

— that if requested by the Secretary of State the whole or part of the grant will be repaid if the property is sold within ten years from the date of the offer of grant.

GRANTS AND LISTED BUILDING CONSENT

Although the proposed works may be accepted for grant by the Secretary of State this does not remove the need for listed building consent if the works affect the character of the property. (Works of alteration, extension or demolition normally require listed building consent.) It is essential therefore that the local planning authority be consulted on the need for such consent as early as possible. Planning permission may also be necessary in appropriate cases. Where such consents are needed, and to avoid unnecessary delay, these should be obtained before an application for grant is submitted.

RATES OF GRANT

Grant is discretionary and there are no fixed rates. The Historic Buildings Council will consider each application separately and recommend an appropriate level of grant.

Grant is offered as a percentage of approved costs. If the actual costs turn out to be less than the amount approved, the grant will remain at the same percentage, calculated on the actual costs. There is no entitlement to grant in excess of the amount offered, but consideration may be given to a request for an increase in grant where costs have subsequently risen. Advice on the likely percentage of grant can be obtained from CADW.

GRANT PAYMENT

Grant will be paid when the works have been completed to CADW's satisfaction. A proportion of grant (normally 10 per cent) will be retained until a final inspection has been made. Interim payments may be made if supported by an architect's certificate confirming that a proportion of the works has been completed to the agreed specification or on submission of a contractor's receipted invoices if an architect has not been employed.

For further information please write to:

CADW: Welsh Historic Monuments,

Historic Buildings Administration,

Brunel House,
2 Fitzalan Road,

Cardiff CF2 1UY

or Telephone (0222) 465511

CADW: Welsh Historic Monuments

November 1990

APPENDIX 3

NOTES

Conditions

i. that an architect/professional adviser is employed to prepare drawings in sufficient detail to illustrate the scheme, to prepare a specification and to supervise the work in progress;

ii. that the works are carried out in full in accordance with a specification, which should be approved by our Architect before work commences (the enclosed note details the works eligible for grant aid which are considered necessary by our Architect, and for which this grant is offered) and that no other works are carried out without our approval;

iii. that this offer is accepted within one month and that work should begin within three months of the date of this letter, unless otherwise agreed by us and that the date of the commencement of work is notified to this office;

iv. that our Architect will have the right to inspect the work in progress and after completion, and that the work is carried out to his satisfaction;

v. that should you receive any other offer of grants or subsidies towards the cost of the works, either from central or local government, or from any other source, you will notify this office immediately;

vi. that the property is maintained in a reasonable state of repair; and that no future major works of repair which may affect the character of the building (eg, re-roofing with different material), alteration, conversion, addition or improvement will be carried out without prior approval from this office;

vii. that the property is adequately insured so that its repair and restoration after fire or other damage will be practicable by means of that insurance. The property must be so insured whilst the grant eligible works are in progress, and you should forward evidence of insurance when accepting the grant offer. Please note also that you are obliged to maintain such adequate insurance for five full financial years (a financial year runs from April to March) after the financial year in which the works are completed. This will be the subject of a random check, and you may be called upon to provide evidence of insurance at any time within the five year period.

viii. that the property is adequately insured so that repair and restoration after fire or other damage will be practicable;

ix. that outside normal church hours reasonable access is permitted to members of the public on request (if necessary accompanied by an officer of the church or member of the congregation) and that notice of these arrangements is displayed in the porch or nearby.

x. that in the event of the sale of the property within a period of 10 years from the date grant is offered, the owner shall immediately notify the Secretary of State.

xi. that this office is notified of any unforeseen increase in costs.

Explanatory Notes

A. If any of the above conditions is contravened or not complied with the Secretary of State may at any time recover from you the whole of the grant or such part of it as he thinks fit (in accordance with section 4A of the 1953 Act, as enacted by the Ancient Monuments and Archaeological Areas Act 1979).

B. Under the provisions of section 4A, the Secretary of State may also recover the whole or part of the grant if, during the period of 10 years beginning with the day on which the grant is made, you dispose of the property, or of any part of it, by way of sale, exchange or lease for a term of 21 years or more.

C. Should you wish to make a gift of the property, directly or indirectly (but otherwise than by will), you should bear in mind that under the provisions of section 4A, the Secretary of State may recover the whole or part of the grant:

    (i) from you, if you make a gift of your interest in part of the property and the recipient disposes of that interest or of any part of it by way of sale, exchange or lease for a term of 21 years or more within the 10 year period specified in Paragraph B; or

    (ii) from the recipient, if you make a gift of the whole of your interest in the property and the recipient disposes of that interest or of any part of it by way of sale, exchange or lease for a term of 21 years or more within the 10 year period in Paragraph B.

D. If you decide to accept this offer, payment of grant can be made either by way of a lump sum on completion of the work, or by instalments as the work proceeds. In either case, it will be necessary to submit architects' certificates, receipted accounts or invoices, fee statements, etc, or some other acceptable form of evidence of expenditure requesting payment as the works or stage works are completed. Provided that the conditions of this grant offer have been met, the schedule of work has been approved by our Architect and the work carried out to his satisfaction, grant-aid calculated on a pro-rata basis on the eligible portions of the submitted certificates, invoices, etc will subsequently be paid direct to the owner of the property unless an alternative method is requested. However, I must emphasise that it is the responsibility of the owner in the first place the meet payment of the full cost of the works together with, where appropriate, fees, VAT and any other associated costs.

E. VAT at the appropriate rate is normally payable on the cost of repairs and architects' fees where appropriate and estimates on which this offer is based take that into account. But in certain cases, eg if the building is in the use for trade or business purposes, VAT may be wholly or partly recoverable. Before grant can be paid therefore, you must certify the amount of VAT that you have been required to pay and that no part of it is recoverable.

F. The Secretary of State reserves the right, at his discretion, to:

(a) alter or cancel this offer of grant if any of the above conditions is contravened;

(b) alter or cancel any grant offered in the light of any other offers of grant or subsidy towards the cost of works concerned which are accepted by you; and

(c) to reduce the grant if the actual cost of grant eligible works considered necessary by our Architect proves to be less than £120,000.

G. Please note that the Historic Buildings Council is under no obligation to recommend further grant aid should the final cost of the works concerned exceed the figure quoted in this letter. You should also note that the Secretary of State's approval to the details of a scheme does not affect the necessity for the owner to comply with the Planning Acts.

APPENDIX 4

ECCLESIASTICAL EXEMPTION FROM LISTED BUILDING CONTROL CONSULTATION PAPER BY THE DIRECTORATE OF HERITAGE AND ROYAL ESTATE (DEPARTMENT OF THE ENVIRONMENT)

1. In March 1989 the Department issued a consultation paper seeking views on proposals to restrict the current exemption of ecclesiastical buildings from listed building control in respect of external demolition work to churches, other than those of the Church of England, and to clarify the position in respect of controls relating to buildings in the curtilage of ecclesiastical buildings.

2. The Department has considered very carefully the responses received to that consultation paper. Whilst some respondents considered that the proposals still left ecclesiastical bodies with a considerable degree of freedom from the listed building controls which was not, in their view, justifiable, church bodies particularly were concerned at the proposal to restrict the exemption. In particular, some denominations have represented to the Department that they have in existence control systems of their own which include some of the key aspects of the secular controls, and that the imposition of further listed building controls would therefore not be justified.

3. The Government considers that retention of the exemption can only be justified where churches have adequate systems of their own for controlling works to their historic church buildings. The Government therefore proposes to make an Order to remove the exemption from all ecclesiastical buildings except those of denominations which can demonstrate that they have in place the necessary administrative mechanisms to implement the principles set out below, or declare their intention to introduce such mechanisms within 12 months from the date of making of the Order.

4. Ecclesiastical bodies which could meet these requirements would remain free of listed building control and would be specified in the Order. Any ecclesiastical body not specified in the Order would however lose the exemption in respect of all external works: it is not proposed to introduce listed building controls over works to interiors of ecclesiastical buildings, as the Department has no wish to interfere in matters of religious worship.

5. It should be noted that, whether or not an ecclesiastical body implements these requirements, total demolition of an ecclesiastical building is already, and will remain, subject to listed building control (except in the case of the Church of England where demolition takes place under the Pastoral Measure provisions).

6. The following draft Code of Practice sets out the basic requirements which in Ministers' view any internal system of control over works to listed church buildings should meet.

7. *Code of Practice: Main Principles*

(a) the church body should have in place a formal system whereby

(i) all internal and external works for the demolition, alteration or extension of a listed church building which would affect its character as a building of special architectural or historic interest; and

(ii) all works of demolition affecting the exterior of unlisted churches in conservation areas,

are submitted for prior approval to a body which is independent of the local congregation or community proposing the works in question.

(b) the decision-making body when considering applications for works should be under a specific duty to take into account, along with other factors, the desirability of preserving historic church buildings, and the importance of protecting their features of architectural merit and historic interest.

(c) the decision-making body should either include, or have arrangements for obtaining advice from, persons with expert knowledge of historic church buildings.

(d) the decision-making process should make provision for consultation with the local planning authority, English Heritage and national amenity societies, and (except in cases of emergency) allow those bodies at least 28 days in which to comment on work proposals. During the same 28 day period a notice should be posted on the building describing the proposed works and inviting comments from any interested persons. Any representations made by these bodies or any other person in relation to such proposals should be taken into account before the decision is made.

[Note: English Heritage will wish to be consulted on all works to churches in London; all works to Grade I and II* churches in the rest of the country; and all works involving demolition of churches of any grade in the rest of the country.]

(e) there should be a clear and fair procedure for settling all disputes between the local congregation or community and the decision-making body as to whether proposals shall proceed.

(f) the procedures of the ecclesiastical body should include arrangements for dealing with any breach of the control system, including provision for reinstatement of works to historic ecclesiastical buildings carried out without consent.

8. The Department will look to the ecclesiastical bodies themselves to ensure that such systems are properly enforced and monitored, and will wish to discuss monitoring arrangements with them. It will wish to review the position three years after making the Order referred to above and consider whether the Code of Practice is successful in securing the proper preservation of historic ecclesiastical buildings.

Curtilage Buildings

9. The question of how far buildings within the curtilage of an ecclesiastical building enjoy exemption from listed building control can frequently cause confusion. The Department therefore proposes to rationalise the situation by providing in the Order that the exemption applies in relation to those who have signed the Code of Practice only in relation to the principal ecclesiastical building. Works to all buildings within the curtilage of that ecclesiastical building would be subject ot listed building control in the same way as they would in respect of secular buildings.

Comments

10. The Department invites comments on

— the proposal to remove the exemption from all bodies except those who can implement the principles set out in the Code of Practice (either immediately or within 12 months of its adoption)—paragraphs 3-4;

— the principles proposed for that Code of Practice—paragraph 5;

— the proposals for monitoring the arrangements for such a Code of Practice—paragraph 6;

— the proposals in respect of curtilage buildings—paragraph 7.

11. Ecclesiastical bodies are invited to indicate whether they would wish to adopt the Code of Practice, either in its present form or with specified amendments. The Department will consider the comments received and will then circulate a final version of the Code of Practice and invite each organisation to provide a formal statement of its adoption by the relevant governing body or bodies.

12. Comments should be sent by 6 April 1992 to Paula Griffiths, Room C9/06, 2 Marsham Street, London SW1P 3EB.

Department of the Environment

February 1992

APPENDIX 5

ECCLESIASTICAL EXEMPTION FROM LISTED BUILDING CONTROL

Note by the Churches Main Committee in response to the DOE Consultation Paper of February 1992

1. This Note is submitted by the Churches Main Committee on behalf of all its member churches other than the Church of England which has a distinct legal position and will be responding separately. In the previous consultation paper of March 1989, the DOE proposed legislative changes to bring into effect Lord Skelmersdale's statement of 1986, which set out the agreement then reached with the Churches, in particular, that listed building consent would be required for partial demolition relating to items such as a spire, tower, or cupola but not for proposals which would have a lesser effect. We recognise the difficulties, exposed in that consultative paper, in legislating in precisely these terms; and we understand why the government wishes to proceed by way of a Code of Practice along the lines discussed in the present consultative paper. But we believe that Skelmersdale accurately reflects the way in which churches should be dealt with for the purpose of government building controls; and we consider that the final outcome of this long drawn out consultation should be fully consistent with the spirit of Skelmersdale.

2. Against that general background, we have the following specific comments on paragraphs 7 to 9 and 11 of the consultation paper.

3. *Internal works* will continue to be excluded from listed building control (paragraph 4 of the consultation paper). Yet the Code of Practice appears to envisage that they should be made subject to the ecclesiastical body's system of control (paragraph 7(a)(i)) and in particular be the subject of consultation with local planning authorities, English Heritage and National Amenity Socieites (paragraph 7(d)). This would have the anomalous effect that an ecclesiastical body which did not adopt the Code of Practice would have complete freedom over alterations to the interiors of its churches, whereas one which adopted the Code would not only have to include internal works within its system of control but would also have to consult the bodies listed in paragraph 7(d) over any such works. The Department recognises the undesirability of interference in matters of religious worship (paragraph 4). Similarly, churches should be free to change their interiors as an aspect of their worship and theology and should not be required to consult over such changes.

4. *Nature of demolitions, etc. to be controlled.* Under paragraph 7(a)(i), works on a listed building affecting "its character as a building of special architectural or historic interest" are to come within the system. Leaving aside the reference to internal works (dealt with in paragraph 3 above), confirmation is sought that this description, taken from the planning legislation, is the most satisfactory legislative means of giving effect to the Skelmersdale distinction.

5. *Consultation with planning authorities and amenity bodies etc (paragraph 7(d))* We recognise the importance of fully taking into account architectural, historical and other such considerations. But we believe that this is sufficiently safeguarded by the proposals in paragraph 7(b) and (c), that the decision-making body should be under a specific duty to take these considerations into account and should include, or obtain advice from, experts. The consultation envisaged in paragraph 7(d) would add considerably to the administrative costs of controlling building works, which for most ecclesiastical bodies already consume a great deal of time and money.

We consider that the legitimate concerns of amenity societies etc. would be adequately met by the requirements imposed by paragraph 7(b) and (c). If, nevertheless, consultation along the lines of paragraph 7(d) is regarded as essential, the period during which comments and representations may be made by these bodies should be *no more than* 28 days, not *at least* 28 days as the consultation paper appears to suggest.

6. *Enforcement* (paragraph) 7(f). The need for enforcement is understood. At least one denomination is uncertain about the precise methods of enforcement, including the exaction of penalties and the provision for reinstatement. But we accept that these aspects will be clarified in the discussions envisaged in paragraph 8.

7. *Curtilage.* (paragraph 9). The definition of ecclesiastical building in this part of the draft Code of Practice is too narrow. In practice, buildings other than the principal place of worship may also have an ecclesiastical function. If an ecclesiastical body establishes a satisfactory system of control in accordance with paragraph 7, this could and should cover curtilage buildings in the same way as the main building.

8. *Ecclesiastical bodies/denominations.* Under paragraph 11 of the consultation paper "ecclesiastical bodies" are invited to indicate whether they wish to adopt the code of Practice. Two points arise on this. First, although for convenience the responses of all denominations other than the Church of England are being channelled through the Churches Main Committee, the Committee will not itself adopt the Code of Practice. It will be for each denomination to decide whether it wishes to do so, and if it does (either in its present form or with specified amendments) to provide a formal statement of its adoption when it is invited to do so. Secondly, whereas the term "denominations" is used in paragraph 2 and 3 of the Paper, "ecclesiastical body" is used in paragraph 11 and elsewhere. We infer from this that, where a denomination may not wish as a whole to adopt the Code of Practice, it will be open to constituent parts of that denomination (eg. provinces or corporations covering specific geographical areas) to adopt it if they so wish.

9. In summary:

(i) Internal works should be excluded from the Code of Practice.

(ii) There should be no requirement under the Code of Practice to consult the bodies listed in paragraph 7(d). If, nevertheless, consultation is thought essential, the period for consultation should be no more than 28 days.

(iii) Before they adopt the Code of Practice, denominations will wish to discuss with the department appropriate methods of enforcement.

(iv) Curtilage buildings should be treated in the same way as the principal church building to which they relate.

(v) Denominations should individually adopt the Code of Practice (or otherwise) and carry on the necessary discussions with the Department to determine whether they should adopt; but where a denomination so wishes constituent bodies should be free to adopt or otherwise, rather than the denomination itself.

Letter from the Chairman of the Representative Body of the Church in Wales to the Clerk to the Committee (HB 8)

I would like to take this opportunity to emphasize briefly what I regard as the salient points included in Mr Samuel's letter* and the attached memorandum.

It should be appreciated in the first place that the over-riding responsibility of the Representative Body is to maintain the Ministry of the Living Church in Wales, which includes both the clergy and the necessary church buildings.

Our means are limited, and it has never been our wish or intention to take on our shoulders the preservation of heritage buildings for their own sake.

Having said this, we were very conscious of the heritage element in our buildings, and wish to work closely with CADW to produce the optimum benefit for the Country as well as the Church.

In trying to achieve this position I would like to draw attention to the following key points:—

1. Our continuing requirement to receive Ecclesiastical Exemption, which we believe to be well buttressed by our Faculty procedures and constant supervision from our Diocesan authorities, as well as expert supervision from the Representative Body itself.

2. The necessity, if more work is found to be needed, of help for Redundant Churches as well as the Cathedrals, for which categories seperate funding is available in England. We feel this should apply similarly in Wales.

3. A fear that there may be future listing of some buildings for somewhat narrow local reasons. There is a great danger here that too many buildings will be chasing too little money, with grave results to the really worthy examples.

Mr Samuel's paper recites much of the background information in admirable detail, but I am anxious to ensure that these main principles are given due emphasis.

23 December 1992

Memorandum by the Free Church Council for Wales

PRESERVATION OF HISTORIC BUILDINGS AND ANCIENT MONUMENTS (HB 32)

1. We accept the need to preserve some of the chapels in Wales because of their significance in the religious and cultural life of Wales.

2. We appreciate that many of the chapels built in Wales are now of architectural importance and need to be preserved.

3. We welcome the setting up of CADW and appreciate the contribution of CAPEL.

4. We express concern that many churches are facing difficulties in maintaining their buildings. The primary reason being the high cost of maintenance and decreasing elderly membership.

5. We note with concern the effect a conservation order has on the sale of chapel buildings, and trust that the Select Committee will discuss this matter fully.

6. We express concern that the burden of maintaining listed closed chapels will be borne by the Denominations themselves.

* See HB7.

7. We appeal to the Select Committee to set up a Working Group consisting of interested parties to discuss the question of preservation and the implications involved.

17 February 1993

Examination of Witnesses

MR J W D McINTYRE, Secretary General, and MR C D SAMUEL, Chartered Surveyor, Church in Wales, were examined; REVEREND P D RICHARDS, Secretary, Free Church Council for Wales, was examined.

Chairman

543. Thank you very much for coming to see us this afternoon. Mr McIntyre, I would be very grateful if you would introduce the gentleman on each side of you.

(*Mr McIntyre*) Thank you, Chairman. My name is David McIntyre, Secretary General to the Church in Wales. On my left is Chris Samuel, the Church in Wales property executive. He is a chartered surveyor. The Committee may be interested to know that he has almost completed a two-year diploma in building conservation. On my right is the Revd Peter Richards who represents the Free Church Council of Wales.

Chairman: As you know, we are looking at the preservation of historic buildings and ancient monuments in Wales. One of the things that has been concerning us is the whole question of redundant buildings, in particular churches and chapels. In terms of the exemption procedures and rules, I will ask Mr Roger Evans—the acknowledged expert in this field—to start off the proceedings.

Mr Evans

544. If the Revd Richards will forgive me, perhaps the "chapel" question can be dealt with separately because it involves different issues. Mr McIntyre, you tell us in your evidence that presently there is a commission sitting on the faculty jurisdiction system in Wales. When is it expected to report?

(*Mr McIntyre*) It has already produced an interim report. We are expecting it to produce a final report in the course of the next 12 months.

545. Is that interim report submitted to us?

(*Mr McIntyre*) Not at the moment, but if we can send it to you if you wish to have it.

546. I think that is extremely important. For example, at paragraph 5.12 of your evidence you appear to be quoting from such an interim report. Is that so?

(*Mr McIntyre*) Yes. At that stage the quotation was taken from a draft.

547. The Victorian Society has complained that no diocesan advisory committee papers, agendas or minutes are at present being sent to amenity societies.

(*Mr McIntyre*) I think that is right.

(*Mr Samuel*) The diocesan advisory committees are under the jurisdiction of the diocesan courts. They (the Amenity Societies) will be relating directly to the DACs as is appropriate. I know that there are a number of architects and a member of the Historic Buildings Council on DACs, but at the moment there is no formal procedure in that regard.

548. One of the complaints also made is that the DACs in the Church in Wales are both smaller in number and less all-encompassing in terms of range of expertise than in England. Everyone accepts that the Church of England has altered its arrangements in the past few years. Is that a fair summary?

(*Mr McIntyre*) I think it is. One of the recommendations in the interim report is to do with DACs. We are minded to model ourselves very much on the new English pattern. Indeed, a member of the English Commission sat on that commission.

549. Can we reasonably expect that the DAC system will be overhauled very much on the lines of modern thinking in England?

(*Mr McIntyre*) Yes.

550. In terms of central expertise for DACs, at the moment in Wales there is no equivalent to the Council for the Care of Churches. Is there any proposal to provide such centralised expert advice?

(*Mr McIntyre*) There is no proposal to mirror the Council for the Care of Churches. Speaking personally, I would like to see the Church in Wales having a much closer relationship with that council. After all, churches in Wales are not greatly different from churches in England, although obviously we do not take directions from the Church of England. I hope that we will have closer relationships with them. If the proposals in the interim report are adopted there will be a provincial advisory committee dealing largely with cathedrals.

551. But is not the point that in England in the case of a faculty application involving something reasonably significant there will be a recommendation from and consultation with the DAC but also consultation with the Council for the Care of Churches which in a sense will have an overall expert view on conservation? Is there no suggestion in the Church in Wales at the moment that at a provincial level such a body should not be set up?

(*Mr McIntyre*) Not at the moment.

552. Why is that? Is it something that the Commission has not considered, has rejected or what?

(*Mr McIntyre*) It is a question of cost.

553. Is it beyond the Church in Wales to get the advantage of that kind of expertise from voluntary sources in Wales? For example, would not such a body be a prestigious matter on which Welshmen would be proud to serve?

(*Mr McIntyre*) I think that the role of our Provincial Commission could well be extended in this area. That combined with relationships with the Council for the Care of Churches in England might well serve the purpose. At the moment we have a

[Mr Evans *Cont]*
number of members of amenity societies on our diocesan advisory committees.

554. In terms of the division of power, I see in your report that, according to the interim (presumably) report, the commission is not happy with the present arrangements for archdeacons' certificates?

(*Mr McIntyre*) For minor works.

555. Is there a recommendation arising out of that?

(*Mr McIntyre*) Yes. The recommendation will be that we do away with "minor works" and that all works go through the same faculty procedure. The reason for that is that it is very difficult to define what is a minor work.

556. The Church of England has been doing it for years. For example, are you suggesting that a small piece of wiring is not a minor work and is something of such importance that it needs to go to the chancellor? Is that not taking an enormous sledge hammer to crack a very modest nut?

(*Mr McIntyre*) That is the recommendation of the commission at the moment.

(*Mr Samuel*) I think that the intention is to make the application go to the diocesan registrar for him to process it to make sure that it is genuinely of a minor nature. Wiring has been mentioned. Wiring may bring with it conduits which in a grade 1 building may prove to be a very serious intrusion.

557. I happily agree with you that it could be. In relation to graveyards, at paragraph 2.09 of your document you say: "The regulations for the administration of churchyards. . .define how burials shall take place. . .and the nature of gravestones. . ." In the Church in Wales at the moment who has control over tombstones in churchyards?

(*Mr Samuel*) The tombstones are causing a problem because they are the property of the families. For example, in the case of Llantrisant we are unable to undertake certain repair works because tombstones prevent us from doing so.

558. My question was inexact and imprecise and that is why you have answered my point not in the way I would wish. Suppose a parishioner wished to erect a memorial in a country churchyard in Wales. Would that memorial be determined by the regulations or by faculty?

(*Mr Samuel*) It is determined by the regulations, but if it is outside what is in the regulations it proceeds via the faculty.

559. One of the more controversial issues in English country churchyards at the moment is the use of polished Italian granite tombstones that are regarded as being wholly out of place. In Wales is that a decision taken by the chancellor or somebody else?

(*Mr Samuel*) It goes via the faculty to the Chancellor. It is not a matter that will be dealt with under the regulations.

560. Is there any general guidance in the Church in Wales? I do not know whether the commission is looking at it. In my part of the world there is an outrageous proliferation of polished Italian granite in traditional churchyards. Is that a matter on which general guidance has been given to chancellors in Wales?

(*Mr Samuel*) I believe so. Again, it is a matter for the diocesan court; it is not directly in our remit. I have to service the property sub-committee that deals with these matters. I know that in your territory, for example, the Archdeacon of Newport has taken steps against certain monumental masons who have put up unacceptable tombstones. Indeed, in one case they had to go a very long way—and I do not know whether it actually got to court—to get the offending tombstone removed.

561. Is not the position that you accept that the preservation of the ecclesiastical exemption depends upon the totality of the success in conservation terms of the system which you are proposing to put into operation? Still on the question of the exemption, I want to turn to the Revd Richards. As far as the free churches are concerned, is the ecclesiastical exemption something that you wish to preserve, or is it too much expense?

(*Revd Richards*) It is very difficult to answer that question. The Free Church Council for Wales represents four main free church denominations in Wales. Two are centrally based, the Presbyterian Church of Wales and the Methodist Church, whilst I am joint secretary of the Baptist denomination and the Welsh independents which are of a congregational nature. From the Baptist, Congregational and Welsh independents' view, they would find difficulty in working within the ecclesiastical exemption. Speaking in general terms, I would like to support the Church in Wales and through that the two main denominations in saying there is value in the ecclesiastical exemption.

562. The problem of the ecclesiastical exemption is that the thrust of the present legislation appears to be that if a denomination sets up its own system of expert assessment, detailed consideration and a proper system of appeal the Secretary of State will allow the exemption to continue; otherwise, he may by statutory instrument remove it. Clearly, that obviously involves both expense and complexity, but presumably large numbers of the bodies you have just mentioned would find that burden too much?

(*Revd Richards*) Perhaps I can speak about my own denomination and the Congregational Church. They would find that to be the case. I cannot speak on behalf of the Presbyterian Church of Wales which is a very large denomination.

563. I want to turn to the question of grants. Mr McIntyre, referring to paragraph 5.22 of your memorandum you say: "On 31 July 1987 the Archbishop of Wales received a letter from the Minister of State of the Welsh Office, proposing that the ownership of a number of redundant churches of special architectural or historic interest should be transferred to the Secretary of State and repaired, maintained and managed on his behalf by Cadw". In the view of Mr Ivor Bulmer-Thomas, director of the Friends of Friendless Churches, that was a very advantageous proposal. Why was it not accepted by the Church in Wales?

(*Mr McIntyre*) Part of the answer is contained in paragraph 5.22. First, obviously the church is concerned largely with mission rather than the buildings. Nevertheless, we are very conscious of the part we play in respect of the architectural and

[Mr Evans Cont]
historic inheritance of Wales. Since we are concerned with mission there may come a time with shifting populations when we need to bring those churches back into use again. Secondly, we were concerned that Cadw might well wish to take into their care the outstanding and exceptional examples—grade 1 and grade 2*—and we would be left with the other ones which would be a problem for us in financial terms, just as they are for the Church of England.

564. Pausing for a moment, you say that obviously the church is primarily concerned with mission, which is right, but you are talking in terms of bringing things back into use; in other words, you are saying that these buildings are not truly redundant for ever?
(Mr McIntyre) I cannot say that they are redundant for ever; they are redundant at this time. Who is to say where the population will be in 200 years' time?

565. That must be right. On the other hand, there is a very real problem particularly in rural Wales in that there has been increasing depopulation over a very long period. You described graphically how the burden would fall on the particular parishes. If the burden is too great is there a not a case for taking it off the shoulders of the Church in Wales?
(Mr McIntyre) Yes. I think that for seven years or so we have been trying to find with Cadw a cost-effective way of working together on this subject. I am sure that Cadw as well as ourselves would like to reach a conclusion. If it were to be suggested that we should have something like the redundant churches fund as in England—which is 70 per cent funded by the State—and I make the assumption that the same would apply in Wales—I believe that we would be very happy.

566. That surprises me. I would have thought that the offer made in 1987 was much more generous.
(Mr McIntyre) We did not think so at the time.[1]

567. Because in England once a church is declared redundant it is redundant for ever? The Friends of Friendless Churches have had experience of situations where there are problems with holding ecclesiastical services in them. If the Minister of State at the Welsh Office was offering to take 100 per cent of the burden off your shoulders in 1987 that would appear on the face of it to be more attractive than the English model under which you would have to pay 30 per cent of the costs?
(Mr Samuel) I think that the point at issue here was that they were dealing with literally a handful of churches. If one refers to paragraph 5.21 one sees that previously there was talk about six being definitely outstanding and 21 possibly outstanding and worthy of preservation. In those early negotiations I was left with the impression that we were talking about more than just five churches and that a lot more redundant churches would be covered by the new regime, whatever it might be.

568. Presumably, that is a good thing, is it not?
(Mr Samuel) Yes, indeed, but that was not offered to us. If one looks at the end of that paragraph one

sees: "It was understood that the matter was to be taken to the Historic Buildings Council in July 1986". Nothing came out of it. The next thing we heard was that on 31 July 1987 the Minister of State was saying, "We have a new arrangement", which related to five or six on the basis of a list prepared in 1985-86.

569. This is very puzzling. If one looks at paragraph 5.21, one sees: "At that time, an analysis of the 62 redundant or closed churches revealed that six were regarded as 'definitely outstanding'. . ." That would bring them within the Cadw grant category?
(Mr Samuel) Yes.

570. ". . .21 being 'possibly outstanding and worthy of preservation'". One of my difficulties in questioning earlier witnesses on the other side of the argument was: What was "outstanding"? How did that relate to the criterion in England for vesting in the Redundant Churches Fund? I am bound to say that I do not think we ever got a satisfactory answer to that. On the face of it, it looks as if six plus 21 may be talked about as being looked after by the Welsh Office for you?
(Mr Samuel) As to the way matters would develop, that was not the impression with which I was left. It came to a stop at the end of paragraph 5.21. There was a change in politics, or whatever, and there was a different approach with effect from 31 July 1987.

571. The impression to be gained from all this is that for reasons which I am bound to say are not entirely clear the Church in Wales and the Minister of State at the Welsh Office, instead of bringing the negotiations to an advantageous conclusion in terms of preservation, have allowed the matter to drag on inconsequentially. Is that fair?
(Mr Samuel) I think not. We have had a lot of discussions to work out a formula acceptable to both sides. For example, under 5.22 we have to go back to committee. The committee has to consider the implications of that. We then relay that back to Cadw and develop negotiations. I may say that there have been three secretaries at Cadw since I went to Cardiff.

572. Referring to 5.22, I can see that there is a management arrangement. Once one has such an arrangement one can understand how the negotiations slide on, because one ends up with the problem about the position of the representative body as trustee and the need to control future occupation. Is there not a case—or has the Church in Wales not reached this stage—for saying that there is a group of churches which in the public interest ought to be preserved but which in the interests of the Church of Wales is really beyond you?
(Mr Samuel) I would say there is.

573. How many are there at the moment?
(Mr Samuel) If we use the word "fundworthy", at the moment I would say that there are five or six, based on the criteria post-31 July 1987.

574. How many closed churches do you have at the moment?
(Mr Samuel) Curiously enough, the list is very close to that produced in 1985. I think it comes to 64.

575. There was criticism from one of the amenity societies because there was a proposal to close St

[1] Note by witness: In fact devesting from the Redundant Churches Fund has taken place in England (eg Didmarton).

115218 H

[Mr Evans *Cont*]

Bride's Wentloog and demolish it. Is that one of the 60-odd?

(*Mr Samuel*) It is on the redundant list at the moment.

576. Is it one of the five or six?

(*Mr Samuel*) Yes, it would be. However, at the moment there is a move in the parish to bring it back from redundancy. Last week I attended a meeting where I said that the parish seemed confident that it would be able to raise well over £200,000 to restore the church.

577. Mr McIntyre, how seriously does the Church in Wales regard the question of redundant buildings? How many buildings are we talking about now and in the next decade which are surplus to the church's use but are too much of a burden for the church to bear?

(*Mr McIntyre*) I do not think I am able to answer you in terms of statistics but I can give some idea of the problems we have. We have 1,450 churches, of which 620 are currently listed. If Cadw list their full 30,000, which from their evidence they regard as an accurate figure, I imagine that since a lot of our churches are between medieval and Victorian a lot more will be listed. The prime responsibility of the church is its mission. I should make clear that the responsibility for upkeep of churches falls on the local parish. In 1991 we spent £7 million on church upkeep and capital, including grants of £1.4 million. That represents 40 per cent of parish expenditure, and the proportion is increasing. It currently equates to about £70 per annum per regular worshipper. It is a major question for us. As a matter of some urgency, we would like to reach a conclusion with Cadw to work with them on this subject.

578. Bearing in mind other considerations, would it be more satisfactory in Wales if Cadw was able to give more grant aid on a wider criterion than the "outstanding" criterion? Is that too restrictive?

(*Mr McIntyre*) Are you referring to living churches?

579. Yes.

(*Mr McIntyre*) That would be extremely welcome, although our impression is that Cadw are not ungenerous to us. When it comes to outstanding churches, we are content with the current level, although we are always prepared to receive more. We have quinquennial inspections of our churches. To offer an opinion, it seems to me that the churches are in a better standard of repair than perhaps they have been since disestablishment.

580. Are quinquennial inspections now universal in the Church in Wales?

(*Mr McIntyre*) Yes.

581. That in itself is an achievement, is it not?

(*Mr McIntyre*) Yes.

Chairman

582. I should like to ask about grants. It has been the experience in England that few Free Church buildings have received grants and a high proportion of the grants offered to non-conformist chapels are not taken up. Do you happen to know how many non-conformist chapels in Wales over the past 10 years have been offered grants and how many have been taken up?

(*Revd Richards*) I cannot give any statistical information regarding that question. I know that many churches have taken up grants. Many are living churches, but the question is how long they will live. Because the grant that Cadw gives is only 50 per cent many of them have refused the grant because they have to find the remainder to upgrade their buildings. Since many are small congregations they are unable to do that.

583. Is there any difference in the level of take-up between grants for outstanding chapels and grants for chapels in conservation areas?

(*Revd Richards*) Not to my knowledge. The problem with many of the free church denominations is that many of the churches are autonomous. Therefore, it is difficult to get information, especially from the congregational denominations, as to how many of those individual churches would take up the invitation. But in general terms it is a matter of concern to all of us that a major element in the situation is that the money goes on maintenance rather than mission.

584. Referring to the chapels in Wales, is there any evidence that the standard of work required under the grant specification in order to be eligible for assistance would be so high that the financial burden would be too great?

(*Revd Richards*) I am sure that that would deter many churches from proceeding with using those grants to maintain their buildings and, in so doing, hasten the time when they became redundant.

585. Is that also the view of the Church in Wales?

(*Mr Samuel*) The fact that certain higher standards are required is commented on from time to time, but I believe the general view is that when Cadw is giving grant aid of perhaps 50 per cent for the repair of a listed church it is not appropriate to put up, say, pvc gutters rather than cast iron gutters. They take perhaps a longer-term view. They like to use Welsh slate perhaps rather than composition slate. Therefore, the standards that they seek are ones which the advisory committees would very much want to endorse. On the subject of cost, the Historic Houses Association a few years ago produced some figures on the additional cost of repairing listed buildings as opposed to those which were unlisted. They came up with a multiplier of 4.7. Whether it is 4.7, 4 or whatever, I believe there is evidence to support the belief that it costs more to look after listed buildings. Another issue that is brought up at this time is the question of VAT on repairs. The other condition that is imposed by Cadw is the subject of insurance. Quite properly, they seek to have the church or chapel fully insured when they have spent a good deal of taxpayer's money on it. We have recently been involved in discussions in the Churches Committee where it has been reported that one English diocese has discovered that its year-on-year increase in insurance premiums has been 250 per cent. The question of terrorism was also thrown into our lap at Christmas time. Insurance is a major factor. Our postbag in Cardiff probably contains more insurance problems than anything else.

[**Chairman** *Cont*]

586. The grants offered are 50 per cent for outstanding buildings and 40 per cent for external work in conservation areas. Does the Historic Buildings Council interpret that very strictly, or do you know of examples where the percentage of grant-aided work has been larger than those limits?

(*Mr Samuel*) A few years ago I remember some 60 per cents coming through. I also have knowledge of work done on St John the Baptist in Cardiff and St Giles at Wrexham where the repairs have been done in phases and grant contributions have been made in phases, so the total figure has risen to that extent. But it still represents a percentage of the overall cost of repairs.

587. Let us assume that one has a church that is an outstanding building and a 50 per cent grant has been secured. Let us further assume that it is done in three phases. Where else would the church, say at parish level, go to in order to top that up? I am thinking first of the transfer of funds to the county and county borough councils on disestablishment. Can you say a few words on that aspect first and then go through what other bodies the church finds helpful in going as close as it can to the 100 per cent it needs when appeals are launched, such as the one in which I am involved in Cheriton in North Gower? I am looking to you for advice.

(*Mr Samuel*) You have touched on the Welsh Church Act grants. Obviously, they are dealt with directly as between the parish and local authority. For example, the Pantyfedwen Trust in Aberystwyth has been very active for a good many years. We have had HCT and a number of other trusts that have helped individually. There are some trusts which deal with specialist fittings and fixtures. I can give you a list of those outside bodies afterwards. Coming back to ourselves, the representative body makes grants through its churches group and the diocesan churches committees also make grants.

588. What about the fund that was transferred to the county councils in Wales for administration? We have heard, though anecdotally, that that fund is administered very differently as between different county councils in Wales. Do you find that there is a greater inclination on the part of some counties to administer that fund favourably to the church and others less favourably?

(*Mr Samuel*) Yes. If you ask me for facts and figures I am afraid that I cannot give them to you. I can give merely an impression.

(*Revd Richards*) First, as a trustee of the Pantyfedwen Trust I can say that it receives many requests from churches in regard to what I call topping up to enable them to reach their target figure. I have to say that the emphasis in the Pantyfedwen Trust has changed considerably over the past few months, especially the past 18 months. We feel that the responsibility of that fund is not to maintain the fabric of a building but to support the living church in its mission and ministry. Therefore, the guidelines adopted by the Pantyfedwen Trust are narrowing, although grants are made to churches who want to maintain the buildings on the understanding that when we are assessing the application they show that the local congregation has made an attempt to raise funds. I also know that the Prince of Wales and the Welsh Church Fund are other sources of funding.

Without any statistical information, the impression I gain when I receive applications from Baptist churches is that many local authorities administer the fund very differently. Some are more generous than others. Some local authorities are much easier and helpful in the administration of the fund. We also have examples where the improvement of churches has been included in an urban aid package. There is a Baptist church in Glanamman which is such a case. The local congregation had to find a large sum in order to carry out that work.

Mr Evans

589. Mr McIntyre, referring to the Welsh Church Fund and the endowment that took place on disestablishment, as I understand it the county councils are entitled to spend those moneys on public purposes which are set out in the Act. Is there any way in which we can see how that series of separate funds has been administered over the past 70 years? Has anybody done a general survey?

(*Mr McIntyre*) We have not, but I imagine that as they are trusts somewhere there must be trust accounts.

590. I believe that in Gwent £5,000 a year is given to church restoration. We have asked for information as to what the rest of the moneys are for. I think that some of it went into a national library, universities and things of that sort. Is there any general view as to where it has gone and how much is left?

(*Revd Richards*) Speaking on behalf of the churches, we would value information as to the criteria used in allocating the funds. Is it because you have a certain local county councillor who is good at arguing the case? Is it general policy? We would value that information so we can advise our churches whether or not they come within the criteria.

Chairman: We have tried to strike a balance. We do not want to spend an enormous time enquiring into the administration of each of those funds, but we are certainly tracing through some of the aspects of those funds to address the issue.

Mr Robinson

591. On the issue of grant take-up, when a church or congregation decides not to take up a grant how much assessment are you able to make as to the reason behind that? One would think that if the congregation was small that might be the obvious reason for the grant not being taken up, yet I know of one church (that is extremely difficult to find) in Llandeilo Graban in Powys where the grant was taken up by a tiny but loyal and hard-working congregation. I just wonder whether you have done any investigations into those churches taking up grants and whether there are any other reasons, including social ones, why grants may not be taken up. Are you saying that the usual reason is the nature of the congregation?

(*Mr Samuel*) The main problem is the size of congregation and the ability of the congregation to match the funds provided and go down that track. When we, as the Representative Body, receive grant applications from individual parishes we process them and see whether Cadw has given a grant. That

[Mr Robinson Cont]

is a specific question on the form. We also ask what other sources of grant have they turned to. That is our means of monitoring what is going on. At the same time, we give them advice as to where they might be able to go for other funds. As to going to perhaps 1,400 individual churches, the task would be virtually impossible for us in administrative terms.

592. Are you able to give any guidance on fund-raising?
(Mr Samuel) We try to do so.
(Mr McIntyre) There may be another reason. Cadw grants come with certain conditions. One of them is that the church has to be insured for the full reinstatement value. That is becoming increasingly expensive, particularly for a small congregation.
(Revd Richards) When one comes to insure a church building the insurance company will always expect one to insure for the replacement value. Surely, in this day and age no-one would build a chapel holding 1,000 people, but that is expected by the insurers. Therefore, for a very small congregation one is often thinking of a building value of about £½ million.

593. Is that a reasonable expectation? I would have thought that in the case of an historic church the replacement value would be almost beyond the limit of most congregations.
(Revd Richards) That is true, but I am thinking now of those which are not even listed. Even if they are grade 2, or in the process of being listed, many would not take up the grant if there was a requirement to take up insurance on the basis of replacement value.

594. Who stipulates that requirement?
(Revd Richards) Usually, the insurance company.

Mr Evans

595. This is an interesting and important point. I can see the force of what you are saying, but an insurance company would not necessarily insist upon that. It would normally require you to be the insurer of the balance. Would it not be possible to come to an agreement that the only risk against which you needed to insure—particularly in the case of a very large Victorian chapel—was the loss of the building on the basis of a nice modern building which was a fraction of the size? Is that something which Lloyds of London cannot provide for you?
(Revd Richards) I do not know. All I know is that if you do not pay the insurance premium on the basis of replacement value there is no guarantee that if the chapel is burnt down, for example, there will be sufficient funds available to rebuild it, even on a modest scale.

596. But that is because of the arrangement under which if you insure for half the value you get only one-quarter under the insurance policy?
(Revd Richards) Yes, but that would deter some people. If Cadw made the requirement that one had to insure for full value or replacement cost it would deter some people.

597. Does the fault lie with Cadw? Is Cadw being unrealistic in the case of large Victorian chapels in requiring more insurance than is really needed to protect the taxpayer's interest or the needs of the congregation?
(Revd Richards) It is difficult to answer that; it is something for Cadw to look into. It is an increasing problem for small congregations.

Mr Sweeney

598. Would it be helpful if instead of insisting on full insurance value Cadw accepted the kind of arrangement that has been adopted at Beverley Minister, following the experience at York Minster where the building was very badly damaged by fire? Having looked at their insurance arrangements, what they came up with was a scheme whereby if half the Minster was burnt down they would receive the total cost of repairing that half; if the full Minster burnt down they would get only half. There would be a maximum payout figure, and yet they would not be deemed to be under-insured simply because they had paid only half the premium.
(Mr McIntyre) This is a difficult area. There is something called a first loss policy that is offered by the Ecclesiastical Insurance Group. The trouble is that generally churches do not burn to the ground. Another factor is that people are very attached to their churches. I cannot speak for the chapels but I assume that the same applies there. Whilst the building is standing they are prepared to say, "We would replace it with a small modern one", when push comes to shove they tend to want it back exactly as it was before.
Mr Ainger: I want to return to the Welsh Church Fund. From the researches that I have done, it seems to me that churches and chapels are involved in a lottery as far as where they are located. For instance, Dyfed in the coming financial year has £168,000 to distribute from the Welsh Church Fund and yet Clwyd has only £30,000. Different formulae are applied. Before the Committee travels to Clwyd next week, can it be supplied at very short notice with some information to give an indication of your understanding of the different formulae throughout Wales that are applied to applications from each of the county or county boroughs?

Chairman

599. That sounds a bit of a tall order!
(Mr McIntyre) We could certainly do that if that was what the Committee wanted, but we would be acting as a post box; we would have to ask the county councils.

Mr Ainger

600. So, you do not know what the formulae are?
(Mr McIntyre) No.

601. Not even for Dyfed?
(Mr McIntyre) No.
Chairman: When we take evidence from Clwyd County Council we will explore that with them in detail and try to get the picture on an all-Wales basis.

Mr Evans

602. Mr McIntyre, to help us get some impression as to what the burdens of conservation are upon the Church in Wales, can you provide us with some

[Mr Evans Cont]

accounts that identify what proportion of your income is related to that?

(Mr McIntyre) Yes.

603. Is that done by simply one consolidated set of accounts for the representative body, or is it a question of parishes accounting separately?

(Mr McIntyre) We have just done it for the first time. The matter has not been to my Governing Body yet. We have tried to consolidate the total financial picture of the church, and it was from there that I took the 1991 figure of £7 million.

Mr Ainger

604. To clarify the position, you have not been informed by any of the county councils what formula or system they are applying to grant aid for churches?

(Mr McIntyre) My understanding is that the fund is applied much more widely than to just churches. That was part of the reason for disestablishment.

Chairman

605. Gentlemen, is there anything you wish to say to correct any misunderstandings we may have had or to supplement anything? Have we missed anything?

(Mr McIntyre) I am conscious that lunchtime is approaching, but perhaps I may make four brief points. First, I apologise for the fact that my chairman, Mr Richard Parkinson, is not here. He very much wanted to attend but I am afraid that he had an operation last week. Secondly, I believe that the problems of the Church in Wales are much the same as those in England, but I have to say that England has a Redundant Churches Fund which is funded as to 70 per cent by the state. It also has the Historic Chapels Trust which is 70 per cent funded by the state. They grant-aid cathedrals. They can move headstones whereas we cannot. The Church of England can pass on closed burial grounds to local authorities, which is something we cannot do. All of those are differences which disadvantage Wales. Thirdly, obviously we are very keen to retain the ecclesiastical exemption. I will not bore you with the reasons for it; they are contained in the document that we will send you. I believe that we have a good system which is at least equal to the state's and relieves local authorities of the cost. We will be abiding by the code of practice. Fourthly, referring to Cadw I wonder about the listing policy. It has been said by Sir Roy Strong that one needs to do some thinking about the past and present, and one wonders whether one should be concentrating on a smaller number of fine examples and making sure that they are in good repair rather than trying to cover everything. That is something for you to consider. Cadw's problems are the same as ours. We are very keen to look after the architectural heritage of Wales but resources as always are a problem. We find that Cadw are helpful to us, and we would dearly like to find a way of working with them in harness particularly on redundant churches.

(Revd Richards) I have two comments. First, the number of redundant churches will probably increase in the next 10 to 15 years due to many factors. Secondly, in the light of that there are and will be many problems relating to burial grounds. Mr McIntyre has touched on some of those issues. It is a problem for the local community and local churches, but it also means that even denominations like ourselves have to face tremendous costs in future.

(Mr Samuel) One major concern that ought to be reflected here and which lands on my desk is Cadw being required to take funds from living churches and apply those to redundant churches. This is brought out in 5.37. If they were required to take funds away from grants to increase staff to accelerate listings that would be a worry. There would also be worries about the increase in the number of listings without a proportionate increase in grants. Picking up the theme of a sustainable conservation policy, one needs to make a distinction between historic buildings with limited or no commercial value—that is, churches where repairs and maintenance are funded voluntarily—and historic buildings with a commercial value such as Mr Evans mentioned—the domestic property—that can be sold on with the cachet of a two-star rating. I think it is essential to bring the church and chapel members along with the conservationists. This was the point I was endeavouring to bring out in referring to the DOE's Circular 8/87, section V. These people are paying out of their pockets not only as members of parishes but also as taxpayers when the money comes through by way of grant. There are some serious concerns about the listing of certain buildings. For example, we have recently seen some rather interesting reports on educational establishments. There is a worry that if those listings continue, as appears to be the case, there will be a message sent out to the trustees of those organisations to the effect, "Do not employ high quality innovative architecture". I think that that is a worry for the architectural profession of which you should be aware. Earlier a point was picked up about the archaeological trusts and the possibility of conflicts of interest. I think there is also a conflict of interest in relation to planning authorities who are obliged to take advice from ADAS, for example, whilst ADAS is advising the applicant on the worth of the particular application and obtaining fees from the applicant—at the same time, obviously taking fees from the local authority. Finally, one of our diocesan inspectors telephoned yesterday and asked whether I knew why there was such a variety of approaches across the province about the provision of discretionary grants for the repair of houses. He was thinking in terms of his parsonages. There seems to be a wide difference in approach for which I cannot account. But the point is that he is sitting on a number of schemes at the moment awaiting decisions on grant applications. If the grant applications were processed it would help the building industry and unemployment in his area considerably. For example, in Bangor diocese they are much more liberal—and I use that word with some care—in providing grant assistance. Perhaps that is something that should be looked into.

Chairman: Gentlemen, thank you very much indeed for your tolerance in keeping with us for this length of time.

Supplementary Memorandum by the Council of Welsh Districts

PRESERVATION OF HISTORIC BUILDINGS AND ANCIENT MONUMENTS (HB74)

1 The authorisation of works affecting listed buildings under Chapter II of the Planning (Listed Buildings and Conservation Areas) Act, 1990, and

2 The prevention of deterioration and damage under Chapter V of the same Act.

The authorisation of works affecting listed buildings

Works for the demolition, alteration or extension of a listed building may be authorised following the submission of an application for listed building consent. The Act (Section 10) requires that applications are made to the local planning authority. Sections 12, 13 and 15 establish a fairly elaborate procedure to establish the relationship between the Local Planning Authorities and the Secretary of State (CADW) as far as the processing of Listed Buildings Consent applications are concerned. Further advice, including directions, is given in Welsh Office Circular 61/81 (Part III).

With some exceptions the legislation requires the referral of applications for Listed Buildings Consent to CADW where the Local Planning Authority intends to grant consent (Sections 13). This mechanism provides CADW with the opportunity to call in the application for the purpose of allowing the Secretary of State to determine the proposal under Section 12. The consequence of Section 13 is to effectively duplicate consideration of the application, and it is therefore inevitably time-consuming. This has sometimes resulted in delay in the determination of applications.

The operation of the system may have other unfortunate consequences. Local Planning Authorities may give less attention to the details of Listed Building Consent applications than they might, because they feel that the matter ultimately rests with CADW in any event. It would appear however that, possibly because of the provisions of Section 12(4), the Secretary of State is unwilling to call-in applications for his determination. In the period 1985 to 1992 a total of 3,391 Listed Building Consents applications were received by CADW from the Local Planning Authorities. Of these, only 89 were called-in. This constitutes just over 2.5 per cent of the total. (See paragraph 16 of CADW's submission to the Welsh Affairs Committee). Such a low rate of called-in applications reflects badly on the purpose and construction of the machinery.

It is therefore suggested the Committee may wish to consider the following recommendation. There would appear to be no reason why CADW (acting as the Secretary of State) should not become a statutory consultee in respect of Listed Buildings Consent applications, in the same way as the Director of Highways (also acting as the Secretary of State) is a consultee in respect of planning applications affecting trunk roads. While it is true that this would result in CADW having to consider an increased number of applications for Listed Buildings Consent, it is suggested that the dangers of inappropriate works being permitted would be reduced. In order to protect CADW's position vis-a-vis Listed Buildings Consent applications, it is further proposed that CADW should be endowed with powers similar to those enjoyed, in effect, by the Director of Highways, under Article 14 of the General Development Order.

It is contended this mechanism would both speed-up the procedure, make it more effective in its objective of protecting the nation's built heritage, and avoid the danger of superfluous duplication.

The prevention of deterioration and damage

Chapter V of the 1990 Act establishes two procedures for the prevention of deterioration and damage, viz., compulsory acquisition following the service of a repairs notice, under Sections 47 and 48, and urgent works notices for unoccupied buildings under Section 54. Part IV of Welsh Office Circular 61/81 gives further advice on these powers.

Both these procedures are complicated and time-consuming, include rights of representation for the Secretary of State or the courts, and, especially in the case of compulsory purchase, can be very expensive.

The Committee's attention is drawn to the comment of Roger Suddards in Chapter 7 of "Listed Buildings". He writes:

"Initially it should be stated that nowhere in the listed building legislation is there an obligation cast on an owner or occupier to keep the building in repair. There are sanctions if a building falls into disrepair but nowhere is there a positive obligation, nor is it primarily a criminal offence to fail to repair..."

It is contended that this is an unsatisfactory state of affairs and that a specific duty of care should be built into the legislation. Given the difficulties associated with enforcing such a duty under Sections 47 and 54 however, it is proposed that Local Planning Authorities should be endowed with a more limited power to make care orders in respect of buildings which they feel are at risk. Such care orders would specify works necessary to ensure the protection of the building from the earliest signs of neglect. This might involve painting, minor roof repairs, window maintenance, gutter and downpipe repairs, repointing or repairs to rendering. The requirements of such care orders are essentially cosmetic, but they could make a useful contribution to protecting and enhancing the quality and appearance of our most important and attractive buildings.

It would clearly be necessary for there to be a sanction to ensure compliance. It is suggested that a fine in excess of an estimate of the costs of compliance with the order would be appropriate. The existence of such a power would perhaps be sufficient to ensure an appropriate level of care for those minority of owners who appear unwilling to commit the necessary level of resources to the care of their buildings.

19 March 1993

TUESDAY 9 MARCH 1993

The Committee met in the Guildhall, Wrexham

Members present:

Mr Gareth Wardell, in the Chair

Mr Nick Ainger   Mr Elfyn Llwyd
Mr David Hanson   Mr Walter Sweeney

Memorandum by the Clwyd-Powys Archaeological Trust

PRESERVATION OF HISTORIC BUILDINGS AND ANCIENT MONUMENTS IN WALES (HB29)

PREFACE

The Clwyd-Powys Archaeological Trust is one of four independent, regionally-based bodies, supported by funding from both the public and private sectors, with broad concerns in the field of heritage preservation, management and interpretation. It maintains an archive and computerised record of sites, finds, historic buildings and areas of archaeological interest in the counties of Clwyd and Powys. It provides information and advice about the archaeology of the two counties to the general public, planning authorities, developers, and local and national organisations for research and interpretative projects, and for gauging the effects of proposed developments upon the archaeological resource. The Trust undertakes a wide variety of projects in the field, often either in response to proposed developments or to enhance the archaeological record. These include rescue excavations, building recording, evaluations, surveys and watching briefs.

The Trust is a registered charity and a limited company registered in Wales. Its activities are managed by a board of trustees, an advisory committee, and by a membership invited from local authorities, museums, historic societies, and other bodies with interests in the archaeology of the region. Some of the Trust's core activities are funded by Cadw/Welsh Historic Monuments and the Royal Commission on Ancient and Historic Monuments in Wales. Fieldwork and desk-top studies are normally funded on a project-by-project basis by local authorities, developers, and other bodies.

The following general comments are pertinent to the inquiry.

— The contribution of historic buildings and ancient monuments to the quality of life should be fully appreciated—their importance in serving education, tourism, leisure, and research interests, as well as the more subtle role they play in creating a sense of time and place.

— Provision for the care, presentation and understanding of historic building and ancient monuments should reflect as far as possible the history and culture of Wales as a well-defined region of Europe.

— Equal attention should be given to the full range of structures and deposits surviving from the remotest times to the more recent past. Policies should be sufficiently broad and flexible to ensure the preservation of what features may be more highly valued in the future.

— The historical, architectural, and amenity value of a proportion of buildings and monuments and their settings is quite obvious. The potential importance of many less spectacular and less well-recorded buildings and monuments can often not be readily quantified, but should not be under-rated.

— Existing legislation perpetuates a misleading distinction between historic buildings and ancient monuments. Provision for the care, maintenance, recording and interpretation of these different aspects of the heritage should be integrated as fully as possible.

— Historic buildings form one element of a broader archaeological landscape which has developed through time. Attention must therefore be given to their setting and archaeological context.

— Only a limited proportion of sites of archaeological importance are statutorily protected as scheduled ancient monuments. Further sites should be scheduled, but adequate provision must also continue to be made for the protection of the majority of known sites by liaison with landowners and as part of the planning process.

— There should continue to be a presumption in favour of the preservation of historic buildings and ancient monuments. Where the case for preservation is outweighed by other considerations, arrangements must be made for "preservation by record".

— An appropriate and realistic balance of public and private sector funding should be achieved for the preservation of historic buildings and ancient monuments. Certain important functions and

---

The cost of printing and publishing these Minutes of Evidence is estimated by HMSO at £★★★★★★.

activities are only likely to be adequately fulfilled and maintained with support from the public sector.

— Preservation, interpretation, display, and research work are of equal importance and should each be adequately resourced. It is not sufficient simply to preserve and display that which is poorly understood.

— A broad range of organisations and consultative bodies are directly or indirectly involved in the issues covered by this inquiry. Effective liaison should be maintained between these bodies. Where public expenditure is concerned it will be appropriate to consider which organisations can deliver which services most cost-effectively.

— Attention must be given to the effects of proposed changes to the structure and functions of local authorities in Wales. Adequate provision must continue to be made for the maintenance of controls over applications affecting historic buildings and ancient monuments by appropriate bodies at local or regional levels.

— For historical reasons, the arrangements for the preservation of historic buildings and ancient monuments have developed along different lines in Wales, Scotland, Northern Ireland and England. It will probably be more appropriate in terms of cost-effectiveness and regional identity to improve and extend the mechanisms which already exist in Wales than to seek uniformity with other parts of the United Kingdom.

— The significance, value and interpretation of historic buildings and ancient monuments are matters of well-informed and sensitive judgment. The care and maintenance of properties depend upon skill and experience. It is important to ensure that the necessary expertise and skills to carry out these functions continue to be maintained at national and regional levels.

1. *Arrangements for the properties in the care of the Secretary of State, as exercised by Cadw*

1.1 Arrangements for the properties in the care of the Secretary of State in the counties of Clwyd and Powys are generally satisfactory.

1.2 In most instances Cadw is at present the only satisfactory custodian of these properties in Clwyd and Powys, given the relatively low level of revenue they might generate, and the high level of expertise and cost essential for their maintenance and presentation.

1.3 There has been significant improvement in the presentation of monuments in care in Wales, but the access, presentation and promotion of a number of the less well known properties in care in Clwyd and Powys remain poor.

1.4 There are a number of other properties of national importance in Clwyd and Powys which are poorly maintained by private owners, which would benefit from being taken into care by the Secretary of State.

1.5 The maintenance and presentation of monuments demand a high level of skill. expertise and local knowledge. It is essential that this skill-base is maintained at least at its present level.

2. *The care exercised by other major owners (such as the National Trust, the churches, and local authorities) over their properties*

2.1 A distinction can be drawn between bodies owning *specific* properties of historic or archaeological importance and those owning properties or estates which *incidentally* include sites of archaeological importance. (Some of the larger properties owned by the National Trust, the national parks, the Forestry Commission, and the privatised water companies would fall within this latter category.) In the present context, comment is restricted to the care exercised by major owners in relation to specific historic buildings and ancient monuments.

2.2 Whilst the *National Trust* is normally exemplary in the preservation and presentation of properties in their care (principally historic buildings), some branches of the organisation in Wales are insufficiently aware of the archaeological value of these properties. The management and recording of this resource would be more adequately catered for by making better use of the archaeological expertise within the organisation, by wider consultation, and by ensuring a stricter enforcement of conditions attached to listed building consents, scheduled ancient monument consents, and grants awarded by the Secretary of State.

2.3 *Church authorities* in Wales are frequently negligent in their failure to appreciate the archaeological value of the properties in their care, particularly with regard to the necessity of carrying out archaeological recording of standing structures and buried deposits in response to repairs and alterations, There is an urgent necessity to require diocesan authorities to establish appropriate consultatory procedures, or to revoke the present exemptions from listed building and scheduled ancient monument controls. The controls exercised by many diocesan authorities at present are not sufficient to warrant these exemptions. Where appropriate, archaeological conditions should be applied to grants awarded by the Secretary of State. Adequate provision should also be made for the preservation or recording of places of worship of historical, architectural or archaeological importance that are declared redundant.

2.4 Arrangements for the properties in the care of *local authorities* (Clwyd and Powys County Councils and a number of district councils and town councils) are generally satisfactory. Few authorities have in-house expertise in building conservation and archaeology, however, and it is therefore important to ensure that appropriate consultatory mechanisms are established with bodies that are able to provide this advice. Grant-aid from the Secretary of State will continue to be needed for the maintenance and presentation of properties in the care of local authorities, and it is again essential that provision should also be made for archaeological recording where appropriate. It appears unlikely that many additional properties will be taken into care in the run-up to local authority re-organisation in Wales. Serious consideration needs to be given to the future management of properties in the ownership of local authorities, following the establishment of unitary authorities.

3. *The listing of historic buildings, the scheduling of ancient monuments and the controls exercised (chiefly through Cadw) on planning consents in relation to them*

3.1 Existing legislation promotes an unnecessary distinction between historic buildings and ancient monuments and fails to cater for the preservation and recording of portable antiquities. A more fully integrated approach to the controls exercised over these diverse elements of the heritage at both national and regional levels would be more cost-effective and in the public interest.

3.2 The re-listing programme of *historic buildings* in Wales has been carried out at a much slower rate than in England, and it appears that additional resources should be made available for this work. Documentation for older listings is often inadequate or difficult to obtain, and the lack of computerised records for listed buildings reduces the ability of organisations to comment on and ensure that adequate controls are exercised over them at national and regional levels. The provision of in-house expertise in building conservation at local authority level is frequently inadequate. In many instances little or no provision is made for carrying out essential recording work before or during the course of works affecting listed buildings, and a proportion of consents are granted without consultation or notification to statutory consultees. Whilst some of these failings are due to inadequacies in the existing legislation, the promotion of better liaison and greater consistency of approach by organisations handling and commenting upon applications affecting listed buildings is in the public interest.

3.3 Despite inadequacies in the existing legislation, scheduling should provide an effective mechanism for the preservation and management of *ancient monuments*. Enhancement of the schedule of ancient monuments has been undertaken at a much slower rate than in England, and would again appear to be under-resourced. In view of class consents permitting normal agricultural activities on a high proportion of monuments in a rural context, scheduling policy will be especially effective it more fully integrated with other conservation measures (the designation of environmentally sensitive areas, agricultural set-aside, and management agreements). In the urban context, greater attention should be given to the definition and protection of the urban archaeological resource. The introduction of the wardening system in Wales has beeen beneficial in establishing better links with landowners, but the long intervals between visits in some areas suggest that this is under-resourced. Effective controls must continue to be exercised over scheduled ancient monuments, but the slowness with which scheduled ancient monument consent applications are frequently handled by the Secretary of State is a cause of concern to landowners and prospective developers.

4. *The grant schemes available for the preservation of historic buildings and ancient monuments, their overall adequacy as well as the effectiveness and fairness with which they are allocated*

4.1 Existing grant-schemes to owners provide an important means of ensuring the preservation of listed buildings and scheduled ancient monuments.

4.2 In instances where there is little or no financial incentive for owners to ensure that properties are adequately maintained it may be appropriate to award a higher percentage of grant than normal, to ensure the preservation of certain monuments or classes of monument. This may be particularly relevant in the case of earthwork and redundant industrial monuments.

4.3 In many instances it appears that grants are only awarded in response to applications from owners. A more proactive policy of promoting awards and in setting up schemes of work involving other agencies will be important in ensuring the continued preservation of buildings and monuments in cases where there is little explicit incentive for owners, and where specialised skills are required for repairs to buildings or monuments.

4.4 Conditions must be applied, where appropriate, to ensure that adequate provision is made for the preservation or recording of archaeological information before or during the course of grant-aided works to historic buildings and ancient monuments.

5. Associated issues

5.1 Only a small proportion of known sites of archaeological interest (about 5 per cent) are designated as scheduled ancient monuments. Whilst a high proportion of unscheduled sites might not meet the criteria for protection as monuments of national importance, they nonetheless represent a vitally important archaeological resource which demands protection as part of the planning process or through management plans drawn up by landowners. The continuing identification of previously unrecorded buildings and archaeological sites clearly shows that only a proportion of these are already known.

5.2 Historic buildings, ancient monuments and other landscape features (whether listed or unlisted, scheduled or unscheduled) are entered into the computerised regional *sites and monuments records* held by the four Welsh Archaeological Trusts. These records need to be kept up to date by adding details of new discoveries, by adding new information or revising the interpretation of existing records, and by extending the scope of the records to include new classes of structures or sites. Apart from their role in providing locally-based sources of information for educational and tourism projects, these records also provide a vital and responsive mechanism for monitoring and controlling the effects of proposed developments on the archaeological resource.

5.3 Given their important role in the planning process, these Welsh records should now be given a similar measure of statutory or official recognition as those maintained by the English counties. The Royal Commission on Ancient and Historical Monuments in Wales is charged by its new Royal Warrant with the responsibility for supporting these records. However, it is a matter of some concern that grossly inadequate resources are made available from central or local government in Wales to ensure that these records are adequately maintained and updated.

5.4 Each of the independent Welsh Archaeological Trusts have long-established links with planning authorities in their areas and play an important role in providing information on historic buildings and ancient monuments for inclusion in local and structure plans as well as advice on the individual planning applications affecting them, in line with planning policy guidance issued by the Secretary of State. They also play an important role in gathering and recording new information and liaising with landowners and developers for the purpose of helping to preserve buildings and monuments, whether or not they are statutorily protected.

5.5 Since few local authorities have in-house archaeological expertise, considerable reliance has been placed for many years on the services provided by the Archaeological Trusts throughout Wales. It is a matter of concern, however, that Cadw has signalled its intention to reduce funding for the development control aspects of work undertaken by the Archaeological Trusts, given that few of the existing local authorities or proposed unitary authorities have or maintain sites and monuments records, or appear to be in a position to fund this work as efficiently or cost-effectively themselves.

Memorandum by Dyfed Archaeological Trust

PRESERVATION OF HISTORIC BUILDINGS AND ANCIENT MONUMENTS IN WALES (HB38)

INTRODUCTION

The Dyfed Archaeological Trust is one of the four identically constituted Trusts established in 1974–75 at the instigation of the then DoE Ancient Monuments Branch (Wales) to provide a complete regional coverage of the Principality. The combination of full-time professional heritage organisations in Wales represented by CADW: Welsh Historic Monuments, RCAHM(W), and the four Trusts is unique to Wales and is widely regarded as structurally and organisationally superior to arrangements in other parts of the UK.

Each Trust is constituted as a private limited company and a registered charity. Management boards and membership are drawn from a wide spectrum of interests within Wales including local authorities, museums, historical and archaeological societies and other bodies with interests in the historic heritage. There are strong links with the universities and currently the chairmanship of three of the Trusts is held by academics (Dyfed: St David's University College, Lampeter; Gwynedd; University College, Bangor; Clwyd-Powys; University College, Bangor).

The Trusts perform a wide-ranging role in the investigation, conservation, interpretation and promotion of Wales' historic heritage. At a regional level they are at the interface between central government policies and local public and private sector practises and initiatives. The Trusts are therefore very much at the "sharp end" of heritage policy, often acting as the "eyes and ears" for the national bodies.

Trust activities are funded from a variety of public and private sources. In 1991–92 the combined income of the four Trusts was £1.5 million of which £840K was provided by Cadw from the Rescue Archaeology vote. 1992–93 income is estimated at £1.6 million (Cadw £853K). Together, the Trusts constitute the largest source of employment for professional archaeologists and related staff in Wales; in 1991–92 the aggregate average number of staff employed by the Trusts was 110.

Levels of current funding represent a considerable decrease in resources available in the 1980's when, on their own initiatives, all Trusts took extensive advantage of Manpower Services Commission schemes to enhance the investigation, conservation and promotion of the historic environment in their regions. Aggregates of MSC income in this period indicate an annual funding peak of £1.6 million, three times the then amount of Cadw income. Given this level of resources it is not surprising that the demise of the Community Programme badly affected the Trust's capacity to conduct large-scale rescue excavation and post-excavation programmes, carry out essential survey and recording work and maintain and enhance the information base on ancient monuments and historic buildings. Educational initiatives, essential to medium and long-term conservation strategies were virtually wiped out. It is only in the last two to three years that the Trusts have been able to re-instate educational and interpretative initiatives, albeit at a much more modest level than previously, using non-Cadw funds generated from a variety of other sources. The information base (Sites and Monuments Records), now the responsibility of RCAHM funding, has however remained static (see paras 5.5—5.4).

The following comments are based primarily on the Dyfed Trust's own regional experience.

1. PROPERTIES IN CARE OF THE SECRETARY OF STATE

1.1 The majority of these properties are well-maintained and protected. Interpretation and other facilities have been considerably improved in recent years (eg, Kidwelly Castle, the Bishop's Palace, St. David's, Strata Florida Abbey).

1.2 For historical reasons, the range of monument types in the care of the Secretary of State is limited. Consideration could be given to extending the range, especially where opportunities for joint management arrangements could be effected.

1.3 There is a number of properties in care in the region which have been subject to investigation and consolidation programmes extending over a very long period, and to which there is still no public access. Some properties are in key tourist locations (Laugharne Castle is a pertinent example). Funds should be provided to enable Cadw to complete programmes of consolidation over a much shorter timescale, so as to generate income from these sites and utilise more rapidly their potential as educational resources.

1.4 The skill levels exercised by Cadw in the conservation and maintenance of the fabric of properties in care are very high. It is important that the experienced work forces should not be diminished. Rather, this reservoir of expertise and experience should provide a basis for training which could be made available to other owners of historic monuments.

2. PROPERTIES IN CARE OF OTHER MAJOR OWNERS

National Trust

2.1 The National Trust has fewer important historic buildings in Dyfed compared with other regions. These buildings are well-maintained and managed. By virtue of its landholdings, the Trust has a substantial number of individual smaller buildings of historic importance and an even greater number of individual archaeological sites, the latter including the extensive complex of the Dolaucothi Mines. The Trust has its own "in-house" archaeological survey team and the Trust's provision for recording of archaeological sites and historic landscape features and the incorporation of information into property management plans is applauded. Sometimes, however, the archaeological expertise and opinions of external specialists are not sufficiently utilised in implementing and monitoring programmes which affect individual sites and buildings. The short- and long-term consequences of visitor pressure are not always taken into account or the necessary remedial action taken.

Churches

2.2 The care exercised by the Church in Wales in relation to the historic, architectural and archaeological importance of its properties is completely inadequate. Alterations, repairs and "improvements" are undertaken both inside and outside churches without reference to professional archaeological advice; licences and faculties are not subject to consultation; there are no adequate voluntary procedures in force which would compensate for the Church's continued exemption from listed building and scheduled monument control. Recent Diocesan reviews remain confidential and there is an urgent need for open debate to establish publicly the extent and scale of the problems, adequate consultative system and measures, and the extent of resources required.

2.3 Redundancy has is own special problems. Procedures are complex and by the time the historic importance of a church is brought within the full scope of planning legislation much damage may have already taken place, not least by neglect. Wales has no equivalent of the English Redundant Churches Fund.

Chapels

2.4 Non-conformist chapels are equally if not more so at risk. Organisational structures vary according to denomination and the responsibility for individual chapel buildings is therefore diverse. There are no consultation procedures for monitoring proposals for closure or "redundancy" nor any formal procedure for recording buildings and fittings when chapels pass out of effective use. The outcome of a recent study commissioned by the Pembrokeshire Coast National Park on the extent of the problems associated with redundant and impending redundant churches and chapels is awaited with interest. RCAHM(W)'s proposed survey of ecclesiastical buildings is also welcome: the Dyfed Archaeological Trust is anxious to support this programme in whatever way it can in order that the survey may be accomplished within a timescale which is commensurate with the immediacy of the problem facing these historic buildings.

Local Authorities

2.5. Local Authorities in Dyfed own substantial and important individual monuments (for example castles at Carmarthen, Haverfordwest, Llandovery, Aberystwyth) and their other properties contain a variety of monuments and buildings of archaeological and historic importance.

2.6. The major monuments are generally subject to grant-aid from Cadw towards their maintenance and repair, and through such arrangements, such monuments are generally well maintained. The lack of in-house expertise in historic buildings and archaeology means that the Dyfed Archaeological Trust is called upon to provide advice and assistance, although lack of consultation and inadequate provision for monitoring has resulted in lack of recording of valuable information in some cases.

2.7. To the Trust's knowledge, no authorities, with the exception of the National Parks, have undertaken a comprehensive "audit" of all historic sites and monuments in their ownership. There are instances where this has led to last-minute difficulties over proposals by authorities for development schemes on their own properties. In addition, the architectural and historic importance of buildings owned by the authorities (including, for example, the Victorian schools largely in the ownership of the County Council) is not generally appreciated and there have been several instances where redundant buildings have been neglected and their details unrecorded prior to demolition or change of use.

2.8. The growing awareness of the contribution that the physical historic heritage can make to the region's economy has led to a much more positive approach by local authorities to the promotion and interpretation, and inter alia, the conservation of ancient monuments and historic buildings. Dyfed County Council's "Historic Resources Initiative" which has been subject to substantial input by the Dyfed Archaeological Trust is but one example. Others are Carmarthen District Council's management and interpretation (with Trust advice) of sites in the authority's ownership, such as the Carmarthen Roman Amphitheatre, the Carmarthen Civil War Earthworks and Newcastle Emlyn Castle.

2.9. This also applies to the National Parks. Brecon Beacons National Park has become, by virtue of its acquisition of large tracts of common land in east Dyfed, a major landowner of nationally important archaeological sites. It has also acquired ownership of a nationally important Iron Age hillfort, Carn Goch, in the Towy Valley. Pembrokeshire Coast National Park has negotiated a lease of Carew Castle, purchase of the important industrial complex at Porthgain on the north Pembrokeshire Coast, and the acquisition of the Iron Age Hillfort at Castell Henllys, Meline. Management plans for all these sites are in force or are being developed in consultation with external professional archaeological or advisory committees.

2.10. Community-based initiatives: see para 5.5.

3. LISTING AND SCHEDULING

3.1. Cadw's record of listed buildings remains paper-based and there is an urgent need for computerisation of the lists. It is often very difficult to obtain information from local planning authorities and many are relying on records and descriptions compiled in the 1950s. Information involving analysis of numbers of listed buildings by type or period is virtually impossible to obtain because of the effort required to abstract data by manual means.

3.2. The re-listing programme needs to be substantially accelerated. Moreover the present re-survey programme focus on towns or former towns means that there is no systematic approach to the rural areas. Information on buildings in the latter areas is reliant on the supplementary lists compiled in 1963. Historic farm buildings and vernacular styles need urgent attention.

3.3 Industrial monuments are poorly represented. Programmes of rapid survey are required to establish the survival of important industrial remains so that criteria for listing can be further developed. The recent disgraceful demolition of substantial sections of an unrecorded historic industrial complex at Pentregwenlais, Llandybie, clearly demonstrated the need to identify such complexes in the first place so that assessments of their relative importance may be made.

3.4 Cadw's Scheduled Monuments enhancement programme is to be welcomed but targets are set at a very low level because of lack of resources.

3.5 The introduction of the Field Monument Warden system and the programme of monitoring scheduled monuments through the air photography programme carried out by the Royal Commission and the Trusts has improved the frequency of monitoring, but there may still be substantial gaps—of up to three or four years, between ground inspections. Moreover, the Trust has noted several circumstances where Field Monument Warden recommendations for remedial action are not subsequently followed up.

3.6 In many cases revisions of the extent of the scheduled area is required to take on board the below-ground archaeological potential associated with upstanding remains. The importance given to "group value" as a criteria for scheduling is often not translated into the extent of scheduling on the ground. For example individual barrows in a group may be individually scheduled but the space between them remains unprotected. If there are legal difficulties in applying the 1979 Ancient Monuments and Archaeological Area Act to these areas, programmes of geophysical survey could be employed to demonstrate archaeological potential.

3.7 The same applies to industrial complexes. Current review by the Trust of historic lead mine sites in Ceredigion has revealed many situations where upstanding structures have been selectively scheduled with little or no attention paid to the complex as a whole and the archaeological potential of elements such as spoil and waste tips—some of which may conceal evidence of working as far back as the prehistoric period. Again it is appreciated that enhancement of scheduling in such situations is hampered by the lack of resources available to Cadw.

3.8 The protection of field monuments under agricultural regimes is a cause of concern. Continued degredation of sites by even occasional ploughing is arguably the largest single threat to these sites. The system of class consents effectively hinders protection and discourages new scheduling. The Trust knows of instances where Cadw understandably have been reluctant to schedule new discoveries, since the scheduling would not be able to prevent further ploughing. At the same time the landowner has refused permission for the site to be recovered by excavation. This situation results in needless destruction of valuable archaeological evidence.

3.9 Existing Ancient Monuments legislation does not cater for the need to protect wider areas of historic landscape, the significance of which in cultural and historic terms is now widely recognised. As a result of the deficiencies in the 1979 Act, conservation and protection is dependant on inducements and restraints afforded through designation of Environmentally Sensitive areas, and other schemes such as the Countryside Council for Wales' Tir Cymen initiative. However the effectiveness of such schemes in protecting areas of historic landscape importance and their individual components is difficult to establish. Monitoring by professional archaeologists is required but confidentiality of grant arrangements appears to be a barrier to this.

3.10 The level of explanation and documentation supplied to individual owners of scheduled monuments remains generally poor. Formal documents concentrate on the statutory obligations and procedures and insufficient attention is given to supplying owners with information which would further stimulate their interest and encourage postitve management. Few field monuments for example have a detailed ground plan at a larger scale than 1:2500.

3.11 In its contacts with owners and developers, the Trust is aware of widespread concern about the slow processing of scheduled monument consent applications. How far the consultative procedures adopted by Cadw contribute to this concern is uncertain, but the Trust considers that the present level of consultation is essential and should be retained.

4. GRANT SCHEMES

4.1 For scheduled ancient monuments, the Trust wholeheartedly supports the use of management agreements and related grants as an essential way of securing the maintenance and protection of monuments. Resources should be made available to extend the number of agreements offered.

4.2 Almost inevitably, a common complaint voiced to the Trust is the low level of payment involved. Since this appears to provide a disincentive to enter into management agreements, there is a case for reviewing the rates per hectare applied.

4.3. In the past, insufficient attention has been given to conditions providing for protection or recording of below-ground archaeology where grants for repair of historic buildings are involved. However, the Trust is pleased to note that Cadw has now remedied this deficiency.

5. ASSOCIATED ISSUES

The Trust wishes to single out three items:

Sites and Monuments Records

5.1 As a result of policy decisions following the 1988 KPMG report on the Royal Commissions on Ancient and Historical Monuments, responsibility for funding the four Trusts Regional Sites and Monuments Records was transferred last year from Cadw to RCAHM(W). The Trusts' SMRs were established in the late

70s at a time when no computerised data bases for historic sites and monuments existed in Wales, either locally or nationally KPMG noted that contrary to the situation in England the regional SMRs in Wales were in advance of the central National Monuments Record in this respect. This remains the situation today.

5.2 The Regional SMRs are essential to the provision of advice to local planning and other authorities concerning the impact of development and other proposals affecting both scheduled and listed and unscheduled and unlisted sites and monuments (the Trusts monitor some 35,000 planning applications per year). The SMRs also provide an academic and educational resource and a body of heritage information invaluable for the development of tourism and other strategies aimed at enhancing regional economies.

5.3 Considerable discussion has taken place between the Trusts and RCHAM(W) with a view to developing a computer-based extended national data-base (END) through which links can be established between the regional SMRs and the National Monuments Record (at present still a paper record). KPMG laid considerable stress on the need for RCAHM(W) to apply modern information technology to its record holdings and this was accepted by ministers. It is therefore a matter of acute concern to the Trusts that the necessary resources to achieve the creation of the END and in the process, the computerisation of core data in the NMR are not being made available. This is especially disappointing in view of the fact that Wales has the opportunity to create the most efficient integrated information system for historic sites and monuments in the whole of Europe.

5.4 In addition, very little enhancement of the Trusts Regional Sites and Monuments Records has taken place since the demise of MSC schemes in the late 1980s. The transfer of responsibility for funding these records to RCAHM(W) was accompanied by assurances that adequate funds would be made available for the Commission to discharge its enhanced responsibilities for SMRs. Again, despite bids from the Commission, the necessary resources have not been made available.

Conservation and Protection through Community-based Initiatives

5.5 The Trust wishes to commend to the Committee the benefits to the conservation and promotion of the historic environment afforded through the government's support of community-based initiatives in rural areas. The Trust developed close links with one such initiative—the Taf and Cleddau Rural Initiative—now extended to the whole of South Pembrokeshire (South Pembrokeshire Partnership for Action with Rural Communities (SPARC)).

5.6 Through the community-based system operated by the Initiative, there has been a considerable raising of the level of awareness and appreciation of individual monuments and buildings and of the historic landscape at large. The Initiative has also been extremely successful in attracting funds from a wide variety of sources (including the EC) to enhance the conservation and interpretation of important sites. Partnership between a variety of public and private bodies has been a major instrument of this success. This has enabled much more to be achieved than is generally effected by individual heritage agencies and interest groups normally working on their own.

Training

5.7 There is an acute shortage of Welsh-trained and Welsh-speaking graduates in Wales with professional qualifications and experience to fulfil the wide range of functions involved in the conservation of the Welsh historic heritage. Whilst there is a variety of courses on offer at undergraduate level, there is no provision for post-graduate training dealing with the Welsh (or other) historic environment and its management. This lack of provision compares badly with the position in England where for example, English Heritage supports in-service training courses organised by the Oxford University Department of External Studies. As a result it is the Trusts' experience that the majority of new staff are recruited from outside the Principality.

5.8 The Trusts are anxious to increase their complements of Welsh speaking staff and make provision for existing staff to acquire proficiency in the Welsh language. Resourcing this is a problem, one that has been brought to Cadw's attention, but without any conclusion.

Letter to the Clerk of the Committee from the Director, Gwynedd Archaeological Trust

PRESERVATION OF HISTORIC BUILDINGS AND ANCIENT MONUMENTS (HB 20)

1. With regard to properties in the care of the Secretary of State for Wales as exercised by Cadw, it appears to us, from our experience, that Cadw are exercising their responsibilities adequately within the resources available. There would seem to be, in the current political climate, commercial pressures to take into guardianship, and manage, monuments which are likely to be self supporting and which, at least generate some income. This should be resisted and, for a public body, funded by the tax payer, the main considerations should be the preservation, management, interpretation and provision of access to monuments of national importance in their landscape or townscape setting rather than financial considerations. On the whole Cadw does this well and local examples might be Dolbadarn Castle, Capel Garmon chambered tomb, Trefignath chambered tomb, Din Llugwy hut group and Hen Capel Llugwy among others. The excessive hype and

commercialisation of monuments which has led to disaster at Stonehenge should be resisted at all costs. The privatisation of monuments should also be resisted. The taking of monuments into State care was a provision for the *care* of these monuments for the benefit of the public and not a profit making exercise at the expense of a national asset—the historic landscape.

2. The care exercised by other major owners is inevitably variable and depends on the owner. In general the National Trust's record with regard to historic buildings is good and the National Trust also make provision for the recording of archaeological sites and landscapes on properties they own. Historic churches, on the other hand, have been very much at the mercy of the attitudes of local incumbents which range from caring to indifferent. "Improvements" which serve the needs of the parish do not always respect the antiquity, and the evidence for the antiquity, of the original foundation. The problem of the preservation and/or recording of the evidence for early churches, graveyards and their development is a major one for which there is little provision in the planning process.

3. The schedule of ancient monuments includes only a small proportion of the total archaeological heritage worthy of record and/or preservation. As an indication of the major monuments defined by site-type within a geographical area it serves a purpose. The criteria by which monuments are selected is in need of review and the schedule barely addresses modern concepts of approaching the past such as the evolution of *landscapes* and the inter-relationship of settlements and other monuments within a complex landscape both spatially and through time. The statutory protection the schedule offers is limited in its provision and the schedule is sometimes misused—not to identify a newly recognised monument of national importance but to confer immediate protection on a site at risk from development. This, however, is sometimes necessary in default of an adequate mechanism for protecting or stalling a threat to archaeological evidence in the face of that threat. Such a mechanism is desperately needed, particularly in areas where most developments (primarily agricultural) escape the planning process.

3 February 1993

Examination of Witnesses

Mr WILLIAM J BRITNELL, Director, Clwyd-Powys Archaeological Trust, Mr GARETH DOWDELL, Director, Glamorgan-Gwent Archaeological Trust, Mr DAVID LONGLEY, Gwynedd Archaeological Trust and Mr DON BENSON, Director, Dyfed Archaeological Trust, were examined.

Chairman

606. Gentlemen, could I on behalf of the Committee thank you very much for coming to see us in this wonderful building this afternoon. In terms of the four archaeological trusts in Wales what we would like to do first of all is to explore your relationship with Cadw, if we may. In their memoranda to us they identify grants to the four trusts in the order of £800,000 for 1991-92 for core and project funding. How would you define the tasks and role required of you as archaeological trusts by Cadw and, broadly speaking, could you tell us what proportion of your grants are devoted to this particular task or to these tasks?

(*Mr Dowdell*) First of all, Mr Chairman, I confirm that figure as being a correct figure. The scope of the work that we cover ranges from the compilation of and enhancement of sites and monuments records on a regional basis, which is very uniform throughout the four trusts—the trusts have identical structures with their sites and monuments record work—and as far as the development control side is concerned, that is the monitoring of planning applications with archaeological implications, that is basically uniform as well in terms of the level of funding provided by Cadw. We also contract to cadw to undertake certain works, mainly those works which are not developer-funded, and Cadw has introduced an initiative whereby three-year programmes have now become possible to deal particularly with non-development type of threats to the archaeological heritage of Wales, and in that I would identify for example

coastal erosion problems, and on top of that problems connected with agricultural activity, ploughing in rural areas, afforestation programmes, and in general, as I say, the non-development type of threat which in many areas of Wales in the rural areas can cover up to 90 per cent of the actual problems that a particular trust could encounter. They all have the same effect eventually, no matter how gradual those problems may be, in destroying part of the archaeological resource of Wales.

607. But in terms of these grants, what grants did you have, for example, in 1991-92?
(*Mr Dowdell*) Off the top of my head, Mr Chairman, in 1991-92 I believe it was £256,000.

608. Do you have an annual report, as a trust, identifying the way in which that money is spent in terms of the break-down and the way that you undertake those tasks which you have mentioned?
(*Mr Dowdell*) Most certainly, Sir, yes. It includes a separate statement of account to Cadw, because obviously each of the trusts do derive income from sources non-cadw, but as one of the conditions of grant we have to submit separate audited statements of account to account for the expenditure which cadw has approved.

609. But in terms of your annual report, is that published and available to the public?
(*Mr Dowdell*) Yes, Sir, it is most certainly.

610. That is the same for all the trusts?
(*Mr Britnell*) Yes.

THE WELSH AFFAIRS COMMITTEE 175

9 March 1992] Mr WILLIAM J BRITNELL, Mr GARETH DOWDELL, MR DAVID LONGLEY and Mr DON BENSON *[Continued*

[Chairman *Cont*]

611. What about the rest of you, gentlemen? What kind of figure did you have in 1991-92?

(*Mr Benson*) I can give you a break-down for the Dyfed Trust. The total rescue archaeology vote allocation was roughly 206,000, and that broke down as follows: core costs, roughly 42,000; post-excavation projects, 81,000; excavation projects, 41,000; and other projects, which included development control work, totalled 41,500. Included in that latter total was the development control funding for the various survey projects which was within a ring-fenced figure set by Cadw as a total, and I think our share of that was a quarter of the total, and that was 29,000, so 29,000 times four was the ring-fenced figure which cadw allocated for development control work in that year.

612. In terms of the break-down of the way you spend that grant money, you heard what Mr Benson said about the way his particular trust in Dyfed sub-divides the expenditure, do you all consistently have the same way of breaking-down that expenditure?

(*Mr Longley*) I would say we are all very comparable.

613. So one could look at your figures and work out the relative expenditure on each item very easily in terms of comparisons and contrasts?

(*Mr Benson*) Yes, that would be a simple thing to do.

(*Mr Britnell*) There may be ups and downs in particular years because a particular trust might have a particularly heavy post-excavation programme in one year, and another trust might have a particularly heavy excavation programme, but in terms of our overall expenditure, the running costs or central administrative costs and the proportion of grant which goes on broadly curatorial work would probably be similar across the trusts.

614. You have mentioned, Mr Dowdell, the additional income, could I run through with each one of you what was the additional income you attracted in the year 1991-92, in addition that is to the grant from Cadw? Have you got the figure there for Glamorgan-Gwent, Mr Dowdell?

(*Mr Dowdell*) It was £338,510.

(*Mr Britnell*) Our non-Cadw income in 1991-92 was £152,800.

(*Mr Longley*) £118,222.

(*Mr Benson*) £90,500.

(*Mr Britnell*) Generally about 50 per cent of our income is non-cadw income.

615. About 50 per cent?

(*Mr Longley*) Slightly under 50 per cent.

(*Mr Benson*) That figure is likely to vary considerably from year to year. It generally is on an upward trend but it does depend on a number of factors. There is a whole range of factors involved, including the amount of pressure and funding which comes from developer-funded projects, and that varies from year to year, they are not all at the same level, and indeed other sources of income, such as in our particular case, doing interpretative work.

Mr Ainger

616. On the funding: I note in the memorandum we had from the Dyfed Archaeological trust that a comment is passed that the "levels of current funding represent a considerable decrease in resources available in the 1980s ..." when Dyfed, and presumably other archaeological trusts, were involved with MSC schemes. What is "a considerable decrease"?

(*Mr Longley*) In the years we were operating in the 1980s using MSC schemes, in our particular experience in Gwynedd, we were not attracting the level of other than cadw funded projects which we are now; we relied very much more heavily on cadw for our total rescue archaeological programme in those years, but we were able to carry out a lot more excavation work utilising MSC resources in those years. I would say in Gwynedd in our strongest year we had something like £100,000-worth of MSC funded work in addition to the cadw budget, and that was probably around 1985, 1986. We are attracting something like £100,000 per annum from other sources now, so the figure has not decreased in that sense. In real terms it has, but in proportion to the amount of funding received from Cadw there is a considerable shift in the balance. That is the difference.

617. Is that the same for you all?

(*Mr Dowdell*) Perhaps to a greater degree. Input into projects in the period between 1 April 1982 and the end of August, 1988, GGAT input into Cadw approved projects, income derived from the Manpower Services Commission, totalled in excess of 3.4 million. The Cadw contribution, by comparison, was some 800,000. So we have witnessed a very substantial drop, a decrease, as Don Benson has pointed out in his paper to you, from the 1980s. We have made good to a certain extent by deriving additional input, as I mentioned previously, from developers, but it is a fair point to make that there were other projects which were supported by the now defunct Manpower Services Commission, particularly in what I call community archaeology; a lot of work was done in the education field which is no longer possible, and there was a considerable input made into the production of education resource packs, for example. All of this, unfortunately, is no longer available to us. There is a gap there which, given the governing instrument of the trust to promote the education of the public in archaeology, we find a very significant gap, and one we would like to rectify if we had the necessary financial support to do so.

618. Chairman, this is obviously quite a large field. Is it possible for us to ask the archaeological trusts to send us a note on the effect of the ending of the MSC schemes both on their total global budget and the various interpretative and educational schemes which they have touched on?

(*Mr Dowdell*) Yes, certainly, Mr Chairman.

Chairman

619. That would be a good idea. In terms of that Manpower Services Commission scheme, have you been able to replace that with any other government scheme which is in place which may be a poorer

[Chairman *Cont]*

substitute? Is there any way that you have geared yourselves up in some other way to get government money to replace those lost funds?

(*Mr Dowdell*) I think, Mr Chairman, you are probably referring to employment training, or more particularly in our instance, environmental action. I can say there has been very little impact on the archaeological scene in Wales from those schemes; very little indeed. Given the very nature of archaeological work, it demands a consistency of approach, a continuous approach, which is not possible under the ET or EA programmes.

620. That is true of all of you? You have a unanimous view on that?

(*Mr Benson*) Yes, I think there has not been anything which has replaced the level of MSC funding. On the other hand, we have been in the position over the last two or three years of gradually building up non-Cadw funding from other sources, and some of these sources include organisations like the CCW who are now taking a much more positive interest in the historic aspects of the landscape. So there are areas which are coming to the fore, or sources which are available now which were not available to us in MSC days, but they are certainly not at the level which we enjoyed during that period.

Mr Ainger

621. I think it would be helpful, for whatever new sources there are, if there was a comparison with a peak period in the 80s when the MSC scheme was of great importance to you.

(*Mr Longley*) Could I add for information that in comparing MSC schemes with the training schemes, we did not just use the MSC schemes as a labour resource, there was an element of training there in the MSC schemes, even though they were not set up as the later training schemes were, to the extent that we are at the moment (and we are talking about eight years on) still employing regularly four people who first joined us on an MSC scheme. One of them is a permanent employee of ours now with the role of project manager, which is one of the key roles in our organisation—he first joined us on an MSC scheme seven years ago.

(*Mr Britnell*) Between us there are many hundreds of people who came through our organisations, who ended up with quite an interest and experience in archaeology, and although each of us have retained staff who started with us on MSC we have unfortunately lost some, but there was a great well of experience which went out into Wales of people who have worked with us.

Chairman

622. Moving on now to the core relationship between you as archaeological trusts and the planning authorities, one of the aspects which has concerned us is that few local authorities in Wales have conservation officers which are designated within the local authorities. Indeed in the Clwyd-Powys memorandum, Mr Britnell, in paragraph 2.4 you say, "Few authorities have in-house expertise in building conservation and archaeology ...". Do you, as archaeological trusts, see yourselves as a Cadw support system trying to compensate for the weak

infrastructure of local authority conservation officials in the area of ancient monuments? Are you a kind of rescue, a lifeboat if you like, for the local authority system?

(*Mr Britnell*) Yes, I think we do see ourselves undoubtedly in that role. The situation in Wales has developed along different lines from that in England. I think also, rather than just seeing ourselves there by default, we do see that we have a strength in working outside the local authority system. If you want me to expand on that, I can. I do not think we see ourselves as just a poor substitute for the lack of local authority staff, but from our position outside central government and outside local government we do see that we have an important role to play as a pressure group in a lot of ways.

623. Mr Longley, do you want to add anything to that?

(*Mr Longley*) I was going to jump in and add something but Bill has covered the points I wanted to raise there. We see our position as a positive one rather than as a fall-back. We are pro-active.

624. Let me put the question in another way: do you think the lack of conservation officers within local authorities is now a weakness, or do you think that it is no longer necessary for the local authorities to employ conservation officers because you in fact are doing the job?

(*Mr Benson*) I think there is a distinction to be made here between conservation officers and, as you then went on to mention, archaeologists in local authorities. This really goes back to the difference in the legislation ultimately between that for historic buildings and that for ancient monuments. I do not think any of us would want to say we would not want to see more conservation officers in local authorities. We would want to see conservation officers in local authorities because generally they deal with very specific areas of activity which by and large I do not think the trusts actually provide. But if we are talking about archaeological officers and archaeological advice, that is a very different matter. Across even some aspects of the broader range of the historic environment we feel at the moment the system we have in Wales is a very good one and in many ways superior to that in England, and we are looking at situations in England now where things might end up the same way as they are in Wales.

625. You deal with local authorities right across Wales, very few of them have got conservation officers. Do you find that those who do have conservation officers have a tremendous advantage in terms of the work that is done regarding ancient monuments in particular relative to those who do not?

(*Mr Benson*) My view on that would be in terms of ancient monuments, as distinct from historic buildings, and the answer to your question is no.

626. Is the same true of you all?
(*Mr Longley*) Yes, Sir.

627. Looking on to April 1995, and let us assume the Secretary of State for Wales gets his way and the unitary authorities which are proposed in the White Paper which came out just over a week ago are in place at that date, would you with the background of

[Chairman *Cont*]

unitary authorities coming along welcome perhaps more local authority provision in terms of conservation officers? What would be your role as trusts if these new unitary authorities were encouraged with pump-priming funding by Cadw, to have both archaeological and building specialists? Do you see, in other words, a possible conflict there? Do you see possibly the end or the reduction at least of your activity? Or put it even another way: do you see the new unitary authorities could pose problems for you in the fields which you yourselves are expert in?

(*Mr Dowdell*) Could I respond firstly to the point about the appointment of archaeological staff, and confine my response to that? I think being pump-primed to appoint archaeological staff would be a very costly option. I say that because we are talking about 21, I believe, unitary authorities which are proposed at present, and I would argue, I believe from a fairly concrete platform, that the sort of figures we would be talking about to maintain one person and perhaps some secretarial support per authority will be in the order of £30,000 a year. That is 30,000 times 21 and that is a substantial sum of money, and that is just for a solitary individual to be employed at a reasonable level of salary. But when you look elsewhere outside of Wales, in England, the cost factors we are talking about for a reasonable number of staff, say three or four, can fluctuate from, say, £109,000 up to £143,000 per district authority, and I think that our position would be that we provide very, very good value for money to the various local authorities which we serve, whether counties or districts. I do not want to labour the point on the financial side of things, but one of the strengths which the trusts have got, and perhaps it should be emphasised, in their advice to local authorities is an impartiality of advice, an independence of advice, and it is a very broad-based series of advice which is given. I am addressing my remarks to the archaeological aspect of it. I do not think it is economically realistic to propose that situation. I know the difficulties which currently local authorities are going through because I have been trying to make representations to them, as indeed my colleagues have in the other trusts, to financially support the development control aspects of our work. So economically, it is not a good thing. Secondly, the trusts, because of their impartiality and independence, can be seen to be best advisers, particularly in the planning processes, and in related conservation matters there is a wealth of expertise.

628. Anything to add?

(*Mr Britnell*) One thing which should be added as far as my understanding goes is that the new unitary authorities would see themselves very much as enabling authorities, and the concept of buying-in specialist services from other bodies is a concept which will gain increasing ground. I know the structures group on economic development and planning which was considering this in Wales, specifically considered the archaeological position, and I think one of the trends that they saw was that rather than having in-house archaeological staff one of the options they could have would be to buy-in these services from organisations such as ourselves. I think this is a trend we are also seeing in England at the moment with various planning functions being contracted out.

629. Mr Benson, do you want to add anything to that?

(*Mr Benson*) The only other thing, Mr Chairman, I would like to add to that is that if archaeologists were appointed within unitary authorities, such appointments would generally invariably be at a fairly low level in the authority, they would tend from previous experience with authorities to be not very well supported in terms of support staff, both in expertise of archaeology and other matters. It seems to us that contrasting that with the position which the trusts are in, they have staff with a wide range of experience across the archaeological spectrum, and are able to apply the whole of that experience and indeed use their members to link into a wider body of experience into the conservation issues which the unitary authorities will be dealing with.

Mr Llwyd

630. Moving on slightly, it is clear that more adequate provision within local authorities in Wales would bring Wales more into line with the present practice in England. As I understand it, that is the case, but in the Clwyd-Powys memorandum, and I refer to page 2, it does say, "It will probably be more appropriate in terms of cost-effectiveness and regional identity to improve and extend the mechanisms which already exist in Wales than to seek uniformity with other parts of the UK." Two or three points I would like to ask on that to all you gentlemen. Firstly, how would you set about achieving this? In other words, more adequate provisions rather than emulating the present practice in England? I think Mr Dowdell made the point earlier that in certain ways there was a preferred system in the Welsh context in any event, but the question is, how would you set about achieving this and how would you set it on foot?

(*Mr Longley*) I think one of the key elements in the relationship between the trusts and the planning authorities is the advice we provide with regard to development control, because this is only one of a large number of works which the trusts carry out. They are able to provide this advice because of the depth of knowledge and experience and stability and regional expertise, they are able to provide this advice I think better than one or two people in a planning department could. But because the SMR is the key to our relationship with local authorities, one way we could provide a better service for local authorities would be to put resources into improving the regional SMRs which the trusts maintain. The trust SMRs at the moment probably have the breadth and depth to equal any comparable record in Wales—I do not think I would be wrong in saying that—but there is more work to be done. These SMRs cannot be left to look after themselves. They need to be maintained and there needs to be enhancement of the SMR, new information is coming up through new field work, new excavations all the time, and this information has to find its way on to the SMR in a way which is accessible and useful. There are ways of interrogating the computer-based SMRs, and we have to look at ways of getting information out of the SMRs in a more appropriate, more usable, way than

[Mr Llwyd *Cont]*

at the moment. There are in the Gwynedd Trust many records which exist in a paper form queuing up to be put on the SMR. This is a resource problem.

631. What I was trying to ask was, given that the Welsh system appears to be adequate, were it extended would it be far more effective? That is what I am trying.
(*Mr Longley*) Extended in what sense? There is room for development within the trusts.

632. An extension of the present system.
(*Mr Longley*) I think resources into the SMR is one of the most important ways that we could improve the trust system.
(*Mr Benson*) You asked how you would set about achieving that, and to a certain extent we have already achieved it in the sense that the system we have at the moment is in place and if you are looking at that in terms of unitary authorities, it is simply transferring our relations between existing local authorities to the new unitary authorities, so the structural framework is there. Obviously the efficiency of that relationship does depend upon the resources which are devoted to it, and my colleague here has drawn attention to one area.

633. Do you other gentlemen have comments to make on that?
(*Mr Dowdell*) I think we would just endorse that. There are areas, obviously, which can be improved upon which have been identified—the record for instance—and there are areas which we believe are under-resourced and we do try to make up the various deficits ourselves from funding other than that derived from cadw. But I would agree with my colleagues, the basis is there for a progression given the changes in two years' time or whenever those changes may be.

Mr Ainger

634. What you are saying is that there should not be a change in the way the system operates at the moment, but if there is going to be an improvement in funds for various ranges of needs, you should be the main recipient of those rather than the new unitary authorities? Is that what you are saying?
(*Mr Dowdell*) I do think we should be the main recipient, I do not think we are being greedy, Mr Chairman, but there should be acknowledgement of the fact that there are services in place which just require a little topping up here and there to make those services more than adequate.
(*Mr Britnell*) Coming back to the point Mr Dowdell was making earlier, at the moment over large parts of Wales, looking at one particular area of development control, we have four organisations, which are the trusts, who are effectively maintaining a service. If you are to go to 21 different units in each of the unitary authorities, the increase in public expenditure (and it is all public expenditure whether it is from revenue support grant or whether it is funded centrally or out of the council tax) is a multiplication by five. So there is a very significant resource implication there, and the disadvantages of it which have been spelt out by Mr Benson are potentially one member of staff operating singly at a low tier in a unitary authority.

635. What you are saying is you agree with me, if there is to be a better service provided then you should be the lead organisation doing that rather than it going to the new unitary authorities?
(*Mr Benson*) Yes, and I think comparisons have been made with England and the difference has been stressed. But, if I may say so, Mr Chairman, we are already seeing developments in England where the archaeological services as part of planning authorities are in some cases already being externalised—they are going out into the private sector. This seems likely to be an increasing trend, and what it seems to us likely to happen is that ironically perhaps over the next five years, England will develop a system of the kind we already have in place here in Wales, so there is no point in reversing the trend.

636. Do you make a charge for this work you do for all the current planning authorities and will do for the new unitary authorities?
(*Mr Benson*) We have been making—and this has come in really since the extra workload which has been placed on our resources as a result of PPG 16, which may come up for further analysis—attempts to try and secure contributions from existing local authorities towards the services which we are providing.

637. You do not send a bill in for the advice you currently give on a particular planning application?
(*Mr Benson*) We do not send a bill to the local planning authority.

638. If we went to a contracted-out basis, of course, that is what would happen. Or are you seeking to do that? Would you prefer it on that basis rather than an annual contribution from a planning authority?
(*Mr Benson*) It depends on the level of resources which in fact the trusts have at that stage to operate that system effectively. At the moment we are put in the position where we are asking, if you like, for voluntary contributions from local planning authorities because we have a deficit in the funding that we get to run the system effectively.

Chairman

639. Can I take that on because Mr Ainger's questioning led into PPG 16, as you mentioned, Mr Benson, and that brings us to the interrelationship between the archaeological trusts and developers. One of the points which has been put to us during this inquiry is that you can be a kind of piggy-in-the-middle organisation. On the one side you could be asked by a developer to give on a fee paying basis advice to that developer wishing to develop on a site where there could be archaeological remains of great importance, on the other hand, you are obliged to give advice to the local authority in that particular area. What I want to explore with you just a little is the interrelationship between you, the planning authority and a potential developer on a particular site. Let me ask you a few questions in relation to that: under Planning Policy Guidance 16 and in other circumstances, do you work under contract to developers who are making applications within the planning system?

[Chairman *Cont]*

(*Mr Longley*) In response to your first statement, where a developer approaches us for archaeological information in support of an application he may be making, we do not charge for that advice. We do not levy a fee for that pre-planning advice. What we might do is provide information from our SMR and that information is available to any member of the public, and we would make that information available to him on the archaeology or the area that he may be seeking to develop, and we will at the same time copy the information to the local planning authority and we will inform them that we have had an inquiry from a developer in this respect. Exactly the same advice will go to the developer as goes to the planning authority. It may be that if the developer wishes to proceed with his development, he will require further work being done in the area of his proposed development, but this would not be work which would be a contract for our curatorial section. What we would recommend to the planning authority, if it was that far on in the planning process, is that further work would be necessary, and in the same way we would recommend this to the developer. We could prepare a brief for him of what work was required, and he would then be able to employ any archaeological contractor to carry out that work; it need not necessarily be us but any archaeological contractor. He would then get that work done if he wished to by an archaeological contractor for which presumably a fee would be charged, but that is not the same as charging a developer for advice and information on the archaeological implications of the proposed development at the pre-planning stage.

640. But presumably at that stage, where let us say your advice to a potential developer would be that he would need to have a detailed examination of that site in an archaeological sense, you would be then one of the organisations that could for a fee carry out that work as one of the consultants which could be in a potential list which the developer could in fact use?

(*Mr Longley*) It is probably appropriate to stress that in our organisation and in all the other trust organisations there has been a strict division of functions between the curatorial side, which provides advice to the planning authority and the developer, and the contracting side which may tender for work, both within Gwynedd and outside Gwynedd in our case. The same is true of the other trusts. So it would not be the same person who would be giving advice as would be tendering for work.

641. I appreciate that in terms of the way you deal with it, that in order to be absolutely fair you have that division of function, but nonetheless is it still the case that part of your function could be on a fee paying basis carrying out the work for a developer in assisting him to make a planning application, which could perhaps lead to a conflict of interest?

(*Mr Longley*) No. No conflict of interest.

642. None at all?

(*Mr Longley*) No.

643. But nonetheless could a situation arise whereby you would be advising the local authority in that area on the appropriate planning constraints in respect of developments where you also have been a consultant to a developer?

(*Mr Longley*) In our pre-planning advice we would give the same advice to the developer as to the local planning authority. Under the guidelines, PPG 16, it is for the planning authority to provide a brief for the developer. We would be in a position to make a brief available to a local planning authority but it need not necessarily be us. The guidelines put the onus on the planning authority to provide a brief for any archaeological work which might arise out of the planning application. The contract section in our trust would be in a position to tender for such work should the developer ask us to.

644. One of the witnesses we had last week put it to us that if he was a potential developer the last thing he would do would be to employ one of the archaeological trusts in Wales to support an application because the probability would be that the developer would run a mile from that report, because it would not be in the interests of the developer to employ one of you. Would you go that far?

(*Mr Longley*) I can only say that any report arising out of any archaeological work we carried out for a developer would be an unbiased, objective report, and an objective assessment of the archaeological implications of that development. I think the reason why we are in a position to say this is because, and this applies to all the archaeological trusts in Wales, the archaeological trusts are regional based trusts whose interest is the archaeology of that region, and that is why there is no conflict of interest. We are not interested in tendering for work in order to make a buck, we are interested in the archaeology of that region, and that is why I can confidently say in a situation like that there is no conflict of interest.

645. Would you find that conflict of interest possibly arising if in fact certain conditions were put on you in terms of a commercial rate of return in terms of the trusts as businesses? Or do you not foresee that happening?

(*Mr Longley*) We as charitable bodies are precluded from making a profit.

646. And there is no indication, as far as you know, of that changing?

(*Mr Longley*) Not as far as I know.

647. Do you want to add something, Mr Dowdell?

(*Mr Dowdell*) I was very glad that my colleague took up the point about the term you used, conflict of interest. The interest we have, whether it is curatorial or contractual, is archaeology and more particularly the preservation of that archaeology. On the curatorial side, obviously the thrust has always got to be preservation in situ. The other major option is of course preservation by record, the excavation of the site and its detailed recording. There is one other option which is open as well on the curatorial side, and that is the introduction of mitigatory measures, and there are a number of very good examples of this current at the moment, where we have in fact insisted, if that is the right term to use, upon the impact of the proposed development being reduced by (a) the development removal into another location or (b) minimising the low ground disturbance by a particular type of foundation being employed, and so forth. So there are three prongs, as it were, here. But I do not believe at any time there is a conflict of interest. On the curatorial side I should draw to your

[Chairman *Cont*]

attention, Mr Chairman, that we do have a curatorial code of practice which is in operation throughout all four trusts, in addition to which there are codes of conduct which are laid down by our own professional institute, the Institute of Field Archaeologists, which are also strictly adhered to. I would like to think in this respect, Mr Chairman, we are squeaky clean. I think we are as impartial as we possibly can be on both sides.

648. In terms of that, can you give us the figure of the income which has been received in the same year that we started off with today, which is the year 1991-92?
(*Mr Dowdell*) £338,000, I think.

649. What I meant was the amount of income you received as trusts from fees when you were asked to provide information for developers within your areas in that year, to give us some idea of the relative importance to your funding of money you received from that? Would you know the figures?
(*Mr Benson*) In my case it is nil.

650. You did no work at all?
(*Mr Benson*) We undertook archaeological excavation. In the particular circumstances that you are describing, I do not think we had one instance where we were involved in having a fee from a developer. We did carry out contract work as a result of a condition of planning consent which related to a development by Dyfed County Council for which they actually contributed some £40,000-odd towards the cost of the excavation.

651. What about the rest of you gentlemen?
(*Mr Dowdell*) The only fees which we have charged in that particular year would be in respect of consultants acting on behalf of prospective developers, but the sum of money is very, very small, only about £100 over the entire year. This is a fee levied for staff time devoted to searching through the record, which is a very·modest fee.

652. So the income of the archaeological trusts for that kind of work forms a very, very small proportion of your total income?
(*Mr Benson*) For that kind of work, yes.
(*Mr Dowdell*) For the initial advice, yes.

Mr Hanson

653. I would like to look at a couple of points relating to the sites and monuments record and your relationship with the Royal Commission and with cadw and try to explore those, if I may. The sites and monuments record was transferred last year from cadw to the Royal Commission, and in the Clwyd-Powys and Dyfed memoranda a series of reservations have been expressed about the level of funding of the SMRs via the Royal Commission. I wonder if Mr Britnell could outline the concern that he has relating to the funding particularly about SMRs?
(*Mr Britnell*) We have become very concerned. I think the trusts see the sites and monuments record as the hub of a lot of work for them, both in development control and educational work and planning work programmes and so on; the sites and monuments record is the basis for a lot of that. At the time when the transfer of funding to the Royal Commission was being talked about there was a

working party group which involved the Royal Commission, Cadw and the trust, and we at that stage identified a figure I believe of £112,000 which we thought was the figure upon which a reasonable service for the maintenance of the sites and monuments record could be maintained in Wales per annum. In looking through some of the other evidence given to you, I think the figure of £60,000 per annum was mentioned, so we are already now talking of a figure which is half that amount. In reality the amount of money going into the sites and monuments record at the moment in Wales is £24,000, so a figure that we had identified of over £100,000 has come down to £24,000. We are all in the situation of having backlogs of information which desperately need to be accessed into the SMR—we have problems with hardware and software development, we have problems with wanting to extend the scope of the record to embrace more monument types which are now considered to be important. It is frustrations of this kind which have been building up.

654. Where do you feel the problem lies? You have mentioned the figure of £112,000 and we are now expecting £24,000, where do you see the need for action and whose responsibility do you see that being? Cadw are funding the Royal Commission who are in turn transferring work and support to yourselves. Where do you see the responsibility?
(*Mr Britnell*) Perhaps it lies with cadw. I am not sure I can answer that.

Mr Ainger

655. Are you saying that it is Cadw's fault because they did not transfer sufficient resources to the Royal Commission? Or perhaps they did in a lump sum and the Royal Commission has kept some of it?
(*Mr Benson*) Can I come in here? As I understand it, the Commission put in a development bid for funding which was connected with the development of the extended national data base, which is the subject of discussion between the trusts and Cadw, and they have not been successful in that bid. So it is not so much the Commission has not asked for the money, as Cadw has not provided it.

656. That is the point of the question I was asking. The Royal Commission have told us they did not receive the level of support and resources they had hoped for from Cadw, but I wanted the situation from you.
(*Mr Benson*) That is our understanding of the position.

657. Is that understanding a gut understanding or is it based on information?
(*Mr Dowdell*) We have been advised to that effect by the Royal Commission, what the finances would be.

658. Do you, each of you, support the transfer of responsibility to the Royal Commission in the first place?
(*Mr Dowdell*) Yes.
(*Mr Longley*) Our concern is the maintenance and enhancement of the record. If funds are made available, I do not mind if they are coming from the Royal Commission or directly from cadw. It is the

[**Mr Ainger** *Cont*]

record itself which is our concern and our responsibility.

659. In terms of that record, do you feel you are getting a better service dealing with the Royal Commission than you would do from dealing directly with cadw or indeed with the Welsh Office or any other body?

(*Mr Benson*) It depends what our ultimate objectives are in Wales. My view is that we need to create a national data base which will have various elements. It will be a combination of nationally available data and regionally available data, data which could be collected at a national level and at a regional level. It is building up a structure which will be accessed from a wide variety of points and be utilised for a wide variety of functions, and in this particular case we are looking at a structural arrangement which involves the Commission as the lead body for records in Wales and the regional trusts. That seems to me to be a sensible way forward.

Mr Hanson

660. It could be argued that there is a proliferation of records at the moment. If you had the option and there was to be only one organisation managing the record, which would it be? Yourselves, the Royal Commission or local authorities?

(*Mr Benson*) The trust and the Commission records have developed in different ways. I would not like to be offered that kind of choice because the Commission has the national monuments record which is certainly greater in depth in some areas than the trust records, for example on architecture, and the trust records, as well as being computerised, have a greater depth in archaeological sites. It seems to me that building a relationship between those two is a sensible way forward. .

Chairman

661. Let us look at that for a minute. In terms of that, are your four SMR data base systems compatible so that in fact the building blocks for having a NMR system, or even having a satisfactory SMR system, are there? Can you, in other words, tell me whether you have that compatibility between each of your systems?

(*Mr Britnell*) I can say when the records were first set up in the late 1970s we went to a great deal of care to ensure that the information which was being put into the records was on a similar structure basis which would allow compatibility of the records throughout Wales. I think we are probably one of the largest regions in Britain where that is possible and there is scope within Wales to amalgamate the records on a national basis.

662. So if I popped into each of your trust offices and looked through your SMRs, I would have no difficulty moving from one office to another in terms of understanding the way it works because they are uniform across the trusts, are they?

(*Mr Longley*) That is correct.

Mr Hanson

663. Just to clarify for ourselves, what functions do you believe the SMR has or might have for other people who might wish to use it?

(*Mr Longley*) In discussing the respective merits of a national or regional data base, while I take every point that Don has made and agree with him, we have to stress the value of the local SMR, the regional SMR which is maintained locally. It is maintained in the region by people with local regional knowledge and it is used in the region by people who want to gain access to that local knowledge. It is used for development control purposes but also by members of the public and it is used for educational purposes and all sorts of things, and in the development control work and when dealing with the general public seeking further information there is a lot of local knowledge which goes into interpretation of the evidence on the SMR in making information available either to planners or in answer to enquiries from the public. So I would stress that while there is value in having a centralised record, there is at least as much value in having that regional component to it, and that is a function which the trusts perform.

664. Is that access common to you all?

(*Mr Britnell*) Yes.

(*Mr Benson*) Can I say in answer to your question about functions, my list would include the contribution which the record can make to conservation policies and the development of strategies. There is an educational dimension to the record, it is also a research tool for a whole variety of individuals and organisations, it also has a value in economic terms if you look at areas where information is required on aspects of historic environment for economic development for example in the tourism industry. I would also add on the question of the information which the records hold, their utility as far as interpretation work is concerned.

665. Do any of you charge the general public for use of the record?

(*Mr Dowdell*) No.

(*Mr Longley*) No.

(*Mr Dowdell*) *Bona fides* research students, interested members of the public, there is no charge, it is free access.

666. Cadw has a background to all the work which is going on in your sphere. In your experience and in your case, each of you, do you think Cadw have a strategic role in the preservation of historic monuments in Wales, and what is your view on what that role is?

(*Mr Longley*) Cadw are increasingly taking on a strategic role. I think that with the onus being placed on developers through PPG 16 to provide information as part of the planning process, this has enabled cadw to move slightly away from the very specific and direct response to developer threat and the funding of developer threat, and to use the rescue resources available to it to look at a more strategic approach to the threats to archaeology in the landscape. I would welcome the initiatives which cadw are currently engaged in, in looking at the non-developer, or the threats which fall outside the planning process such as agricultural threats, in a

[Mr Hanson *Cont]*

strategic way, such as the project we will soon be engaged in in Gwynedd, which is looking at the threats to non-scheduled hut groups in the landscape, one of the major monument types in the Gwynedd landscape in North Wales—the Iron Age stone wall hut groups—many of which are on agricultural land and subject to processes which fall outside the PPG 16 develop control side of things. I can say at the same time that in a rural environment such as Gwynedd and this probably applies to Clwyd, Powys and Dyfed as well, something like 90 per cent of the threats to archaeology fall outside the planning process, and this is an area of development control which is sometimes overlooked which trusts do perform.

667. In a very short statement do you feel you have an input into what Cadw's strategic role is in Wales? Do you believe you are consulted by Cadw? Do you feel part of the process of development policy in Wales?

(*Mr Benson*) For the most part, yes.

(*Mr Dowdell*) For the most part, yes.

(*Mr Longley*) We would like to be consulted at an earlier stage on some of the initiatives.

Chairman

668. Like what?

(*Mr Longley*) There is a very important initiative which will begin in April which will, in partnership with CCW, ICOMOS and Cadw, be looking at the historic landscape of Wales, and it will be a study which will begin to look at the criteria and parameters for defining historic landscapes in Wales. This is a very important initiative and it is one to be welcomed, and it has the support of the trusts and the trusts will be consulted to a great degree during the progress of this initial study, but some of my colleagues feel that involvement at an earlier stage in defining the brief for the project might have been welcomed. That is one example.

669. Have you been involved by now? It starts in April, you say?

(*Mr Longley*) It starts in April, yes. We all will be involved. I have perhaps a slightly more direct involvement than my colleagues because one member of my staff in Gwynedd is being seconded to the CCW for a 12 month period to carry out this exercise, so I have known a little more about it at the earlier stages than my colleagues. But my colleagues have communicated to me they would have liked to have been consulted and to have had an input into the definition of the brief for this project at an early stage. I cite that as an example. But having said that, the strategic approach which cadw is now making, and I feel increasingly, is one which (and I hope I speak for my colleagues here) is to be welcomed and we look forward to seeing the results of some of these initiatives.

670. Mr Dowdell, you were nodding?

(*Mr Dowdell*) I certainly endorse those remarks. We have welcomed these initiatives, as Dave Longley has just mentioned, and we saw it last year as well with the Tir Cymen scheme across Wales, and that is continuing. There are problems there but these will gradually iron themselves out. The only main criticism we have is that we would prefer to be involved at the word go rather than coming in a little along the line, because we do feel we have positive contributions to make and to assist and co-operate with cadw in these initiatives.

671. We are coming to the end of this session but can I ask you about the listing side? In terms of the slowness with which the re-survey programmes are occurring across Wales, certainly not in Wrexham but certainly across Wales, for both scheduled monuments and listed buildings, does that slowness of the re-survey programme cause any particular problems for you in the management of conservation archaeology?

(*Mr Dowdell*) I am a little concerned, to say the least, Mr Chairman, as indeed my colleagues are. We hear of the projected figure in terms of how many buildings can be listed within the existing and on-going programme, and we think the target is far too low. Given the timescale involved I most certainly, and I think the rest of my colleagues, will never see the end of that programme. I do feel it needs to be accelerated and there should be more input. Having said that, it is easy to be critical, but again we would collectively welcome an approach from cadw to assist in this programme. It has been done elsewhere in England and I know there have been criticisms. For example, if a site has been scheduled because it is a Bronze Age burial mound, you do not dig the site up to find out what is inside, you schedule the mound (and as far as I am concerned, list the building) and if at sometime in the future it is under threat from demolition or whatever, then is the time to do that. It is an early warning system which is adopted within the planning process by identifying it as a listed building. As I say, one can be critical of the approaches, but at the same time I would like to be constructive and say we would like to assist if the necessary resources are there, and it does not have to be a very substantial resource.

672. Would the four of you agree with that? That you would welcome an approach from cadw to assist in speeding up that process?

(*Mr Benson*) Yes, we think we could be involved in a way, providing the resources could be made available, which would assist very much in that process. There is no doubt the slowness of both these programmes does cause problems as far as conservation is concerned, because we are losing buildings where we should not be losing buildings, and we are losing archaeological sites where we should not be losing archaeological sites.

673. You say in your memorandum, Mr Benson, there have been several instances where redundant buildings in local authority ownership have been neglected and their details unrecorded prior to demolition or change of use.

(*Mr Benson*) Yes, I was thinking particularly I suppose, because some work which I am doing at the moment brought it to mind, of examples like Victorian school buildings, some of which, although they may be redundant in terms of the requirements of today, are in fact significant architectural pieces in their own right, and whatever their future may be in many cases they should be recorded. I can think of several examples where in the process of these buildings become redundant and let for a long time

[**Chairman** *Cont*]

without any change of use, they have gone from bad to worse, and there has been no provision made for recording the important and interesting architectural detail.

674. Would it be difficult for you to let us have the names of those schools?

(*Mr Benson*) I can let you have the names of a few, yes. It is a thing I have not surveyed in detail, but I know of a number of examples where this has occurred.

675. One of the difficulties we are having in this inquiry is finding a sufficient number of examples of cases in order to illustrate the problem. That comes to the last part of my question which relates to churches and chapels. One of the things which has been very much to the fore in our inquiry is the extent to which congregations are falling throughout Wales and increasingly over the next few years we are going to have the problems of redundant buildings, particularly chapels and churches. When we questioned the Church in Wales and the Free Church in Wales about their present exemption from planning controls, we were told they wanted to retain the exemption that they have got. Your trust, Mr Benson, described the care exercised by the Church in Wales in conservation terms as "completely inadequate". What kind of problems have you encountered with this issue in the past? Again it is examples we are short of because the strange thing is that we hear sometimes that there are as many as three chapels a week in Wales actually closing, and yet at the same time we are having great difficulty identifying the scale of this problem. Have you encountered problems in the past with this whole question of the exemption from planning controls of churches and chapels? Mr Longley?

(*Mr Longley*) Yes, we have; we all have. I can give you some examples. At St Mary's, Talyllyn, in November 1991 we were contacted by the vicar there when bones were discovered during the course of digging the floor up. The church had a grant to carry out this reflooring work but there was no archaeological notification that this was the case, and there was no recognition of the archaeological implications of this particular piece of work. The trust responded as best it could under the circumstances, but by the time we got to the site the damage had been done. I can give another example: Llangylennin in the Conway Valley, back in 1986 there was a Manpower Services Commission scheme to re-point the church. Llangylennin is a very attractive and very important church in an upland landscape; very, very important with a holy well, which is probably pre-Christian and Celtic in origin. The scheme was to re-point the church, dig a trench right round the church for drainage purposes, tidy up the graveyard and dig out the holy well. This was a tidying up Manpower Services scheme. The trust returned to the site on as many occasions as it could, as it was able to find the resources, and it recorded a number of burials as they were disturbed during the course of these excavations around the outside of the church, and it identified the site of a side chapel which had been demolished some considerable time previously, the foundations of which were no longer visible above ground and had been turfed over. These tidying up schemes cut right across the foundations

of the side chapel. Those are two examples but I can give you others if you want them.

676. Would you from your experience, Mr Longley, wish the Church in Wales to retain its exemption from planning controls in the light of what you have just said?

(*Mr Longley*) I can see no reason whatsoever for churches to be exempt from the same kind of planning controls as any other historic monument.

677. What they told us was that in return for more consultation, which they were prepared to give, they wanted to retain that exemption, but you think they should lose it?

(*Mr Longley*) I think if we are genuinely interested and concerned for our historic buildings, of which churches are an important element, I can see no reason to maintain the exemption.

678. I am really glad to be given those examples and if you other gentlemen could supply us with examples of that kind, that would be helpful. The difficult point for us is if we find some examples from the past, and then we recommend, let us say, the Church in Wales should lose its exemption, we are just worried those examples may be very few and far between, or that there has been an improvement in the way the Church in Wales consults. So if in fact the church is moving quickly in the right direction and wishes to retain that exemption, we would find ourselves in a bit of a difficult position. Do you think that the problem has not got any worse? Or, do you think the Church in Wales still does not consult enough?

(*Mr Longley*) If the Church in Wales is genuinely interested in the implications of its development work, and is prepared to consult in order to safeguard the integrity of the historic buildings, then it has nothing to fear from putting its applications through the normal planning channels, has it?

679. That is the view of you all, is it? You all unanimously believe that the Church in Wales should lose its exemption and should be subject to normal planning controls like every other owner of buildings?

(*Mr Benson*) I have a slight reservation over that because we are not dealing with the kind of building which can readily be put to alternative use. It is not like an historic building which is a dwelling house which has the opportunity if necessary of several purchasers who might be interested in it. There is a problem about what to do as a result of declining congregations. I am not saying this in any way is a defence against their obligation to look after important historic buildings, but I do think they are in circumstances which are slightly different from the average private owner of an historic building. Therefore my own view would be given those circumstances perhaps one ought to allow an opportunity to see whether effective consultation procedures can be brought in. But having said that, my own experience up to now leads me to believe that is unlikely because the track record is simply not there.

(*Mr Britnell*) I would like to endorse what Mr Benson said there. If a timescale could be set within which the churches could provide evidence that they

[Chairman *Cont*]

had set procedures in motion, that would be acceptable. But I think a timescale has to be set.

680. Do you agree, Mr Dowdell?

(*Mr Dowdell*) I agree more with David Longley. I do not see any reason why this situation should continue. A church is yet another historic building type and I do not see why it should be outside the planning legislation at all. My experience, and I will list them for you, Mr Chairman, is a catalogue of disaster with churches, both the damage which has been caused to the actual churches and to the immediate environs. It is not a pretty document to read and I will certainly submit these instances which you require.

681. Mr Dowdell, you use the term "a catalogue of disaster", is that continuing? You are adding to that catalogue, are you?

(*Mr Britnell*) Yes, we have got examples which are coming to light now.

682. They are still coming in?

(*Mr Dowdell*) Almost certainly.

(*Mr Britnell*) We had one last week, and there was one a couple of weeks before that, of works in relation to church sites which should really have had archaeological consultation.

(*Mr Longley*) I would add a slight modification to that, that the situation has changed in the last 12 months in that Historic Building Council grant-aided work which may have an archaeological implication is being identified by cadw, and they are identifying the threat and diverting some of the rescue vote into any archaeological work which might be necessary arising out of the Historic Building Council grant-aided work. But my understanding of the situation is that this alerting of the archaeological bodies, the trusts, is after the grant has been awarded, so it does not actually allow the situation whereby we can prevent a threat or modify it or divert it, all we can do is respond to the threat by what we call, in the jargon, preservation by record.

(*Mr Britnell*) The other anomaly from our point of view is that if the Church in Wales is wanting to build a new vestry or a church hall or whatever, that would have to go through the normal planning process, and we would pick it up and can comment on it, and try

to ameliorate the effects of that, but if it is works which do not require planning permission, or repairs to the structure and it is not grant-aided by cadw, the archaeological implications of that are not going to be picked up at the moment unless the church itself has some mechanism for identifying that.

683. Would you say this change in the procedures would really save a great deal of important archaeological remains for Wales, if this consultation procedure had been in place over the last ten years?

(*Mr Britnell*) I think you can contrast, looking at it in academic terms, the knowledge increase there has been in England in church archaeology over the last ten or fifteen years, which really has not developed in Wales. There has been a considerable amount of church archaeology in England, a lot of it stemming from the consultation procedures which the Church of England goes through which do not operate to effect in the Church in Wales.

684. If that system operated in Wales, would you be happy for the churches to retain their exemption?

(*Mr Britnell*) I probably would.

685. Mr Longley would not?

(*Mr Longley*) If the consultation is effective then it would have the same effect as going through the normal planning process, so I do not see why we have to take a chance on relying on effective consultation. I do not really see why it cannot be put to the test in the planning process.

Chairman: Gentlemen, thank you very much for coming to see us. We have learnt a tremendous lot. Perhaps you could give us some of the information which we asked for—we would be very interested in having four catalogues of disaster because nothing pleases us more than information like that! Thank you very much indeed. I hope that you will accept from us that we did not in any way try to impugn your integrity when we looked at the possible conflict of interest with regard to development, we simply wanted to explore the way you have dealt with that matter, and we are very much better informed as a result of you coming before us. Thank you very much.

Examination of Witnesses

MR PHILIP EYTON-JONES, Director of Architecture, Planning and Estates, DR IAN W BROWN, County Heritage Officer, MR STEPHEN GRENTER, Archaeologist, and MR JON JAMES, Conservation Officer, Clwyd County Council; MR RON DOUGLAS, Conservation Architect, Snowdonia National Park; and MR CHRISTOPHER J THOMAS, Head of Planning Services and MR WILLIAM J TWIGG, former Conservation Officer, Delyn Borough Council, were examined.

Chairman

686. Gentlemen, I apologise for the lateness of our start. I thank you very much for coming. It is going to be difficult to ask questions with so many of you here but we will have a go. In terms of expertise, the Assembly of Welsh Counties has pointed to the shortage of trained conservation officers among Welsh local authorities. Mr Twigg, you are a former conservation officer?

(*Mr Twigg*) Yes.

687. Is it correct, as far as you know, only two county councils in Wales employ full-time conservation staff?

(*Mr Twigg*) As far as I am aware, yes.

688. Is this a matter of concern for you?

(*Mr Twigg*) Yes, indeed it is. I am also concerned about the lack of conservation officers in district councils particularly. We are dealing with buildings of specific interest and the knowledge required is fairly esoteric, and really a level of expertise is needed

THE WELSH AFFAIRS COMMITTEE

185

9 March 1992]

MR PHILIP EYTON-JONES, DR IAN W BROWN,
MR STEPHEN GRENTER, MR JON JAMES, MR RON DOUGLAS,
MR CHRISTOPHER J THOMAS, AND MR WILLIAM J TWIGG

[Continued

[Chairman Cont]
to interpret buildings of that type and the lack of that expertise is a considerable concern.

689. Can I turn to Mr Douglas, you are the conservation architect for the Snowdonia National Park?
(Mr Douglas) Correct.

690. Could you describe for us what that position involves and how it has developed?
(Mr Douglas) First of all I was a development control officer, I am an architect and planner and I have spent 20 years in development control. Then in 1988 I agreed to become the conservation architect so we could start enhancement and protection of listed buildings. At the moment I have an assistant who has just been appointed, so there are two of us, qualified architects, and we have also an in-house archaeologist.

691. In terms of Delyn, does Delyn Borough Council employ a conservation officer?
(Mr Thomas) Mr Twigg, until 31st December, was our conservation officer, having been employed since the local government reorganisation in 1974. He has taken early retirement but we are retaining him on a consultancy basis, effectively one day a week for the time being, to tide us over as it were. I am not sure what the long term arrangements will be in the light of the White Paper which has recently been published, but at the moment the arrangement is working quite well and Mr Twigg is able to advise and help us in his consultancy capacity on matters which are arising in the conservation field.

692. Thank you. The Assembly of Welsh Counties states that only one county council in Wales employs an archaeologist. Presumably, Mr Grenter, who are that man?
(Mr Grenter) I am it, yes.

693. In England, county councils are obliged to employ archaeological staff. By what arguments would the Clwyd County Council try to persuade other county councils in Wales that they should also employ an archaeologist?
(Mr Grenter) I think you need to look at the range of activities which the Clwyd archaeology service carries out. We see ourselves as a very broad historic conservation body, and we carry out in Clwyd a curatorial role in terms of development control, and we have a sites and monuments record to carry that function out. We undertake conservation work on a wide range of sites for a variety of periods throughout the county, and we are able to go out to look at sponsorship and grant-aid in order to carry that conservation out. We also carry out a large amount of site management work, which is a new field, and something which we are taking an increasing interest in. Underlying the whole of that conservation effort (and this is something which is particular to local authorities because we have very much in mind we are employed by the local population, that the work we do is predominantly funded by the taxpayers of the county) is public participation and telling people exactly what we have been doing and why we have been doing it. I think the county council archaeology service over the years has pioneered, in Wales at least, the concept of public archaeology, and that is backed by our mailing list.

Our mailing list has been going since the mid-70s and it now has something over 2,500 people within Clwyd on it, and they receive newsletters and are invited to various events, et cetera. So in terms of a role of a sort of agent provocateur, if you like, in carrying out site preservation, we have had a significant effect on the archaeological and historical environment in Clwyd. I would say that to other county councils in Wales. I think the other thing is something which you touched on with your previous witnesses, and that is the curatorial function in terms of development control. We see that very much as a local authority role and function, and we also would see it as an enabling function. We are enabling contractors, and we would possibly look at the trusts in that regard, as archaeological contractors and we are enabling those organisations to carry out archaeological work providing independent and objective advice to the local planning authorities in order the contractors can be employed by the developer.

694. How do you relate to the local archaeological trust?
(Mr Grenter) We are obviously independent of the trust. We consult the Clwyd-Powys Archaeological Trust in Clwyd regarding planning applications because what we want to avoid is the Clwyd-Powys Trust and ourselves giving conflicting advice to the local planning authorities. That would not be good for anybody. So because we exist and because we have existed since 1975 and because the Clwyd-Powys Trust has existed for the same period, we consult at a very early stage in the planning process, and consider what the best archaeological response is. We would then write a brief for any archaeological work which would go out, and it is then up to the local planning authority to advise developers as to which contractor they would use. The other point I would mention, which I know did not come up during your last witness session, is the monitoring of the archaeological work which is carried out. It is extremely important in our view that the monitoring, cost effectiveness, the quality control, of archaeological work on sites where there has been planning permission granted, is carried out by an independent body and not in the situation at present in most of Wales by the same body carrying out the work.

695. In terms of the historic landscape and fabric of the principality, do you think, Dr Brown, we may be suffering from a lack of trained personnel employed by local authorities in these areas?
(Dr Brown) In terms of the historic landscape as such, it is probably not as bad as in pure archaeological work. As you say, Stephen is the only county council archaeologist. In terms of the historic landscape, the traditional role of the local authority planning departments is well developed throughout Wales. In regard to the archaeological implications of historic landscapes, that is something different, I think, and certainly our archaeological sites management officer is, or was, unique in Wales—I understand Brecon Beacons now is appointing such an officer. So in terms of the site management role in historic landscapes, the answer to your question is yes, there are not many officers around in regard to the archaeological implications of historic landscapes.

[Chairman *Cont*]

696. Going back to Mr Grenter, in terms of the archaeological trust, do you think that there is a potential conflict between the role of the archaeological trust in giving advice to the planning authority on the one hand and to a potential developer on the other?

(*Mr Grenter*) I think there is. If there is not a real conflict of interest, I think there is a perceived conflict of interest, and as far as developers are concerned that amounts to the same thing. In the majority of Wales outside of Clwyd, outside of the national parks, there is not an option; the archaeological trusts at present are the only organisations in existence who are there to carry out both roles, so that is pragmatically the situation we are in at the moment. However in Clwyd we are in a situation where we could have the ideal of the local authorities carrying out the curatorial role and the trust acting as an archaeological contractor. We do not believe, and I certainly do not believe, that the trusts can be in a position where they advise the local planning authority as to how much work needs to be carried out on an archaeological site and then be one of the people bidding in order to carry that work out. The trusts are small organisations, unlike the situation in England where these two roles do happen in some local authorities where they are very large authorities; the Clwyd-Powys Trust for example only has a permanent staff of four or five. I do not believe in an organisation that small these socalled Chinese walls can really function properly.

697. Mr Douglas, would you go along with that view?

(*Mr Douglas*) In our case, our archaeologist consults directly with the development control officers. As regards planning applications, we automatically send a weekly list to the Gwynedd Archaeological Trust, and then if they wish to raise any point they will raise it directly with us as the planning authority.

698. But what about that conflict of interest?

(*Mr Douglas*) I would hope if they are professionals they would be able to keep that at bay.

699. Is hope enough, Mr Douglas?

(*Mr Douglas*) As an architect I would hope it would be, yes.

Mr Ainger

700. Can I clarify what Mr Grenter is saying to us? Is he saying in every planning authority—and after unitary authorities come in if the number of authorities is unamended in Committee Report Stage and Third Reading will be 21, plus the Snowdonia National Park, plus the Brecon Beacons, and plus the Pembrokeshire Coast National Park, which to my mind makes 24—there should be a conservation officer or an archaeologist giving advice rather than the current four archaeological trusts? Is that what you are saying?

(*Mr Grenter*) I am saying ideally after reorganisation that would be the option we would most favour, but as I am sure you have heard that would cost a great deal of money. The other option which I know was discussed by the committee dealing with local government structures after reorganisation, is the concept of lead authorities, and

I know this is very much suggested as a means of organising strategic services such as museums and archives. Because Clwyd is divided into four or three and a half areas, we would see this as a good possibility, that one of those new authorities could act as a lead authority and employ archaeological services which would be jointly funded by the boroughs in that area. So we are not talking about 21 or 24 archaeological services but at least half that number at most.

701. Twelve?

(*Mr Grenter*) Perhaps twelve, perhaps ten, it depends on the area that they would cover. In South Wales the new unitary authorities are very small and therefore you could have at least half a dozen of these covered by one archaeological service which is jointly funded by those new authorities.

702. But it would still represent a significant increase?

(*Mr Grenter*) Yes, certainly on what it is at the moment.

703. And all because you believe there is a conflict of interest?

(*Mr Grenter*) Yes.

704. Have you any particular instances where you think a conflict of interest has taken place?

(*Mr Grenter*) No.

705. So it is just a belief.

(*Mr Grenter*) It is a belief but also, to be fair, developers have come to us and said, "What has happened here? The trusts are carrying out both roles, are the trusts leading us up the garden path so to speak in specifying work which does not need to take place?" So developers have this problem about conflict of interest.[1]

Mr Hanson

706. Delyn Borough Council's memorandum to the Committee said in relation to the role of Cadw as far as Cadw's operations were concerned, there is a basic feeling that its headquarters' location in Cardiff is too remote to give a fully satisfactory service to North Wales. Certainly representing Delyn, that is a feeling I have picked up from a number of the community councils who have sites within their community council areas which are the responsibility of cadw. Mr Eyton-Jones, could I ask you whether you would share the view of Delyn's officers with regard to cadw's "remoteness"?

(*Mr Eyton-Jones*) I think I would. Certainly from a North Wales perspective you do not really see cadw officers up in North Wales as much as we could

---

[1]Note by witness: Although I see the problems regarding the conflict of interest as significant ones, I believe that the range of conservation work which the Clwyd Archaeology Service undertakes, justifies the additional expenditure that would be needed to set up similar bodies throughout Wales as the result of local government reorganisation. It should also be remembered that should the Trusts be asked to carry out the Curatorial function after reorganisation, they would not do so for free. Since, therefore, there are significant cost implications for the new Authorities whatever happens, I believe the case in favour of the establishment of broad based Conservation Services, including archaeology, within the new Unitary Authorities is an excellent one.

[**Mr Hanson** *Cont*]

expect. We realise, and I have not read the evidence which has been presented so far, that Cadw is under-resourced, but I think possibly a greater presence in the north would give us more reassurance that we would get a greater feed-back and a quicker response, particularly on the site and things we are looking at. I have only once been to visit cadw in Cardiff, and it is quite an effort to arrange meetings, et cetera. I am not being over-critical of their service to us, we believe we get a good service from cadw, but in combination with the under-resourcing and the distance, I would agree with Delyn's comments about that.

707. Would anybody not agree with Delyn's comments on that? Does anybody have any strong views in the opposite direction?

(*Mr Douglas*) I do feel that if there were enough professional officers who would be travelling in the north, probably the situation in the south does not matter so much. I find there is a shortage of professional officers.

708. I am led to understand there was an office in Conway which was closed recently. Does anybody wish to comment on the effect of that closure on the service?

(*Mr Twigg*) Talking now purely about the situation of listed buildings, town schemes rather than the archaeological side of matters, my experience as a working officer at that time was that we were served by an officer working from the Colwyn Bay area, prior to that office being closed, and contact was swift and good. I would not criticise the quality of service we get from the officers, their expertise, their knowledge and willingness, certainly I would compliment that, but it is really this problem of the distance between north and south, and the difficulty of travel between north and south Wales which affects not just this particular matter but many others. If I can give you one specific instance, there was a time when I was waiting for a visit on town schemes from a Cadw officer and it was some time before I could get a meeting on that and the reason I was told was that Cadw at the end of the year, towards December, had run out of money allowed for travelling and there was a three month moratorium on travel. This sort of situation does not really suit the needs of north Wales.

709. One site we are going to visit tomorrow which is close to my heart, is Flint Castle, and I know the chief planning officer, Mr Thomas, has said in his memorandum that there is a disappointment about the way in which cadw works with Flint Castle. Could you for the benefit of the members of the Committee who do not know the site, give your views so that when we meet tomorrow at Flint Castle we can have a background and an example of how Cadw operates with one of the sites within its control, within the Delyn Borough Council area?

(*Mr Thomas*) I think the situation basically as far as Flint Castle is concerned, is that there is a general feeling within Delyn and particularly within Flint itself, that here we have a national monument which cadw does not appear to have a very high opinion of, if I can put it that way, because the perception is that the monument is left very much to its own devices in terms of its care. There is no permanent presence

there by cadw on site, the site is exposed and is liable to vandalism, and even during the summer when one would expect there to be a regular presence to help interpretation and visitors to the site, there is very little in the way of a presence from Cadw. So there is the whole perception that Flint Castle is cut off from the sort of mainstream, as it were, as far as Cadw's involvement and marketing of the site and its care of the site is concerned.

710. To illustrate the point of remoteness from North Wales, could you perhaps indicate to the Committee what representations have been made to cadw with regard to Flint Castle and what has been the response of that body in terms of physical presence, physical support, to the borough councils and town councils and to the community, as an example of a cadw operation of a minor site admittedly—major historical importance but a minor site in relation to the other major sites in North Wales?

(*Mr Thomas*) I have not got the details with me but from memory I think the borough council and certainly as far as I am aware Flint Town Council have made representations to Cadw to improve the character of the surrounding area, around the castle, to improve the level of representation by people to help with interpretation, et cetera, on the site, and really there has been very little response from cadw to those requests. We have had meetings with them but in practical terms there has been very little which has come out of that sort of request directly to Cadw.

711. Obviously we will talk about Flint Castle in much more detail tomorrow, because Mr Carr, the chief executive, is coming tomorrow. The borough and the town council have requested him to do that for many years and it has taken the Select Committee visit to get that visit to take place, so I am pleased about that. In relation to some of the monuments, such as Flint Castle or Basingwerk Abbey, as typical examples of "minor" Cadw-held monuments in Wales, do you feel there is ever a case for, with appropriate resources, the transfer of the care and maintenance and development and marketing and operation of those monuments from a centrally-held Cardiff-based body directly reporting to the Secretary of State, such as Cadw, to a local authority such as the county, the borough, or the new unitary authorities?

(*Mr Eyton-Jones*) Deep in my heart I would like to say yes, but having had the experience of some of the buildings which Clwyd has handled over the last few years, I think the tide of our loss of income and other factors which have affected the way we have been able to look after these, leads me to worry that we would not be able to do that with the thoroughness we should do, to be able to involve possibly the voluntary sector and other people. There may however be a case for such a transfer. In fact Mr James and I have been deeply involved with a debate with English Heritage on behalf of the County Planning Officers Society, in a similar debate as to how they can discharge some of their functions out to the councils or local authorities or some other bodies. We saw organisations such as the National Trust had the experience, the advisers, the organisation, the support in the public domain, to be able to support that sort of monument or building in the community

[Mr Hanson Cont]

with fund-raising, technical expertise, on-going organisation et cetera. I am not sure, given the state of local authorities at the moment and the reorganisation procedures, whether a local authority should be given all the type of Flint Castle monuments you are talking about to put into its care, unless it has guaranteed financial support to back it up.

712. Would it be appropriate if, for example, a local authority such as Delyn or the county council in Flint, felt a particular monument in the care of a nationally organised body was not being sufficiently maintained, developed or marketed, that there was scope for not a wholesale transfer but a specific bid for a specific monument which the local authority felt it could manage better than a nationally-based body? Would you support that?

(Mr Eyton-Jones) I have to say that Clwyd has taken on Castle Dinas Bran as a monument and has put resources into that, and I am sure Dr Brown wishes to say, yes, he would definitely support that, but as a general policy I would be worried that without the ability to raise the finances in the future we would be unable to sustain that role.

(Dr Brown) Can I agree with Mr Eyton-Jones on this. It is very much a question of resources. We have taken over Dinas Bran and you will be seeing it tomorrow and we will tell you just how much it is going to cost. We feel, particularly with monuments with up-standing masonry, like castles, it does cost a lot of money and it is a question of resources. In relation to our relationship with Cadw, can I say how very pleased I am at the response of Cadw to the Clwyd Archaeology Service. Its inspectors advice I find is excellent, and I would not like as far as the Clwyd Archaeology Service is concerned, for us to feel as though we are criticising Cadw. They do pump an awful lot of money and resources into us.

(Mr James) May I say that guardianship implies care and maintenance. One of the things which local authorities would not have would be the pool of expert craftsmen who are needed to restore these buildings and keep them in good repair. I do not think there is the equivalent in Wales of the English Heritage moveable workforce which can travel around and keep these monuments in good order. There used to be a very well established one down in Cardiff, with again a branch in Colwyn Bay, but they are being diminished all the time, and the pool of special craftsmen and contractors who are needed to keep monuments in good repair and therefore in guardianship is very, very limited indeed.

(Mr Twigg) I would certainly back that up. We are talking about the expertise in local authorities, conservation officers, and that expertise would be needed as well. The great strength of Cadw is that it is dedicated to the conservation of the built environment. The problem with local authorities is that their funding is under bids from so many other different services, probably equally important, but it is only one part of the total pot we are talking about. With dedicated resources and the right expertise, yes, there would be a great potential for the transfer of some monuments, and one which comes to mind in our area is Basingwerk Abbey, which is at the lower end of a greenfield valley where we do have a heritage park and farm museum and the location is ideal, but

I would certainly wish to see us having the expertise and dedicated resources to handle that properly before that was done.

Mr Sweeney

713. In the absence of in-house expertise, plainly there is a need for local authorities to seek other sources of advice, and from your replies you do avail yourselves of the services of Cadw, how frequently in the case of Delyn do you actually use the services of Cadw?

(Mr Twigg) It is a question of which particular part of the service we are talking about. I stand at the moment with a foot in both camps! Our major involvement with Cadw as a district authority has not been so much on the ancient monuments side because the control of ancient monuments is with cadw and the county council services is so good so we are left out, it is with the work of the control of alteration to listed buildings and the operation of town schemes that we have been mostly involved. With the town schemes we have used their expertise, it is a partnership, as far as that is concerned it has worked very well, their help, their assistance, their expertise has been absolutely invaluable to us. As far as listed buildings are concerned, this again has worked very well at the sharp end. As an officer with Delyn, I was quite able to pick up the phone and ring my counterparts in Cadw, get good advice, support, help and information whenever needed. So at an officer level at the sharp end, it has worked extremely well, and the assistance has been there whenever it has been required. Subject, I will add, to the problems of travel from north to south Wales, which, whichever way you tackle it, is a recurring thing. But, yes, we use them whenever we need them, and we have had a good response all the way down.

714. What is the situation as far as Clwyd is concerned?

(Mr Eyton-Jones) I must say I have always had tremendous support from Cadw whenever we have asked for help. If I have asked for help on a particular problem, I have certainly had that, and I know my officers have too had support. I can only add to this question on remoteness, I am sure we would have greater involvement in this work if there was somehow a closer involvement.

715. Mr Hill of Cardiff City Council told us last week that there has been a change in the last 18 months in cadw and they "now make themselves more available for giving advice to local authorities where listed buildings are concerned." Have you found any difference so far as listed buildings are concerned?

(Mr Twigg) Yes, the operational situation has changed slightly. Cadw does not process applications, they give advice to the planning department of the Welsh Office. I do not think there has been a great deal of difference inasmuch as the original operation and expertise and help was so good, and it would take a great deal to improve on what was offered in the first place.

(Mr Eyton-Jones) I am involved with a particular project on a day by day basis, and personally, with Mr Douglas Hogg, I do find their service and help is invaluable.

[Mr Sweeney *Cont*]

716. So what you are saying, apart from the fact they are too far away in Cardiff, they provide a good service?

(*Mr Twigg*) Otherwise the system is great and does not need amending.

717. Mention has been made to English Heritage and comparisons drawn with that. We have had our attention drawn to specialist publications produced by them, and Mr Bowen of Dinefwr Borough Council told us he believed that cadw should be providing a similar service. Do you agree with this?

(*Mr Twigg*) Is this referring to the technical conservation handbooks which were published recently?

718. Yes.

(*Mr Twigg*) An excellent series. They are a bit heavy possibly but otherwise excellent. Possibly, yes, it would be an advantage if they could do so. My only worry on this is that there is one deficiency which does come to mind with Cadw and that is keeping up-to-date with information in official circulars. For example, we are working in local authorities still on Circular 61/81 which was a Welsh issue of Circular 23/77, and as you are aware the legislation was reorganised in 1990 and circulars were issued at that time under the English numbers and we are still waiting for an up-date of the more recent circulars to be issued in Welsh form. I would quite honestly prefer to see Cadw first of all bring itself up to date on the official information, but if there is spare capacity to produce anything like the excellent series of information which we have had—and I bought a set from English Heritage—and also the publication of the Georgian Group and the Victorian Society which was another model, that sort of information would certainly be welcomed, and particularly if local authorities are not able or willing to take on conservation officers, to have that advice available to development control officers would certainly be very, very useful.

719. If Cadw did at some future date find resources to produce such publications, do you believe the type produced by English Heritage are suitable for Wales, or would you like to see any differences?

(*Mr Twigg*) They are suitable inasmuch as they address themselves fully to the problems, particularly on the matter of building construction and the detailing. Obviously the particular detailed advice would differ in Wales because the vernacular construction and design of buildings in Wales is different, so it would have to be more tailored towards the Welsh experience, construction and detailing. But the way it has been produced is excellent. The price is perhaps a little high—I think that is an appeal everybody would make—but the format is fine. They take a basic subject per book, deal with it in a great deal of detail and I have certainly found them very useful in my own work within Wales even though they are addressing the English situation.

720. Does Clwyd have anything to add on that?

(*Mr Eyton-Jones*) It is a matter of scale, and obviously English Heritage has the advantage of scale in that circumstance.

Chairman

721. Could I turn to conservation areas for a moment? In terms of the 399 of those in Wales—funny how it is always £3.99 and not £4.00 or 399 and not 400—do you find the county council has any role whatever in taking initiatives in designating conservation areas?

(*Mr Eyton-Jones*) We certainly did have in the early days of the designation of conservation areas, and particularly Mr James played a great part in that in those days. Since the districts have taken that on more directly, our role is more an advisory role, and Mr James is consulted when the districts are thinking of designating conservation areas.

722. But, Mr James, you do not actually establish the conservation areas, do you?

(*Mr James*) No, we do not. We leave that role to the districts. We advise them, we walk the conservation areas with them, we locate where we think the boundaries of the conservation areas ought to be, we feed in any documentary or historical evidence or architectural reports on the conservation area, and let them prepare their own report to committee. Our role is very much an advisory role to the district councils.

723. And when conservation areas are established, there are then no financial implications for the county either?

(*Mr James*) No. We have had financial implications when we have designated town schemes within conservation areas, and Clwyd County Council has in the past supported town schemes in designated conservation areas, but unfortunately that funding has had to be withdrawn because of the stricture of local government finance. We have had to pull out of the Wrexham town scheme, the Denbigh town scheme and the Corwen town scheme.

724. What benefits do county councils see in those town schemes?

(*Mr James*) It is pump-priming, is it not? For instance, if the county council is able to put £10,000 into a town scheme, the local authority, the district council, will put in £10,000, and you have £20,000. Cadw will match that pound for pound, and will put £20,000 in, so you have £40,000. That £40,000 is matched by the equivalent amount from the private sector, the person actually applying for the grant, which is a 50 per cent grant. So by putting in £10,000 you get £80,000 restoration work done. That is the essence of a town scheme.

725. Mr Douglas, in terms of your area, do you contribute anything at all to town schemes in your area?

(*Mr Douglas*) We are the body which designates them and we have about fifteen.

726. You fund those?

(*Mr Douglas*) Yes. We have two town schemes and we allocate £25,000 to Dolgellau and £10,000 to Maentwrog.

727. Does Delyn have any problems raising its share for the schemes?

(*Mr Thomas*) No, Chairman. I hope I am not sounding too proud of our record, but I think Delyn has had a good record in terms of the funding of conservation grants generally and its town schemes

[Chairman *Cont*]

over the last few years, and certainly we have put substantial sums into the four town schemes now in Delyn. We have seen a considerable improvement in Holywell town centre, in Mold, and more recently in Flint and the town scheme in Caerwys, and Delyn has been quite far-sighted in its support for the town scheme concept and the level of resources which it has actually put in to these town schemes.

728. Mr Douglas, turning to you in terms of rural conservation areas, the National Parks Review Panel's report "Fit for the Future" advocated extending the conservation area concept to protect built features in the landscape. Can you suggest how this should be done and what benefits it could bring?

(*Mr Douglas*) I cannot think of any particular area within the Park at present where we could do it. The one which probably people are thinking of is in the Dales, Swaledale, and we have not got that same sort of situation.

729. And you do not think there will be a situation arising in the future as far as you know where that would be helpful?

(*Mr Douglas*) I cannot think of one at the moment. I assume you are not referring to historic gardens or formal landscapes.

Chairman: No.

Mr Llwyd

730. Mr Morris of the Council for British Archaeology told us a while ago, "whole stretches of the barren Snowdonia hillside, when investigated closely, turned out to be laid out by people in the Iron Age." He suggested that such discoveries called for "a new type of designation, which is less powerful than scheduling." What I would like to ask is, would a developer of the conservation area concept be able to meet these requirements?

(*Mr Eyton-Jones*) Perhaps I can lead on that, Chairman. I think possibly Mr Llwyd may be referring to the only thing we can do, which is in structure plan and local plan terms make sure our structure plans reflect the CCW's vision of the countryside. Obviously we are now looking at the second revision of our structure plan and very much to the fore will be how we can preserve landscapes; the gardens and buildings of our landscape. I think only in getting the right structure plan policy can we attempt to ensure what you are asking, Sir, and possibly Mr Thomas at local level would add his plan is trying to seek to specify those. Again we in Clwyd have the Clwyd Range area of outstanding natural beauty, and in administering that, Dr Brown, through our own joint working would seek to ensure these policies were carried out.

731. I do not know whether Mr Thomas wants to comment on that point?

(*Mr Thomas*) I would endorse what Mr Eyton-Jones has said. In local terms we will be looking to see what policies would encourage the type of development you are referring to, and obviously specific development control policies and local plan policies to accomplish that would be included in the local plan. We already have a conservation section, landscape section, in our existing Delyn local plan which does seek to address those sort of issues.

732. Are you satisfied with the strength behind the policy? Are you able to implement it as tightly as you would like?

(*Mr Thomas*) I suppose one would say you are never wholly satisfied that you have everything under control, but I think we have had success to a certain extent.

733. Referring to my constituency of Merionnydd, as you probably all know there is a scheme called Tir Cymen, which in essence of course is to bring back the old form of agriculture, less intensive, and bring in certain aspects of conservation, eg stone-walling, et cetera. I do not know if you have any views on the possible contribution that kind of scheme, were it broadened out or made more general, would have in this field?

(*Dr Brown*) I think that there is a substantial benefit in these types of schemes within the rural areas for archaeological sites, and perhaps taking it into the wider context in historic landscapes, archaeological landscapes. I think the Tir Cymen scheme is one that will be taking archaeological considerations into account, but I think there is definite scope for a much more specific, homed-in scheme such as Tir Cymen for the historical heritage.

(*Mr James*) It is a one-off, of course, but there was an instance only about a month ago when, if we are looking at sound conservation management in the agricultural field, the advice given by Clwyd County Council's conservation and environment section resulted in one of our landowners winning the prestigious national award for conservation work in agriculture. I think it is called the Golden Lapwing Award, and it received a great deal of publicity in *Country Life*. So we are working at this level with landowners. They are the custodians of the countryside and when they adopt sound conservation practices within their agricultural production it can result in really quite splendid environmental schemes related to agriculture and conservation, and this one was *the* national award to win.

734. Was this Mr Wileyman?

(*Mr James*) Yes.

735. Following closely on what you said, there is a great feeling in agriculture nowadays that there is a need for conservation and farmers themselves admit and accept it, and there is also a need for under-pinning financing and resourcing of the agriculture sector. I take it then that you would be in favour of a more broad approach towards further designations of ESAs, for example? May I ask whichever gentleman decides to answer, how the extension of the ESA designation has affected, hopefully for the better, the Clwyd Range environment?

(*Dr Brown*) As far as I am aware, Sir, the actual designation has not come into operation as yet but is going to, I hope, when resources are available. I would think that the ESA designation of the Clwyd Range would have a significant effect on the landscape. I would hope that the Clwyd Range AONB and the mechanisms we have in place would help in perhaps guiding and advising how the money that would go into the ESA schemes should be spent to conserve the historical landscape. There are certain provisions in the Ancient Monuments and

9 March 1992]

Mr Philip Eyton-Jones, Dr Ian W Brown,
Mr Stephen Grenter, Mr Jon James, Mr Ron Douglas,
Mr Christopher J Thomas, and Mr William J Twigg

[Continued

[Mr Llwyd Cont]

Archaeological Areas Act 1979 which we actually operate under—sections 17 and 24—to provide the restoration of sites, but it is this landscape as a whole which I am concerned about, and I would hope that the ESA principle in Clwyd would assist us very greatly in historical conservation.

736. Just one final question to Mr Douglas, I understand some parts of the National Park are actually putting the Tir Cymen scheme into effect. Do you know about the take-up of that scheme?

(Mr Douglas) Very good, Mr Llwyd. I would say in terms of landscape conservation this is probably the best approach. I do not see how one can control the landscape with general development order provisions—you cannot control agriculture, and the landscape is changing anyway. It seems to me the best way of controlling the landscape is by management. This is an experiment at present but I would say it is probably the way to go.

Mr Ainger

737. Coming back to the point about ESAs, have you been consulted by MAFF or anybody else? My understanding is that the ESAs should be starting in August. Secondly, are you aware which organisation, which body, will actually make the recommendations for grant aid?

(Dr Brown) In terms of archaeology, we have not been consulted specifically, just a general telephone conversation with myself. As regards the second point, no.

Chairman

738. To ask a general question which is a bit off-beam, in terms of the local plans, Mr Eyton-Jones, how many of the district councils in Clwyd have not yet got their local plans in place?

(Mr Eyton-Jones) I am taken aback, Sir! Can you help, Chris?

(Mr Thomas) All the districts are in fact working towards adoption of their formal local plans now. Some obviously are further advanced than others. Wrexham, I know, have a formally adopted local plan and they are working on a revision of that. We ourselves are about to adopt our local plan. Alun and Deeside, Rhuddlan are at about the same stage—Alun and Deeside, Glyndwr and Colwyn have adopted a district plan for the coast but not for the rural hinterland. So we are all at slightly different stages but all working towards getting local plans in place as quickly as we can.

739. But under the legislation you have to do that, do you not? I know you have your local plan but one of the things which has struck me is the completely unsatisfactory situation where many district councils in Wales did not have local plans when the legislation was brought in. Do you think that that is a very unsatisfactory state of affairs, that the legislation had to be introduced to compel local authorities to bring in those local plans?

(Mr Thomas) I suppose that it was unfortunate that the cajoling and advice of the Government was not sufficient, that they had to enact legislation to achieve that. Yes, that is unfortunately the situation, but I think as far as Clwyd is concerned, my experience is that most of the authorities in Clwyd were working towards formal local plan designation in any case, and the legislation really was not necessary in terms of prompting us to work towards that goal.

740. I am sorry to ask you that question but our next inquiry is into planning in Wales, so I thought I would just give you a little taster now because we will be turning to that subject in the very near future! As you had mentioned the local plans I could not resist the temptation just to remind you, if you did need reminding, that is our next study, which I am going to find fascinating. Turning to the listings situation, we have heard a lot in our inquiry about the length of time that the re-listing survey will take. Do you think that the local authority could do this re-listing or at least help in accelerating this?

(Mr James) I think only where they have appropriate staff. I think it could be done in Clwyd and in fact I have listed about 500 buildings which I think ought to be listed which are not listed and which I keep on sending down, district by district, to cadw. They are there for them to look at and they are simply recommendations which they could take on. But I do feel if you have an experienced conservation officer who knows his patch well, he may be of great assistance in providing cadw with a fairly accurate list of buildings which should be listed, complete with documentary and architectural evidence, and I think that can be done.

741. If that job was given to the county council, how quickly do you think it could be done and how much do you think it would cost?

(Mr James) The rural areas I think are going to be the major areas. I think this is probably why Cadw have tended to concentrate on re-surveys within the urban envelope. They have been doing the borough surveys because those are fairly tightly drawn and constructed and there are lots of buildings but in a very small area. My argument as conservation officer has always been if anybody does anything untoward to a listed building in a town, planners and conservation officers soon find out because there are 20 people on the telephone complaining, but it is those buildings in the rural hinterland, the ones which have been left, those are the ones which should be given attention because those are the ones we are losing quickly. So if I was to concentrate on doing a re-survey, I would be concentrating on the rural hinterland of Clwyd. That is going to take a little longer because of the travelling element but with the amount of information which I already have I think I could re-survey the rural hinterland of Clwyd within two, three years.

742. Mr James, you have raised a very interesting point there. Do you think that in terms of the so-called vernacular buildings of Wales in the rural area, the traditional long houses, for example, we are losing, or maybe have lost, most of those traditional Welsh buildings because the listing re-surveys have not been put in place?

(Mr James) Yes, I am sure we are losing some because that survey has not gone into the rural areas. There are people who share my concern because a new building preservation trust has been established now to, hopefully, acquire some of those smaller vernacular agricultural buildings and try to put them

[Chairman Cont]

to good use. So the concern is not only mine but is coming from other organisations as well. Many of them are so remote you do not even know they have gone, or you do not know they have been altered beyond recognition, and that is the problem.

743. Do you know of any such buildings which have been identified which are in fact in danger of being lost now, at this moment in time, because there are not the financial resources in place to purchase those buildings?

(*Mr James*) Yes, there is one particular building in Colwyn Borough Council known as Dolbelidr, which is a Grade 2 listed building. It is almost completely landlocked and what is needed there is the willingness of the owner to sell it and whoever buys it to have sufficient money to provide a long road or drive or bridge over the river to enable that building to be restored and maintained. It is a classic 15th century house, a splendid example, but its roof is off, its gable end is falling in and yet no one seems to have either the resources or the willingness to step in and save it.

(*Mr Eyton-Jones*) I have been under pressure to try and find a way for someone to purchase it, and purchasers have been coming forward, and one came forward last month, but there has been, as Mr James said, an unwillingness by the owner to sell because of its position and its location on his estate, that is the problem, and how we can find a way through that in legalistic terms, I do not know, but we are trying to find a way.

(*Mr James*) What concerns me even more is not so much listed buildings which are already there and have been identified, but that vast pool of buildings which are unlisted but ought to be.

(*Mr Twigg*) In front of me I have four buildings, all Grade 3, in a derelict state, three of which I know the owners have resisted sale of and they have gone further down hill. I would add to Mr James' catalogue a large number of small cottages—the mining area, two-roomed cottages—which are under considerable pressure for alteration to modern day standards, and very few of them are listed. A whole class of buildings is being, in my phrase, "bungalised" out of existence.

744. It could very well be, as we do not know of their existence or non-existence, that we might in fact be losing a catalogue of buildings which may be unique in our heritage because this survey is not taking place?

(*Mr Twigg*) Yes. Mr James and I together on Holywell came out with our own list which is 95 per cent of what Cadw came up with, so the expertise is there, but so many of the buildings we had at risk are borderline cases where we could not be certain they would be listed. I know Cadw is getting more sensitive to the 19th century terraced cottages but we are not in a position to know where the dividing line would fall at present and, as I see it, the small vernacular cottage at the moment is in a very parlous situation.

Chairman: Changing the subject, I will ask Mr Ainger to ask about churches.

Mr Ainger

745. Mr Eyton-Jones, last week we had the churches up with us in the House and we asked them about the Welsh Churches Act Fund and what their knowledge of it was and it seemed to be very little. Could you tell us what the rules are which Clwyd applies to giving grant to churches and chapels?

(*Mr Eyton-Jones*) In Clwyd, first of all, the buildings must be listed, they must have a grade, and as far as that is concerned then we advise our local department as to the question of whether a grant should be given on at particular building. Then, of course, a grant via the finance sub-committee is usually given but the maximum grant is £500 in each case. There can be multiple applications, and certainly Wrexham's St Giles, which you have seen today, received multiple awards of £500 during its renovation recently, but they must be listed.

746. They have to be listed, so a chapel which is not listed would receive nothing?

(*Mr Eyton-Jones*) It will not receive a grant.

747. Are you aware from the Welsh Assembly of County Councils that you are applying different rules from other county councils?

(*Mr Eyton-Jones*) I am not aware of that. Certainly we have not had consultation among my colleagues in Wales on that matter but I can look into that and let the Committee know.

Mr Ainger: Would it surprise you to learn that my evidence is that it is totally different from other county councils? The others do not ask for listing as a requirement.

Chairman

748. Can we explore that a little just to check we have understood what Mr Eyton-Jones is saying? Are you saying in terms of the administration of this fund by the county council that the entire fund is only used for the purposes of listed buildings?

(*Mr Eyton-Jones*) No, sorry, we are talking about buildings. There are grants from the Welsh Church given for very many other things but as far as buildings are concerned, the grant must be given to a listed building.

Mr Ainger

749. That is Clwyd County Council's policy?

(*Mr Eyton-Jones*) Yes.

750. That is not a policy related to the rest of the Welsh Church Fund spread throughout the rest of Wales?

(*Mr Eyton-Jones*) That is the one we have applied over the years.

751. What proportion of the Welsh Church Fund does go on churches and chapels?

(*Mr James*) Probably 50 per cent. They are grants going to cultural organisations which are involved with the Welsh language or books or Welsh culture, and sometimes further education youth services will apply for grants.

Mr Ainger: That is 50 per cent of what? Per annum?

9 March 1992]

Mr Philip Eyton-Jones, Dr Ian W Brown,
Mr Stephen Grenter, Mr Jon James, Mr Ron Douglas,
Mr Christopher J Thomas, and Mr William J Twigg

[Continued

Chairman

752. Do you know what you are spending in the current financial year?

(*Mr James*) I think we are operating on something between £30 and £40,000 in the financial year.

(*Mr Eyton-Jones*) £28,000 in the financial year.

753. In the Church Fund altogether?

(*Mr Eyton-Jones*) No, to spend from the fund.

Chairman: The total amount of money you have to spend is about £28,000.

Mr Ainger

754. What proportion of that goes on administration?

(*Dr Brown*) About £6,000 above that, so it is £34,000 in all.

755. What has puzzled me in the research I have done is the enormous difference in the capital lump sum from which the interest on whatever it is—34,000—accrues between authorities. For instance, Dyfed tell me they have £1.3 million but from my investigations with Clwyd you have only got just over £300,000. Is there an explanation for that, because obviously it directly affects the policies you follow?

(*Mr James*) I think it was part of the carving up following disestablishment when there were pro rata awards made between the former county of Flintshire and the former county of Denbighshire, and they pooled together on a pro rata basis what they had got and they gave us that figure as lump sum capital.

756. It does concern us as the Welsh Select Committee that there are apparently totally different policies and totally different funding levels between the councils, when this is one of the major sources of funding particularly for chapels, grant aid for roof restoration and so on; basic structural things. Have you any comment on the differences between yourselves and Dyfed?

(*Mr Eyton-Jones*) It is a hard one to answer. We administer the fund and I am not sure there have been many refusals. Probably that is one of the things which we could say, that where churches and other establishments have applied for funds then most of those would have been met with either, from my recollection of seeing the committee reports, £250 or £500 grants.

(*Mr James*) In this day and age with restoration costs being so much, the maximum level of grant at £500 is something of a pittance, especially in the case of chapels when their income is being so drastically reduced. I am afraid Wales has suffered from interdenominational rivalry since about 1860 when even a small village will have four enormous chapels and maybe one family supporting each one.

Mr Ainger: But in Dyfed the maximum grant is £3,000 not £500 and you do not have to be a listed chapel in order to qualify. Could you perhaps let us know how many chapels for instance are listed and what that represents as a proportion?

Chairman

757. On top of that, in terms of the chapels and churches, would you know how many are falling into disuse or becoming redundant now within Clwyd in a year?

(*Mr Eyton-Jones*) Mr James is doing a survey and writing a book on that.

(*Mr James*) I am writing a book on that and of the 535 chapels which I have carried out a survey of in the county something like 75 to 80 per cent of them are either derelict, converted or have got for sale notices on them. It is an alarmingly high percentage.

758. How soon is this book going to be produced?

(*Mr James*) I was hoping to get it produced for the next visit of the Welsh National Eisteddfod to Colwyn Bay, Sir!

Mr Llwyd

759. How much will it cost?

(*Mr James*) It depends how much help I get from the Welsh Churches Act Fund!

Chairman

760. Is there anything you would like to add which we have missed today?

(*Mr Eyton-Jones*) Can I pick up on the ecclesiastical exemptions? I was fascinated to hear the archaeologists' comments before and I have read some of the transcripts of evidence, and from a personal point of view, having applied during the course of my lifetime to do works in various churches, including St Giles, and in fact having seen the workings of the diocesan advisory committee, Wales has certainly lagged behind England in the way churches have been inspected on a national basis in Wales. I suppose it is only in the last six years that we have had a quinquennial inspection by the Church of Wales of the churches. We are now seeing the first of those five year repairs going on to those churches, greater concentration of consultation with cadw and in consequence the archaeological societies. I believe that in doing that the Church in Wales did get its act together to look at the question of exemption, and that it forms a good data base for the Church of Wales for doing its future work on churches. Furthermore, the awareness within the diocese, particularly on the composition of the advisory committee, is much greater than it ever was. I personally believe on the question of seeking permission to change anything, particularly within churches, there is a great degree of delicacy with regard to the denomination concerned, the feelings of the congregation, the parish, and I feel that how the system proceeds at the moment is to my mind satisfactory. I accept and I believe that the advisory committees will follow and will seek to follow new guidance on consultations, and I believe that it is an on-going process of enlightenment throughout Wales as far as its buildings are concerned. I have the strong feeling this will meet the criteria that all of the bodies would like to see without having statutorily listed building consents which we would normally be involved with for planning procedures, which to my mind would possibly interfere with the ethos of the religion concerned.

[Chairman Cont]

761. So would you like the churches to retain their exemption?

(*Mr Eyton-Jones*) I would.

762. Anything else, gentlemen, before we finish?

(*Dr Brown*) In relation to cadw and the role of cadw, I also have responsibility for the countryside service and the museum service. I have compared the way the Countryside Council and the Council of Museums in Wales provide specific grant aid for officers, and regretfully cadw does not give grant aid in quite the same way, it is funded via project work, but with CMW and CCW grant aid it supports an officer to 40 per cent, 45 per cent or 50 per cent for example for a short period of time. This can be usually three years now or five years on a tapering basis. What that does allow local authorities to do is to employ the required staff, to have this pump-priming mechanism, and the pump-priming role is so important; the CCW and CMW do this, and this is just a plea that there would be great benefit if cadw was able to pump-prime us, or whoever, in the same way.

Mr Ainger

763. What posts are you specifically thinking of?

(*Dr Brown*) I am not necessarily thinking of a great number of posts. As a local government man I see the important of an archaeological service within the local government framework, just as we have a countryside service, just as we have a museum service. The archaeological service is looking to the historic heritage and with this pump-priming role I do feel we would be able to appoint perhaps a specialist, such as Andre Berry[1] for instance who deals with historic landscape sites. It does not necessarily have to be an archaeologist. He was part-funded by CCW to start with but that funding now has gone. I see as part of the archaeological service as a whole perhaps an education officer—I would love an education officer to deal with our fast expanding role on the interpretation of the heritage to the public, especially to young people; I would love a part-funded grant aided educational officer to deal with that. That is just an example, Sir.

Chairman: Gentlemen, could I thank you very much for spending this length of time with us. I would like to thank Clwyd County Council's archaeological service for the tremendous effort they have taken in helping us put this programme together, and taking us round, and for the good offices of the borough council in giving us this splendid building, and I hope by the time we come here next they will have got the microphones working! Thank you very much.

[1]Note by witness: Andre Berry is the Archaeological Sites Management Officer with Clwyd Archaeology Service, Clwyd County Council.

Supplementary memorandum by Clwyd-Powys Archaeological Trust

PRESERVATION OF HISTORIC BUILDINGS AND ANCIENT MONUMENTS IN WALES (HB83)

This supplementary memorandum comments upon some other evidence taken before the Welsh Affairs Committee in Wrexham on Tuesday 9 March 1993.

1. *Relationships with planning authorities*

1.1. Contrary to the impression which may have been given, it should be stressed that the Trust endeavours to work closely with staff of County Council in *jointly* providing advice on archaeological matters to local planning authorities in Clwyd. The Trust is also recognised by planning authorities in Powys as a principal body providing archaeological advice. Officers of both County Councils sit on the Trust Committee.

1.2. The value of *independent* role of the Trust is highlighted by the many instances where the local authority is itself the developer or has interests in a development. In 1990, for example, the Trust formally objected to the coastal route for the Flint Bypass, proposed by the County Highways Department and supported by the County Council, on the grounds that it would severely affect the setting of Flint Castle. The scheme was subsequently rejected following a Public Inquiry by the Secretary of State. In 1993, for example, the Trust has been asked by Clwyd County Council to take a lead role in providing archaeological recommendations about the proposed development of the industrial complex at Pennant Mine near Dyserth, where the County Council is involved in applying to grant aid to the WDA.

2. *Relationships with developers*

2.1. Contrary to other evidence taken before the Committee, the Trust would like to stress that no conflicts of interest arise in its relationships with developers. The Trust's Curatorial Section provides local planning authorities in both Clwyd and Powys with independent and impartial advice on archaeological matters and makes recommendations on specific planning proposals submitted to the authorities. Planning authorities decide whether they will act upon this advice, taking a variety of other considerations into account. Developers who, as a consequence of this advice, are required by a planning authority to undertake archaeological work in order to obtain planning consent have freedom to chose which competent archaeological contractor they wish to engage. A decision is normally made on the basis of competitive tenders from appropriate contracting bodies, which may include the Trust. Planners and developers may take advice from a third should they consider this necessary. Developers may appeal against planning decisions to the Secretary of State.

2.2. The Trust has no evidence which suggests that its integrity in these matters is not fully respected by both planning authorities and developers.

2.3. Contrary to other evidence taken before the Committee, the Trust would like to state that it currently employs a staff of 19, of whom incidentally 11 are graduates in archaeology or allied disciplines and 4 of whom are Members or Associate Members of the Institute of Field Archaeologists. In addition the Trust engages the services of 3-4 other workers in specialist areas (draughting, building recording, building conservation, field survey) on a part-time basis.

2.4. The number of staff employed by the Trust is equivalent to or indeed considerably greater than that number of county-based units in England which combine curatorial and contracting functions. The Trust experiences no difficulties in clearly separating these two functions within the same organisation.

25 March 1993

Letter from the Director Glamorgan-Gwent Archaeological Trust to the Clerk of the Committee

WELSH AFFAIRS COMMITTEE MEETING—WREXHAM, 9 MARCH 1993
MINUTES 653–665 (HB85)

We would respectfully refer you to the above Minutes concerning the Welsh Trusts' Sites and Monuments Records and in particular the effects that the current and proposed funding levels have had upon staffing resources.

As previously stated, the current and proposed funding levels, £6,000 per Trust per annum, are wholly insufficient to adequately resource the maintenance and enhancement of the Record. Such a low level of funding has resulted in this Trust having to dispense with the services of its Sites and Monuments Record Officer last September. It is a matter of most serious concern that the individual concerned, who had been in our employ since 1983, is a registered disabled person whose prospects of alternative employment are negligible. We are equally concerned that neither Cadw-Welsh Historic Monuments nor the Royal Commission on Ancient and Historical Monuments (Wales) was willing to assist with payment of redundancy monies, a different situation from that where English Heritage is concerned.

It is our understanding that currently the Dyfed Archaeological Trust does not employ a Sites and Monuments Record Officer, owing to the same financial restrictions. Within the Clwyd-Powys Archaeological Trust the position is currently occupied by another registered disabled person whose further employment prospects are undecided. The Gwynedd Archaeological Trust advises that the current occupant of the post will be transferred in due course to non-Sites and Monuments Record duties.

25 March 1993

Letter from the Director Glamorgan-Gwent Archaeological Trust to the Clerk of the Committee

WELSH AFFAIRS COMMITTEE MEETING—WREXHAM, 9 MARCH 1993 (HB 84)

I would respectfully refer you to the Minutes of the above meeting, specifically Nos 616–618.

I would confirm that the total income derived from the now defunct Manpower Services Commission for the period 1 April 1982 to 31 August 1988 was £3,578,665. Within that time this Trust acted as an Agency for the Manpower Services Commission (MSC). Prior to 1 April 1982 it had acted as a sponsor for various temporary employment programmes from 1 April 1976; total income £600,308. The maximum non-Cadw income in any year derived from the MSC being £871,063 for 1987–88. The funding provided by the MSC enabled this Trust to fulfil a variety of educational and community projects. With regard to the former, educational officers were appointed whose tasks included the preparation of archaeological educational resource work-packs for distribution to various school and teacher resource centres in the Glamorgan and Gwent counties. A wide range of archaeological guides and brochures, fact-sheets, questionnaires and other related literature was produced and distributed. A major educational (and tourism) facility was created with the reconstruction of the deserted Medieval village at Cosmeston Lakes County Park. This project was recognised nationally in 1986–88 by achieving the highly prestigious "Heritage in Britain Award". In 1988 this project was granted further recognition in the receipt of a "Prince of Wales' Award".

In addition, provision was made for schoolchildren and students of visit ongoing archaeological excavations, and to participate in "hands-on" activities both on site and in the classroom. All of the above work has now ceased due to a total lack of funding since the demise of the MSC. It is noteworthy here to state that, unlike English Heritage, Cadw does not provide funding for Trust in-house/external training, let alone fund any other educational projects.

Community Archaeology

Funding by the MSC also enabled this Trust to produce various publications that were intended to increase the awareness in the general public of their archaeological heritage—the book *South Glamorgan's Heritage* being an excellent example. This work was compiled and illustrated by personnel exclusively employed under a project funded by the MSC.

Travelling and static exhibitions were mounted at numerous locations on a regular basis. One exhibition, the largest non-museum display ever mounted in Wales, stood within the Canal Underpass, Kingsway, Cardiff, for nearly three years and was viewed by millions of local people and visitors.

Large numbers of MSC-employed staff gave talks and lectures on subjects relating to all aspects of archaeology, both within the Trust's area and beyond. As many as twenty different venues per week were being attended upon, together with regular Workers' Educational Association and Extra-Mural classes. Our ability to provide such services is now severely impaired by Cadw's current project-funded "agreement" with this Trust.

24 March 1993

WEDNESDAY 24 MARCH 1993

Members present:

Mr Gareth Wardell, in the Chair

Mr Nick Ainger
Mr Alex Carlile
Mr Jonathan Evans
Mr Roger Evans
Mr David Hanson

Mr Elfyn Llwyd
Mr Rod Richards
Mr Mark Robinson
Mr Walter Sweeney

Examination of Witnesses

SIR WYN ROBERTS, a Member of the House, Minister of State, Welsh Office, was examined. MR JOHN CARR, Chief Executive, and MR RICHARD HUGHES, Director, Policy and Administration, Cadw: Welsh Historic Monuments Executive Agency, were further examined.

Chairman

764. Minister, good morning to you and to your colleagues. Before making the opening statement that you wish to make, Sir Wyn, would you like to introduce the colleagues you have with you this morning?

(*Sir Wyn Roberts*) Yes, indeed. Thank you, Mr Chairman. I have with me John Carr, the Chief Executive of Cadw, whom I believe you have already met, and probably too Richard Hughes, our Director of Policy at Cadw. May I say I am grateful to you for consenting to my making an opening statement. This contains views and facts that I think would be helpful to the Committee. May I begin by saying that the transfer to the Welsh Office of responsibilities for the built heritage was completed in the late 1970s with the assimilation of the skilled workforce caring for ancient monuments in Wales. With regard to the estate in care, our view was that there were opportunities for better conservation and presentation and we decided to establish Cadw to put new impetus into these policies and their implementation. The Cadw Steering Committee, which I chaired from 1984 until the Agency was established in 1991, also ensured a cohesive approach to built heritage issues. Since 1984 Cadw has drawn on a range of skills and, working closely with the Wales Tourist Board, it has sought to make the monuments more accessible and attractive to visitors and the people of Wales. There have been important developments, for example in presenting the Roman Baths at Caerleon, in the facilities for visitors at Conwy, Tintern, Criccieth and Chepstow and in major conservation projects at Rhuddlan, Laugharne and Dinefwr. In what I believe the Wales Tourist Board would acknowledge to have been a volatile market, Cadw has sustained visitor numbers of the order of 1.3 million and that has brought benefit, of course, to local economies. Visitors to Cadw sites are expected to generate more than £2.2 million in the current financial year. The estate in care is, however, demanding and in the coming year we expect to invest more than £2.5 million in caring for it. Additional monuments have become our responsibility, including Rug and Llangar churches in Clwyd, which I shall be opening shortly, and most recently Plas Mawr in Conwy and soon Wiston Castle in Dyfed. Cadw has developed a very positive education programme for school children and I am pleased to tell the Committee that school visits to the monuments have increased from around 50,000 in the early years to over 120,000 last year, and these are, of course, free visits. We have increased Cadw's support for owners of historic buildings, for town schemes and conservation areas and increased spending on these activities from £1.5 million in 1984 to nearly £4 million in the current financial year. Our response to archaeology has also resulted in increased funding for the four Welsh Archaeological Trusts, and in the current year this is more than £850,000. We have also supported the core funding of the Civic Trust for Wales, enhanced our support for the National Trust—a significant employer in the Principality—launched our modest, but welcome, Civic Initiatives (Heritage) Grants Scheme and most recently embarked on a closer relationship with the Architectural Heritage Fund, which is involved in setting up building preservation trusts and set to be more involved in Wales with financial support from us. In putting forward Cadw as the Welsh Office's first Executive Agency, our expectation was, and is, that while it would not produce immediate dramatic changes, the new management regime would enable the Department to set a clearer framework for what Cadw should be doing and Cadw to develop systems to do it better. We are also keen to see Cadw as a more responsive and accessible part of the Welsh Office, able to deal closely with the many interested bodies and individuals with which it must work. To underpin this, as the Secretary of State has announced, we shall publish a Heritage Charter in the spring. Cadw's reservoir of professional expertise is unique in Wales and it must be there to be tapped. These are all things we are looking to Cadw's Chief Executive, Mr John Carr, to do. In setting a framework for Cadw, its resources and annual targets, we are aware of the need to balance the many priorities of the built heritage. The state can never provide the answers to all the problems that arise— indeed the Committee has seen some of these during its inquiry. But in Cadw we are seeking to promote solutions through setting a planning framework, backing that with specialist expertise, encouraging and supporting voluntary groups and in supporting private individuals, with whom much of the day-to-day responsibility inevitably rests. The Committee has heard of unmet expectations and disappointments at Cadw's progress in some areas.

[Chairman Cont]

We share some of those sentiments, as does Mr John Carr. Cadw has, however, benefited from a better-than-average provision of resources over the years. To illustrate that, more than £12.5 million is being made available to the Agency for the forthcoming financial year, an increase of 16.4 per cent. over the Agency's out-turn of £10.765 million in 1991-92, but even so, hard choices have had to be made. We are fortunate to have had the help of our independent advisers, the Ancient Monuments Board and Historic Buildings Council, to guide us in the decisions we have taken. Perhaps I should finish, Chairman, by referring to three of the concerns of which the Committee has heard. The listing re-survey of Wales is far short of completion. The Committee heard that, mathematically, the indications were that it might take 55 to 60 years to complete. In fact, the steady acceleration of this work has already seen that time span reduced, with the Agency having issued 14 re-survey lists so far this financial year against a target of 12. For the next year a higher target will be set. The need for more effort in this task is well appreciated, as the Agency's Corporate Plan for 1992-93 acknowledged. The fate of redundant churches and chapels is something with which we have wrestled without resolution yet, though the Committee has heard, first, that a generous offer was made to the Church in Wales in 1987, and second, that examples of the loss of architecturally or historically important ecclesiastical buildings are not easy to find. We are keen to deal with this issue, however, and the Agency knows that this must be done—but, of course, other parties need to agree. Finally, the Agency has as a central task an education initiative aimed at improving the appreciation of Wales' built heritage and ways in which it should be protected and managed with sympathy. This work is being taken forward, gaining impetus, and we anticipate it will be underpinned by a new Planning Policy Guidance Note on historic buildings in the near future. Much has been done, Mr Chairman, but much remains to be done and we believe that the Agency is on course to make an increasingly effective contribution to this area to which the Committee has helpfully devoted its attention in recent months.

765. Thank you, Sir Wyn. What we would like to do, first of all, if we may, is to turn to the area of conservation strategy and to look at the Government's policy and the way it interacts with Cadw's aims and objectives. How does that occur in terms of the objectives, Minister, that is, how do Government policy and objectives relate to Cadw's aims and objectives?

(*Sir Wyn Roberts*) They are really one and the same because, of course, we begin with the Framework Document which sets out the relationship between Cadw and the Government and others, too, and it is from that Framework Document that Cadw has evolved its Corporate Plan, which is agreed with Ministers. It is within that Corporate Plan that not only is there a mission statement, which you will be well aware of, but, in fact, the tasks are identified there, some eight tasks spelt out and, similarly, the role of Cadw, its specific aims and its principal objectives occur in that Corporate Plan. Of course, the Corporate Plan results in an Annual Report which again is studied by Ministers and reviewed by Ministers. If any change of direction is needed, then that is the time to do it. Meanwhile, of course, you will be aware that Cadw has its Advisory Committee which monitors its performance in terms of the achievement of its objectives and again that ensures that Cadw is keeping to its Corporate Plan and to its objectives as far as possible.

766. Thank you. Apart from specifically agreeing Cadw's Corporate Plan and setting its annual targets, how much of your time is devoted to this issue in your busy life?

(*Sir Wyn Roberts*) It is very difficult indeed to put a time on it. Of course, when I was chairman of the Steering Committee I was very close indeed and in touch with day-to-day events almost at Cadw—although I must pay tribute to Mr Carr at this point because he, of course, was responsible for the day-to-day working of Cadw. Since Cadw has become an Agency, then obviously the relationship has changed and I am certainly not involved in day-to-day issues, but clearly responsible to Parliament for the performance of Cadw. I am also responsible for its policies and, similarly, I think in terms of day-to-day operation, I rely on Cadw to bring matters to my notice that require my attention, that may be controversial, that may involve Parliament, but, as you will know, Members now correspond with the Agency direct and, at the same time, I bring to Mr Carr's notice anything that I see which calls for his attention and the attention of the Agency. In terms of time, I regret to say it is impossible, but far less time than I used to devote to Cadw in its early days.

767. In terms of the work you do, say, on the re-survey programme, which is presumably an operational matter for Cadw, do you make any political decision on the nature or the speed of the programme other than through setting the annual target?

(*Sir Wyn Roberts*) I would be involved. I am involved in the sense that obviously I approved of the statement in the Corporate Plan which says: "The Agency regard it as essential to reduce the timescale for the completion of the listing re-survey from an unacceptable 60 years to a more realistic period." I am very well aware of the need to press on with the re-survey and I am aware of the progress that has been made in England, what the situation is in Scotland and when we come to discuss Cadw's future policy, there is no doubt about it that I shall be laying considerable stress on the need to proceed with the re-survey programme.

Mr Roger Evans

768. Sir Wyn, we asked a number of questions on this of Mr Carr on a previous occasion and just so that we are quite clear whom really we should be asking these questions, it might be suggested, for example, that the failure to survey large areas of Wales at all could unkindly be put as a failure to discharge basic statutory obligations upon Ministers. At the end of this, is this really an issue which we should ask you questions of, in the sense that you are responsible for the amount of resources and priority given to relisting, or is it a matter which we should ask Mr Carr?

[Mr Roger Evans *Cont*]

(*Sir Wyn Roberts*) I think you should probably ask both of us. If I may take up your first point, I think the legislation requires us to compile lists of buildings of special architectural or historic interest for the purposes of the 1990 Act and for the guidance of local planning authorities but it does not actually lay a timescale upon us. Nevertheless, we are very conscious indeed of this requirement under the 1990 Act and having started on the re-survey, you will have noticed that there has been quite a significant acceleration; I think I am right in saying that the figure I gave in the opening statement as being 14 completed this year instead of the 12 targeted, should actually now be 15. We do intend to accelerate it further. That does, of course, involve resources and I have certainly looked into this and it is our estimate that we would need to spend an additional half a million pounds per annum in order to complete the re-survey in a period of, let us say, ten years.

769. Sir Wyn, accepting the force of that argument, the difficulty is this, is it not, we have received evidence to the effect that by failing to have up-to-date lists, in fact, other costs have been incurred. In other words, the cost of spot-listing, the imperfections in the process are simply because there is no basic database. Has any attempt been made to assess those costs?

(*Sir Wyn Roberts*) I think there are costs both ways. One must remember, too, that as we re-survey and list, then there will be additional costs involved in the consultations that have to be carried out before the lists are published and then, of course, we come to listed building consents. We could imagine that there will be more such consents sought, so that there would be costs as a result of re-surveying as well. You are talking about the costs of spot-listing. I cannot see—but I would like to hear Mr Carr's views—that spot-listing will not be necessary until the survey is completed.

770. Maybe I have not explained the evidence with sufficient clarity and I apologise for that, the point that has been made to us is that because the listing is inadequate at the moment, the mere business of having to chase through what records there are, trying to find out what the information is when it is not there in a full up-to-date record, that in itself has posed excessive administrative burdens upon the system and there ought to be a proper cost-benefit analysis of, on the one hand, the costs which are being occasioned by the failure to have an up-to-date database and, on the other hand, the cost of bringing it up to date. Has any such survey been done by the Welsh Office?

(*Sir Wyn Roberts*) Let me turn to Mr Carr on that. I am not aware of that.

(*Mr Carr*) A survey has not been done on that basis. It is a very valid point, but I would just like to return, if I may, to your point about the cost of spot-listing. Spot-listing will need to continue anyway, as I think you probably understand. We have been an Agency for two years and it has taken some time to get our systems in place. It is, during the course of the next couple of years, our intention to be able to pinpoint costs precisely on all our operations.

771. Mr Carr, you will accept this, would you not, that spot-listing is a result of not having an up-to-date database as well as these buildings which are fit to be listed?

(*Mr Carr*) Not really, no. As I think I mentioned in my earlier evidence, Chairman, fashions change, time passes and new criteria are developed and, therefore, there is a rolling base or database or reservoir of structures.

772. But, Mr Carr, should that not with a proper, up-to-date database, be very much at the margin?

(*Mr Carr*) I could not disagree with that.

773. Sir Wyn, it is fair to say that in the early 1980s the lists for the border counties were at least as much of a shambles as anything in Wales and we saw in England an initiative by Michael Heseltine in the early 1980s to bring the English lists up-to-date. What are the prospects of that in Wales, as a matter of political judgment and decision?

(*Sir Wyn Roberts*) I think the prospects are very good but I do have to bring to your notice our estimate of the costs as being of the order of an additional £½ million a year, that is, over a period of ten years, and I do not think that it will have escaped your notice that this means that we would have to step up the rate at which we re-surveyed from the current 15 to something of the order of 65 to 66 per annum in order to accomplish the work in ten years. At the same time one has to say that yes, there are over 700 communities in Wales and we are surveying by community and there will be some communities where there is not as much work as others. We have concentrated so far on the urban areas. Nevertheless, this is an area that we are looking at with a view to accelerating the programme. You referred to England as having progressed. Yes, I understand that they are coming to an end of their survey but they are, in fact, checking up still on some of the earlier work done. As far as Scotland is concerned, I believe that they intend to complete their re-surveys by about 2005.

774. Sir Wyn, you still are talking, however, even under that accelerated suggested programme, of a period of ten years. Is that not, in fact, significantly slower than the period and timescale which Michael Heseltine introduced in England?

(*Sir Wyn Roberts*) I think that overall they took about ten years to do it. I think the initial completion was after eight years but then, as I say, some surveys of the re-surveys have had to be done. If I may stress this point, it is absolutely essential in these re-surveys that the work done is, of course, of very high quality.

775. Sir Wyn, would you agree that one of the most significant achievements of British scholarship and the appreciation of the built environment has been the "Buildings of England" series begun by Professor Pevsner?

(*Sir Wyn Roberts*) Indeed, very important.

776. What can the Welsh Office do to accelerate the publication of the "Buildings of Wales" comparable volumes, because we have received evidence that this is not going to be completed for really quite some years?

(*Sir Wyn Roberts*) May I ask John Carr to deal with that?

[Mr Roger Evans *Cont*]

(*Mr Carr*) The same question was put to me previously, Mr Chairman, Minister. We already support the costs of research and authorship of the "Buildings of Wales" series. I do not think, if I may say so, that the Welsh Office can influence the commercial decisions of the current publishers of the book in terms of the timescale taken to produce it. I regret their absence, as I have stated previously, and they would be a tremendous reservoir of knowledge for our visiting inspectors as well as for the general public.

777. What I do not understand, Mr Carr, from that answer is how far you are suggesting the delay is as a result of lack of resources provided by the Welsh Office or how far it is a result of commercial decisions made by the present publishers?

(*Mr Carr*) I do not think the delay can be laid at the door of the Welsh Office.

Chairman

778. Sir Wyn, coming back to your costs and your estimate of costs of the re-survey, I think we have a problem here in terms of conflicting evidence. Dr Wools in his evidence to us says that he estimates that to re-survey Wales in a three-year period would cost £250,000 per annum, which gives us a figure of £¾ million. Your figure of an additional £½ million over ten years would give us a figure at current prices of £5 million. How do you explain your estimate that it is going to cost that much money when Dr Wools, in fact, is saying that it could be done for so much less?

(*Sir Wyn Roberts*) I understand Dr Wools actually operated in a somewhat rich part of England in terms of its architectural heritage and I am sure that there is a certain amount of optimism hidden within his figures. I do not think that they are applicable to Wales but John Carr has made a study of this and could enlighten you further.

(*Mr Carr*) Yes, as the Minister has stated, Chairman, Dr Wools was working in a particularly rich and compact area of Yorkshire. His costs identified at £250,000 for each of all three years related solely to the cost of engaging contract listers to undertake the work. What he did not include in that sum was the necessary back-up administrative support, the in-house support, which is where we reach our figure of £500,000 per annum for each of ten years in addition to what we spend already.

779. Is that not a very small part of the total cost, though?

(*Mr Carr*) The administrative costs?

780. Yes?

(*Mr Carr*) It is roughly equivalent to the same again.

(*Sir Wyn Roberts*) I think what Mr Carr is obviously referring to is the extent of the consultations that have to take place before the lists are actually issued.

781. But can I ask you, Minister, how was that figure of an extra £½ million actually derived? Who did the costing for that?

(*Sir Wyn Roberts*) We estimate that it costs us about £6,000 per re-survey and then we worked it out largely from that basis. Each contractor or lister is estimated to do about 3½ re-surveys a year, and I

think if you build up that equation plus the internal costs of Cadw you will arrive at that figure of the £½ million.

782. Do you think it is possible for us to have a note from you on the method of calculation in detail of how that was worked out? I think that would be helpful.

(*Sir Wyn Roberts*) Yes, certainly.

(*Mr Hughes*) Could I perhaps help the Committee. I think a key overhead cost that has not entered the equation is the question of professional supervision. There is a heavy on-cost in ensuring that the standards of the contract listers you employ are maintained and the need to have national criteria observed is terribly important in undertaking this exercise.

Mr Roger Evans

783. Mr Hughes, I have no doubt that is absolutely correct but what you are suggesting is the enormous size of, if we use the defence argument analogy, tail to teeth. Whereas in England outside contractors have been used, the costs, as we understood Dr Wools' evidence, of making sure they were of sufficient standard and uniformity was nothing like as great as is now being suggested.

(*Mr Hughes*) I am not sure his figures took account of the supervisory costs.

(*Sir Wyn Roberts*) I think the best answer to this, Mr Chairman, is if we may indeed meet your request and provide these figures, and hopefully we shall have been in touch with all our English colleagues to check on the figures that Dr Wools gave you to see exactly what they included and what they excluded.

Chairman

784. Thank you very much. In terms of your opening statement, Minister, on page 6, lines 6 and 7, you say: "in Cadw, we are seeking to promote solutions through setting a planning framework". Of course, that links in with what I was asking you earlier on. In terms of that, how do you actually go about producing or setting that framework? Do you, for example, go to public consultation in establishing that framework, or not?

(*Sir Wyn Roberts*) Not specifically, no. Can I ask Mr Hughes to come in on this?

(*Mr Hughes*) I think that what we are referring to there is the guidance that is issued for local planning authorities and before the guidance becomes firm, certainly with the upcoming planning policy guidance note that we hope will be issued for consultation in the near future, the need to take the views of those involved is something that is important and we would wish to do.

785. Fine, thank you, Mr Hughes. In terms of the estate in care, Minister, we looked at this in detail with Mr Carr in an earlier session. How would you reply to the accusation that far too many English castles are in care in proportion to the small number of monuments and buildings which have meaning to the Welsh nation, such as chapels and rural vernacular houses?

(*Sir Wyn Roberts*) I do not regard the native Welsh heritage, shall we put it that way, as not being

[Chairman *Cont]*

included, of course, in the estate in care. In fact, there are quite a number of Welsh castles, although overall there are fewer within the estate simply because there are fewer native Welsh castles anyway. We do have, of course, Dolbadarn, Dolwyddelan, Criccieth, Castell Y Bere, Ewloe, Dryslwyn, Dolforwyn, Dinefwr—Dinas Bran has now been taken into care by Clwyd County Council, as you know, with Cadw's assistance—and there is also Caergwrle. We should not forget either the Welsh abbeys that were patronised by the Welsh princes, Penmon—which I recommend for a visit because it has the only medieval pin up that I know of carved on the lintel there—Cymer Abbey, Valle Crucis, Talley, Strata Florida. So that is quite a collection of predominantly, medieval, of course, buildings in care. With regard to chapels—I know that this does concern you—but we are somewhat constrained by the need to preserve outstanding buildings, architecturally, historically and many of the chapels, as I recall, were in fact built to a standard pattern and they are not particularly distinguished buildings. I know that they do have associations in some cases with great preachers and so on, but there are not all that many of them in existence that are in fact worth preserving or that call for preservation. There is in England a redundant chapels fund which is just coming into existence and I understand that it has four chapels under consideration at the moment. We would be anxious to look at the possibility of establishing a similar sort of trust.

Chairman

786. Sir Wyn, what about vernacular rural houses because certainly in evidence to us in Clwyd, great concern was expressed that because the listing of the re-survey programme is so slow, there may be a number of these buildings that are being lost to the Welsh nation because of that very slow re-survey programme? Do you think that that is the case, that there are buildings being lost that are of very great value to the Welsh nation because they are indigenous to the Welsh nation because of that in rural areas specifically?

(*Sir Wyn Roberts*) What I must point out to the Committee is, of course, that local authorities do have the power to issue Building Preservation Notices. If my memory serves me right, last year there were only 32 such notices issued by some ten local planning authorities in Wales. I cannot believe somehow that we are actually losing buildings at a significant rate.

787. But, of course, you would not know, would you?

(*Sir Wyn Roberts*) We have to depend to a considerable extent on the expertise of local authorities and their knowledge and Clwyd is one of the best informed of local authorities. They are the only ones who have an archaeological service, for example.

788. Which is, of course, why they say that they are losing quite a few?

(*Sir Wyn Roberts*) I would have thought that if that was the case, then they would certainly be aware of the possibilities of stopping any such loss as there

may be by the issue of these Building Preservation Notices.

789. But the problem is, as you know, that these Building Preservation Notices are fraught with difficulties because if in fact the building is, for example, occupied, there are problems and, if it is unoccupied, there are problems. It is not an easy situation for the local authority if in fact those notices are issued because under the legislation they can in fact be landed with large bills themselves should they do that. But the issue is not that; the issue that I was asking you about is the fact that unless the re-survey programme, particularly in the rural areas, is accelerated substantially, we could, at the end of the ten-year period, if in fact it takes that long, have lost buildings and we will not even know about them because the local authorities, for example, do not even have many conservation officers in Wales to do that job and that I think is the issue that was raised with us in Clwyd?

(*Sir Wyn Roberts*) I would certainly like to look into that point rather more carefully but I would also urge upon you that it is of course open to anyone to approach us for spot-listing if indeed they believe that a particular building of value is in some danger.

Mr Llwyd

790. In your opening statement, Minister, you referred in part to unmet expectations and disappointments about Cadw's progress in some areas. You also said that there were hard choices to be made. During the last few months, we have had evidence from many witnesses, many of whom have said the very point that the Chairman has just raised that the slowness of re-surveying appears to be a very critical issue. We understand that the chief executive of Cadw has admitted that his organisation does not employ any structural engineers or legal advisors, though English Heritage has both. We have also been told by the Royal Commission and the Archaeological Trusts that Cadw has not provided them with resources needed to maintain and develop the SMRs and the NMRs. Another critical matter which has been raised is the absence of a Cadw regional office in North Wales. There used to be one, there is not any more. What I would like to ask you, Minister, is do you accept that the current underfunding of Cadw is to such an extent that it is unable to carry out its full range of responsibilities at an appropriate level because this is what we have heard time and time again from very informed opinion?

(*Sir Wyn Roberts*) I am sure that that is what you would have heard, in short, that pretty well everyone involved could do with more resources, but we have to live within our means and Cadw's record of allocation is a very good one, as I implied earlier, and, indeed, its record of achievement. But yes, I certainly accept that both rescue archaeology trusts could probably do with more money and, indeed, so could other parts of the entire structure such as the Royal Commission and so on, but we have to live within our means and, as I say, I do think that Cadw does get a fair share of resources annually and its record proves that, and it is able to carry out and meet the targets as far as the resources are concerned set out for it in the Corporate Plan. But that is not to

[Mr Llwyd *Cont]*

deny that we could always spend more money on different aspects. You referred to the records and so on and the work of the trusts but, as I said earlier, there has been a considerable increase, now up to £850,000, in the money that is available for the Trusts and we have, as far as the National Monuments Record is concerned, given considerable assistance to the Royal Commission to computerise that record. We have also channelled support through the Royal Commission to the Trusts to build up their local records as well.

791. Minister, we had a very graphic example in Flint a fortnight ago of what appears to be lack of resources as far as Cadw is concerned. One gentleman came to us and said, "This castle used to be virtually twice its size when I was a youngster." With some incredulity we all looked at him, including Mr Carr, and then subsequently we were shown photographs and that is exactly the point. If Cadw are doing such a good job, there is one example where a castle is virtually disappearing.

(Sir Wyn Roberts) I have to intervene very sharply there because I am aware of the considerable work that has been carried out on Flint Castle in order to conserve it. In the early 1980s it had been very subject to vandalism and so on and we have actually done a great deal to restore it. We are, however, engaged in further work in conjunction with the local community council and I will ask Mr Carr to say a few words about this.

(Mr Carr) Mr Chairman, I enjoyed very much my not infrequent visits to Flint when I was able to meet you there and I was aware that in the early part of this century a great deal of removal of later structures had taken place. That was within the ethic of conservation of ancient monuments at that time. For example, the old jail was removed. That has not diminished the size of the monument. If I can disagree with Mr Llwyd, what it has done is to expose the medieval remains, but that was the policy at the time. The monument as it now stands—and I was grateful for Members' comments—is now in a very good condition. As to the amount of money spent upon it, that is variable from year to year depending on the state of conservation or decay of monuments. We do not take a budget and divide it by the number of monuments we have. We apply money as the need arises and we do this on the basis of quinquennial inspections and annual inspections by our expert inspectorate and conservation architects.

Mr Hanson

792. Flint Castle is in my constituency and I have raised that issue on a number of occasions with Mr Carr and I do welcome, and am grateful, for the visit and comments he has made after the visit to the local council and to myself. But in general, Sir Wyn, on the point that Mr Llwyd mentioned earlier about the lack of a north Wales regional office—there was one in Conwy which was recently closed—and about the perception of authorities such as mine in Delyn Borough Council of Cadw, I would welcome a view—I am not endorsing the view given but the view or the perception in north Wales that Cadw is a south Wales-based organisation in Cardiff which is distant from local people in North Wales. That is a view which has been expressed in Committee and in evidence, and I think the instances and feelings about Flint Castle from my local community are evidence of that. I am not endorsing that view necessarily. I am just saying that is a view that has been expressed. I would like your view on that perception.

(Sir Wyn Roberts) As a North Waleian myself I am very conscious of the views of north Wales. Cadw is very much a national Wales-wide organisation. It is true we did have an office in north Wales. It is true that our conservation staff are divided and there is one headquarters in Caernarfon but we are considering this and shall consider it further in the context of the Heritage Charter that we shall produce, where obviously we will be considering the quality and standard of conservation that we will be able to offer to local authorities, visitors and so on. I think that is the proper place in which to consider this issue of whether there should be a North Wales focal point for Cadw. It all requires, and will require, additional resources. I think we would all accept that. On that issue, it may interest you, Mr Chairman, if I can say that we have some comparative figures which I think we ought to look at, with the usual caveats, and these are spending per head figures on heritage in Wales, England and Scotland. In 1991-92 we appeared to spend some £4.12 per head, England, £2.12 per head, Scotland, £5.09 per head, but I would use those figures with considerable reserve. Nevertheless, they are worth perhaps putting into the record.

Chairman

793. Going back to the point about the distribution of the funds—and I am thinking of Flint Castle as an example of that—one criticism of Cadw that we have received is that it has not directed adequate resources to the development and marketing of, as it were, the second division of its monuments in care, of which Flint Castle would be one. Yet the relevant 1992-93 target given to Cadw was to increase its market share of visitors to the top 20 heritage sites in Wales. By setting a target like that are you, in fact, obliging Cadw to concentrate on its principal sites to the detriment of the remainder?

(Sir Wyn Roberts) Perhaps I may explain that. Of the top 20 heritage sites that we are talking about, 13 of them belong to Cadw anyway and they attract just over 1 million visitors. The aim of setting that target of some 65 per cent. share of the total visitors to the sites was to ensure that Cadw was setting itself an acceptable standard which bore comparison with non-Cadw sites. That was the aim but I will turn to Mr Carr, if I may, to deal with your other point about the secondary sites.

(Mr Carr) Mr Chairman, we do not in fact classify sites as primary, secondary and tertiary. They all have, as I think I have explained previously, the same value to the nation as any other one. In terms of the presentation and promotion, it is more a question of handling the number of visitors who we know go to certain sites and visitor pressure does need to be controlled and managed very carefully. You will have seen our marketing leaflets where you will see that all sites get a mention, all sites in the north get a mention in the North Wales leaflet and, similarly, in the south. The objective behind those marketing leaflets, as we call them, we could call them

[**Chairman** Cont]

promotional leaflets, is to make the general public aware of the range and the totality of the estate in care, so that they can make their own choices as to what they want to go to see. What we have also done—if I may remind the Committee—is produced a number of thematic volumes which include the monuments in private ownership, in other public ownership and so forth, as well as our gazetteers on ancient and field monuments which came out last year. All of this is designed to promote the ideal of understanding and thereby having an interest in protecting the generality of the built heritage. We do have in certain of the sites, as you will be aware, specific promotions in the form of events, but these are held not solely on the major sites, they are also held on the minor ones. If I may also just take up the Committee's time a little further, our education programme would, I think, identify that most of the specialist education events that we put on are held on what you would describe as the secondary or the smaller sites. So we have a very very broad approach to the promotion of the estate.

794. In terms of the evidence we have had, we have been told that Cadw takes a too exclusive view of its marketing activities, in particular, you have mentioned some of the points there in answer to this, that it advertises its properties and it tends to even in the literature like the one that you have provided us with here, say on south and west Wales, to emphasise the properties that you in fact yourself or Cadw owns. Yet on the map itself, for example, the very important castles such as Pembroke Castle which you say is undoubtedly one of the greatest castles in Britain, is marked with a grid reference J4 for the map, but is not in fact marked on the map itself and, therefore, as a tourist when looking at this, would tend to mean or suggest that these are your main sites and that these at the bottom part of the page are less important. What do you think of that? Is that a fair criticism or do you think it is unfair?

(*Mr Carr*) I think there may well be some fairness in it, Chairman. What I should also like to point out in relation to Pembroke Castle, is that we recognised this difficulty in conjunction with the trustees some eight years ago, and we have agreed with them, and the system has been going on, as I say, for eight years, that we will have reciprocal promotion from our sites adjacent to Pembroke and he in turn handles leaflets appropriate to our sites in West Wales.

795. In terms of the map for South and West Wales that you have got here, this is a very recent map, I would just like to check with the Minister that I think he mentioned before that Dr Wools had been rather optimistic perhaps in his assessment of the cost of doing a re-survey. Do you think, Minister, that Cadw has been a bit optimistic in plotting the M4 as, first of all, having been completed and, secondly, having been extended to Carmarthen? Could you give an opinion as to whether in fact it is meeting targets or policy objectives that you were setting by in fact extending the M4 to Carmarthen and in fact bringing the entire missing gap into production almost instantly the minute that the map was produced?

(*Sir Wyn Roberts*) I am sure that Cadw is right to anticipate the completion of the M4.

796. And its extension?

(*Sir Wyn Roberts*) You have the advantage over me in that you have the map, Chairman, but I accept your interpretation of the map and I am sure that you would agree that we do want to bring as many visitors as possible to the monuments of West Wales and perhaps a little poetic licence is allowed as far as the ease with which you can get to West Wales is permitted. If I may just say that, apropos of Pembroke Castle, there are one or two problems of which I am well aware but, at the same time, it has got to be pointed out that Cadw is involved, as far as marketing is concerned, with some 18 other bodies in joint marketing efforts. I think that Cadw is right to expect the major monuments to contribute to the cost of marketing literature of the kind that you have there if they are to be featured as prominently as they would wish.

Mr Jonathon Evans: I also note on the back of the leaflet to which you refer the very pleasing note that the Shrewsbury to Swansea railway line appears, which does not appear in fact on British Rail advertising. So that is at least something worthwhile appearing in the leaflet.

Mr Carlile

797. Sir Wyn, the jewels of the Welsh built environment are owned by three sources, broadly speaking, the National Trust, places like Erddig which is a wonderful example of what has been done in recent years in terms of restoration, Cadw for example, Harlech Castle which is accessible on a touring holiday and privately owned places like the Felin Crewi restored flour mill near Machynlleth which has been restored at considerable private expense with some statutory funding. So we have three examples of different ownerships of jewels of the Welsh built environment. Are you satisfied that information is provided to the holiday making public which enables them to make a fair assessment of the respective value of each of those three types of building? Because whilst the Cadw promotional leaflet and map which we have been given for North and mid-Wales is helpful and attractive, and I would not wish to criticise it in itself, it does not even attempt to bring a balance between the various options from which the tourist can choose.

(*Sir Wyn Roberts*) As I said, Cadw is involved with 18 other bodies and organisations in joint promotions. I think what one has to say is that there is a certain amount of competition between the different attractions but, nevertheless—and obviously the choice must finally be exercised by the visitor—as far as Cadw is concerned, there is considerable support from Cadw, for example, to the National Trust, and also to the privately owned monuments through restoration grants and so on. So I do think that there is a fair balance struck but at the same time one has to bear in mind that, after all, Cadw is interested in securing visitors to its sites in care and does spend money marketing those sites, and it could be expected of others involved, such as the National Trust and, indeed, private owners, to do similar marketing on behalf of their own sites.

798. Do I detect, Sir Wyn, from what you have said that there is some tension between Cadw and the National Trust which may not redound entirely to the benefit of the visitor, and do you not think that

[**Mr Carlile** *Cont*]

there is still room for improvement of the range of objective information provided to the visitor, particularly through the Wales Tourist Board?

(*Sir Wyn Roberts*) It is certainly a matter for the Tourist Board to consider the promotion of all the heritage attractions that it believes will attract visitors and interest visitors when they come to Wales, and there have, of course, been many efforts along the years in this direction. But I do want to tackle, if I may, the point that you made about the rivalry—

799. Tension?

(*Sir Wyn Roberts*) No, there is no tension between Cadw and the National Trust. In fact, if you look at our record, the support that has been channelled through Cadw to the National Trust for the conservation of its buildings has been very extensive indeed.

Mr Ainger

800. Sir Wyn, in your opening statement, you referred to the tourist figures and the amount of money generated by visitors to the estate in care and to the local communities. Would you accept that the growth area for tourism throughout Wales, and certainly throughout Britain, is rather than trying to increase visitor usage during the traditional season but actually in what are termed the shoulder periods of the season, spring and autumn? If you accept that—and that is certainly the view, I know, of the Wales Tourist Board and all other authorities concerned with tourism—how can you square that with the fact that staffing is now being cut in the estate in care—Lamphey Bishops Palace is an example—from a full-time all-year staffing to a six-month or even less staffing per year?

(*Sir Wyn Roberts*) I will ask Mr Carr to deal with that latter point, which is very much an operational matter, but, of course, I agree that certainly the early and later part of the season and so on have a great deal of potential in terms of attracting tourists to Wales, but I think that the pattern of visitors generally—which has been reflected, I might say, in visitor figures to Cadw sites—has been somewhat disturbed by the recession and that is why we did not have a particularly good year in 1991-92. All this reflects upon the numbers of visitors attending individual sites and, of course, we seek to justify whatever manning is required at those sites in terms of visitor numbers. I will ask Mr Carr to deal with the particular case.

(*Mr Carr*) The Minister has expressed our view very clearly, I think, Mr Chairman. It always surprises me how quickly those thoughts that we may have in Head Office are translated into facts out in the regions. That is a fact of life. In relation to Lamphey, we have had a long-serving custodian who was dedicated to his job. He has, unfortunately, had to retire early and we are currently looking at the manning for that site. It was a full-year manning. The site itself attracts some 8,000 visitors per annum but if you take it as a single operating unit that number of visitors does not produce sufficient revenue to cover the costs of a full-year operation. That does not mean to say we have yet concluded that the site should not be open at specific times of the year and, of course, West Wales has a different visitor pattern

to that of North Wales or even South Wales and that is what we are currently looking at. As to St David's, the monument itself is manned all year round and it will continue to be manned. What Mr Ainger is referring to here, I think, Mr Chairman, is our consideration of the continued manning of the *Domus Juxta Pontem* that we restored some few years ago and have on lease from the cathedral authorities, where we were looking at the costs of continuing to man that shop. What I can tell Mr Ainger is that that will be manned through this forthcoming season. The point about the shoulder seasons is very well taken. It is one, I know, that is shared by the Wales Tourist Board. It is most certainly shared by us because we would like to be able to attract more people in those off-seasons when the weather is very equable at many times of the year, but it has not proven so far to be possible to do so. If it does prove to be possible to do so then we shall continue to review our manning requirements at the site.

Mr Robinson

801. Could I turn now, Sir Wyn, to Cadw's role as an Executive Agency? My understanding of an Executive Agency is that it exercises a considerable degree of autonomy from its parent ministry and is basically within the parameters and guidelines set by the parent ministry. One of the advantages of becoming an Agency is that it is able to operate executively as a separate entity. That does not, however, quite seem to be squaring with what we have heard in evidence. In his evidence Mr Carr said to us and stressed that Cadw remains inside the Welsh Office and legally inseparable from the Secretary of State. That I am sure is the technical position but you in your statement, Sir Wyn, this morning say that you are also keen to see Cadw as a more responsive and accessible part of the Welsh Office, able to deal closely with the many interested bodies and individuals with which it must work. Would it be a fair criticism in all of this to say, therefore, that Cadw's establishment as an Executive Agency is purely cosmetic?

(*Sir Wyn Roberts*) I do not think that is a fair description at all, bearing in mind the relationship between myself as a Minister and Cadw in the early days when, as I referred to in my opening statement, I was Chairman of the Steering Committee. My recollection of the meetings of that Committee indicate to me that I was fully involved in an enormous amount of detail, ranging from the handling of individual monuments such as Dinefwr and what we were doing there, the development of facilities at Conwy, Criccieth and so on, and also the production of the excellent guide books that we finally published for the most important monuments. I was very much involved in considerable detailed work as a Minister. When Cadw became an Agency and it was clearly a compact and separate organisation within the Welsh Office and ripe for setting up as an Agency, then I withdrew, certainly from the chairmanship of the Steering Committee, but I also withdrew from day-to-day responsibility for the work of Cadw. That, of course, has been the responsibility since then of the chief executive with his progress in the implementation of his Corporate Plan being checked on a quarterly basis by his

[**Mr Robinson** *Cont*]

Advisory Committee. Nevertheless, at the end of the day, the Agency has to be accountable somehow or other to Parliament because there may well be adjournment debates as we had recently over St Quintin's Castle, for example, and a Minister has to reply to such a debate and, therefore, he must acquire such knowledge as is necessary from Cadw sources. So far from being cosmetic, I would say that there is certainly a reality about the agency status of Cadw as far as the relationship with Ministers is concerned. That is not to say that possibly because of my experience as Chairman of the Steering Committee up to 1991, I may be referred to rather more frequently than another minister might be. Reciprocally, I may be in touch with Cadw rather more than might otherwise be the case because I am particularly interested in its activities and I know only too well of the political sensitivities related to the built heritage, but it is very difficult to make any kind of division. On the whole, I think that the situation is very clear that the Agency is independent within the framework, within its Corporate Plan and within the scope given to it by the advisory body and within the terms of the Annual Report and any Ministerial policy guidelines that may result from examination of that report and, indeed, as a result of decisions relating to resources because Cadw does have its own PES line and has to bid like other sections of the Welsh Office for any funds that it requires from year-to-year.

802. You are happy to see Cadw develop a distinct identity, at least as far as the outside world is concerned?

(*Sir Wyn Roberts*) I think it was always our intention that Cadw: Welsh Historic Monuments should have a very distinct identity and may I at the risk of being too historical, just simply recall the lack of cohesion that there was before the establishment of Cadw. There was a great deal of work being done, listing, scheduling and so on. An Historic Buildings Council was in existence, so too was the Ancient Monuments Board, so too was the Wales Tourist Board, and it was a very significant step when we formed Cadw, that we brought in all these bodies and cohered them within the Cadw framework.

803. But you would not, of course, see Cadw going on from that and developing a separate identity, at least in the context of planning applications and appeals?

(*Sir Wyn Roberts*) Without changes in legislation I do not think that that would be possible and one area where there is concern, which I know that we all share, is in the area of political accountability. Someone has got to be answerable for Cadw's activities to this House and that pre-supposes that whoever is answering for Cadw does have some fairly extensive knowledge of what Cadw's activities are.

804. Perhaps we could turn this round then, and you could enlighten the Committee on what differences the establishment of Cadw as an executive agency has actually made and what these extra freedoms and responsibilities that go with being an agency actually translate into being?

(*Sir Wyn Roberts*) I think that Cadw would say that it has had considerably more flexibility and I think one of the major developments, as far as Cadw

is concerned, which I know the Agency values, is that in fact the budget that is allocated to them is allocated net and they are allowed to add to their net allocation other receipts from the monuments and that, of course, enables them to have a larger gross budget, but if I may turn to Mr Carr for his experience of the Agency as compared with previously.

(*Mr Carr*) Thank you, Minister. Chairman, we touched on this quite early on in your inquiry. I think that the principal freedoms that I would point to are the ability to use excess receipts towards whatever activity we identify in-year. We also have the freedom to engage our own staff without having to go through the personnel division of the Welsh Office up to certain grade levels, which can be very useful, because we can directly engage, for example, our direct labour organisation, our custodians and some administrative support and, also, some of the professionals. We take the initiative and we can move perhaps just a touch faster than might have been the case otherwise. We have also developed separately our accounting system which is on an accruals rather than a cash basis and that means that we are able to identify just the sort of management information that Mr Evans referred to earlier as the systems are progressing and I think that that is a very considerable gain to us. We also have within the Framework Document a much greater clarity of what the Department or Ministers expect of us through the Framework Document, the Corporate Plan and the setting of these annual key targets. Of course, there is my own personal accountability, which I do not resent in any way, but I am exposed if I fail to deliver what is required of me. There is a degree of freedom from the line management within the Department. We are given the cash, we are given the framework and we essentially get on with it with, as the Minister has identified, advice from the Advisory Committee and, of course, Ministerial inquiries from time to time. I think that we are also—and I think this is very important in terms of the forthcoming Heritage Charter and the discussion we have had on that—more accessible to the general public. We can advise in a rather more open way than we were previously able to do because what we have been able to do is separate out some of the decision-making on planning issues, which are now undertaken by the planning division of the Welsh Office, which enables our expert professional staff to discuss issues with applicants before the formal application has been set before the local authority. I think that those are very meaningful developments.

805. Sir Wyn, that leads me nicely on to the issue of the role of the Corporate Plan, which, of course, you are responsible for agreeing?

(*Sir Wyn Roberts*) Yes.

806. And also for the setting of targets each year. How important do you take the achievement of the targets that you set and how do you measure them?

(*Sir Wyn Roberts*) Very important indeed, is the answer to that question, but, of course, circumstances beyond Cadw's control can sometimes affect the achievement or otherwise of these targets. That is certainly true of the first year of Cadw as an Agency in 1991-92, when they achieved some four out of the nine targets set, but the failure to achieve was also not unconnected with the recession and with

[Mr Robinson *Cont]*

the effect that that had on visitors to the monuments. So I think that setting targets has to be realistic and it is so because they are discussed within the Welsh Office with Cadw and presented to Ministers, who may then express their own views, and so the targets are evolved.

807. Can you explain, therefore, why the 1992-93 targets were not announced until July 1992, three months after the start of the period to which they applied, because surely that must make management's task rather difficult?

(*Sir Wyn Roberts*) I seem to recollect that we had an election somewhere around that time but perhaps Mr Carr may refresh my memory.

808. Could I perhaps then add to that, are you in a position to tell us what the 1993-94 targets are or when they will be announced?

(*Sir Wyn Roberts*) Not at the moment but they will be announced by the end of April, we hope.

(*Mr Carr*) I have nothing to add, other than that the election did delay the announcement of the targets for this current year.

809. You would normally expect to get them by the beginning of the year?

(*Mr Carr*) I would expect to go through the discussion process progressively with the Department from around November of the previous year and as the provision of resources became more and more apparent, so the talks would become more easily definable and by the end of the financial year— and we are very close to it—we should have notification of our resource provision, which then enables us to be able to put up draft targets to the Department. The Department itself suggests draft targets to us. When we have a measure of agreement on our ability to deliver—and, of course, we have to balance the budgets and the resources very carefully—then we agree the final draft targets which are put to the Minister.

810. When you have those final targets, you obviously at that stage also know what your resources are. How much freedom do you have to allocate those resources to what you perceive as the requirements of the targets or how much do you have also to do that in consultation with the Welsh Office?

(*Mr Carr*) No, I am given a block of money. The Advisory Committee is important here also, but I have freedom to set my programmes against the targets and to use the financial resource to the best effect.

811. So you are your own Financial Officer, in effect, are you not?

(*Mr Carr*) I am the Accounting Officer for the Agency, yes.

(*Sir Wyn Roberts*) That again, if I may stress, was a major change as a result of Agency status.

Chairman

812. Sir Wyn, in terms of these targets, why is it that it is going to take you to the end of April, you hope, actually to produce them? Here we are on 24 March. Why do you not have the goods available today?

(*Sir Wyn Roberts*) I think that some of the things that I am hearing at this Committee and in your evidence, the various stresses that are being given, for example, to the re-survey programme, may lead us to adjust our targets in that area. We are very conscious and very flexible as far as these targets for the Agency are concerned, partly because of its Agency status. As Mr Carr was saying, I think it is one of the virtues of the Agency status that the Agency can react and be much more flexible.

813. Mr Carr, what initiatives has Cadw taken as an Agency which they would not have taken before?

(*Mr Carr*) I think that is a rather difficult question to answer, Chairman, because there was not a sudden break. Cadw when it was first established—and I think the Minister might endorse this—was not of the normal Welsh Office Division variety. It did have certain activities given to the Director (as he then was) to enable him to act reasonably freely but within rather tighter constraints than we currently have. So the Agency has progressed from an organisation which was partway towards "agencification", as we understand it.

(*Sir Wyn Roberts*) Could I add to that because it does occur to me that an example of an initiative which Cadw has certainly taken has been the development of relationships with the Countryside Council for Wales in relation to historic landscapes. That is something quite new and was certainly not dealt with during the time when I was Chairman of the Steering Committee. I think the progress being made in connection with historic landscapes is a good example of an initiative really taken by Cadw.

(*Mr Carr*) If I may add to that—forgive me, my memory is actually at fault!—we have also been able to be far more reactive and helpful to the public, as I mentioned earlier, in terms of advice than we were hitherto.

814. In terms of that, Mr Carr, do you mean that the public can actually turn up at the Agency office in the Welsh Office and simply ask for advice? There is no problem with that, is there?

(*Mr Carr*) It depends on the volume of people who come, Mr Chairman, but yes, indeed, that does occur.

815. The link question then is, would you feel a new breath of fresh air if physically your office could be taken out of the Welsh Office and be in a different physical location so that not only would you be at arm's length but you would be at an even better length from the people to whom you are accountable, or the person, I should say, sitting next to you?

(*Mr Carr*) On a matter of fact, Mr Chairman, we are already located outside the Welsh Office in Cathays Park. We are in Brunel House.

816. And you find that the relationship between you and Brunel House and the public is all right, apart from volume?

(*Mr Carr*) Perhaps I should expand upon that. There has been over the years a steady stream of people enquiring about such matters as listing or grant cases and so on, which are dealt with there and then, if possible, by members of my staff. Where a matter is more complicated then, of course, we seek to have an appointment system because, as I have already given evidence to the Committee, my professional colleagues do spend an awful lot of time

[**Chairman** Cont]

going around Wales assessing buildings, advising local authorities, scheduling monuments and so on.

(Sir Wyn Roberts) I do think, if I may just add to that, Chairman, that the whole question of Cadw's relationship with the public, indeed, the wider public and I include planning authorities, local authorities and so on, as well as visitors to monuments, that will be the subject of the Heritage Charter which we are currently considering and I am sure that as a result of the definitions in that charter that Cadw's relationship with the public will become closer than they now are.

Mr Roger Evans

817. As part of that Heritage Charter, would, for example, burdens be placed upon Cadw which we have been hearing evidence of, have not been entirely fulfilled, namely, the range of advice which Cadw publishes of a technical nature giving detailed and specific guidance to applicants, that has been criticised in some of the evidence before us. Is it the intention that the charter should widen Cadw's obligations?

(Sir Wyn Roberts) I think that it will do that inevitably. It is of the very nature of defining what services you are prepared to give and the citizens' rights in that area. But as far as guidance and information is concerned, we are in fact providing more detailed information through best practice pamphlets, pamphlets relating to the use of materials and so on. This is on-going work. We do realise that there are gaps in the information provided and that some would appreciate more guidance than we are currently giving, but we are building up this guidance.

818. How would you assess Cadw's present publication of a technical advisory nature compared to the range published by English Heritage, for example?

(Sir Wyn Roberts) It is not something that I have actually done, but I do have occasion to know that some of Cadw's guidance is in fact very very detailed indeed, guidance to local authorities, for example, in certain areas, but then I am thinking of a small 18th century bridge near my home which the county are rebuilding and very very detailed guidance has been provided to the county as to how the bridge is to be pointed and so on, very detailed indeed. We do want to extend that kind of information and, of course, we could call upon some of the work done by English Heritage, but then you would be the first to realise that patterns of building and materials and so on are very different in Wales.

819. No, but one of the criticisms made to us, bearing in mind the rapid growth of scholarship in depth on a lot of these issues whether it is 18th century bridges, medieval glass or rain water goods in 18th century buildings, the criticism made is that Cadw's technical publications are nothing like on balance as detailed or as broad as those published by English Heritage. I do not know whether Mr Carr is a more appropriate person to answer that question?

(Mr Carr) I think, Chairman, that I could safely say we very much admire the technical publications that English Heritage has produced. We envy, to a degree, the speed with which they have been able to produce them. It is our intention during the course of the next two to three years, as I previously advised the Committee, to produce our own best practice guides and, as the Minister says, many of these will need to have particular relevance to the types of materials and the types of structures which exist in Wales which are very much different to those of England.

820. Mr Carr, the fact that English Heritage has appeared to have done rather more, is that a result of greater resources available?

(Mr Carr) It is a large organisation.

821. Is it also the case that when we come to the question of dealing with listed building consents, the more detail and broad the specific technical guidance notes published, in fact the easier it is for the public to know what is expected and indeed for Cadw to decide on a consistent basis?

(Mr Carr) I am not sure that I would agree to any suggestion of inconsistency, but I would agree entirely that if the owner had access to fully illustrated comprehensive technical information, that would put him or her in a better position to review the works to a structure which they would have to do with their own professional advisers. Now the professional advisers themselves, the architects and so forth, would need to have their own technical expertise and our leaflets would help to boost that expertise and knowledge.

822. Mr Carr, that was one of the criticisms made that because of the lack of the comprehensiveness which is suggested is desirable of your technical literature, the standards of drawings submitted by surveyors and architects in Wales left something to be desired in the case of listed buildings and the dialogue could have been improved by greater publication by Cadw?

(Mr Carr) I would not deny that.

(Sir Wyn Roberts) I think one has got to bear in mind the point that Mr Carr made earlier that, of course, English Heritage have got considerable resources which means that they do have their own laboratories, I am told, obviously being a larger organisation. However, one cannot but agree with the point that you are making that certainly the information contained in the re-surveys should enable us to give a more practical guidance to those who wish to improve the condition of their buildings or alter them in a way that is acceptable.

823. For example, the Heritage Charter which you are contemplating at the moment, would that perhaps include guidance to Welsh local authorities really as to the need to have conservation officers of importance and of sufficient scholarship?

(Mr Carr) I think that there has obviously been a growing interest in conservation and local authorities are well aware of it. Nevertheless, there is, as we said, only one county authority in Wales which has an archaeological service and I think that there are very few, five local planning authorities who have conservation offices.

Mr Ainger

824. Sir Wyn, to return to what Mr Robinson was inquiring into earlier and that is the relationship between Cadw and the Welsh Office. You have said

[Mr Ainger *Cont*]

that you want to develop this separate identity between Cadw and the Welsh Office. You want to push more public advice. You drew the analogy that Cadw now lies closely with the Countryside Council for Wales and so on. When members of the public seek assistance from Cadw when faced with a major problem of conservation, the issue I am referring to is the bypass of the lower town of Fishguard which is in fact a Welsh Office, when they seek help and advice from Cadw on the conservation issues, they are told that as it is a Welsh Office issue, they cannot give any assistance and they certainly are not prepared to be represented at a public inquiry. When the public really need Cadw in that particular issue, they are told quite clearly, "sorry, we are shutting up shop on this one. We cannot help you." Can you address that issue in the future?

(*Sir Wyn Roberts*) Can I just say this, there are indeed many areas where Cadw is obviously acting on behalf of the Secretary of State. Indeed, the powers that Cadw has are powers that are derived from the Secretary of State. As far as the separation of Cadw is concerned as an agency, it always has been, as I have described, a separate organisation within the Welsh Office. The extent to which we could make it even more separate is rather dependent on the kind of function that Cadw is involved in in any given situation as to whether Cadw is in fact acting on behalf of the Secretary of State, but I am sure that Mr Carr would like to say something on this and, in particular, about the situation in Lower Fishguard.

(*Mr Carr*) I am concerned, Mr Chairman, that a misapprehension has occurred with regard to the by-passing of Lower Fishguard. One of my conservation architect colleagues was involved in a number of consultative meetings regarding the route of that by-pass. There were two buildings, if I recall correctly, which were listed within that conservation area which might be the subject of removal as a result of that line of the by-pass. That colleague also attended a PLI when the issue came before the Inspector in Fishguard. If I could explain that, whether it is professional advice, expert professional advice, that is available, particularly available to the Highways Directorate of the Welsh Office as it is to a local authority or a private individual. That advice is available up to a point when that advice is specifically related to the professional expertise in relation to the quality, setting and so forth of buildings, and I think that that advice was freely available to all the people involved and it is again available in other instances throughout Wales. So I think there has been something of a small misapprehension, if I may say so.

825. Coming back on that, we are talking about the difference between an opinion and advice. You can advise somebody but at the end of the day what the people of Fishguard were looking for was the expertise, the experts employed by Cadw who had already given them advice actually to give an opinion to the inquiry, and they were prevented from doing so. I understand the reasons and obviously you referred earlier to the fact that there may well be legislation required if you accept that it is something that Cadw should in the future be able to do, and that

this arm's-length position which currently exists in relation to planning, there should not be any connection; there should be Chinese walls or whatever it may be developed so that your experts can actually pass an opinion.

(*Sir Wyn Roberts*) I think that probably there is a distinction to be drawn here between the role of an Executive Agency and a statutory body, for example, like the Countryside Council for Wales, who have a specific duty to advise the Secretary of State on various matters and who frequently make that advice known. It may well differ from the advice that has been given to the Secretary of State by other bodies but I think we shall have to look at this rather more carefully in terms of the Heritage Charter.

Mr Roger Evans

826. Could I ask you this, because that is an astonishing example, I suggest. English Heritage is a non-departmental public body and I understand the position. For example, if the Department of Transport comes up with some revoltingly barbarous by-pass scheme which is highly controversial, English Heritage would take a public position and would, indeed, appear before a planning inquiry, would it not? Is that the case, Mr Carr?

(*Mr Carr*) Yes, they would, but if I could perhaps stem your flow, we also gave evidence to a by-pass inquiry in Flint, professional advice.

827. Mr Carr, let me clarify this for a moment. I accept that but I want to ask you why that is different from Fishguard. The position in England is that because English Heritage is a NDPB they always, if asked, take a public position and if they deemed it appropriate they would appear at an inquiry to support that condition. What I understood from the answers which have just been given is that Cadw's independence to take a position, because it is wearing two hats and is the creature in a sense of the Secretary of State for Wales, is different. Is that the case? You are caught between your responsibilities to the Welsh Office and what your independent professional view might be?

(*Sir Wyn Roberts*) I drew attention to the status of the Countryside Council for Wales, which does take an independent stance that is similar to that taken, for example, by English Heritage because of its NDPB status. At the same time one has to point out that Cadw can certainly object to various schemes and so on put forward and I am very well aware of the fact that it has done so. There was, if we may move away from Fishguard for a moment, the case of a road development near Flint Castle to which Cadw objected and Cadw appeared at the public inquiry and made its view publicly known.

828. But the position as I would understand where we have got to is that there is a fundamental structural difference in respect of the position of English Heritage and the position of Cadw in relation to this type of public inquiry?

(*Mr Carr*) If I may, Mr Chairman, Minister, when our professional advisers appear in front of public local inquiries, which they do fairly regularly each year, they are giving their professional advice as to the impact of a particular development upon the heritage. That advice is, in my own instance, firmly

[Mr Roger Evans *Cont*]

stated but it is given without prejudice to the Secretary of State's final decision and that final decision is guided by a planning inspector's report in the same way as would occur in England. What we are not able to do in the same way as English Heritage might be able to do, should they be so minded, is to set up campaigns.

829. It is not Mr Ainger's constituents but whether it be the exmaple which Mr Ainger put or another one, the difference is simply this, is it not, that whereas in England, whether it is Oxleys Wood, Twyford Down or whatever controversy it might happen to be, those who object can look to English Heritage and seek to persuade English Heritage to put the heritage argument independently. Your position is not so open?

(*Mr Carr*) Correct.

(*Sir Wyn Roberts*) That is right. It is the difference between Agency status and NDPB.

830. Sir Wyn, would this be a matter which you might consider reviewing?

(*Sir Wyn Roberts*) I would certainly like to look at the arguments, yes. Could I simply add that, of course, the position of other bodies related to Cadw is not quite the same in that the Ancient Monuments Board, I think, could make their view very publicly known; so too could the Historic Buildings Council, although they are essentially advisory bodies to the Secretary of State. It depends on the strength of their feeling on any particular issue.

Chairman

831. I would like to take another example, if I may, Minister, of a similar kind of problem that could arise because of the difference between English Heritage and Cadw. I think I would like to do it in terms of a piece of evidence we had from the principal planning officer of Cardiff City Council when he said that there had been a recent change of procedure in Cadw where they now make themselves more available for giving advice to local authorities where listed buildings are concerned. Can you explain exactly what that change of procedure is?

(*Sir Wyn Roberts*) I think that Mr Carr has already referred to this obliquely as one of the consequences of agency status. I would like to ask him to expand on the reference that he has already made.

(*Mr Carr*) With your permission, Chairman, I know that Mr Hughes is very familiar with this particular area.

(*Mr Hughes*) In the run up to Cadw becoming an agency, we did review the way some of the planning functions were dealt with and the decision to which Mr Carr referred to earlier was that some of the decision-making functions should pass to the planning division of the Welsh Office. The legal position has not changed. The legal position is that Cadw is the Secretary of State. In relation to planning matters, an applicant may feel very bruised if with one hat the Secretary of State is taking a very strong view and with another hat the Secretary of State is performing his quasi judicial planning settling role. So what happens is that we now assess applications for listed building consent and provide advice to the planning division and we have arrangements whereby our professional conservation architects can

give a professional assessment that is shared with an applicant and other parties involved if that application is called in for determination by the Secretary of State and, subsequently, the architect would attend a public local inquiry. That was a major change because prior to that change on 1 May 1991, Cadw did not attend public inquiries and the professional assessments were not made known and that was a source of considerable complaint.

832. In terms of a specific example, Mr Hughes, we have had evidence of the Victorian Society suggesting to us that in formal evidence by Cadw's professionals had contributed to the loss of the interior at the Old Guild Hall in Swansea and the Victorian Society then provided us with detailed correspondence relating to that case. They argue that the lack of a structural engineer in Cadw can render its advice incomplete. Do you accept their point there?

(*Mr Hughes*) I think that the way that that is dealt with within Cadw, Chairman, is that the conservation architects have a broad experience of historic buildings and, if necessary, they would draw on specialist expertise.

833. But what about the structural engineer? That would include that, would it?

(*Mr Hughes*) If they needed to consult a structural engineer, I am sure they would, Chairman.

Mr Roger Evans

834. Could I just ask this, one of the other criticisms allied with that particularly in the case of serving various forms of notice, was the lack of in-house lawyers in Cadw?

(*Mr Hughes*) The position, Chairman, is that Cadw uses the legal services of the Welsh Office. In fact, the particular point there I think arose in relation to Leighton Hall in Powys where the local planning authority was looking for support in dealings with the removal of fixtures and fittings and they did approach us and asked for our help in taking the case forward. The difficulty for Cadw is again the legal position because they were initiating procedures which have a route of appeal to the Secretary of State.

835. That is another ambiguity in the role of Cadw which is different from English Heritage?

(*Mr Hughes*) That is a difference between an executive agency and an NDPB.

(*Sir Wyn Roberts*) Could I just say, apropos of this point, that of course Cadw has been set up as an Executive Agency and the situation will be reviewed according to the Framework Document in three years, of which one has already gone, and we are into the second. Obviously these differences as between an executive agency and an NDPB and what one can do and not the other, and so on, is something that we shall have to consider.

Chairman

836. What I would like to do now is to move on to the grants situation, and to ask you, since in fact the Secretary of State has to approve the recommendations of the Historic Buildings Council when they look at applications for repair and maintenance of historic buildings; on how many

[Chairman *Cont*]

occasions have you actually turned down an application that the Historic Buildings Council has suggested that should be approved and on how many occasions have you actually done the opposite? That is, in fact, approved one that they turned down?

(*Sir Wyn Roberts*) I begin with your opening words, the Secretary of State does not have to approve. In fact, the recommendations are submitted to us for approval, but personally I do not recollect a particular case where I did not approve of a grant recommended by the Historic Buildings Council, although there could well have been a reduction in the amount that was recommended. We would have to check back on the years for that, but the point is that the Historic Buildings Council does comprise considerable experts in this area. They do know the quality of the buildings and, indeed, their recommendations clearly bear out their knowledge and is confirmed by one's own knowledge of the buildings on the ground. Coupled with that is the fact that all the buildings that are recommended for grant have been visited by Cadw's conservation architects, again for whom I have the very highest respect. Therefore, if we are in fact in receipt of the very best advice available and have no clear reason for rejecting it and every reason for approving the advice that we get, then I see no reason for dissenting with the advice given by the Historic Buildings Council, but I am always prepared to do so and I always do look most carefully at their recommendations.

837. How many times have you overturned their advice when they say that an application should be refused but you, in fact, have decided that they are wrong, in your view, and the Secretary of State has granted the money?

(*Sir Wyn Roberts*) Very seldom. I cannot recall any cases where we have tried to second guess them.

838. So, in fact, you could be said to be a rubber stamp of the Historic Buildings Council because you have so much confidence in them that basically you rubber stamp the decision. Accepting the possibility you look at them, but you have never in your recollection actually dissented one way or the other from what in fact they advise you?

(*Sir Wyn Roberts*) The quality of the advice that we have been given from the Historic Buildings Council over the years has been very high indeed and one has also got to bear in mind that the essence of that advice is published in their Annual Report. Not only have we, to the best of my knowledge, not dissented from them on this matter of advice but I am not aware of any public reaction either, public dissent from the advice that they have given, the basis of which has been published in the Annual Report. Could I also say this, that, of course, the Chairman for a considerable number of years was Lord Anglesey. He was in all a member of the Historic Buildings Council and Chairman for a period of 40 years and it was well-known to us that the Historic Buildings Council did not simply wait for applications for grant but where they knew that there were buildings in need of repair they did go to considerable lengths to encourage the owners of those properties to put forward applications because, indeed, the grants were for the benefit of the buildings, not for the benefit of the individual owners.

Mr Roger Evans

839. Are you saying there in effect Lord Anglesey's very considerable reputation in this field was an important factor?

(*Sir Wyn Roberts*) Tremendous, very important, as, indeed, is the experience of the present Chairman, Mr Thomas Lloyd, who, as you know, has written a book entitled "The Lost Houses of Wales", so that we have been very fortunate in that both Chairmen have had a very deep commitment to the built heritage of Wales and I have certainly never been able to fault them, although I am quite prepared to do so.

Chairman

840. You have a problem here, though, Minister, in so far as if I take a couple of examples perhaps you could assist the Committee in understanding the application of the criteria for these grants where, in the ultimate, of course, you have the power to change the advice, not ignore it but actually to have a different view. I want to take the example we have only just had in from Felindre near Swansea of the old corn mill. Mr Carr, in listing the building on 4 December 1989, says: "This building has been listed primarily for this mill's importance as one of the last two examples in Glamorgan with sufficient of the existing machinery to be capable of restoration on site to working order." That was the schedule that Mr Carr signed on 4 December 1989 and yet the Historic Buildings Council actually decided to recommend that this was not, in fact, an outstanding historic building and you agreed with them. What is the basis of your decision not to disagree with the Historic Buildings Council when Mr Carr says that it is one of the last two examples in Glamorgan that could, in fact, with existing machinery come back into use? I would be very interested to know why you did not decide, as Minister responsible, to override the Historic Buildings Council advice in that case?

(*Sir Wyn Roberts*) I really would have to look into the individual circumstances of that particular case.

841. I am interested, though, because this letter from Cadw giving the decision to the owner of the mill was dated 3 March this year. Therefore I would imagine that you were involved in this decision very recently and, therefore, as that decision was yours and you made it very recently, would you not remember that particular case?

(*Sir Wyn Roberts*) I really would have to look at the detail of the advice that I was given by the Historic Buildings Council and the listing given by Cadw. But, of course, they are two quite different issues and it may very well be that the listing is, of course, correct but that the circumstances for grant-aiding were not there. Very often we are dependent on the bona fides of the owner of the property and so on. All that has to be taken into consideration by the

[Chairman Cont]
Historic Buildings Council when deciding whether to recommend a grant or not and it is a question of whether the owner can actually meet his or her part of the cost required.

842. What in fact is interesting me is, how does the Historic Buildings Council decide on what is outstanding, because that is the key problem here? There is another example of a letter that I recently had from the Rector of St Mellons Vicarage, where he finds it extremely hard to understand why it is that one of the churches in his particular parish has been eligible for grant-aid from Cadw and yet the other one, Michaelston-y-Fedw parish church has been made ineligible, and he and his parishioners find it extremely hard to understand why, in fact, one has been considered to be outstanding and the other one not. So the real question, Minister, is, how does the Historic Buildings Council distinguish between one outstanding building and another and how closely does it follow the listing grades or should it, in fact, be based, as at present, only on an independent assessment by the Council and its architectural assessor?
(Sir Wyn Roberts) I think that the re-survey situation does have a bearing on that final point. I believe that in England only grade 1 and grade 2* buildings are in receipt of grant, but because of the situation with which we are very familiar in Wales that re-surveying is by no means complete, we do not have that limitation on grant-aiding. I am sure that the Historic Buildings Council is aware of the listing given to any particular building, but as far as grant-aiding is concerned, as I have tried to indicate, I think that a considerable number of factors do enter into it, including the ability of the owner to carry out the works and finance his or her element of the works. As to whether they are suitable persons to be in receipt of grant and so on, that is just one element. With regard to the two churches, again we would have to look at the particular circumstances and listings or otherwise of those churches. I do, you will appreciate, hesitate to make comments on particular cases without having a very thorough knowledge of them and I would like to refresh our memory on those cases.

843. Could we have a note on both those cases then, Minister?
(Sir Wyn Roberts) Yes, indeed.

844. Thank you for that. Is there any means by which you could give grant-aid to a historic building other than on the basis of a Historic Buildings Council recommendation?
(Mr Hughes) It may be possible for a historic building to be fitted under some other scheme in the Department but that would not be a scheme specifically for the built heritage. The Council's advice is made in the strict context of the 1953 Act and the 1990 Act and we are, as a Department, not permitted to offer a grant without consulting the Council in those cases.
(Sir Wyn Roberts) I think that the answer, the more I think about it, is yes, in that we are able to help in the restoration of buildings if they are within conservation areas, for example, and in certain cases where the buildings can be used for other purposes. I am thinking, for example, of that chapel at Cefn just

beyond Merthyr, Tabor, which has been restored and is used as a community centre. I was very happy to endorse such financing as was required to improve the appearance of that chapel because it dominated the A470 at that point. Its refurbishment did have not only an effect on the local community but on the appearance of the whole of that area and this has been of importance in the Valleys Initiative too because it was recognised that churches, chapels, do occupy dominant positions in the localities and it is part of the renovation of a community that its church or chapel may be restored visually.

Mr Roger Evans

845. Does that not operate against rural country churches in Wales which fall below the outstanding category because in the countryside there are no conservation areas and none of the town schemes which you have referred to?
(Sir Wyn Roberts) Yes. There is a lot of consideration being given to the idea of rural conservation areas but some of our urban programmes certainly apply to what you and I would call perhaps rural towns, but there is some validity in the point that you make.

Chairman

846. We were told by the Chairman of the HBC that their grants were made for the benefit of the building, not of its owner. We were also told that although access conditions were imposed on the recipients of grant aid, no subsequent check was made to establish whether grant-aided buildings were being opened to the public, nor did the HBC produce a handbook detailing grant-aided properties and their access facilities. In fact, the owner of one grant-aided Georgian mansion told us on our tour in north Wales that although he opened his house to local organisations, he had never once been approached by a member of the public with a request for access. The questions therefore obviously follow from that such as where is the benefit in the existence of grant aid to outstanding buildings? Is it to buildings thus preserved or is it to the taxpayers? That is one of them. The thing is, how important do you believe, Minister, is it that the right of public access should be tied in with the giving of such grants, otherwise, in fact, the money that is being spent is not in fact then being spent to the advantage visibly of people who can visit?
(Sir Wyn Roberts) We do indeed require access as a condition of a grant but, of course, it has got to be reasonable in whatever the circumstances may be, but the grant is certainly in order to preserve the building and, as far as a register of property is concerned, you will know, Chairman, that the Historic Buildings Council does in fact publish the titles of the properties that it has grant aided and access is certainly featured and described in relation to those buildings. I am looking at Appendix B of the 35th Annual Report where varieties of access from one to five are ascribed to various grant-aided buildings.

847. But not many people would actually get hold of that annual report, would they? Say you were going around Wales as a tourist, it would not be a

[Chairman *Cont*]

case whereby people would know that and it is not cumulative either and so there is that fundamental problem. The question has to be, how does, let us say, the tourist coming into Wales actually know as to which buildings are accessible and how to go about getting accessibility and, of course, whose responsibility is it, Cadw or the Historic Buildings Council, to give that publicity to people who obviously need to know if they can go to a building or if they cannot?

(*Sir Wyn Roberts*) I think that the knowledge is public because it is published in the Annual Reports of the Historic Buildings Council and the type of access is also known. It is simply a question of whether it would not be advisable to publish this information in a more coherent and readable form.

848. But you cannot get that in the high street, can you, in the newsagents? It is very important that people actually get that information, that it is incorporated by other bodies then using that Annual Report, for example, the Tourist Board or however, in order to ensure that that information is there. For example, has thought been given to some indication on a building, or at least outside it somewhere or perhaps even outside the permit of the building, so that the public can know from outside that building that that building has received a grant and is therefore available in terms of public access because the taxpayer has in fact contributed to its upkeep?

(*Sir Wyn Roberts*) I think we have got to be careful that we do not interfere too much with the rights of the owner who may well have received a grant. Nevertheless, we have to respect the fact that he has applied for a grant and also made a significant contribution himself. It is always, as far as a grant is concerned, a matter of negotiation as to what terms the grant is given on and on what basis it is accepted, but I can reaffirm that access is certainly one of the conditions, but the nature of the access will vary as reported by the Historic Buildings Council in their Annual Report. I do think that there is merit in the suggestion that we should consider producing—it might have to be on a regional basis but certainly overall—a guide to grant-aided properties in Wales where access is available.

Mr Roger Evans

849. Sir Wyn, I do not understand your last answer. You refer to the right of owners, but no owner is under any obligation to apply for a grant, let alone to receive public money and it is a condition of the grant that there be reasonable access. Why is it not a simple matter because the owner has voluntarily entered into it simply to expect him to allow only reasonable access? Nobody says every day from nine to six, but reasonable access surely means that if I write to a named owner I ought to be allowed on appointment to inspect?

(*Sir Wyn Roberts*) This is why I referred to the different types of access and it is clearly identified in each case in the annual report. For example, access type 1, "these buildings are open to the public for a minimum of 30 days each year"; access type 2, "these buildings may be inspected by appointment with the owner", and so on. I do think that we have to be careful, as far as the owner is concerned and the type of property. For example, I do know of one property

which has been grant-aided in Wales which is open to the public and does, in fact, have one of the most valuable Rembrandts in the country. When it comes to access at all times and so on, one has to take all interests into account.

850. Yes, Sir Wyn, but if you own a very valuable Rembrandt you balance that asset against the disadvantage of accepting public money for access, do you not?

(*Sir Wyn Roberts*) In this case it was the National Trust.

851. Sir Wyn, is not the really serious criticism, however, in this area this, that we were told by the Historic Buildings Council that the condition of access is purely a private contractual matter between the owner who applies and receives the grant and the Welsh Office and there is no system of imposing an obligation upon somebody who buys the property? In other words, you can receive public money, sell your building next year and the public are suddenly excluded?

(*Sir Wyn Roberts*) You cannot sell it within a period of ten years that we cannot recover the grant, but after ten years the situation that you have described is, in fact, so. If an owner sells on after ten years then access would have to be renegotiated.

852. No, it is not a question of renegotiating. If the owner sells after one year the public thereafter cannot get in. You may or may not succeed in claiming back your grant from an owner in Grand Cayman or somewhere else?

(*Mr Hughes*) The Act allows the Secretary of State to recover the grant paid within ten years and the sale of the property is one of the things that would certainly trigger consideration of recovery of grant. The question that I think we got on to before is the question of a land charge so that there is a continuing obligation on successors to keep the property open. The difficulty is, of course, that in some grant cases I think we see that there could be a case for that but a great number of grants are of a much smaller amount. You as a Committee visited a restored building that had had a considerable amount of grant-aid and I think that the question of whether some continuing obligation is needed in cases where a very substantial grant has been given is something we would want to look at, but equally quite a number of grants given are actually for a comparatively small amount.

853. But still what the machinery does not provide for at the moment is either on disposal any continuing public right of access or assurance that public money will be recouped?

(*Sir Wyn Roberts*) It does provide for the recoupment of money.

854. Not by a land charge, Sir Wyn, not by something which is enforceable against the proceeds of sale.

(*Sir Wyn Roberts*) But I think you would be the first to acknowledge that the imposition of any kind of covenant of that type might affect the value of the property.

855. No more than a private mortgage affects the value of the property. Why on earth cannot this be a case simply of a charge on the property which, upon

[Mr Roger Evans *Cont*]

sale, you would recoup, and you may or may not, on sale, decide to persuade your purchaser to accept an on-going public obligation to let the public in? There seems a gaping hole in these arrangements?

(*Sir Wyn Roberts*) I can only reiterate that the purpose of grant is, of course, to restore and carry out essential repairs to the buildings that qualify for grant and that access is a condition of grant and, in the event of sale, we can recover the grant but the access position remains as we have stated.

Chairman

856. In terms of the recovery, have you ever had any problem getting your money back, Sir Wyn? Have you lost cash?

(*Sir Wyn Roberts*) I do not think we have.

Mr Roger Evans

857. Have you ever been told of sales?

(*Mr Hughes*) Yes, we have been told of sales, Chairman.

858. How many, Mr Hughes?

(*Mr Hughes*) I do not have the figure with me, sir, but perhaps we may send you a note on that.

Chairman

859. Have you successfully recouped all grant moneys that have been paid where, in fact, that property has been sold on?

(*Mr Hughes*) I am not certain enough of that to answer, sir. Perhaps we could cover that.

Chairman: Let us know in detail, thank you. Mr Sweeney?

Mr Sweeney

860. Would you agree, Sir Wyn, that it would be sensible to have a land charge system to protect the public purse so that any purchaser of a property would be placed on notice that the property had been in receipt of a grant, and would you also agree that to go any further by, for example, putting labels on the outside of a house to indicate that it had been in receipt of a grant in order to encourage public access might deter people from going for the grant in the first place and, therefore, be counter-productive?

(*Sir Wyn Roberts*) I agree with that second point. It is certainly one where we have to be very careful and we have to balance. We must remember that in all cases it may be a fine judgment on the part of the owner as to whether to apply for a grant or not. What we have in mind, our first concern, is, of course, the preservation of the building, so I do think that we have to take the views and the interests of the owner very much into account and we may well be faced with a situation where, in the event of some identification being put on the building as being in receipt of grant, the owner might very well turn round to us and say, "In those circumstances I am not going to have a grant," and the building might then deteriorate, which is not what our wishes would be. I am quite prepared to look at this idea of a land charge. It would certainly be right obviously to try to ensure that access is preserved after a grant has been made.

861. Would it not also be desirable to ensure that nobody would apply for the grant simply to enable them to sell their property on quickly at a profit? Surely that is not what is intended by the provision of grant and any such speculator should know that he or she will have to repay the grant if he or she sells within ten years?

(*Sir Wyn Roberts*) I do not think that is automatic because again the emphasis is on the building and the preservation of the building. It does not matter really who owns it because, do not let us forget that the grant only covers a proportion. It is a 40 per cent. grant and, therefore, the owner has to put in 60 per cent. and in return for that we dictate how the grant will be spent and the standard of work required and so on. So the owner does have a very significant role in this and there is some danger, I think, in overplaying our hand, as it were, as the giver of grant. It is a matter of balance.

Mr Ainger

862. I am a little confused by what Sir Wyn is saying. First of all, he is telling us there is this access condition put into the grant—and we are not talking about percentages, we are talking about, in some cases, hundreds, well over £100,000 in the case of the property we inspected—and he is virtually saying to us it is done on a nod and a wink basis to the owner, that, "Whilst there is an access condition, we promise not to tell anybody about it." That is really what you are saying. Other than its being published in the Historic Buildings Council Annual Report, where else is it published? How can visitors know that just up the line from perhaps where they are staying there is a property which has had £150,000 of government money spent on it and they actually have a right to go and look at that building?

(*Sir Wyn Roberts*) I am not saying that at all. What I am saying is that it is public knowledge when a grant has been given and not only through the Annual Report of the Historic Buildings Council but we usually issue a press notice drawing the attention of the public to these grants.

Chairman

863. But you could not say whether it is reported or not. You could not really, Minister, say that public knowledge is a combination of what is in the Annual Report of the Historic Buildings Council plus a press release? Surely that does not make anything public knowledge. Public knowledge would be that something is widely known, easily accessible and that if a member of the public, whether within Wales or from outside, comes to Wales, that it is easily recognisable as a place that they can go to and it is in the literature. That is public knowledge, is it not?

(*Sir Wyn Roberts*) If we did publish this very interesting information about buildings that are in receipt of a grant, it would perhaps interest you and I and certain others, but one has got to accept the fact that even a publication of that kind, which contains all the details, I would guess, would have a very limited circulation, but it is the principle that I am stating, that it is public knowledge and it is simply a question of how you convey that public knowledge. It is simply a matter of presentation and I have

[Chairman *Cont*]

already agreed that we shall give further consideration to the presentation of this otherwise public information, but there is no guarantee that having published this information, albeit in a more attractive form and so on, that the knowledge therein will necessarily attract people, but there will be a better chance, obviously.

Mr Llwyd

864. Sir Wyn, I think the publicity angle is really like the old *London Gazette*, is it not? There is the legal fiction, amongst lawyers anyway, that the *London Gazette* is read by all and sundry but, in fact, nobody ever buys or reads the document. I think what we are talking about is not so much whether grant aid has been given—are we not talking about making the public aware of the accessibility or the access to these buildings and, in that case, is there not a case for some joint enterprise with the Tourist Board and other organisations to make it absolutely clear to the public that access is freely available to these buildings? The question of grant is one thing, it is important of course, but I think in terms of letting the public see these jewels, as Mr Carlile described them, is it not incumbent upon everything to make sure the public are aware of their privileges in this regard?

(*Sir Wyn Roberts*) There are, of course, many hundreds of these buildings. The best known of them are already patronised by the public. I think, for example, of Penrhyn Castle in my own constituency which has been in receipt of a substantial grant over the years. That belongs to the National Trust and is very much visited and that is true of the most important buildings that are grant aided. There are, as you will know, many other buildings of not necessarily equal importance or equal attraction to visitors which are listed here and I think it is a case of simply elevating the level at which this knowledge which is already public is indeed available to people who are interested.

865. How does one do that?

(*Sir Wyn Roberts*) I think it is simply a matter of presentation. The knowledge is there to be culled from these reports and it is a matter of presentation and style.

Mr Roger Evans

866. Why could it not be inserted in the well known annual guidebook, *Houses and Gardens open to the public in England and Wales*? Why could the Department not simply provide a list available to commercial publishers to publish?

(*Sir Wyn Roberts*) I do not want to get bogged down in this issue. I think that we have conceded the principle. It is simply the methodology of how you present this information to interest a wider public. I would say in reply to the last remark that I do think in some of these cases you do need to provide rather more than a list of names and addresses, as it were, because the interest lies in the description which is essential in many of these cases.

867. But do you, for example, in these access conditions lay down what amount of public access should be given?

(*Sir Wyn Roberts*) Yes, we do. There is the categorisation from one to five.

868. Is that imposed by the Welsh Office as opposed to a voluntary arrangement with the owner?

(*Sir Wyn Roberts*) It is imposed—negotiated would perhaps be the better word.

Chairman

869. In terms of another area, Sir Wyn, completely different and that is the way that the improvement grants system works in Wales in relation to unlisted but historic and valuable vernacular Welsh cottages. We have had some evidence to show that large sums of money, up to £50,000 per building can be involved and the allegation is that the works required for these grants are frequently excessive, that is, re-building when sensitive repair would be adequate, and unsympathetic where inappropriate materials, UPVC windows and so on are in fact put in. Are you aware of this problem?

(*Sir Wyn Roberts*) I am aware of the problem of UPVC windows and Cadw's very strong view is that they should not be used in historic settings and, indeed, vigorous action is taken to ensure that that is so. I do think that housing renovation grants and so on, the applications have to be made to the local authorities and they are well aware of the character of the buildings that are being applied for and there is a special guidance which we have issued in Circular 15/90. We are dealing with people's homes and I think that we have to have, again, considerable respect for the kind of improvements that they wish to carry out, but we must, at the same time, in the case of a historic building and in the context of the townscape or conservation area, seek to ensure, as do the local planning authorities, that whatever improvements are carried out are consistent with the architectural and historical character of the area. We have got no evidence, I might say, of large numbers of very expensive grants in Wales. The average cost of grants in Wales is about £15,000.

Mr Roger Evans

870. The evidence we have got is that you can do a great deal of damage for £15,000 to vernacular cottages, particularly in Pembrokeshire and the evidence that has been put to us is simply the planning authority is wasting public money in a destructive fashion. Is there any review by the Welsh Office as to whether damage is being done?

(*Sir Wyn Roberts*) We are certainly not aware of damage.

871. Mr Martin Davis has published a well known book on this subject which has also been precised in other national journals. Is Cadw aware of this problem, Mr Carr, in Pembrokeshire?

(*Mr Carr*) That is a very open question. There have been some unfortunate alterations to a particular town that I am aware of, yes.

872. Is this a matter which Cadw is looking at?

(*Mr Carr*) Yes, it is a matter we are looking at and it is also a matter where particularly my professional colleagues seek to work closely with the local planning authority so that the character of the particular conservation area can be as little altered as

[Mr Roger Evans *Cont]*
possible by the sympathetic use of the right sort of materials in the improvement grant scheme.

873. Mr Carr, perhaps this is more a question for Sir Wyn, but the same question was put to us. It is all very well talking about respecting people's homes and choices but if they are to be given generous amounts of public money should this not be carefully monitored to ensure that there is not heritage damage and so on?

(*Sir Wyn Roberts*) As I say, we are not aware of damage being done. There is certainly a role for the local planning authority in this. They know the properties that are being applied for in terms of grant and the actual giving of grants is, indeed, a matter for them at the end of the line, although, of course, we fund them.

Mr Ainger

874. Again I am a little confused in that part of the problem which was identified for us is, first of all, the building regulations, which are not worked out at a local level but are worked out nationally. In other words, if you want to qualify for a grant you have to abide by all the building regulations and that may well mean putting far larger windows into a cottage. That is the first problem. The other problem is that many owners of these properties do not want to have such an extensive grant and they are happy to receive it at the end of the day but their problems are that because of the building regulations, because of the restrictions placed on them as applicants by the local authority and ultimately by the Welsh Office, they have to have this extensive work done to comply with all the building regulations. There seems to be this total conflict, on the one hand between the Department and the Welsh Office saying, "Let us preserve our heritage," and on the other side, "Let us radically improve the housing stock and give grants to individual owners to do that"?

(*Sir Wyn Roberts*) I do not think that there is the incompatibility or inconsistency that you are referring to. What we are talking about here are home renovation grants in particular, which are grants given by the local authority, but yes, whatever work is done has to conform with building regulations and again it is a matter for the local authority to ensure that that conformity is obtained. Yes, the regulations are worked out by central government and approved. When these grants are given, they are home renovation grants. Applications are made. If they relate to buildings within a conservation area—and it is, after all, a matter for the local authority to decide what is a conservation area or a townscape and so on; it is for them to decide—then that property and any architectural value that it may have will be taken into account in so far as grant-giving is concerned. Again the responsibility actually falls on the local authority.

Mr Ainger: But from my own direct experience as somebody who did renovate a Pembrokeshire cottage, in fact I was forced to do things I did not want to do because of the building regulations, for instance, the size of windows. If you qualify for grant you have to abide by all the building regulations. For a certain size of room you need a certain size of ventilation, therefore, you need a certain size of window. All these sorts of things are constantly forcing owners of vernacular cottages not in conservation areas—because they are in rural areas where there are no conservation areas—to destroy the appearance of their properties in order to qualify for grant, and I do think it is something that needs to be looked at very seriously.

Chairman

875. Mr Carr, do you have experience of that yourself?

(*Mr Carr*) Not direct experience, Chairman. I regret I am not a professional architect or planner.

876. What about Mr Hughes? Do you have anything at all in that line where you are finding a conflict?

(*Mr Hughes*) I can only speak in this case as Secretary to the Historic Buildings Council perhaps and say that the Council has discussed on occasions the difficulties that might be being caused by over-enthusiastic application of the improvement grant scheme. We have as a result from our secretariat been in touch with our colleagues elsewhere in the Welsh Office who are responsible to ensure that they are aware of these concerns and that guidance to local authorities does take account of conservation issues.

(*Sir Wyn Roberts*) May I add that my experience, which certainly does not relate to Pembrokeshire, is, of course, of members of the public complaining of the excessive demands made upon them because of the character of the properties that they wish to improve.

877. I wonder, Mr Carr, if it would be possible for you to give us a note on what your view would be of that book by Martin Davies regarding these Pembrokeshire country cottages in terms of the points he makes?

(*Mr Carr*) If the Committee request that, Chairman, I can do a book review. It is a very difficult question to answer without knowing the content of the book or the subject matter. I do not know it personally. I can certainly consult with my colleagues and I am sure that you would respect the fact that the Minister would wish to know what it was we were going to say.

Chairman: I do not mind if you write it together!

Mr Roger Evans

878. It has been very widely reviewed in the national press and it is an important work and important that we at least know what the alternative argument is.

(*Sir Wyn Roberts*) We will certainly have a look at it.

Chairman

879. Thank you very much. You mentioned the Welsh Office Circular. I wonder whether you can say a few words on the point that witnesses put to us that Welsh Office Circular 61/81 is now outdated and they have pointed to the 1987 Department of the Environment Circular on changes in the law relating particularly to conservation areas. Do you think that circular needs to be updated?

(*Sir Wyn Roberts*) Yes, and I am glad to say I am well aware also of the English document of 1987 and

[Chairman *Cont*]
we shall be consulting on a new policy guidance note
on historic buildings very shortly. We are aware of
the growing interest of local authorities and we do
want to respond positively to that interest.

880. Will you have that in place before the
establishment of the unitary authorities in 1995?
(*Sir Wyn Roberts*) I think we will.

881. In terms of Article 4 directions, these must be
confirmed by the Secretary of State and we believe
there are none in Wales?
(*Sir Wyn Roberts*) There I think you are wrong, Mr
Chairman. There have, in fact, been four confirmed
in 1992. I believe that all four were in Cardiff and
Swansea.

882. And in terms of that, were there any before
that year?
(*Sir Wyn Roberts*) I do not have that information.

Mr Roger Evans

883. Sir Wyn, one of the arguments that has been
pressed upon us by the amenity societies is that
conservation areas are much weakened because of
the location of, and control over, certain visual
features such as doors and windows, and unless
Article 4 directions are made, would you be prepared
to consider being sympathetic to making these a
fairly standard procedure in all conservation areas?
(*Sir Wyn Roberts*) I think that these Article 4
directions do interfere, do they not, with the General
Development Order and our feeling is that they
ought to be used sparingly but in a way that does
successfully protect the features of conservation
areas. I think that to get down to the kind of detail
quite clearly that you have in mind could involve us
in excessive and laborious interference which might
be very much resented, but I do know that we are very
stiff on certain matters like windows in conservation
areas and we are insistent on that particular score.

884. Sir Wyn, I am very surprised to hear you use
the phrase "some resentment", because it is a very old
fashioned 1960s view, I suggest. I suggest in the 1990s
people who live in conservation areas are very well
aware of the fact that being in a conservation area
with the kind of ruthless detailed control actually
enhances the value of their properties and their
environment at a stroke and it is the lack of social
control over anti-social neighbours which down
values their properties.
(*Sir Wyn Roberts*) I am sure that there are many
who would agree with you, but I have a feeling that
there would be a lot of people who would resent
interference from outside. Nevertheless, we do it very
extensively, as far as windows are concerned and
other features too, but I am just wary of where this
interference occurs it could become excessive.

885. Sir Wyn, one of the mysteries of the evidence
we have received is dealt with at page 8 of your
opening statement, when you say: "a generous offer
was made to the Church in Wales in 1987" in the case
redundant churches and, indeed, it is not disputed
that the generous offer was made in 1987. What we
have not had any complete explanation of is why has
nothing come of it?
(*Sir Wyn Roberts*) I think the short answer is that
those who deal with eternity take a long time to
answer letters and that may be the answer. It was a
generous offer from myself to the then Archbishop
that we would actually take care of any churches that
should be considered for preservation and so on, but
we have not had a direct response. We have, in fact,
grant aided a number of churches in Wales and we
have enabled them to be kept in working order.

886. Sir Wyn, we have also had evidence that that
is indeed the case and obviously it is. Is it the case that
those perhaps who are concerned with eternity
should be a little more concerned with immediate
judgement because it is implicit in what you are
saying, that really I suggest what you are saying is
that the Church in Wales has been dragging its feet
on this very important issue?
(*Sir Wyn Roberts*) Not only that, but there is the
matter of exemption as well and again we have put
the situation on exemption to the Church in
December of last year and that was done not only by
the Welsh Office but by the Department of the
Environment as well and the situation there is that if
they abide by the Code of Practice then exemption
from listed building consent can continue. If not,
then there is clearly a case, which has been pressed
upon us, for churches having to abide by the same
rules as apply to secular buildings.

887. Has the Welsh Office seen or considered the
interim report of Judge Michael Evans, QC, which is
a report for the Church in Wales on this matter, or is
that a matter which you are going to wait until the
final report is produced?
(*Sir Wyn Roberts*) We have not as yet considered
it. We shall obviously when the final report is
produced.

Chairman

888. Minister, gentlemen, could I thank you very
much for coming to see us. If perhaps we have got any
supplementary questions to put to you, would it be
all right that you could answer those in writing, Sir
Wyn?
(*Sir Wyn Roberts*) Indeed.

889. Thank you very much indeed, gentlemen.
(*Sir Wyn Roberts*) Thank you.

Supplementary evidence by the Minister of State, Welsh Office

HISTORIC BUILDINGS AND ANCIENT MONUMENTS (HB 93)

Q. 778

Costs relating to any acceleration of the resurvey of buildings of special architectural/historic interest.

The Committee drew to my attention evidence from Dr Wools which suggested that this task might be undertaken in a three year period at a cost of some £0.75 million. The Committee was concerned at the disparity between this estimate and the costs we gave, as an example for a 10 year programme, of the order of £0.5 million per annum. By way of background, it is important to bear in mind that the resurvey fieldwork undertaken by English Heritage formed only part of the whole task. Draft lists prepared by them were referred to the Department of the Environment for consideration as the statutory power to list rests with the Secretary of State. Costs, therefore, arose there in addition to the costs of fieldwork, professional supervision and contract management incurred by English Heritage.

We understand from colleagues in England that the costs quoted by Dr Wools related to fieldwork in the Vale of York, Humberside and the Wold. These are areas rich in built heritage which contrast markedly with most of Wales where problems of accessibility and geography add to fieldwork costs. We have considered the costs of fieldwork in England for areas where the work is more comparable with the Welsh scene and these tend to be higher than those areas where concentrations of historic buildings feature.

In framing our estimates of fieldwork costs we have assumed that we shall need 16 contract listers to produce about 70 (new or updated) lists for each year of a 10 year programme. This would represent an additional cost of £350,000 per annum on the 1992–93 base and at current prices. To this must be added central, professional supervisory costs to ensure uniformity of standards, the costs of contract management, consultation with local planning authorities, processing and publication (including informal notification of owners). We estimate that, allowing for supporting services, these functions will add some £150,000 per annum (on the 1992–93 base and at current prices) to Cadw's costs.

The figures quoted do not include the costs of reordering the work priorities of staff at more senior levels and, allowing for some rise in costs each year, would take the total estimated beyond £5 million over a 10-year period.

Q. 824.

Participation in Public Local Inquiries.

The Committee enquired about the position Cadw took at Public Inquiries concerning road proposals at Lower Fishguard and Flint.

Cadw's role in such matters is to ensure that information about historic buildings and ancient monuments is available and, through professional assessments, that the effects on them of development proposals are understood. The Agency is consulted on all emerging road schemes promoted by the Welsh Office (as in the case of Lower Fishguard) and by other highway authorities (in the case of Flint, Clwyd County Council).

Cadw can then bring forward appropriate professional advice to ensure that information on built heritage matters is available. Where an Inquiry is necessary, Cadw provides its assessment and appropriate professional officers attend.

Contrary to information apparently given to the Committee, Cadw's Superintending Conservation Architect did give evidence to the Inquiry at Lower Fishguard, as had his Inspectorate of Ancient Monuments colleagues in the case of Flint.

What Cadw could not do is to join a public campaign lobbying against a particular development, though Cadw's professional assessments would be available to parties to any Inquiry.

Q. 825, 826, 827 and 834

Cadw's status as part of the Welsh Office and English Heritage's position as an NDPB

The Committee noted that Cadw's status as an Executive Agency did not permit it to take as independent a line as English Heritage—a NDPB—might adopt.

While the judgement has been that the creation of a NDPB best met the needs of England, our judgement— both when we first established Cadw in 1984 and when we made it an Executive Agency in 1991—has been that the distinctive needs of Wales would be well served by keeping Cadw as part of the Welsh Office, but with independent advisers—the Historic Buildings Council and Ancient Monuments Board.

Cadw enjoys close relationships with other parts of the Department (such as Planning Division) and in a multi-functional Department this brings with it the real benefit that policy advice can be guided by in-house experts whose counsel arguably can be applied more constructively than if it came as lobbying from without.

The status of the Agency, as I said to the Committee, is however kept under review.

Q. 840, 842

Advice from the Historic Buildings Council re grants: The Old Cornmill Velindre. St Mellons and Michaelston y Fedw Parish Churches

The Committee was concerned to know why the Old Cornmill and the parish church of St Michael had not been judged to be buildings of outstanding historic or architectural interest (by the Historic Buildings Council) and so had not been offered grant aid. I said I would wish to re-examine both cases.

At the outset I think it is important for the Committee to appreciate that the listing of buildings as being of special architectural or historic interest—with the associated grading of I, II* and II—and grant aid under the Historic Buildings and Ancient Monuments Act 1953 are not directly linked. The outstandingness test of the 1953 Act is an exacting one and while the listed status of a building can help to guide the Council in its deliberations, it does not fetter them.

In examining whether any structure under consideration for grant aid and, on which we consult them, should be judged outstanding, the Council weighs the merits of the individual case. They are guided by a report from their Architectural Assessor—and each structure is visited by him or by a conservation architect colleague—by advice from the Inspectorate of Historic Buildings and information from the applicant. The Council is made up of independent experts chosen for their knowledge of the many aspects of the built heritage and they consider the case in the context of others of similar type and vintage of which Council members have developed a close appreciation. The standard maintained is high and inevitably involves a measure of subjective judgement on the Council's part. The Council's independence and expertise offers me invaluable guidance in seeing that standards are maintained without fear or favour.

At my request, the Council has reconsidered the two cases raised by the Committee and has reaffirmed its advice that neither building should be judged to be outstanding. Whilst the parish church of St Mellons was accepted to be of clear architectural merit, its sister church of St Michaels, Michaelston y Fedw did not reach the standard required. Although being of 13th century origin, later Victorian alterations have compromised the architectural integrity of the structure which suffered also from damage by fire in 1898. The fittings of the church were felt to be unexceptional. I regret that the incumbent feels that he has not been given sufficient explanation of this and Cadw's Chief Executive will write to him.

In the case of the Old Cornmill, Velindre, you drew to my attention the list description associated with the building's 1989 listing (Grade II). After reconsidering this case at some length, the Council holds firmly to its view that the structure is not outstanding. That it is of special interest is acknowledged by the listing, but the Council has drawn to my attention the ordinary architecture of this essentially utilitarian structure which has no particular historical association. Its interest lies in its comparative rarity as a mill with machinery in situ, but even allowing for this the Council is of the view that the building is not of outstanding historic or architectural interest.

Q. 846

Public access to grant aided buildings

The Committee was concerned that better arrangements be made for public access to historic buildings which had received grant aid.

As I said to the Committees I am sympathetic to the idea and I have asked Cadw to consider how best this might be achieved. I understand that the Historic Buildings Council had also asked for this to be looked at. I think, however, we must keep all this in perspective. National Trust property we grant aid is clearly available, church property the same. Our grant programmes under the 1990 Act only address external works. The balance of grant aided structures where improved publicity and continuing access after change of ownership need to be considered involves a comparatively small part of expenditure on this grant scheme. We shall certainly consider this further, however, with the Council.

Q. 856

Grant Recovery

The Committee wish to know if the Secretary of State's powers to recover grant aid were being used and in how many cases.

As we told the Committee, these powers are being used. In the past 3 years we have had to review 3 cases and grant aid has been recovered (the proportion depending on the outstanding pre-emption period) and a further three cases are currently under consideration.

Q. 869

Renovation Grants

The Committee reviewed with me the question of the possible adverse impact of housing renovation grants—particularly in the Pembrokeshire area. The Committee also drew to our attention a book by Mr Martin Davies on traditional qualities of the West Wales cottage.

Insofar as renovation grants relate to historic or architecturally important properties, as I said to the Committee our policy guidance to housing authorities does point up the need for sensitivity.

More broadly, where a housing authority may be looking at grant giving to unlisted properties and to those outside Conservation Areas it seems to us that there is a balance to be struck. But this is very much a matter for housing authorities, their grant officers and those responsible for building control. We must not lose sight of the fact that these are peoples' homes and we must be careful how we seek to regulate the choices individual home-owners make.

In this respect the Committee suggested that building regulations compelled some home-owners to take on works they would not normally have wished to. In the first place I think I should say that the building regulations are important to ensure that adequate building standards are achieved. The implementation of building regulation control is, however, a matter for local authorities' building control officers, but if an owner believes that regulations are too onerous then local authorities do have powers to relax these. In certain circumstances, where agreement cannot be reached, there is also provision for appeal to the Secretary of State.

I think these are all important considerations we should not lose sight of. That said, however, Wales does have a rich stock of vernacular buildings and we appreciate the contribution they make. Our statutory advisers—the Historic Buildings Council for Wales—have expressed certain concerns on this front and we will want to consider what further advice can be given to local authorities on this issue in any new policy guidance.

Turning to Mr Martin Davies' pamphlet—Traditional Qualities of the West Wales Cottage—I read this with interest. It seems to me to be a well written dissertation by an author who clearly has a close interest in and regard for such buildings. Cadw professional staff think that Mr Davies' work points up important considerations in the development of such property which in some cases need to be sensitively dealt with by home owners. I do hope that he has sought to make it available to local authorites in the area he writes of.

Supplementary memorandum by Cadw

WELSH HISTORIC MONUMENTS RESPONSE TO ADDITIONAL QUESTIONS FROM THE COMMITTEE (HB 95)

Church Act Funds

The Committee asked about Welsh Church Act Funds.

The Department does not monitor the use of County Councils' Welsh Church Act Funds. It is for the Councils themselves to administer the funds within the terms of the scheme (or schemes) governing them. Our policy on allocating Welsh Church Act Funds to the new unitary authorities has not yet been decided. In any arrangement we would be careful to ensure, as far as we were able, that any administrative costs would be kept to a minimum. The option of retaining the funds on broadly their current basis, but administered by lead authorities, is therefore one option being considered.

Historic Landscapes

The Committee has asked what consultations there has been on the subject of historic landscapes.

By way of background, I think it is important for the Committee to know that, although the decision to embrace an evaluation of historic landscapes was taken at the same time as we originally decided to embark on the preparation of a Parks and Gardens Register, it was on the understanding that this was a complex area and would need to be reviewed in the light of the results of the first, pilot register—that for Gwent. We also asked the consultant who was preparing that register to include an evaluation of work on landscapes in order to help to inform our broader thinking. The contractor discussed the pilot project with English Heritage and drew on their experience and benefited from their preliminary work on defining historic landscapes. Nevertheless, the evaluation demonstrated that a different, broader approach would have to be taken towards landscapes than that being adopted for parks and gardens.

Cadw reviewed the position with its partners in the compilation of the register, ICOMOS UK, and decided that landscapes should be dealt with as a separate exercise preferably as a joint project with the Countryside Council for Wales who, obviously, have a very broad interest in the historic landscape.

As I am sure the Committee will appreciate, it was felt preferable to establish the framework and funding base for this new project before opening a broader dialogue. When the CCW and Cadw did reach broad agreement on the desirability of the scheme this was reviewed in detail at the earliest opportunity with the Archaeological Trusts who were invited to join in the project and are represented on the project's Steering Group. There was no question of excluding the Trusts from our thinking—it was simply a question of timing—and we were pleased that they were able to participate, along with the Royal Commission in helping to formulate the detailed brief for the project. In this respect the Committee will be interested to see the attached consultation letter which the Countryside Council for Wales have recently issued on this project.

The Record

The Committee is interested in what it terms "The Record" which we take to mean the various records of archaeological sites, landscapes and historic buildings in the Principality. The Committee identifies an important role for such information—in the planning process—but this of course is not the exclusive use of such information.

Local records are compiled and maintained by the four Welsh Archaeological Trusts and form the basis of the regional Sites and Monuments Records. At the national level this information is held in the National Monuments Record by the Royal Commission on Ancient and Historical Monuments and in addition we have the Department's (Cadw's) record of scheduled sites. Your Clerk's letter suggests that wider conservation will require a more subtle form of record but I have to say that we are not altogether clear what is meant here. In terms of protecting important archaeological sites a comprehensive record exists—both at regional and national level—which is available to interested parties. Indeed, in this respect it is interesting to note that since the introduction of our strategic planning guidance on archaeology—PPG 16—Welsh local authorities have taken even more advantage of the locally held record.

In this respect the Committee is interested to know what steps we have taken to ensure that local planning authorities have their own full access to a properly maintained record.

It may be helpful for me to explain that historically, with the exception of Clwyd County Council, Welsh local authorities have not chosen to keep such information in-house. In England the majority of local planning authorities similarly do not hold such information but rely instead on county-based Sites and Monuments Records.

In the mid 1970s in response to a gap in archaeological coverage in Wales the Department fostered the establishment of the 4 regional—county-based—Trusts. This in turn led to the development of the 4 regional Sites and Monuments Records which fulfil a range of functions most notably in the field of development control.

As the importance of our built heritage has become more keenly appreciated this seemed to us, and we believe to local planning authorities, to be the most effective response to the needs of archaeology in the Principality. In obtaining their advice from the Trusts local planning authorities do, of course, have access to properly maintained records. Furthermore, I understand that the Trusts, when giving evidence before your Committee, emphasised how cost effective this system was if compared with any system based on the greater number of local planning authorities holding such records. Having said that I think I should add that we are still firmly committed to encouraging the development of conservation expertise in the heritage field within local authorities.

In the context of planning and development control, the most recent consultation we can point to on the importance of archaeology, the need for strategic consideration and of the importance of using the "records", is our consultation on the draft PPG on archaeology and planning. This was widely welcomed and was subsequently published by the Department in November 1991. We are currently consulting both local government and the Trusts on the effectiveness of this guidance.

As to the future of "the record" the Department continues to seek to support the Royal Commission in its recently redefined role as the lead body responsible for the maintenance and enhancement of the record at local and national level and welcomes the Commission's new Extended National Data Base Index [ENDEX] initiative. The main objective of this initiative is to link the National Monuments Record, the Sites and Monuments Records and Cadw's Scheduled Ancient Monuments Record into an extended national database index and a strategy to this end will be formulated following the Commission's information strategy study and a detailed analysis of the archaeological site indices of the National Monuments Record and the Sites and

Monuments Records. The intention is to build ENDEX from the available data sets and the Commission's funding of the Sites and Monuments Records will be targeted to achieve this end.

Insofar as the Royal Commission is concerned it is, perhaps, an over-simplification to seek to categorise it as either primarily a conservation body or a research institute. As the principal body charged with surveying and recording archaeological sites (including landscapes) and historic buildings in Wales, it fulfils a particular role of its own. The results of its work may be used for a variety of functions including conservation (eg informing the listing and scheduling process) and providing information for research either through its published work or the National Monument Record.

As stated in their Warrant, one of the Commission's main priorities is the compilation and maintenance of the National Monuments Record of Wales. While the collection of information is vitally important it is not, on its own, sufficient unless the data is in a readily retrievable form and available to those who may need to see and use it. The Commission has, therefore, been given responsibility for developing and maintaining an effective database which is to be computerised.

Additionally, the Commission has now assumed responsibility for the coordination and sponsorship of the local sites and monuments record.

Archaeological Trusts

The Committee asks if there is a conflict of interest within the Archaeological Trusts between their commercial operations and their role within the planning process.

We recognise that there is potential for conflict where an Archaeological Trust might be fulfilling a contractual and curatorial role. However, the difficulty we face to some degree in Wales relates to the availability of archaeological expertise to which a developer may look for advice and a local planning authority for guidance on the importance of archaeology.

The Trusts are well placed to provide this. However, to regularise the potential for the very conflict you have identified, the Trusts have created separate advisory and contractual sections and have adopted a code of practice which seeks to separate these two roles.

It seems to us that this is a sensible way to proceed particularly in the early days of the introduction of our strategic planning guidance to local planning authorities—Planning Policy Guidance Note 16 (Wales) Archaeology and Planning. However, it will clearly be important for us to monitor the situation to see how these arrangements work in practice.

Dear

CADW (WELSH HISTORIC MONUMENTS) AND CYNGOR CEFN GWLAD CYMRU (COUNTRYSIDE COUNCIL FOR WALES) JOINT INITIATIVE—REGISTER OF LANDSCAPES, PARKS AND GARDENS OF SPECIAL HISTORIC INTEREST IN WALES (PART 2)

On behalf of the above organisations, it is my great pleasure to invite your organisation to participate in this new initiative which is a first but significant step forward in formally recognising the tremendous importance of the Welsh historic landscape and the urgent need to bring it within the mainstream of conservation policy and practice. Your organisation is cordially but specifically invited to become a specialist participant because of its acknowledged specialist knowledge and expertise in certain aspects of the Welsh historic landscape.

The initiative stems from Cadw's joint project with ICOMOS/UK to produce a Register of Landscapes, Parks and Gardens of Special Historic Interest in Wales and is jointly funded by Cadw and CCW, with the participation of the RCAHM (Wales) and the Welsh Archaeological Trusts, who will provide key pieces of information for the study.

The initiative takes the form of a one year project based at CCW's Headquarters in Bangor led by Mr Richard Kelly, seconded from his post of Principal Archaeological Officer (Contracts) with the Gwynedd Archaeological Trust.

Representatives of the funding and participating bodies sit on a Steering Group which has decided on the following objectives for the project:

(a)   propose the principles and criteria for selecting types of historic landscapes drawing on the current awareness and experience of a broad spectrum of specialists;

(b)   using these criteria identify, with justification, an initial list of historic landscapes with at least indicative geographical boundaries. These historic landscapes should be particularly significant from cultural (archaeological, historical, architectural, artistic and literary) and/or physical (landform, ecology and land use) points of view;

(c) recommend the issues and criteria for a more detailed assessment of Welsh historic landscapes in the future, commenting on the appropriateness of the Register of Historic Landscapes being compiled by ICOMOS and English Heritage;

(d) produce a report for the steering group on:
   — the methodology
   — the findings and recommendations
   — a critique of the methodology.

The objectives will be achieved on the basis of a thorough desk-based study, supported by an input of information and limited fieldwork by the Welsh Archaeological Trust and the widest possible commentation, with the time available, among specialists and organisations currently working or involved with the Welsh historic landscape and its study.

I would like to emphasise that we are very much aware of the practical limitations of such an exercise and that it is a 'top-down' as opposed to a 'ground-up' study which would take many years to complete. I am nevertheless extremely confident that the study will arrive at a valid and worthwhile consensus, and with your valued participation it can achieve the stated objectives and attain the success it so rightly deserves.

Once again, I would be most grateful of your agreement to participate. As soon as I have received your reply Mr Richard Kelly will be writing to you to suggest a suitable time to visit you. In the meantime, I would be pleased to receive your views or to answer any queries you may have.

Yours sincerely

Mrs E Hughes

Chief Planner

APPENDICES TO THE MINUTES OF EVIDENCE

APPENDIX 1

Memorandum by the Ancient Monuments Board for Wales. December 1992

PRESERVATION OF HISTORIC BUILDINGS AND ANCIENT MONUMENTS IN WALES (HB4)

1. The Ancient Monuments Board for Wales is the Secretary of State for Wales' independent advisory body on matters relating to ancient monuments in the Principality.

2. The Ancient Monuments Board for Wales was originally constituted under section 15 of the Ancient Monuments Consolidation and Amendment Act 1913. It is currently constituted under section 22 of the Ancient Monuments and Archaeological Areas Act 1979 and is charged with providing advice to the Secretary of State with respect to the exercise of his functions under the 1979 Act. These range from the management of monuments in his care to, for example, the identification of ancient monuments designated as being of national importance and the treatment of archaeological remains.

3. Members of the Board are drawn from the disciplines and specialisms involved in this field and include historians, archaeologists and architects. The legislation does not prescribe the size of the Board but does require the Secretary of State to include nominees from:—

   (i) The Royal Commission on Ancient and Historical Monuments (Wales);

   (ii) The Royal Institute of British Architects;

   (iii) The National Museum of Wales;

   (iv) The Cambrian Archaeological Association.

Efforts are always made to ensure that all the main geographical areas of Wales are adequately represented and that there is a reasonable balance of age and experience among members.

A list of current members of the Board is at Annex 1.

The Board takes a keen interest in Cadw's work and its Chairman is a member of the Secretary of State's Cadw Advisory Committee.

4. The Board's Secretariat is provided by Cadw: Welsh Historic Monuments Executive Agency and includes a secretary and assistant secretary, archaeological adviser and conservation adviser.

5. Under section 23 of the 1979 Act the Board is required to submit an annual report to the Secretary of State which he is required to lay before Parliament.

6. The Board meets in full session twice a year. Each December there is a business meeting and in midsummer a 2/3 day tour of ancient monuments in private, local authority and State care followed by a business meeting. Members also meet on other occasions to consider specific matters on which guidance is sought or to consider issues of concern. They are also consulted individually on issues which arise between meetings, where their professional experience is considered helpful.

7. The Ancient Monuments Board for Wales believes the ancient monuments in the Principality present an invaluable and irreplaceable resource and that:—

   (i) the importance of this must be recognised both in respect of locally important monuments and those scheduled ancient monuments;

   (ii) conservation is the best way of ensuring the preservation of such monuments;

   (iii) identification and monitoring of monuments' condition is a vital task;

   (iv) the estate in the care of the Secretary of State for Wales is a national treasure;

   (v) such monuments must be conserved to the highest standard;

   (vi) such monuments should be made available and interpreted to the best effect and benefit of visitors both from home and abroad;

   (vii) such monuments are a unique educational resource which should be capitalised upon by those involved in this field; and

   (viii) the State has an indispensable part to play in the conservation and management of ancient monuments.

THE ESTATE IN CARE

8. The Board takes a keen interest in the management of the estate in the care of the Secretary of State. This includes consideration of monuments which might be taken into care, major developments at existing sites such as the provision of visitor centres, Cadw's conservation programme, the provision of guidebooks and other publications and a close interest in Cadw's education programme.

9. The range of monuments in the care of the Secretary of State is as rich and diverse as is the historical evidence of man's presence in Wales. There is a wide span of prehistoric sites and monuments, fine remains of the Roman occupation of Wales, castles of the Welsh Princes, the World Heritage Sites of Edward I and remains from the Industrial Revolution. The demands of this estate are many and varied.

10. In 1988 Cadw introduced the mechanism of its quinquennial review of properties in the estate in care. By this process, Cadw's professional staff evaluates the condition of monuments and identifies areas which require attention. The Board strongly endorsed this initiative. It believes that this is an effective mechanism for periodically assessing the condition of these buildings in order to guide and prioritise maintenance programmes. In terms of maintenance, the Board has 3 principal concerns: the proper conservation of the built heritage; making it available to be enjoyed and understood by visitors from home and abroad; and ensuring that while there is full concern for a commercial return, this should not take precedence over the needs of conservation. The difficulty of conserving ancient monuments should not be underestimated, however. Monuments have distinct needs. Conservation of medieval tiles at Strata Florida Abbey is a different challenge from that to be faced with nineteenth-century iron furnaces at Blaenavon. Drawing on its expertise the Board is able to guide Cadw's work in the use of certain materials, the provision of historical information and the conduct of archaeological excavation etc.

11. The Board considers that the proper presentation of and access to monuments in the Secretary of State's care is a matter deserving of high priority. The board is glad to note that the estate in care continues to attract a large number of visitors both from home and aborad. In terms of engaging visitors' interest— and this perhaps is particularly relevant to young people—the Board has helped guide the way in which the monuments are presented. This extends from the provision of exhibitions such as that at Chepstow Castle on the Civil War to jousting displays at Caerphilly Castle. While the latter may have less historical relevance, this seems to us a very positive way of engaging people's attention and providing them with an enjoyable day out. There is, however, in all this a balance which has to be struck between making monuments available and the accuracy and skill with which they are presented. From field monuments to the majestic remains of Caerphilly Castle the estate in care has a certain dignity which the Board has always felt should be maintained. That it should be readily available, particularly to the people of Wales, is self-evident. There is, however, an important balance which must be struck between the conservation and long-term needs of these sites and any short-term benefits which might arise from over-popularising monuments. In this area, the Board thinks that Cadw's guidebooks, for example, should be of a high standard and manage to capture the interest of both the casual visitor and the more serious scholar in interpreting particular monuments. Cadw's guidebooks and other publications have achieved national standing and won several awards; they are also now regarded as a prime educational resource for the schools of Wales.

MONUMENTS OUTSIDE STATE CARE

12. There are many monuments in the Principality scheduled as being of national importance and of local interest which are in the care of local authorities and private owners. The demands and pressures which these owners face are no less exacting than those of the estate in care. Drawing on individual Board Members' knowledge of these and on information which it asks Cadw to provide, the Board takes a close interest in such monuments. Examples of this include individual cases such as Eastington Manor House in Dyfed or a more strategic review of Offa's and Wat's Dykes. In respect of such monuments the Board welcomes the positive approach of Cadw's professional staff working with owners to provide technical guidance. In recent years Cadw has developed a positive programme of grant aid to owners and provision for this has been increased from £150,000 in 1987–88 to more than £290,000 in the current financial year. Such funding, though modest in the overall allocation of resources to the built heritage, has secured the conservation and preservation of many such monuments. In this respect it must be borne in mind that the question of investment by a private individual in an ancient monument is often a demanding financial commitment. Such an outlay, unlike that in an historic building, may not be to the material advantage of the person putting up the funds other than in the satisfaction of knowing that the future of the monument has been secured. In this respect the Board applauds the dedication and commitment of private and local authority owners who have adopted such an enlightened approach. Preservation and conservation are the most effective tools in ensuring that Wales' rich built heritage is to be available for future generations. The Board continues to encourage the Agency to develop this work and to keep a vigilant eye on such scheduled monuments.

13. In 1985 Cadw appointed six part-time Field Monument Wardens. This was a development which we very much welcomed as the Wardens provide an essential point of contact between Cadw and the owners and occupiers of scheduled ancient monuments. The Board has taken the opportunity to meet each of these officers and we value very highly the effective contribution they make. We have been very concerned to ensure that the condition of monuments is carefully monitored and have encouraged Cadw to use the Wardens to produce county-by-county reports assessing the condition of monuments by both type and period.

STATUTORY PROTECTION AND PLANNING CONTROL

14. Monuments scheduled as being of national importance within the meaning of the Ancient Monuments and Archaeological Areas Act 1979 enjoy protection against development. The presumption is against development for obvious reasons. There can be, however, circumstances in which positive programmes of works to ancient monuments are desirable or where development—in the planning context—might have an

impact on scheduled ancient monuments. To guide those who are considering such works the Secretary of State has issued policy guidance—Planning Policy Guidance 16 (Wales): Archaeology and Planning—which describes the essential considerations in respect of this important resource. Where works are proposed to an ancient monument the specific consent of the Secretary of State for Wales is required—scheduled monument consent. The Board is not involved in the day-to-day conduct of this regulatory control, which is exercised through Cadw, but its advice and guidance can be sought in cases where this is thought desirable.

IDENTIFICATION OF MONUMENTS

15. The identification of monuments which might be designated as being of national importance is an important task for the Agency. Currently there are nearly 2,700 scheduled ancient monuments in the Principality, but Cadw has embarked on a most welcome programme of expanding the schedule. To date palaeolithic caves, medieval castles and moated sites have been critically reviewed and, where appropriate, added to the schedule. This work continues, with Roman military sites being considered next. Most recently, with the Board's encouragement, the Agency has set in hand preliminary work to examine the statutory protection of twentieth-century military structures.

GENERAL

16. The Board recognises that it has its own specific duties and functions to perform, but it also sees itself as part of a team, led by Cadw, which is concerned with the care and maintenance of the built heritage. It seeks to co-operate, wherever desirable, with bodies like the Royal Commission on Ancient and Historical Monuments (Wales), the Historic Buildings Council, local authorities and private owners. It also takes a very close interest in the work of the four Welsh Archaeological Trusts, which were established in the mid 1970's. The Trusts are limited liability companies with charitable status. They are independent of Cadw but the Agency provides core and project funding. Based on the Regional Sites and Monuments Record which they maintain, the four Trusts provide archaeological advice and guidance to local authorities and developers. In addition the Trusts conduct archaeological excavations and watching briefs where the destruction of archaeological features is unavoidable.

17. The Board enjoys a very close association with Cadw: Welsh Historic Monuments Executive Agency. It was consulted when Cadw was established in 1984 and again in 1991 when the proposal to change the status of Cadw to that of an Executive Agency was brought forward. On both occasions it drew the Secretary of State's attention to the need to ensure that the conservation and proper presentation of monuments in his care should be given high priority in any policy decisions taken and that this obligation should in no way be threatened or diluted. It is pleased to note that such has been the case to date. The Welsh Office's continued commitment to the preservation and conservation of ancient monuments in the Principality, be these in private or State care, seems to us to have remained constant and we have confidence in the Agency's ability to continue to take this work forward.

ANCIENT MONUMENTS BOARD FOR WALES

LIST OF MEMBERSHIP

CHAIRMAN

Emeritus Professor Glanmor Williams, CBE, FBA, MA, DLitt, FSA, FRHistS

Former Vice Principal and Professor of Welsh History, University College, Swansea. Member and Chairman of the Board since 1983. Current period of appontment ends 31 March 1995.

MEMBERS

Mr Robert Barclay Heaton, BArch, FRIBA

Architect. Former partner now consultant to the Anthony Clark Partnership, Wrexham. Member of the Board since 1983. Nominee of the Royal Institute of British Architects. Current period of appointment ends 31 March 1995.

Professor William H Manning, BSc, PhD, FSA

Professor of Archaeology University of Wales College of Cardiff. Member of the Board since 1990. Current period of appointment ends 31 March 1993.

Professor Robert R Davies, FBA, BA, DPhil, FRHistS

Professor of History, University College of Wales Aberystwyth. Member of the Board since 1979. Current period of appointment ends 31 March 1993.

Professor Jenkyn Beverley Smith, MA, FRHistS

Head of Department and Professor of Welsh History, University College of Wales, Aberystwyth. Chairman of the Royal Commission on Ancient and Historical Monuments (Wales). Member of the Board since April 1992. Nominee of the Royal Commission. Current period of appointment on the Board ends 31 March 1995.

Dr Peter Smith, PhD, FSA

Former Secretary of the Royal Commission on Ancient and Historical Monuments (Wales). Member of the Board since 1987. Current period of appointment ends 31 March 1993.

Dr Stephen H R Aldhouse-Green, BA, PhD

Keeper of Department of Archaeology and Numismatics, National Museum of Wales. Member of the Board since 1990. Nominee of the National Museum of Wales. Current period of appointment ends 31 March 1993.

Mr Richard Keen

Historic Buildings Representative, National Trust (South Wales Region). Member of the Board since 1986. Current period of appointment ends 31 March 1995.

Mrs Frances Lynch Llewellyn, MA, FSA

Lecturer in Archaeology, University College of North Wales, Bangor. Member of the Board since 1986. Current period of appointment ends 31 March 1995.

Mr Donald Moore, BA, MA, MEd, FSA

Former keeper of Prints, Drawings and Maps National Library of Wales, Aberystwyth. Member of the Board since 1983. Nominee of the Cambrian Archaeological Association. Current period of appointment ends 31 March 1993.

APPENDIX 2

Memorandum by Assembly of Welsh Counties

PRESERVATION OF HISTORIC BUILDINGS AND ANCIENT MONUMENTS IN WALES
(HB 26)

1.0 GENERAL OBSERVATIONS

1.1 In many respects the scope of activity promoting the preservation of historic buildings and ancient monuments in Wales lags behind that which is generally found in England. The present arrangements are generally only skimming the surface of this important part of our national heritage, and meanwhile buildings and "monuments" are continuing to suffer from neglect or from inappropriate "improvements", and even destruction. This is particularly evident in industrial South Wales where a culture of architectural and archaeological conservation amongst property owners has barely been established.

1.2 As a consequence, many historic buildings and ancient monuments in Wales suffer neglect from their owners. Greater pressure could be exerted by local authorities upon owners to keep structures in basic repair or to take reasonable steps to secure them from theft or vandalism.

1.3 No clear advantage appears to have been gained from the different statutory arrangements that have evolved since 1984 nor from the different constitution of Cadw in comparison with English Heritage.

1.4 For example, whereas conservation procedures in Wales are determined by Welsh Office circular 61/81, England has benefited from the more extensive circular 8/87 and amendments. The recent PPG16 on Archaeology and Planning, published in similar forms in England and Wales, is a welcome development, and it is hoped that a similar approach will be adopted in the preparation of the forthcoming PPG on historic buildings.

1.5 As a manager of historic properties, Cadw has a good public image, produces publications of the best quality, and operates an excellent membership scheme.

1.6 However, in the exercise of its statutory functions, Cadw appears to be seriously under-resourced and is generally perceived to be too civil service oriented in the culture and timid in its dealings with the public. Its effectiveness would almost certainly have been enhanced had it enjoyed the greater independence and budget of English Heritage. In Wales, Cadw should be the primary focus of conservation debate and technical expertise but, unlike English Heritage, Cadw for example publishes neither a regular bulletin, nor technical reports, nor even staff lists setting out responsibilities in each section. In particular, Cadw is remarkably reticent in publishing its policies and programmes of activity.

1.7 An inhibiting factor in the promotion of good conservation practice is the shortage of trained conservation officers amongst Welsh local authorities. Very few district councils and only two county councils employ full time conservation staff, and this is reflected in the quality of control and advice that is available to developers and the wider public.

1.8 Similarly, only one county council in Wales employs an archaeologist, a situation which is in stark contrast to that prevailing in England where county authorities are obliged to employ archaeological staff. In Wales, archaeological advice is generally only available from the county archaeological trusts who are under-resourced in relation to the number of local authorities which they serve, and in some cases also geographically remote for the same reason. This latter point makes regular face-to-face contact difficult to achieve. The Trusts are now moving towards a contracting role in addition to their long-standing advisory function. It is clearly necessary if their advice is seen to be unbiased for these two functions to be kept clearly distinct and there remains some concern among local authorities that this might be difficult to achieve in practice.

1.9 A further example of the poor state of conservation in Wales is the limited development of building preservation trusts, which in England and increasingly in Scotland are a useful mechanism for the restoration of historic buildings. There are only six Building Conservation Officers in Wales and very few architects that specialise in historic buildings, with virtually all builders being ignorant of historic techniques. Recent efforts by the Architectural Heritage Fund to increase BPT activity in Wales have to date been relatively unproductive.

2.0 PROPERTIES IN CARE OF SECRETARY OF STATE

2.1 The management and preservation of properties in the care of the Secretary of State appear to be exercised satisfactorily by Cadw with no obvious deficiencies in comparison with English Heritage or the National Trust. The marketing of the properties to the public, for example through its Heritage membership scheme, is one aspect of its role in which Cadw does appear to enjoy a public profile.

2.2 Should consideration be given to passing over some properties of lesser importance into local management (in the manner proposed in *Managing England's Heritage*), it is essential that adequate finance to maintain the properties should be made available by the Welsh Office. Careful consideration would also need to be given to the appropriate successor owner, whether it be a specially created trust or the local authority.

3.0 PROPERTIES IN CARE OF MAJOR OWNERS

3.1 Local authorities, in the present economic climate, are finding maintenance of historic buildings in their ownership beyond a very basic level to be extremely difficult. Local authorities are increasingly finding themselves in the ownership of historic buildings which are redundant, expensive to maintain, and difficult to market.

3.2 The National Trust is able to call upon its prestige and massive membership to sustain a level of care and maintenance which is impressive and exemplary. However, they have previously tended to pick up stately homes, although there now seems to be a more flexible approach. Nevertheless, in the Pembroke area, for example, the only building open to the public is the Tudor Merchant's House in Tenby. It would be helpful if they were to pick up more buildings with public access, particularly residential buildings to which the public can more easily relate, i.e. from the 17th Century onwards.

3.3.1 The various religious denominations share common problems arising from ownership of historic buildings which can be expensive to maintain with limited resources which often they would rather spend on needier causes. Whereas most churches are listed and, therefore, qualify for Historic Buildings Council grant aid, very few non-conformist chapels are listed.

3.3.2 The preponderance of non-conformist chapels, most of which date from the nineteenth century, is a distinctive element which contributes to the unique character of Welsh townscape. Many are currently under threat, and their survival in many instances depends upon the efforts of small and often elderly congregations. Similar problems affect Church in Wales churches, although the tendency for medieval buildings to be listed does provide access to grant assistance not available to most chapels. Few non-conformist chapels are listed, and although the Royal Commission is currently undertaking a national survey, wider action needs to be taken to ensure the survival of significant numbers into the next century. The redundant buildings study being undertaken by the West Wales Task Force will be a field leader within Wales. It is worth noting that Cadw refused to contribute towards it.

4.0 LISTING OF HISTORIC BUILDINGS AND SCHEDULING OF ANCIENT MONUMENTS

4.1 The serious under-resourcing of Cadw is particularly evident in the progress being made in the resurvey of both listed buildings and scheduled monuments.

4.2 Whereas in England a comprehensive county by county resurvey of listed buildings was undertaken during the 1980s, in many parts of Wales the statutory lists still date from the 1950s. Again, whereas in England the 1980s resurveys were undertaken by consultants, in Wales a very small core of staff and limited contract staff are undertaking the surveys on a community by community basis which it is perceived may take decades to complete, by which time much will have been lost or irrevocably altered.

4.3 The consequence is that there are in Wales very many buildings of listable quality which do not enjoy statutory protection, and are therefore undervalued and very often under threat. The number of listable buildings that have been demolished in recent decades is incalculable. The problem can be grotesque, for example in Rhondda, where an urban conglomeration which had a population of 163,000 people at its greatest extent only possesses 17 listed buildings. The result is a commonplace attitude which, often out of ignorance, fails to respect the quality of the historic built environment.

4.4 Similar problems exist with the scheduled monuments enhancement programme which appears to have barely commenced in Wales.

4.5 Cadw has recently made a significant step in the appointment of an inspector specialising in the listing and scheduling of industrial buildings and monuments. Although praiseworthy, this appointment has been made long after many significant buildings and monuments have been demolished. For all building and monument types, priority needs to be given to accelerating the resurvey programmes to prevent further losses.

4.6 A comprehensive resurvey of listed buildings is also essential in order to rectify current statutory records of existing listed buildings, many of which have inadequate descriptions and gradings and omit location maps, thereby limiting their usefulness.

4.7 in its exercise of listed building and schedule monument controls, Cadw could be more sensitive to the views of local authorities and more mindful of the constraints within which local authorities function. For example, on sites which are to be the subject of comprehensive redevelopment a proposal for listing or a refusal to consider demolition of a listed structure, can create serious problems for urban regeneration. Examples in Gwent are i) the former Six Bells Colliery Site, where the listing of the colliery buildings (despite the local authority's insistence that other structures on the site should be listed instead) resulted in these structures being given listed building consent to demolish only after considerable delays; and ii) the Dunlop Semtex buildings at Brynmawr are proving to be an eyesore and detrimental to the area. In such circumstances, it would be helpful if Cadw could show greater willingness to consider representations from local authorities and to take more account of these wider issues.

4.8 Cadw is to be applauded for its participation in the survey leading to a national register of Historic Parks, Gardens and Landscapes. This is one area in which Cadw can be seen as setting the pace ahead of English Heritage.

4.9 There is widespread perception that Listed Building Consent and Scheduled Monument Consent applications, when required to be processed by Cadw, can be subject to unreasonable delays. Again, insufficient resources is probably a major contributing factor. Delays can be irksome for all developers, but no less for local authorities who often have tight time limits within which the project expenditure can be incurred.

4.10 Another area of concern, in relation to the controls exercised on planning consents, is that Cadw say that they are statutorily prevented from advising formally, or having informal site inspections prior to decisions being made on particular development proposals. This is particularly unhelpful, and goes completely against rhyme or reason in seeking to achieve a better understanding and concern for the historic environment, and leaves local planning authorities in a very difficult position in the absence of the very technical advice which is sought. It is difficult to understand the reluctance to provide informal assistance, as it is no different from the position of local authority planners who provide professional advice to members of the public and potential planning applications, and then adjudicate fairly and impartially applications when they are received.

5.0 Grant Schemes

5.1 Because of a growing number of buildings and monuments which are elibible for grant aid, it is inevitable that there will be insufficient funds to assist all applicants. However, even limited grant aid can be detrimental to the preservation of the historic built enviroment if it is not allocated with care in accordance with good conservation practice. It is therefore essential that properly qualified staff administer grant schemes, and local authorities in particular are often unable to employ them.

5.2 Although limited, the grant aid provided by the Historic Buildings Council for Wales and Cadw appears to be distributed on a fair basis. However, those schemes which require listed status or a high listed grade as a prerequisite are not available to many worthy historic buildings. With so few buildings actually listed and so much of the Welsh heritage being more modest, ie, vernacular, there is need of a national scheme to care for vernacular buildings, and the ability to offer them grant aid.

5.3 The grant regimes of the HBCW and Cadw do not have the flair and innovation displayed by English Heritage; where resources are limited, creative targeting of grant aid is necessary.

5.4 Local authorities have very limited financial resources either to promote their own grant schemes under section 57 of the 1990 Act or to participate in agreements such as section 79 Town Schemes, even though there is often considerable desire to do so.

5.5 There is a perception that popular ancient monuments, including those in the care of Cadw, receive disproportionately large amounts of grant aid.

5.6 A presumption that grant allocation should be biased towards those structures at immediate risk. If a building or monument is spot listed or scheduled because it is of national interest, there should be an obligation upon Cadw to provide some grant assistance to the property owner.

5.7 Much work towards the preservation of the historic built environment is assisted by means of grant schemes which are not specifically conservation oriented. Examples are Commercial Environment Area grants and Town Improvement Grants, which can be available for the repair and improvement of historic buildings in town and village centres, and Derelict Land Grant which can be available for the consolidation of ancient monuments on derelict land. Specifically Welsh grant schemes include the Welsh Church Act Fund and various schemes managed by the Prince of Wales Committee. The success of such grant aid often depends on its being administered by qualified staff who can exercise the necessary technical and design expertise.

6.0 CONCLUSIONS

6.1 Cadw is under-resourced and lacks independence. At present, building and archaeological conservation in Wales suffers from a lack of leadership. Cadw should be strengthened, allowed to evolve into an independent body and encouraged to be the focus of conservation expertise and debate in Wales. It should be required to publish its policies and its staff should be significantly more accessible.

6.2 Urgent priority should be given to a comprehensive resurvey of listed buildings and scheduled monuments throughout Wales. Cadw should be required to establish and publish its resurvey programmes.

6.3 Local authorities should be strengthened with more conservation staff.

6.4 Welsh statutory circulars and policy guidance should be co-ordinated with those prevailing in England.

6.5 Greater financial resources for conservation in Wales are desperately needed, as well as a significant change in attitudes towards the preservation of the historic built environment.

January 1993

APPENDIX 3

Letters from the Society of Welsh District Planning Officers to the Clerk of the Committee

PRESERVATION OF HISTORIC BUILDINGS AND ANCIENT MONUMENTS IN WALES (HB10)

Your letter of 26 November 1992, refers; my Society took the opportunity at their last meeting to discuss the topic generally and the particular points set out in the terms of reference.

Firstly then in general it was strongly felt that a National body of expertise and advice was essential to ensure the consistent application of best techniques developed by and through the management of buildings and monuments of similar age or construction. This being so, sufficient resources, both in terms of skilled personnel and finance should be available separately from the competing pressures that affect Local Government. It was felt that currently insufficient of both of these was available, which was bound to produce a slow but noticeable deterioration in Wales' stock of historic monuments and buildings.

Turning to the particular points raised:

1. The charging of entrance fees in appropriate cases to provide for their management and maintenance, should not deter full availability to all sections of the community and visitors to Wales. Value for money as expressed by the detailed care of the site and in the quality of its interpretation should be the goal. However, surpluses arising from the most visited sites should be applied to other, perhaps more remote, monuments. Notwithstanding the above, the aim should be to set charges, if any, to the lowest possible level, to avoid denying access to the grander sites simply to raise income to balance the account. Admission income should be treated as a welcome but small part of the financing arrangements for this very important part of our culture.

2. generally the advice given to private owners is of the highest quality, but especially where the property has no fund raising potential, the cost of the work, albeit supported by grant in some cases often (and noticeably in these difficult financial circumstances) results in work being delayed or even abandoned in favour of short term ameliorative measures. Two points arise here; firstly a case could be made for increasing the percentage or amount paid as grant and secondly to ensure that the increasing list of buildings and monuments is ranked to ensure that the most important examples nationally receive the best attention, however, allowing more locally important sites to be supported by application to the Local Authority, or where appropriate by a local rolling fund administered by a Building Preservation Trust. The increasing number of redundant churches and chapels is going to require a dispassionate analysis of their national and local importance.

3. Whilst it is, of course, of the first importance to know in detail the resource available in terms of the built heritage and to ensure that adequate records of locally and nationally important buildings and sites are kept, this does not mean that all these buildings should be kept for ever. This means a categorisation of the resource through the listing procedure which perhaps should have more "grades" in it—the lower classifications only requiring the local planning authority to take their value into account—without reference to Cadw or the Welsh Office. There should be a duty to consult and inform of the local decision.

A problem arises where listed buildings are also scheduled monuments. Enforcement efforts are not focused and are therefore confused. The purchase of listed buildings, in the ultimate by local authorities, deters action where resources are scarce, as does the uncertainty of the ultimate cost and thereafter the maintenance costs.

4. As noted above grant schemes should be generous enough not to deter owners from undertaking work—whether the grant arises through the status of the building itself or through a townscheme. Townschemes were generally agreed to be a good basis for affording a local democratic input into local heritage, although the geographic extent of these areas are generally thought to be too confined. The criteria applied to grant aid in townschemes ensures fairness and consistency, and it may be that a scheme could be devised which would allow similar grants to be allocated in rural areas, where listed buildings and monuments are perforce more scattered.

I am asked to make one other point on behalf of the Society, and this relates to the speed with which listed building applications are processed. As is now well known, local authorities are being beset with performance targets of all sorts, not the least in handling planning applications. Whilst we continue to be impressed with the diligence and expertise of the professional officers in handling these matters, the deficiency in their numbers makes their performance, especially when relatively small matters are being dealt with regrettably slow. This part of the planning development control system needs review (which may lie outside your Committee's terms of reference) to allow perhaps many more applications to be handled exclusively by local authorities, especially where these are classified as being only of local importance, and perhaps where local authorities are charged with an appropriately worded duty to manage this important resource.

Finally, in order to fill out the above broad points, I attach a copy of a letter written by Mr C J A Thomas, Head of Planning Services at Delyn Borough Council, to Mr Geraint Price-Thomas. I am sure that similar letters could have been written by many colleague Planning Officers referring to local examples, but perhaps this one more local view will serve to illustrate some of the deficiencies and plus points that arise.

23 December 1992

CYNGOR BWRDEISTREF DELYN BOROUGH COUNCIL. DEVELOPMENT AND ENVIRONMENTAL SERVICES

ANNEX

Geraint Price-Thomas
Under Secretary (Wales)
The Association of District Councils
Atlantic Wharf
Cardiff
CF1 5LN

WELSH AFFAIRS COMMITTEE—INQUIRY INTO PRESERVATION OF HISTORIC BUILDINGS AND ANCIENT MONUMENTS IN WALES

Thank you for your letter received 2 December, and the opportunity to comment on the subject of the preservation of historic buildings and ancient monuments.

My comments below follow the paragraph numbering of the letter from Mark Hutton.

(i) As far as Cadw's operations are concerned, there is a basic feeling that its headquarters location at Cardiff is too remote to give a fully satisfactory service to North Wales. A mid-Wales relocation would probably be more satisfactory for personal access and communication generally. Alternatively a stronger sub-regional presence at, say, Colwyn Bay would make day-to-day access to Dadw more acceptable.

Properties in the care of the Secretary of State in the Delyn area consist of Flint Castle, Basingwerk Abbey, St. Winefride's Well Chapel, and Maen Achwyfan wheel cross.

For the first two, whilst their condition is fair and basic upkeep appears to be adequate, their low public profile, and the apparent lack of enthusiasm to implement ways to "market" them imaginatively as tourist attractions, are disappointing.

St. Winefride's Well Chapel has a complex ownership and occupation pattern, with the property in the ownership of Delyn, the Chapel in the quardianship of Cadw, and the Well leased by the Roman Catholic Church. Its condition gives cause for concern, but Cadw is undertaking repairs at present, and a project by Delyn to improve access facilities and presentation is in hand. I therefore look forward to an improved situation as far as this particular monument is concerned.

Maen Achwyfan is in a peaceful rural setting. Whilst it has a fairly low visitor level, this is in harmony with its character and setting. I feel it would be inappropriate to encourage high visitor numbers in this case.

(ii) I have no comment to make on the National Trust's care of its properties.

As far as churches are concerned, the ecclesiastical exemption in Section 60 of the 1990 Act has potential for regrettable alterations to Listed churches. An example of the kind of damage that could ensue can be seen locally in the case of the church at Pantasaph Friary. This building contains work by Pugin, which has been badly compromised by alterations. Due to the outdated nature of the Statutory Lists this building is not yet Listed, but even if it had been this damage could not have been prevented.

(iii) Probably the greatest matter for concern, and one that needs urgent action towards its solution, is the outdated nature of the Statutory Lists, and the length of time that completion of the full national resurvey is taking. The present forecast of some 40 years to completion of the resurvey is quite intolerable.

This should not be taken as criticism of the officers of Cadw discharging this duty. Their helpfulness and diligence at this task is admirable. The fault lies with a failure to match staff allocation to policy aims.

The two areas in Delyn, Mold and Holywell, which have been resurveyed showed tenfold and threefold increases respectively in their number of Listed Buildings. Pro rata this suggests that between 600 and 2,000 possible candidates for Listing are being denied that protection in Delyn alone.

Of the 151 Grade 3 buildings in Delyn on the Provisional Lists, (of which about 80 per cent appear to qualify for upgrading), 22 have been totally demolished, and 60 have suffered the type of unsympathetic alterations which are allowed under the GDO but which could be prevented by Listing. These figures suggest that a promptly updated List could have saved up to 17 of these buildings from total loss, and 48 from unsympathetic alteration.

The Lists are supposed to be for the guidance of Local Authorities. Delyn has already had to work for 18 years with an outdated List and, if existing plans for Local Government Reorganisation go ahead as planned, will indeed have spent the whole of its existence without this "guidance" having been brought fully up to date.

Local Government Officers are left to cover this deficiency by the use of Building Preservation Notices where appropriate. This requires skills which (by the assumption that they need a List to guide them) they are presumed not to possess.

The present staffing levels allocated to the resurvey appear to be quite inadequate to completion of the task within a reasonable time scale. Urgent attention should be given to providing sufficiently skilled staff, whether by increases in Cadw staff, by use of suitably knowledgeable external expertise or by whatever other means is available, to enable the resurvey to be adequately completed within the next five years at the most.

In the case of Ancient Monuments, an excellent database of statutory and non-statutory monuments is to hand, predominantly through the actions of Clwyd County Council and the Clwyd-Powys Archaeological Trust. This may well suggest a model for an alternative approach to updating the statutory Lists of Buildings of Special Architectural and Historic Interest. The operation of Ancient Monument Consents appears to be working adequately.

The GDO tolerances, particularly in respect of changes to windows, doors and roofing materials in Conservation Areas, continue to give cause for concern, particularly in Conservation Areas containing a significant proportion of terraced 19th century housing. In Delyn the character of the Conservation Areas of Ffynnongroyw, Gwespyr, Cadole Caerwys and Northop has suffered badly from unsympathetic alterations of this nature.

(iv) The grant aid available from Cadw provides a very useful input, and Delyn has benefited considerably from this source in the Town Schemes at Holywell and Mold.

For individual properties, grant aid under the 1953 Act has also proved to be most helpful, within the limits of its statutory restriction to buildings of Outstanding Interest, and much good work has been done. Overall the scheme appears to be well run, effective and fair, though an increase in the percentage level of grant aid from its current 40 per cent figure would be beneficial.

Since 1974, Delyn has run its own scheme of grant aid, under the powers contained in what is now Section 57 of the 1990 Act. This has been of considerable positive benefit to the cause of the survival of historic buildings. It has complemented both the controls against unsympathetic change, and the grant input of Cadw, enabling many schemes of repair and maintenance to go ahead where they would ortherwise have been impossible, or at best badly underfunded. The aim has been to concentrate grant aid on buildings which could not qualify for aid from Cadw, thus ensuring help to the upkeep of historic buildings at all levels of interest.

The scheme has also been of value inasmuch as it gives an opportunity to combine financial help with advice and explanation of the building's interest and the way it should be cared for thus helping to raise the standard of awareness of owners.

I would accept that available funds to deal with the repair needs of historic buildings generally will almost always be felt inadequate to the task in hand. This particularly applies in difficult economic times such as the present, and downward pressure on local authority expenditure and staffing will inevitably have a negative effect on the future survival of historic buildings. In Delyn the last two to three years have been particularly difficult, with demand for grant aid exceeding available funds, and constraints on expenditure preventing sufficient allocation of funds and staffing to fully answer the problem.

The future will, no doubt, include further cutting back on available resources. Whilst this may well conform to overall national expenditure policy, it will be to the disbenefit of the buildings concerned. At the worst this could cause further losses, and at the best deferred expenditure on maintenance will cause costlier problems in future.

In conclusion, I hope the above will be helpful in compiling your memorandum. I have concentrated mainly on the deficiencies of the system in the interests of future improvement. However, looking back to 1974 there has been a significant improvement in national awareness of the need to preserve and care for the stock of historic buildings, and in appreciation of their significance and interest. Whilst there is still a long way to go, progress has been made and will no doubt continue once the economic climate has improved.

APPENDIX 4

Letter from the Countryside Council for Wales to the Clerk to the Committee

PRESERVATION OF HISTORIC BUILDINGS AND ANCIENT MONUMENTS (HB41)

Thank you for your letter of 27 January 1993 inviting me to provide a memorandum of evidence for the Welsh Affairs Committee inquiry into the preservation of historic buildings and ancient monuments.

The Countryside Council for Wales is the Government's statutory adviser on wildlife and countryside conservation matters in Wales. It is the executive authority for the conservation of habitats and wildlife. Through partners it promotes the protection of landscapes, opportunities for enjoyment, and the support of those who live and work in, and manage the countryside. It enables these partners, including local authorities, voluntary organisations and interested individuals to pursue countryside management projects through grant aid. The Council is accountable to the Secretary of State for Wales who appoints it and provides its annual grant in aid.

It recognises that one of its leading partners, CADW, has the primary role in the matter before the Committee to which this letter refers.

The Countryside Council for Wales i required to play the lead role in conserving and enhancing the natural beauty and amenity of the whole countryside in Wales. The value placed on individual landscapes often reflects, at least in part, the extent to which they have been developed, how and when, and the historic interest associated with land uses, works and buildings. The Council therefore recognises the need to conserve that part of the historic and built heritage of Wales which is an integral and attractive feature of the Welsh landscape. It recognises, in particular, that:

i. the character of our landscape and enjoyment of it by the public, particularly the designated areas, is greatly enhanced by vernacular designs, settlement remains, field patterns and enclosure systems, planted woodlands, more recent industrial features and historic buildings which reflect their landscape setting, local materials and customs;

ii. small settlements and buildings of historic interest can complement and add to the natural beauty of the countryside itself, and the experience of visiting and being in the countryside.

I set out below a brief resume of the Council's current work, and work with other agencies, which has a bearing on the task of preserving historic landscapes and a description of the relationship with CADW and other relevant organisations.

1. INFLUENCING DEVELOPMENT PLANS

CCW is a prescribed consultee for all development plans in the making. The Town and Country Planning Act 1990 requires structure and local plans prepared by local authorities to include policies for the conservation of the natural beauty and amenity of the land. CCW is therefore concerned to ensure that the new development plans, required as a consequence of the Planning and Compensation Act 1991 and Planning Policy Guidance Note 12 "Development Plans and Strategic Planning Guidance in Wales", include policies relating to maintaining the character and quality of the environment. The Council is concerned to ensure that development plans include policies which recognise not only the historic dimension of the landscape, but also the value of historic buildings and ancient monuments and the items noted in sub-para (i) above.

Such policies should provide for:

— protection to sites of archaeological importance and their setting, and landscapes which are known to be of specific historical importance, thus reflecting advice in PPG16 (Wales) "Archaeology and Planning";

— protection to be afforded to the landscape setting of scheduled ancient monuments, listed buildings, conservation areas and other sites of cultural importance in rural areas;

— recognition that designed landscapes, such as parks and gardens—and also "landscaped" farm settings—are also important both in their own right and in their absorption of earlier features such as ancient woodlands. They frequently contribute to the wider landscape and can included important wildlife resources;

— identification of sites of special historic importance (with reference to CADW's Register of Historic Landscapes, Parks and Gardens in Wales) and inclusion of a policy for their protection, including protection from development which would intrude on key vistas from the site;

— policies to ensure that new developments should respect the character of their surroundings (in accordance with Annex A of PPG 1 "General Policy and Principles") in the case of designated areas, including Conservation Areas, and in rural villages in the countryside, where additional development may be appropriate.

2. DEVELOPMENT RELATED CASEWORK

CCW has a role in advising local authorities in Wales (including National Park Authorities) on the management of protected areas such as National Parks and AONBs and is also concerned to ensure, through the development control process, that LPAs consider the setting of historic buildings and settlements when considering new development proposals, and that they promote sensitive conservation of the built environment in rural areas.

CCW encourages local planning authorities, inter alia, to aim for:

— better design and landscaping of new development in and around villages;

— better conservation of vernacular architecture, buildings, bridges, etc;

— better conservation of man-made patterns in the rural landscape;

—more active conservation of old trees, exotic trees, orchards, parkland fields and historic landscapes, gardens and parks.

CCW is also concerned to promote improvement in the design of new buildings and other built development in the countryside. To this end it has commissioned Chapman Warren to prepare a design guide for new, modern, energy efficient houses of appropriate style for rural Wales.

3. OTHER CASEWORK

CCW advises CADW where it encounters rare and protected species of wildlife on land which has been notified as being an area of archaeological importance and/or a Scheduled Ancient Monument.

4. INFORMATION

—CCW is currently assessing how landscapes in Wales should be described and analysed so that they may be protected and enhanced.

—CADW will begin work during 1993/94, in partnership with CCW, on the mapping of Historic Landscapes in Wales. This will entail an initial appraisal of the historic landscapes of note in Wales to inform Part II of the Government's Register of Parks and Gardens and Landscapes in Wales. This will ensure that a wide range of historic landscapes are identified quickly so as to:

(i) protect them from inappropriate development;

(ii) trigger consultation on proposals affecting them;

(iii) assist CCW/CADW in refining a definition of historic landscapes in order to move away from a provisional to a definitive list of historic landscapes in Wales.

—CADW supplies CCW with information on all scheduled sites whilst CCW in turn supplies CADW with information relating to SSSI affecting Scheduled Ancient Monuments and their subsequent management.

—The Wildlife and Countryside Act 1981 gives priority in terms of protection to the retention of sites or features (eg buildings) which support species protected by law. Better known species so protected include Bats and Barn Owls whose habitats are often found in historic buildings. CCW provides advice to Local Planning Authorities on the management of such buildings to sustain their nature conservation value.

5. LIAISON WITH OTHERS

The Council seeks a high quality of care for the Welsh landscape and, to that end, it pursues partnership with other organisations, provides advice, encourages joint working schemes and gives grant aid.

6. WORKING WITH CADW

As the Secretary of State's advisor on matters affecting the historic/built environment in Wales, CADW is one of CCW's key partners. The Council's relationship with CADW advances on three levels:

(i) Policy/Procedural: This involves an annual liaison meeting, joint dealings with National Park Authorities, and Chief Executives' bilaterals.

(ii) Operations: Consultation on casework, exchange of information, joint projects and joint funding.

(iii) Research: as necessary.

The South Wales Region of CCW also holds annual liaison meetings at regional level with CADW staff.

Part of the context for this relationship is provided in a "Statement of Intent" by NCC, CADW, English Heritage, Historic Scotland, the Council for British Archaeology, and the Council for Scottish Archaeology. The document was adopted by NCC in March 1991, prior to CCW's formation, and provides a framework for land management practices by the bodies concerned, to reconcile archaeological and nature conservation interests. (A copy is attached: see *Appendix I*).

A revision of this document, for Wales only and in respect of CCW's wider remit, is currently being undertaken. This should improve and broaden its scope.

The annual liaison meeting provides an opportunity to discuss emerging policy initiatives, joint schemes and projects, staff training and the review of liaison/consultation arrangements, relating to the exchange of information on SSSI and Scheduled Ancient Monuments.

At operations level, contact relates in the main to the exchange of information/advice relating to SSSI/SAMS and historic and listed buildings and scheduled monument consents. CCW has undertaken to consult with CADW prior to giving consent to any potentially damaging activity on SSSI land, or concluding a management agreement on SSSI land, or when drawing up a management plan for a nature reserve, where the land in question has been notified by CADW as being an area of archaeological importance. Further, CCW has agreed to consult with the appropriate County Archaeological Trust prior to consenting to any potentially damaging activity on SSSI land or concluding a management agreement on SSSI land.

CCW is the advisory body to the Capital Taxes Office in cases of Inheritance Tax, Conditional Exemption, and Maintenance Funds and liaises with CADW, where appropriate, regarding these matters.

7. HISTORIC BUILDINGS COUNCIL FOR WALES

The Historic Buildings Council for Wales brings to the attention of local authorities those buildings/areas which are in most need of protection. CCW has started to discuss with HBC the concept of "rural conservation areas"—the adaptation of the Conservation Area concept to the protection of certain built features scattered in the rural landscape and their setting. Conservation Areas, as such, are designated in built-up areas, towns, villages and isolated terraces in rural areas. Conservation Areas, as designated, rarely explore the full scope for designation, embracing open spaces, trees etc as advised in para 28 of Welsh Office Circular 61/81 'Historic Buildings and Conservation Areas—Policy and Procedure'. More generous interpretation of para. 28 (or its refinement) would not, however, be sufficient in itself. There would still be a need for a mechanism to conserve small, precious areas of rural landscape with characteristic and distinctive walls, barns, etc.

CCW, HBC and CADW have important roles to play in respect of maintaining and enhancing landscape character. This may be particularly so where CADW and/or HBC can supply information on rural areas which may coincide with an important landscape, especially one designated statutorily or in development plans. In fact, the National Parks Review Panel's report "Fit for the Future" drew attention to this link between the countryside and buildings and recommended that the government examine how the Conservation Area concept might be extended to cover, or be adapted to, the protection of built features of historic or other significance in enclosed farm landscapes.

In its response to the Review Panel the Government recommended that National Park Authorities ensure that archaeological considerations form an integral part of the conservation of National Park landscapes. This is a complex multi-agency issue which requires, and merits, further discussion.

8. ROYAL COMMISSION ON ANCIENT AND HISTORIC MONUMENTS IN WALES

At a policy level, CCW is represented on a forum to review the direction and standard of research relating to the Uplands Initiative—A Strategy for Archaeology in the Uplands of Wales. This initiative was begun by CADW and is now sponsored by RCAHMW, its aim being to promote a wider and deeper understanding of the archaeology of the uplands in Wales and to provide a framework for archaeological work in such areas for the foreseeable future.

As a first stage in this process field studies will be selected which will have the greatest potential for incorporating the archaeological results into existing casework strategy, such as the association with areas lying within Environmentally Sensitive Areas (ESAs) or the Tir Cymen programme (see para 11 below).

9. GRANT AID

The Council may, under Section 9 of the Local Government Act 1974 and Section 134 of the Environmental Protection Act 1990, give financial assistance by way of grant or loan to attain any of the purposes of the Countryside Act 1968, or the National Parks and Access to the Countryside Act 1949, or towards work which is conducive to nature conservation, or which will foster the undertaking of nature conservation. CCW also provides grant aid to local authorities to enable them to offer "Landscape and Conservation Grants" to assist the conservation of the rural landscape. An outline of the Council's Grant Aid Scheme is attached (see Appendix II).

The grant aid budget is a vital tool for implementing the policy and proposals of the Council.

CCW has a "partnership" scheme with the Welsh Historic Gardens Trust whereby WHGT receives a grant towards the costs of undertaking a programme of activities and reporting back to CCW from time to time.

10. NATIONAL PARKS AND AONB

CCW offers advice to National Park Authorities and local authorities on the management of these areas and in doing so, encourages the conservation of historic features in the landscape. CCW has a statutory role in the formulation of NPA budgets and functional strategies, which can allow it to influence the spend, and the staffing, for historic and archaeological purposes.

11. TIR CYMEN

Tir Cymen is a whole-farm environmental management scheme, which is being pursued on an experimental basis in three pilot areas—Dinefwr, Meirionnydd and Swansea districts. Entry into the scheme requires farmers to safeguard stone walls, slate fences, hedges and earth banks, archaeological and geological features, traditional stone built features and traditional farm buildings, which are still waterproof, in return for a basic payment. Additional payments are available for positive management of selected stone walls, hedges, earth banks and slate fences, and capital grants for certain items of landscape enhancement (see Tir Cymen Booklets enclosed).

13. OTHER ISSUES

As farmers readdress farm economics and the scope for diversification, there is a danger that very unusual farm buildings (eg Edwardian poultry houses in half-timbered style) may be converted or disappear. The listing of such unusual farm buildings, their restoration and maintenance needs further consideration as a matter of some urgency if they are not to be lost.

19 February 1993

APPENDIX 1

NATURE CONSERVANCY COUNCIL (NCC) AND CADW, ENGLISH HERITAGE, HISTORIC SCOTLAND, COUNCIL FOR BRITISH ARCHAEOLOGY, COUNCIL FOR SCOTTISH ARCHAEOLOGY

A STATEMENT OF INTENT

PREAMBLE

Many British landscapes, including areas of high nature conservation value, are not natural but owe their present distinctive character to a long history of human activity. This leaves traces in the form of archaeological sites and the biological evidence (eg, pollen) they contain. Such evidence can show how and when the present landscape came into being, and this better understanding of its history can contribute to the formulation of effective nature conservation management policies. Thus it is important from a joint archaeological and natural historical perspective that Sites of Special Scientific Interest (SSSIs) and Nature Reserves are managed in a way which is not detrimental to archaeological evidence. This statement establishes procedures to safeguard the archaeological interest of such sites and reserves, and provides also for reciprocal arrangements where such areas are also managed for their archaeological interest.

1. This statement relates to those areas of land or water (onshore and offshore) which have:

   (a) been notified under S23 of the National Parks and Access to the Countryside Act 1949 or under S28(1) of the Wildlife and Countryside Act as Sites of Special Scientific Interest, or

   (b) been declared as nature reserves under S19 of the National Parks and Access to the Countryside Act 1949 or S35 of the 1981 Act, or

   (c) been designated as marine nature reserves under S36 of the 1981 Act;

   or which are so notified, declared or designated in the future.

2. CADW

Cadw: Welsh Historic Monuments is the division of the Welsh Office which advises the Secretary of State on matters affecting the built heritage. Cadw is responsible for the operation of the Ancient Monuments and Archaeological Areas Act 1979, which includes the maintenance of a Schedule of Ancient and Historic Monuments of national importance. The Secretary of State for Wales also has a number of sites in his own Guardianship which are on display to the public.

3. ENGLISH HERITAGE

English Heritage is the statutory body established under the National Heritage Act 1983 to promote the preservation of ancient monuments and historic buildings and areas in England and to enhance the public's understanding and enjoyment of them. Its functions include the management and presentation of monuments and historic buildings in state care; advice to the Secretary of State on the selection of monuments and buildings for statutory protection and on the exercise of his statutory powers in relation to scheduled monuments and listed buildings; advice and financial assistance to private owners and other bodies to secure the proper conservation of historic sites and buildings; responsibility for rescue funding of threatened sites of archaeological importance.

4. HISTORIC SCOTLAND

4.1 Historic Scotland (HS) is part of the Scottish Office and is responsible for administering the Secretary of State's policies on the protection of ancient monuments and historic buildings, conserving and managing the 330 monuments and the Royal Parks in State care and advising on the conservation, maintenance, preservation and management of ancient monuments, whether or not legally protected (scheduled), and listed buildings.

4.2 HS is concerned with the protection and management of all monuments not in State care, whether or not they are scheduled, and liaises widely with other Scottish Office departments and external organisations to ensure the protection of ancient monuments in the countryside. HS is also responsible for rescue archaeology, the recording of monuments under threat of destruction. Within HS specialist advice on all matters relating to ancient monuments, archaeology and architectural history is provided by the Inspectorate of Ancient Monuments.

5. COUNCIL FOR BRITISH ARCHAEOLOGY

The Council for British Archaeology (CBA) exists to advance the study and practice of the archaeology of Great Britain, and in particular to promote the education of the public in British archaeology and to conduct, and publish the results of, research therein. In furthering this object the Council is empowered to coordinate and represent archaeological opinion in Britain.

6. COUNCIL FOR SCOTTISH ARCHAEOLOGY

The Council for Scottish Archaeology is a voluntary and charitable association of institutions, societies and individuals concerned with the promotion of archaeology in Scotland. The work of the Council is primarily facilitative and its activities and publications serve both an educational purpose and aid the general dissemination of information about archaeology. The Council for Scottish Archaeology is a member organisation of the Council for British Archaeology.

7. NCC

7.1 The Nature Conservancy Council is the statutory body established by Act of Parliament to promote nature conservation in Great Britain. The NCC has a duty to notify owners and occupiers of any area of land (generally above low-water mark) which is of special interest by reason of its flora, fauna, geological or physiographical features. These areas are known as Sites of Special Scientific Interest (SSSIs). Owners and occupiers of SSSIs are required to give the NCC written notice before carrying out an operation on that land which has been specified in the notification.

7.2 The NCC is empowered to consent to operations proposed by owners and occupiers under 7.1 above, or, alternatively to enter into management agreements with such persons for purposes conducive to the conservation of the special interest. The NCC is also empowered to establish, manage and maintain nature reserves on land above low water mark, and is required to manage areas designated as marine nature reserves within territorial limits.

8. ARCHAEOLOGICAL INFORMATION

8.1 Insofar as is practicable and feasible *Cadw* undertake to notify the NCC of all scheduled archaeological sites in Wales lying within the designated areas referred to in paragraph 1 above and to advise the NCC on the archaeological implications of new designations.

8.2 Insofar as is practicable and feasible English Heritage undertakes to notify the NCC of all scheduled archaeological sites in England lying within the designated areas referred to in paragraph 1 above and to advise the NCC on the archaeological implications of new designations.

8.3 Insofar as is practicable and feasible HS undertakes to notify the NCC of all known archaeological sites in Scotland (whether scheduled or not) lying within the designated areas referred to in paragraph 1 above and to advise the NCC on the archaeological implications of such designations.

9. NATURE CONSERVATION INFORMATION

NCC undertakes to supply Cadw, English Heritage and HS, as appropriate, with details of all sites designated under paragraph 1 above in a manner sufficient to enable them to comply with the undertakings given under paragraphs 8.1 to 8.3 above.

10. CONSULTATION BY ARCHAEOLOGICAL BODIES

Subject to any legal or other essential limitations:

10.1   Cadw, English Heritage and HS will endeavour to ensure that the advice they give to owners and occupiers of land within the designated areas referred to in paragraph 1 above does not lead to damage to the nature conservation importance of the area.

10.2   Cadw, English Heritage and HS will, in addition to any statutory obligation, endeavour to consult with the NCC prior to authorising or undertaking any works likely to damage the nature conservation importance of the area.

11. CONSULTATION BY NCC

Subject to any legal or other essential limitations:

11.1   The NCC will endeavour to consult with Cadw, English Heritage and HS, as appropriate, prior to consenting to any potentially damaging activity on SSSI land likely to be damaging to archaeological interests or concluding a management agreement on SSSI land or when drawing up a management plan for a nature reserve or marine nature reserve, where the land in question is land which has been notified to the NCC by Cadw, English Heritage or HS, as the case may be, as being an area of archaeological importance.

11.2   The NCC will endeavour to consult with the appropriate County Archaeological Officer or Regional Archaeologist or Regional Archaeological Trust (as appropriate and insofar as individual counties and regions have made such appointments) prior to consenting to any potentially damaging activity on SSSI land likely to be damaging to archaeological interests or concluding a management agreement on SSSI land or when drawing up a management plan for a nature reserve or marine nature reserve.

11.3   The NCC will endeavour to ensure that when granting authorisations, concluding management agreements or carrying out management, proper regard is had to the views of consultees referred to in 11.1 and 11.2 above and to the need to conserve features of archaeological interest.

12. FURTHER MEASURES OF AGREEMENT AND GRANTS

The parties to this statement undertake to consider further what measures could be taken which would be conducive to their mutual interests and, in particular, the potential for improved co-ordination in respect of management agreements and grants.

13. FACILITATION

The Council for British Archaeology and the Council for Scottish Archaeology will use their best endeavours to facilitate the effective implementation of the Statement of Intent and, in particular, the provisions of paragraphs 11.2 and 12 above, and 16 below.

14. LIAISON

Council members and senior officers from each party organisation will meet annually to consider issues of mutual interest including research programmes, and to review working arrangements. The party organisations will encourage regional and local liaison between respective officers.

15. LEGISLATION

15.1   The appropriate archaeological organisation and NCC will consult through their headquarters when advising Government or other bodies on legislation which affects their mutual interests. They will seek to further such interests when making a case for improvements in legislation to protect sites of archaeological and nature conservation importance.

15.2   NCC, Cadw, English Heritage and HS will endeavour to ensure their relevant staff are familiar with the staturory protection afforded to important archaeological and nature conservation sites.

16. TRAINING AND EDUCATION

NCC will follow a policy of improving the understanding of its staff in the sympathetic management of sites containing important archaeological features. The appropriate archaeological bodies will assist and cooperate with the NCC in the preparation of educational material which may be needed. NCC will consider how best to enhance the awareness of nature conservation among the archaeological bodies.

CONCLUDING REMARKS

This statemtnt sets out a framework for the safeguard of the archaeological interests of designated nature conservation sites. It will be for the NCC's successor Councils, established by the Environmental Protection Act, and subsequently Scottish Nature Heritage, to agree with the relevant archaeological bodies, the appropriate detailed procedures for the implementaion of this framework.

APPENDIX 2

OUTLINE OF CCW'S GRANT SCHEME

A detailed scheme has recently been submitted to the Welsh Office, and is awaiting approval. In the meantime, the following considerations apply.

1. RATIONALE

A grant is intended to be a contribution towards expenditure incurred by "a person" carrying out a project or programme meeting the purposes of the relevant parts of the Acts governing CCW's work and specific CCW policy objectives, whilst also allowing the partner to realise some of its own objectives.

2. TYPES OF GRANT

Grants are awarded to assist:
— wildlife and landscape conservation;
— access and enjoyment;
— environmental education and awareness;
— meeting policy objectives common to the various countryside agencies;
— other innovative projects.

3. TARGETS

Council agrees priorities and specific targets, and allocates resources annually as part of CCW's Corporate Planning activity.

4. DECISION MAKING

Each application for grant is assessed according to its contribution to meeting CCW's published objectives, and specific criteria for each policy area.

5. PUBLICITY

CCW will publish information on its grant scheme, the resources available to it and CCW's policy objectives.

6. MONITORING

Each grant aided scheme is closely monitored.

APPENDIX 5

PRESERVATION OF HISTORIC BUILDINGS AND ANCIENT MONUMENTS (HB59)

(Memorandum of the Wales Tourist Board)

The Importance of Historic Buildings and Ancient Monuments to the Tourism Industry in Wales

1. The market research undertaken by the Board consistently shows that in our main holiday market, England, it is the perceived quality of our natural environment which is the main motivating factor for visits to Wales. Significantly however "visiting heritage sites" defined as castles, monuments and churches scores very highly among the activities pursued by visitors. The United Kingdom Tourism Survey for 1991 listed the following among the main activities pursued by the 6.7 million holiday visitors to Wales in that year.

	per cent of visitors engaging in this as a main holiday activity
Hill walking, hiking, rambling	21
Swimming	19
Visiting Heritage sites	14
Visiting artistic or heritage exhibits (museums, art galleries, heritage centres)	6
Visiting a theme or activity park	6
Fishing	6

2. It will be noted that visiting artistic and heritage centres shared fourth place as the most popular activity with visiting theme/activity parks and fishing. Combining visiting "heritage sites" with visiting "artistic and heritage exhibits" makes visiting heritage attractions the second most popular activity for holiday visitors.

3. For Wales' key overseas markets our heritage portfolio has a particular significance. Together with the Welsh language and the distinct culture reflecting it, our heritage portfolio gives Wales a distinct identity as one of the constituent countries of the United Kingdom. As will be noted below this is reflected in the way we market Wales overseas as a visitor destination in conjunction with the British Tourist Authority.

4. In the last 20 years there have been significant additions to the number of heritage attractions, many of them reflecting Wales' industrial past. We now have a number of centres which reflect slate working, coal mining, iron making and non-ferrous metal industries together with additional "great little train" experiences. Other developments have involved the restoration and interpretation of old houses. (e.g. Tredegar House, Newport and Llancaiach Fawr in the Rhymney Valley) or the complete interpretation of an area (e.g. Oriel Ynys Môn). Some of the new heritage attractions have been private sector lead, but the majority by local authorities or local authority lead trusts. There have also been significant enhancements to long existing heritage attractions (e.g. by the National Trust through an Exhibition of the Clive Collection at Powys Castle and a new interpretation centre at the Dolaucothi Gold Mine and Cadw at Caerphilly and Chepstow Castles).

5. While the market for visits to heritage attractions has grown during the course of the eighties, it is apparent that visitors to Wales now have a far wider range of choice. Cadw has certain inherent advantages in its appeal to visitors; the media profile of the major monuments remains almost naturally high, especially in English speaking markets overseas, and Cadw benefits from a unique system of signposting its attractions throughout Wales. However it is competing with heritage attractions which in many cases may not be as constrained as Cadw over the physical aspects of interpretation and which because they are new have the benefit of modern interpretive facilities and techniques which are perhaps of greater appeal to the public.

Marketing Wales' Historic Buildings and Ancient Monuments

6. The Wales Tourist Board markets the historic buildings and ancient monuments of Wales as an integral part of its overall strategy to persuade visitors to come to Wales. It gives the owners and operators of these buildings and monuments a variety of opportunities to participate in its marketing. In addition further opportunities are afforded by the three Regional Tourism Companies (North Wales Tourism, Mid Wales Tourism and Tourism South Wales) whose marketing activities complement those of the Board.

7. For the past 6 years the Board has assembled a database of names and addresses of people in the United Kingdom who request information about Wales. This now numbers some 1.5 million names and addresses. This list is updated and duplicate entries removed each year and analysed to establish the marketing profile of our customers. We then use it to mail promotional brochures to past customers and to send solicitation material inviting brochures to likely new customers. The latter is done by door to door distribution in defined geographic areas that we know offer good prospects of positive response, by including postcard response inserts in magazines which have been identified as having readers with some disposition to holidays in Wales and by mailing to known individuals identified in a variety of ways as having a similar marketing profile to previous visitors to Wales.

8. So that members get some idea of the scale of marketing activity involved in the above activities, they might care to note that the campaign run by the Board in December 1992-February 1993 aimed at persuading early commitment to holidaying in Wales in 1993 involved:

— Mailing 170,000 copies of the main Wales Holiday brochure to past customers in the week prior to Christmas;

— The distribution "door to door" of 1.2 million pieces of solicitation material in targeted areas in January/February;

— 1.9 million postcard inserts in magazines in January/February;

— Mailing solicitation material to 60,000 named potential visitors.

The target response requesting brochures from the last three activities was 87,000, a target set having regard to the amount being spent and past performance. The campaign has in fact generated some 117,000 responses at a cost per response of under 50p, continuing the significant reductions in cost per response that the Board has achieved in recent years.

9. The purpose of the above campaign is to persuade potential customers to request a promotional brochure and it is that document which is designed to "convert" the enquiry into a firm booking to stay on a visit to Wales. In 1992–93 for the first time for many years the Board was also in a position, through an increase in budget provided by the Secretary of State, to back up the direct mail campaign with an image building campaign. This is not directly intended to generate requests for a brochure but to raise an awareness of Wales as an attractive destination among residents of targeted market areas who do not currently put Wales on their "menu" for possible holiday destinations. The Board has constructed an image building campaign which has involved very large poster advertising (500 "48 sheet" sites in January/February) with striking images showing the quality of our environment together with a television commercial on Granada, Central, HTV and London.

115218 L

10. Enclosed in the wallet at *Annex A* are copies of some of the promotional brochures currently being used by the Board. Members attention is drawn first to the "1993 Holidays and Short Breaks—All year Round" brochure. Members will find extensive reference to Wales Heritage attractions in the introductory editorial sections, pages 2-7, which are categorised on a regional basis. In addition pages 12-13 gives specific coverage to Industrial Heritage, which is to be the subject of specific promotional activity this year by both the English and Wales Tourist Boards. Elsewhere in the brochure which mainly consists of over 800 paid advertisements, the opportunity is taken subject to design constraints to remind the reader of our built heritage eg the view of Harlech Castle on page 47, Manorbier Castle on page 52, Tintern Abbey on page 65, Powys Castle on page 86. Attention is also drawn to the opportunity given to local authorities and other organisations to advertise in the brochure, pages 134-136, 450,000 copies of this brochure have been produced together with additional copies of individual accommodation sections.

11. Members will also wish to note the focus given to Wales' historic buildings and ancient monuments in the main Wales Tourist Board/BTA overseas brochure for 1993. The front cover features Carreg Cennen Castle and Mr Bernard Llewellyn who has a management agreement with Cadw for the castle, while the back cover features Chirk Castle. Members attention is drawn to the specific coverage given to the heritage of Wales from its earliest years in the editorial pages on pages 4 and 5 and to the further coverage given on pages 14 and 15 dealing with the Capital and pages 20-25 dealing with the various regions. 400,000 copies of this brochure have been produced in 8 different languages for use in our key overseas markets.

12. Members attention is also drawn to the coverage of our heritage which is given in the 16 page image building brochure which has been produced to support our image building advertising campaign and for use in the various promotions in which the Board is engaged. Wales heritage attractions also feature in the saleable Accommodation guides which are currently published by Jarrolds in association with the Board and there are also extensive references in the Regional Visitor guides (reference copies included).

13. The wallet labelled *Annex B* contains publications relating to specific promotions overseas in which Cadw together with other heritage attractions operators are participating. Attention is drawn to the "Wise Wales" initiative with USA travel agents, 800 of whom have now joined the network who have professed readiness to promote visits to Wales. 200 of these agents have already paid visits to Wales for week long educational visits. It will be noted that Cadw have contributed to the costs of this promotion, have a double page spread in the brochure which USA agents issue to prospective visitors, four pages in the travel agents guide and that Cadw were represented on a WTB/BTA "road show" to meet agents on the North Eastern seaboard of the USA in December 1992.

14. Members will also wish to note that the A5 colour brochure "On the Wales Heritage Trail" produced in 1991–92 involving participation by Cadw, the National Trust, the National Museum and BTA. This was produced in seven overseas languages and is still in use.

15. Turning to the UK market Cadw and other operators have participated with the Board in the Valleys Marketing Campaign and in the Board's annual Groups Travel Manual and in the marketing campaign conducted by the Board for schools visits. Reference has already been made to the specific promotion of Wales' industrial heritage. Cadw and other industrial heritage operators will feature in the brochure and in the subsequent campaign which will be launched in Swansea on 6 April and in Wrexham on 7 April.

16. The wallet at Annex B also contains a copy of "Castles & Historic Places". This is a joint publication of WTB and Cadw, 40,000 copies of which were printed in 1990/91 retailing at £5.95 per copy.

17. While our historic buildings and ancient monuments are integral to the marketing which the Board undertakes to attract vistors to Wales, the responsibility in respect of individual heritage attractions rests with the owners/operators. One of the main ways in which Cadw attracts visitors to its properties (para 54 of its recent Memorandum of Evidence to the Committee) is "the widespread distribution of attractive full-colour marketing leaflets and show cards to Tourists Information Centres and to tourism accommodation ......, other attractions and local marketing consortia". In this context the creation by the Board as of 1 April 1992 of a national TIC network involving some 78 centres working to uniform operational criteria will have helped Cadw and other attractions operators.

18. In the location of TIC's the local authority, which generally speaking owns or leases the TIC building, frequently has regard to the proximity of a nearby heritage attraction which attracts significant numbers of visitors. This was certainly taken into account in relocation TIC buildings in Caernarfon and in Conway, the latter forming part of Cadw's Conway Castle Visitor Centre. The location of the new TIC at Pont Nedd Fechan, near Glyn Neath, reflected the proximity of the National Trust's Aberdulais Falls property while the new TIC at Chepstow was located in the car park which serves Chepstow Castle. The Board invariably supports the capital cost of TIC developments.

The Distribution of Heritage Tourism in Wales

19. One of the interesting differences in the distribution of main tourism attractions in England, Scotland and Wales is the concentration of main attractions in England in London, in Scotland in Edinburgh and Glasgow and the much wider dispersion in Wales. Eight or nine of the 10 main tourism attractions in England and Scotland are concentrated in those cities. In Wales only Cardiff Castle features in the 10 most visited

historic properties and only the Castle, the National Museum and the Folk Museum if the list is widened to include all heritage type attractions. It follows, therefore, that the advantages of heritage tourism in terms of the income generation and employment to which it gives rise are widely spread throughout Wales.

Tourism and Conservation Priorities

20. Wales' environment, natural and man-built, has an intrinsic value and needs to be preserved for the benefit of future generations. Maintaining the environment is also important for the wellbeing of tourism; it is what people come to enjoy. The income and awareness created by tourism can foster conservation ideals.

21. The Board will be addressing these issues in its forthcoming Tourism Strategy for Wales to be published in draft in May which will succeed its present five Year Framework Development Strategy. However, it is significant to record that the Board's current mission statement is:

> To develop and market tourism in ways which will yield the optimum economic and social benefit to the people of Wales. *Implicit within this objective is the need to sustain and promote the culture of Wales and the Welsh language and to safeguard the natural and built environment.*

This mission statement has underpinned our environmental concern without prejudicing the Board's primary purpose. It has found expression in a number of ways:

> While encouraging measures to enhance the appeal of our built heritage insisting that developments must be sensitive and of the highest possible standards of design and materials.

> Provision of relevant information to planning authorities to enable them to take more informed decisions about proposed developments which bear on the tourism industry.

> Recognition of the particular sensitivity of the National Parks and areas of particular designation.

> In the context of that part of our five Year Development Strategy which has been executed in partnership with local authorities in the Local Enterprise and Development Initiative (LEAD), the deployment of grant aid to assist in improvements to the built environment.

22. Improvements to road communications within Wales over the last 20 years have lead to some dramatic improvements in the environment of many of our foremost heritage attractions. Most recently, for example, the completion of the A55 Conway Tunnel has taken through traffic out of the historic walled town, which has been the beneficiary of Board financial assistance under the LEAD scheme. Wales has not for the most part experienced the disbenefits of heavy congestion around heritage sites which has been experienced in parts of England but tourism traffic does require improved management in a number of resorts. The new strategy will offer a partnership approach between the Board and other interested partners to explore new methods of vistor management to address these problems.

23. While recognising the potential disbenefits of tourism to our built heritage, the scope for increasing visitor numbers in an acceptable way by better interpretation, improved facilities and more imaginative packaging and marketing of the product also needs to be recognised. Cadw, for example, have run pageants at some of their properties; the Pembrokeshire Coast National Park had a very successful reenactment at Carew Castle while Rhymney Valley District Council's ongoing living interpretation of the Llancaiach Fawr Tudor Manor House is successfully pioneering "first person interpretation" in Wales. All heritage attractions operators need to keep under review appropriate ways of interpreting their properties. For its part the Board will be addressing in its new strategy ways of developing in an appropriate manner the visitor potential of Wales' historic towns.

The Board's Relationship with Heritage Attractions Operators

24. As will be clear from earlier comment the Board's marketing activities support heritage attraction operators:

— In attracting visitors to Wales in part by highlighting the attractions on offer;

— By offering specific joint marketing opportunities to individual heritage attractions;

— Through its National Tourist Information Centre Network which provides outlets for the information literature of attractions.

25. In addition the Board provided financial support for the development of many heritage attractions. For example, the National Trust has been a major beneficiary with support being provided for the display of the Clive Collection at Powys Castle, for the development of interpretive facilities at Dolaucothi Gold Mine, for Dinefwr Park, for Aberdulais Falls and the restoration of properties at Cmwdu Llandeilo. In addition the Board has supported a feasibility study into the development of the National Trust's Llanaeron Estate. Local authorities and local authority lead trusts have also benefited, for example the authorities involved with the Rhondda Heritage Park and Blaenavon Big Pit, both of which have received Board grant aid as has Wrexham Borough Council for the Kingsmill development and Ynys Môn Borough Council for Oriel Ynys Môn. Private sector developments which have benefited include the Llechwedd and Inigo Jones Slate Works and the Sygun Copper Mine.

26. Through a special dispensation given by the Welsh office some years ago it has also been possible for the Board to consider providing financial assistance to capital expenditure on the improvement of tourism

facilities by the National Museum and Cadw. This facility has been activated in the case of the former body with assistance having been provided for the deveopment of No 126 Bute Street (a reconstruction of a Ship Chandlery) and for the Power of Wales Exhibition at Oriel Eryri, Llanberis.

27. Members will be aware by reference to the recent Welsh Office Financial Management and Policy Review of the Board that there is a recommendation to withdraw the right of the Board to consider assisting in the provision of tourism facilities by other central government organisations. That is an issue to be considered further.

28. The Board has a very constructive relationship with the operators of heritage attractions. By virtue of the number of sites there is very frequent contact with Cadw, the National Trust and the National Museum. The relationship with Cadw was and to an extent remains unique. Upon the inception of that body all Cadw's commercial staff were drawn from and employed by the Board and seconded to Cadw. The Board did not, however, have any managerial responsibilty for them or for the operational policies. That arrangement ceased when Cadw became an Executive Agency when it decided that staff would be directly employed. The Board's Chairman continues to serve as a Member of Cadw's Advisory Committee and as such to offer advice on the evolution of Cadw's policies.

March 1993

APPENDIX 6

Memorandum by The Architectural Heritage Fund

Preservation of Historic Buildings and Ancient Monuments (HB14)

1. INTRODUCTION

The Architectural Heritage Fund has seventeen years' experience of making low-interest loans for projects undertaken by buildings preservation trusts and other organisations with charitable status in every part of the United Kingdom. It has long been concerned by the slow growth in demand for loans for projects in Wales, and by the comparatively small number of buildings preservation trusts there. Policy and practice in respect of the listing of historic buildings and the controls exercised on planning consents in relation to them, and on grant schemes (points (iii) and (iv) of the Committee's terms of reference) have a bearing on this. The Architectural Heritage Fund is not qualified to comment on arrangements for the properties in the care of the Secretary of State, as exercised by Cadw, or on the care exercised by other major owners (such as the National Trust, the churches and local authorities) over their properties (points (i) and (ii) of the Committee's terms of reference).

2. THE ARCHITECTURAL HERITAGE FUND (AHF)

The Architectural Heritage Fund is a national charity which operates throughout the United Kingdom. It was established in 1973 "to promote the permanent preservation for the benefit of the public generally of buildings, monuments or other edifices or structures . . . of particular beauty or historical, architectural or constructional interest; to protect and conserve or promote the protection and conservation of the character and heritage of the cities, towns and villages in and around which such buildings, monuments or other edifices or structures exist; and to advance public education and interest" in such matters.

Although this "objects" clause is very widely drawn, both the government (which has contributed most of the AHF's working capital over the years and which appoints 50 per cent of the members of the Council of Management) and the AHF itself have always understood that its principal role is to provide low-interest loan finance for projects undertaken by local preservation trusts and other charities. Between May 1976, when it opened for business with a potential working capital of £1 million, and 31 December 1992 when its working capital stood at £6.6 million, and the AHF made low-interest loans amounting to just under £14.5 million in support of 250 preservation projects. In the same period, 200 loans amounting to almost £10 million were repaid.

The majority of projects undertaken with The Architectural Heritage Fund's assistance involve historic buildings which are listed Grade II or are in a conservation area, and whose importance is local rather than national. Individually, or taken out of context, many of these buildings might appear insignificant. Collectively, however, they give each town or area its distinctive character, and there should be a presumption in favour of their preservation. To achieve the repair and rehabilitation of such buildings requires constructive co-operation between central government, local authorities and the community. Charitable preservation trusts, with or without the AHF's assistance, have proved one of the most effective agents for success in this field.

3. BUILDINGS PRESERVATION TRUSTS

In 1976, there were 30 "revolving fund" buildings preservation trusts in the United Kingdom. Revolving fund trusts are charities constituted to acquire, repair, rehabilitate and dispose of historic buildings, devoting any surplus from one project to the working capital required for the next. By the end of 1992 there were 120 organisations on The Architectural Heritage Fund's Register of revolving fund buildings preservation trusts.

The majority of buildings preservation trusts operate within a narrowly defined geographical area. Because they are charities, their overheads are minimal, they do not have to budget for a profit margin, and they can raise funds from sources which are not available to the private sector. As a result, preservation trusts can often restore and rehabilitate historic buildings which might otherwise be beyond economic repair.

4. BUILDINGS PRESERVATION TRUSTS IN WALES

Until 1992, there were only two revolving fund trusts in Wales, and only one of these had ever undertaken a preservation project. In the course of 1992, four further revolving fund trusts in Wales registered with The Architectural Heritage Fund, bringing the total to six. Several more are in the process of formation.

5. ARCHITECTURAL HERITAGE FUND LOANS FOR PROJECTS IN WALES

The AHF's first loan for a project in Wales was disbursed in 1987. Since then the AHF has disbursed five more loans in Wales; a further loan, offered in December 1991, is expected to be taken up early in 1993.

By the end of 1992, the total amount loaned by the AHF in Wales was £450,000 for six projects. One of these loans was to a revolving fund preservation trust based in Wales. One other was to a preservation trust based in England but empowered to operate throughout Britain. The remaining four loans went to charities undertaking eligible projects but established for other purposes.

6. BUILDINGS PRESERVATION TRUSTS AND AHF LOANS IN THE REST OF THE UNITED KINGDOM

By far the majority of The Architectural Heritage Fund's loans go to projects in England, where there are currently just over 100 revolving fund preservation trusts. But there is strong demand for AHF loans in Scotland, where the AHF has supported 30 projects with loans amounting to £2.2 million since 1981, and where there are now twelve revolving fund preservation trusts. Although there is only one revolving fund trust in Northern Ireland, that trust has undertaken six projects with the aid of AHF loans amounting to £350,000 since 1982 (the AHF has not made any loans to other organisations in Northern Ireland).

7. GOVERNMENT GRANT TO AHF AND VOLUME OF ACTIVITY

Most of the AHF's working capital (which stood at £6.6 million on 31 December 1992) has derived from central government grant. Over the years, the AHF has received £750,000 from the Department of the Environment, £1.8 million from English Heritage, £1.4 million from the Secretary of State for Scotland and £60,000 from the Secretary of State for Wales. The rest of its working capital has derived from donations from the private and charity sectors, and from interest on loans and bank deposits.

The AHF first received grant from the Secretary of State for Scotland in 1988 (in two tranches, of £100,000 and £200,000), when it had made loans amounting to £381,000 for seven projects in Scotland. Since then, the Secretary of State for Scotland has made further grants amounting to £1.1 million, and the AHF has made 23 further loans in Scotland amounting to £1,854,000.

The first (and so far only) grant to the AHF from the Secretary of State for Wales was £60,000, disbursed in December 1992. The Architectural Heritage Fund hopes this will both boost the buildings preservation trust movement and encourage other eligible organisations in Wales to undertake projects involving the repair and rehabilition of historic buildings.

8. EFFORTS TO INCREASE BPT ACTIVITY IN WALES

During the last two years the AHF has stepped up its efforts to stimulate the formation of new buildings preservation trusts in Wales. Discussions have taken place with Cadw, with the Historic Buildings Council, at meetings convened by the National Trust in South Wales, with the Association of Preservation Trusts, with several local authorities, and with a number of local civic and amenity societies. The AHF was therefore delighted by the establishment in 1992 of the Clwyd Historic Buildings Trust, Cyfeillion Cadw Tremadog, Cywaith (The Gwynedd Building Preservation Trust), and Mongomeryshire Building Preservation Trust, and by the fact that two of these new trusts have already applied for AHF feasibility study grants for their potential first projects. Likely to obtain charitable registration in 1993 are the Carmarthenshire & Llanelli BPT, Hendref (Welsh Traditional Houses at Risk), and a BPT for the Vale of Glamorgan, and the possibility of establishing a BPT for Gwynedd National Park is also being explored.

9. FACTORS IMPEDING BPT ACTIVITY IN WALES

The low level of activity by buildings preservation trusts in Wales is largely a product of a general lack of interest in and appreciation of vernacular buildings. As far as the AHF is aware, almost nothing is being done, either by the Welsh Office or by individual local authorities, to enhance awareness of the importance and feasibility of preserving and rehabilitating vernacular buildings and using traditional materials and techniques in their repair. Very few local authorities employ conservation officers. Because many such buildings are neither listed nor in a conservation area, they have no protection against demolition or inappropriate alteration, nor are they eligible for statutory historic buildings or conservation area repairs grants. The re-listing survey is far from complete. Because of this, the survival of a number of important historic buildings is dependent upon action by a concerned official or individual to obtain their "spot listing" as a matter of urgency. There is no Welsh equivalent to English Heritage's "Buildings at Risk" campaign or system of grants towards the cost of emergency repairs to listed buildings at risk. Unlike English Heritage and Historic Scotland, Cadw does not have a proactive approach to buildings preservation trusts and did not until 1992 make available any grant to The Architectural Heritage Fund.

10. ACTION TO ACHIEVE CHANGE

A. Enhancing Awareness

The Secretary of State's decision in August 1992 to award a grant to The Architectural Heritage Fund was welcome in itself, and especially welcome as evidence that higher priority than hitherto may now be given to efforts to stimulate an increase in activity of the kind the AHF can support. Although the grant was publicly announced, the AHF is not aware of any campaign by the Welsh Office to disseminate information about the contribution buildings preservation trusts can make to the repair and rehabilitation of vernacular buildings and the assistance available from the AHF. The Architectural Heritage Fund sends every chief planning officer a copy of its annual report and supplies of its information leaflets, and all members of the Association of Conservation Officers receive not only the AHF's annual report but also its biannual newsletter, *Preservation in Action*. Nevertheless many local authorities, as well as most members of the public, are wholly ignorant of the existence and purpose of buildings preservation trusts and The Architectural Heritage Fund and give low priority to the care and preservation of vernacular buildings. Action to enhance interest and awareness is urgently needed, and should in the longer term prove to be highly cost effective.

B. Re-listing, and Buildings at Risk

Equally important and even more urgent is completion of the re-listing survey, to which additional resources ought to be devoted. This survey could also provide valuable information about historic buildings at risk in Wales, and this initial information might then form the basis for a new policy of action designed to save such buildings. Preservation trusts could contribute in various ways to a vernacular buildings at risk campaign, for example by undertaking surveys, mobilising local support for action, and ultimately by acquiring individual buildings at risk for repair and rehabilitation, either direct from their owners or following their compulsory purchase by local authorities.

C. Grants

Statutory grants are almost always critical to the viability of projects undertaken by buildings preservation trusts. There should be a presumption in favour of offering the maximum possible grant for every eligible project submitted by a preservation trust. When assessing the financial resources of the applicant and potential "profitability" of the project, account should be taken of the fact that the applicant is a charity established for the sole purpose of preserving historic buildings and with the intention of undertaking a programme of such projects. Clawback should be enforced only in the event of a substantial surplus of income over expenditure when a building is sold after repair and rehabilitation.

D. Seek to Encourage a Community Solution

The importance of a change of attitude—official as well as popular—both towards buildings preservation trusts and to the preservation of vernacular buildings in Wales can hardly be overstated. The AHF was surprised and disturbed to learn in December that listed building and conservation area consent for the demolition of buildings in Bridge Street, Carmarthen, had been confirmed by the Secretary of State, even though the Camarthen & Llanelli Buildings Preservation Trust (which expects to register as a charity in a matter of weeks) was formed largely in order to undertake their repair and rehabilitation.

Most of the arguments in the Inspector's report were in favour of retention of the Bridge Street properties. The case for demolition included the statement that little progress had been made in establishing the Trust. Establishing a trust takes time, and those prepared to do so should be given all possible support and encouragement. A local authority's decision to apply for consent to demolish in the face of the declared intention of a fledgling trust to acquire and rehabilitate the buildings concerned suggests that the local authority has no interest in the economic, environmental and social benefits to be obtained through co-operating with a local historic buildings trust.

The Inspector also made the point that demolition would "bring into greater prominence part of the earlier history of medieval Carmarthen". Although this could be argued both ways, it is difficult not to interpret the

Bridge Street decision as further evidence of the lack of importance attached to the preservation of vernacular buildings in Wales.

5 January 1993

APPENDIX 7

Memorandum by the Cambrian Archaeological Association

PRESERVATION OF HISTORIC BUILDINGS AND ANCIENT MONUMENTS (HB16)

INTRODUCTION

The Cambrian Archaeological Association is a voluntary Society which has since 1846 campaigned for the preservation of the ancient monuments and the built heritage of Wales (a full account of its interests is given in the accompanying leaflet).

The Association has long realised that this task is immense and that voluntary effort, whether by individuals or by societies, is inadequate to meet the needs of the situation. It believes that the State has a leading role to play, and in the Welsh context it welcomes the delegation of responsibility for ancient monuments and historic buildings to the Secretary of State for Wales.

The meetings of the Association are held in different parts of Wales in turn, drawing members' attention to all types of antiquity and historic buildings. They are invariably impressed by the high standard of conservation and presentation of monuments in the care of the State, and by the scholarship of the Inspectors and Architects of Cadw who described the sites to them and who are responsible for the guide books.

The Association believes in prompt and full publication of the results of archaeological research, and it devotes virtually the whole of its current subscription income to the publication of its Journal, Archaeologia Cambrensis. It welcomes the subventions given from time to time by Cadw towards the cost of publishing certain papers dealing with excavations in which Cadw has been involved. This is a fruitful partnership between statutory and voluntary endeavour.

Cadw officials (although many are members of the Association) have not been involved in the preparation of this memorandum.

The Association believes it is important to look at areas of countryside as a whole and not to concentrate narrowly on buildings and monuments alone. Such an approach could also include the scheduling and preservation of areas where the views are outstanding (as is already occasionally done in England). Hafod in Dyfed and Conway in North Wales come to mind as examples.

Indeed we believe that conservation areas in the countryside, as with conservation areas in urban areas, are already possible under existing legislation, but that the possibilities have not been realised up to the present.

THE WORK OF CADW.

This received very high praise from our members and was thought to have been a major improvement on the situation that obtained before Cadw was established.

Particular praise is due for their presentation of sites and for the excellent and attractive guides they produce. Their proceedures for scheduling buildings and monuments was praised, although there was some concern at the delays involved. This delay was often a reflexion of the detailed and careful preparatory work carried out, necessarily time consuming. Their Field Wardens have been a great success and are seen as "user friendly".

There are some minor criticisms of Cadw. The Association wonders whether Cadw could do more to help threatened churches and chapels of significance, whilst realising the financial constraints under which they work. Perhaps occasionally, they should take direct ownership of historic churches and chapels.

There are concerns over the diminution and dilution of Cadw's uniquely skilled direct labour force. The Association is aware of the value of competitive tendering but feels that more allowance should be made for the highly specialised abilities required of a workforce doing this sort of preservation work on historic buildings.

We wonder, too, whether adequate induction training is available for administrators coming to an organisation like Cadw, which would help them in dealing with outside enquiries and with their own highly specialised staff, to whom they have to delegate much of their work.

Some concern was expressed at "translated bilingualism" as opposed to more natural bilingualism in dealing with some parts of rural Wales.

There is concern over the predatory use of metal detectors in Wales, although the problem is not thought to be widespread.

We regret the cessation of acknowledgement payments to owners/tenants of scheduled ancient monuments, however small. They are now only available if changes or developements occur. The Association appreciates the increased funding received in recent years, but would like to see more resources made available to Cadw to enable expansion of its work to occur.

THE CARE OF CHURCHES AND CHAPELS

Here major anxieties were expressed by our members who regard the present situation as unsatisfactory. Churches and chapels often cannot raise enough money for preservation work even when grants are made. Some work done is quite unsuitable, no doubt due to both lack of resources and of the skilled knowledge needed to plan such work. The introduction by Cadw of a "Code of Practice" into the arrangements for ecclesiastical exemption is a major step forward. The Association would like to see better research and documentation carried out when repairs are effected.

We are aware of the good work done by voluntary bodies such as the Historic Churches Preservation Trust, the Incorporated Church Building Society, the Friends of Friendless Churches and Capel who all help financially and in other ways in Wales. However, it is felt that this an area that the Welsh Office should look at with a view to increasing financial help in to coming years.

It was suggested that the standard set for Cadw intervention in the case of churches and chapels was too high, so that less "glamorous" but still valuable buildingds were not eligible.

Many believe that a Redundant Churches Fund is needed in Wales.

THE NATIONAL TRUST

Their work in Wales is highly regarded by the Association.

THE NATIONAL PARKS AUTHORITIES

There is high praise, too, for the enlightened and cooperative attitude shown by the National Parks to buildings in their ownership and to their surrounding environment.

THE ARCHAEOLOGICAL TRUSTS

The Association believes that the setting up of the four Archaeological Trusts in Wales was an inspired move that has produced extremely valuable results in their local areas, often operating at a different level from Cadw. We are pleased that the cooperation between Cadw and the Trusts is good.

THE LOCAL AUTHORITIES

We see the record of Local Authorities in this field as variable. Some have an excellent reputation – others are not so good. The creation of Archaeological Trusts has helped the work of Local Authorities enormously.

Only one Local Authority in Wales has an Archaeological Officer and the Association feels that much of the problem lies in the absence of Local Authority staff with adequate professional knowledge to judge issues as they arise. We compare unfavourably with Scotland who have a system of "Nominated Officers" with designated powers.

SITES IN PRIVATE OWNERSHIP

There is concern about monuments in private ownership. This is by no means of criticism of the owners, but reflects the difficulties they have in carrying out maintenance and repair work professionally.

Grants are available but seldom cover more than half of the cost of this necessarily expensive work. The anomalous situation arises that poorer owners (most in need of help) refuse grants because they feel they cannot afford their share of the cost. Grants in any case, are only given for essential repairs and not for alterations, services, decorations or moveable fittings.

We feel that this is an area that Government should look at. Possible solutions are 100 per cent interest-free loans, repayable on death or when the property is sold, or tax relief arrangements for the cost of necessary work.

January 1993

APPENDIX 8

Memorandum by the Civic Trust for Wales

PRESERVATION OF HISTORIC BUILDINGS AND ANCIENT MONUMENTS (HB33)

INTRODUCTION

1. The Welsh Affairs Committee of the House of Commons is currently inquiring into the preservation of historic buildings and monuments in the Principality. It is considering in particular:

— the arrangements for properties in the care of the Secretary of State, as exercised by Cadw,

— the care exercised by other major owners over their properties,

— the listing of historic buildings, the scheduling of ancient monuments and the controls exercised on planning consents in relation to them, and

— the grant schemes available for the preservation of historic buildings and ancient monuments.

2. The Civic Trust for Wales has been asked to supply evidence covering the following:

— the role of the Trust and its associated civic societies in the preservation of historic buildings, and

— the Trust's experience of Cadw, particularly in respect of its statutory functions (*e.g.,* in the listing of buildings and scheduling of monuments, and in its administration and distribution of grants).

The Trust has also been asked to express a view on whether the civic societies in Wales have a contribution to make to the relisting survey, and to put forward issues that it considers relevant to the inquiry.

THE CIVIC TRUST FOR WALES

3. The Civic Trust for Wales was established in 1964. The Trust is a registered charity (registration number 242672). The Trust's objectives, as set out in its *Declaration of Trust,* are *inter alia,* to:

— encourage high quality in architecture, building and town and country planning in Wales,

— assist and encourage the preservation of buildings of historic and architectural interest, and

— encourage a sense of civic pride in Welsh communities.

The Trust pursues these aims as part of the wider Civic Trust movement. It is one of three regional bodies affiliated to the Civic Trust (UK), which was founded in 1957 by Duncan Sandys. However, the Civic Trust for Wales is financially and organisationally autonomous and receives no direct support from the national body.

4. The Trust's objectives commit it to the development of environmental understanding and improvement. Historically, its commitment is primarily to the urban environment and the relationship between town and country. The Trust's role is to act as a force for positive change in improving the quality of the places where people live and work; to encourage and promote community environmental action; and to raise awareness and understanding of issues relating to the built environment and its context. The Trust's Strategic Plan identifies three key areas of activity through which its objectives will be pursued:

— the continued development and support of the civic society network,

— the promotion of environmental awareness to a wider audience, and

— the maintenance of an advisory and policy role.

5. The Trust's *Report to the Welsh Office* for 1992 is annexed to this memorandum. During the year, its main activities were represented by:

— its daily advice and support to affiliated civic societies, including public inquiry work,

— observations to national and local government on planning and environmental issues,

— a publications programme, including a series of advisory notes and a newsletter,

— consultancy, represented by the *Llanidloes Town Study,*

— a major conference on urban regeneration, and

— the organisation and promotion of National Environment Week in Wales.

6. The Trust is staffed by a Director and a part-time administrator. Since 1988 it has been supported by an annual grant from the Welsh Office, channelled through Cadw. Other income is derived from society registrations, income from events and consultancy, and from private sector donation and sponsorship. Without the significant support received from the Welsh Office, the Trust would not have been able to develop with the success that has been achieved over the past four years. In 1992, the Welsh Office was able to increase

its level of funding to take account of the impact of inflation since 1988. The Trust meets annually with Cadw to review its work.

7. Sixty-four civic societies are currently registered with the Civic Trust for Wales. The character and activities of each are a reflection of the community in which it is established. There is no prescriptive model setting out what a civic society should do, although the constitution of each is based on the advice of the Trust. Some societies emphasise practical environmental or educational projects, others focus on local planning issues. All, however, have a general concern with the conservation and interpretation of the built environment.

THE CIVIC TRUST AND THE PRESERVATION OF HISTORIC BUILDINGS

8. The Trust is committed by its *Declaration of Trust* to encourage the preservation of historic buildings. Often this is undertaken through advice to affiliated civic and amenity societies. Most civic societies are adept in monitoring threats to historic buildings in their communities, and have experience in making representations to the local authorities and to Cadw when a problem occurs. The Trust will often make supportive observations to a planning authority or Cadw in particular instances.

9. The Civic Trust for Wales has recently published detailed advisory notes on *Conservation Areas* and *Listed Buildings* to assist civic societies and similar bodies in these areas of interest.

10. Civic societies regularly draw to Cadw's attention buildings that are at risk from development and which could merit spotlisting. For example, Sully Hospital was listed Grade II following representations made by the Barry Civic Society and the Penarth Society; more recently, the Porthcawl Civic Trust, supported by the Civic Trust for Wales, urged that Jennings Warehouse and associated structures at Porthcawl Old Dock be listed. The local knowledge of civic groups is frequently of assistance in documenting the historic importance of buildings.

11. Where appropriate—normally where an issue is of more than local importance—the Civic Trust for Wales will press its concerns about particular buildings at public inquiry. In 1991, for instance, the Trust presented oral evidence opposing the demolition of two Grade II Georgian houses to facilitate the extension of Gwynedd County Hall. Also in 1991, the Trust submitted extensive written evidence to a public inquiry (and gave considerable legal advice to the local civic society) dealing with a proposed marina and housing development at Porthcawl that would impact on a conservation area and lead to the loss of buildings that were considered worthy of listing (and were subsequently spotlisted, despite the opposition of the developer and the district council). In 1992, the Trust worked closely with the newly formed Fishguard Civic Society to oppose a planned diversion to the A487 at Lower Fishguard. This road scheme, if approved, will lead to the demolition of a Grade II listed former public house and a Grade II listed bridge, as well as generally harming the character and appearance of the local conservation area and the setting of numerous listed buildings. A copy of the Trust's evidence to the latter inquiry is appended to this memorandum.

12. The Trust's work in Llanidloes, for clients headed by Llanidloes Town Council, Montgomeryshire District Council, Powys County Council and the Development Board for Rural Wales deals extensively with opportunities to conserve the historic townscape of the settlement. The report includes proposals for a town scheme in Llanidloes, prioritising buildings at particular risk; it also provides the client group with illustrated design guidance on general matters, windows and doors, and shop fronts.

13. The Trust does not own or manage property; neither has it the resources (or the wish) to make grants towards the maintenance or acquisition of historic buildings. However, it is currently assisting a newly formed building preservation trust, *Hendref,* which is seeking support for a feasibility study in connection with the acquisition and repair of a property in Narberth. It has also drawn the attention of the Montgomeryshire Historic Building Trust to the derelict Bridgend Mill at Llanidloes, a property that has potential for conversion to a variety of uses.

THE CIVIC TRUST'S EXPERIENCE OF CADW

14. The Trust is directly assisted by Cadw and liaises closely with its staff. The Trust is impressed by the capability and dedication of the small team within Cadw that has responsibility for the survey and listing of historic buildings. It is understood that this team currently comprises four persons, and that there are in addition three persons carrying out listing work on a sub-contract basis. The Trust perceives the size of this team to be a function of the resources made available to Cadw by government. While the Trust and its affiliated societies are impressed by the responsiveness of Cadw in responding to requests for spotlisting, it would be fair to say that we have always regarded this as too small a team in relation to its role.

15. Notwithstanding the above comments, the achievement of Cadw (post 1984) in increasing the number of listed buildings in Wales from 8,000 in 1979 to approximately 15,000 currently is substantial. The form in which the updated lists is published is regarded as convenient and helpful.

16. Comments are made below on the lack of data regarding the degree of risk to listed buildings, the level of local authority resources dedicated to conservation, and the rate of demolition of public buildings. Cadw would be the appropriate body to collate and publish such information, perhaps in an Annual Report.

17. Comments are also offered below on the administration of grants made by Cadw. The Trust's principal observation is the lack of available statistics relating to need against which to measure the application of grant aid.

ASSOCIATED ISSUES

18. The Trust is of the view that the Welsh Affairs Committee should be concerned not simply with the issue of the efficiency of Cadw, but with larger issues regarding the existing system of protection of historic buildings as it operates in England and Wales. It is one matter to ensure the steady progress of a resurvey, but is the process of listing any form of guarantee that a building of recognised importance can be protected from falling into disrepair? If it is not in fact possible to maintain the buildings that are listed to date, is there any point in adding day on day to the statutory list?

19. In Wales there is as yet no counterpart to the recent English Heritage *Buildings at risk* survey. This revealed that over twenty percent of the stock of listed buildings in England were likely to be "at risk" or vulnerable because of neglect or decay. Buildings were most likely to be at risk in areas of social and economic decline. It would be a useful exercise were a comparable survey to be undertaken in Wales. It is inherently likely that the scale of the problem revealed in England may obtain in Wales, and that parallel questions need to be asked regarding the nature and targeting of resources towards conservation.

20. It is understood that in 1993-4 in the order of £4M has been allotted to Cadw to make grants under the 1953 and 1990 acts on the advice of the Historic Buildings Council. This is a significant increment on the £2.8M devoted by government to the repair of the "built heritage" in Wales in 1989-90, but the problem remains that the extent of disrepair probably outstrips the state's ability to help. The Trust's experience is that Town Scheme grant is a proven and effective method of targeting listed and unlisted properties in conservation areas, achieving its impact by combining local authority and government resources and expertise, and unlocking matching investment by owners. Outside town schemes it is generally only the outstanding properties that can be assisted, and only a selection of those. However, the character of the Welsh countryside and the landscape of towns is generally determined more by ordinary rather than extraordinary properties, and it is the run-of-the-mill Grade II category that inevitably contains most properties at risk.

21. In the paper on "Urban conservation" published by Welsh Office as a guideline report within the Strategic Planning Guidance in Wales exercise (1991), it is stressed that while national organisations can provide a measure of funding and expertise targeted at the most important structures, effective implementation and local commitment to conservation depends on the local authorities. Government looks to the local authorities for development control, as custodians themselves of monuments and buildings, as suppliers of expertise, and as partners with Cadw and HBC in deploying grant aid. These are onerous duties in view of the contraction in resources available to local authorities. Conservation is one of the most vulnerable areas of local government finance. By no means all local authorities, either at country or district level, employ conservation officers or architects with specialist skills.[1]

22. Without detailed Welsh statistics it is impossible to do more than suggest that there obtains in Wales a situation comparable to that which English Heritage has shown to be the case in England: that the integrity of many historic buildings may be under threat owing to the limited resources available for the conservation of buildings which the state has determined to be of special interest and the reluctance or inability of owners themselves to spend money on repair and maintenance. In this context an assessment of the degree of risk to the Principality's increasing stock of listed buildings would be of use in targeting government assistance. It would be useful to know how many listed buildings are demolished or heavily altered annually, and helpful were information on the deployment of local authority resources assessed and published.

23. In the Trust's advice note on Listed Buildings attention is drawn to ambiguities in both statute law and circular guidance relating to development control and listed buildings. It is desirable that government consolidates and updates its advice in the form of Planning Policy Guidance.

CIVIC SOCIETIES AND THE RELISTING SURVEY

24. The Comment has been made above (para. 10) that civic societies frequently draw Cadw's attention to buildings under threat that could merit spotlisting and from time to time offer useful documentation on the historic importance of particular buildings. The level of expertise obviously varies from society to society, but there are many civic groups that include among their active membership professional or lay persons with skills in architecture and architectural history.

25. It could well be helpful were a civic society consulted before the undertaking of relisted work in a community. It is understood that this does happen informally from time to time. The degree of assistance that a civic society could offer would vary. There are several societies that would be capable of drawing up a draft list of buildings meriting listing, and providing the inspectorate with architectural and historical appraisals of

[1] Many councils feel that the work of conservation area review, designation and management is likewise constrained by lack of resources with little cash to spare for enhancement schemes. More than one authority has told the Trust that it would take more interest in conservation area work if money were available to buy officer time. Other councils feel handicapped by lack of expertise. One result of this situation is that little use has been made of article 4 directions in Wales; it has been suggested more than once to the Trust that the lack of staff time to prepare the extensive justifications required for such directions is a problem.

each. Others would certainly be able to indicate to the inspectorate buildings that should be assessed, though with less technical competence. The Trust's *Annual Report to the Welsh Office* contains a list of societies currently in compliance with the Civic Trust.

M. Griffiths, MA, DPhil
Director
The Civic Trust for Wales

11 February 1993

APPENDIX 9

Letter from the Country Landowners Association to the Clerk of the Committee

PRESERVATION OF HISTORIC BUILDINGS & ANCIENT MONUMENTS (HB42)

1. CLA Wales welcomes the opportunity to comment on the preservation of historic buildings and particularly the listing of such. I apologise for the lateness of this reply but hope that the comments are of some use to the Committee.

PRESERVATION RESTRICTIONS & RESPONSIBILITIES PLACED ON OWNERS BY LISTING

2. Inevitably there is a variation in the importance attached to listed buildings and in the funds available to landowners to maintain them. There is widespread concern that too many buildings are listed as of historic interest. Such listing often appears to have resulted from the most cursory of external inspections from nearby highways. It is therefore questionable as to whether many buildings listed in this way would have been listed following internal inspections. There is also a suggestion that sometimes the staff involved are "over-qualified and under-experienced".

3. The framework which is used in listing buildings is not well-known and it is not often clear to landowners why many buildings are deemed to merit listing. It is suggested that the criteria for listing should be reviewed.

4. There is also concern over provisions for authentication and the lack of opportunities for landowners to appeal to Cadw or an independent authority over listing decisions.

5. Cadw, local authorities and the owners of listed buildings often disagree over the action needed to preserve them. New uses should be found for many listed buildings if they are to continue to have a role in the economy of rural areas, yet planning policies are so often restrictive. A wider range of new uses for redundant listed buildings should be encouraged.

6. The CLA believes that full information should be provided to planning authorities on the specific reasons for listing a historic building. When proposals for changes of use or conversion come forward, there is a danger that local authorities assume that any change will be detrimental, simply because the building is listed. Planning committees should instead be provided with the information needed to make an informed judgement on the impact of any proposals on the specific features of interest in the building.

7. Buildings which are occupied and serve an economic use are far more likely to be maintained than those which are simply a cost to the owners. The prime consideration should be to give such buildings a new lease of life.

8. Where listed buildings are not occupied or not capable of economic use, then Cadw or the local authority should undertake maintenance works to ensure that such buildings are kept in repair. Landowners could of course be contracted to take on this role.

FINANCIAL & ADVISORY ASSISTANCE

9. The CLA questions whether the existing Cadw grant schemes are effective. There is often confusion among landowners and others as to the sources and levels of grant aid available. Grant levels generally are too low to affect decisions on future maintenance.

10. Landowners should not be expected to suffer the consequences of listing, such as the refusal of planning permission for a new economic use, without grant aid to help maintain the building in the public interest.

11. There is concern over the Historic Buildings staff favouring more expensive maintenance options to achieve "authenticity" where a cheaper alternative is available. CLA also wish to draw attention to the problems associated with the imposition of VAT at the standard rate of repairs to listed buildings.

12. Clearer guidance on objectives, linked to the availability of expert advice and grant aid, is especially needed in Conservation Areas.

13. Too many buildings are designated without giving thought to the consequences of management and change. Consideration should be given as to how best to maintain listed buildings that were rarely designed to last for eternity particularly with the difficulties and expense of obtaining matching materials.

14. An attempt should be made by Cadw to produce a consensus of priorities for listed buildings and then priorities for funding could be defined once the objections are clear.

15. The CLA would object most strongly to any attempt to widen the circumstances to compel landowners to "put their property in order". This would alienate responsible owners and could encourage some to demolish unlisted buildings for fear of future listing.

16. The future maintenance of historic buildings will depend on the goodwill of their owners and the partnership between Cadw and landowners to find solutions to maintenance problems which are acceptable to all interests.

18 February 1993

APPENDIX 10

Memorandum by the Friends of Friendless Churches

PRESERVATION OF HISTORIC BUILDINGS AND ANCIENT MONUMENTS (HB1)

This memorandum is submitted in response to Mr Mark Hutton's letter of 26 November and deals with his numbered paragraphs. There are subjects in his letter that are outside the Society's experience and we comment only on such matters as are within our competence.

(i) We are unable to comment on this matter.

(ii) This Society is the owner of Llanfair Kilgeddin church in Gwent and Llanfaglan old church in Gwynedd in fee simple, and has a 999-year lease of Llantrisant old church in Anglesey from 1 November 1978 and a 999-year lease of Bayvil church in Dyfed from 7 October 1983. The churchyards of Llanfair Kilgeddin and of Llanfaglan remain in ecclesiastical ownership and use, but our lease of Llantrisant and Bayvil includes the churchyards.

The Society has also rescued from dereliction, and continues to carry out any necessary repairs at, the following churches which remain in ecclesiastical ownership and to some extent in use: Llangua in Gwent, for which we hold a Fabric Fund sufficient to maintain it in the foreseeable future; Llanelieu in Powys; Tal-y-Llyn in Anglesey; Cwm Pennant in Gwynedd. We also rescued from dereliction Llandeilo Talybont church in West Glamorgan, but this has now been moved to the Welsh Folk Museum at St Fagan's.

All the churches owned by or leased to the Society and those others in which we take an interest even though they remain in ecclesiastical ownership are regularly inspected by us and repairs are carried out as necessary.

We used to have a high regard for the care taken by the Church in Wales over its parish churches, but in recent years we have become disappointed. The Representative Body now seems anxious to dispose of very large numbers of churches, even some of high architectural quality. This has one advantage in that the Church in Wales has never made any difficulty about handing over churches to this Society such as we have occasionally encountered in England, but there is a limit to the number we can accept. The most disappointing feature is that the Church in Wales has neither accepted nor rejected, as we understand, the very advantageous proposal offered to it a few years ago by the Secretary of State on the advice of the Historic Buildings Council for Wales and CADW. The reason is presumably that the Representative Body would not wish to have any continuing responsibility for such churches and would prefer to dispose of them outright. As for the churches that remain in use, the great majority, there has been a decline in the care they receive and their maintenance is becoming a serious problem. This is due in part to deteriorating economic conditions.

The loss of Nonconformist churches in Wales is even more serious, mitigated only by the fact that relatively few have architectural pretensions, and those that are architecturally important appear to have been preserved. The Nonconformist denominations became in the 19th century and until the First World War remained closely bound up with the Liberal party, and the two have collapsed together. A large number of former Non-conformist chapels have been turned into shopping centres, which must be distressing to those who have worshipped in them but does not in general raise architectural questions.

There does not as yet appear to be any Roman Catholic problem in Wales.

We are not able to comment on the care exercised by the National Trust and local authorities over their properties.

(iii) The listing of historic buildings and the scheduling of ancient monuments in Wales appears satisfactory to us, but we have only a limited knowledge and no knowledge at all of the controls exercised on planning consents as we do not seek to make changes in the buildings in our care.

(iv) We are very favourably impressed by the consideration our applications for grant aid have received, by the promptness in reaching decisions, by the amount of aid promised and by the speed in payment when the work is completed. Our experience in Wales compares very favourably with our experience in England.

Our answer to this last question prompts us to make the general observation that we are glad that in Wales the ultimate responsibility of the Secretary of State, advised by the Historic Buildings Council and CADW, has been retained. We find this much more satisfactory than the system which has been adopted in England.

It is, of course, a truism that no organization can be better than its members, and both the Historic Buildings Council for Wales and CADW have been extremely well served.

10 December 1992

APPENDIX 11

Letter from the Lamphey Estate to the Clerk of the Committee

PRESERVATION OF HISTORIC BUILDINGS AND ANCIENT MONUMENTS (HB69)

I understand that on 22nd February members of the Welsh Affairs Select Committee visited the Bishop's Palace at Lamphey.

Are the Committee aware that an issue regarding the extent of scheduled land around the Palace has arisen as a result of Planning Applications by Lamphey Estate to create, in an area east of the monument, a new interpretive and cultural centre. The land in question was last in use as a camp in WWII, since when it has reverted to rough pasture and unmanaged woodland.

The original Applications were submitted to South Pembrokeshire District Council in June 1992. At Cadw's request the Applications were withdrawn, although subsequently resubmitted, to enable informal discussions to take place between themselves and the Estate regarding the implications of the proposal, and to explore a possible joint management arrangement of the Palace.

Following a meeting between the project team, at their request, and Mr Rick Turner of Cadw the scheduled area of the monument was extended, on the 18th June 1992, to the area east of the monument; thereby including the centre of the proposed project, its sculpture park and visitor facilities.

The scheduled zone was further enlarged to include two more areas, first of which is the silted fish pond directly south of the Palace. The land involved belongs to David Cole of Court House Farm, Lamphey. The pond and the land around it has not been exploited or damaged in any way by the farming activities taking place there.

The second extension took in a further pond and land to the north west of the Palace belonging to Mr A. W. Lain of Hill House, Lamphey, proprietor of Lamphey Court Hotel. The southern boundary of the hotel borders the stream flowing past the Palace, meaning that land between the stream and the southern edge of the newly scheduled area enjoys no statutory protection.

In fact extensive built remains linked to the water management system are clearly evident in the unscheduled area, indeed there are more features of obvious archaeological significance in it than its scheduled neighbour. Nor does protection extend to the causeway and the bridge, with the result that a section of wall shown in the Nathaniel Buck print of Lamphey Palace, 1740, has been removed to facilitate access to tennis courts now under construction by Mr Lain. Members may well have noticed the work going on. Already a not insignificant part of the unprotected site has been back-filled, and new trees planted on land not submitted to any acheological field evaluation.

The issue is that extension of the scheduled zone was prompted by Lamphey Estate's proposed project, not consideration of the ancient monument, its context and interpretation. As a result artefacts relating to the historic watercourse have been removed or damaged, with the certainty of more destruction to come. Furthermore, a private initiative designed specifically to preserve and enhance the landscape has been put in doubt by a vociferous campaign of objection largely directed by Mr Lain, the person directly responsible for the degradation of all the habitats in the vicinity of the Palace.

Perhaps members would care to give consideration to the matter in their deliberations.

18 March 1993

APPENDIX 12

Letter from the Director General the National Trust to the Clerk of the Committee

PRESERVATION OF HISTORIC BUILDINGS AND ANCIENT MONUMENTS IN WALES (HB19)

Thank you for your letter of 25 November informing me of the proposed inquiry by the Welsh Affairs Committee into the preservation of historic buildings and ancient monuments in Wales. The National Trust is grateful for the opportunity to give evidence to the Committee and I enclose a written submission accordingly.

The enclosed submission deals primarily with the purpose, powers and general functions of the National Trust, its sources of income and specific initiatives in relation to the built heritage in Wales. In the process it sets out the Trust's relationship with other conservation bodies, both public and non-governmental; describes what we believe to be the principal benefits of the Trust's work to the economy as much as the cultural heritage of the Principality; and relates the Trust's concerns with respect to a number of issues including the small buildings and industrial history of Wales, planning controls, VAT on repairs to historic buildings and, inevitably, funding considerations. A summary of conclusions is also provided.

In common with rural areas in the north of England, the west country and Northern Ireland, the buildings and monuments of Wales, in particular the vernacular tradition and associated social and economic influences, form vital components of its landscape. The theme which emerges from the Trust's submission is the complexity and the importance of historic landscapes in Wales, both in themselves and as settings for historic buildings and ancient monuments.

The fragility of those landscapes demands that measures be taken to protect them and ensure their adequate management. It is a great strength of the Trust that it recognises and is able to protect sites of historic interest and natural beauty as integrated units. This feature of the Trust's work is also conveyed in our submission.

The Trust, however, cannot and does not presume to achieve its objectives in isolation. Instead, our experience leads to the conclusion that there is a need to harness financial resources, administrative effort, appropriate expertise and land use planning more effectively in the protection of historic landscapes and their component parts. The Trust would wish to play a full role in such a combined effort.

It is the perception of what is important in historic terms which has a determining influence on attitudes towards preservation. The Trust hopes very much that the Committee shares its perception of what is important and that the Committee will feel able to adopt similar conclusions as part of its report to Parliament.

Finally, should the Committee consider it appropriate, the Trust would be willing to give oral evidence in support of its written submission. If this is the case, I look forward to receiving details in due course. Thank you once again for the opportunity to submit evidence to this inquiry.

12 January 1993

THE NATIONAL TRUST

EVIDENCE TO THE WELSH AFFAIRS COMMITTEE INQUIRY INTO THE PRESERVATION OF ANCIENT MONUMENTS AND HISTORIC BUILDINGS IN WALES

JANUARY 1993

Section 1—Background to the National Trust's submission

GENERAL

1. The National Trust for Places of Historic Interest or Natural Beauty was founded in 1895 as an independent charity to hold and manage in perpetuity for the benefit of the nation countryside and historic buildings in England, Wales and Northern Ireland. The Trust fulfils its statutory responsibilities, as laid down in the National Trust Acts, through ownership and direct management and its prime concern is therefore for the conservation and management of the properties in its care.

2. As a consequence, the Trust is the largest private landowner in the United Kingdom with an estate of about 235,000 hectares (ha) of land and 756 kilometres of unspoilt coastline in its ownership in England, Wales and Northern Ireland. The Trust protects a further 32,000 hectares and 83 kilometres of coastline under restrictive covenants which help to ensure long term conservation of areas outside our ownership. Though the majority of the areas owned are freely open to the public, the Trust also provides admission at specified times or at a charge to some 320 properties, including 190 historic houses and castles.

3. The Trust is the largest conservation organisation in Europe, supported by over 2.1 million members. Its properties open at a charge receive in excess of 10 million visitors annually.

INALIENABILITY

4. The Trust has the right, enshrined in its Acts of Parliament, to hold land inalienably. This means that land held in such a fashion cannot be freely sold or mortgaged but, also, that it may be protected against the threat of acquisition by a public body for the purpose of development. This is a right which the Trust shares only with the National Trust for Scotland. Should the Council of the Trust so choose, it can call on Parliament to support this right by invoking Special Parliamentary Procedure.

COMMITTEE AND STAFF STRUCTURE

5. The general policies of the Trust are determined by its Council, half of whose members are nominated by institutes such as the British Museum, National Museum of Wales, Ramblers' Association and Royal Horticultural Society while half are elected by Trust Members at their annual general meeting. The Council appoints an Executive Committee which, in turn, appoints a Finance Committee and a Properties Committee (see Appendix 1). Day-to-day administration is carried out by executive staff at the Trust's Head Office in London, and 16 regional offices of which North and South Wales comprise two. Regional Directors are responsible to the Director-General who is in turn responsible to the Trust's committees and Council. The Trust employs nearly 2,400 permanent members of staff in Wales, England and Northern Ireland.

FINANCE

6. The National Trust, as a charity, operates without public core funding. This independence is an important factor in the stance it is able to adopt towards preservation and conservation but the costs of running such a large charitable trust are substantial and the trusts needs, as a consequence, to be fully aware of opportunities for and future constraints upon income generation. An extract from the Trust's 1991 accounts which is attached (Appendix 2) shows how income and expenditure have increased over the last five years (figures for 1992 are not yet available).

7. However, changes resulting from the economic climate project a worsening period, as a diminishing operating surplus in 1989 becomes a deficit in 1995 (Appendix 3). Fiscal changes outside the control of the Trust pose a significant threat to its income while the general downturn in the economy has resulted in a levelling off, and in some instances a decrease, in visitors to admission charging properties.

Section II—The National Trust in Wales

GENERAL

8. The first property acquired by the National Trust in 1895 was Dinas Oleu—four and a half acres of cliff land near Barmouth. In Wales, the Trust now protects over 50,000 hectares, including over 180 kilometres of coastline, 17 historic properties open to the public, nearly 13,000 hectares of farmland, 175 agricultural tenancies, 1,400 hectares of woodland, and 1,200 vernacular buildings. It owns over 5,000 sites of archaeological importance, of which 70 are Scheduled Ancient Monuments, ranging in type from prehistoric caves in Gower to Segontium Roman Fort. The Trust is responsible for 85 listed buildings, including three Grade I, and eight grade II*. We elaborate upon some of these categories of property below.

9. There were 54,000 National Trust members in Wales in 1992, a figure which has been increasing at an average of 10 per cent per annum. Properties open at a charge in Wales received some 700,000 visitors in 1992. This is in addition to the millions who visit and enjoy the Trust's open spaces properties in areas like the Snowdonia, Brecon Beacons and Pembrokeshire Coast National Parks.

COMMITTEE AND STAFF STRUCTURE

10. The Trust's Committee for Wales consists of 17 members drawn from a wide range of professions and interests, with membership distributed equally between North and South Wales. Each member is appointed by invitation for a three year period, with provision for a further three years. The Trust's regional committees supervise the overall management of regions and approve and monitor regional strategy within the framework of national policy. Regional Directors in North and South Wales have a responsibility to the Committee for Wales in this respect.

11. For administrative purposes, Wales is divided into two regions, North and South, managed from offices in Llandudno in Gwynedd and Llandeilo in Dyfed. The Trust in Wales employs a total of 550 staff in the various fields of expertise which its work requires in addition to seasonal staff. This includes 193 permanent full time staff, 10 fixed term permanent staff, 28 permanent part time staff, 133 temporary full time and 186 temporary part time staff. We deal with volunteers in detail below.

12. Within the next two to five years it is hoped that every region of the Trust will have a full time qualified conservator responsible to the Historic Buildings Representatives. The person appointed in South Wales will be expected to have skills related to conservation of industrial archaeological artifacts and be in a position to advise other regions accordingly.

13. At the core of the National Trust's operations in Wales are its regional plans and management plans for individual properties. Constantly reviewed and updated, these plans are backed by extensive survey work prior to adoption and provide the basis for a continuing programme of conservation and management.

FINANCE

14. In terms of legacies and sponsorship, Wales is relatively poor and relies very heavily upon central funding within the Trust for its deficit properties. The total operating deficit for Wales in 1991 was £3,305,900, and essential repair work is dependent upon grant aid. Any diminution in the availability of grant assistance from public bodies would have serious short and long term implications.

15. As a consequence, European Commission funding has become increasingly important in assisting projects at properties which meet the existing criteria for eligibility. Grants from the European Social Fund and European Regional Development Fund have been awarded to National Trust projects. The National Trust in Wales works closely with EC Welsh Office staff, and continues to build upon its relationship with the EC in Brussels.

16. The National Heritage Memorial Fund (NHMF) has, over the last decade, played an increasingly important role in providing financial assistance for preservation and conservation in Wales. The Trust in Wales considers it very significant that the first major grant by the NHMF for smaller buildings was given to

a National Trust property in 1990. The role that the NHMF plays cannot be over-emphasised but the Trust is all too aware of the demands on its limited resources. To enable the NHMF to meet these demands will require adequate funding provision in the future.

Section III—Principal activities and initiatives

HISTORIC HOUSES

17. Historic Buildings Representatives based at Llandudno and Llandeilo advise on the conservation and presentation of the Trust's historic buildings and their contents, archaeological sites and landscapes, and on the aesthetics and historical context of every aspect of the Trust's management. The Trust owns and manages the major national "treasure houses" of Wales in Powis Castle, Erdigg, Penrhyn Castle and Plas Newydd.

18. Chirk Castle is also owned and managed by the Trust under special arrangements of which the Committee should be aware. Transferred in 1981 without endowment, the property is held by the Trust under a maintenance deficit agreement with the Welsh Office which undertook the initial programme of capital repairs. Funding for the remaining programme of capital items is now based on an agreed list which is discussed annually with Cadw alongside future arrangements for the maintenance deficit. The future of these arrangements after 1996 is now receiving consideration.

THEFT, VANDALISM AND FIRE

19. Of direct concern to the National Trust are theft and vandalism. The theft of statuary from a number of our properties is particularly disturbing because of their vulnerability and the difficulties involved in their protection. The Trust employs full time specialist security advisers and instals a complex array of theft and fire prevention measures and alarm systems for houses, garden furniture and statuary.

20. The major fires at Uppark in Sussex and Windsor Castle have drawn attention to fire hazards in our larger houses. The Trust is in the process of upgrading fire prevention measures in all its properties including the elimination of hot work, and careful control of other potential risks. There has been a major upgrading of fire detection equipment and the National Trust emergency procedures, involving special trained staff, are well in advance of most other organisations. It is significant that Trust training courses are attended by personnel from museums and other conservation organisations.

ARCHAEOLOGY

21. Two full time archaeologists are employed by the Trust in Wales to survey properties and potential acquisitions, and provide data for management plans. In addition to permanent archaeologists, a number of property based staff are qualified archaeologists. Permanent Archaeological Advisers with a remit for the whole of the National Trust are based at Cirencester, Gloucestershire. All archaeological work throughout the Trust is overseen both on a regional basis and by the permenent Archaeological Advisers. Of the scheduled ancient monuments in the Trust's ownership in Wales, three—Cilgerran Castle, Skenfrith Castle and Segontium Roman Fort—are managed by Cadw.

SMALL BUILDINGS, COMMUNITIES AND THE LANDSCAPE

22. The majority of the small, vernacular buildings in the ownership of the Trust have been acquired as part of large estates such as the 14,800 ha Ysbyty Estate, transferred with Penrhyn Castle and the 1,000 ha Dolaucothi Estate in Dyfed. These contain widely scattered rural cottages as well as concentrations of traditional dwellings in villages such as Ysbyty Ifan and Pumpsaint.

23. The architectural integrity of such buildings and their settings are paramount considerations in the Trust's overall management of its estates. They involve the Trust in the management of the landscape as a whole as opposed to single monuments or defined "honey pot" areas. Some, such as Bishop Morgan's birthplace of Ty Mawr, in Gwynedd, have sufficient historic, cultural or architectural merit in their own right to be subject to separate management plans involving detailed restoration and conservation work and special provision for public admission.

24. To improve understanding and knowledge in this respect, a series of landscape studies is being undertaken by the Trust covering archaeology, vernacular buildings and biological sites. The results of the surveys will be incorporated with information from other sources in the management plans.

25. As a consequence of this pattern of ownership, the Trust fulfils a major landlord role in Wales with acknowledged responsibilities for farming and local community interests. We are fully aware that the areas in the Trust's protection are also places where people live and work. The Trust believes, however, that the language, lifestyles and attitudes of the people who live on the land are indivisible from their environment. A careful balance has therefore to be maintained between socio-economic needs and preservation. The Trust in Wales is also committed to a policy of bilingualism which is evident in its publications and property presentation. Wherever possible, Welsh language speakers are employed.

EDUCATION

26. The Trust seeks to promote public understanding and support of historic properties by developing the educational potential of its buildings and sites. Hands-on experience can be gained by children at Erddig, Chirk, Penrhyn, and Lower Treginnis. Education officers in Beddgelert and at Aberdulais Falls deal with industrial archaeology. At Dolaucothi Gold Mine a comprehensive education package has been tailored to meet the demands of the National Curriculum. The only residential school camp in the Trust is accommodated in former estate buildings on the Stackpole Estate on the Pembrokeshire coast. Depending upon the availability of funds, adult education courses in skills associated with historic buildings may be developed at the newly acquired Llanerchaeron estate in Dyfed.

VOLUNTEERS

27. For the last decade the National Trust has acknowledged the increasing importance of volunteers. The present financial climate necessitates more than ever the development of volunteer activity in all aspects of the Trust's work. Volunteers already make and important monetary contribution to the Trust. The North Wales region has a full time Regional Volunteers Co-ordinator and South Wales a part time Co-ordinator on a temporary appointment. In 1990–91 over 86,000 hours were worked by volunteers for the Trust throughout Wales. The notional benefit of all volunteer work for the two regions has been estimated at £477,000 over the same period. The use of volunteers has been successfully applied to the conservation and care of historic buildings and their contents.

LIAISON WITH OTHER BODIES

28. Close contact is maintained at all levels with other conservation organisations in Wales. Archaeological records and building surveys are deposited with the Royal Commission for Ancient and Historical Monuments at Aberystwyth. Very close contact is maintained with the executive staff of Cadw, the Ancient Monuments Board and the Historic Buildings Council. Specialist advice is sought from and given to individual archaeologists, University Departments and Archaeological Trusts. The Trust also liaises with specialist staff in the National Museum for Wales and the National Library of Wales.

ECONOMIC BENEFITS OF THE TRUST'S WORK

29. In addition to the direct employment of 550 people in Wales, the Trust in 1991 spent a total of £7,072,220 on the conservation and presentation of its properties. This figure includes coast and countryside properties but many of these also contain important archaeological sites. This expenditure has an important multiplier effect on local economies and on the economy of Wales as a whole insofar as it attracts visitors to the Principality and is a major source of inward investment.

30. The Trust's commercial arm, National Trust Enterprises, also operates shops and catering outlets at the majority of properties open to the public. A policy of buying British wherever possible and allowing a certain amount of local discretion in the range of items offered for sale means that a high proportion of goods sold in Trust shops and restaurants originate in Wales while a number of local entrepreneurs benefit from franchise operations.

31. Historic buildings and archaeological properties also require specialist skills. The Trust in Wales makes a positive commitment to ensuring continuity of the standards required through the appointment of full time craftsmen and project based, short term, contract craftsmen who are suitably qualified and trained. It is hoped that by training short term, contract employees in historic building conservation their techniques and skills will be made available to wider markets. The Trust also monitors suitable contractors to ensure that high standards are available and can be maintained for the purposes of this work.

32. In April 1993 the new government training initiative called Training for Work commences. This programme replaces Employment Training, Employment Action and Higher Technical National Training with the National Vocational Qualifications in Environmental Conservation. One of its objectives will be training in the conservation and preservation of historic buildings. The National Trust in Wales will be taking a lead in this initiative, using its current experience and expertise.

Section IV—Specific concerns and conclusions

A number of specific issues arise from the foregoing.

CADW AND THE HISTORIC BUILDINGS COUNCIL

33. *The National Trust is pleased to acknowledge the successful development of Cadw which, since its inception in 1984, has raised the standards of presentation and promotion of its properties in Wales.* It says much for the commitment of Cadw staff that the backlog of listing and scheduling continues to diminish and that response times to listed building and scheduled monument consent applications are very rapid.

34. As already mentioned, there are three Trust properties in the guardianship of Cadw. This arrangement works successfully and all the properties are well cared for. *The Trust does not foresee the need for major change in this respect.*

35. As has also been mentioned, however, the Trust, in common with other owners of historic buildings, is reliant upon grant aid for repairs. The Trust consequently applauds the understanding fashion in which the Historic Buildings Council (HBC) has helped to fund phased capital works, particularly on its major properties such as Penrhyn Castle, Powis and the Conwy Suspension Bridge as well as Chirk.

36. The cost of upkeep has nonetheless increased and is likely to continue to do so. It is therefore all the more imperative that the Government continues to provide sufficient funds to enable Cadw to fulfil its statutory responsibilities for buildings and archaeological sites so that standards of conservation may also improve. *We note, however, the impact of financial trends on the availability and timing of Historic Building Council grant aid, and view the cumulative effect of postponing essential repair work with concern.* Until 1991-92, for example, the HBC awarded a grant of £280,000 per annum towards repairs at Penrhyn Castle. For the current financial year the figure was reduced to £199,500. *The Trust therefore questions the efficacy of the core funding to Cadw having to cover both Cadw's statutory responsibilities for its monuments in care and grant aid towards historic buildings and scheduled monuments in the ownership of others.*

HISTORIC LANDSCAPES, GARDENS AND CONSERVATION AREAS

37. The establishment of the Welsh Historic Gardens Trust, and the work of Cadw on the register of historic gardens and landscapes in Wales, has focused attention on an important aspect of landscape history. Having been given little consideration in the past, recent research now indicates that Wales has some of the most important examples of formal gardens and landscapes in Britain. In addition to the well known and well preserved, such as Powis, Bodnant and Plas Newydd, the "rediscovery" of Hafod, Dinefwr and Llanerchaeron raises important questions about their future protection and management.

38. Gardens and formal landscapes are very fragile creations, in constant need of attention. The delay of a few months can result in the loss of important species and features. The very nature of a landscape requires that protection is provided for the whole. At the moment, however, it is not possible to apply protective controls other than the application of conservation area status. Furthermore, it raises the question of providing statutory protection to large areas of land.

39. A sense of place is similarly dependent upon the interplay of several elements, including the use of sympathetic materials and localised skills. It is very often the case that it is only when these essential qualities have been lost that their importance is recognised. For example, the application of proprietory stone cladding and the insertion of UPVC windows on a row of terraced houses in a mining village or slate quarrying community can diminish the integrated quality of that particular locality. In this respect, planning controls and guidance are often quite ineffective in protecting our built heritage.

40. The Trust welcomes the recent increase in the number of conservation areas in Wales, although it is fully aware that compared to other parts of Britain much has yet to be achieved. We are also concerned about the paucity of qualified conservation officers within local authorities in Wales. Even within conservation areas no guarantees of protection can be given, and the work of a sympathetic owner on one structure may easily be offset by misguided planning decisions and lack of attention to detail in adjoining properties. At much greater risk are those buildings not covered by specific control categories such as conservation areas or listed building status, but which are individually or collectively important to the historic and cultural landscape.

41, *The Trust therefore urges the Government to set clear and co-ordinated policies, backed by adequate incentives and controls, to protect historic, cultural and rural landscapes. In particular, we believe local authorities should be encouraged through guidance to undertake surveys in selected areas with a view to identifying landscapes worthy of special protection; establishing the funds, in the form of grant-aid, required to carry out restoration work; and designating them accordingly with a view to incorporation within local plans.*

SMALL BUILDINGS

42. There are discrepancies in the understanding of Welsh historic buildings and archaeological sites. Certain aspects are well recorded and protected by listing or guardianship, such as castles and larger houses. Other aspects however are being lost or damaged by default. Especially vulnerable are the smaller buildings, and structures and sites from the industrial period. Two examples may serve to illustrate the Trust's concerns in this matter.

43. In the first instance, a small building has recently come to light which has been described by a leading authority on vernacular buildings in Wales as "an unflowed gem of an archaic vernacular Carmarthenshire farmhouse in an unspoilt landscape setting of outstanding merit". The property, which is late medieval in origin, has remained unchanged, along with its largely unimproved landscape, since the mid-nineteenth century. Yet it was unknown until a potentially disastrous fire brought it to the attention of the local authority in 1989 and, so far at least, no major source of funds for its purchase and future protection has been found.

44. A second example relates to the Trust's proposal to establish part of the Llanerchaeron Estate as a training centre in rural skills development, which will include building skills training. The decline in demand for new buildings and the concomitant increase in unemployment lends emphasis to the re-use of existing buildings, especially in rural areas. The Trust has been disappointed by the lack of grant aid available for such purposes.

45. *The Trust accepts that no single organisation or group of public bodies can be expected to carry the burden of conservation throughout the country. We believe, however, that the lack of core funding as well as the failure to appreciate the importance of smaller buildings may be better resolved through the promotion of locally based trusts.* In an attempt to improve the awareness of conservation of small buildings the National Trust has therefore been active in establishing Hendref—Building Preservation Trust for Wales. It is hoped that Hendref, working with private and public bodies alike, may be able to make inroads into the general decline of conservation standards which are outside the control of specifically dedicated conservation bodies. *The Trust would welcome the Government's endorsement of this approach.*

VAT on Repairs to Historic Buildings

46. In common with all the representative heritage bodies, the Trust is greatly concerned about the continued imposition of VAT on repairs to historic buildings, while new building is zero rated. This is a severe disincentive to owners to carry out even essential repairs, and tends to militate in favour of new construction. *We favour the abolition of VAT on repairs to historic buildings.*

Industrial History

47. Wales has some of the best examples of industrial archaeology in Britain, including the first cast iron railway bridge in the world. Much has been lost over the past two decades, but some of the industrial landscapes still extant are vitally important. It is here that attention needs to be focused, as much is still being lost because of ignorance and prejudice. *In the opinion of the Trust, more effort and resources need to be devoted to the preservation of our industrial heritage now, as sufficient time has not yet elapsed for a wider appreciation and perspective to be developed of the importance of this period in our history. The Trust therefore applauds the recent appointment by Cadw of an inspector for Industrial Archaeology, who has been active within the former industrial valleys of South Wales.*

Importance of Liaison

48. The Trust believes that close liaison between the major bodies in the conservation field is vital to the continuing understanding of historic buildings and archaeological properties. An awareness of the needs and responsibilities of other organisations is imperative if the challenge of upkeep and presentation is to be met.

49. In similar fashion, *the Trust believes there is a need for closer co-ordination between government agencies and private bodies whose remit encompasses the landscape in various forms such as the Countryside Council for Wales, Welsh Development Agency, Development Board for Rural Wales, Wales Tourist Board, Cadw, Welsh Office Agricultural Department, Forestry Commission and local authorities.*

Tourism

50. The National Trust welcomes the Wales Tourist Board's consultative paper, Tourism 2000—A Strategy for Wales, and is presently considering a detailed response. It is pleased to note the acknowledgement that historic buildings and gardens are significant tourist attractions within Wales, and that emphasis will continue to be placed on the Welsh heritage in future marketing. Grant aid from the Wales Tourist Board is often a key element in the funding of National Trust heritage tourism related projects. The Wales Tourist Board has consistently shown a positive stance towards the National Trust.

Section V—Summary of conclusions

Cadw and the Historic Buildings Council

— The successful development of Cadw and, in particular, its standards of presentation and the promotion of its properties in Wales is acknowledged. *(para. 33)*

— The Trust does not foresee the need for major change with respect to arrangements for the three guardianship properties in the care of Cadw. *(para. 34)*

— The impact of financial trends on the availability and timing of Historic Building Council grant aid is noted and the cumulative effect of postponing essential repair work is viewed with concern. *(para. 36)*

— The Trust questions the efficacy of the core funding to Cadw having to cover both Cadw's statutory responsibilities for its monuments in care and grant aid towards historic buildings and scheduled monuments in the ownership of others. *(ibid)*

Historic Landscapes, Gardens and Conservation Areas

— The Government is urged to set clear and co-ordinated policies, backed by adequate incentives and controls, to protect historic, cultural and rural landscapes. Local authorities should be encouraged through guidance to undertake surveys in selected areas with a view to identifying landscapes worthy of special protection; establishing the funds, in the form of grant-aid, required to carry out restoration work; and designating them accordingly with a view to incorporation within local plans. *(para.41)*

SMALL BUILDINGS

— The Trust accepts that no single organisation or group of public bodies can be expected to carry the burden of conservation throughout the country. It believes, however, that the lack of core funding as well as the failure to appreciate the importance of smaller buildings may be better resolved through the promotion of locally based trusts. The Trust would welcome the Government's endorsement of this approach. *(para.45)*

VAT ON REPAIRS TO HISTORIC BUILDINGS

— We favour the abolition of VAT on repairs to historic buildings. *(para.46)*

INDUSTRIAL HISTORY

— More effort and resources need to be devoted to the preservation of our industrial heritage now, as sufficient time has not yet elapsed for a wider appreciation and perspective to be developed of the importance of this period in our history. The Trust therefore applauds the recent appointment by Cadw of an Inspector for Industrial Archaeology, who has been active within the former industrial valleys of South Wales. *(para.47)*

IMPORTANCE OF LIAISON

— The Trust believes there is a need for closer co-ordination between government agencies and private bodies whose remit encompasses the landscape in various forms such as the Countryside Council for Wales, Welsh Development Agency, Development Board for Rural Wales, Wales Tourist Board, Cadw, Welsh Office Agricultural Department, Forestry Commission and local authorities. *(para.49)*

APPENDIX 13

Memorandum by the Roman Catholic Archdiocese of Cardiff

HISTORIC BUILDINGS (HB28)

The Catholic Church in Wales exercise a considerable amount of central control over all of its buildings, and in the case of its listed building stock always endeavours to maintain this to the highest possible level. However, it must always be borne in mind that the various Dioceses are charities and as such have both only a limited income and a large number of calls on this income.

The Church has at this moment only a limited number of buildings that are listed, all of which are in regular use either as places of worship or as residences for clergy. It is an important point to bear in mind that the Church has historically only built and maintained churches where they are pastorally and economically viable entities. Where primarily there has been either of these lacking, then the Church has closed and disposed of the buildings: to have done otherwise would have been to act in a manner, especially in the light of the recent Charities Act, contrary to good sense.

Equally where we have the above two conditions present, be it in a listed building or not, then it is in our basic interest to maintain that building to as high a standard as possible. This is done through using the best possible professional advice that we can afford and acting on it when financially possible. Also, at the moment all major works both internally and externally have to be approved by the Trustees of the charity involved.

At the moment, as I understand it, Regligious Bodies are exempt from the main controls exercised by CADW, these controls being mainly concerned with the exterior of the building and the question of repairs. Bearing in mind all that has been said before about the charitable status of the Churches, I would feel that this should remain basically the same. However, regarding external alterations, there is most certainly a case for the statutory bodies to have a very active voice to ensure that not only the character of the building is not adversely affected, but also that of the surrounding area.

If we now move on to the interior of the building, where I believe it is intended stricter controls should be enacted, then we would feel very aggrieved by this. Roman Catholic worship is conducted along very specific lines; yet the "liturgy" of the Church is a living breathing thing, and our modern churches have been designed with this in mind. However, our earlier churches were designed to cope with an earlier understanding of this living breathing entity, and must therefore be brought, as far as we are able, into sympathy with the new understanding.

Sympathy is the key word here. If any building is to work then all must be in sympathy; the structure, the internal decor, the internal positioning of fittings, the choice of internal fittings, and the people themselves; all must be in sympathy and harmony as far as possible.

To seek to say that one or more of the above factors must take precedence is not only to damage that sympathy, but is also a good way of destroying the community that uses the building. Thus I would argue that giving precedence to architecture and fittings—a precedence that will be decided by people who will not necessarily have any understanding of the other elements—is to do damage to the whole, and to interfere with religious freedom to worship as we wish. It must never be forgotten also that the State has not borne the cost of these buildings, they are paid for by the people that use them.

As regards grants, all we have to say is that the amount of money put up by the statutory bodies should be the decider in the amount of voice they have in what should, or should not, be done. In recent cases we have experienced statutory bodies offering a grant and then insisting on so much unplanned extra work, or different quality of work, that the cost has far exceeded the grant on offer.

21 January 1993

APPENDIX 14

Letter from the Society for the Protection of Ancient Buildings to the Chairman of the Committee

HISTORIC BUILDINGS (HB 78)

As I mentioned to you after Philip Venning and I gave evidence to your committee on 17 February, there were a number of further points we would have liked to have had time to make.

The first is that we have the strong impression, and this a view shared by Dr Eurwyn William the Director of the Welsh Folk Museum, that vernacular buildings are under-represented on the statutory lists of buildings of historical and architectural importance. The only way of testing this view would be to carry out a sample listing in certain areas. One of the differences between Wales and England is the relatively greater importance of vernacular buildings as part of the Welsh heritage and this should be reflected in the lists.

As was mentioned at the hearing of the Select Committee. Conservation Areas throughout the United Kingdom lack real teeth. The effectiveness of rural conservation areas was also mentioned. Another of the differences between England and Wales is the relatively greater importance of rural areas in Wales and therefore the increased importance of buildings as part of the "cultural landscape". The procedure for making Article 4 directions is too cumbersome to be effective in preventing the degrading of conservation areas by minor changes in the character of buildings. We suggest that Wales could experiment with a new type of conservation area which not only designates the area but also, at the time of designation, defines alternations for which conservation area consent would be needed. Conservation areas could be "tuned"in this way to ensure that their essential character is not eroded whilst being less restrictive than listing all the buildings in the area. "Tuning" could include landscape elements overcoming some of the problems of rural conservation. This system would also have the benefit of giving a greater degree of control to vulnerable areas while the re-listing process is carried out.

Finally we think that the experience of English Heritage as an organisation independent of government is a good one, and would suggest that your committee should consider whether CADW should become independent of the Welsh Office. Some of the advantages we feel could come from this area that CADW would be seen to be giving disinterested advice on listing, that advice from CADW would not compromise the position of the Secretary of State in making decisions and finally that staff would no longer be moved from CADW to and from different sections of the Welsh Office, which is a problem in developing knowledge and skills.

You asked us to provide examples of district councils failing to notify us of listed building applications. As was stated at the hearing, this type of negative evidence is quite hard to find but we are making enquiries and will write to you again if we find suitable examples.

5 March 1993

APPENDIX 15

Memorandum by Welsh Historic Gardens Trust

HISTORIC BUILDINGS & ANCIENT MONUMENTS IN WALES (HB27)

1. This memorandum has been prepared at the invitation of the Clerk of the Committee and it sets out for the consideration of the Inquiry the work of the Welsh Historic Gardens Trust in relation to the *Register of Landscapes, Parks and Gardens of Special Historic Interest in Wales,* which is being compiled by Cadw under the auspices of ICOMOS.

2. The catalyst for the founding of the Trust in 1989 was concern for the fates of two sites in the Twyi valley, but it soon became apparent that there were many other gardens and landscapes in Wales, once renowned for their beauty and splendour, that lay neglected or even forgotten, the victims of indifference, ignorance or unsympathetic development; and the growing acceptance that they are as much a part of the Welsh heritage as the buildings and natural landscapes, and as worthy of conservation for generations to come.

3. The Trust is an enabling organisation, specialising in research, management planning, restoration and interpretation of gardens, parks and designed landscapes,[1] and draws upon professional and voluntary skills available throughout Wales in close co-operation with both the public and private sectors. It therefore exercises its powers as a charitable trust on behalf of owners, local authorities, developers and other concerned individuals and agencies. For that reason the commitment by Cadw to the compilation of the Register was warmly welcomed as an acknowledgement of the importance of the garden landscape heritage of Wales.

4. Substantial data have been contributed, largely through the voluntary work of its members, and the Trust's nascent Gazetteer exercise will provide much further information. In return Cadw has undertaken to make its Register site dossiers available for use by the Trust in its advisory service on the conservation of the garden landscapes of Wales; an exchange of information in the furtherance of what the Trust sees as a complementary and cost-effective role for the benefit of local authorities, owners, developers and other concerned individuals.

5. Given the resources to complete it there is little doubt that the Register will be of inestimable value in establishing a definitive record of sites of special historic interest in Wales in the early nineties. However there is cause for concern for the "after-care" of the Register. Firstly, the completed Register (like the garden landscapes themselves) will be ephemeral; as a result there will be a long-term—if intermittent— requirement to take account both of changes in condition as well as new knowledge, a point well demonstrated in the cases of the English Register and Scottish Inventory. Secondly, the listing of sites inevitably leads to the type of casework which is already offered by the Trust through its advisory service. Such work always entails research and usually site visits, as well as a readiness to submit proofs of evidence. The fact that listed garden landscapes (unlike listed structures) lack protection under statute adds particular force to the requirement for a capability for effective and timely casework.[2]

6. Clearly, because the Register has been compiled in response to statute, its "custodianship"—and all that entails—must continue to rest with Cadw. However, when there is not already a casework service in being, on the lines of that provided by English Heritage, there are grounds for suggesting that that function should be quite separate. Firstly, experts in historic buildings are unlikely to have specialised knowledge of garden landscapes and their conservation. Even if they did there could be instances where the best interests of structures and their settings might well conflict and, because of the lack of protection already referred to, there is a risk that gardens will be regarded as the "soft option" in planning matters. Experience elsewhere indicates that this may well be the case when other government departments are involved, eg in road schemes. Finally, the costs of providing an advisory service by an organisation such as this charitable Trust are likely to be lower than those incurred by an official body.

7. Because the Trust is well placed and qualified to take an objective view of the conservation of the garden landscape heritage of Wales, and already plays a complementary and cost-effective role in its provision of an advisory service, the Committee is invited, therefore, to consider the proposal that the casework that is already being generated by the Cadw Register should be undertaken by this Trust.

---

[1] The term "garden landscapes" is used hereafter to cover all three categories of site.
[2] The case for statutory notification, using the procedure recently adopted in Scotland, is being pursued with the Welsh Office through Cadw. In the meantime the Trust is offering model policies for development plans and entering listed sites in the relevant Sites and Monuments Records.

Printed in the United Kingdom by HMSO
19585   C6   6/93   115218

ISBN 0-10-020973-4